Bernhard A Koch (ed)
Medical Liability in Europe

Tort and Insurance Law
TIL 29

Tort and Insurance Law

Vol 29

Edited by the
European Centre of Tort
and Insurance Law

together with the

Institute for European Tort Law
of the Austrian Academy of Sciences

De Gruyter

Bernhard A Koch (ed)

Medical Liability in Europe

A Comparison of Selected Jurisdictions

With Contributions by

Ewa Bagińska
Suzanne Carval
Ondřej Dostál
Esther Engelhard
Massimo Foglia
Ivo Giesen
Bernhard A Koch
Miquel Martín-Casals
Attila Menyhárd
Philip Mielnicki
Herman Nys
Franz Michael Petry
WV Horton Rogers
Alessandro P Scarso
Mårten Schultz
Ruth Sefton-Green
Josep Solé
Corinne Widmer Lüchinger

De Gruyter

European Centre of Tort and Insurance Law
Reichsratsstraße 17/2
A-1010 Vienna
Tel.: +43 1 4277 29650
Fax: +43 1 4277 29670
E-Mail: ectil@ectil.org

Austrian Academy of Sciences
Institute for European Tort Law
Reichsratsstraße 17/2
A-1010 Vienna
Tel.: +43 1 4277 29651
Fax: +43 1 4277 29670
E-Mail: etl@oeaw.ac.at

ISBN 978-3-11-026010-6
e-ISBN 978-3-11-026016-8
ISSN 1616-8623

Bibliografische Information der Deutschen Nationalbibliothek

Die Deutsche Nationalbibliothek verzeichnet diese Publikation in der Deutschen Nationalbibliografie; detaillierte bibliografische Daten sind im Internet über http://dnb.d-nb.de abrufbar.

Druck: Hubert & Co. GmbH & Co. KG, Göttingen

Gedruckt auf säurefreiem Papier

Printed in Germany

www.degruyter.com

Die Idee

Immer wieder bewegen ärztliche Leistungen oder Fehlleistungen die Medien, die Politik und die Bevölkerung; amerikanische und europäische Verhältnisse werden unscharf unterschieden und Erneuerungsbedürfnisse werden geweckt, auch wenn objektiv Bedarfe fehlen.

In der Diskussion über die Qualität im Gesundheitswesen sind sich die Akteure auf internationalen Symposien einig über die Notwendigkeit gleicher Standards, einer qualitativ hochwertigen Medizin und gleichwertiger Risiko-Managementsysteme. Danach gebe es kaum etwas zu verbessern oder zu verändern. Die Gesundheitsleistungen und die Rechtssysteme der Länder in Europa sind aber so unterschiedlich, dass es auch auf absehbare Zeit keine einheitlichen Regelungen geben wird.

Bereits 2001 ist in der Diskussion um die Notwendigkeit von Patienten-Unfallversicherungen in verschiedenen Ländern Europas eine erste europäische Vergleichsstudie[1] zu konkret identifizierten Arzthaftungsschadenfällen aus Deutschland auf Basis der Rechts- und Entschädigungssysteme in Belgien, Deutschland, Frankreich, den Niederlanden, Österreich, Portugal und der Schweiz erstellt worden. Franz-Michael Petry, Rechtsanwalt in Detmold, hat seinerzeit die Fälle identifiziert und Prof. Dr. Michael Faure, Universität Maastricht, sowie Prof. Dr. Helmut Koziol, Europäisches Zentrum für Schadenersatz- und Versicherungsrecht, Wien, haben mit Länderreferenten die Studie durchgeführt und eine Bestandsaufnahme sowie Weiterentwicklungstendenzen dokumentiert und dabei auch Standards in der finanziellen Kompensation von eingetretenen Gesundheitsschäden nach ärztlichen Behandlungen auf sehr hohem Niveau aufgezeigt, z. B. in Österreich und Deutschland. Den Anstoß zu dieser Studie gab seinerzeit die Deutsche Krankenhausgesellschaft Berlin und die Ecclesia Gruppe in Detmold.

---

1 Der ärztliche Behandlungsfehler – Eine Fallstudie im Vergleich europäischer Rechtssysteme, auf Englisch veröffentlicht: Springer-Verlag Wien/New York unter dem Titel „Cases on Medical Malpractice in a Comparative Perspective“, ISBN 3-211-83595-4, sowie im Eigenverlag der Gesellschaft für Risiko-Beratung, Detmold, in deutscher Sprache.

Wie haben sich die Systeme entwickelt in den letzten 10 Jahren? Die Diskussion um Arzthaftungsschäden und die Schwierigkeit der Patienten, Kompensation und Genugtuung zu erhalten, ist nach wie vor hoch aktiv. Werden durch die Ärzte und Krankenhäuser wirklich mehr Fehler begangen? Wovon profitieren Patienten mehr, von vollständigem Schadenersatz nach festgestelltem Verschulden oder von Ausgleichssystemen, wie sie in einigen Staaten anzutreffen sind? Wird die Höhe eines zu leistenden Schadenersatzes mit vom politischen Willen einzelner Staaten bestimmt, z. B. bei der Möglichkeit von Regressen der Sozialversicherungsträger?

Prof. Dr. Koziol stellte seinerzeit in Wien fest:

Vom Arzt geht grundsätzlich kein Risiko aus

und sprach sich damit gegen eine verschuldensunabhängige oder Gefährdungs-Haftung aus.

Auf Anregung der GRB – Gesellschaft für Risiko-Beratung mbH, Detmold, die für die Ecclesia Gruppe schon über 120 000 Arzthaftpflichtschäden in Deutschland ausgewertet und lehrbar gemacht hat – ist die jetzt vorliegende Studie entstanden, die ihre Erhebung auf 13 Länder erweitert hat und auch Aufschluss über die tatsächlichen Rechtsverhältnisse, Gesundheitssysteme und vorliegenden Erfahrungen in den einzelnen Ländern gibt. Nur vor dem politischen, sozialen und tatsächlich rechtlichem Hintergrund sind Entscheidungen verständlich, mit denen die Bevölkerung und damit auch die Patienten im Übrigen ja schon lange leben. Die Frage, ob die Systeme verbesserungswürdig sind, kann nur in den Ländern selbst entschieden werden. Ganz herzlich danken wir Herrn Prof. Dr. Bernhard A. Koch, Universität Innsbruck, der mit den einzelnen Länderreferenten die Studie für das European Centre of Tort and Insurance Law, Wien, erstellt hat und selbst den österreichischen Länderbericht sowie die zusammenfassende vergleichende Beschreibung gefertigt hat. Wir bedanken uns aber auch bei Franz-Michael Petry, Ecclesia Gruppe Detmold, der das gesamte Werk inhaltlich und fachlich begleitete, wieder die Fragen mit identifizierte und selbst den Länderbericht Deutschland verfasste.

Die Studie ist eine wichtige Arbeit und eine Entscheidungsgrundlage in der politischen Diskussion. Arbeiten wir gemeinsam fachkundig an der Weiterentwicklung der Systeme – vielleicht ist dann in 10 Jahren der Bedarf nach einer weiteren Überarbeitung geben.

Detmold, im Juni 2011

Manfred Klocke

CEO Ecclesia Versicherungsdienst GmbH

Preface

In 2001, the European Centre of Tort and Insurance Law (ECTIL) published its very first book entitled 'Cases on Medical Malpractice in a Comparative Perspective' edited by Michael Faure and Helmut Koziol. It contained the outcome of a research project undertaken at the initiative of Ecclesia Versicherungsdienst GmbH and the Deutsche Krankenhausgesellschaft. Six actual cases were analysed from the perspective of nine different jurisdictions, coupled with an economic as well as a comparative analysis of key issues. At least one aim of the project at the time was to identify potential deficiencies of German law in this field.

Ten years later, ECTIL was approached by Ecclesia again and asked to produce an update to this first study, though with some differences. The list of jurisdictions covered was amended and expanded, and the task now was no longer to evaluate the German legal system in comparison to other countries, but rather to put all thirteen countries selected into perspective. While the original idea of working on the basis of hypothetical cases was maintained in order to again provide a more practice-oriented approach, this time the sponsors and the project leader agreed that a theoretical perspective should also be added. Therefore, in contrast to the previous volume, country reporters in this present study first address a series of general points before turning to the case analyses. With the exception of one case that was already used in 2001, five new hypothetical cases, again inspired by actual lawsuits, have been selected for the purpose of this research in order to address further facets of medical liability. The range goes from obstetrics to paediatrics, from orthopaedics to surgery, addressing classic malpractice as well as informed consent issues and such diverse problems as wrongful conception and infections.

As mentioned, this follow-up project was also initiated and financed by Ecclesia Versicherungsdienst GmbH. The cooperation with its CEO Manfred Klocke and his team, in particular Hendrik Dammann and Franz Michael Petry, has been as pleasant as before. Both ECTIL and I would like to take the opportunity of this preface to express our sincere gratitude for such exemplary support of our research work.

At the occasion of concluding this research endeavour with the publication of its outcome, I would like to thank all authors for participating and for providing us with such knowledgeable insight into their respective jurisdiction. Several individuals have provided assistance at various stages of this project, including in particular Colm McGrath and Petra Pipkova, who has also produced the index to this book. Fiona Salter-Townshend, Donna Stockenhuber and Emma Witbooi have taken care of proof-reading the contributions as perfectly as always. Kathrin Karner-Strobach has checked the citation and style uniformity also for this volume. I am particularly grateful to all of them for their support in bringing about this volume.

The contributions were finalised in February 2011. Developments thereafter could no longer be taken into account.

Bernhard A Koch

Innsbruck, March 2011

Table of Contents

List of Contributors

Ewa Bagińska
Nicolaus Copernicus University, Torun, Poland

Suzanne Carval
University of Le Havre, France

Ondřej Dostál
Charles University, Prague, Czech Republic

Esther Engelhard
Utrecht University, the Netherlands

Massimo Foglia
University of Bergamo, Italy

Ivo Giesen
Utrecht University, the Netherlands

Bernhard A Koch
University of Innsbruck, Austria

Miquel Martín-Casals
University of Girona, Spain

Attila Menyhárd
ELTE Faculty of Law, Budapest, Hungary

Philip Mielnicki
Stockholm University, Sweden

Herman Nys
Katholieke Universiteit Leuven, Belgium

Franz Michael Petry
Ecclesia Versicherungsdienst GmbH, Detmold, Germany

WV Horton Rogers
University of Nottingham, United Kingdom

Alessandro P Scarso
Università Bocconi, Milan, Italy

Mårten Schultz
Uppsala University, Sweden

Ruth Sefton-Green
Université Paris 1 Panthéon-Sorbonne, France

Josep Solé
University of Girona, Spain

Corinne Widmer Lüchinger
University of Basel, Switzerland

Questionnaire

General Questions

A. The Health Care System Framework

I. General Introduction

1. Please describe your health care system in broad overview, focusing in particular on the role of public and/or private hospitals, the availability of one or more national health care provider(s), as well as other general features which may have an impact on the way medical malpractice cases are being treated in your jurisdiction.

II. Social Welfare Provision

2. What role is played by public health care provision in your jurisdiction? How is it organised, and how do patients receive medical treatment (by way of individual contracts with practitioners/hospitals, by way of assignment through the social security carrier, ...)?

3. If something goes wrong in the course of (at least partially) publicly funded medical treatment, are the patient's claims handled differently in comparison to other personal injury cases? What internal review/claims management systems, if any, are there in your national social security system?

4. If another social welfare agency contributes to the care or well-being of a patient who has suffered harm in the course of medical treatment, does it have a right of recourse against those providing the treatment? Do your social welfare agencies actually exercise this right of recourse in practice, or are there limitations?

III. Private Insurance

5. What is the role of private health insurance in your country, particularly in comparison with public health care provision? Do private health insurers have a right of recourse against medical professionals or institutions whose services have caused harm to patients?

6. Are doctors, hospitals and/or others required to take out liability insurance? Can you give some details on the liability insurance market for medical professionals and institutions in your jurisdiction?

IV. Professional Standards

7. What professional standards apply to the medical profession and the provision of medical services in your jurisdiction? Do they describe the standard of care more generally, with reference to some national or international regimes, and/or with a higher degree of detail? How are violations of such standards treated if they lead to harm?

8. Are your doctors and/or hospitals required to adhere to some quality and/or risk management systems? Are there mandatory certification procedures in your jurisdiction?

B. Tort Liability

9. Please describe very briefly the fundamentals of tort liability in your jurisdiction, focusing primarily on aspects which have specific importance in cases of medical malpractice beyond those addressed specifically below.

10. In medical malpractice cases, who has the burden of proving:

(a) a loss (ie the patient's deterioration in health)?

(b) causation?

(c) fault?

11. How does your jurisdiction deal with problems of uncertain causation, eg if it is unclear whether the patient's situation deteriorated because of the treatment or in the ordinary course of his or her pre-existing condition? What if it is unclear which member of a hospital's staff caused the loss?

12. Is the loss of a chance of recovery recognised as a separately compensable type of harm in your jurisdiction?

13. In cases where more than one individual was involved in the provision of medical services to the patient, who is liable for whom and in what circumstances? Is the hospital liable for its staff, and if so, can the patient still sue an individual staff members nevertheless? If a private doctor performs surgery in a hospital, is he liable for (a) the hospital's staff who assist in the operation and/or (b) those who take care of the patient before or after the operation (such as nurses)?

14. Are there any strict liability regimes in force in your jurisdiction which apply to any aspect of medical liability (eg the use of certain technical equipment or to infections incurred while in a hospital, blood transfers, pharmaceuticals, etc)? To what extent do these regimes deviate from the general law of delict?

C. Contractual Liability

15. Do patients receive medical services on a contractual basis? If so, with whom do they enter into a contract? What is the impact of the social welfare regime on their relationship with medical professionals or hospitals? Are there specific features of contracts in the health care sector that distinguish them from ordinary private law contracts?

16. If patients are injured in the course of medical treatment offered on a contractual basis, are their compensation claims treated differently from claims based on (general) tort law, eg when it comes to the burden of proof or to the standard of due care? Can they choose between contractual and delictual liability as a basis for their claims?

17. If patients do not themselves contract with the doctor or hospital, can they nevertheless base a claim on the violation of contractual duties between (eg) the hospital and the doctor, or between a social welfare agency and the doctor?

18. Is the doctrine of informed consent of any relevance for medical malpractice claims in your jurisdiction? If so, please give details on its definition and scope as well as its practical importance.

D. Public Liability

19. In case your jurisdiction treats cases differently if they occur in public hospitals or in some public health care context, what are the key differences from cases involving private hospitals or doctors?

E. Alternative compensation regimes

20. Are there any funds and/or other alternative compensation regimes in your jurisdiction which offer at least partial compensation to victims of medical malpractice? How are they organised, and how do they interact with the liability regime(s) just outlined?

F. Extent of Liability/Remedies

I. Pecuniary loss

21. Please describe very briefly how pecuniary loss is being indemnified in your jurisdiction in general tort cases, and how compensation is calculated. Are there any deviations from these general rules in cases of medical malpractice?

22. Are only loss of earnings indemnified based on actual (or expected) income or also loss of earning capacity without reference to any actual employment (in particular in case of students/trainees/homemakers/…)?

23. Are losses indemnified on a periodic basis or by lump sum?

24. Are there caps on the amounts available as compensation, or thresholds (minimum damage)?

II. Non-pecuniary loss

25. Please describe very briefly how pain and suffering and/or loss of amenities and other types of non-pecuniary loss are indemnified in your jurisdiction in general, and how compensation is calculated. (Please also quote the maximum amount you are aware of that was attributed so far in your country.) Are there any deviations from these general rules in cases of medical malpractice?

26. Who can claim compensation for non-pecuniary loss in your jurisdiction? Only the direct victim or also relatives and/or other indirect victims? Can the latter get compensation for the mere fact of their bereavement if the direct victim has died? If the direct victim has survived, can third parties claim compensation because of the effect on them of the direct victim's injuries?

G. Procedural Matters

27. Are there any specific rules of jurisdiction or procedure which apply to medical malpractice cases?

28. Are there any special institutions handling malpractice claims (at least temporarily) out of court? Who pays for them, and how are they organised?

H. Outlook

29. Are there any plans for a reform of medical liability in your jurisdiction, eg with a view to the introduction of strict liability, no-fault or other alternative regimes?

Cases

Please give analyses from your own jurisdiction's perspective of the following case hypotheticals, whose facts are based on actual court cases in Germany. You may of course rely on cross-references to your replies to the general questions above wherever suitable.

Case 1[1]

A and B had a joint gynaecological practice and both were also affiliated doctors in a hospital run by C. A and B also always stood in for each other whenever one of them was away, in particular on holidays.

X was attended by B in the joint practice during her pregnancy with twins. On 24 February 1989, X was admitted to C's hospital because of preterm

1 Based on OLG München 20. 6. 2002, 1 U 3930/96, OLGR München 2003, 269–270.

contractions and treated by B and other doctors with intravenous tocolysis. On 15 March 1989, A took over X's treatment acting as a locum for B during his holiday.

On 17 March 1989, the midwife D, who was employed by C, took a CTG starting at 6:35am, the results of which were so abnormal that she ought to have sent for a doctor immediately. However, she only informed A by telephone at 7:20am. A did then come around briefly but did not take the medical action required at this point in time. Instead he immediately thereafter treated another patient although there was no necessity for him to do so. During his subsequent round of the patients at 8:30am, he should have carried out further investigations on the basis of said CTG and ordered a caesarean section; he omitted however to do so. At 9:40am X was transferred to the delivery room, where A also appeared at 10:00am. At 10:06am, Y was born with Apgar scores of 1, 2 and 5. Y's twin brother was subsequently delivered stillborn.

Y suffers from serious, permanent impairments, in particular spastic tetraplegy (paralysis of all four limbs), central hypotension (muscular atony) as well as optic atrophy with extensive visual impairment (blindness). Y cannot sit on her own or stand or walk. She must be fed. She suffers from secondary damage like deformation of the spine. She also has a cognitive disability, in particular she is unable to speak. Y lives in her parents' household and is looked after there by day by professional nursing staff. The associated costs are nonetheless greater than if Y lived in a care home. X looks after her in particular during the night and at weekends.

It cannot be ascertained whether, prior to the events which happened around the time of her birth, Y already had a pre-existing problem which could at least partially have contributed to her present condition. While it is probable that a considerable part of her impairments happened before the delivery, it is also possible that A and D's conduct were the sole cause of Y's impairments.

Y seeks an order for A, B and C to pay for the pecuniary damage sustained up until now and which will be sustained in the future as a result of the alleged mistakes in treatment during the pregnancy and the birth, insofar as such has not been passed on to the social insurance agencies or other third parties. Furthermore, she seeks damages for non-pecuniary loss from the defendants.

X seeks an award of compensation for the care that she herself provides to Y, assessed according to the standard wage of a qualified nurse, as well as damages for her own non-pecuniary loss from the distress arising from the stillbirth of her son and the serious damage sustained by her daughter Y.

Case 2[2]

The gynaecologist A gave his patient X at her own wish and at her own expense the long-acting contraceptive implant 'Implanon' in January 2002. This is a plastic tube about 3mm wide and a few centimetres long, which is inserted under the skin above the inside of the elbow. In July 2002, A diagnosed that X was in the 16th week of pregnancy. It was no longer possible to locate the 'Implanon' implant and its active agent could no longer be detected in X's blood.

X was unable to take on a position she had been offered because of the pregnancy and having to care for the child. Y, the father of the child, who the plaintiff had known for about half a year at the time of the conception, acknowledged paternity. However, he does not live with the plaintiff. He fulfils his maintenance payment obligations towards their son Z.

X now seeks compensation from A for the damage sustained up until now and which will be sustained in the future as a result of the parental obligation to support the child both in her own right and on the basis of the assigned right of the father Y.

Case 3[3]

X was born on 26 August 1997 in the hospital run by A. About two to three hours after his birth, a blood sugar test was carried out and the results were under the norm threshold. After sugar had been administered orally and two control tests were carried out, X was discharged after about 8 hours.

X ought definitely to have been classified as a high-risk newborn at his birth. He should, therefore, not have been discharged at a few hours old, even subsequent to the short-term pickup in his blood sugar level due to the oral glucose. In the year 1997 it had long been established paediatric knowledge that overweight children with hypoglycaemia need to have

2 Based on BGH 14.11.2006, VI ZR 48/06, VersR 2007, 109.

3 Based on HansOLG Bremen 13.1.2006, 4 U 23/05, OLGR Bremen 2006, 745–748 = MedR 2007, 660–663.

their sugar levels monitored for a minimum of 24 hours. Because of the serious long-term effects which failure to treat such hypoglycaemia has for the child, the obstetrician who attends babies directly after the birth must also be familiar with the condition. It is not necessary for him to know in detail how to treat it but he is under a duty to seek the advice of a paediatrician.

In this case, however, no paediatrician examined the child and neither X's mother nor her midwife B were informed of the necessity to monitor his blood sugar level.

B took over the care of X in his mother's home. She visited him still on the 26 August 1997 and after his mother told her of the hypoglycaemia after the delivery, she recommended that he be given tea with grape sugar and she also gave him a homeopathic sedative the next day. On the basis of her education and experience as a midwife and independently of any references from the birth clinic, B ought to have recognised the risk posed to X and have acted accordingly without delay. She should have sought the advice of a paediatrician by the afternoon of 27 August at the latest.

On the morning of the 28 August the parents went to the paediatric clinic run by C because X looked as if he was dead; they arrived at 8:30am.

In C's clinic there was neither a consultant in attendance nor were there any directions as to when either the nurse handling admissions or a doctor who was still inexperienced had to call in an experienced doctor. There were not even any directions that or whether the nurse handling admissions had to call on a doctor at all. Neither were there any binding regulations to the effect that a detailed case history (questioning of the mother) had to be carried out and recorded, that the child be thoroughly examined or that a consultant then be brought in within a reasonable length of time. Moreover, in the case of alarming findings, valuable time should not be wasted as in this case with having to phone around to see which ward could admit the child before treatment could be started.

In the absence of such organisational structure, it happened that more than one and a half hours passed from when the child and his parents reached the hospital to when X had his first blood sugar level check and blood gas analysis. In these first one and a half hours, the nurse handling admissions, D, only initiated a breast-feeding attempt. An exact case history was not taken by the inexperienced doctor E, who arrived at about 9:00am in admissions. Questioning the mother could have led quickly to a complete diagnosis. Without having documented such a detailed case history, E proceeded to only organise the first examination at about

10:00am; however she clearly did not believe the alarming result. The very first recording of a blood sugar test in the documentation of the case was at 10:25am. At this point in time, the child had a serious hypoglycaemia of 17 mg/dl, on re-check 20 mg/dl (a usual result would be 40–45 ml/dg). Yet despite this, still no immediate action was taken. X was only admitted to a ward after 11:00am, where he was finally examined by a consultant physician. According to the patient's file, the next acid-base status was not evaluated until 11:15am. Shortly thereafter, X suffered cardiac arrest during the consultant's attempt to place an IV line and had to be resuscitated. Ever since then X has been severely disabled. He cannot perform any targeted movements and can only communicate at the basic level. In addition, he is practically sightless.

Even in the year 1997 such an organisational structure fell below the medical standard for a full-service hospital such as the C clinic. Evaluation of the condition of a newborn baby who has been brought in by his parents without a doctor's referral cannot be left solely in the hands of a nurse handling admissions, even if said nurse is experienced. Equally, the fact that the child was not immediately examined by a doctor and no precise medical history was taken and documented failed to meet the required standard. Moreover, it ought to have been ensured that a doctor on duty, who was inexperienced, be required to secure a specialist's standard of care for the final assessment of the patient's condition. Those responsible for the organisational structure of the medical service may not rely on an admissions nurse, even when experienced, to reliably recognise the health problems of a newborn brought in without a doctor's referral. If the clinic cannot be attended at all times by an experienced doctor who can attain the required standard of care, there must be directions requiring that a child at least be examined thoroughly and a detailed medical history taken. Then, the advice of an experienced doctor must still be sought.

Even in the event that there was pre-existing damage to X's brain by the time he had arrived in the paediatric clinic, it is no longer possible to establish the extent of such damage. The longer hypoglycaemia is allowed to continue, the higher the risk of such damage. In retrospect it is no longer possible to establish what degree of damage had already been sustained and to what extent more damage was sustained during X's treatment in the C clinic. On the basis of how things continued it can be assumed with a very high degree of probability that the organic damage was sustained in the C clinic.

X seeks compensation from the defendants A, B, C and E on the basis of joint and several liability for all damage sustained up until now and which will be sustained in the future and which is a result of the care provided in the aftermath of his birth from 26 August until 28 August 1997. Besides the costs of nursing care and the expenses caused by his increased needs, he seeks compensation for his prospective loss of capacity to earn in the amount of € 2,000 per month (as of his 21st year of life capitalised until his 65th year of life). Additionally, he seeks compensation from the defendants for non-pecuniary loss.

Case 4[4]

The Iranian citizen X came to live in the Federal Republic of Germany in April 1987, at which time he did not speak German, his mother tongue is Persian. Four months later it was also not possible to communicate with him through English.

X was referred on 9 June 1987 to the neurosurgical department of A clinic, subsequent to treatment as an in-patient in another hospital because of problems over a long period of time including severe pains in his legs and an occasional weakness of the right leg. In the clinic, a disease of the spinal cord (myelopathy) with transverse spinal cord symptoms was diagnosed and an operation recommended.

In the course of his examination upon admission to the A clinic on 9 June, a weakness of the right leg when going up stairs was noted. After he had been examined comprehensively, surgery to treat a process which was causing the compression of the bone marrow was proposed.

On 24 June 1987, X and B, a doctor who worked at the A clinic, signed a form for 'consent to a medical procedure'. This included inter alia the declaration 'I have been informed that it is intended that the above-mentioned procedure be performed on me, about the type, purpose and manner of proceeding as well as about its main advantages and disadvantages and the risks also in comparison to other methods of examination/treatment/operation and I was informed orally/by the leaflet … with respect to the option of not carrying out the procedure … Particular problems of mine were discussed in detail, especially *infection, deterioration, paralysis, secondary bleeding*.' The words in italics were added in handwriting by B. This doctor had already noted in his admissions report: 'The case

4 Based on OLG Oldenburg 25.6.1996, 5 U 170/95, VersR 1997, 978 = ArztR 1997, 205

history was taken through the patient's interpreter. The patient himself can hardly speak German'. It could not, however, be established whether and how B had used a Persian dictionary during his talk with X. In any case, no interpreter was present during this consultation with the patient.

If X had been informed in a manner understandable to him about the risk of paralysis associated with the operation, he would have found himself in a state of conflict as to the decision and would probably not have had surgery at all. His symptoms were not so serious as to make an operation absolutely necessary.

On 25 June 1987, the operation was carried out by the surgeon C as a laminectomy of the 9th and 10th thoracic vertebrae. Alternative to the dorsal approach which was selected for the operation, it would also have been possible to make a transthoracic opening (through the breastplate). Both paths of access are possible from a medical point of view. Both involved a risk of death as well as of paralysis. The risk of death is higher in the case of the transthoracic opening. However, in the case of the dorsal approach the risk of paralysis is higher. The fact that there was a choice of these two approaches was, however, not discussed in the preoperative consultation.

After the operation, X suffered complete paralysis of the lower extremities accompanied also by almost complete loss of sensitivity and a bladder/rectum malfunction. The operation led to complete motor and vegetative paralysis with partially retained sensitivity. X can no longer control his anal sphincter muscle. He can no longer perform intentional movements with either of his legs. There is a definite loss of sensitivity below the level of the navel; the right side is worse affected. X will need a wheelchair for the rest of his life. He is henceforth dependent on care and assistance in many areas of life.

Nonetheless X, who was 47 when he underwent the surgery, already suffered from myelopathy with paralysis symptoms. As of the 9th thoracic vertebra, the pyramidal pathways and the posterior bundle were most affected. While this myelopathy did not continually restrict his movement, his well-being had been seriously impacted during the five years prior to the operation. He had also had to use crutches sometimes. Without an operation this state would at the least have remained unchanged.

X seeks inter alia compensation from A and C for the conversion of his house to provide wheelchair access, for the purchase of a new car with wheelchair access and for additional increased needs arising from his paralysis. Moreover, he also seeks appropriate damages for non-pecuniary loss.

Case 5[5]

X underwent surgery in a hospital operated by A because of fractures. Directly after the operation, X had pain and numbness in the left side of the hand and in the area of the fourth and fifth finger. He suffered damage to the nervus ulnaris and consequently had restricted movement in the left hand. He was no longer able to pursue his occupation as a bricklayer.

During the three-hour operation, X was placed in a supine position, his arms were cushioned and secured so that they did not stick out. The damaged arm was turned to his back, laid on a splint with a standard rubber cushioning, which was splayed out at an angle of 90 degrees to the patient's body.

According to an agreement between the national professional association of anaesthetists and the professional association of surgeons, the positioning of the patient on the OP-table during and after the operation as well as the monitoring of the positioning is the responsibility of the surgeon and the anaesthetist. The actual positioning is, in principle, the surgeon's responsibility. He must instruct the nursing staff on how to position the patient and equally, he must check such positioning before beginning the operation. The anaesthetist must point out any errors to the operating surgeon. The anaesthetist, on the other hand, is responsible for the positioning of those extremities which he requires for the monitoring and administration of the anaesthetic, infusions and medication, ie also for X's arm in this case. Equally, the anaesthetist must monitor the positioning of the extremities during the operation. While the patient is under the anaesthetic, the anaesthetist must observe the positioning and communicate any eventual change in position to the operating surgeon.

The surgeon B states that he was only able to make observations directly before the operation. Thereafter, his view of the patient's arm was blocked by the surgical drape, which is why B was unable to see any eventual changes in position.

---

5 Based on OLG Köln 2.4.1990, 27 U 140/88, VersR 1991, 696.

It has been established that the damage to the nervus ulnaris could not have occurred as a direct result of the positioning at the beginning of the operation but can only have been sustained due to compression during the operation, which moreover must have lasted for some time. It is not possible to establish whether the arm was so unpropitiously positioned, partly because there is no corresponding reference in the documentation of the operation. Furthermore, it cannot be established whether the anaesthetist C monitored the proper positioning of the arm on a sufficiently cushioned abduction splint during the long operation, taking into consideration the shaking of the body caused by the surgical procedure, in order to make sure it was positioned so as not to suffer any damage. C was an intern at the point in time of the operation and was only three months into her residency. The responsible chief resident D had to supervise procedures in six operating theatres at the same time as X's operation and thus only appeared once an hour to check on anaesthetist C.

Besides damages for non-pecuniary loss, X seeks compensation from A and its employees B, C and D for his loss of income, including the loss of income from moonlighting at the weekend. He refuses to consider retraining as a sales person in a building supplies store.

Apart from that, X wants to be awarded the costs for a private medical injuries assessment which he commissioned from an 'institute for the assessment of medical injuries' to clarify the facts. He could have had the facts evaluated free of charge by an assessment commission at the medical council.

Case 6[6]

In June 1999, X went to A and B's joint orthopaedic practice, in which C and D worked as locums at the time. C gave X an injection in the neck area on 9 and 11 June 1999, D did the same on 15 June 1999.

In the aftermath, a syringe abscess developed, making it necessary for X to be treated as an in-patient for two weeks. The syringe abscess derived from a staphylococcus infection. The infection originated from the medical assistant E employed by A and B, who was suffering from hay fever at the time and assisted with the administration of the injections. Other patients at the practice acquired similar infections during the same time period,

---

6 Based on BGH 20.3.2007, VI ZR 158/06, NJW 2007, 1682 = VersR 2007, 847 (cmt *Jungbecker*) = BGHZ 171, 358 = MDR 2007, 951 = ArztR 2008, 153.

the first cases were on 2, 8 and 10 June 1999. It is not possible to establish whether it would have been possible for the doctors to recognise the staphylococcus infection of the medical assistant E.

An investigation by the Health Authority in mid-June 1999 revealed that the hygiene standards in the doctors' practice for the medical assistants were not communicated and supervised by the doctors to the extent necessary. Disinfectants were not kept in their original containers but moved to others. Vials with substances for injection were used over several days. Furthermore, disinfectants for working surfaces, which had a long exposure time, were wrongly used as disinfectant for skin. Additionally, it was not usual for the medical assistants to disinfect their hands before drawing up a syringe and working surfaces were not disinfected every day as required but only once a week.

X was the manager of a catering business and initially resumed this work. However, as she suffers ongoing pain, insomnia and depressive moods as a result of the syringe abscess, she is unable to work. Besides appropriate damages for non-pecuniary loss, she seeks compensation from A, B, C, D and E for her pecuniary damage, in particular also costs for cleaning assistance. However, since the infection her daughter has been helping her with household tasks, which she performs for her mother in addition to her own.

Variation 1: The carrier of the bacteria cannot be identified. It could have been the medical assistant E, another patient in the waiting room or someone who accompanied patient X.

Variation 2: No hygiene shortfalls in the doctors' practice can be proved, the usual standards were observed.

Medical Liability in Austria

Bernhard A Koch

General Questions

A. The Health Care System Framework

I. General Introduction[1]

1. The health care system in overview[2]

In the federal system of Austria, the competence to ensure public health 1
care is split between the federation and the nine *Länder* (provinces). While public health as such generally falls under the legislative and executive competence of the federation, this is only true for sanitary supervision when it comes to hospitals and other health care institutions (Art 10 para 1 no 12 of the Federal Constitution, B-VG).[3] For the latter, legislation only as regards principles is the business of the federation, whereas the issue of implementing laws and execution remains the business of the *Länder* (Art 12 para 1 no 1 B-VG).

There is no national health care provider comparable to the English NHS. 2
Instead, there are independent hospitals and other health care institutions that are paid at least in part via the social insurance scheme.[4]

---

1 When citing a decision of the Austrian Supreme Court (*Oberster Gerichtshof*, OGH) or other courts below, apart from its date and publication the case number will also be given in order to allow retrieval of the full original text at <http://www.ris.bka.gv.at/Judikatur>, where it can be entered under '*Geschäftszahl*'. If the option '*Rechtssätze* (RS)' is marked on this search form (as it is by default), the key rulings will show first, with all other decisions following them listed.
If only the case number is cited below, no publication of the decision could be found.

2 See also Bundesministerium für Gesundheit (ed), The Austrian Health Care System. Key Facts (2010, available at <http://bmg.gv.at/cms/home/attachments/3/4/4/CH1066/CMS1291414949078/the_austrian_health_care_system_2010_e1.pdf>)

3 With the exception of military and prison hospitals (3.8 % of all Austrian hospitals).

4 On the latter, see infra question 2.

3 The division between public and private hospitals is not so easy to make in Austria because it depends upon a combination of ownership and status criteria. As to the latter, one distinguishes between hospitals with public law status and those for public benefit. According to the Federal Hospitals Act (*Bundesgesetz über Krankenanstalten und Kuranstalten,* KAKuG), the latter do not necessarily have public law status, but at least operate on a non-profit basis and admit any patient for whom they can provide the appropriate treatment with adequate means (§ 16 KAKuG, around 12.5 % of all hospitals). They may be granted public law status if they meet the conditions of the provincial plan for hospitals (*Landeskrankenanstaltenplan*) and some further statutory requirements (§ 15 KAKuG, almost half of all hospitals). Around 40 % of all Austrian hospitals fall under neither of these two categories because they are run for profit. All this is independent from the type of ownership,[5] so there are privately owned hospitals which have public law status just as there are provincial or municipal hospitals which do not.[6]

4 Hospitals for public benefit, with or without public law status, are financed by the provincial health funds (*Landesgesundheitsfonds*; this applies to roughly half of all Austrian health care institutions), whereas private hospitals run for profit (around 16.3 % of all Austrian health care institutions) can draw monies from the private hospitals fund (*Privatkrankenanstalten-Finanzierungsfonds,* PRIKRAF), which serves as a kind of clearing house between private hospitals and the social insurance providers. The latter pay into the fund according to the services provided by these hospitals and determined eligible by the fund administration according to the same DRG-based funding system (*leistungsorientierte Krankenanstaltenfinanzierung* or in short LKF[7]) that applies to the afore-mentioned institutions which are directly publicly funded. Finally, long-term care or

5 Apart from the federal hospitals mentioned in fn 3, 33 % of all hospitals are owned by the provinces, 7.6 % by municipalities, 15.2 % directly by social insurance providers, 15.5 % by religious orders or congregations, and 25 % are owned by private persons or companies: *Bundesministerium für Gesundheit, Familie und Jugend,* Krankenanstalten in Österreich (7th edn 2008, <http://www.bmg.gv.at/cms/site/attachments/6/9/9/CH0786/CMS1039007503101/ka-verzeichnis_2008_gesamt_internet.pdf>) 21.

6 Krankenanstalten in Österreich (fn 5) 20 f.

7 *Bundesministerium für Gesundheit und Frauen,* Die Funktionsweise des österreichischen LKF-Systems (2004, <http://www.bmg.gv.at/cms/site/attachments/1/4/8/CH0718/CMS1098272734729/lkf-broschuere_internet.pdf>); see also for a comparative overview the European Hospital and Healthcare Federation's HOPE Report on DRGs as a Financing Tool (2006, <http://www.bmg.gv.at/cms/site/attachments/3/9/5/CH0721/CMS1182951248070/hope_drg_report_20061.pdf>).

other specialised institutions in particular organise their funding directly with the social insurance providers (about one third of all health care institutions).[8]

Irrespective of status, ownership or funding, all hospitals' relationships with their patients are governed by the same rules for the purpose of this survey. Furthermore, there are no separate courts for public health care providers, and the same procedural rules apply as far as claims of interest here are concerned. 5

Doctors (both general practitioners and specialists) as well as dentists can be approached directly by patients at the latters' free choice. However, most of them tend to select among those doctors who are in a contractual relationship with the patient's social insurance provider[9] which reimburses these practitioners directly (so-called 'Kassenärzte' or contract physicians) without any immediate contribution by the patients themselves. If patients instead see a doctor whose fees are not paid directly by a social insurance provider (so-called 'Wahlarzt' or 'doctor of choice'[10]), or if they enter into a special contractual agreement with a 'Kassenarzt' for preferential[11] or additional treatment otherwise not covered by their health plan, the doctor will bill the patients directly who in turn will have to seek (typically only partial) reimbursement from their (social and/or private) health insurer. These latter patients are referred to as 'Privatpatienten' (private patients). 6

Most doctors practice on their own. Apart from sharing space and/or equipment while retaining independence, they may now instead team up in a so-called 'group practice' (*Gruppenpraxis*), which may also be established as a limited liability company since 2010. 7

All doctors are mandatory members of one of the nine provincial Medical Chambers (*Landesärztekammer*), who in turn constitute the Austrian Medical 8

8 Krankenanstalten in Österreich (fn 5) 18 f, 21.

9 This relationship is actually tripartite, as the contract with the social insurance provider is concluded by the competent Medical Chamber, which in turn selects those among its members who may benefit from this arrangement. About one third of Austria's physicians practising on their own are 'Kassenärzte'. See The Austrian Health Care System (fn 2) 14 f.

10 This does not mean that patients have no choice among the 'Kassenärzte', the choice refers to the reimbursement procedure.

11 In the case of specialists or dentists, this means in particular that appointments will be much sooner than with regular patients of this 'Kassenarzt', which makes a substantial difference for those specialisations where doctors tend to have a long waiting list for non-acute patients.

Chamber (*Österreichische Ärztekammer*).[12] Dentists are united in the Austrian Dentists Chamber (*Österreichische Zahnärztekammer*). These chambers represent the interests of their members and are in charge, inter alia, of organising their training.

9 Apart from courts of law, Austrian doctors are also answerable to the disciplinary commission in their region, which operates under the supervision of the disciplinary council of the Austrian Medical Chamber (§§ 135 ff *Ärztegesetz,* Act on the Medical Profession). A rather vague statutory provision defines disciplinary offences as any conduct which may adversely affect the reputation of Austrian doctors, or any violation of professional duties (§ 136 *Ärztegesetz*). As express examples of such misbehaviour, the statute mentions disobedience of a professional ban as well as criminal conduct which has been sanctioned by any national or foreign court with a sentence of at least six months of imprisonment or a minimum fine of 360 daily rates (or exceeding € 36,340). Apart from temporary injunctions, possible sanctions range from written reprimands to a permanent ban on practising medicine. If a doctor works for a legal entity of public law, only the disciplinary rules for civil servants apply (to the exclusion of the afore-mentioned provisions of the *Ärztegesetz*). Unfortunately (or fortunately for the doctors concerned), decisions of the disciplinary commissions are not publicised, so their impact on liability issues cannot be properly assessed.

II. Social Welfare Provision

2. The role of public health care

10 99 % of all Austrians are currently covered by social insurance, which is organised via several providers installed for different groups of the workforce and the self-employed.[13] The regime is financed by contributions from

---

12 These institutions are to some extent comparable to medical boards or associations. They are organised under public law, both on the provincial as well as on the national level; §§ 65 et ff *Ärztegesetz*) and intended to 'safeguard and enhance the common professional, social, and economic interests of medical pracitioners, including professional associations of medical practitioners, as well as to ensure the protection of the professional honour and the professional duties of medical practitioners' (§ 66 subs 1 *Ärztegesetz*).

13 There are 19 social health insurance providers: one each for the self-employed, for farmers, for civil servants, one for employees of the Austrian railways and the mining industry, six occupational health insurance funds, and for the general workforce not falling under one of the specialised providers one health insurance fund for each of the nine provinces.

the insured, who cannot choose among the various providers, but are assigned to one (or more) of them according to their professional status or other statutorily defined characteristics. In case of employees also their employers pay a certain share. Needless to say, the state has to co-finance the system (currently up to 13 %), which it takes from general tax monies.[14]

Social health insurance provides benefits irrespective of the cause triggering the need for treatment, therefore also in cases of bodily harm tortiously inflicted by a third person.[15] In such a case, the victim's tort law claims are assigned by law to the competent social insurance provider.[16] Social health insurance primarily grants benefits in kind in the form of medical treatment by physicians or doctors who are under a contractual relationship with the social insurance provider and are reimbursed directly by the latter.[17] If the insured chooses a medical professional not covered by such a contract, the latter's bills are directly paid by the patient herself who can subsequently seek at least partial reimbursement from the social insurance.[18] Further benefits in kind include medication, therapeutic aids and appliances, hospital and nursing care, and, to a more limited extent, dental treatment.[19] In case of inability to work during an illness and once the employer's duty to continue wage payment has ended, social health insurance also covers a certain percentage (between 50 and 75 %) of the employee's income up to a time limit of 52 weeks (*Krankengeld*).[20] 11

In a medical malpractice scenario, the injured patient will therefore receive treatment as well as other support from her social insurance provider who in most cases will already have covered the initial treatment where something went wrong. 12

---

14 *Hauptverband der österreichischen Sozialversicherungsträger* (ed), Die österreichische Sozialversicherung in Zahlen (25th edn 2010) 9, 13. On the Austrian social insurance system, see eg *W Holzer*, The Interaction of Tort Law and Social Security under Austrian Law, in: U Magnus (ed), Tort Law and Social Law (2003) 7. See also the information leaflet distributed by the Main Association of Austrian Social Security Institutions: Well Insured – Social Security in Austria (2010, available at <http://www.sozialversicherung.at/mediaDB/697831_Gut_versichert_englisch_2010.pdf>).

15 *Holzer* (fn 14) nos 11, 20.

16 Ibid no 13.

17 Certain varieties of social insurance require the insured to pay a certain (rather nominal) contribution per event to the social insurance provider in addition to the monthly premia.

18 Costs exceeding the amount reimbursed may be covered by private health insurance, which therefore allows patients to freely choose from all medical professionals irrespective of their affiliation with a social insurance provider.

19 *K Grillberger*, Österreichisches Sozialrecht (7th edn 2008) 37–39. Certain types of treatment are not covered by social insurance, particularly even rather common varieties of dental treatment such as tooth caps or bridges.

20 *Grillberger* (fn 19) 43–45.

3. Differences in treating patient's claims

13 As a matter of principle, medical malpractice claims are not treated differently in comparison to other personal injury cases. However, there may be certain practical variations due to the specific nature of the tort, eg with respect to determining causation,[21] or in light of the buffers provided by the Medical Chambers and the *Patientenanwaltschaften*.[22] These differences will be addressed below.

4. Right of recourse

14 If someone who has received benefits from a social insurance provider has a legal claim against a third party such as a tortfeasor to recover the monetary equivalent of such benefits, this claim is subrogated by law to the social insurance provider (§ 332 *Allgemeines Sozialversicherungsgesetz*, General Act on Social Insurance or in short ASVG).[23] It seems that recourse actions based on such subrogated claims are taken more systematically nowadays.

15 Hospitals also benefit from a statutory subrogation of their patients' tort claims that arise from the incident triggering the treatment, though of course only to the extent it has not yet been paid otherwise, in particular by a social insurance agency (§ 48 KAKuG).[24]

III. Private Insurance

5. The role of private health insurance

16 About one third of Austrians had taken out (supplementary) private health insurance in 2008,[25] which does not necessarily mean better treatment, but – depending upon the type and scope of policy – benefits such as free choice of doctor as *Privatpatienten* (not limited to those in contract with the

21 See infra at question 10.
22 See infra at question 28.
23 *Holzer* (fn 14) no 13.
24 A possible conflict between social insurance providers and hospitals may arise due to this concurrent subrogation of tort claims; see *P Steiner/G Fleisch*, Zur Legalzession im Krankenanstaltenrecht, Österreichisches Anwaltsblatt (AnwBl) 1998, 614.
25 *Versicherungsverband Österreich*, Jahresbericht 2008 (2009) 133.

patient's social insurance provider) and more pleasant conditions during a hospital stay (upgrade to the so-called *Sonderklasse*).[26]

According to § 67 subs 1 of the Insurance Contract Act (*Versicherungsvertragsgesetz*, VersVG), any claim against a third party that has caused the victim's loss is subrogated by law to the insurer to the extent that the latter has paid out compensation, which shifts the role of the active party, also in medical malpractice cases, to a different player – from the immediate victim to her insurer. **17**

6. Liability insurance

A recent amendment to the *Ärztegesetz*, to the *Zahnärztegesetz* and to the Hospitals Act (KaKUG) introduced the requirement of a liability insurance for all practising doctors, dentists and hospitals, with a minimum cover of € 2 million per incident (§ 52d ÄrzteG, § 26c ZahnärzteG, § 5c KaKUG).[27] Patients and others harmed have a statutory direct claim against the liability insurer of doctors. The *Ärztegesetz* also provides in its § 58a para 2 that the insured can contribute to the objective finding of the facts without risking to thereby violate an obligation under the liability insurance.[28] **18**

Some doctors already have concluded framework contracts with a commercial insurer, as have some professional organisations of specialists.[29] Hospital staff are typically (but not always) covered by their institution's insurance policy.[30] At least so far, doctors do not seem to have a hard time finding insurers on the Austrian market, with plenty of companies willing to underwrite both specific liability or at least combined policies that include cover considerably beyond the statutory limit.[31] Premiums are **19**

26 Patients can opt for treatment by the senior medical staff. Rooms typically have no more than two patients, are better equipped, and there are other conveniences.

27 Minimum annual cover is € 6 million for doctors and dentists, in case of a group practice € 10 million, which also applies to hospitals. This obligation will enter into force in August 2011. Hospitals owned by a public entity need not have such insurance, in which case the victim can sue the hospital's carrier directly (§ 5c para 1 KaKUG).

28 See infra no 102.

29 See the forms available for download at <http://www.dr-rinner.at/Downloads.71.0.html>.

30 See *A Fenyves/Ch Hirsch*, Zur Deckung der Ansprüche aus ‚wrongful life' und ‚wrongful birth' in der Arzthaftpflichtversicherung, Recht der Medizin (RdM) 2000, 10 (16 fn 74).

31 Cf the following quotation from the Ärztemagazin 46/09 (<http://www.aerztemagazin.at/dynasite.cfm?dsmid=101247&dspaid=831299>): 'Es gibt am Markt jede Menge Auswahl an Anbietern, die außerhalb der Rahmenvereinbarungen Einzelverträge im Bereich der Ärztehaftpflicht offerieren.' See also news4docs 02/2008 (<http://mein-doktor.at/n4d 2 2008 netz.pdf>) 14–16.

typically calculated according to the area of expertise (with plastic surgeons, gynaecologists, radiologists, and anaesthetists in the most expensive group) and the professional status (trainee, general practitioner, specialist).[32]

20 If both the hospital and its employed doctors have taken out liability insurance, but from different insurers, and a risk materialises which is covered under both policies (in case of the hospital due to its vicarious liability, in case of the individual doctor due to her personal liability), the insurer who covers the losses of the patient in full can seek recourse from the other according to § 59 para 2 Insurance Contract Act (*Versicherungsvertragsgesetz*, VersVG), corresponding to the ratio of the insured amounts, but only if the loss does not exceed the combined maximum insured amounts.[33]

IV. Professional Standards

7. Applicable professional standards

21 Apart from requiring doctors to pursue continual professional training, the Austrian Act on the Medical Profession refers to professional standards in a rather broad and unspecific way, pointing to medical science and experience in general (Art 49 para 1 *Ärztegesetz*).[34]

22 A 2005 federal statute (*Gesundheitsqualitätsgesetz*, Act on the Quality of Health Services) foresees amongst other measures the development of national quality standards for specific areas. These standards can either be mere guidelines or mandatory by way of federal regulations, violations of which can be sanctioned with administrative fines. So far, however, no such standards have been adopted.[35]

---

32 See the market overview for 2008 in News4Docs 02/2008, 14–16 (available at <http://www.mein-doktor.at/pdf/MD0208n4d_net.pdf>) and a current application example at <http://www.aerzteservice.com/PDF/AS_Haft.pdf>.

33 See eg OGH 17.4.2002, 7 Ob 52/02a, Entscheidungen des österreichischen Obersten Gerichtshofes in Zivil- und Justizverwaltungssachen (SZ) 2002/49.

34 'Ein Arzt … hat sich laufend im Rahmen anerkannter Fortbildungsprogramme der Ärztekammern in den Bundesländern oder der Österreichischen Ärztekammer oder im Rahmen anerkannter ausländischer Fortbildungsprogramme fortzubilden und nach Maßgabe der ärztlichen Wissenschaft und Erfahrung sowie unter Einhaltung der bestehenden Vorschriften und der fachspezifischen Qualitätsstandards das Wohl der Kranken und den Schutz der Gesunden zu wahren.'

35 See the homepage of the competent institution, the Federal Institute for Quality in the Public Health System (*Bundesinstitut für Qualität im Gesundheitswesen*, BIQG), at <http://www.goeg.at/en/Area.html>.

8. Quality and/or risk management systems[36]

The Federal Hospitals Act requires the provinces to foresee adequate quality control measures in their legislation (§ 5b KAKuG). They have implemented this, however, by merely copying the text of said provision into their provincial hospitals statutes with more or less trivial adjustments but without any further qualifications.[37] **23**

Due to recent amendments to the laws governing the medical professions, quality control mechanisms are now mandatory for medical doctors and dentists.[38] The chosen method for both is self-evaluation based on online questionnaires.[39] **24**

There is no mandatory certification procedure, but the market for optional/voluntary certification of doctors seems to be expanding.[40] **25**

In November 2009, a nationwide[41] CIRS pilot project was started, initiated by the Austrian Medical Chamber and the Federal Ministry of Health.[42] **26**

Apart from promoting a checklist for surgical procedures, the Austrian Medical Chamber in association with the Austrian Network for Patient Safety have also just recently launched a campaign to improve communica- **27**

---

36 See, eg, *L-M Marzi/A Leischner/R Kempf*, Integriertes Risikomanagement im Krankenhaus – eine Notwendigkeit? RdM 2008, 68.

37 § 23 Burgenland Hospitals Act; § 24 Carinthia Hospitals Act; § 16c Lower Austrian Hospitals Act (but see eg the report of the Lower Austrian Audit Office at <http://www.landtag-noe.at/service/politik/landtag/LandtagsvorlagenXVI/04/492/38B.pdf>); § 27 Upper Austrian Hospitals Act; § 33 Salzburg Hospitals Act; § 11d Styrian Hospitals Act; § 9b Tyrolean Hospitals Act; § 31 Vorarlberg Hospitals Act; § 15b Viennese Hospitals Act.

38 As to medical doctors, see §§ 49 paras 2a and 2b, 118a–118c *Ärztegesetz*. For dentists, see § 22 *Zahnärztegesetz* (Dentists' Act); §§ 50–52 *Zahnärztekammergesetz* (Act on the Chamber of Dentists).

39 See <http://www.oeqmed.at/> for further details concerning quality control of doctors. The questions they have to answer themselves (!) can be found at <http://www.oeqmed.at/fileadmin/Downloads/Muster_Evaluierungsfragen.pdf>.
In the case of dentists, there are apparently not even random spot checks by external auditors, which evidently raises the question of validity and usefulness: See <http://www.zahnaerztekammer.at/download.php?id=2652>.

40 Cf <http://www.medical-tribune.at/dynasite.cfm?dssid=4170&dsmid=95849&dspaid=736124>.

41 A few other such systems are already operative at a smaller scale. The Austrian Association of Family Doctors (*Österreichische Gesellschaft für Allgemein- und Familienmedizin*) instead promotes the German platform at <http://www.jeder-fehler-zaehlt.de>, see <http://www.oegam.at>.

42 See <http://www.cirsmedical.at>.

tion between patients and medical professionals based upon the model of the Massachusetts Coalition for the Prevention of Medical Errors.[43]

B. Tort Liability

9. Fundamentals of tort liability

28 Tort liability in Austria is traditionally based on fault, as expressed by § 1295 para 1 ABGB: 'Everyone is entitled to demand compensation from the person who did him harm by fault.' Fault presupposes wrongfulness, as indicated by § 1294 ABGB. Furthermore, it is still prevailing opinion in Austria that fault is a subjective concept, so that in principle the personal abilities of the tortfeasor are decisive.[44] However, according to § 1299 ABGB, the conduct of experts has to be assessed according to an objective standard instead, which is crucial for the cases under survey here. Therefore, medical professionals are supposed to have the knowledge and abilities of their peers and have to account for any failure to meet that standard.[45]

29 According to the Austrian Supreme Court (*Oberster Gerichtshof*, OGH), the state of medical science is decisive irrespective of local customary usages that might be lagging behind. A typical formula describing the expected standard may read like the following: 'A doctor has violated his duties of care owed to his patient if he failed to act in accordance with medical science and experience or if he neglected to exercise the usual prudence of a conscientious average doctor in the actual situation. He is not at fault, however, if the method of treatment that he chose is in accordance with the practice of well-respected doctors who are familiar with this method, even if other experts may have chosen a different technique. In such case, the doctor has to take the safest measures according to the state of medical science in order to prevent known risks of such treatment'.[46]

---

43 See <http://www.aerztekammer.at/print.php?type=module&aid=xhtml&id=00000000 0020091209113016> with further links and references.

44 *W Wilburg*, Die Elemente des Schadensrechts (1941) 17, 43 ff; *R Reischauer*, Der Entlastungsbeweis des Schuldners (1975) 201 ff; *H Koziol*, Liability Based on Fault: Subjective or Objective Yardstick? Maastricht Journal 1998, 111 ff.

45 Cf *BA Koch/H Koziol*, Austrian report, in: M Faure/H Koziol (eds), Cases on Medical Malpractice in a Comparative Perspective (2001) 57 (72 f). See also *E Pitzl/G Huber/M Lichtenegger*, Der Sorgfaltsmaßstab des behandelnden Arztes: Wissen, Können und Bemühen', RdM 2007, 4.

46 OGH 25.1.1994, 1 Ob 532/94, SZ 67/9; cf also OGH 16.3.1989, 8 Ob 525/88, SZ 62/53.

In contrast to most legal systems, the extent of compensation depends upon the degree of fault (§ 1324 ABGB): As a general rule, lost profits or non-pecuniary harm must only be compensated if the harm was caused with gross negligence or intent (§§ 1323–1324 ABGB). In cases of bodily injury and therefore in the cases under survey here, however, the degree of fault has hardly any impact upon the range of available remedies: The injurer has to indemnify the costs of medical care and loss of earnings; in addition, she must pay damages for pain and suffering (§ 1325 ABGB). 30

10. Burden of proof

(a) **Damage.** As a general rule, it is up to the claimant to prove the requirements to hold the defendant liable. She therefore has to substantiate not only the medical condition she complains of with sufficient evidence, but also the financial and other implications thereof. However, § 273 ZPO (*Zivilprozessordnung*, Act on Civil Procedure) eases that burden with respect to the amount in dispute if it cannot be proven in every detail or if such proof were unreasonably difficult. In such a case, it is in the judge's discretion to assess the loss in light of the circumstances. 31

(b) **Causation.** As a rule, the patient also needs to convince the court that her (further) injuries or diseases were caused by the defendant hospital or doctor.[47] Prima facie proof suffices, so if the alleged course of events linking proven facts is typical and not unusual, causation is established even if its probability is not considerably high (which is the common standard of proof),[48] but just 'clearly outweighs' the opposite.[49] 32

Courts also tend to waive standard requirements of proving causation if it is evident that something was objectively wrong within the sphere of the defendant, which increased the likelihood of adverse effects upon the patient more than just insignificantly. While the latter has to be established by the claimant,[50] it is up to the defendant to rebut this by proving 33

47 Eg OGH 16.3.1989, 8 Ob 525/88, SZ 62/53; 25.1.1994, 1 Ob 532/94, SZ 67/9; 31.1.1995, 4 Ob 509/95, JBl 1995, 453 (cmt *J Steiner*); 4 Ob 554/95, SZ 68/207.

48 The previous standard of 'probability close to certainty' is no longer valid: Eg OGH 12.12.2007 7 Ob 255/07m, Zivilrecht aktuell (Zak) 2008/212

49 OGH 31.5.1990, 6 Ob 702/89, SZ 63/90; 8.7.1993, 2 Ob 590/92, JBl 1994, 540 (cmt *R Bollenberger*); 12.12.2007 7 Ob 255/07m, Zak 2008/212.

50 OGH 31.5.1990, 6 Ob 702/89, SZ 63/90; 7.8.2007, 4 Ob 137/07m, SZ 2007/122; 4.8.2009, 9 Ob 64/08i, EvBl 2010/9.

'with highest probability' that her misconduct did in fact not cause the patient's loss.[51]

34 Lack of adequate documentation may come to the patient's aid as well: Her contract with a doctor or a hospital undoubtedly obliges them to document at least key aspects of diagnosis and treatment.[52] Furthermore, § 51 *Ärztegesetz*,[53] inter alia, requires doctors to record the 'type and degree of ... diagnostic and therapeutic services' and to preserve such documentation for at least ten years.[54] This provision was at least in part enacted in order to facilitate the patient's proof of causation in cases of damage.[55] Any breach of such a duty can reverse the burden of proof, since a person who acts in violation of the law shall not benefit from such conduct.[56] If there is no documentation of a certain measure, eg information being given to the patient, it is therefore presumed that this did not take place.[57]

35 **(c) Fault.** Apart from damage and causation, the claimant also needs to rebut the presumption of § 1296 ABGB that 'the loss was caused without the fault of another'. However, since fault is a question of law, all the claimant needs to prove are facts to support such a judgment, not fault as such.[58] § 1297 ABGB comes to the rescue inasmuch as it contains a further presumption according to which anyone is expected to possess ordinary skills supporting her diligence and attention.

---

51 Eg OGH 29.1.2008, 1 Ob 138/07m, Zak 2008/244; *T Juen*, Arzthaftungsrecht (2nd edn 2005) 241.

52 OGH 23.5.1984, 1 Ob 550/84, SZ 57/98; 25.1.1994, 1 Ob 532/94, SZ 67/9; 12.8.2004, 1 Ob 139/04d, SZ 2004/122; *Juen* (fn 51) 143 ff, 229 ff with further references.

53 This rule was already included in the predecessor statute of the present 1998 law (§ 22a *Ärztegesetz* 1984).

54 A similar provision is contained in § 10 KAKuG for hospitals, which are required to store their patients' medical history for 30 years.

55 *Juen* (fn 51) 229.

56 *H Koziol*, Der Beweis des natürlichen Kausalzusammenhanges, in: A Koller (ed), Haftpflicht- und Versicherungstagung 1999 (1999) 79 (91). Cf OGH 25.1.1994, 1 Ob 532/94, SZ 67/9: 'If a doctor fails to fully comply with his duty to record the treatment and thereby makes it more difficult for the patient to prove any wrongdoing, such proof will be made easier corresponding to the difficulties caused by the lack of documentation in order to ensure a fair distribution of evidentiary positions in the relationship between doctor and patient.' See also OGH 7.11.1995, 4 Ob 554/95, SZ 68/207; 1.12.1998, 7 Ob 337/98d, RdM 1999/12.

57 Eg OGH 25.1.1994, 1 Ob 532/94, SZ 67/9; 1.12.1998, 7 Ob 337/98d, RdM 1999/12; 16.8.2001, 8 Ob 134/01s, RdM 2002, 27; 20.2.2002, 9 Ob 6/02a; 12.8.2004, 1 Ob 139/04d, SZ 2004/122.

58 *H Koziol*, Österreichisches Haftpflichtrecht I (3rd edn 1997) no 16/15.

The burden of proving fault is reversed according to § 1298 ABGB if the conduct complained of constitutes a breach of a duty arising out of some pre-existing special relationship between the parties, in particular in cases of breach of contract. However, this reversal only applies for plain negligence, whereas gross negligence and intent have to be proven by the claimant.[59] **36**

According to Austrian jurisprudence, § 1298 ABGB also applies to so-called protective laws (*Schutzgesetze*) as addressed by § 1311 ABGB.[60] These are rules of conduct prohibiting specific behaviour because of its general (abstract) dangerousness. While fault otherwise has to take into account the first ensuing loss, in case of a protective law it only needs to extend to its violation (and not the harmful consequences thereof).[61] If a protective law was infringed, proving causation can also be easier – if the loss is of a kind that is to be prevented by the protective law, this is deemed to be prima facie evidence of the causal link.[62] **37**

11. Uncertain causation

Where it is established that the loss must have been caused by either one of two or more external sources, but it remains unclear which of them, an undisputed analogy to §§ 1301 f ABGB foresees joint and several liability for all these alternative causes (irrespective of whether they intervened jointly or independently). This is also true if two causes concur of which each alone would have triggered the full loss (cumulative causation).[63] **38**

59 In case of a contractual exclusion of liability but for gross negligence of the party in breach, the latter has to prove the absence of such qualified fault.

60 This is disputed, however. While courts are in favour, it is denied by leading scholars. See E *Karner*, in: H Koziol/P Bydlinski/R Bollenberger (eds), Kurzkommentar zum ABGB (KBB) (3rd edn 2010) § 1298 nos 3–4; *Koziol* (fn 58) no 16/40.

61 KBB/*Karner* (fn 60) § 1311 nos 3 ff. However, qualified fault (gross negligence or intent) needs to extend to the consequences of the tortfeasor's behaviour even if such has violated a protective law.

62 KBB/*Karner* (fn 60) § 1311 no 6. Particularly older case law tended to go even further, contra *Koziol* (fn 58) nos 16/36 ff.

63 See H *Koziol*, Causation under Austrian Law, in: J Spier (ed), Unification of Tort Law: Causation (2000) 11 (13–15).

39 Austrian courts have adopted[64] a proposal by Franz Bydlinski[65] to split the loss in cases where the defendant may have caused the claimant's injuries, but where another possible cause for the (full) same loss lies in the latter's own sphere. He found support for this in the aforementioned analogy to the provisions on alternative causation read together with § 1304 ABGB (contributory negligence). Since it seems unfair either to let the defendant bear the full risk of liability by (further) lowering standards of proof or to leave the full loss with the claimant, Bydlinski proposed spreading the risk between the two parties according to the ratio of the respective probabilities,[66] but only if it is proven that the defendant violated a duty of care and behaved highly dangerously under the circumstances. Therefore, in the medical liability scenario, if a patient suffers injuries in the course of some treatment and it remains unclear whether this happened due to some precondition of the patient herself or whether these injuries were alternatively caused by the (undisputedly) negligent behaviour of the physician, both sides will have to share this uncertainty and therefore the loss.[67]

40 If it is certain, however, that a precondition of the patient would have led to the same harmful result as the faulty conduct of the doctor, but only at a later point in time (though not too far in the future, but within a reasonable context), the doctor is only held responsible for the fact that such damage has occurred earlier than anticipated under the (now) hypotheti-

---

64 OGH 9.11.1989, 7 Ob 648/89, JBl 1990, 524 (with critical cmt *W Holzer*); cf also OGH 7.5.1985, 2 Ob 544/85, JBl 1986, 576 (cmt *E Deutsch*); 4.6.1993, 8 Ob 608/92, Evidenzblatt der Rechtsmittelentscheidungen (EvBl) 1994/13; 7.11.1995, 4 Ob 554/95, SZ 68/207 (only distribution of the damage ensures 'a solution to the problem which is in accordance with principles of justice'); 12.3.1997, 6 Ob 2144/96d, Recht der Wirtschaft (RdW) 1997, 394; 15.3.2001, 6 Ob 36/01i; 26.7.2006, 3 Ob 106/06v; 28.2.2008, 8 Ob 121/07p ('no longer significant question of law'). Others have initially expressly rejected his theory: OGH 10.10.1991, 6 Ob 604/91, JBl 1992, 522; 8.7.1993, 2 Ob 590/92, JBl 1994, 540 (cmt *R Bollenberger*).

65 Probleme der Schadensverursachung nach deutschem und österreichischem Recht (1964) 86 ff; Aktuelle Streitfragen um die alternative Kausalität, in: Festschrift Beitzke (1979) 3 (30 ff); Haftungsgrund und Zufall als alternativ mögliche Schadensursachen, in: Festschrift Frotz (1993) 3. See also *H Koziol*, Problems of Alternative Causation in Tort Law, in: H Hausmaninger et al (eds), Developments in Austrian and Israeli Private Law (1999) 177 (180 ff).

66 *R Bollenberger* in his comment on OGH 8.7.1993 JBl 1994, 540 (545); *Koziol* (fn 56) 97, 99 ff; *Koch/Koziol* (fn 45) 78–80, with further references. But see *W Holzer*, Die Haftung des Arztes im Zivilrecht, in: W Holzer/W Posch/P Schick (eds), Arzt- und Arzneimittelhaftung (1992) 1 (15 ff).

67 *F Bydlinski*, Probleme der Schadensverursachung (1964) at 89.

cal course of events.[68] If, for example, a wrongful and faulty treatment brings about the same symptoms that would have arisen anyway due to the patient's predisposition, liability only covers the damages incurred in the time period starting from their actual occurrence until the predicted moment when their cause would have manifested itself anyway (so-called *Verfrühungsschaden*) or – if the tortious act has aggravated a precondition – *Verschlimmerungsschaden*.[69] All this has to be proven by the defendants, who have to meet high standards of proof as imposed by the Austrian courts for such defence.[70]

If neither the patient's precondition nor the faulty treatment of the doctor alone would have triggered the deterioration of the patient's health, which instead was caused by the combined impact of these two causes (*summierte Einwirkungen*), the solution depends upon whether it is possible to identify a portion of the loss only attributable to the conduct of the doctor. If so, the doctor will only be liable for the part of the loss corresponding to this share, otherwise the loss is split between the doctor and the patient evenly in analogy to § 1304 ABGB.[71] **41**

12. Loss of a chance

In light of alternative approaches to spreading the risk of uncertainties as developed by Franz Bydlinski,[72] there is no need for Austrian law to consider the French concept of a *perte d'une chance* for cases where a predisposition of a patient coincides with potential harmful conduct by a medical **42**

68 *R Reischauer*, in: P Rummel (ed), Kommentar zum Allgemeinen Bürgerlichen Gesetzbuch II/2a (3rd edn 2007) § 1302 nos 14 ff; *F Harrer*, in: M Schwimann (ed), ABGB Praxiskommentar VI (3rd edn 2006) § 1302 nos 35 ff; *Koziol* (fn 58) nos 3/58 ff (all with further references, the latter arguing at no 3/78 that Bydlinski's theory mentioned above no 39 should be applied).

69 OGH 3.9.1996, 10 Ob 2350/96b, SZ 69/199; 5.5.1998, 4 Ob 23/98f, JBl 1999, 246 (cmt C *Bumberger*). Cf *Juen* (fn 51) 44; *R Reischauer*, Ärztehaftung in der Rechtsprechung, Versicherungsrundschau (VR) 1997, 141 (144).

70 It is therefore not sufficient if the parties to the patient's contract can only prove a 'preponderant probability' of the intervening predisposition as to the injuries at issue. Instead, such probability must almost amount to certainty (insofar as possible): OGH 5.5.1998, 4 Ob 23/98f, JBl 1999, 246 (248, cmt C *Bumberger*); 3.9.1996, 10 Ob 2350/96b, SZ 69/199.

71 OGH 10.6.2008, 4 Ob 75/08w, Interdisziplinäre Zeitschrift für Familienrecht (iFamZ) 2008/124. The second alternative leads to a different outcome as it would in Germany, cf BGH 1.10.1996, VI ZR 10/96, VersR 1997, 362 (quoted by the OGH in this decision).

72 See supra no 39.

professional.[73] There is no indication in the decisions of the Austrian Supreme Court that it was ever taken into account as such.

13. Multiple persons involved

43 **(a) No delegation of treatment as a general rule.** Generally, a practitioner must not delegate her duties under the contract without the patient's consent.[74] If she nonetheless does so, she will be held responsible for all negative consequences which would not have materialised had she performed her obligations herself. If the patient agrees to substitution or if it becomes unavoidable, the doctor will only have to account for fault in selecting the substitute (*culpa in eligendo*), not for the latter's fault in executing the substituted task.[75] The latter is true, for example, if a doctor refers the patient to another specialist in a different field (eg a radiologist),[76] but also if she sends away patients to another doctor whom she recommends while on holiday (with the designated doctor retaining her own practice).[77]

44 **(b) Vicarious liability in general.** Notwithstanding liability for personal fault in selecting an auxiliary (*culpa in eligendo*), (true) vicarious liability for torts committed by employees and other staff outside of special (in particular: contractual) relationships (then referred to as *Besorgungsgehilfen*) is limited to rather rare cases in Austria: According to § 1315 ABGB, a principal will be held responsible without personal fault for any

---

73 See *BA Koch*, Der Verlust einer Heilungschance in Österreich, European Review of Private Law (ERPL) 2008, 1051 (1057 ff) with further references.

74 According to § 49 para 2 *Ärztegesetz*, doctors have to exercise their profession 'personally …, at most in cooperation with other doctors.' A doctor can, however, employ helpers who have to act under his exact orders and permanent supervision. § 49 para 3 *Ärztegesetz* allows doctors 'in individual cases' to delegate certain duties vis-à-vis their patients to other health service professionals or to trainee doctors, but the delegator bears full responsibility for such delegation. See generally *P Steiner/G Fleisch*, Ärztliche Substitutionsbefugnis, AnwBl 1997, 702. Cf infra no 104 on the various options on teaming up with other doctors.
Patients may also implicitly consent to being treated by another doctor, the longer the treatment or consultation is meant to last, the more likely this is (and vice versa); cf Rummel/*Reischauer* (fn 68) § 1299 no 30.

75 Rummel/*Reischauer* (fn 68) § 1299 no 30; *Holzer* (fn 66) 54.

76 In this case, the patient enters into a separate contract with the designated expert: OGH 19.12.2001, 3 Ob 237/00z, RdM 2002/20. An exception may be the case where the original doctor asks another expert for the latter's advice internally, with the second doctor not charging the patient directly for his services. In such a case, the original doctor is liable for the second expert's misjudgment by way of vicarious liability.

77 *Juen* (fn 51) 188 ff; *Steiner/Fleisch*, AnwBl 1997, 704 f. But see infra no 48.

misbehaviour of a dangerous or unfit helper within her sphere.[78] In the former variety, the victim needs to establish that the principal had known about the dangerousness of the helper whom she had employed. In the latter case, there is no need to show that the principal was aware of the fact that her helper is not capable of or suitable for the job with which she is entrusted. If a helper falls under either of these two categories, the required qualities themselves justify the principal's liability for harm caused by such risks. Therefore, it is not necessary to claim that the latter herself was at fault.[79]

If the auxiliary was charged with the fulfilment of contractual duties of her principal, however (as a so-called *Erfüllungsgehilfe*), the principal will be held vicariously liable for her auxiliary's behaviour irrespective of the qualifications required in tort law proper just mentioned (§ 1313a ABGB).[80] Furthermore, a special relationship of social or economic dependency between the principal and her auxiliary is not of the essence, so that the latter may also be a mere independent contractor. **45**

(c) Liability for (other) doctors and other medical professionals. A hospital may therefore be vicariously liable for its employees (including doctors, nurses etc.) if and to the extent these act within the scope of their employment in order to fulfil the hospital's obligations vis-à-vis its patients and third parties to whom the duties are extended.[81] If the hospital entrusts a junior doctor or even an intern with tasks that should be assigned to a specialist, or if a specialist in a different field would be required, as far as the hospital's vicarious liability is concerned, the conduct of the employee actually performing the task will be assessed according to the standard of care to be expected from the expert required.[82] **46**

If a doctor operates in a hospital without being employed there, instead simply renting the space and equipment, and contracts for temporary support services of hospital staff (so-called *Belegärzte*), she may be liable for the latter if these assisted her in fulfilling her obligations towards her **47**

78 See, eg, *H Koziol*, Österreichisches Haftpflichtrecht II (2nd edn 1984) 352 ff.

79 Ibid 358.

80 On vicarious liability in general, see *Koziol* (fn 78) 163 f. For the area of health care, see *K Stellamor*/*J Steiner*, Handbuch des österreichischen Arztrechts I (1999) 149 ff; *C Markl*/*R Pittl*, Ausgewählte Fragen der Erfüllungsgehilfenhaftung beim ärztlichen Behandlungsvertrag, Österreichische Juristen-Zeitung (ÖJZ) 1997, 774.

81 See infra no 61.

82 Rummel/*Reischauer* (fn 68) § 1313a no 12; OGH 25.1.1994, 1 Ob 532/94, SZ 67/9 (intern).

patient.[83] In addition, the Austrian Supreme Court also held a *Belegarzt* liable for the negligence of a fellow specialist (in the case at hand an anaesthetist), even though the latter was not employed by the hospital but selected by the defendant.[84] In that case, the court argued that anaesthetist had acted under the defendant surgeon's (at least general) direction and control, which was particularly disputed since both were independent specialists acting exclusively within the scope of their expertise.[85]

48 A doctor may also be vicariously liable for another under § 1313a ABGB if the latter steps in as the former's substitute, eg while on leave or vacation. However, merely nominating another doctor does not suffice,[86] the substitute must typically work in the holidaymaker's practice temporarily or otherwise signal to the patients that she is acting as a temporary replacement for the doctor on leave.[87]

49 **(d) Liability of the auxiliaries themselves.** While the same damage can of course only be covered once, the fact that a hospital or practitioner is vicariously liable for the behaviour of its or her staff does not exclude the possibility that these auxiliaries can also be held (jointly and severally) responsible for their own personal acts and omissions. The major difference concerns the scope of duties that fall to mere assisting personnel. While this has hardly any effect in case of tortious liability, it is most important in contract cases. Obviously, auxiliaries themselves are not bound by the contractual obligations entered into by their employer,[88] so they, for example, do not personally owe the patient ex ante information about the risks of her treatment, even if it is they who have to talk to her in the course of their employment. Therefore, auxiliaries can only be held personally liable for delicts in violation of duties owed to everyone, which, apart from the protection of a person's bodily integrity, includes, inter

83 OGH 27.10.1999, 1 Ob 267/99t, RdM 2000/7 (cmt *E Pitzl/G Huber*). In addition, the hospital may be jointly and severally liable for the same misconduct of its staff if the duties owed to the patient by the *Belegarzt* and the hospital overlap: OGH 29.9.2009, 8 Ob 103/09v.

84 OGH 23.11.1999, 1 Ob 269/99m, RdM 2000/8 (cmt *C Kopetzki*).

85 See the comment by *C Kopetzki* (fn 84) and the critical remarks by *H Bruck/H Pfersmann*, Wie weit reicht die Haftung des operierenden Chirurgen? JBl 2001, 64. On the general notion of who should count as an assistant in the meaning of § 1313a ABGB: Rummel/*Reischauer* (fn 68) § 1313a no 9 (on independent contractors); *Koziol* (fn 78) 340–342.

86 Cf supra no 43.

87 See eg OGH 22.1.2008, 4 Ob 210/07x, JBl 2008, 651 (cmt *S Dullinger*); 10.3.2008, 10 Ob 119/07h, JBl 2008, 654 (cmt *S Dullinger*); *Steiner/Fleisch*, AnwBl 1997, 705 f.

88 Rummel/*Reischauer* (fn 68) § 1299 no 24.

alia, the duty to skilfully complete a task undertaken inasmuch as necessary to avoid further harm. Such duties might, on the other hand, be extended by particular statutes governing the profession of the assistant only (and not the practice of medicine in general),[89] which might count as *Schutzgesetze* within the meaning of § 1311 ABGB.[90]

In a labour law relationship, there are certain limits to direct liability of the employee in cases of minor degrees of negligence.[91] **50**

(e) **Recourse.** If a hospital has been ordered to pay compensation based on vicarious liability for the behaviour of its staff, it has a right of recourse based on § 1313 ABGB to the extent that the employees have violated personal obligations vis-à-vis the hospital (in particular those arising from their employment contracts).[92] **51**

Depending on the degree of the employee's fault, the hospital's contribution claim can be reduced or even denied:[93] If, for example, the nurse's or doctor's behaviour attributed to the hospital was hardly negligent at all (a so-called *entschuldbare Fehlleistung* or excusable slip within the meaning of § 4 subs 3 DHG), the hospital will not recover any damages paid to the patient. In other cases of negligence, the judge may mitigate the hospital's claim in light of several equitable aspects listed in § 2 subs 2 DHG.[94] **52**

---

89 See, eg, §§ 4, 5, 7 and 8 Act on Practical Nursing (*Gesundheits- und Krankenpflegegesetz*, GuKG) §§ 4, 6 and 9 Midwives' Act (*Hebammengesetz*); §§ 5–7 Act on Cardiotechnicians (*Kardiotechnikergesetz*, KTG); §§ 11, 11a Act on the Practice of Medical-Technical Services (*MTD-Gesetz*). On delegating duties to such professionals, see *T Radner*, Die Ausübung medizinischer Tätigkeiten durch MTD, MTF, Sanitätshilfsdienste und Hilfspersonen im Sinne des Ärztegesetzes, RdM 1998, 137, 175.

90 Supra no 37.

91 The contribution claim of the employer may be reduced or even inapplicable according to § 4 DHG; see infra (e).

92 *Koziol* (fn 78) 350. The right of recourse mentioned in § 1313 ABGB is already founded in the employment contract.

93 *H Koziol/K Vogel*, Vicarious Liability under Austrian Law, in: J Spier (ed), Unification of Tort Law: Liability for Damage Caused by Others (2003) nos 58 f; *W Brodil*, Arzt-haftung und Dienstnehmerhaftpflichtgesetz, RdM 1994, 50; *Stellamor/Steiner* (fn 80) 153 f.

94 The judge has to take into account: the skill of the employee; the degree of responsibility which the work implied; the dangerousness of the work and the question of whether the employee was paid (extra) for it; finally, also the degree of blameworthiness of the employee's behaviour. Cf *W Brodil*, Mäßigung der Haftung nach § 2 DHG im ärztlichen Bereich, RdM 1995, 34.

53 If a doctor in a direct tort law action has to pay damages to a patient of the hospital that she is working for (the reverse scenario), she might have a contribution claim against the hospital according to analogous principles if she merely has to account for some minor degree of negligence.

14. Strict liability

54 The ABGB only provides for liability without fault in exceptional cases. However, there is quite a range of special legislation introducing strict liability, typically addressing the keeper of dangerous objects. A few of these statutes may be relevant for establishing liability in the health care sector.

55 The Austrian Product Liability Statute (*Produkthaftungsgesetz*, PHG)[95] implements the corresponding EC Directive and improves the situation of victims harmed by defective products in many respects, though not as far as causation is concerned.[96] It may be relevant in this context if medical devices or other products used in the course of the treatment fail to meet the safety expectations.

56 According to § 9 Nuclear Liability Act 1999 (*Atomhaftungsgesetz*, AtomHG), the keeper of a radionuclide is liable for any damage resulting from ionising radiation. She can avoid liability by proving that she and her staff have observed all due care necessary to avoid harm under the circumstances. The standard of care is not just the ordinary care that has to be exercised, but the utmost care ever possible to an experienced expert in a similar case.[97] If the radionuclides are used for medical therapy, it is sufficient to prove that the substances and equipment used were state of the art at the time, and that the damage was not caused by some failure of the equipment (§ 9 subs 2 AtomHG). The statute does not prescribe maximum amounts.

95 It may be disputed whether product liability really qualifies as 'strict liability' *stricto sensu* since it strongly relates to the conduct of the producer; see *H Koziol*, Grundfragen der Produktehaftung (1980) 17 ff, 53 ff.

96 On problems relating to the loss of the harmful products, see *G Aigner*, Behandlungsschäden durch Produktfehler – Beweisnotstand des Patienten? RdM 2006, 80.

97 § 9 AtomHG has the same wording as § 9 of the Act on Liability for Keeping Railways and Motor Vehicles (*Eisenbahn- und Kraftfahrzeughaftpflichtgesetz*, EKHG), and the latter statute is interpreted in the sense just described; cf *P Apathy*, Kommentar zum EKHG (1992) § 9 no 16; *M Schauer*, in: M Schwimann (ed), Praxiskommentar ABGB VII (3rd edn 2005) § 9 EKHG nos 19 ff.

A different kind of strict liability was introduced by the Act on Harm Caused by Vaccination (*Impfschadensgesetz*): The state has to compensate any harm caused in the course of certain vaccination campaigns.[98] 57

C. Contractual Liability

15. Basics of contracts in the health care sector

(a) Contracts in the health care sector in general. All patients are typically[99] treated on the basis of a contract with a doctor or a hospital.[100] This is not only true for patients who pay out of their own pocket (so-called *Privatpatienten* or private patients),[101] but also for (the majority of) patients whose treatment is paid for by social insurance. While the reimbursement of the health care professionals is based upon contracts between them and the social insurance provider via the competent provincial Medical Chamber, patients are nevertheless considered to enter into their own contractual relationship with the doctors or hospitals.[102] 58

Contracts in the health care sector are not treated differently from other contracts apart from the fact that the nature of the services contracted for may impact the actual duties between the parties. There was a lengthy debate in Austria on whether contracts for medical treatment are contracts for works (*Werkvertrag*) or for services (*Dienstvertrag*), the former aiming at a certain success, the latter at the provision of services over time. The discussion was fuelled by a widespread misunderstanding of what the 'success' of medical treatment should be, confusing such with the healing process to which the treatment merely contributes. If the success owed under a contract for works is rightly seen as the completion of the treatment due according to medical standards rather than the complete recovery from the illness or condition requiring the treatment, it is fairly 59

98 Claims governed by the *Impfschadengesetz* have to be raised before an administrative body and not in the regular (civil) court.

99 Exceptions are emergency situations, for example, where the legal basis of the treatment may be benevolent intervention (*negotiorum gestio*); see eg *P Steiner*, Der Notarzt – Geschäftsführer ohne Auftrag? Zeitschrift für Verkehrsrecht (ZVR) 1998, 38.

100 *S Völkl-Torggler*, Die Rechtsnatur des ärztlichen Behandlungsvertrages, JBl 1984, 72; *F Bydlinski*, Verträge über ärztliche Leistungen, in: Festschrift Kralik (1986) 345; *D Engljähringer*, Ärztlicher Behandlungsvertrag, ÖJZ 1993, 488; *id*, Ärztliche Aufklärungspflicht vor medizinischen Eingriffen (1996) 16 ff; *Juen* (fn 51) 52 ff; all with further references.

101 See supra no 6.

102 *Völkl-Torggler*, JBl 1984, 73 f.

easy to categorise the contract as one for works (though some specific contracts in the health care sector may indeed be for services over time, particularly for longer-term therapies).[103]

60 (b) **Contracts with individual medical professionals.** A contract for medical treatment obliges the doctor to exercise reasonable and comprehensive professional care and skill, which is determined objectively as is the case with respect to any expert behaviour (§ 1299 ABGB).[104] Medical practitioners are therefore required to come up to the standard of a prudent and experienced specialist in their respective area of expertise,[105] which is determined according to the state of science at the time the injurious behaviour occurred.[106]

61 The protective scope of the contract not only covers the contracting parties themselves, but extends to all persons affected by the treatment. This includes in particular (at first) unborn children, who are clearly also at the focus of a gynaecologist's contractual duties primarily owed to the mother,[107] but also the father[108] or spouse[109] may be protected. As a consequence, such third parties can themselves raise direct claims for breach of contractual duties even though these were promised to another.

62 (c) **Contracts with hospitals.** If it is a hospital rather than an individual practitioner alone that the patient has contracted with, the hospital carrier can be held responsible for any breach of duties arising from such contract according to the same principles applicable to the doctor individually. In particular, the burden of proving fault is also shifted to the hospital if the

---

103 *Völkl-Torggler*, JBl 1984, 72.

104 On the liability of experts in general, see *Koziol* (fn 78) 182 ff; *id*, Characteristic Features of Austrian Tort Law, in: H Hausmaninger et al (eds), Developments in Austrian and Israeli Private Law (1999) 159 (173 f).

105 Rummel/*Reischauer* (fn 68) § 1299 no 25; *K Hofmann*, Qualitätsmängel bei der medizinischen Behandlung als Tatbestand in der Rechtsprechung, Österreichische Richterzeitung (ÖRZ) 1999, 82; *Juen* (fn 51) 164 ff. Cf § 49 subs 1 *Ärztegesetz*.

106 *Holzer* (fn 66) 9 ff.

107 Cf OGH 7.11.1995, 4 Ob 554/95, SZ 68/207. Such a contract involving the treatment of third parties (here: children) is considered a 'Vertrag mit Schutzwirkung zugunsten Dritter', which in general does not protect the pure economic interest of the third party as such, but only his absolute rights. See *Koziol* (fn 78) 87 f; contra Rummel/*Reischauer* (fn 68) § 1295 nos 33 ff. For special aspects of 'wrongful life', see *Koziol* (fn 58) no 2/33.

108 OGH 25.5.1999, 1 Ob 91/99k, SZ 72/91.

109 OGH 30.6.2010, 9 Ob 83/09k, EvBl 2010/132.

patient succeeds in establishing that her injuries were caused by a breach of the hospital's contractual duties (§ 1298 ABGB).

The contractual relationship between a patient and a hospital, however, can fall under a broad range of varieties, from an 'all-inclusive' contract covering all services connected with the patient's stay at the hospital (including medical treatment) to mere 'lodging' contracts where the patient merely rents the room and the medical facilities which are then used by one or more internal or external medical professionals that the patient hires separately.[110] Accordingly, the hospital's contractual duties do not necessarily include all aspects of the patient's treatment. In particular, it will generally not be held responsible for malpractice of an out-house surgeon that the patient has contracted with individually. **63**

However, it is not always easy to draw a line between the responsibilities of the hospital (which provides at least for the equipment, but typically also for assistants and nurses) and those of the non-employed surgeon. While the latter might be held vicariously liable under her own contract with the patient for misconduct of the hospital's staff to the extent that they are under her control,[111] the hospital might also be jointly and severally responsible for the acts and omissions of its personnel.[112] Common opinion holds that such issues of attributing liability to the respective contractual duties should not impede on the patient's procedural position, so that such shall not be burdened with proving who is responsible for the cause of the injuries.[113] **64**

If a patient is admitted to a hospital, she has no contractual claim to be treated by any specific staff member, eg a particular surgeon, unless she is a so-called *Privatpatient*,[114] in which case her special contractual arrangement typically foresees such an option. Therefore, the hospital can freely decide whom to assign to any patient. However, if a patient declares that she only wants to be operated on by one specific staff member, her consent to treatment[115] is limited to that individual. If another surgeon is assigned **65**

---

110 Eg as *Belegärzte*, supra no 47. On the various options see *Engljähringer* (fn 100) 51 ff; *Stellamor/Steiner* (fn 80) 55 ff; *P Steiner*, Zur inhaltlichen Unterscheidung zwischen Belegarzt und Konsiliararzt, RdM 1998, 70.

111 See supra text accompanying fn 83 ff.

112 OGH 29.9.2009, 8 Ob 103/09v.

113 *Holzer* (fn 66) 57.

114 Supra nos 16 and 58.

115 On the significance of informed consent, see below at nos 72 ff.

to her, she has to be specifically informed about such change in order to extend her consent to that other doctor.[116]

66 A particular kind of duty that usually only hospitals and entities of similar complexity have to account for is their obligation to provide for adequate personnel and equipment as well as to make sure that all resources can be used efficiently.[117] If they fail to come up to such organisational requirements, hospital carriers will have to indemnify any harm resulting therefrom, even if the ultimate staff members involved directly with the patient's treatment did not do anything wrong (so that the hospital would not be vicariously liable for their behaviour).[118]

67 Hospital visitors and family members accompanying a patient are not entirely out of the protective scope of the latter's contract.[119] If they are injured while on a visit, they might, however, (in addition) base their claims on a violation of general *Verkehrssicherungspflichten* (ie duties to maintain safety and to protect others against risks created).[120]

16. Differences to tort law

68 Subject to certain qualifications, the tort law section of the Austrian General Civil Code (§§ 1293–1341 *Allgemeines Bürgerliches Gesetzbuch*, ABGB) equally applies to contractual liability.[121] Nevertheless, these two varieties differ in several important respects.

69 In essence, it is easier for the claimant to succeed with a claim for contractual liability: Apart from the fact that contractual duties of care go much further, it is up to the defendant to prove that she was not at fault when violating her contractual obligations (§ 1298 ABGB).[122] Furthermore, a contractual defendant is vicariously liable for all auxiliaries that she used in performing her obligation (§ 1313a ABGB), whereas in the law

116 OGH 26. 9. 2003, 3 Ob 131/03s, RdM 2004/37.
117 *Juen* (fn 51) 60 ff.
118 *Landesgericht* (provincial court, LG) Innsbruck 16.2.1992, 1a R 50/93, ZVR 1993/100; *Holzer* (fn 66) 52 ff.
119 OGH 27.11.1984, 2 Ob 657/84, JBl 1985, 293; contra OGH 13.11.1985, 1 Ob 661/85, SZ 58/4; *G Gaisbauer*, Schutzpflicht des Krankenhauses gegenüber Besuchern und Begleitern des Patienten, RdM 1998, 75.
120 *Koziol* (fn 78) 160. Cf OGH 23.4.1996, 10 Ob 2048/96s, RdM 1997/11 (visitors slipping on wet staircase).
121 Cf *H Koziol,* The Borderline Between Tort Liability and Contract, in: H Koziol (ed), Unification of Tort Law: Wrongfulness (1998) 25.
122 See already supra no 36.

of delict proper, her auxiliaries must have fulfilled certain (stringent) qualifications.[123] These advantages can also be decisive in a medical malpractice case, eg when a patient is treated by an employed doctor: The latter will only be liable in tort if she has not contracted with the patient directly, whereas the hospital (or any other employer) will be vicariously liable for violations of contractual duties of care which extend to the doctor if she performs such duties on behalf of her employer.[124]

While there is obviously no possibility for double recovery, victims can **70**
choose the basis of their claims, they are not mutually exclusive.

17. Contractual claims in the absence of direct contracts?

It is generally acknowledged that third parties may be protected by certain **71**
duties arising out of a contract, whose scope therefore extends beyond its actual parties.[125] The link between the contract and the third parties must have been foreseeable at the time the contract was concluded, which is of course particularly true if they are the ultimate beneficiaries of the contract performance.[126]

18. Informed consent[127]

The doctrine of informed consent is of utmost importance for medical **72**
malpractice claims in Austria, as it at least traditionally seems to have served as a cushion for those cases filed against health care providers where the deviation from medical standards cannot be proven for whatever reason, but where the suspicion remains that something went wrong during treatment.

The contract for medical treatment requires the doctor or hospital to **73**
inform the patient not only about the diagnosis[128] and the recommended

---

123 Supra no 44.

124 See *BA Koch/H Koziol,* Compensation in the Austrian Healthcare Sector, in: J Dute/M Faure/H Koziol (eds), No-Fault Compensation in the Healthcare Sector (2004) 89 (nos 1 ff); *BA Koch,* Austrian Cases on Medical Malpractice, European Journal of Health Law (EJHL) 2003, 91.

125 See, eg, supra no 61.

126 See, eg, KBB/*Karner* (fn 60) § 1295 no 19.

127 *K Prutsch,* Die ärztliche Aufklärung (2nd edn 2004).

128 Eg OGH 29.1.2001, 3 Ob 87/00s, RdM 2001/21.

therapy,[129] but also about all possible risks of the treatment[130] and to offer her adequate and proper medical care. If she subsequently rests her claim solely upon the breach of the doctor's or hospital's duty to inform, she must not only prove that such breach indeed occurred, but also that it led to the damage which she has suffered.[131] Instead, she might follow another line of reasoning which helps to avoid potential difficulties that such a burden of proof could produce: She can alternatively sue on the grounds that she was physically injured through the acts of the practitioner, hospital, or its staff. Such effect by itself indicates wrongful behaviour on their part since it implies that they have acted in violation of the claimant's interest in her own bodily integrity. This interest is not only protected under general principles of delict, but further specified by contractual duties. The doctor or hospital could still justify such acts by claiming that the patient had validly consented to the treatment beforehand, but in this case they would have to prove that fact since this argument now would serve as defence.[132] Consequently, the hospital would further have to establish that the patient previously had received sufficient information about the upcoming treatment and the risks involved therewith, which is a prerequisite to her informed choice. Without such consent, the doctor or hospital is liable for the claimant's damage even if caused accidentally in the course of proper and careful treatment.[133]

74 If a patient is treated without her approval, those providing the service violate § 110 of the Austrian Criminal Code (*Strafgesetzbuch,* StGB), which penalises the treatment of another 'without that person's consent, even if

---

129 So-called *Therapieaufklärung* or *Verlaufsaufklärung*. See *Juen* (fn 51) 118 ff. In the case of a hospital, it must under certain circumstances also inform the patient of the staff member assigned to treat her, see supra no 65.

130 Eg OGH 25.1.1994, 1 Ob 532/94, SZ 67/9; 3.9.1996, 10 Ob 2350/96b, SZ 69/199; 11.12.2007, 5 Ob 148/07m, JBl 2008, 521; 4.8.2009, 9 Ob 64/08i, EvBl 2010/9; *Engljähringer*, ÖJZ 1993, 498 ff. On the issue of whether this is a primary or collateral duty of the contract see *id* (fn 100) 59 f.

131 For further questions regarding burden of proof see also supra nos 31 ff.

132 There is consequently no 'shift from contract to tort liability' as suspected by *K Hofmann*, Die Aufklärungspflicht des Arztes im Lichte der Rechtsprechung des Obersten Gerichtshofes, ÖRZ 1998, 80 (81 f).

133 Established practice, eg OGH 19.12.1984, 3 Ob 562/84, SZ 57/207; 7.2.1989, 1 Ob 713/88, SZ 62/18; 25.1.1990, 7 Ob 727/89, EvBl 1990/87; 12.9.1990, 1 Ob 651/90, SZ 63/152; 12.11.1992, 8 Ob 628/92, RdM 1994/2 (cmt *C Kopetzki*); 25.1.1994, 1 Ob 532/94, SZ 67/9; 31.1.1995, 4 Ob 509/95, JBl 1995, 453 (cmt *J Steiner*); 11.1.1996, 2 Ob 505/96, RdM 1996/11; 30.1.1996, 4 Ob 505/96, RdM 1996/24; 3.9.1996, 10 Ob 2350/96b, SZ 69/199; 11.11.1997, 7 Ob 355/97z, JBl 1998, 443 (cmt *E Bernat*).

completed according to common standards of the science of medicine'.[134] Tort law holds this provision to be a so-called *Schutzgesetz* (protective law, cf § 1311 ABGB).[135] This is also true for § 8 subs 3 KAKuG, which provides that a patient who is admitted to a hospital must specifically agree to any action taken if there is enough time to ask for such consent without imminent danger to her life or health.[136] These special provisions are designed to protect the patient's right of self-determination, whereas the infliction of bodily harm as such has to be judged according to the more general principles of wrongfulness.[137]

Information must be given early enough so that the patient can thoroughly consider the pros and cons of the treatment,[138] which enables her to decide on the basis of ample background knowledge whether she wants to go ahead with the planned treatment or not. A mere standard form letter or leaflet including printed information is not enough: The patient must have the option of asking questions.[139] **75**

---

134 Subs 2 leg cit rules out prosecution if consent was not sought because one could expect that life or health of the patient would be in imminent and 'serious' danger otherwise. According to subs 3 leg cit, the patient has to request prosecution.

135 Established court practice, eg OGH 23.6.1982, 3 Ob 545/82, JBl 1983, 373 (cmt *W Holzer*); 23.1.1986, 6 Ob 683/84, SZ 59/18; 7.2.1989, 1 Ob 713/88, SZ 62/18; 26.9.1989, 4 Ob 113/89, SZ 62/154; 12.9.1990, 1 Ob 651/90, SZ 63/152; 25.1.1994, 1 Ob 532/94, SZ 67/9. On *Schutzgesetze* in general, see supra no 37.

136 OGH 23.6.1982, 3 Ob 545/82, JBl 1983, 373 (cmt *W Holzer*). Further code provisions which require a medical practitioner to inform his patient are eg § 5 AIDS Act (*AIDS-Gesetz*), § 8 Veneral Diseases Act (*Geschlechtskrankheitengesetz*), § 7 Reproductive Medicine Act (*Fortpflanzungsmedizingesetz*), § 3 Blood Donor Regulation (*Blutspenderverordnung*), as well as § 8 Blood Safety Act (*Blutsicherheitsgesetz*). See *R Resch*, Zur Rechtsgrundlage der ärztlichen Aufklärungspflicht, RdM 1996, 170.

137 *W Holzer*, in his comments on OGH 23.6.1982, JBl 1983, 376; *id* (fn 66) 4; *E Karner*, Der Ersatz ideeller Schäden bei Körperverletzung (1999) 111.

138 If there is no imminent danger, a rule of thumb might say that the higher the risks involved, the more time the patient will need. *Engljähringer* (fn 100) 166 ff; *W Holzer*, Schadenersatzrechtliche Konsequenzen der ärztlichen Aufklärungspflicht aus österreichischer Sicht, in: Festschrift Gitter (1995) 375 (382); *id* (fn 66) 32; *J Schramm/M Stempkowski*, Die zahnärztliche Aufklärungspflicht, RdM 1997, 138; *A Heidinger*, Die ärztliche Aufklärungspflicht in der Rechtsprechung des Obersten Gerichtshofes, in: F Harrer/A Graf (eds), Ärztliche Verantwortung und Aufklärung (1999) 17 (37 f). See also OGH 23.6.1994, 6 Ob 555/94, RdM 1995/1 (cmt *C Kopetzki*): Information given on the eve of the operation still timely. Similarly OGH 14.4.1998, 10 Ob 137/98i, RdM 1998/21.

139 See, eg, OGH 31.1.1995, 4 Ob 509/95, JBl 1995, 453 (cmt *J Steiner*); 30.1.1996, 4 Ob 505/96, RdM 1996/24. Cf *Holzer* (fn 138) 384 f; *E Pitzl/G Huber*, Behandlungsaufklärung – Risikoaufklärung – Aufklärungsbögen, RdM 1996, 113, *Schramm/Stempkowski*, RdM 1997, 136 (138); *Heidinger* (fn 138) 39 ff.

76 Since the patient's approval serves as an argument in favour of the doctor's position, it is up to the latter to prove it.[140] If she herself is under no personal obligation to inform the patient (as she would be under a contract),[141] she can avoid liability merely by establishing that she had reasonably relied upon her belief in the patient's valid consent to the treatment. This might be endorsed, for example, if she is part of the medical staff of a hospital to which the patient was admitted. Such proof is bound to fail, however, if she personally was in charge of informing patients under the hospital's internal assignment of duties, but in fact did not disclose the risks to the plaintiff and could further not assume that such information had been given to the patient elsewise.[142]

77 While there are no generally applicable criteria for determining what complications need to be disclosed, the OGH has developed a few guidelines on how to observe the patient's right of self-determination while still respecting the superior goal of her well-being.[143] The more urgent it is for the patient's health, the less extensively she has to be informed, especially if an overly anxious patient might opt against the treatment, which in turn would constitute a much higher risk to her health.[144] On the other

---

140 Eg OGH 12.11.1992, 1 Ob 651/90, RdM 1994/2 (cmt *C Kopetzki*); 11.1.1996, 2 Ob 505/96, RdM 1996/11; 12.3.1996, 10 Ob 1530/96, RdM 1996/25; 20.3.1997, 6 Ob 2391/96b, RdM 1997/29. See further *G Gaisbauer*, Zur Beweislast für Einwilligung des Patienten und Erfüllung der ärztlichen Aufklärungspflicht, JBl 1994, 352; *Holzer* (fn 138) 385; contra Rummel/*Reischauer* (fn 68) § 1299 no 26j (but see *id*, VR 1997, 146); *A Haslinger*, Probleme der ärztlichen Aufklärung und Patienteneinwilligung, AnwBl 1994, 866 (871); *Hofmann*, ÖRZ 1998, 80; *S Dullinger*, Zur Beweislast für Verletzung/Erfüllung der ärztlichen Aufklärungspflicht, JBl 1998, 2 (9 ff, 16). *Dullingers* arguments were expressly rejected by OGH 23.2.1999, 4 Ob 335/98p, RdM 1999/11 (cmt *A Kletečka*); 11.3.1999, 6 Ob 126/98t, RdM 2000/2; 30.3.1999, 3 Ob 314/97s, RdM 2000/4; 23.11.1999, 1 Ob 254/99f, JBl 2000, 657 (cmt *P Jabornegg*). See further *Karner* (fn 137) 114 ff; *A Kletečka* in his comments on OGH RdM 1999, 120 ff; *P Jabornegg* in his comments to OGH JBl 2000, 662 ff. But see OGH 7.8.2007, 4 Ob 137/07m, SZ 2007/122: No reversal of the burden of proof if the risk not disclosed concerns the chance of a relapse or the failure of the treatment, since doctors do not owe the success of the treatment.

141 Contra *Resch*, RdM 1996, 173 ('duty to inform based on delictual protection of legal interests'); *Heidinger* (fn 138) 26. Sec 49 subs 2 and 3 *Ärztegesetz* specifically consider (and do not rule out) the case that some or all of the doctor's duties are delegated. This is typically true for hospitals. Consequently, there are not only practical reasons speaking against a strict duty of each and every doctor to inform every single patient without exceptions.

142 On delegating the duty to inform see eg *Engljähringer* (fn 100) 137 ff; *Heidinger* (fn 138) 27 ff.

143 See in particular the landmark case of OGH 23.6.1982, 3 Ob 545/82, JBl 1983, 373 (cmt *W Holzer*). Cf the overview given by *Hofmann*, ÖRZ 1998, 80; see further *Heidinger* (fn 138) 24 ff; *Koch/Koziol* (fn 45) 61–65.

144 *Holzer* (fn 66) 26 ff; *Engljähringer* (fn 100) 215 ff with further references.

hand, if treatment is not imperative (such as purely diagnostic measures),[145] information has to be given as extensively as possible.[146] Typical risks always have to be disclosed, even if chances of such complications are remote.[147] Statistical probabilities thereby play a role, but are just one factor amongst others:[148] The paramount test is whether the patient might be specifically interested in the particular risk at stake[149] and to what extent knowing thereof might influence her decision.[150]

Even if the patient was not sufficiently informed and could therefore not give any valid consent to her treatment, she will nevertheless have to bear her own loss if the defendant can prove that the patient would still have gone ahead with the treatment had she known all possible complications thereof.[151] **78**

---

145 *Holzer* (fn 138) 383 f; OGH 23.1.1986, 6 Ob 683/84, SZ 59/18; 18.10.1991 8 Ob 620/91; 20.5.1998, 2 Ob 124/98v; 23.2.1999, 4 Ob 335/98p, RdM 1999/11 (cmt *A Kletečka*); 16.9.2009 1 Ob 80/08h RdM 2009/62 (cmt *A Leischner*).

146 Eg OGH 12.9.1990, 1 Ob 651/90, SZ 63/152; 7.9.1993, 10 Ob 503/93, RdM 1994/1 (cmt *C Kopetzki*); 25.1.1994, 1 Ob 532/94, SZ 67/9; 3.9.1996, 10 Ob 2350/96b, SZ 69/199; 10.7.1997, 2 Ob 197/97b, RdM 1998/18; 27.2.2009, 6 Ob 122/07w; see further *G Gaisbauer*, Ärztliche Aufklärungspflicht bei kosmetischen Eingriffen, ÖJZ 1993, 25.

147 Eg OGH 26.9.1989, 4 Ob 113/89, SZ 62/154; 25.1.1994, 1 Ob 532/94, SZ 67/9; 29.1.1997, 7 Ob 12/97h, RdM 1997/18; 17.1.2001, 6 Ob 318/00h, RdM 2001/16; *Engljähringer* (fn 100) 189 ff.

148 This does not mean that rare risks never have to be disclosed: OGH RdM 1994/1 (cmt *C Kopetzki*). Even if the risk of infection is close to one in a thousand, the patient still has to be informed if the doctor realises that the patient would otherwise believe that the treatment is without any danger at all. See also OGH 7.8.1997, 8 Ob 230/97z, RdM 1998/19 (2 %). But see *Engljähringer* (fn 100) 201 ff.

149 OGH 29.1.1997, 7 Ob 12/97h, RdM 1997/18.

150 OGH 24.10.1996, 6 Ob 2211/96g, RdM 1997/28.

151 OGH 23.1.1986, 6 Ob 683/84, SZ 59/18; 21.9.1989, 8 Ob 535/89, SZ 62/154; 12.9.1990, 1 Ob 651/90, SZ 63/152; 4.7.1991, 6 Ob 558/91, JBl 1992, 520 (cmt *P Apathy*); 14.1.1992, 5 Ob 1573/91, JBl 1992, 391; 31.1.1995, 4 Ob 509/95, JBl 1995, 453 (cmt *J Steiner*); 14.5.2009, 6 Ob 71/09y; 9.6.2009, 5 Ob 111/09y. But see *Koziol* (fn 58) no 8/72, who does not grant the doctor such a possibility to justify his acts if 'the practitioner has substantially violated his duties,' for example if he 'completely failed to disclose risks'. In contrast to Germany, Austrian courts do not require patients to substantiate a decisional conflict whether they would have gone ahead with the treatment had they been fully informed: OGH 14.10.2008, 4 Ob 155/08k, ecolex 2009/77.

D. Public Liability

19. Key differences from cases involving private hospitals or doctors

79 Only one quarter of all Austrian hospitals are privately operated, the rest being run by legal entities under public law.[152] Nevertheless, liability of all these entities vis-à-vis their patients is considered to be of a contractual nature.[153] Therefore, cases involving private health care professionals do not differ from those dealing with liability of public health care providers.

E. Alternative Compensation Regimes

20. Funds and/or other alternative compensation regimes

80 (a) **Patient compensation funds of the provinces.** A federal law introduced in 2001[154] initiated the creation of compensation funds (*Patientenentschädigungsfonds*) for hospitals.[155] As this falls under the jurisdiction of the provinces themselves, the federal legislator can only lay down the principles for its provincial counterparts; thus there are some differences in the models ultimately adopted by the various provinces.[156] The fund is financed by contributions from the patients (ie the potential victims!) themselves, who must pay an extra € 0.73 per day spent in hospital.[157]

---

152 See fn 5.

153 Supra no 58.

154 § 27a subs 5 and 6 KAKuG. To some extent, this was modelled after the Viennese fund created earlier; see *B Jahn*, Außergerichtliche Konfliktlösung im Gesundheitswesen (2009) 133 ff. The Viennese fund (*Freiwilliger Wiener Härtefonds*, ex gratia fund for hardship cases) continues to exist alongside the general fund and offers payments up to € 50,000 for people domiciled in Vienna who have suffered damage in the course of a treatment in a Viennese hospital (see <http://www.wien.gv.at/gesundheit/wppa/haertefonds.html>).

155 Practitioners outside hospitals are not covered by this fund.

156 *W Kossak*, Der Entschädigungsfonds gem § 27a Abs 5 und Abs 6 Krankenanstaltengesetz, RdM 2002, 25; *E Pitzl/G Huber*, Verschuldensunabhängige Patientenentschädigung, RdM 2003, 100.

157 The fund's means vary from province to province: In 2003, the funds in Vienna and Lower Austria stood at almost € 1 million each (with payments totalling about € 400,000 in the latter province during that year). In comparison, the monies collected in the same period in the Burgenland amounted to only one tenth. See the report by the Patientenanwalt of Lower Austria at <http://www.patientenanwalt.com/pdf/Patientenentschaedigungsfonds_Taetigkeitsbericht_2003.pdf>.

The fund was created for patients who have suffered material or immaterial harm in the course of medical treatment (or the omission thereof) at a hospital.[158] It is not meant to replace liability regimes, quite the contrary: The prime focus of the fund are cases of hardship, where liability cannot be clearly established (particularly due to problems involved in proving causation or fault),[159] or if a rare, but severe ('catastrophic') complication has occurred (even if the patient had been warned of its possibility before). Patients may still try to pursue their claims in court, even if already (partially) indemnified by the fund, but have to return payments in case of success.[160] The application process is suspended, on the other hand, while a court trial is pending, or as long as the parties try to find an out-of-court settlement. **81**

As cases typically do not reach the commission before the *Patientenanwalt*[161] has decided on the tort law merits of the cases in the negative, the success rate of these filings is rather high.[162] Payments out of the fund are capped, but the threshold amounts vary from province to province.[163] **82**

---

158 On details of this causation requirement, see *Pitzl/Huber* (fn 156) 103.

159 As expressly stated in the guidelines of the Viennese fund, for example, payments out of the fund are excluded if the facts are clear (whether in the patient's favour or not). See <http://www.wien.gv.at/gesundheit/wppa/patientenfonds-richt.html>, no II.1.

160 This works either way, so if a patient is awarded € 10,000 by the fund and subsequently obtains judgment in the amount of € 5,000, she only has to pay back the latter amount, whereas if the court award in her favour exceeds € 10,000, this is the maximum she has to repay. Repayment may be waived in cases of social hardship. See <http://www.wien.gv.at/gesundheit/wppa/patientenfonds-richt.html>, no II.3.

161 See infra no 98.

162 The 2008 statistics show that 94 % of applications were successful in Vienna (<http://www.wien.gv.at/gesundheit/wppa/pdf/bericht-2008.pdf> p 57), 76 % in Lower Austria (<http://www.patientenanwalt.com/fileadmin/dokumente/04_publikationen/taetigkeitsberichte/noe_patienten_entschaedigungsfonds/Patienten_Entschaedigungsfonds_Taetigkeitsbericht_2008_Publikationen_Taetigkeitsberichte.pdf.pdf> p 5), and 75 % in Tyrol (<http://www.tirol.gv.at/fileadmin/www.tirol.gv.at/themen/gesundheit/patientenvertretung/downloads/TPF_Taetigkeitsbericht2008.pdf> p 12).

163 While the maximum in Vienna currently stands at € 100,000 (exceptions possible, see <http://www.wien.gv.at/gesundheit/wppa/patientenfonds-richt.html>), awards in Lower Austria generally must not exceed € 21,801.85 (in cases of extraordinary hardship € 36,336.417, but in special cases of permanent harm of extraordinary dimensions, the exceptional ultimate maximum is € 150,000, see <http://www.patientenanwalt.com/fileadmin/dokumente/02_ihre_rechte/Geschaeftsordnung_08_NOE_Patienten-Entschaedigungsfonds.pdf>). In Tyrol, the general maximum lies at € 35,000, in extraordinary cases of grave permanent impairment this amount may be doubled <http://www.tirol.gv.at/fileadmin/www.tirol.gv.at/themen/gesundheit/patientenvertretung/downloads/Richtlinien_TPF-11-07.pdf>. There are no caps in Carinthia (*Pitzl/Huber*, RdM 2003, 109).

83 **(b) Solidarity fund of the Austrian Medical Chamber.** After unsuccessfully fighting the relevant provision of the *Ärztegesetz* after its introduction in 2006,[164] the Austrian Medical Chamber has installed a *Solidarfonds* (solidarity funds). It is meant to absorb losses that are not recoverable despite a valid claim, particularly due to a lack of liability insurance cover. Eligible claimants are patients who have been harmed by wrongful and faulty medical treatment provided by doctors in private practice.

84 **(c) Special funds.** Apart from the general solutions mentioned before, there have been two instances of special funds which have been created in order to handle the peculiar problems of large-scale infections of a multitude of victims: The first fund was initiated in 1988 in favour of patients infected with the HIV virus in the course of blood transfusions.[165] The second fund (modelled after the prior one) was installed for people who contracted hepatitis C while donating blood plasma.[166]

F. Extent of Liability/Remedies

I. Pecuniary Loss

21. Introduction to indemnifying pecuniary loss

85 As already indicated, the Austrian law on damages is peculiar inasmuch as the extent of compensation for property losses depends upon the tortfeasor's degree of fault. However, there are no conduct-related differences when it comes to indemnifying personal injuries.[167]

86 Damages can be calculated objectively or subjectively. In the case of property losses caused with merely slight negligence, only the former method is available, which entails looking at the market value of the

---

164 An attempt to quash this provision before the Austrian Constitutional Court failed: *Verfassungsgerichtshof* (VfGH) 10.10.2007, G 187/06 <http://www.vfgh.gv.at/cms/vfgh-site/attachments/0/2/9/CH0006/CMS1197022513092/aerzte-entschaedigungfonds_g_187-06.pdf>. Cf also <http://www.ots.at/presseaussendung/OTS_20060701_OTS0012>.

165 'Unterstützungsfonds für Personen, die durch medizinische Behandlung oder Tätigkeit mit HIV infiziert worden sind, und ihre Angehörigen.' See <http://www.bmg.gv.at/cms/site/standard.html?channel=CH0742&doc=CMS1038915386478>.

166 'Unterstützungsfonds für Personen, die durch die Spende von Blut oder Blutbestandteilen mit dem Hepatitis-C-Virus infiziert wurden.' See, eg, <http://www.parlament.gv.at/PG/DE/XXII/AB/AB_03821/fname_059687.pdf> on the practice of this fund.

167 Supra no 30.

damaged object. The subjective loss of the claimant is assessed by way of the so-called *Differenzmethode*, where the actual value of the victim's patrimony after the harmful event is deducted from its hypothetical value without the damage.[168] As regards personal injury, the victim can choose between these two approaches.[169]

Austrian law bears no surprises when it comes to the list of compensable heads of damage:[170] Apart from expenses for medical treatment,[171] medication, medical aids, nursing, rehabilitation and the like, even the costs of relatives incurred visiting the victim and other comparable extras can be recovered.[172] The same is true for increased expenses such as adaptations of the house and loss of income.[173] If the victim can count on relatives to take care of her voluntarily and for free, she can still recover the (fictitious) expenses of a professional nurse, because the gratuitous services offered by third parties are not meant to benefit the tortfeasor.[174] **87**

A special head of damage is recognised by § 1326 ABGB, the so-called *Verunstaltungsentschädigung* (compensation for disfigurement). While it seems to constitute non-pecuniary damage at first sight, it is meant to indemnify reduced chances of future income and other pecuniary consequences, including weaker prospects of finding a marital partner,[175] whereas the emotional effects of disfigurement may (additionally or instead) be claimed as non-pecuniary loss. A merely slight possibility of an impact upon the advancement of the victim suffices to give her a claim **88**

168 *H Koziol*, Damages under Austrian Law, in: U Magnus (ed), Unification of Tort Law: Damages (2001) 7 (nos 39 ff).

169 *K-H Danzl*, in: H Koziol/P Bydlinski/R Bollenberger (eds), Kurzkommentar zum ABGB (KBB, 3rd edn 2010) § 1325 no 4.

170 Cf *BA Koch/H Koziol*, Comparative Analysis, in: BA Koch/H Koziol, Compensation for Personal Injury in a Comparative Perspective (2002) 407 (nos 40 ff).

171 This may include the additional costs for treatment by a private doctor who is under no contract with a social insurance provider and/or a stay in the hospital's *Sonderklasse* (see fn 26), if appropriate to the patient's situation, or if it is otherwise adequate under the circumstances of the case (eg if treatment by a specialist working for a private hospital is required by the patient's medical condition): OGH 24.4.2003, 2 Ob 284/01f, ZVR 2004/38. In the medical malpractice scenario, this is obviously the case, inter alia, if the deterioration of the patient's condition happens while staying in the *Sonderklasse*, but also otherwise if the more expensive treatment is expected to lead to a more satisfactory result: OGH 28.6.2005, 10 Ob 24/05k, RdM 2005/106.

172 This may even include tips for the nursing staff of a hospital or flowers and other small presents: KBB/*Danzl* (fn 169) § 1325 no 7.

173 Ibid § 1325 nos 10 f, 12 ff.

174 KBB/*Danzl* (fn 169) § 1325 no 8.

175 Not the emotional bonds are at focus here, but the fact that a spouse at least contributes to the family income and assumes maintenance duties.

under § 1326 ABGB; such also need not be permanent. The highest award under § 1326 ABGB so far amounted to € 30,000.[176]

89 If medical malpractice causes the death of the patient, § 1327 ABGB is the statutory basis for claiming not only funeral expenses and other costs relating to the death as such (including unsuccessful efforts to safe the life), but also for maintenance claims of surviving relatives if recognised by law.[177] The latter are calculated on the basis of the deceased's income after taxes. The tortfeasor also has to indemnify the loss of services that the deceased would have provided in fulfilment of her maintenance duties (eg childcare or household activities).[178]

90 There are no deviations from these general rules in the special case of medical liability.

22. Loss of earnings vs loss of earning capacity

91 Apart from the reduction of previous income, loss of earning capacity is also compensable due to the objective approach to calculating the damage. Therefore, even if the victim suffers no actual loss of earnings, her reduced ability to theoretically generate income according to her educational background and other circumstances determining said ability has to be indemnified by the tortfeasor.[179] The costs of housekeeping and childcare also have to be compensated according to labour market value to the extent the injuries prevent the victim from rendering such services herself.[180] A so-called *abstrakte Rente* (abstract annuity) has to be paid for any likely diminution of future income[181] due to the victim's lasting handicap, or if her physical or mental efforts to maintain the previous level of income have to be increased, both criteria in light of her deteriorated standing when competing with others on the labour market.[182]

---

176 OGH 7.5.2003, 7 Ob 36/03z, ZVR 2004/39. Like non-pecuniary loss, it is typically compensated by way of a lump sum payment, exceptionally it may also be in the form of an annuity: KBB/*Danzl* (fn 169) § 1326 no 9.

177 KBB/*Danzl* (fn 169) § 1327 no 5. This excludes, inter alia, fiancé(e)s or lifetime companions, and also those whom the deceased had contractually promised to provide support.

178 KBB/*Danzl* (fn 169) § 1327 nos 11–18.

179 *Koziol* (fn 168) no 47; KBB/*Danzl* (fn 169) § 1325 nos 12 ff.

180 KBB/*Danzl* (fn 169) § 1325 nos 24 f.

181 It cannot be claimed for additional efforts made in the past; eg OGH 29.4.2009, 2 Ob 234/08p, ecolex 2009, 1057 (with detailed analysis of further aspects).

182 KBB/*Danzl* (fn 169) § 1325 no 21.

23. Periodic payments or lump sum?

While the ABGB is silent on the matter, common opinion holds that loss of earnings typically have to be awarded in the form of an annuity and only exceptionally as a lump sum.[183] **92**

24. Caps and thresholds

No caps or thresholds apply in the area of (delictual or contractual) fault liability.[184] **93**

II. Non-Pecuniary Loss

25. Introduction to indemnifying non-pecuniary loss

Irrespective of whether the claim is based on contractual liability or on tort law, persons suffering personal injuries are entitled not only to compensation for their pecuniary losses, but also for pain and suffering 'as adequate under the circumstances' (§ 1295 ABGB). Even if it does not amount to a medical condition in itself (such as a shock, trauma or depression), significant mental suffering is included in the notion of 'personal injury', either as a consequence of actual bodily harm or due to a massive threat to the physical integrity,[185] which is why, for example, under certain circumstances the fear of dying can also constitute a compensable immaterial loss.[186] Damages for non-pecuniary loss are calculated on the basis of the duration and intensity of the actual suffering. Since the latter can hardly be measured, the assessment in practice primarily focuses on more objective criteria like the type and seriousness of the injury.[187] While one could **94**

---

183 *Koziol* (fn 168) no 63.

184 Compensation for harm caused by vaccination under the statutory regime mentioned supra no 57 is limited, but not strict liability under the Nuclear Liability Act (see no 56).

185 KBB/*Danzl* (fn 169) § 1325 nos 28; *Karner* (fn 137) 106 ff; *H Koziol*, Die Bedeutung des Zeitfaktors bei der Bemessung ideeller Schäden, in: Festschrift Hausheer (2002) 597, 601 ff.

186 OGH 14.1.2010, 6 Ob 248/09b Zak 2010/197. Cf § 1316 par 3 no 6 of the draft for a new Austrian tort law, which provides that compensation shall also be had 'insofar as serious grounds for imputation exist, for the fear of dying or of being seriously injured if such fear has been caused by a concrete endangerment.' A translation of the draft is available in the annex to *BC Steininger*, Austria, in: H Koziol/BC Steininger (eds), European Tort Law 2007 (2008) 134, 158 ff.

187 *Koziol* (fn 58) no 11/19 ff.

imagine further including subjective elements like sensitivity of the injured person (to the extent objectively assessable), most courts decline to do so.[188] Neither do they take into account the degree of the defendant's fault when calculating non-pecuniary loss.[189] Personal (in particular economic) circumstances of the victim are generally not considered either;[190] this is subject to substantial criticism.[191]

95 Damages are typically awarded in the form of a lump sum for all pain and suffering sustained.[192] Nevertheless, in practice courts consider statistical data, which is published regularly on the basis of prior awards.[193] Such tables list average 'rates' determined according to the severity of pain ('agonising', 'severe', 'medium', and 'slight') as well as its duration (given in days). While such rates are certainly not used as mathematical constants, they at least regularly serve as guidelines for the assessment of damages for pain and suffering.[194] The maximum currently attributable as compensation for non-pecuniary loss probably ranges around € 250,000.[195]

---

188 Rummel/*Reischauer* (fn 68) § 1325 nos 45 ff; *Karner* (fn 137) 123 ff. (Only) more recent cases award damages despite lack of sensitiveness: OGH 23.4.1992 Ehe- und familienrechtliche Entscheidungen (EF) 69.111; 14.1.1993, 2 Ob 66/92, ZVR 1993/150; *K-H Danzl*, in: K-H Danzl/K Gutiérrez-Lobos/O Müller (eds), Das Schmerzengeld in medizinischer und juristischer Sicht (9th edn 2009) 144 ff. Contra Rummel/*Reischauer* (fn 68) § 1325 no 45; Schwimann/*Harrer* (fn 68) § 1325 no 80.

189 Eg OGH 11.4.1956, 3 Ob 162/56, ZVR 1957/6 and many more; see also *Danzl* (fn 188) 105–107. But see *V Steininger*, Minderung der Erwerbsfähigkeit ohne Verdienstentgang, in: Festschrift Wilburg (1965) 181 (202); *Koziol* (fn 58) nos 11/23 ff; cf Rummel/*Reischauer* (fn 68) § 1325 no 48.

190 OGH 7.3.1928, 3 Ob 201/28, SZ 10/44; more recent cases are eg OGH 15.11.1989, 1 Ob 43/89, SZ 62/176; 19.12.1990, 1 Ob 27/90, SZ 63/223; contra OGH 9.5.1985, 7 Ob 566/85, SZ 58/80.

191 *A Ehrenzweig*, System des österreichischen allgemeinen Privatrechts II/1 (2nd edn 1928) 630 f; *H Wenusch*, Überlegungen zur Höhe des Schmerzengeldes, AnwBl 1997, 706; *Koziol* (fn 58) nos 11/21 ff; cf also Rummel/*Reischauer* (fn 68) § 1325 no 46; contra Schwimann/*Harrer* (fn 68) § 1325 nos 75, 81; *Danzl* (fn 188) 119 ff.

192 Rummel/*Reischauer* (fn 68) § 1325 no 49. Exceptionally, annuity payments are also possible in case of severe bodily injuries with particularly grave and lasting painful consequences: OGH 21.11.1968, 2 Ob 330/68, SZ 41/159; 8.8.2002, 2 Ob 145/02s, ZVR 2002/95; Schwimann/*Harrer* (fn 68) § 1325 no 89. On the practice of compensation of future pain, see eg *Ch Huber*, Globalbemessung, Teilbemessung und Teilglobalbemessung bei zukünftigen Schmerzen, ÖJZ 2008, 83.

193 *R Fucik/F Hartl*, Schmerzengeld für seelische Schmerzen, ÖRZ 1994, 148 (151), cf the latest list eg in *F Hartl*, Schmerzengeldsätze in Österreich, Zivilrecht aktuell (Zak) 2011, 47 (with € 100–120 per day of light pain, € 200–250 per day of medium pain, and € 300–360 per day of severe pain).

194 Schwimann/*Harrer* (fn 68) § 1325 no 72; *K-H Danzl*, Schmerzengeldsätze in Österreich? ZVR 1990, 295; *id* (fn 188) 132 ff; *Juen* (fn 51) 16 f; *Karner* (fn 137) 91 f.

195 The highest published award so far was around € 218,000 in 2002: OGH 18.4.2002, 2 Ob 237/01v, SZ 2002/50. Cf OGH 23.9.2004, 2 Ob 180/04s, ZVR 2004/113.

26. Who can claim compensation for non-pecuniary loss?

Apart from the immediate victim, Austrian courts have meanwhile acknowledged that close relatives and loved ones[196] can claim damages for bereavement in fatal accident cases.[197] However, so far courts insist on qualified fault on the side of the tortfeasor, therefore claims based upon merely slight negligence or strict liability do not extend to such third parties. Furthermore, until recently only damages for bereavement, ie in fatal cases, were granted. However, the Supreme Court has already indicated obiter that it may more favourably look upon cases in the future where the immediate victim has survived, but suffered severe and lasting injuries, though still only if caused by qualified fault.[198] **96**

G. Procedural Matters

27. Specific rules of jurisdiction or procedure

There are no specific rules of jurisdiction or procedure which apply to medical malpractice cases. **97**

28. Special institutions handling malpractice claims

(a) Patient advocacy. As required by § 11e KAKuG, all provinces have installed so-called *Patientenanwaltschaften*[199] (patient advocacies) offering, inter alia, free advice and support to patients who believe they have been **98**

---

196 So far, courts have recognised parents, children, siblings, and life-time companions as eligible for such claims. Amounts awarded are, for example, € 20,000 for each parent and up to € 15,000 to siblings; cf OGH 26.6.2008, 2 Ob 55/08i, ecolex 2008, 907.

197 KBB/*Danzl* (fn 169) § 1325 no 29. This has to be differentiated from cases where the relatives have suffered a shock when learning about the (fatal) injuries of one of the family, which leads to a medical condition and therefore personal injury of themselves (*Schockschäden mit Krankheitswert*). On both types, see *E Karner*/*H Koziol*, Der Ersatz ideellen Schadens im österreichischen Recht und seine Reform (Verhandlungen des 15. Österreichischen Juristentags Innsbruck 2003, vol II/1) 74 ff.

198 Eg OGH 14.6.2007, 2 Ob 163/06v, SZ 2007/96.

199 Though misleading in light of the missing right of representation before courts, this German term is used in five provinces (Burgenland, Carinthia, Lower Austria, Vienna, Vorarlberg), whereas others speak of 'Patientenvertretung' (Salzburg, Tyrol, Upper Austria) or 'PatientInnen- und Pflegeombudsschaft' (Styria). On the history, see *Jahn* (fn 154) 16 ff. See generally *G Bachinger*, Patienten helfen – The System of the Patient Advocacies in Austria, <http://www.patientenanwalt.com/fileadmin/dokumente/09_english_documents/legal_information/0510legalinfo_patient_advocacies_DrBachinger.pdf>.

wronged in the course of medical treatment at a hospital.[200] These independent bodies are not competent to represent patients before courts, but their services may prevent cases from going there inasmuch as they offer guidance to patients about their options, negotiate on their behalf with liability insurers, appoint experts to assess the facts and so on. The patient advocacies serve an important buffer function, filtering out unsubstantiated cases, while at the same time at least offering an official place to be heard to these complainants.[201]

99 **(b) Conciliation bodies of the Medical Chambers.** All provinces with the exception of Salzburg[202] have established so-called *Schiedsstellen* or *Schlichtungsstellen* (conciliation panels)[203] in order to provide a forum for both patients and doctors to resolve disputes arising from or in the course of the treatment. They can therefore not only be called upon by patients, but also by doctors.[204] These panels are typically organised at the seat of the respective Medical Chamber.[205] The number of members varies and typically includes at least one doctor and one judge each.

---

200 In Burgenland, Carinthia, Lower Austria, Styria, Vienna, and Vorarlberg, the patient advocacy is also competent to handle claims concerning individual doctors: <https://www.gesundheit.gv.at/Portal.Node/ghp/public/content/Patientenanwaltschaften_LN.html>.

201 In 2008, of all 673 complaints filed with the Lower Austrian patient advocacy, for example, 563 (84 %) upfront turned out to be unsubstantiated from a liability perspective. However, of the remaining 110 cases, 98 led to compensation payments, either through direct talks with the insurers (75 cases) or after consulting the Medical Chamber's conciliation panel (23 cases). See the 2008 activity report of the Lower Austrian Patient Advocacy <http://www.patientenanwalt.com/fileadmin/dokumente/04_publikationen/taetigkeitsberichte/noe_ppa/T%C3 %A4tigkeitsbericht_2008.pdf> 27 f. While the number of patient complaints has doubled over the past ten years in Vorarlberg, only eight cases on average go to court each year: <http://vorarlberg.orf.at/stories/422006/>.

202 In Salzburg, the *Patientenvertretung* (patient advocacy, see supra no 97) is entrusted with similar functions. See *Jahn* (fn 154) 74 f.

203 The litteral translation would be 'arbitration panel'. Despite their name, however, they do not offer arbitration in the formal sense since their decisions are not binding: *Jahn* (fn 154) 67; ibid 68 ff on the history.

204 On details see *M Leitner*, Schiedsstelle in Arzthaftpflichtfragen, RdM 1998, 7; *M Roth/J Sperl*, Außergerichtliche Konfliktlösung in medizinischen Schadensfällen, AnwBl 2000, 387.

205 This is true for Burgenland, Lower Austria, Styria, Tyrol, Upper Austria and Vienna. In Carinthia and Vorarlberg, they are seated at the offices of the patient advocacy. The same is true for Salzburg with respect to hospitals, whereas the competent body for self-employed doctors is at the seat of the Salzburg Medical Chamber.

The proceedings are entirely voluntary for both sides[206] and can be initiated by an informal request. The panel tries to resolve the matters in dispute by offering a forum for discussion. In some cases, it will request a formal independent expert opinion.[207] The decisions of the panel are mere non-binding recommendations, so that the patient can still file suit at a regular court of law. The decisions (if in the patient's favour) primarily recommend lump-sum payments. **100**

§ 41 *Zahnärztegesetz* requires the Austrian Dentists' Chamber to install its own conciliation panels in all provinces.[208] **101**

As expressly stipulated by law (§ 58a para 2 *Ärztegesetz*, § 48 para 4 *Zahnärztegesetz*) doctors or dentists who participate in the fact-finding process of the conciliation procedure are not deemed to violate their obligations under their liability insurance policy, which otherwise might lead to a release from the obligation to cover the incident. **102**

H. Outlook

29. Reform plans

While a reform of medical malpractice law has been discussed repeatedly over the past decades,[209] there is no reform plan in sight which has any chance of immediate legislation. **103**

Cases

Case 1

1. Contractual aspects

The facts do not state whether X had entered into a contract with B alone or with the joint practice of A and B, which may be a separate legal entity. In Austria, doctors may team up informally (without external effects), also **104**

206 In some provinces, hospitals have filed general ex ante-submissions so that it is entirely up to their patients whether they want to have their cases heard before the competent conciliation panel or go straight to court. Cf *Juen* (fn 51) 294.

207 In Tyrol, this is true for about half of all cases handled: *Juen* (fn 51) 296.

208 On their predecessors and the reason for establishing a separate structure, *Jahn* (fn 154) 76 ff.

209 See, eg, *Jahn* (fn 154) 96 ff.

by way of shared practices or equipment (*Ordinationsgemeinschaft* or *Apparategemeinschaft*, § 52 *Ärztegesetz*),[210] or they may jointly open a *Gruppenpraxis* (group practice, § 52a f *Ärztegesetz*),[211] which so far could only be done in the form of a partnership (*offene Gesellschaft*) within the meaning of § 105 *Unternehmensgesetzbuch* (Enterprise Code, UGB).[212] From 2010 onwards, a group practice can also be established as a limited liability company. If it is a shared practice, the patient enters into a contract with each doctor individually, whereas in the latter case, it is the *Gruppenpraxis* as such that is competent to conclude contracts with its patients. In that case, X and Y would have to direct their contractual claims against the group practice, whereas A and B individually would have to be sued on a tort theory. They would nevertheless also be personally liable as partners for the contractual duties of their *Gruppenpraxis* unless it is a limited liability company.

105 In the following, it is assumed, however, that X had contracted with B individually, in which case A had acted as an *Erfüllungsgehilfe* for B within the meaning of § 1313a ABGB.[213] This leads to a follow-up question whether B could shift his contractual duties onto A while on holiday. This has to be answered in the affirmative under the circumstances, since the fact that A and B teamed up must have been known to X, and it is to be assumed that she had tacitly or even expressly consented to A's stepping in while B was away. This is further supported by the fact that the treatment in the instant case was by its nature meant to last for a longer period of time.

106 Even though A and B use the facilities and staff of hospital C (apparently as *Belegärzte*),[214] X will have entered into a separate contract with C, which may be vicariously liable for its staff (including D) depending upon the

---

210 In this case, the *Ordinations-* or *Apparategemeinschaft* as such has external effects, but only with respect to the acquisition (or rent) and maintenance of space and/or equipment. Doctors may alternatively also enter into a mere *Gemeinschaftspraxis* (joint practice), which has no external effects at all and constitutes a purely internal arrangement between the doctors. See *Juen* (fn 51) 55.

211 Doctors may also form a *Gruppenpraxis* with dentists.

212 While being a separate legal entity externally, the *offene Gesellschaft* is marked in particular by the fact that all partners must retain full personal liability for the partnership. There is a third alternative without external effects: Doctors may, for example, also form a limited liability company (*Gesellschaft mit beschränkter Haftung*) or any other form of legal entity for the mere operation of the practice, in which case the investment risk (costs of establishing the practice, equipment etc) is borne by the company, whereas the doctor rents space and equipment from his or her own company. They nevertheless contract individually with their patients.

213 See supra no 45.

214 Supra no 47.

scope of said contract. B will also be vicariously liable for D if his contract with X included all medical assistance during birth (which is not clear under the facts given).

Y is clearly within the protective scope of X's contracts with B and C and can therefore raise her own claims on the basis thereof.[215] Her twin brother was stillborn, so his conditional rights as *nasciturus* never materialised.[216] 107

2. Compensable losses

Subject to further conditions, Y's impairments as described are all generally compensable under both tortious and contractual liability. As far as pecuniary damage is concerned, the tortfeasor(s) have to cover all expenses Y would not have to incur in the absence of her condition caused by the tortfeasor(s). This includes, for example, necessary adjustments to the home, a suitable wheelchair and added costs of transportation (eg a special car), expenses for suitable and adequate therapy,[217] and of course also the costs of the professional nurses.[218] The fact that the costs of taking care of Y at home are higher than if she stayed in a professional care centre is irrelevant – there is no duty to mitigate the loss by moving into a nursing home just because it is cheaper there.[219] With respect to already predictable future losses, she will *have to* file for a declaratory judgment in order to avoid prescription; she *may* ask for declaratory relief also for other potential future losses, even if unlikely.[220] 108

Apart from compensation for disfigurement,[221] Y may also have a claim for non-pecuniary damage. The former may amount up to € 30,000; the latter may be worth around € 200,000 in light of a recent decision with 109

215 See supra no 61.

216 According to § 22 ABGB, even unborn children are protected under law from the moment of conception onwards. However, if they are stillborn, for the purpose of these rights they are treated as if never conceived.

217 This may even include alternative methods not (yet) recognised by orthodox medicine if proven to be promising or successful: OGH 19.5.2009, 3 Ob 283/08a, AnwBl 2009, 368 (dolphin therapy).

218 Cf KBB/*Danzl* (fn 169) § 1325 nos 10 f. Claims for loss of future income would be premature: OGH 26.1.1988, 2 Ob 69/87, ZVR 1988/148.

219 OGH 10.12.1999, 2 Ob 338/99s, ecolex 2000, 282.

220 W *Dehn*, in: H Koziol/P Bydlinski/R Bollenberger (eds), Kurzkommentar zum ABGB (KBB, 3rd edn 2010) § 1489 no 4.

221 Supra no 88.

seemingly similar birth defects.[222] The fact that she may not (fully) sense pain due to her condition is irrelevant.[223]

110 Parents of the immediate victim may in their own right claim compensation for all expenses they incur in the fulfilment of their parental duties of maintenance. There is consequently no need for them to prefinance such expenses and wait for a refund via their child's claims against the tortfeasor. Parents can secure their future claims by asking for a declaratory judgment confirming the duties of the tortfeasor vis-à-vis them upfront.[224] X's claim for services provided to Y therefore need not necessarily be filed by the latter, even though the defendant(s) will obviously not have to compensate twice.[225] The extent of compensation will be measured according to the (fictitious) costs of a professional nurse, but only for the time X actually spends taking care of Y, therefore not only discounting the time Y is looked after by the professional staff, but also the time X would have spent with Y anyhow without nursing her (in particular at night and during other activities in the household than taking care of Y).[226] Furthermore, if X has to give up a previous employment or cut her working hours in order to take care of her daughter, and if this reduction of income also leads to a lower pension claim after her retirement, not only the difference between her previous and present income are compensable, but also the negative effects on her future pension.

111 If the defendant(s) had acted with at least gross negligence X may have a claim for bereavement with respect to her stillborn son,[227] whereas the non-pecuniary loss of a mother with respect to a surviving daughter (despite the latter's deplorable condition) is not yet recognised as compensable under Austrian law.[228]

3. Causation

112 The fact that it remains unclear whether Y's current condition was caused by the treatment or instead due to a precondition she had, and that misconduct by A and D appears to be out of the question, seems to make

222 OGH 19.5.2009, 3 Ob 283/08a, AnwBl 2009, 368.
223 KBB/*Danzl* (fn 169) § 1325 no 27.
224 See, eg, OGH 29.4.1997, 1 Ob 2201/96z, SZ 70/84; 5.4.2005, 4 Ob 15/05t, SZ 2005/50; 30.7.2009, 8 Ob 27/09t, ecolex 2009, 947.
225 OGH 5.4.2005, 4 Ob 15/05t, SZ 2005/50.
226 OGH 16.7.2009, 2 Ob 137/09z; 21.4.2010 7 Ob 63/10f Zak 2010/427.
227 In light of recent judgments, it may amount up to € 20,000.
228 See no 96.

this a perfect case for Franz Bydlinski's proposal to split the loss between the claimants and the defendants according to the probability of each side's contribution to causation.[229]

Furthermore, even if A and B are not vicariously liable for D's behaviour, they may still be held jointly and severally liable if it remains unclear whether Y's condition was caused by the misconduct of either A or D.[230] **113**

Case 2

1. Wrongful conception

The Austrian Supreme Court has had to deal with three cases of wrongful conception so far.[231] Despite significant criticism in academic literature, the Supreme Court in all three decisions denied the parents' claim to compensation of their maintenance costs, arguing that the birth of a healthy (though unwanted) child does not constitute a compensable loss. Consequently, the monetary consequences thereof cannot be indemnified in tort law either. **114**

In the case at hand, therefore, X would not be successful before an Austrian court. **115**

2. Wrongful birth

In contrast, the Supreme Court has acknowledged the right of parents to claim compensation for wrongful birth, ie cases where a child is born with abnormalities that could have been diagnosed at an earlier stage of pregnancy so that the parents could have opted for an abortion. **116**

229 Supra no 39. See in particular OGH 7.11.1995, 4 Ob 554/95, SZ 68/207 (perinatal asphyxia either due to malpractice or to precondition – umbilical cord slung around neck).

230 Supra no 38.

231 OGH 14.9.2006, 6 Ob 101/06f, SZ 2006/133 (vasectomy); 30.11.2006, 2 Ob 172/06t, ecolex 2007, 169 (occlusion of Fallopian tube); 7.8.2008 6 Ob 148/08w, JBl 2009, 108 (triplets after in-vitro fertilisation despite express wish of parents to insert only two embryos in order to avoid multiple pregnancy). *D Hinghofer-Szalkay/C Hirsch*, Wrongful Conception die Zweite – (k)ein Ende in Sicht, Zeitschrift für Ehe- und Familienrecht (EF-Z) 2007, 89; *iid*, Wrongful birth/Wrongful conception quo vadis? ÖJZ 2007, 519; *iid*, Wrongful Birth – Wrongful Conception: Die Diskussion geht in die Verlängerung, iFamZ 2008, 120; *E Karner*, Unerwünschte Zeugung und ungeplante Geburt – (k)eine Rechtsprechungsdivergenz? EF-Z 2009, 91.

117 In the first such case in 1999,[232] the Supreme Court confirmed that the abnormalities should have been detected during ultrasound screening at the hospital whose carriers were subsequently held liable for such malpractice. The key question remaining in dispute was whether the parents had suffered a compensable loss due to said malpractice, also in light of the fact that the abnormalities as such had not been caused by the defendants. Since an abortion would have been possible and legal if the ultrasound screening had been performed properly, the mother was deprived of her freedom to opt for terminating the pregnancy. One of the major motivations for the legislator to allow abortion for medical reasons was precisely in order to protect parents from the consequences of all mental, physical and social problems a life with a severely handicapped child can entail. The Supreme Court also pointed to the additional financial aspects which puts further pressure onto the parents. These economic consequences of the failure to properly inform the parents in time have to be seen as distinctly separate from any other aspects, which also rules out that acknowledging the negative financial consequences for the parents as compensable losses is equated with a value judgment on the child as such. The Court therefore awarded the parents the additional costs of raising and bringing up a handicapped child (only those and not the full maintenance costs were asked for in that case), which may well extend over the whole lifetime of the latter. While there may be a duty of the parents under family law to come up for such costs, this obligation cannot reduce the defendants' liability under tort law.

118 In a more recent decision, the Austrian Supreme Court went even further and awarded full maintenance costs to the parents, not just the added expenses due to the child's handicap.[233] After thoroughly analysing the manifold reactions in academic writing to the afore-mentioned first case of wrongful birth, the Court repeated that the existence of the child as such is not damage and emphatically denied that its jurisprudence was pointing in that direction. Proceeding from the undisputed understanding that a person's death may trigger monetary consequences in tort law without putting a price-tag on the person as such, the Court argued that

232 OGH 25.5.1999, 1 Ob 91/99k, SZ 72/91; *C Hirsch*, Arzthaftung infolge unerwünschter Geburt eines Kindes, RdM 1999, 163; *R Rebhahn*, Schadenersatz wegen der Geburt eines nicht gewünschten Kindes? JBl 2000, 265; *M Schauer*, 'Wrongful birth' in der Grundsatzentscheidung des OGH, RdM 2004/5; *J Cornides*, Zur Haftung des Arztes bei fehlerhafter pränataler Diagnose, JBl 2007, 137.

233 OGH 11.12.2007, 5 Ob 148/07m, JBl 2008, 521; *R Pletzer*, 'Recht auf kein Kind?' JBl 2007, 490; *BC Steininger*, Wrongful birth revisited, ÖJZ 2008, 436; *H Koziol/BC Steininger*, Schadenersatz bei ungeplanter Geburt eines Kindes, ÖRZ 2008, 138.

faulty conduct at the beginning of life may also lead to pecuniary losses distinct from the affected person.

While the outcome of the latter case as compared to the former is at least conceivable, the continuing denial of any compensation for wrongful conception is inexplicable (and the Court did not even try, playing the conflict down by simply pointing to the different facts). In particular, this aggravates the ethical problem the Court tried to resolve: On the one hand, the Court denies compensation for an unwanted, but healthy child, on the other, it grants full (!) maintenance costs as damages for an unwanted, but handicapped child. As the Austrian Bioethics Commission stated, 'the impression was created of a discriminatory valuation of children with and without a disability.'[234] **119**

3. Wrongful life

In the first decision on wrongful birth cited above, the Court was also asked to decide upon the child's own claim for compensation. This was categorically denied, pointing (again) to the German jurisprudence. No one has a claim to prevent his or her own existence, and there can never be a duty of another to intervene and to take action against someone else's life, irrespective of how miserable the latter's condition may be.[235] **120**

Case 3

1. Contractual aspects

X is protected under his mother's contract with A, which includes protective duties also vis-à-vis X as a third party.[236] The same is true for his mother's contract with midwife B, while he himself is the contractual partner of hospital C, entered into after his birth. X can therefore avail himself of the advantages of striving for contractual liability of the defendants.[237] **121**

---

234 <http://www.bundeskanzleramt.at/DocView.axd?CobId=23689>.
235 OGH 25.5.1999, 1 Ob 91/99k, SZ 72/91.
236 See supra no 61.
237 Supra no 69.

2. Failure to monitor blood sugar level

122 According to the facts, proper treatment of X at hospital A in light of established paediatric knowledge at the time would have included the continuous monitoring of his blood sugar level. This would have revealed the need for immediate action, which in turn would have prevented the subsequent deterioration of X's condition. This failure to adhere to contemporary professional standards[238] clearly amounts to negligence which triggers the vicarious liability of hospital A for its obstetrics staff.

3. Failure to consult other expert(s)

123 As stated in the facts, both hospital A's obstetrician and midwife B should have sought the advice of a paediatrician (though at different times) but failed to do so, which constitutes a failure to meet the standards to be expected by X in light of their contractual obligations.

124 The same is true for doctor E at hospital C, who should have referred X to a more experienced doctor. Assuming he was a junior doctor (intern, *Turnusarzt*), he would, inter alia, be subject to § 3 para 3 *Ärztegesetz*, which restricts the scope of permissible activities for *Turnusärzte* and essentially requires them to work under the supervision of a more senior doctor.[239] If they exceed their spectrum of permissible activities, this may amount to *Übernahmeverschulden* (or *Einlassungsfahrlässigkeit*). This means that they are to blame for assuming a duty whose proper fulfilment is beyond the scope of their abilities, of which they are aware.[240]

4. Lack of proper organisation

125 One aspect indicated by the facts that may trigger the liability of hospitals A and C directly concerns flaws in their respective organisation.[241]

---

238 Supra no 29.

239 See *J Steiner*, Rechtsfragen der Rufbereitschaft, RdM 1997, 80, on the status of the *Turnusarzt* and the responsibilities of his hospital, his instructor, and the specialists on call while the *Turnusarzt* is on duty.

240 *Juen* (fn 51) 175 ff (in particular 178 f). See, eg, OGH 9.9.1986, 2 Ob 599/85, JBl 1987, 104 (trainee anaesthetist).

241 *W Mazal*, Haftung, Haftungsüberlagerung und Organisationsverantwortung, RdM 2000, 65.

As far as A is concerned, it seems evident that a paediatrician should have been available at least on call, but either no such specialist was present or could be reached with reasonable efforts, or hospital A did not even have such expert staff on its payroll at all. **126**

According to § 3 para 4 lit e KAKuG, a permit to run a hospital can only be granted if appropriate senior staff have been named and if there is convincing assurance that the hospital also otherwise will be adequately staffed, with further details in §§ 7 ff KAKuG. § 8 KAKuG sets the minimum standards for the organisation of a hospital's medical staff, requiring, inter alia, that professional medical help has to be available at any given time immediately (no 1), with enough specialists present in all fields covered by the hospital (no 2). Exceptions are permissible at night and on weekends for special areas, but even then specialists must be on call. In light of the circumstances of the case, it appears that hospital A either did not come up to these standards or had failed to establish a compulsory system of referrals between its specialists in different fields. Either way, A can be held liable for such (own) failure without the need for attributing this vicariously via the misconduct of one of its employees or executives.[242] **127**

In the case of C, the facts spell out that there was no adequate organisational structure in force regulating the competences at the various staff levels and how these should interact. Suitable control mechanisms as well as measures to ensure the exchange of information among medical staff were equally missing. All that shows that C is also to blame for its lack of proper organisation. **128**

Both A and C could only escape liability by proving that X would have suffered the harm in question anyhow, even if their staff had been perfectly organised.[243] **129**

In a case with comparable legal issues, the Austrian Supreme Court also had to deal with the issue of delayed referral to another specialist within a hospital.[244] The four-year-old plaintiff was diagnosed with mumps meningitis by his family doctor and referred to the defendant's hospital, where neither the junior doctor at the reception nor the senior internist realised that the plaintiff's symptoms in fact originated from an acute epiglottitis. **130**

---

242 Since a few years ago, enterprises and other legal entities can be held liable for inadequate structures etc also in criminal law (*Verbandsverbindlichkeitsgesetz*), which in turn underlines their exposure to civil liability. See *W Mazal*, VbVG, Haftungsdrohung als Chance, RdM 2006, 1; *J Steiner*, Krankenhausmanagement und Verbandsverantwortlichkeit, RdM 2007, 175.

243 Eg OGH 9.9.1986, 2 Ob 599/85, JBl 1987, 104.

244 OGH 3.12.1985, 5 Ob 608/84, *Konsumentenrecht-Entscheidungssammlung* (KRES) 9/8.

Only after the plaintiff's cardiac arrest was he transferred to the hospital's intensive care unit. Spontaneous breathing did not resume before nine days later. The plaintiff suffered major brain damage due to the lack of oxygen, resulting in most severe permanent mental and physical handicaps very similar to X in the case at issue. While the Court acknowledged that the internist herself was not to blame for failing to recognise the epiglottitis, she should have consulted a specialist in intensive care much sooner in light of the symptoms; the Court also saw this as a blameworthy flaw in the hospital's organisation. There was no need to identify any individual employee for whom the hospital was vicariously liable; it was rather its own failure to provide for adequate and efficient structures and organisational plans for such emergency situations which triggered the hospital's liability.

5. Multiple tortfeasors

131 Since X sues A, B, C and E, let us briefly address the question of how Austrian tort law deals with multiple actors contributing to causing harm.

132 As mentioned above, hospitals A and C have to account for flaws in their organisation in addition to being vicariously liable for their staff (in the case of C including doctor E). B and E may have to account for their individual behaviour, but only B can be sued for violations of contractual duties, whereas E is not in any personal contractual relationship with X or his mother and can therefore only be sued in tort.

133 The interplay of all these defendants is relevant when it comes to establishing causation. One key question relates to the time span in which X's condition deteriorated or, in other words, at what stage the delay in having him examined by an expert had a causal impact on the injuries he sustained. Even though there may be a high probability that the ultimate organic damage was sustained while in hospital C, this effect must not be confused with its cause, as there may have been a possibility to prevent such harm already at an earlier stage (even making the admission to hospital C unnecessary). On the other hand, this fact makes it very difficult for C and E to argue that X's loss had already been caused in its entirety before he was admitted to hospital C; furthermore, they cannot argue that X's condition should have been detected earlier, as they were also consulted to examine his state of health and were (also) under a duty to provide expert help to diagnose and treat him.

The facts leave it open, however, whether at this point in time at least part of the damage had already been caused, with C and E merely contributing to a (further) deterioration or aggravation of X's condition.[245] As the facts state, 'it is no longer possible to establish what degree of damage had already been sustained and to what extent more damage was sustained during X's treatment in the C clinic'. 134

Therefore, in light of the dangerousness of each contribution to the chain of causation, it seems very likely that all four defendants may end up being liable jointly and severally for the entire damage due to the impossibility of resolving individual quotas or excluding one or more of them because their respective conduct had no (further) deteriorating impact upon X's physical condition. 135

6. Remedies

(a) Future loss of earnings. Assuming that X is below even school-age at the time of filing suit, he will not be able to claim monetary compensation for his future loss of earnings, as determining the amount of (hypothetical) income is not possible yet, even if he were already close to the end of his school education.[246] This does not prevent him from asking for declaratory relief, however, determining the defendants' liability for future losses. 136

(b) Non-pecuniary loss. In light of the afore-mentioned decision,[247] where the Austrian Supreme Court awarded the highest amount of damages for pain and suffering to the claimant, non-pecuniary loss for X in the instant case could well reach € 200,000 or even € 250,000. 137

245 In such case, C and E could only be held liable for the additional harm caused, cf supra no 40.

246 KBB/*Danzl* (fn 169) § 1325 no 13.

247 Supra fn 244.

Case 4

1. Informed consent issues

138 **(a) Language.** If the patient does not properly (or at all) speak the language used by the doctor to communicate the risks of the treatment and therefore fails to understand the information given by the doctor at least in crucial parts or even entirely, the patient is obviously not in a position to make an informed decision which could justify the treatment, no matter how precise the doctor had been in describing the risk in his own language.

139 Generally speaking, doctors must communicate possible complications to their patients, and in doing so must adapt to the latters' language skills as well as their intellectual abilities.[248] Patients may, of course, at the doctor's or at their own initiative call in confidantes who themselves must know the language spoken at least insofar as they should be able to understand and translate medical information.

140 Since none of this happened in the instant case, the patient was obviously not sufficiently informed, so that he did not validly consent to his treatment despite his signature on the consent form.[249]

141 **(b) Who has to inform the patient?** The fact that it was not surgeon C himself who discussed potential risks of the procedure with the patient, but doctor B instead, would itself not be sufficient to establish liability – it lies in the nature of modern-day division of labour also among medical staff, particularly in a hospital, that the information may be given by someone else than the ultimate surgeon. However, the latter is obliged to make sure that the patient has been previously informed by his referring colleague(s) or some other doctor consulted in the course of the preparatory examinations. Depending upon the circumstances of the case, the range of risks to be warned of may be narrower if the patient had undergone comparable treatment before, which may rightfully lead the current doctor to believe that the patient has previous knowledge which need not be brushed up.[250]

---

248 In case of foreign-language patients, a colleague or other staff member, a confidante of the patient, or an interpreter who speaks the relevant language must assist: *Schramm/Stempkowski,* RdM 1997, 137; see further *Engljähringer* (fn 100) 140.

249 See *Heidinger* (fn 138) 43.

250 Eg OGH 23.6.1982, 3 Ob 545/82, JBl 1983, 373 (cmt *W Holzer*).

(c) Use of standard forms and documentation. While pre-printed material or other media may certainly be used in order to support the process of conveying information to a patient, it is of course not enough simply to hand over a sheet of paper without further comments – a conversation with opportunities for the patient to ask questions is indispensable. The form used in the instant case may, however, serve to prove that an exchange between doctor and patient had taken place, even though it may be difficult in practice to convince a court that all items on the form had indeed been addressed, let alone that the patient was in a position to understand the information.[251] **142**

In light of the hospital's contractual duty to properly alert its patients of the risks associated with their treatment,[252] it is in its own interest to produce and preserve all evidence possible documenting the process of informing its patients. The fact that the consent form used by B did not specify whether a dictionary was used during his talks with X, the contrary will be assumed by the court (which may correspond to the experience of life anyhow).[253] **143**

(d) Information about alternatives of treatment. While the facts of the case indicate that the failure to effectively communicate the risk of paralysis to the patient was already decisive, it may be worth further addressing the range of available alternative procedures, which – if not notified to the patient in advance – may also be a trigger for the hospital's liability. **144**

However, a doctor does not always have 'to discuss all theoretically possible techniques of treatment or operation with the patients'.[254] Various possible kinds of treatments only have to be mentioned if they involve less pain or risks, if the success rate varies or even just because another cosmetic result can be reached.[255] It is therefore fair to conclude that the patient in the instant case did not have to be informed about the second possible approach which included a lower risk of paraplegia, but had a higher mortality risk, which is much more substantial. **145**

---

251 *Juen* (fn 51) 134 ff.

252 Supra at fn 130.

253 Supra no 33.

254 OGH 12.9.1990, 1 Ob 651/90, SZ 63/152; *Juen* (fn 51) 113–115.

255 OGH 12.9.1990, 1 Ob 651/90, SZ 63/152; 7.9.1993, 10 Ob 503/93, RdM 1994/1 (cmt C *Kopetzki*); 23.2.1999, 4 Ob 335/98p, RdM 1999/11 (cmt *A Kletečka*).

146 **(e) Conclusion.** Hospital A is vicariously liable for the failure of its staff to fulfil its contractual duties[256] to adequately alert the patient of potential risks in order to allow the latter to make a well-founded decision.

2. Intervening causation in case of a predisposition of the patient

147 As stated in the facts, the claimant already suffered from a myelopathy before he underwent the surgery in question. Even though his condition deteriorated in the course of the operation, such aggravation was not unlikely to happen even (entirely) without the treatment in dispute, though most likely later (if at all).

148 If a precondition of the claimant intervenes with the tortious conduct of the defendant, the solution depends upon the way these two causes coincide.[257] According to the facts, the paralysis was indeed triggered by the operation, so it is certain that at this point in time, the patient's precondition had not yet led to the same result.[258] If the hospital can prove with a high degree of probability that the course of events hypothetically would have led to the same or comparable loss even without the treatment within a foreseeable time, the hospital can only be held liable for speeding up the process, so to speak, ie for the pain suffered in the interim.[259]

3. Personal liability of surgeon C?

149 The second defendant might be liable in tort only, eg for negligence in the course of the operation. He was under no personal duty to inform the patient, who had not contracted with the surgeon, but with his employer, the hospital.[260] On the basis of the facts before us, it is highly unlikely that the second defendant would be liable under Austrian law. According to the hospital's organisation, it was another employee (B) who was inter-

---

256 Supra at fn 130.

257 Supra nos 39–41.

258 If so, ie if it remained unclear whether the paralysis was triggered either by the operation or by the precondition, the loss would be split between the hospital and the patient according to Bydlinski's theory presented supra no 39. If, on the other hand, neither the operation nor the precondition alone had caused the paralysis, but it remained unclear which percentage of this condition is attributable to which partial cause, the hospital would only be liable for half of the patient's loss (supra no 41).

259 Supra no 40.

260 Supra no 49.

nally in charge of informing the patients about potential risks of the treatment contracted for. Only in case of doubt would the surgeon C have had to verify himself that the claimant in fact did receive such information.

In the instant case however, he could rely upon the document signed by X, **150** which in itself did not raise any suspicion as to the claimant's actual knowledge. C would have had to inquire this matter further if he had actually known (or reasonably should have known) about X's lack of language skills, which would have rebutted the first-hand inference based on the patient's written statement of consent.

4. Range of available remedies

The heads of pecuniary damage listed in the facts are all compensable **151** under Austrian law.[261] As to X's non-pecuniary loss, a full assessment might range around € 80,000.[262]

Case 5

1. Liability of A for its employees

(a) Liability for C and D. If C performs duties which should have been **152** carried out by a fully qualified specialist such as D instead,[263] C's behaviour will be assessed according to the standards to be expected from D, even if she herself does not yet come up to this level of expertise.[264] However, the mere fact that C is still an intern does not in itself yet trigger her employer's liability, her failure to come up to the standard of a fully qualified anaesthetist is not presumed, even though proof of the latter may be easier under the circumstances.

The facts indicate that X's arm should have been monitored throughout **153** the operation, so that any malpositioning could have been detected in time. This would have prevented the complications from which X suf-

261 Cf supra no 87.

262 Cf OGH 23.9.2004, 2 Ob 180/04s, ZVR 2004/113.

263 On the question of who is in charge of the positioning of a patient's arm during surgery see *T Schmiedbauer*, Lagerung im OP: Wer verantwortet was? RdM 2005, 166.

264 Supra no 46.

fered. C's failure to do so therefore clearly constituted fault, for which A is vicariously liable.

154 **(b) Lack of proper organisation.** The fact that a fully qualified specialist in anaesthesia was not present throughout the operation may also indicate a flaw in the hospital's organisation, for which it can be held liable directly.[265]

2. Liability of intern C individually

155 Since it will be presumed that C did not in fact monitor X's arm throughout the operation, she will probably be held liable individually in tort for such failure to adhere to acknowledged professional standards (which the facts seem to indicate), even though she will not have to come up to the standard of expertise owed by the hospital to the patient as only the latter two are bound by their contract. If C did not violate the standard owed by an intern of her degree of training by failing to monitor the position of X's arm, she may still have to account for assuming the *de facto* primary responsibility as a fully-fledged anaesthetist, which qualifies as *Übernahmeverschulden* as explained elsewhere.[266]

3. Liability of anaesthetist D individually

156 D personally neither owed a duty to X to attend his surgery nor specifically to supervise C. D can therefore only be held liable personally if the protective scope of his duties as superior and/or instructor of C extends to X as a person immediately affected. This depends in particular on the interpretation of § 3 para 3 *Ärztegesetz*, which generally requires an instructor to monitor the delegated work of the intern or other doctor in training assigned to him. However, if the hospital where these doctors work is not required to have a fully qualified specialist on duty all the time, interns who already have a certain degree of expertise and training

265 See also supra no 125 ff, in particular no 127, referring to § 8 KAKuG, which will be decisive with regard to which experts at what time have to present at the hospital at issue.

266 Supra no 124 at fn 240.

may temporarily act even without the supervision of their instructor.[267] In the latter case, the temporary absence of D may hardly trigger his liability, whereas in the former case the provision has to be seen as a *Schutzgesetz*[268] which, inter alia, (if not primarily) was meant to ensure the safety of patients.

4. Liability of surgeon B individually

As it seems that B was not responsible for the positioning of X's arm under **157**
the circumstances, he will not be liable individually (as also his employer A will not be held vicariously liable for B's conduct since it did not amount to malpractice).

5. Lack of documentation

As mentioned above,[269] the failure to adequately record the positioning of **158**
the claimant's arm in the documentation of his surgery will be held against the defendants, as this fact can only be ascertained with evidence from within their sphere. If it is therefore disputed whether X's arm was in an adverse position or not during his operation, the court will most likely presume the former to be a given unless the hospital can produce evidence (such as documentation) that the opposite was true.

---

267 § 3 para 3 *Ärztegesetz* reads: 'Die in Ausbildung zum Arzt für Allgemeinmedizin oder zum Facharzt befindlichen Ärzte (Turnusärzte) sind lediglich zur unselbstständigen Ausübung der im § 2 Abs 2 und 3 umschriebenen Tätigkeiten … unter Anleitung und Aufsicht der ausbildenden Ärzte berechtigt. Sofern krankenanstaltenrechtliche Organisationsvorschriften keine dauernde Anwesenheit eines Facharztes erfordern, können Turnusärzte, die bereits über die entsprechenden Kenntnisse und Fertigkeiten verfügen, vorübergehend auch ohne Aufsicht eines für die Ausbildung verantwortlichen Facharztes tätig werden.'
See also § 49 para 3 *Ärztegesetz*: ' (3) Der Arzt kann im Einzelfall an Angehörige anderer Gesundheitsberufe oder in Ausbildung zu einem Gesundheitsberuf stehende Personen ärztliche Tätigkeiten übertragen, sofern diese vom Tätigkeitsbereich des entsprechenden Gesundheitsberufes umfasst sind. Er trägt die Verantwortung für die Anordnung. Die ärztliche Aufsicht entfällt, sofern die Regelungen der entsprechenden Gesundheitsberufe bei der Durchführung übertragener ärztlicher Tätigkeiten keine ärztliche Aufsicht vorsehen.'

268 Supra no 37.

269 Supra no 33.

6. Compensable losses

159 **(a) Loss of income.** X can claim compensation for any reduction of his actual income, including the proceeds of moonlighting that he would have generated, despite the fact that the latter violates the norms of a different area of law.[270]

160 **(b) Refusal to re-train – duty to mitigate the loss.** Subject to the circumstances of the case, victims are expected to contribute to reducing their loss of income by accepting reasonable[271] alternative jobs or by committing to re-training in order to get back onto the job market.[272] This duty is based upon § 1304 ABGB, which not only deals with contributory negligence, but also lays the statutory foundation for the victim's duty to mitigate the loss. Generally, it is up to the tortfeasor to prove that the victim had an actual offer to return to work, a merely abstract possibility does not suffice.[273]

161 **(c) Non-pecuniary loss.** In light of recent case-law, it appears likely that the non-pecuniary loss of X will be compensated with up to € 50,000.[274]

162 **(d) Costs of private expert opinion to clarify facts.** Reasonable expenses to clarify the facts in preparation of a trial can not only be recovered as pre-trial costs (§ 41 ZPO) in the main proceeding,[275] but can even be pursued independently if the main claim has already been satisfied, as in case of an out-of-court settlement, for example.[276]

---

270 OGH 25.3.1999, 2 Ob 289/97g, SZ 72/54; critical *G Iro*, Entgeltsanspruch für Schwarzarbeit, RdW 1999, 453; contra *Ch Huber*, Der Erwerbsschaden des Schwarzarbeiters, ZVR 2000, 290.

271 The reasonableness depends upon various factors such as social status, abilities, talents and interests of the victim, previous type of training and working experience, working environment, compatibility with the victim's family life etc. The current situation on the job market is also relevant. Cf OGH 4.2.1976, 8 Ob 505/76, SZ 49/19.

272 OGH 7.12.2000, 2 Ob 324/00m, ZVR 2002/5; 28.4.2008, 2 Ob 227/07g, ZVR 2009/10 (cmt by *G Kathrein*; higher income after re-training not to the tortfeasor's advantage).

273 OGH 20.12.1988, 2 Ob 110/88, ZVR 1989/203.

274 OGH 27.9.2007, 2 Ob 166/07m, Zak 2007/716.

275 Eg OGH 7.2.2006, 5 Ob 212/05w, Zak 2006/335.

276 Eg OGH 24.2.2003, 1 Ob 302/02x, JBl 2003, 857.

In light of the fact that participation in a conciliation proceeding before the competent body[277] is completely voluntary, X's expenses incurred to assess his physical condition seem to be recoverable (as long as and to the extent they are reasonable in light of market prices for such an expert opinion) despite the fact that there would have been no such costs if he had first filed his claim before the conciliation panel. **163**

Other costs incurred before court proceedings may also be compensable if incurred in order to prepare or to avoid a trial, eg the fees of an attorney[278] who represented the patient before a conciliation panel.[279] **164**

Case 6

1. Contractual aspects

As outlined with respect to case 1,[280] there are several means of cooperation between doctors. The facts do not state how A and B have teamed up in their joint practice, so their patients may either conclude contracts with either one of them individually, with both individually, or – if the joint practice is in the form of a legal entity – with the latter. This is obviously decisive for the question of who they can sue for violations of contractual duties. Since X sued A and B individually, it seems that she contracted with the two rather than with their practice, so this is assumed in the following. **165**

2. Liability for infections

Unlike some other jurisdictions, Austria has not (yet) introduced strict liability for nosocomial or other infections in the health care sector. Therefore, standard rules of tort and contractual liability apply, though with a slight modification: § 8a KAKuG requires hospitals to fulfil certain minimum requirements with regard to hygiene standards. This provision clearly has to be considered a *Schutzgesetz* within the meaning of § 1311 ABGB, since its prime purpose is to protect staff, patients and visitors **166**

277 Supra nos 99 ff.

278 Eg *Oberlandesgericht* (Court of appeal, OLG) Innsbruck 26.9.2000, 1 R 193/00t. § 1333 para 2 ABGB explicitly declares the 'necessary costs of appropriate measures of out-of-court collection of debts' recoverable.

279 Supra nos 99 ff.

280 Supra nos 104 ff.

from infections. Therefore, if it is violated, the burden of proving fault is shifted onto the defendant, and a causal link between the violation of the rule and the damage is prima facie proven if the latter is of a kind that § 8a KAKuG intends to prevent.[281]

167 § 56 *Ärztegesetz* and § 36 *Zahnärztegesetz* contain no equivalent requirement for doctors or dentists, but at least foresee control mechanisms for practices with respect to hygiene standards.

168 Apparently the only case concerning infections in the context of health care to reach the Supreme Court concerned E Coli and Klebsiella pneumoniae bacteria which the claimant probably, but not necessarily, acquired while staying at the defendant's hospital. Apart from further complications when treating the infection, the initial (possible) exposure to the bacteria was deemed already to represent fault as the hospital had failed to take adequate preventive measures after the first few cases of infections had occurred. In light of such omissions, the Court was satisfied with the claimant's proof of mere probability of causation. The defendant could have (but had not) refuted this by proving that the claimant's infection may already have occurred before being admitted to the hospital, or even that proper hygiene measures would not have prevented the infection. Since the causal link between the hospital's omissions and the claimant's infection was therefore proven, there was no remaining uncertainty which might have prompted a possible risk sharing.[282]

169 In the case at hand, proper hygiene standards also seem to have been disregarded. These omissions will be deemed violations of the contractual duties owed to X. The burden of proving fault is therefore shifted onto the obligor(s) who is (are) vicariously liable for auxiliaries C and D.[283] Direct claims in tort law against C, D and E would seem to be unsuccessful.

170 Apart from her loss of income, X can also recover the costs for cleaning assistance in the form of an annuity, calculated on the basis of the gross pay due to someone hired on the labour market. The fact that her daughter has in fact taken over these tasks cannot reduce X's claims against the defendants because her daughter is not acting in their favour, but out of generosity to her mother. X could recover these costs even if she had hired no one.[284]

---

281 Supra no 37.

282 OGH 17.6.1992, 2 Ob 538/92, JBl 1993, 316.

283 Apart from the fact that E was apparently not involved in fulfilling contractual duties vis-à-vis X, it seems unlikely on the basis of the facts given that E's conduct amounted to fault.

284 KBB/*Danzl* (fn 169) § 1325 nos 24 f.

3. Variation 1

Under these specific circumstances, one possible cause within the defendants' sphere coincides with two potential sources of the claimant's infection within her own sphere. If the violation of hygiene standards in the orthopaedic practice constituted qualified fault and was significantly likely to cause the claimant's infection in the absence of the two competing causes, under Bydlinski's theory[285] A and B as owners of the practice would be jointly and severally liable for one third of the loss. However, if the claimant convinces the court that the infection was caused by the defendants' omissions with high probability, this will be seen as ample proof of causation (to the exclusion of the alternative causes) which can only be rebutted by defendants as outlined by the Austrian Supreme Court in the above-mentioned decisions.[286] 171

4. Variation 2

Since Austrian law does not foresee strict liability for infections in the health care sector, X would not successfully claim compensation in a scenario without faulty conduct. 172

285 Supra no 39.
286 Cf supra no 33.

Medical Liability in Belgium

Herman Nys

General Questions

A. The Health Care System Framework

I. General Introduction[1]

1. The health care system in overview

Delivery of ambulatory health care in Belgium is mainly private and based on the principles of independent medical practice; that is, independent medical practitioners and paramedics are remunerated via fee-for-service payment and there is free choice of doctor by the patient. The vast majority of physicians work as independent, self-employed health professionals. Medical specialists can work in institutions (mostly hospitals) and/or on an ambulatory basis in private practice. General practitioners (GPs) mostly work in private practice; they are not allowed to work in hospitals except to perform deliveries in maternity units and in emergency care units. Because there is no referral system in Belgium, specialists often form the first point of contact with the patient in the health care system. Patients in Belgium can visit GPs or specialists in their surgeries; they can also visit a specialist in the hospital or in a polyclinic. 1

The functions and roles of many health care personnel have not been clearly defined. There is a lack of distinction between the roles of GPs and specialists. Patients have free choice of the first doctor to contact, can change doctor at any time, and can even consult several at a time. The free choice of doctor is an important right granted to patients in art 6 of the law on the rights of patients of 22 August 2002, but it does lead to patients shopping around for care and to overconsumption of medical care and 2

---

1 *H Nys*, Belgium, in: H Nys (ed), International Encyclopaedia of Laws. Medical Law (2009) 23 ff.

consequent increases in health care expenditure. This explains why the average number of physician contacts per person in Belgium is relatively high.

3 Hospitals can be classified into two categories: general and psychiatric. In 2005, there were 215 hospitals, of which 146 were general and 69 were psychiatric. The general hospital sector consists of acute (116), specialised (23), and geriatric hospitals (7). Specialised hospitals concentrate on one or a few health care specialties, such as cardiopulmonary diseases, locomotive diseases, neurological disorders, palliative care, chronic diseases, and psychogeriatric care. Some acute hospitals have psychiatric departments that only treat psychiatric cases for short stays. The majority of hospitals in Belgium are private hospitals (151, equal to 70 %). Most private hospitals are owned by social-profit associations, whereas the remaining are owned by universities or sickness funds. Public hospitals are for the most part owned by a local public welfare centre, a municipality or an inter-municipal association (which is a legal form of association that groups together local authorities and public welfare centres and, in some cases, the provincial government or private shareholders). Both private and public hospitals are non-profit organisations. Hospital legislation and financing mechanisms are the same for both the public and private sectors. The only differences are that for public hospitals, internal management rules are more tightly defined and their deficits are covered, subject to certain conditions, by local authorities or inter-municipal associations. The acute hospitals include seven university hospitals, which have special status owing to their teaching and research functions. The 'university' label does not necessarily mean that a university owns the hospital; however, it does mean that a certain proportion of beds are registered as university beds. Each university has a certain number of beds, which are distributed among different hospitals.

4 Until the early 1980s, the number of hospital beds in Belgium increased by an average of 1,000 per year to a record number of 92,686 or 9.4 per 1,000 inhabitants in 1981. Since then the Belgian hospital sector has been restructured in order to respond to evolving needs: more geriatric provisions, shorter stays, expansion of day hospitalisation, scaled-up capacity, reduced maternity care, admission of elderly people in need, alternative provisions in the psychiatric sector, etc. The number of acute beds has shown overall decline since the mid-1980s. A process of scaling up the capacity accompanied the measures introduced to reduce the number of beds. In 1989, the minimum bed capacity was fixed at 150 beds for general hospitals. Mergers and closures were supported financially. These meas-

ures were successful in reducing the number of hospitals and beds per population of 1,000. Between 1980 and 2005, the number of hospitals dropped from 521 to 215, and the average capacity of a Belgian hospital rose from 177 to 329 beds. Partly because of the lack of referral structure between types of hospitals in Belgium (or precise distinction among primary, secondary, and tertiary care), the location of hospitals and hospital services is more the result of historical evolution than of well-thought-out geographical planning.

Hospital accreditation is regulated by the federal government and implemented by the three communities (Flemish, French-speaking and German-speaking community). The system of accreditation is primarily concerned with aspects relating to safety, hygiene, quality, and continuity of care. In recent years, hospital accreditation has been moving away from considering the hospital as an overall infrastructure unit towards defining it in terms of its various medical and supportive services. They have coined the descriptive terms *care programme* and *function*. A programme is a coherent intervention for a well-defined target patient group. The programme is first defined by the case treated and the type of care given. Then norms describing infrastructure, number of personnel, minimum activity level, and so on are allocated to this programme. A distinction is made between basic programmes for regular conditions and specialised programmes for more rare conditions, which will not be available in every hospital. A function describes a set of hospital services, which are not aimed at a specific patient group. They are not provided in a defined unit; that is, they are not directly linked to hospital beds and all the programmes and services of the hospital can use them. The idea is that hospitals would be completely made up of a series of basic programmes and basic functions (which would have to be present in every hospital) as well as some specialised functions and programmes. **5**

Art 144, § 1, 1 of the Hospital Law imposes an obligation upon every hospital to determine a so-called general regulation of the legal relationship between the hospital and its physicians, as well as the organisational, working, and financial conditions thereof. With reference to this general regulation, the rights and obligations of every hospital physician and the hospital governor and more specifically his working conditions have to be laid down in writing, either in a contract between both parties or in a unilateral act of appointment. The Hospital Law has not determined the legal nature of this contract. This can be either a labour contract or a contract of work. In the former case, the physician performs his medical activities according to the directions of the hospital manager and receives **6** a salary; in the latter case, he performs his activities independently and is paid by a fee for service. According to the jurisprudence, the contract between a hospital physician and the hospital is in most instances a contract of work. In university hospitals however, physicians work mostly as employees. The distinction between the two types of contracts may be of importance for the liability of the physician in case of a medical fault. A contract between physician and hospital may exist both in a private and a public hospital, whereas by nature the unilateral act of appointment is limited to public hospitals. In this case the physician works as a civil servant. This has become rather exceptional nowadays.

II. Social Welfare Provision

2. The role of public health care

7 Belgium has a system of compulsory health insurance with a very broad benefits package that covers almost the entire population. Health insurance is one of the six sectors of the social security system, which include old age and invalidity pensions, unemployment insurance, work accident insurance, work-related health and occupational diseases, family allowances, and sickness and disability insurance. Almost 99 % of the population is covered by compulsory health insurance. There are two main schemes: (i) the general scheme, which covers major and minor risks for the whole population (except for the self-employed); and (ii) the scheme for the self-employed, which only covers major risks. Major risks include hospital care, child delivery, elective surgery, dialysis, rehabilitation, implants, and specialist care. Minor risks include physicians' visits, dental care, minor surgery, home care, and pharmaceuticals for outpatient care. The basic principle for health insurance coverage in both schemes is that people benefit in accordance with their actual or past professional activity. Both schemes cover active and non-active people and their dependents. The primary insured members are entitled to health insurance based on their current or previous profession. Dependents are covered on the basis of their relationship with the primary entitled person: for example, a member of the family of the entitled person living in the same main place of residence. In 2005, 9,369,424 people (89.1 %) were insured under the general scheme and 983,605 (9.4 %) under the scheme for the self-employed. Individuals have the right to health care only if contributions have been paid and equal a minimum amount. In 1998, insurability rules were alleviated and the principle of an annual entitlement was introduced. In

2004, the government decided to abolish the distinction between the health insurance scheme for the self-employed and the rest of the population. As a first step, as of 1 July 2006, minor risks were included in the compulsory cover for those starting self-employment and for the self-employed with the lowest pensions. From 1 January 2008, all self-employed are compulsorily insured against minor risks.

The services that are covered by compulsory health insurance are described in the nationally established fee schedule (the 'nomenclature'), which is extremely detailed and lists more than 8,000 services. The identification number, contractual fee, and reimbursement rate are specified for each service. Services not included in the fee schedule are not reimbursable. Sickness funds are legally bound to reimburse any claim from their insured members for care delivered by any accredited health care provider at the agreed fee levels. The fee schedule is negotiated yearly or biennially between representatives of the sickness funds and of the health care professionals. **8**

3. Differences in treating patient's claims

If something goes wrong in the course of a medical treatment listed in the 'nomenclature' of reimbursable treatments, the patient's claim is not handled differently in comparison to other personal injury cases. There is no internal review or claims management system within the national health insurance system. However, the sickness funds which are private organisations all have one or other type of 'ombudsperson' and a legal service. Members who are dissatisfied regarding the result of a diagnostic procedure or a treatment can make a complaint and receive legal support if the case is considered serious enough. **9**

The National Institute for Sickness and Invalidity Insurance that runs the compulsory health insurance system (RIZIV-INAMI) is responsible for the evaluation of medical practice with regard to quality criteria. Specifically, the RIZIV-INAMI oversees the system of ongoing training of physicians by means of the accreditation system and peer review. This quality accreditation system should be distinguished from normal physician accreditation, ie licence to practice within the public health insurance system. The quality accreditation of physicians and dentists was introduced in 1995, and has the following objectives: promotion of both the quality and cost-consciousness of care and the quality and efficiency of relations between physicians; exchange of patient data to prevent duplication of effort; ongoing training of physicians to promote quality of care. Within the **10** framework of the compulsory health insurance, quality accreditation is granted to a physician when he/she meets the following conditions: follows an acknowledged programme of ongoing training; maintains a medical file for each patient and exchanges data with other physicians; has achieved a minimum level of activity; collaborates with initiatives for evaluation of quality of care organised by physicians; has not received repeated negative feedback during the evaluation of his/her medical profile. These conditions are related to prescribing and the implementation of diagnostic and therapeutic supplies according to criteria determined by the quality accreditation committee at the RIZIV-INAMI. The efforts involved are rewarded by the granting of a fee supplement to the accredited physicians. Patients are encouraged to obtain services from accredited physicians by means of lower out-of-pocket payments. An important extension of the accreditation was the development of a first form of peer review through the creation of Local Medical Evaluation Groups (LOK-GLEMs). Set up in 1996, LOK-GLEMs are monodisciplinary local or regional groups of 8–25 physicians that meet on an annual basis. The physicians who want to obtain accreditation must join one of these groups and take part in the evaluation of their own practice and those of their peers. The National Council for Quality Promotion is responsible for managing the system of peer review, determining recommendations for good medical practice and supplying feedback data to physicians. From an evaluation in 2003, it was observed that as a result of the accreditation process both the quality of and participation in the extra training has improved. Physicians are more aware of their role regarding ethics, economy and quality, and medical practice has improved due to peer review, a higher level of knowledge and more interdisciplinary discussions.[2]

4. Right of recourse

11 Compensation paid by the public health insurance does not prevail over other compensation. The public health insurance will only compensate damage which is not effectively compensated on the basis of tort law or any other Belgian or foreign law. The compensation by the public health insurance is determined according to its own principles and does not depend on the extent of any effective compensation on another basis. No party will be granted civil immunity because damage is compensated by

2 *D Corens*, Health systems review: Belgium, World Health Organisation (2007) 149–151.

the public health insurance. As long as the damage has not been compensated otherwise, victims can claim a so-called anticipating compensation. If paid, this anticipatory compensation is not of a provisional nature, but has to be considered as permanently obtained by the victim. Compensation can only be paid after the victim has met the obligation to inform the public health insurance about certain aspects of his case (in practice, this rule is not always taken into account). The mirror image of the anticipatory compensation is found in the public health insurer's right to bring a recourse action against the responsible tortfeasor.[3]

III. Private Insurance

5. The role of private health insurance

Mutualities offer their affiliated members complementary insurance to cover additional services not covered by the compulsory insurance system, such as transport to receive treatment or co-payment on home nursing care. The terms and coverage of this insurance differ from one mutuality to another. This part of their service has become popular in the last few years, apparently as a reaction to reductions in the reimbursement coverage of the compulsory scheme. Another form of insurance offered by the mutualities is hospitalisation insurance. This would cover, for example, the extra charges for a single room during an inpatient stay or for pharmaceuticals. This part of the insurance market has recently grown steadily. About 18 % of the population are covered by hospitalisation insurance. **12**

Risk-based private health insurance offered by private for-profit companies remains very small in terms of market volume but has also risen steadily as compulsory insurance coverage has diminished. Belgians seem to take out private insurance in particular to cover hospital costs and the statutory co-payments required of patients (which the compulsory insurance system is legally barred from covering); and companies in Belgium increasingly include private health insurance as a fringe benefit in salary packages. In 1999 about 30 % of Belgians had additional private health insurance, particularly for hospital care costs. Yet apart from these market **13**

---

3 *H Cousy/M de Graeve*, Belgium, in: M Faure/H Koziol (eds), Cases on medical malpractice in a comparative perspective (2001) 92; *H Cousy/D Droshout*, Compensation for personal injury in Belgium, in: BA Koch/H Koziol (eds), Compensation for personal injury in a comparative perspective (2004) 48 f.

niches it is unlikely that private insurance will pose a real threat to the statutory system, because the mutualities have the advantage of benefiting from significant tax relief and economies of scale.[4]

6. Liability insurance

14 Art 8 of the Law of 15 May 2007 regarding the compensation of damage resulting from health care obliges physicians and hospitals to take out liability insurance. However, this law has not (yet) entered into force (see for more details on this, no 57). Meanwhile there is only a 'deontological' obligation imposed by the national council of the order of physicians, a professional body organised by law of which all physicians have to be a member in order to have the right to practice medicine. However, this obligation cannot be legally enforced.

15 Due to the evolution in medical liability, some problems have arisen on the insurance level. Some insurers have left the market or no longer offer insurance policies for the physicians with the most risky activities, like anesthesiology and surgery. Other insurance companies have raised their insurance premiums drastically. In the mid eighties surgeons paid an annual liability premium of € 500; in the nineties the premium was raised to € 1,500 and nowadays the premium is about € 4,000 to € 5,000 or even more. Moreover, the cover of the insurance policy has been limited. Some insurance policies contain a list of non-covered examples of gross-negligence. Furthermore, the cover has been limited in time.[5]

IV. Professional Standards

7. Applicable professional standards[6]

16 According to art 5 of the law on the rights of patients of 22 August 2002, the patient has the right to receive high-quality health care that meets his needs, with respect for his human dignity and his self-determination, and without any discrimination on any grounds whatsoever. The precise implication of the expression 'high-quality health care' is further ex-

4 *Corens* (fn 2) 25 f.

5 *T Vansweevelt*, A no fault-system for medical accidents in Belgium, Paper presented at the 18th World Congress on Medical Law, Bejing 2008.

6 *Nys* (fn 1) 96.

plained in the explanatory memorandum to the law, requiring a physician to act according to 'the applicable standards and the current state of scientific knowledge'. In other words, art 5 makes it mandatory for a physician to act as a '*bonus medicus*'. However, what does 'acting in accordance with the applicable standards and the current scientific knowledge ("*bonus medicus*")' mean? The applicable standards refer, *inter alia*, to guidelines and protocols set up by the medical profession. They contain rules concerning the medical profession as well as technical rules that can be used either as a standard or as guidance in malpractice cases. When deciding whether a physician acted as a '*bonus medicus*' would have, a judge needs to establish what the physician should have done in the particular case and not what is commonly done. Thus, when making a decision on the case, the judge can rely on protocols and guidelines issued by medical organisations, but he is not bound to do so. The significance of clinical practice guidelines in judging the quality of care was already apparent in case law before the development of the patients' rights law. The Brussels Court of Appeal, for example, assigned a decisive role to recommendations formulated in medical literature. The court judged that an expert's report cannot be followed if this report deviates from the recommendations in the literature. In *casu*, it concerned recommendations about which a broad consensus existed in medical science. Moreover, it became clear from the recommendations that the intervention carried out by the physician was not without risk. The importance of observing safety regulations issued by a professional organisation became clear from the decision of the Civil Tribunal of Liège on 20 October 1998.[7] The case concerned the liability of an anaesthetist, who had neglected to personally carry out essential controls, entirely in contrast to what is prescribed by the Belgian safety rules concerning anaesthesia (Safety-First norms). It concerned, in particular, the inspection of the respirator and monitoring alarm. Moreover, he performed different anaesthesias simultaneously and, as a result, he neglected to constantly watch his patient. The Tribunal found the anaesthetist to be at fault because he had not observed the Belgian Safety-First norms, which were enacted for the safety of a patient during anaesthesia. These standards had been approved by the Belgian Professional Association of Specialists in Anaesthesia and Reanimation (BSAR) and had been in effect since 1 January 1995. The Tribunal also stated that these safety rules merely confirm the usual practice as well as some elementary requirements that each careful and devoted physician would have observed in the same circumstances. These cases clearly show

7 See Tijdschrift voor Gezondheidsrecht 1998–1999, 405 with observations by *T Vansweevelt*.

that courts do refer to standards/norms issued by a medical professional organisation when verifying whether the physician has acted carefully.

8. Quality and/or risk management systems

17 There are a variety of accreditation norms for hospitals. Organisational norms relate to staff requirements and responsibilities (eg hygiene, ethical requirements); architectural criteria (eg the number, size, comfort and hygiene standard of hospital rooms); functional standards (eg convenience, accessibility); additional norms relating to minimum activity (eg they stipulate that hospitals should have no fewer than 150 beds; diagnosis/surgical units no fewer than 30 beds; intensive neonatal units no fewer than 15 beds); setting minimum facility standards; and expected staff numbers. Accreditation criteria are developed at federal level and implemented at community level. There are also specific accreditation norms for certain medical services (eg radiology with computed tomography (CT) and magnetic resonance imaging (MRI), radiotherapy, renal dialysis, nuclear medicine, non-urgent patient transport, centres for human genetics) and for certain hospital functions (eg hospital pharmacy, local neonatal care, regional perinatal care, palliative care, surgical day hospitalisation, initial relief of emergency cases, specialised emergency care, intensive care, mobile urgency groups and psychiatric family nursing). Since 1999, the regulation and accreditation of medical hospital services and functions have gradually been replaced by the accreditation of 'care programmes'. A care programme is the collection of several hospital activities which are organised around a certain pathology. For each care programme legal criteria are set related to the target group, nature and content of care, minimum activity level, necessary infrastructure, required medical and non-medical staff and their required expertise, standards concerning quality and quality monitoring, economic standards and geographical accessibility criteria. At present, there are care programmes for reproductive medicine, cardiac pathology, oncology, and geriatric and paediatric activities.[8]

18 Alongside accreditation standards, the Hospital Act contains several requirements which can promote quality of care, such as requirements concerning the organisation of medical and nursing activity; the description of the tasks of the medical manager; the obligation to maintain a medical file; the establishment of an ethical committee, a committee for

8 *Corens* (fn 2) 44.

hospital hygiene, a medical pharmaceutical committee, a committee for medical material and a committee for blood transfusions, as well as other specialized committees. Since 1999, the medical manager of each hospital must produce a report concerning the internal evaluation of the quality of medical activity. This report must be transferred to the Colleges of Physicians, established at the Federal Ministry of Public Health. The objective of these colleges is to promote quality of care by consensually developing indicators of quality and evaluation concerning good medical practice; recording and reporting activities and giving feedback to the hospitals and physicians concerned. These Colleges of Physicians were established in several fields: cardiac pathology, specialised emergency care, intensive care, renal dialysis, mother and newborn, radiology and nuclear medicine, radiotherapy, reproductive medicine and oncology. The appointment of the members of the colleges is generally based on the advice of the scientific associations of the respective disciplines.

With the creation of the Health Care Knowledge Centre (KCE) in 2003, **19**
another step was taken in bridging the gap between policy-oriented research on health care and policy-making in this field. The KCE is active in producing policy papers, recommendations and research on health technology assessment, the evaluation of medical practice in hospitals, the development of new reimbursement and financing systems, recommendations for hospital admission policies and the development of evidence-based medicine and policies.

Several electronic databases, such as Pharmanet, provide information on **20**
the medical practice of individual physicians. The prescription behaviour of individual GPs and specialists is evaluated against objective scientific standards, for pharmaceuticals, diagnostic and technical services and physiotherapy. Individual physicians receive feedback on their prescription patterns taking into account the pathologies of their patients. These data are peer-reviewed in Local Medical Evaluation Groups. Also, hospitals receive feedback on the activities of the physicians practicing in their institution, compared with other hospitals. Here again, systems of peer review are set up to compare practices and outcomes both amongst each other and against internationally accepted standards. Information campaigns are also launched towards target groups of physicians. Physicians can be requested to explain and substantiate their deviating prescription behaviours. Procedures are in place to penalise physicians whose profile is not in accordance with the parameters, or to reclaim unjustified amounts from physicians in case of obvious over-prescription.

21 Over the past several years, a patient safety policy within the hospitals is being developed through pilot projects on issues such as incident reporting in the case of medication mistakes and the development of patient safety indicators based upon the Clinical Minimum Data Set. A law on patient safety in hospitals that will set up committees for quality and patient safety in hospitals involving a coordinator who will set up and follow the incident reporting in order to create a 'no shame, no blame' culture within each institution is actually under preparation.

B. Tort Liability

9. Fundamentals of tort liability

22 Tort liability is relevant in the case of damage to a third party or where services are rendered to a patient who is not in a position to give consent to the treatment in the case of an emergency or when it appears that he has given an improperly informed consent. Tort liability is governed by arts 1382-1383-1384 Civil Code (C civ).[9]

> 'Any act of a person, which causes damage to another, makes him, by whose fault the damage is occurred, liable to compensate the damage' (art 1382 C civ).
>
> 'Everyone is responsible for damage caused not only by his act but also by his negligence and carelessness' (art 1383 C civ).

23 According to art 1382 and art 1383 C civ, the physician is liable for his own negligent acts or omissions. A physician has an obligation to deliver care that meets the so-called professional standard. This means care that does not lie below the level that would be shown in the circumstances by a reasonable, careful physician. Deviation from the professional standard is to be considered fault in the practice of medicine. This criterion of professional negligence is a so-called objective one. It means that the conduct of a physician is compared not with that of any specific person but with a model (the so-called *bonus medicus*) or standard of the prudent and competent physician. In defining this standard, account is taken not of the individual qualities of any specific physician, but of the typical qualities, skill, and learning commonly possessed by members of the medical profession in good standing. The standard of care is not subjec-

9 *Cousy/de Graeve* (fn 3) 89.

tive. If a physician does something that a physician of ordinary prudence would not do, he is negligent, even though he himself may have regarded his action as reasonable.[10]

10. Burden of proof

The burden of proof mostly constitutes an important and very often decisive issue. The patient who wants to sue a physician or a hospital has to prove the loss (the deterioration of the health status of the patient), the causation between this loss and a fault, and the fault. The burden of proof is not divided between the patient and the physician. The patient always has to furnish the appropriate evidence (art 1315 C civ: *actori incumbat probatio*).[11] In civil procedures based on offences, eg a physician who carries out an intervention without informed consent and violates art 392 of the Criminal Code, the criminal law principle according to which a defendant (the physician) is innocent as long as his guilt is not proven (art 6 European Convention on Human Rights) must be applied. In a judgment of 14 December 2001, the Belgian Court of Cassation decided that the burden of proof with respect to the issue of improperly informed consent remains on the patient. The Court reasoned its decision by referring to the principle of presumption of innocence in criminal cases. As a consequence, in a civil case like the one that was the object of the procedure before the Court of Cassation, whereby a patient introduces a claim based on a transgression, the patient must still prove that all the factors constituting the transgression are present.[12] **24**

11. Uncertain causation

In Belgium, according to the 'equivalence of conditions' theory, any factor that has necessarily contributed to the existence of damage in a case, has to be considered a *sine qua non* cause of this damage. The standard of proof is high because the causal relation must be established with near certainty. **25**

To alleviate the difficult burden of proof of the patient, the judge may use the criterion of 'the thing speaks for itself' or the 'judicial presumption' or '*res ipsa loquitur*' doctrine. Usually this criterion will be used when the **26**

10 *Nys* (fn 1) 82.

11 *Cousy/de Graeve* (fn 3) 91 f.

12 *S Callens*, Medical civil liability in Belgium. Four selected cases, European Journal of Health Law 2003, 126.

physician has left one of his instruments in the body of the patient or when the result of the treatment is strange, as compared with the normal result of the treatment.[13]

27 In applying the theory of equivalence, the judge has hypothetically to reconstruct the events leading to the damage and to imagine away the fault of the defendant. If the damage remains the same, the fault was not a necessary condition for the damage. It may be hard to apply this reasoning in cases where it is uncertain what would have happened if a certain fault had not been committed. If a doctor had applied the correct treatment, the patient still might not have recovered. Here, the courts find a way out by compensating the victim for the loss of a chance of recovery[14] (see no 28).

12. Loss of a chance

28 The 'loss of a chance' theory is often used as an instrument to compensate patients in the event that a causal link between fault and physical damage cannot be established. The loss of a chance theory has long been established in Belgian law, including in medical malpractice law. The Court of Cassation applied the theory for the first time in medical malpractice in its judgment of 19 January 1984. A patient who had many fractures of the legs had been hospitalised. In spite of the fact that, during the weekend, one of the plaster casts showed a brown colour, his toes had swollen and he had complained about pain in his legs, the doctor left the patient to fend for himself. The patient developed gangrene and consequently his right leg had to be amputated. The Court of Appeal of Brussels sentenced the doctor to compensate 80 % of the damage, because he was responsible for the fact that the patient had lost his chances of recovery. Although the physician argued that, even if there had been appropriate medical care, there was a good chance that the leg would have had to have be been amputated, the appeal to the Court of Cassation was dismissed. Scientific literature shows that gangrene is the consequence of wrong treatment or treatment that is delayed too long. According to the Court of Cassation, accepting a causal relation between the mistake and the fact that the patient had lost a chance of avoiding amputation or of undergoing a less serious one was justified. Because his chances of recovery were estimated at 80 %, the physician could be sentenced to pay compensation for 80 % of the damage.[15]

---

13 *Cousy/De Graeve* (fn 3) 92.

14 *H Bocken*, Tort law, in: H Bocken/W de Bondt (eds), Introduction to Belgian law (2001) 265.

15 *Callens*, European Journal of Health Law 2003, 121.

Because the application of this theory in a context of uncertain causation is highly controversial, questions were raised about its future in Belgian medical malpractice law. Recent case law of the Court of Cassation shrouded the precise scope of the theory in uncertainty. A woman assaulted by her ex-partner claimed damages from the local city because of the lack of preventive police intervention after she had expressed her fears on several occasions. The Court of Appeal agreed that the police department should have taken preventive measures to protect the woman and that therefore she had lost a chance of avoiding the violence. The Court of Cassation squashed the decision because the woman actually claimed damages for her physical injury and the Court of Appeal did not exclude the hypothesis of the damage being unchanged if the police had intervened in time.[16] Because the events of this case were situated outside of a medical context, it was impossible to predict if and how the Court of Cassation would apply this theory in medical malpractice cases. However, the many comments on the scope of application of the loss of a chance theory incited by this particular case showed that the theory was clearly under pressure even in the context of medical malpractice. Compensating the loss of a chance of a better medical result is sometimes considered to be a false application of the theory, since it artificially conceals the uncertain causal link between the fault and the real physical damage of the patient.[17] However, on 5 June 2008 the Court of Cassation accepted that the loss of a chance for a horse to be cured or to survive, due to the negligence of a veterinarian, could be compensated under certain conditions. By doing so, the Court confirmed its previous jurisprudence of 1984 and a long-standing tradition in Belgian law.[18] **29**

13. Multiple persons involved

In principle, a physician is only liable for his own acts or omissions. But if the physician employs others to help him perform his duties, he will be treated as the person answerable for them according to art 1384, 3 C civ, ie for the wrongful acts or omissions of his own staff (vicarious liability). Also, the physician may be liable as the superior on the particular occasion **30**

16 The Court of Cassation decided likewise in two decisions related to the same case on 19 June 1998 and 1 April 2004. It confirmed its reasoning in a decision of 12 October 2005.

17 *S Lierman*, A death horse named Prizrak and the loss of a chance theory, Paper presented at the 17th World Congress on Medical Law, Bejing, 2008 and the literature cited in footnote 31 of the paper.

18 *Lierman* (fn 17) 1.

for the acts of the nursing and paramedical personnel that a hospital has made available to him on condition that the physician had control over and supervision of this personnel at the time an accident happened.

31 A typical characteristic of modern hospital medicine is that a patient is not confronted with only one physician but with a medical team consisting of doctors, nurses, technicians, assistants, and others. Modern surgery involves many highly specialised, independent and dependent persons, and a complex organisation. The surgeon no longer controls the entire organisation. Instead, the hospital provides a trained staff of nurses, the supervision of whom may be the responsibility of the surgeon or of the head nurse. This depends mainly on the factual situation: Who was really competent to control and instruct the nursing personnel at the time an accident happened? The surgeon, the anaesthesiologist, the head nurse? While going to and from the operating room and during post-operative care, the patient is in the hands of entirely different personnel. Most of the period before, during, and after the surgery, the patient is unconscious and will be unable to determine which of these many people caused his injury. Matters are further complicated by the fact that in many hospitals a surgeon may employ his own nursing personnel, whereas an anaesthesiologist can make use of nursing personnel employed by the hospital.

32 The law on the rights of patients of 22 August 2002 has amended the Hospital Law in order to ameliorate the position of a patient who suffers medical damage during hospitalisation by introducing the principle of the so-called 'central liability' of a hospital for damage caused by health care professionals working within its remits. In principle, the patient who suffered damage during hospitalisation is not confronted anymore with the difficult task of determining who caused the damage. However, the legislature has created the possibility for a hospital to escape this central liability by informing beforehand and in a clear way the (potential) patients that it will not take up responsibility for the acts or omissions of a health care professional, having regard to the legal relationship between this health care professional and the hospital. In practice, this possibility is mainly used with respect to physicians who deliver their medical services in a hospital on the basis of a so-called contract of work (and not a labour contract) (see supra no 1).

14. Strict liability

33 The main text governing strict (objective) liability in Belgium is the Act of 25 February 1991 on liability for defective products which implemented the EU Directive 85/374 on liability for defective products. This Act came into force on 1 April 1991. It was slightly modified by an Act of 12 December 2000 implementing Directive 1999/34. Under the Act of 25 February 1991 (the Product Liability Act), the producer is automatically liable for damage caused by a defect in his product. This liability without fault exists with respect to any injured person (the buyer or another party). According to art 7 of the Product Liability Act, the burden of proof of the defect, the damage and the causal link between the defect and the damage belongs to the injured person. If there are several producers of one defective product which led to just one injury, the producers will be held jointly and severally liable for this damage, without prejudice to the recourse between the producers to obtain full or partial reimbursement of the damage paid. If it is impossible to determine the identity of the producer, the injured party is allowed to act according to art 4 § 2 of the Product Liability Act against the supplier. Art 8 of this Act enumerates six defences for defective product liability. One of them is the state of the art/development risk defence which can be relevant for pharmaceuticals in particular. It allows the producer to prove that the state of scientific or technical knowledge at the time when the product was put into circulation was not such as to enable him to discover the defect.

C. Contractual Liability

15. Basics of contracts in the health care sector

The Belgian courts, as well as the majority of legal writers, have acknowl- **34**
edged the possibility of a contract for medical services existing between a physician and his patient (the so-called medical treatment/services contract) or between a hospital and a patient (the so-called admission contract). The classical decision of the French Cour de Cassation of 20 May 1936 endorsed the view that the relationship between the physician and his patient is contractual. Breach of his professional obligations entails liability of a contractual character. This interpretation is the most plausible one, because a contract of medical services has all the features of a normal contract and there is no reason to exclude it from contract law.[19]

The contract between the physician and his patient results in an obligation **35**
not to cure the patient but to offer him medical help conscientiously and diligently, in conformity with the current data and advances of medical

19 *Nys* (fn 1) 81.

science, in the sense that the current level of scientific progress should be taken into consideration. The Court of Cassation has accepted this view in its judgment of 7 September 1976. Nevertheless, the courts have made some exceptions to this rule. For example, when the physician uses a known treatment of which the outcome is certain, the physician may be expected to achieve a specific result. In these cases the physician is held liable for failure to achieve the specific result, unless he can prove that the failure is not attributable to him.[20]

36 When the patient has a treatment contract with the physician, his relation with the hospital will be governed by an admission contract of the 'physician-out' type. The hospital is responsible for the accommodation of the patient in the broader sense: nursing care; nourishment; infrastructure. In university hospitals where physicians are employees of the hospital, the patient will most of the time have an 'all-in contract' with the hospital, in which case the hospital is not only liable for the accommodation of the patient in the broader sense, but also for the medical treatment.

37 The compulsory health insurance has an influence on the contractual relation between a patient and his physician or the hospital in the sense that the obligation of the patient to pay a fee for the medical services and to pay for the hospital accommodation is to a large extent fulfilled by the health insurance scheme. The freedom of physicians and hospitals to determine the price of their services is also limited by the health insurance scheme.

38 Formally speaking, contracts in the health care sector do not differ from ordinary private law contracts. However, the obligations deriving from contracts in the health care sector are mainly determined by the law on the rights of patients of 22 August 2002.

16. Differences to tort law

39 There is little practical difference as regards the possible consequences between tort liability and contractual liability. The Court of Cassation has excluded the concurrence of contractual and tort liability. The patient has no option as to whether he should proceed in contract and/or in tort. Art 1382 C civ is inapplicable to the fault committed in the execution of a contractual obligation. The main part of the Belgian legal doctrine holds the thesis that the concurrence of contractual and tort liability is impos-

20 *Cousy/de Graeve* (fn 3) 85.

sible unless the fault of the physician or the hospital is not considered a breach of contract but merely a deviation from the reasonable care standard. Also, the damage has to be caused by this deviation from the reasonable care standard and not by a breach of contract. Moreover, if the breach of contract may be considered a criminal act (for example, under art 418 Criminal Code), an action in tort remains possible.[21] In many cases, the fault of a physician causes bodily harm to the patient and consequently may be qualified as a criminal act in the sense of art 418 of the Criminal Code.

According to art 1150 C civ, damage which results from breach of contract **40**
is dealt with in a different way than damage under tort law. The debtor under a contract only has to compensate for foreseeable damage, unless the breach of the contract follows from an intentional act of the debtor. Moreover, the notion of foreseeable damage is interpreted in a very broad way. 'Foreseeable' points only at the possibility of the occurrence of any damage and not at its possible extent.

17. Contractual claims in the absence of direct contracts?

Not applicable. **41**

18. Informed consent

The doctrine of informed consent was developed first by the jurisprudence **42**
and is now firmly established in art 8 of the law on the rights of patients of 22 August 2002. Consent must be given expressly except when the physician, after having informed the patient adequately, can reasonably infer consent from the patient's behaviour (art 8, 1°, para 2). Consent not given expressly is also referred to as implicit, tacit, or non-verbal consent. The consent shall be recorded and added to the patient's medical record at the patient's or physician's request and with the physician's or patient's approval (art 8, 1°, para 3). The information supplied to patients for the purpose of giving the consent referred to in art 8, para 1, relates to the objective and nature of the medical service, to the degree of urgency, the duration, the frequency, the patient specific contraindications, side effects, and risks involved in the service and to the after-care, the possible alternatives, and the financial consequences. In addition, this information

21 *Cousy/de Graeve* (fn 3) 84.

relates to any other clarifications that the patient or physician deems fit to make, including, if necessary, the legal provisions to be complied with in relation to a medical service (art 8, 2°).When, in an emergency case, there is uncertainty as to the will of the patient or his representative, physicians shall immediately deliver all necessary services in the interest of the patient's health. The physician shall record this in the patient's medical record and shall act as soon as possible in accordance with the provisions of the preceding paragraphs (art 8, 5°). Patients have the right to refuse or withdraw their consent for any intervention (art 8, 4°, para 1).

43 The law on the rights of patients does not provide any sanction when the right to informed consent has been violated by a physician. When according to a patient, a physician acted upon an improperly informed consent, the only way to obtain relief is to introduce a medical liability claim (based on tort). The burden of proof is on the patient: he has to prove that he would have refused a diagnostic procedure or a treatment if all the information especially related to the risks, had been communicated to him. The 'transfer-of-risk-theory' defended by some scholars is not accepted in jurisprudence. According to this theory, the risks of an intervention are shifted towards the physician in the case of an improperly informed consent.

44 With regard to the obligation to inform the patient of the risks of an intervention, the law on the rights of patients has initiated an interesting evolution. Traditionally the courts accept that a patient has to be informed of the so-called 'normal and foreseeable' risks. According to this rule, information on abnormal or exceptional risks does not have to be communicated to the patient. For many years, scholars have criticised the 'normal and foreseeable' risks criterion as being too vague and too abstract and have proposed replacing it by the so-called 'relevant-risk theory'. This means that a physician has to inform the patient about the risks that are deemed relevant for the patient in the particular case. According to art 8 § 1 of the law on the rights of patients, the information supplied to patients for the purpose of giving their consent should relate among other elements to the risks involved in the intervention as far as they are deemed of relevance for the patient. After some hesitation in the beginning, the literature considers this provision more and more as an indication of the will of the legislator to accept the 'relevant-risk theory'.[22] A recent judgment of the Court of Cassation has annulled a decision of the Court of

22 *E Delbeke*, De informatieplicht over de relevante risico's van een medische ingreep: draagwijdte, determinerende factoren en gevolgen bij miskenning, Tijdschrift voor gezondheidsrecht 2007-08, 357 f.

Appeal of Antwerp that by not informing a patient about an exceptional risk the physician did not behave wrongly. Although the Court of Cassation did not refer *expressis verbis* to the 'relevant-risk theory', this judgment can be seen as an implicit acceptance of it.[23]

D. Public Liability

19. Key differences from cases involving private hospitals or doctors

The differences between cases involving private and public hospitals are negligible nowadays. **45**

E. Alternative Compensation Regimes

20. Funds and/or other alternative compensation regimes

See infra no 57 on reform plans. **46**

F. Extent of Liability/Remedies

I. Pecuniary Loss

21. Introduction to indemnifying pecuniary loss

No statutory definition of recoverable pecuniary loss is given under Belgian law. Whereas a victim's entire damage has to be covered to the full extent, defining the concepts and the different subdivisions of damage appears to be a rather academic exercise. The words pecuniary and non-pecuniary loss are not frequently used in Belgian legal language. Normally, one distinguishes between patrimonial and non-patrimonial damage or between material and moral (immaterial) damage. Many authors use the concepts of moral damage and extra-patrimonial damage interchangeably, as if they were fully synonymous. **47**

Elements external to the damage, which would increase or decrease compensation, may not be taken into account (ie the objective method is **48**

23 Court of Cassation, 26 June 2009, <www.cass.be>.

applied to calculate the recoverable damages). To calculate the recoverable damage, the damage as it was actually (*in concreto*) incurred, is taken into account.

22. Loss of earnings vs loss of earning capacity

49 To assess the pecuniary damages following incapacity to work, the judge will use the capitalisation method based on the victim's earnings, unless there are insufficient data to establish the earnings accurately enough or unless the actual loss of income by the incapacity to work is considered to be very minor. It is said that in those circumstances, damages will be evaluated *ex aequo et bono*. This method is also applied if the capitalisation method leads to an under-estimation or an over-valuation of the damages. The application of the *ex aequo et bono* method requires the judge to justify why the mathematical calculation proposed by the victim cannot be applied and to conclude that it is impossible to establish the recoverable damages otherwise because of lack of sufficient criteria. It also occurs that capitalisation is applied starting from an *ex aequo et bono* assessed calculation base, eg for the assessment of compensation for a young child for the loss of earning capacity, had he not been injured.[24]

23. Periodic payments or lump sum?

50 The calculation of the amount of damages starts out from the situation at a moment close to the moment of the actual compensation, ie at the time of the judgment. In order to be able to assess future damage at that moment, capitalisation coefficients are usually applied. These coefficients take the following elements into account: the capitalisation interest rate, the foreseeable time the damage will endure and the risk of decease. This mathematical 'actualisation' of future damage is an application of the principle of full compensation in concreto. The aggrieved party, however, can claim the granting of '*une rente*' (in the sense of periodical payments at equidistant intervals), if this seems the most adequate form of full compensation.[25]

---

24 *HA Cousy/A Vanderspikken*, Damages under Belgian law, in: U Magnus (ed), Unification of tort law: Damages (2001) 32.
25 Ibid 33.

24. Caps and thresholds

Not applicable. 51

II. Non-Pecuniary Loss

25. Introduction to indemnifying non-pecuniary loss

No statutory definition of recoverable non-pecuniary loss is given. The *Court of Cassation* defined moral damage in a positive way. It explicitly considered such loss always to be recoverable damage: 'the claim for compensation of non-material damages aims to mitigate one's pain, grief or any other non-material suffering and, to that extent, to repair damage'. Pain refers to any bodily manifestation of suffering, physical as well as mental. Grief points at all non-physical kinds of suffering, eg the sorrow that one feels as a result of the decease of a close relative. Any other non-material suffering results from the moral (dis)appreciation of a tortfeasor's acts by his victim or others. The victim needs to be aware of such feelings: they constitute a minimal requirement to accept the occurrence of non-pecuniary loss. 52

To establish a successful claim for damages, the plaintiff must prove that the damage satisfies three requirements. In order to be legally recognised as being recoverable, damage has to be (i) certain, (ii) personal and (iii) legitimate (ie following from the violation of a legitimate interest). 53

26. Who can claim compensation for non-pecuniary loss?

The requirement that the damage must be personal should not be misunderstood. First, this requirement does not preclude that non-pecuniary damage is claimed *ex herede*. This refers to the damage which is suffered by the victim before dying, and which is claimed by the successor *iure hereditario*. The right to claim non-pecuniary loss belongs to the estate and is transferred after the victim's death. Secondly, non-pecuniary damage may not only be suffered by the primary victim, but also by persons who are not directly harmed. This damage is called damage by repercussion (reflection). It refers to the damage caused to someone who sees a loved one suffering or witnesses his or her death. Doctrine points out that this head of immaterial damage has to be distinguished from the direct immaterial damage suffered by eg the partner of the primary victim 54 because his or her life will be totally different after the occurrence of the damage (one thinks of the unavailability of eg free time, sex life).[26]

G. Procedural Matters

27. Specific rules of jurisdiction or procedure

55 Not applicable.

28. Special institutions handling malpractice claims

56 Not applicable.

H. Outlook

29. Reform plans

57 As the civil liability system was found inappropriate as a compensation mechanism in the context of medical malpractice (eg risk of so-called defensive medicine; liability risks that can no longer be insured; prejudice to confidentiality and trust between patient and physician) the Act of 15 May 2007 was meant to introduce a system of compensation of medical damage based on solidarity instead of liability. The inspiration came from the Scandinavian so-called no fault (although it is more correct to use the term no blame) insurance schemes. The Act of 15 May 2007 was characterised by the following elements: no proof of negligence was required; the individual civil liability of the physician was to be abolished and he could no longer be sued by the patient before a civil judge except in the case of intentional or serious error; for certain types of damages thresholds and caps were planned; compensation of the damage was to be paid by a fund which was to have been financed by the State and the health care professionals. However, the entrance into force of this Act had been postponed several times because of doubts as to its financial viability, and it was finally repealed by the Act of 31 March 2010. This latter Act which at the moment of writing has not yet entered into force will introduce a system inspired by the French regime embedded in the 2002

---

26 *H Cousy/D Droshout*, Belgium, in: WVH Rogers (ed), Damages for Non-Pecuniary Loss in a Comparative Perspective (2001) 31.

Act which combines in a rather unique way the classic liability system as a rule with compensation of very severe damage caused by an unavoidable risk and based on national solidarity with the victim.

Cases

Case 1

The liability of C, who employed midwife D, raises questions regarding the legal competence of midwives in taking and interpreting a cardiotocography (CTG). The practice of the health care professions in Belgium is regulated in the law on the practice of the health care professions of 14 November 1967. According to art 2 of this law, midwives have only a very limited competence to practice medical activities in an autonomous way: the so-called 'normal' delivery. In all other regards midwives have a legal status that is comparable to that of the nursing profession which means that they may not practice medical activities without instruction by a physician. A Royal Decree of 1 February 1991 regarding the practice of the profession of midwives determines in more detail the activities that may (not) be practised by midwives. In is original version, this Decree did not dealt with CTGs and according to the jurisprudence only a physician had the legal competence to interpret the results of a CTG.[27] A Royal Decree of 8 June 2007 has amended the Decree of 1 February 1991 as a result of which a midwife is responsible for detecting high risk pregnancies by 'supervision by means of CTG' (art 4 § 2, 8°). Whether supervision only implies the taking of a CTG or also the interpreting of its results is not clear. There is no jurisprudence on this point yet. However, as interpreting the results of a CTG is a medical act, my opinion is that even after the amendment midwives are not legally competent regarding this. This means that according to Belgian medical law, midwife D has not behaved wrongfully by not informing the physician of the abnormal results she was not supposed to detect. However, according to art 7 of the Royal Decree of 1 February 1991, a midwife who detects pathological signs during a pregnancy or in the course of a delivery has to call a physician. According to the jurisprudence, a hospital has to make available to a 58

27 Criminal Tribunal Antwerp, 24 November 2000, Rechtskundig Weekblad 2000–2001, 1423 with a comment by *H Nys*, Over de bevoegdheid van de vroedvrouw (On the Competence of the midwife); Civil Tribunal Gent, 14 April 2006, Tijdschrift voor Gezondheidsrecht 2006–2007, 282.

physician midwives who have the expertise to detect such signs.[28] The case description does not contain any information that the hospital has failed to do so. So it is questionable whether the liability of C for its own behaviour or the behaviour of the midwife it employed is at stake in this case.

59 There was a treatment contract between B and X. At the moment that A took over the treatment from B, a contractual relationship also started to exist between A and X. The professional mistakes committed on 17 March 1989 by A cannot be attributed to B, unless a *culpa in eligendo* can be demonstrated on the part of B in letting A take over his contractual responsibilities.

60 It makes in principle no difference whether Y already had a pre-existing condition which could at least partially have contributed to her present condition prior to the events which happened around the time of her birth or not. The burden of such a pre-existing condition falls on the liable person: 'the wrongdoer must take the victim as he finds him'. The liable person has to compensate all the damage except for such damage as would also have occurred in the absence of any fault of the liable person.[29]

Case 2

61 This is an example of a so-called wrongful pregnancy claim where the parents of a child claim compensation for the assumed damage caused by the fact that the contraception they used failed. Contraception is in general considered an obligation of means, not an obligation of result. However, the Court of Appeal of Liège in a recent case concluded in favour of the existence of an obligation of result in a case where the gynaecologist had told the patient that the contraceptive method he applied (so-called Hulka clips) since 1982 had never failed and because he had not advised the patient to use another method of contraception.[30] In such a case it is up to the physician to prove that he did not make a mistake and that the failure is due to an external cause. In general, however, it is up to the patient to prove a fault. Jurisprudence in Belgium is rather reluctant to award compensation for the costs to care for and to raise a healthy child. A

---

28 Civil Tribunal Gent, 14 April 2006, Tijdschrift voor Gezondheidsrecht 2006–2007, 282.
29 Court of Cassation, 6 January 1993, Arr Cass 1993, 11.
30 Court of Appeal Liège, 17 April 2008, Revue Générale des Assurances et responsabilités 2009, 14.460, confirmed by Court of Cassation, 15 january 2010, www.cass.be.

recent illustration is another judgment of the Court of Liège that refused compensation for these costs when a healthy child was born because a termination of pregnancy had failed.[31]

A different situation occurs when the child that is born due to the failure of a contraceptive method is the carrier of a genetic disorder. This happened in a case decided upon in a judgment of the Civil Tribunal of Leuven.[32] A couple with two children did not want any more children because one of their children suffered from a serious genetic defect (the so-called Occipital Horn Syndrome). Thus, the physician of the woman implanted the contraceptive 'Implanon' on 26 February 2000. The physician had not attended the training courses offered by Organon, the producer of 'Implanon'. Instead he had been instructed on the use by a sales representative of Organon. The physician did not check the position of the implant immediately after its implantation. Three weeks later the physician himself expressly invited the woman to check the position of the implant. Because he could not detect it, an appointment was made to implant a new contraceptive. During this appointment, the physician again checked the arm of the patient and thought he felt the previously implanted contraceptive and therefore no second one was implanted. On 20 June 2000 the woman discovered she was pregnant. An amniocentesis revealed that the baby was a girl and thus could not suffer from the genetic defect as it is an X-linked recessive disorder. However, a girl can be a carrier of the gene that causes the defect and this can only be established once she is pregnant herself. So, this is not a wrongful birth case (the parents claim compensation for the birth of a severely handicapped child after failure of contraception) but rather a wrongful conception case because the girl is in good health although possibly a carrier of the gene for the genetic disorder her brother suffers from. The Tribunal concluded that the physician had made a professional mistake by not implanting the contraceptive in the right way and not checking it immediately. Rather atypical for Belgian jurisprudence but probably influenced by the specific circumstances of the case, the Tribunal also accepted that this mistake had caused pecuniary (costs for caring and raising the child) and non-pecuniary (moral) damage to the parents. To evaluate the moral damages, the Tribunal expressly referred to the serious genetic defect of the son and the possibility that the girl will be a carrier of the gene. The parents also **62**

31 Court of Appeal Liège, 22 January 2009, Jurisprudence de Liège, 2009, 1161 with observations of G *Genicot* who remarks rightly that this judgment reflects 'une jurisprudence très majoritaire'.

32 Civil Tribunal Leuven, 16 April 2008, not published.

claimed damages on behalf of their daughter because she is possibly a carrier of the gene. This claim however was not granted because being a carrier – if it happens to be the case – is not a result of the physician's fault.

Case 3

63 By application of the doctrine of equivalence of conditions, once the necessary conditions for damage are established, liability arises as soon as a fault appears among these conditions. If faults of more than one person were a necessary condition for the damage, the victim can claim full compensation from each of them. Thus, joint and several liability arises in the event of plurality of defendants,.[33]

64 In the case of minor patients, the patient's rights are exercised by the parents asserting authority over the minor or by the patient's guardians (art 12, 1° law on the rights of patients). The minor patient will be involved in the exercise of his rights, bearing in mind his age and level of maturity. Minor patients who are deemed capable of reasonably grasping their situation may exercise their rights on their own behalf (art 12, 2°). Nowhere is it explicitly stated who is to judge whether the minor patient can be deemed capable of reasonably grasping the situation, but the most obvious course of action would be to leave it up to the physician. He may only act provided he has obtained valid consent. It is up to him to decide whether the conditions for a valid consent are present. In the case of X there is no doubt that his rights had to be exercised by his parents. The relation between X and hospital A is of a contractual nature based on the admission contract that existed between X (his parents) and the hospital. The hospital is held centrally liable (see supra) for not respecting the rights of the patient, in this particular case the right to receive high-quality care (art 5 law on the rights of patients).

65 According to Belgian medical law, the fault of B is not only that she did not act as a normal and prudent midwife in the same circumstances should have done. Besides this, she did not respect her own legal competence as regulated in the law on the practice of health care professions of 14 November 1967 in that she prescribed a homeopathic sedative. This is a medical act falling within the legal monopoly of physicians. The legal status of B is not clear. Apparently she was working as a self-employed midwife, in which case a contractual relationship existed between her and X (his parents).

33 *Bocken* (fn 14) 267.

The relationship between X (his parents) and hospital C is also of a contractual nature. C is also responsible for the damage caused by D who has no contractual relationship with X (his parents) based on art 1384 § 3 C civ: masters are liable for the damage caused by a fault of their servants committed in the course of their occupation. The same is true with regard to E if she acted as an employee of the hospital. If E acted as a self employed physician, a treatment contract existed between her and X (his parents). **66**

Future damage which is the continuation or development of an existing condition can be compensated provided it is sufficiently certain. The prospective loss of capacity to earn resulting from bodily injury will generally be awarded in the form of a lump sum assessed after capitalisation on the basis of cash value tables.[34] However, when the victim is a young person and concrete data as to his future capacity to earn cannot be provided, some jurisprudence favours awarding compensation through a lump sum[35] while others do not.[36] Future damage can also be compensated by an indexed annuity which is only exceptionally granted.[37] The Indicative Table 2004 promotes the use of this method in the case of grave damage caused to young victims.[38] For example, a 19 year old tetraplegic received an annuity of € 992 per month until the age of 65 year and from then onwards of € 744 per month.[39] Because he was totally and always dependent upon a third person for assistance and care, he received an annuity of € 7,678 per month. For *genoegenschade/pretium voluptatis* he was awarded a lump sum of € 12,395 and for sexual damage a lump sum of € 49,579. **67**

Case 4

According to art 7 of the law on patient rights, a patient has to be informed in 'clear' language about his health status. Art 8 that requires an informed consent for any medical intervention refers to art 7 which means that the information concerning the characteristics and risks of a **68**

---

34 *Bocken* (fn 14) 270.

35 Police Tribunal Brussels, 10 February 2004, Revue Générale des Assurances et Responsabilités 2005, no 14.046.

36 The Police Tribunal Gent, 14 April 1997, De Verzekering 1998, 283.

37 *Bocken* (fn 14) 270.

38 *A van Oevelen et al*, Overzicht van rechtspraak. Onrechtmatige daad: schade en schadeloostelling (1993–2006), Tijdschrift voor Privaatrecht 2007, 1226.

39 Police Tribunal Niveles, 2 January 1996, Revue Générale des Assurances et Responsabilités1999, no 13.055.

procedure or treatment also has to be given in 'clear' language. The governmental bill for the patient rights law required not only 'clear' but also 'understandable' language. During the parliamentary discussions, the latter requirement was deleted in order to prevent patients expecting to be informed always in their mother tongue, even if this language is not commonly used in Belgium. 'Clear' language denotes language that corresponds to the level of intellectual comprehension of the patient in a particular case. There is no legal obligation for physicians in Belgium to give information to the patient in his own mother tongue. However, in practice many physicians and hospitals do make reasonable efforts in order to inform patients as much as possible in their own language or a language they understand, by calling in interpreters. Arts 7 and 8 of the law on patient rights also provide that a competent patient can call upon a so-called person of confidence – who should not be confused with the legal representative of an incompetent patient – when he is informed by a physician. Such a person of confidence can be a relative of the patient and can be a minor person. It frequently happens that a patient of migrant origin is assisted by his minor child in the consultation room.

69 The use of written informed consent forms is not widespread in Belgium. According to art 8, 1°, § 2 of the law on patient rights, consent must be given expressly except when the physician, after having informed the patient adequately, can reasonably infer consent from the patient's behavior. Such consent is also referred to as implicit, tacit, or non-verbal consent. An express consent can be given either orally or in writing. In the latter case, however, both parties have to agree that consent is given in writing in order to prevent the physician making up a written consent without the knowledge of the patient. This is a clear indication that the legislator also wanted to discourage the use of written consent forms in daily medical practice. As the burden of proof rests upon the patient also in the case of improperly informed consent (see supra no 10,) physicians are not inclined to use written informed consent forms as a means of legal protection. Anyhow, a written informed consent has no superior legal value as compared to an oral or an implicit consent. In order to be valid the consent always has to be informed. If the patient did not understand the information given by the physician, there is no valid informed consent.[40]

70 According to art 8 § 1 of the law on the rights of patients, the information supplied to patients for the purpose of giving their consent should relate to the objective and nature of the medical intervention, to the degree of

40 *Cousy/de Graeve* (fn 3) 95.

urgency, its duration, its frequency and the contraindications, the side effects, and the risks involved in the intervention as far as they are deemed of relevance for the patient in the particular case as well as to the post-care, the possible alternatives, and the financial consequences. In addition, this information relates to any other clarifications that the patient or physician deems fit to make. With regard to the risks, a rule of thumb that is frequently used in the literature is that a risk of more than 1 % must always be disclosed to the patient except when the consequences are negligible. However, even if a risk is less than 1 % but its consequences are very serious (ie: death or paralysis), the patient has to be informed about it in order to take an informed decision.

The patient will have to prove in the first place that the physician did not **71** inform him about the risk of death or paralysis associated with the laminectomy, nor of the alternative procedure. If this proof succeeds, the loss of a chance theory comes in. The patient will have to prove that the lack of information prevented him from taking an informed decision and from refusing the laminectomy. If he succeeds in this, he will have a right to get compensation that corresponds to a percentage, representing the extent of the lost chance, of the damages that would have been awarded if he had been entitled to full compensation.

Case 5

The 'captain of the ship' theory according to which the surgeon is **72** responsible for the organisation of a surgical procedure and overall supervision of the patient during the procedure has been followed in the past by the jurisprudence.[41] It reduced the role of the anaesthetist to a mere 'servant' of the surgeon and therefore is considered unacceptable. Nowadays, the anaesthetist's medical-organisational responsibility in the operation room has increased. There is, however, no formal agreement between the professional organisations of surgeons and anaesthetists regarding the positioning of the patient as well as the monitoring of the positioning. On the website[42] of the Belgian Professional Association of Specialists in Anaesthesiology and Reanimation (BSAR), Professor Dr E Vandermeersch who is the medical director of the anaesthetic service of the University Hospital in Leuven stated the following. First, the patient has to be

41 See for example Criminal Tribunal Leuven, 30 June 1992, Vlaams Tijdschrift voor gezondheidsrecht1992–1993, 113 with comments by *F Dewallens*.

42 <www.sarb.be/nl/vragen/professionelen> accessed 10 October 2009.

informed beforehand of the possible disadvantages and risks of a given position. The required position of the patient on the OP table is primordially determined by the requirements of the surgical procedure and is therefore the exclusive responsibility of the surgeon. He is therefore also responsible for supervising the correct positioning of the patient by the nursing personnel. He has to take into consideration the consequences of prolonged immobile positioning and to take the measures to remedy them. When the position preferred by the surgeon may have negative consequences for important physiological systems (circulation and ventilation), the surgeon and the anaesthetist should together look for an acceptable solution respecting the patient's safety. Body parts that do not require a special position from the point of view of the surgical procedure are to be positioned under the responsibility of the anaesthetist. Any change in the 'ideal' position of the patient as a consequence of the surgical activities has to be corrected. If this is not possible, the surgeon should be warned about the possible dangers so that he can take adequate measures. A conflict of opinion has to be documented in a clear and complete way.

73 Regarding simultaneous anaesthetic procedures the Belgian professional guidelines and jurisprudence are extremely severe. Already in 1982 the National Council of the Order of Physicians prohibited the simultaneous performance of anaesthetic procedures. In 2008 the National Council confirmed this prohibition.[43] The Belgian Professional Association of Specialists in Anaesthesiology and Reanimation (BSAR) published in 1989 for the first time the Belgian Standards for patient safety in anesthesia, also called the Belgian Safety-First norms. They have been in effect since 1 January 1995 and were updated in 2003. The importance of observing these safety regulations became clear in the decision of the Civil Tribunal of Liège on 20 October 1998.[44] The case concerned the liability of an anaesthetist, who had neglected to personally carry out essential controls, entirely in contrast to what is prescribed by the Safety-First rules. It concerned, in particular, the inspection of the respirator and monitoring alarm. Moreover, he performed different anaesthetic procedures simultaneously and, as a result, he neglected to constantly watch his patient. The judge blamed the anaesthetist because he had not observed the Belgian Safety-First norms. The judge also stated that these safety rules merely confirm the usual practice as well as some elementary requirements that

43 Decision of the National Council of the Order of Physicians, 6 December 2008; <www.ordomedic.be> accessed 10 October 2009.

44 Tijdschrift voor Gezondheidsrecht 1998–1999, 405 with comments by *T Vansweevelt*.

each careful and devoted physician would have observed in the same circumstances.

B, C and D are employees of the hospital A, which places the patient in a **74** more comfortable position as he does not has to prove who exactly made a mistake in the positioning and the monitoring. As an employer A will be held liable according to art 1384 § 3 C civ according to which masters are liable for the damage caused by the fault of their servants committed in the course of their occupation. Employees are the largest group of servants, but not the only one. The fact that the servant who committed a fault cannot be identified exactly does not preclude liability on the part of the master.[45] Moreover, the law on the rights of patients of 22 August 2002 has amended the Hospital Law in order to ameliorate the position of a patient who suffers medical damage during hospitalisation by introducing the principle of the so-called 'central liability' of a hospital for damage caused by health care professionals working within its remits. In principle, the patient who suffered damage during hospitalisation is not confronted anymore with the difficult task of determining who caused the damage (cf supra no 32).

The gain of income from moonlighting is considered an unjustified **75** advantage and the loss of the capacity to earn such income cannot be compensated.[46] It is, however, important to stress that not every infringed interest becomes illegal just because the victim finds himself in a wrongful situation. For example the injuries and other material damages of a smuggler caused by an accident will be compensated, his loss of earnings (gained through smuggling) will not.

According to the jurisprudence of the Court of Cassation the victim has no **76** general, positive obligation to limit the damage caused to him. It follows from the principle of the right to full compensation that the victim is not obliged to mitigate the damages as much as possible. However, he has to take all reasonable measures in order to limit his damage if a normally prudent person in the same circumstances should have done so.[47] It will depend on the appreciation of all the facts in the concrete case by the judge whether the refusal to consider retraining as a sales person in a building supplies store is reasonable or not.

---

45 *Bocken* (fn 14) 263.

46 Court of Cassation, 14 May 2003, Rechtskundig Weekblad 2005–2006, 743; *van Oevelen et al*, Tijdschrift voor Privaatrecht 2007, 1154.

47 Ibid 968.

77 There is no consensus in the jurisprudence as to whether or not the costs of a medical assessment by an advisory physician can be regarded as damage that has to be compensated by the wrongdoer. Some jurisprudence refuses to consider these costs as damages because the victim is not obliged to ask for such a medical assessment while other jurisprudence considers the intervention of an advisory physician a necessity.[48] The facts of the particular case will be decisive in this respect. The provincial councils of the Order of Physicians do not provide a free assessment of the facts to victims of medical malpractices and nor do other organisations.

Case 6

78 A staphylococcus infection is a so-called nosocomial infection that can originate in a hospital setting but also, as in this case, in a private medical practice. There is no specific legislation regulating the compensation of damage caused by such infection. The law of 15 May 2007 on the compensation of damage caused by health care expressly provides that such damage falls within the field of application of this law (art 4, 3°) (cf supra no 57). Neither is there jurisprudence on the liability for an infection that originates from a health care professional. However, some jurisprudence is emerging concerning infections that have been caused by the use of medical devices that have not been sterilised or at least not sufficiently.[49] This jurisprudence makes use of the theory of the so-called safety obligation regarding medical devices. This theory is derived from art 1135 C civ that stipulates that a contract not only creates obligations to what has been expressly convened (the so-called principal obligation) but also to the consequences added to it by reasonableness, commonly accepted practice or the law (the so-called accessory obligations). The safety obligation is an example of such an accessory obligation. The reasoning behind it is that a hospital and a physician are together the stronger party in relation to the patient who is often in a weak and dependent position. This justifies putting a safety obligation upon the hospital and the physician. In the context of an infection caused by a medical device, this safety obligation ought, in correspondence with the French jurisprudence, usually to be considered an obligation to produce a particular result (obligation of result) and not an obligation merely to use reasonable care and skill

48 Ibid 1325.

49 Civil Tribunal Gent, 16 April 2007, Tijdschrift voor Gezondheidsrecht 2007–2008, 370 with comments of *C Lemmens*.

(obligation of means). Unlike the performance of a surgical procedure, where damage can occur due to risks that cannot be prevented even by a prudent and careful surgeon, the use of a safe medical device does not represent such uncertainty. This means that a patient who suffers damage caused by the use of an infected medical device does not have to prove a fault: he is entitled to trust that the hospital or the physician use safe medical devices.[50]

Variation 1

The patient does not have to identify the person who carried the bacteria in order to get compensation for her damage. She will have to demonstrate that the safety obligation has been violated and this clearly follows from the syringe abscess she developed after she received an injection in the neck. In order to escape liability, A and B will have to prove an external cause. Given the use of a syringe under the circumstances described in the case this proof will be extremely difficult: it was not usual for the medical assistants to disinfect their hands before drawing up a syringe and working surfaces were not disinfected every day as required but only once a week. The patient also has to demonstrate her non-pecuniary and pecuniary loss. **79**

Variation 2

In this case too the safety obligation has clearly been violated. The fact that all the usual hygiene standards in the doctor's practice have been respected will not prevent A and B from being held liable as the safety obligation is considered to be an obligation of result and not an obligation to act according to the standards at stake. They will have to prove an external cause eg that the patient already had the infection at the moment she entered the orthopaedic practice. Demonstrating that the infection came from the medical assistant E will offer no relief to A and B: according to art 1384 § 3 C civ they are responsible for the acts of their servants. **80**

50 *S Callens*, Gezondheidsrechtelijke bedenkingen bij ziekenhuisinfecties, Recht in beweging 2006, 237; *C Lemmens*, Medische hulpmiddelen, veiligheid en nosocomiale infecties: een inspannings- dan wel een resultaatsverbintenis, Tijdschrift voor gezondheidsrecht 2007–2008, 375.

Medical Liability in the Czech Republic

Ondřej Dostál

General Questions

A. The Health Care System Framework

I. General Introduction

1. The health care system in overview

(a) **General.** Up until 1989 Czechoslovakian health care was based on the Soviet model of centralised health care (the so-called Semashko system). The state took over all health care coverage and financed it through taxes. At the same time, all health care providers were nationalised. This system offered comprehensive health coverage, almost completely free of charge. Forty years of this experience created an almost universal perception of health care as a public good to which one was entitled without having to bear the costs thereof, but in terms of which patients' abilities to make autonomous decisions regarding the health care that they received were severely restricted. 1

Shortly after the 1989 revolution, the health care system was liberalised, switching from the old model to a compulsory health insurance system (Bismarck model). At the same time, there was an almost complete privatisation of primary health care, the pharmaceutical industry, pharmacies, and a great number of hospitals. The right to choose a physician and a health care facility was introduced. The Constitutional Bill of Rights[1] maintained the principle of unpaid access to the health care package as defined by law.[2] 2

---

1 Constitutional Act 2/1993 Coll, Charter of Fundamental Rights and Basic Freedoms, Art 31.

2 L *Bryndová et al*, Czech Republic: Health System Review (Health Systems in Transition vol 11 no 1, 2009) 102.

3 **(b) Public health insurance.**[3] As from the end of 2009 there are nine public health insurance funds (PHIF). The PHIFs are legal persons *sui generis*, with public, non-profit status, but distinct from the state and with their own budgets.[4]

4 The financing of the system is based on solidarity and equity. It is financed by contributions from individuals and employers. The mandatory public health insurance premiums are set by law. The state pays premiums for all economically inactive citizens,[5] including unemployed, pensioners, children, students, and women on maternity leave, which amounts to approximately 56 % of the population.[6] Any person with permanent residence in the Czech Republic is entitled to health insurance. Health insurance funds are obliged to accept all clients who meet the conditions for participating in statutory health insurance.[7]

5 The Charter of Fundamental Rights guarantees each citizen a right of unpaid access to a basic package of treatment, drugs and medical aids as defined by law and covered by the public health insurance. Each PHIF has a statutory duty to maintain a network of contractual health care providers (hospitals, ambulatory, rehabilitation, emergency care providers etc) and to allow their insured citizens unpaid, non-discriminatory access to the list of health services described in the law via this network.

---

3 In accordance with the established economic terminology, it might be more appropriate to use the term 'social health insurance'; however, an exact translation of the Czech statutory term '*veřejné zdravotní pojištění*' is 'public health insurance'.

4 The largest PHIF, the General Health Insurance Fund (*Všeobecná zdravotní pojišťovna* ČR, VZP ČR) is created by the law 551/1991 Coll and controls around 60 % of the health insurance market. The other PHIFs are created according to the law 280/1992 Coll. The former idea was to create industry-specific PHIFs resembling the insurance funds in Austria and the names of these insurance funds carry often the titles of professions, but due to the free choice of insurance fund, this feature does not apply anymore.

5 The State contribution, which is set by law on a relatively low level, is often criticised as inadequate, especially because it covers the higher risk groups – children, old-age pensioners, disabled persons incapable of work etc. Currently, the health insurance law includes sophisticated redistribution mechanisms between PHIFs, with a purpose to compensate the PHIFs with high-risk members.

6 Contributions are defined by law as a pre-tax percentage of wages, of which employees pay 4.5 % and employers 9 % (13.5 % altogether), with a ceiling on contributions. The self-employed pay the same total percentage (ie 13.5 %) but only on 35 % of their profits. For the state-insured, the Ministry of Finance contributes the same percentage (13.5 %) of the monthly minimal wage set by statutory order.

7 The citizen, rather than the employer, chooses the PHIF, and may choose a different PHIF once a year. There are now nine insurance funds, of which the largest one, the General Health Insurance Fund, controls around 66 % of the market. The insurance funds are legally required to accept any applicant. Since the Czech Republic is now a member of the European Union, those insured by Czech health insurance funds are entitled to demand services in other European countries and vice versa according to European law. Opting out of the insurance system is not permitted in the Czech Republic.

The Czech health insurance system strictly separates the roles of payer (PHIF) and provider (health care facility). The PHIFs are not allowed to own or control health care providers;[8] their relationship is in theory strictly contractual. However, since the public insurance system is the prevailing source of finance and the PHIFs are often in a position of monopoly purchaser, the health care providers are usually dependent on the contracts and the PHIFs enjoy a significant degree of factual authority over the providers' decision-making, both in an economic and a medical sense. These economic pressures often have a marked effect on the quality of care and thus also on liability issues. 6

(c) **Hospitals and other health care facilities.** There are currently more than 27,000 health care providers in the Czech Republic, most of which are private.[9] The Czech Ministry of Health is the operator of teaching (faculty) hospitals and specialised tertiary-care facilities. Most hospitals in the country before the end of 2002 were set up by district offices. State administration at district level was abolished at the end of 2002. Hereafter, the role of operator was transferred to the regional self-governments. In certain cases, communities are the owners and operators of small hospitals. Several dozen hospitals have been privatised in the form of commercial companies, but continue to be financed from statutory health insurance. The network of outpatient services and pharmacy services has been almost entirely privatised. 7

Non-state health care facilities include a diverse range of provider types, including integrated systems of several regional hospitals, individual hospitals, ambulatory care groups, and individual self-employed health care professionals.[10] 8

There is a grey area between health care providers and other entrepreneurs in the field of personal services, such as life-style consultants or natural healers; while the latter often provide services concerning health care issues, 9

8 Since the vertical integration of providers and PHIFs is prohibited by law, the concept of HMOs (health maintenance organizations) as known for instance in the United States, cannot be applied in Czech Republic. Recent unsuccessful attempts of health system reforms however intended to change the status of PHIFs to commercial companies and allow their integration with hospitals and ambulatory care systems.

9 *Bryndová* (fn 2) 81.

10 Interestingly, the same regulatory framework under the law 160/1992 Coll applies to a large joint-stock company integrating several hospitals and to a practice of a single self-employed doctor or midwife. Even those self-employed physical persons have the status of a 'non-state health care facility'.

they are neither registered nor regulated as health care providers, which is potentially detrimental to the legal certainty and safety of their clients.[11]

10 Health care facilities can be classified according to:

- *Ownership.* The health care facility may be operated by a public body in the form of an allowance organisation, receiving subsidies from the public budget; typical examples are teaching hospitals operated by the Ministry of Health, or hospitals run by municipalities. Alternatively, the health care facility may constitute some form of a business organisation, typically a limited liability company or a joint stock company, fully owned by a public body; this is the case with many regional hospitals. Finally, the health care facility could be a privately owned business entity; this is the case with some hospitals and most ambulatory care providers.
- *Status.* A health care facility may take the form of non-profit organisation, a non-profit business organisation or a for-profit business entity.
- *Relation to public health insurance funds.* Generally, a contract with a PHIF entitles the health care facility to receive reimbursement directly from the relevant PHIF fund for the care that it provides its members, and binds the 'contractual' health care facility to provide care to the insured of this PHIF fund free of charge. In absence of the contract, the health care facility can bill the PHIF only the urgent and necessary services provided to its insured patients.[12] A health care facility may contract with each of the nine PHIFs, with only a few, or with none of them. The contract with a fund does not necessarily have to cover the full range of services offered by the health care facility.[13]

11 In practice, the classification 'public – private' is less important than the classification 'contractual – non-contractual'. Health care facilities, both public and private, which contract with a PHIF, have a broad range of statutory duties towards their insured members, including the duty not to

11 The liability regime for natural healers is uncertain, and the possibility of medical malpractice compensation claims against such persons is questionable. Czech law does not have any specific legislation for this type of providers.

12 Act 48/1997 Coll, on Public Health Insurance, § 17 (1).

13 Therefore, the fact that a health care facility is privately owned does not necessarily mean that it has a for-profit status or that it provides services for direct payments; to the contrary, most of the privately owned, for-profit facilities have contracts with PHIFs and therefore provide care free of charge at the point of delivery for their insured. Conversely, a public non-profit health care facility does not necessarily have to have contracts with all health insurance funds; the citizens insured by a non-contractual fund would not be entitled to receive unpaid non-urgent services even in such a hospital.

refuse them medical care,[14] including in non-urgent cases.[15] Contractual health care facilities have the right to receive payment for care directly from a third party, namely the PHIF, but are subject to limitations on reimbursement imposed by the PHIF. They are prohibited from receiving direct payment from patients.[16]

Private, for-profit non-contractual clinics, which are directly reimbursed **12**
by patients, are typically found in the fields of plastic surgery, assisted reproduction and spa treatment or luxury care, which are frequently directed at foreign clientele.

Typically, the doctors and other health care personnel in hospitals are **13**
employees of the hospitals. Self-employed ambulatory care doctors who also work in hospitals are usually part-time employees of the hospital, ie they do not act as independent contractors.[17] The health care facilities are vicariously liable for the acts of their employees. Therefore, plaintiffs in civil medical malpractice case involving hospital care typically sue the hospital rather than the individual doctors responsible for the care.

Current trends include privatisation, utilisation of e-health instruments[18] **14**
and the horizontal integration of health care providers (ie the creation of hospital groups and ambulatory care systems). The impact of these trends in the area of medical malpractice liability can not yet be assessed.

II. Social Welfare Provision

2. The role of public health care

Under the centralised health care system before 1989, health care provid- **15**
ers were financed based on pre-set budgets. The health care system was state directed. As such, it severely limited patient autonomy by restricting

14 Act 48/1997 Coll, on Public Health Insurance, § 11 (b).

15 In case of urgent care, every provider has a duty to accept the patient and claim reimbursement from the patient's PHIF, even in absence of contract of the provider with this PHIF.

16 Act 48/1997 Coll, on Public Health Insurance, §11 (d).

17 'Visiting' doctors or 'consultants with hospital privileges', as known in some Western jurisdictions.

18 These instruments include the recent implementation of Central Database of Electronic Prescriptions intended, among other purposes, to prevent abuse of controlled substances. Another e-health instrument is the electronic health records project IZIP, which enables treating physicians and patient himself or herself to access the medical file using Internet. According to official information, more than million patients and over 15,000 physicians subscribed to IZIP, despite some concerns involving privacy and data protection.

patients' choice of medical procedures and providers. The pre-set budget financing strongly encouraged paternalism of the health care providers, as they exercised almost exclusive control over both medical and financial decision-making. The guidelines for their conduct were set by the state administration.

16 The post-1989 reforms abolished many existing direction and allocation mechanisms. Control mechanisms relating to supply and demand were removed. By privatising health funds and providers, the state lost its statutory power to directly create and control network of health care facilities. The new health insurance funds received few tools to regulate this expansion – in the early 1990s the funds were obliged to contract with every willing provider, resulting in a current network which shows signs of over-servicing in the big cities and under-servicing in other parts of the country. This is despite the fact that all citizens participate equally in funding the system and are equally entitled to its benefits.

17 The guarantee of unpaid access to health care was promulgated as a part of the Charter of Fundamental Rights and Basic Freedoms, which is a Constitutional norm. In the Czech legal system, Constitutional norms cannot be amended by any norm of a lower order; the Constitutional norms that provide economic rights provide for further clarification by a 'simple' act of parliament, but cannot be limited by executive power decrees. As yet, the Czech parliament has not restricted the scope of Constitutional entitlement. The attempts of the executive branch were ruled unconstitutional by the Constitutional Court.[19]

18 In 1997, as a reaction to the health-funding crisis, Parliament enacted a law providing for regulation on the supply side. This statute enabled the health funds to replace the existing fee-for-service reimbursement system with a flat-amount reimbursement system. This was intended to curtail the inflation of health care costs. The flat-amount payment rates were usually computed on the basis of past years' expenses; this had the effect of exacerbating the unequal regional health service provision as providers continuously received less funds based on their low 'historical basis'. The law introduced a collective negotiation procedure between health funds and provider groups for the purpose of setting the flat-amount payment rates and creating framework contracts.[20] This procedure is overseen by the Ministry of Health; in cases where no agreement can be reached or the

19 Decision of the Constitutional Court of 10 June 1996, Pl ÚS 35/95; Decision of the Constitutional Court of 4 June 2003, Pl ÚS14/02.

20 Act 48/1997 Coll, on Public Health Insurance, § 17.

agreement contravenes 'public interest', the Ministry of Health has the power to set the result by a decree. The Ministry of Health has also empowered to assign (by decree) a list of point values to various medical performances in terms of which reimbursable interventions are identified and their values are set in points.[21] These legislative changes and actions of the Ministry of Health provided the PHIFs with the means to exercise relatively strict cost control over the providers.

The 1997 legislation attempted to limit health care costs by restricting **19**
supply while maintaining broadly defined unpaid care entitlement on the side of demand. The new legal definition of 'health services package' includes almost all health care related needs, with only a limited number of services excluded from the statutory health care system, in the form of a negative list.[22] In theory, any medical care that is not legally excluded from the benefits package should be freely available to all patients without discrimination. On the other hand, the duties of insured persons are mostly proclamatory, with no real sanction mechanism in place.[23]

These changes in the reimbursement of contractual providers altered the **20**
incentive structure for health care supply. Whilst they removed the tendency for unnecessary, exaggerated care and procedures, they at the same time often created incentives for providers to minimise care. Although the law specifies what procedures, pharmaceuticals and medical equipment are to be provided under public health insurance, it does not specify which of them is to be used in any given case of a patient with a given illness. Clinical guidelines for individual medical conditions are thus not established, and even when they are, they are not universally recognised by all practitioners and health insurance managers. This is because the guidelines are frequently based on medical considerations only, not economic, which makes them impractical, especially in under-financed health care facilities.

21 Act 48/1997 Coll, on Public Health Insurance, § 17.

22 For instance, cosmetic surgeries for non-medical reasons; furthermore, a few types of services require co-payment, including certain kinds of dental care; Act 48/1997 Coll, on Public Health Insurance.

23 These duties include especially the duty to follow the treatment regime prescribed by the physician, to abide by the measures intended for prevention of disease and to avoid actions knowingly detrimental to health. The absence of a real sanction mechanism, however, provides the patients with little incentive for responsible behaviour. Act 48/1997 Coll, on Public Health Insurance, § 12.

21 Both hospitals and ambulatory care providers bear the burden of discrepancies between citzens' statutory entitlement to modern health care,[24] and the regulated reimbursements that they receive from the public health insurance system. Since most hospital physicians are employees, they have to follow the orders given by management, whose ultimate responsibility is to maintain the hospital's financial viability. The doctors often face the adverse choice of either knowingly providing insufficient care and thereby risking criminal prosecution and/or a civil lawsuit against their health care facility, or providing care contrary to their employers' orders and risking job loss or salary reduction. Furthermore, the insufficient financing of hospitals sees many of them under-staffed. The level of care that the patient actually receives in both hospital and primary care settings is therefore often dependent on the subjective micro-level decisions of individual physicians.

22 The Czech Republic also has no formal legal regulation of medical intervention waiting lists.[25] The hospital physicians themselves thus plan and manage waiting lists for non-emergency surgeries. Although the lists are largely based on equality, typically using criteria of first-come-first-served and medical necessity, there is no legal control of this process. Since patients may have to wait several months for a procedure, and anecdotal evidence suggests that patients make under-the-table payments in order to jump the queue, especially in the field of orthopedic surgeries.

23 This goes hand-in-hand with persisting physician paternalism and an information deficit on the patient's side. The 2001 Biomedicine Convention[26] introduced strict rules regarding informed consent and risk disclosure into Czech law which precede any health care intervention. However, compliance with this new law is relatively poor. The patient seldom requests and rarely receives full information about all available treatment options and their associated risks. In turn physicians almost never disclose their level of experience and possible competing interests regarding reimbursement.

24 Finally, medical malpractice litigation, which would otherwise act as a disincentive to under-servicing or under-informing patients, does not adequately fulfill this role. For a patient who has suffered harm, access to justice is frequently very complicated due to the poor quality of medical

---

24 Act 20/1966 Coll, on Health Care of the People, § 11.

25 With an exception in the 2002 Act on Organ and Tissue Donation, 285/2002 Coll.

26 Convention for the Protection of Human Rights and Dignity of the Human Being with regard to the Application of Biology and Medicine: Convention on Human Rights and Biomedicine, Act 96/2001 Coll Int Treaties, Art 4–10.

records, the slow and ineffective court system, litigation costs, medical expert crisis (see no 136) and the inadequately defined duties of health care providers. Cumulatively, these result in uncertainty concerning the health care benefits stipulated by law.

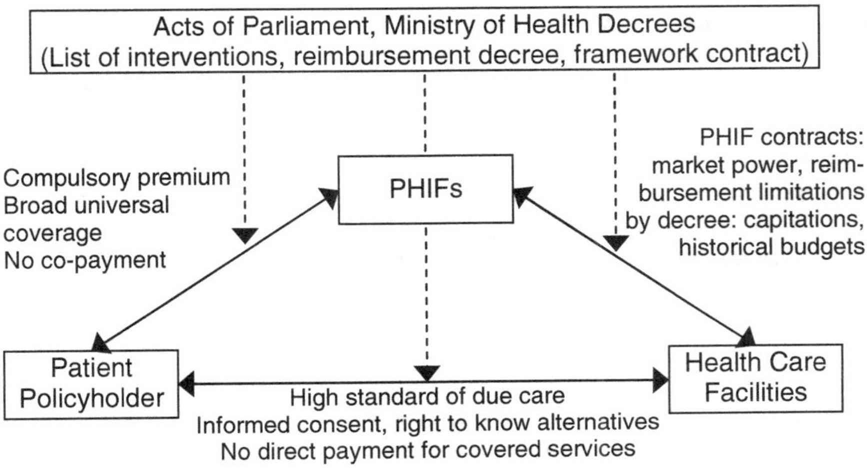

FIGURE 1

25 The causes of the current unfavourable state of affairs arise from an imbalance between rights and conditions for fulfilment of the correlative duties in the triangular relation between citizens, providers, and health funds.

26 The fundamental problem is the relation between citizens and health funds. The resources collected from mandatory premiums do not match the extensive duties imposed on the health funds, which correlate to patients' entitlement to unpaid care. The 1997 legislation, which allowed cost regulation on the supply side, but maintained the level of entitlement on the demand side, effectively transferred the problem to the health care providers. However, the non-existence of binding standards of care and the passivity of most patients enable the providers to restrict the amount or quality of care that they provide to any given patient.

27 The causes of medical liability cases thus often do not arise from the incompetence of health care workers, but rather from the economical context within which they operate, including the difference between the *de iure* entitlements of the citizen, and the *de facto* capabilities of health care facilities as defined by the pre-set reimbursement limitations.

28 The description of the general environment would not be complete without brief reference to the influence of manufacturers and distributors of

pharmaceuticals and medical aids, whose aggressive marketing techniques often adversely influence the physicians' duty to act in the best medical interest of the patient.

3. Differences in treating patient's claims

29 The public financing of medical treatment does not influence the handling of potential malpractice cases.

30 The Act 48/1997 Coll on Public Health Insurance allows the policyholder to raise a complaint or initiate an internal review at the PHIF level. If the policyholder is of the opinion that she is not being afforded due health care from the health care provider, she may:

- submit an application for verification to the health care facility manager or its administrator,
- refer her complaints to the Czech Medical, Dental or Pharmaceutical Chamber if the deficiency relates to the professional or ethical conduct of a doctor or pharmacist,
- refer to her health insurance company, in particular if the health care professional refuses to perform an act included in the covered health care,
- or refer to the competent state authority that registered the health care facility in question.[27]

31 Theoretically, the policyholder may exercise her right to public health care against a PHIF in court. Such cases are however very rare due in particular to the length of court proceedings.

4. Right of recourse

32 The Act 48/1997 Coll on Public Health Insurance provides the PHIF with a right to reimbursement of costs against any third person if it has funded health care arising from their intentional illegal conduct towards a policyholder. For the purpose of the reimbursement, health care facilities are obliged to report accidents and other health impairments of the persons to whom they provide health care to the PHIF if there is a reasonable

27 Act 48/1997 Coll, on Public Health Insurance, § 11 (2).

suspicion that such an accident or impairment of health was caused by intentional conduct of a third person.[28]

This rule is typically concerned with injuries caused by intentional violent **33** crimes. Despite the reporting duty of health care workers, the PHIFs do not regularly pursue these reimbursement claims in practice.

III. Private Insurance

5. The role of private health insurance

The market for private health insurance in the Czech Republic is inher- **34** ently limited by the broad definition of the public health insurance coverage, and by the legal prohibition to ask private supplemental payments for care already covered from public health insurance. The public contribution, however limited or insufficient, cannot be matched by private funds provided by a patient or by his private insurance. The patient therefore cannot legally have a 'basic quality' service paid for by the public health insurance system and add his or her own funds in order to obtain the services of a more experienced physician, receive a more comprehensive diagnosis, more expensive implants or any other advanced service directly connected with covered health care. The patient can only legally purchase such services outside the public health insurance system, usually at a private clinic, by paying the whole advanced procedure costs rather than the difference between the cost of basic services and the cost of additional services. Such a patient thereby completely loses the advantage of the universal coverage system to which she contributes on a compulsory basis.[29]

Private insurance is therefore used typically for coverage of health risks in **35** travel, or less frequently for coverage of health care-related services not covered by the compulsory insurance, such as appointments at a specific time without the need to wait.

---

28 Act 48/1997 Coll, on Public Health Insurance, § 55.

29 For further discussion, see *O Dostál*, Regulation of direct supplemental payments for services covered by the public health insurance in a comparative perspective, Medicine and Law 2007, Dec 26(4), 663–676.

6. Liability insurance

36 According to the law, professional liability insurance is compulsory for every health care facility. Without such insurance, health care facilities cannot obtain or keep the necessary registration.[30] This insurance is provided by commercial insurers active in the Czech Republic.

37 The law however does not specify either the scope of coverage or the minimum insurance limits. Due to the development in personal injury jurisprudence, which led to a significant growth in the number of claims and of compensation amounts, many providers, including even large teaching hospitals, found themselves insufficiently insured.

38 Furthermore, many health care providers recently faced a problem arising from the dual characteristics of malpractice claims – liability for personal injury on one hand, and personality protection liability[31] on the other hand. Although most health care providers insured themselves against the traditional personal injury liability, many providers have insufficient or no protection against the personality protection liability; this type of liability is decided according to different rules before different courts, and as such is often excluded from the list of insured risks.

39 Both these problems are increased by the 'retroactivity factor' – the fact that the recent increase in malpractice liability awards does not result from statutory amendments, but rather from judicial interpretation of the existing law. Due to the combination of the length of limitation periods and the average duration of court litigation, cases decided in 2009 often concerned medical errors which occurred in the early 2000s. As medical malpractice litigation was relatively underdeveloped and multi-million medical malpractice claims were extremely rare at this time, maximum amounts of liability insurance seldom exceeded CZK 5 million, which at that time could reasonably be regarded as sufficient to cover even the most severe cases of harm. But when similar matters come before the current courts, it is not uncommon for compensation to be awarded in excess of CZK 10 million, particularly in the area of immaterial damages. Hospitals accordingly find their 2002 or 2003 liability insurance wholly inadequate to meet the damages awarded by the courts. The same applies jurispru-

---

30 Act 160/1992 Coll on Health Care in Non-State Health Care Facilities, § 16.

31 The personality protection liability refers to the specific set of rights described in § 11 Civil Code, including family life, privacy, freedom, bodily integrity etc, with a specific sanction mechanism different from the 'classical' liability for damage under § 420 ff Civil Code.

dence dealing with personality protection, which has only come to the fore in the medical field in recent years.

Finally, the medical malpractice litigation costs also have a potential impact on the health system's stability. Most health care providers are economically dependent on the reimbursements from the public insurance system, with a strict regulation of health care intervention prices. The providers are therefore unable to pass on the higher litigation costs (higher liability insurance costs) to consumers. Instead, they have to deduct these losses from their general income earmarked primarily for the care of the sick, with a resulting negative impact on health care availability, waiting times and the quality of their services. **40**

IV. Professional Standards

7. Applicable professional standards

The definition of professional standards *(lex artis)* is a complicated problem with legal, medical, ethical and economic aspects. According to the Constitutional Charter of Fundamental Rights and Basic Freedoms, everyone has the right to the protection of her health.[32] According to the Biomedicine Convention, any intervention in the health field, including research, must be carried out in accordance with relevant professional obligations and standards.[33] **41**

These general requirements are further specified by law. According to the Act 20/1966 Coll on Health Care of the People, health care is provided by health institutions of state, municipalities, natural and legal persons in accordance with contemporary knowledge of medical science.[34] Every worker in health care must above all execute her duties in the manner and to such an extent as laid down by principles determined by the Ministry of Health in cooperation with professional organisations.[35] According to the Act 220/1991 Coll on the Czech Medical Chamber, Czech Dental Chamber and Czech Chamber of Pharmacists, these professional self-governing associations with compulsory membership have the power **42**

---

32 Art 31 of the Constitutional Act 2/1993 Coll, Charter of Fundamental Rights and Basic Freedoms.

33 Convention for the Protection of Human Rights and Dignity of the Human Being with regard to the Application of Biology and Medicine: Convention on Human Rights and Biomedicine, Act 96/2001 Coll Int Treaties, Art 4.

34 Act 20/1966 Coll on Health Care of the People, § 11 (1).

35 Act 20/1966 Coll on Health Care of the People, § 55 (2).

to determine whether their members perform their occupation with due skill or not and whether they do so in conformity with medical ethics, law and the regulations of the given Chamber.[36] The Chamber is entitled to issue statements binding to its members in the matters of professional aspects of health care provision.[37]

43 The Ministry of Health issues a range of methodical instructions published in its Bulletin, which describe recommended practice. Similar documents are issued by the Medical and other Chambers.[38] Another source of guidelines are the professional societies associated in the Czech Medical Association of Jan Evangelista Purkyně, a voluntary organisation of experts from all fields of medicine. Finally, the meaning of the statutory definition of *lege artis* is often interpreted by reference to medical textbooks and journal articles, including foreign texts.

44 In court practice, the decisive role in determining the standard and assessing the performance of the defendant physician is played by the medical experts appointed by the parties, by court-appointed expert or by the medical expert institute.[39] The courts are theoretically empowered to critically evaluate the expert opinions in the same way as other evidentiary instruments, but are usually very deferential towards them and seldom challenge the experts' opinion on what is *lege artis*.

45 A frequent problem is that many professionals, including medical experts, confuse the notions of 'professional standards' and 'reimbursement standards'. From the viewpoint of a physician working in the environment of public health insurance and its limitations, these notions merge – the technical level of care provided by the health care facilities is determined to a large extent by the contractual conditions and limitations imposed on reimbursements from by PHIFs. From the purely legal point of view, however, the current statutory definition of professional standard only

36 Act 220/1991 Coll on the Czech Medical Chamber, Czech Dental Chamber and Czech Chamber of Pharmacists, § 2 (1) (a).

37 Act 220/1991 Coll on the Czech Medical Chamber, Czech Dental Chamber and Czech Chamber of Pharmacists, § 2 (2) (i). These guidelines are definitely not binding, as confirmed also by the recent decision of the Supreme Court of the Czech Republic of 22 March 2005, 7 Tdo 219/2005. Due to the representative nature of the Czech Medical Chamber, however, its recommendations usually enjoy a high level of persuasiveness.

38 These documents are issued on the basis of the aforementioned legal authorisations, but are not generally binding and cannot prejudice statutory rights of citizens. Their nature is therefore rather recommendatory than binding.

39 Appointed expert institutes are typically medical schools or teaching hospitals. Institutional expertise is usually sought in situations of contradictions between statements of individual medical experts.

takes medical not economic considerations into account.[40] Theoretically, the fact that the health insurance funds do not reimburse some generally accepted medical interventions (eg modern, very expensive diagnostics), does not mean that such interventions cease to be *lege artis* or that physicians are relieved of their duty to be aware of these interventions and to offer them via disclosure as alternatives to patients who may subsequently decide to pay to undergo them outside the public health insurance system. In practice, however, the medical experts tend to evaluate not only the medical aspects of treatment but also the economic and organisational aspects. The result is that even if a physician applies somewhat obsolete or less intensive treatment than that which is regarded as optimal by current medical science with adverse results she is not *non lege artis* and liability does not arise because of the necessity to consider the economic and organisational constraints of the given health care facility. However understandable this might be, especially with regard to potential criminal liability when evaluating the fault of an employed physician who acted within the constraints of unsatisfactory conditions in his hospital or department, it is inappropriate in civil litigation, for the following reasons:

- *Strengthening of the regional discrimination in access to care.* A plaintiff in a 'poor' region would have less chances of success in a lawsuit concerning outdated, substandard care than a plaintiff from a 'sufficiently funded' hospital.
- *Wrong incentive both to PHIFs and providers concerning quality improvement:* instead of having an incentive to improve their quality, even at higher costs, the PHIFs and providers would be able to continue to contract for low-cost, obsolete, poor quality care without fear of civil liability.
- *Violation of patient's autonomy in deciding between treatment alternatives and their costs.* The fact that some treatment types cannot be provided safely in a given hospital does not mean that a patient should not be informed about them; the patient has the right to choose another provider in the Czech Republic or abroad, within or outside of the public insurance system.

---

40 Act 20/1966 Coll on Health Care of the People, § 11: 'Health care is provided by health institutions ... in accordance with contemporary available knowledge of medical science.' The contrary view is held by *J Mach et al*, Zdravotnictví a právo, komentované předpisy (2nd edn 2005).

8. Quality and/or risk management systems

46 Physicians and other health care professionals have to fulfill the conditions dictated by law in order to perform their work.[41] These conditions generally include professional qualifications, acceptable health status and criminal blamelessness. Competencies of specific health care professions are set out in the law.[42] In most areas of health care, the professionals become fully autonomous and competent only after a certain time-limit; junior professionals typically have to work under supervision. The positions of medical chiefs of departments require a specific license. All health care workers have a legal duty of continuing professional education.

47 All physicians, pharmacists and dentists are compulsorily registered with their professional Chamber. These Chambers also fulfil a disciplinary role against their members, acting upon complaints from patients or other persons.

48 Health care facilities, both hospitals and ambulatory care providers, are compulsorily registered.[43] Registration is conditional upon the fulfilment of the specified conditions for the provision of health care services, including qualified personnel, technical equipment, hygiene and other requirements. If these requirements are not adhered to, registration must be withheld. The registering administrative institution, typically a Region, retains some degree of control, including management of patients' complaints.

49 Many health care facilities in the Czech Republic have undergone accreditation.[44] Accreditation of health care facilities is a voluntary process of external assessment as to whether the activities performed in the health care facilities guarantee a sufficient quality of intervention necessary to provide a good quality and safe level of care. Several hospitals have also obtained international accreditation. Such certification processes are not required by law and the standards prepared by the accreditation organisa-

---

41 Act 95/2004 Coll, on the Conditions for Acquiring and Recognising Qualifications for the Performance of the Medical Occupations of Physician, Dentist, and Pharmacist; and Act 96/2004 Coll, on the Conditions for Acquiring and Recognising Qualifications for the Performance of Non-Medical Occupations in Health Care and for the Execution of Activities Related to the Provision of Health Care.

42 Decree of the Ministry of Health 424/2004 Coll.

43 Non-state health care facilities are registered pursuant to Act No 160/1992 Coll on Health Care in Non-state Health Care Facilities.

44 For reference, see the webpage of the national accreditation organisation, Joint Accreditation Committee of the Czech Republic (*Spojená akreditační komise* ČR, <www.sakcr.cz>).

tions are not legally binding. However, these accreditation standards have persuasive force in interpreting the general preventive duty set in the Civil Code.[45]

B. Tort Liability

9. Fundamentals of tort liability

According to the Czech Civil Code, two kinds of remedies for personal injury or other violation of rights caused by medical malpractice are available: 50

- Liability for damage (§ 420 ff Civil Code),
- Liability for breach of personality protection (§ 11 ff Civil Code).

Ad 1) Liability for damage

The cases of personal injury and causing of death are specifically targeted under the heading of liability for damage (§ 420 ff), which covers not only material damage but also some immaterial damage headings such as pain and suffering and lump-sum compensation for relatives in case of death. All variants of the liability for damage are resolved before the District (lowest-level) Court. In cases of actions for personal injury, the court fee is waived. According to the Czech law, employers are vicariously liable for the act of their employees. 51

The general liability for damages is fault based. The fault is presumed, but the defendant can exculpate himself if he proves that there was no negligence. The plaintiff has to prove: 52

- An unlawful act (a legal duty and a breach of this duty),
- the amount of damages,
- the causal connection between the breach of duty and the damage.

The Civil Code describes several no-fault exceptions, such as damage caused by an instrument (§ 421a), or damage caused by operational activity (§ 420a); attempts to apply the latter in the context of medical malpractice litigation were however rejected by the courts. 53

45 Act 40/1964 Coll, Civil Code § 415.

Ad 2) Personality protection

54 According to § 11 of the Czech Civil Code, an individual shall have the right to protection of his or her personality rights, in particular of his or her life and health, civic honour and human dignity as well as of its privacy, name and expressions of personal nature.[46] In case of violations, the individual is entitled in particular to demand that unlawful violation of his or her personality rights be ceased, that consequences of this violation be removed and that adequate satisfaction be given to him or her.[47] Such satisfaction can be moral or financial; its scope is in the discretion of the court.[48]

55 This broad definition of personality rights in § 11 allows personal injury cases to fall not only under the general liability for damage heading, but at the same time under the heading of personality protection. Recent jurisprudence found in several landmark cases that causing death or severe health impairment is also a breach of personality rights, especially when the damage has a significant negative impact on the future life of the victim him-/herself, or on family rights of the deceased victim's relatives. A liability for damage case can run parallel to a personality protection case, which takes place at a different court level (regional court) and under different conditions, despite the fact that the evidence is usually very similar. In recent jurisprudence, the courts granted monetary awards in personality protection cases even in situations where the plaintiff had already received damages for pain and suffering from a different court in a liability for damage case.

56 The liability conditions for a breach of personality rights, which is a no-fault liability matter, are:

- a breach of a legal duty capable of violating the personality rights,
- an actual violation of personality rights, and
- a causal relation between the above.

---

46 Act 40/1964 Coll, Civil Code § 11.

47 Act 40/1964 Coll, Civil Code § 13. This shows the difference to §§ 420 ff Civil Code. According to court jurisprudence, there is a difference between these two; in personality protection litigation, the courts do not 'compensate' a damage, but provide 'satisfaction' for a harm which is immaterial and therefore cannot be calculated. The monetary 'satisfaction' award therefore does not reflect any actual amount of damage, but rather strives by monetary payment to balance the immaterial loss which cannot be repaired – thus 'satisfies', not 'compensates' the victim.

48 Act 40/1964 Coll, Civil Code § 13.

After the death of the individual, the right to protection of his or her personality may be asserted by his or her spouse or children, or if there is no spouse or are no children, by his or her parents.[49] 57

10. Burden of proof

According to the Civil Code § 420, everyone shall be liable for damage caused by violating a legal duty. A person who proves that he did not cause the damage shall be relieved of the liability therefrom. 58

Under this general liability heading, the plaintiff has the duty to claim and prove: 59

- An unlawful act (a legal duty and a breach of this duty),
- the size of damages and
- the causal connection between the breach of duty and the damage.

The fault is presumed. The defendants can however exculpate themselves if they prove that there was no negligence. 60

According to the Civil Code, § 421a, 'everyone shall be liable also for damage caused by circumstances originating in the nature of a tool or other thing used in performing of an obligation. The liable person can not relieve himself of this liability in any way.' 61

Under this special type of liability for damage, which is based on the no-fault principle, the plaintiff has to claim and prove that: 62

- the event that caused the damage originated in the nature of a tool or other thing used in performing the obligation,
- the size of damages and
- the causal connection between the event and the damage.

In a case dealing with personality protection case, the plaintiff has to claim and prove: 63

- breach of a legal duty capable of violating the personality rights,
- actual infringement of personality rights, and
- a causal relation between the above.

This is a no-fault type of liability. 64

49 Act 40/1964 Coll, Civil Code § 15.

65 Typically, the most important pieces of evidence in medical malpractice cases are medical records and expert statements. According to the Civil Procedure Code,[50] the judge is empowered to freely evaluate the evidence. This power is important especially in situations where the medical records are grossly inadequate, or in situations of multiple contradictory expert opinions presented by the parties to the court. As a rule, such situations are detrimental to the plaintiff who has the burden of proof; the judges can however alleviate this burden by accepting that the plaintiff's claim is based on indirect evidence.

11. Uncertain causation

66 Causation is a necessary condition of liability. According to jurisprudence, a causal link between negligent breach of duty on the side of defendant and damage to health on the side of plaintiff must be proven with certainty; a mere probability is insufficient. The burden of proof concerning breach of duty and causation is on the plaintiff.[51]

67 If there are more relevant causes, it is necessary to evaluate their influence and gradation in relation to the harm. Causation is present if the harm is according to its general nature, general course of events and experience adequate consequence of an unlawful act.[52] At the same time, it is necessary to prove whether the harm would take place also in absence of such an unlawful act. The causal link is not excluded, however, simply because the unlawful act of the defendant was the final cause of the existing adverse health status of plaintiff.[53] Especially in the field of damage to health, an existence of a pre-existing condition does not as such exclude the causation.[54]

68 **What if it is unclear which member of a hospital's staff caused the loss?** According to § 420 para 2 of the Civil Code, the damage is caused by a legal entity or by an individual also if it was caused by persons used by the entity or individual to carry out such activity. These persons shall not be liable themselves for the damage according to this Act.[55]

---

50 Act 99/1963 Coll, Civil Procedure Code.

51 Decision of the Supreme Court of the Czech Republic of 25 November 2003, 25 Cdo 168/2003; Case R 21/1992.

52 *J Švestka et al*, Občanský zákoník – komentář (2nd edn 2009) 1066.

53 Case R 21/1992.

54 *Švestka* (fn 52), Case R 1/1963.

55 Act 40/1964 Coll, Civil Code § 420 (2).

From the viewpoint of a plaintiff in a civil case, it is therefore usually irrelevant which member of staff of a health care facility caused the loss. The defendant is almost always the health care facility,[56] not the health care worker in the position of an employee or a contractual partner who was fulfilling the activities of the health care facility.[57] **69**

12. Loss of a chance

The medical law loss of chance lawsuits are not specifically mentioned by Czech law or established in Czech judicial practice,[58] despite the fact that they have been discussed for several years in legal theory.[59] In liability for damage (§ 420 Civil Code) lawsuits, the compensable damages headings are listed exhaustively in the Civil Code. Adding a new type of damages, such as loss of chance of recovery, is not possible. **70**

However, if the existing statutory conditions of liability are sufficiently claimed and proven, ie the plaintiff successfully claims, firstly, that the unlawful act of a defendant is causally linked to an impossibility of recovery, and secondly, that recovery would be in absence of the unlawful act almost certain, then the plaintiff would most probably succeed. Such claim would however probably be very hard to prove. **71**

The plaintiff might however find a remedy for loss of chance in the area of personality protection. According to § 13 of the Civil Code; the individual shall be entitled in particular to demand that unlawful violation of his or her personality be ceased, that consequences of this violation be removed and that an adequate satisfaction be given to him or her; if such satisfaction under paragraph 1 appears insufficient due to the fact that the individual's dignity or honour has been considerably violated, the individual shall also have a right to pecuniary satisfaction of the immaterial **72**

---

56 Exceptions to this rule are quite rare and typically involve employees who caused damage by their acts (often criminal in its nature), committed exclusively in their own interest and without any relation to the activities of their employer. In such rare situations, the defendant is the employee him- or herself, not the employer.

57 Outside of civil law, for instance in the area of criminal law or in the area of disciplinary offences, the person responsible is always the physical person who caused harm, for instance an employed physician or nurse, not the hospital. Czech law so far does not acknowledge institutional liability in criminal law. In practice, this fact may complicate the defense tactics and extrajudicial settlements, due to the differing interests of an institution and its employees.

58 Decision of the Supreme Court of the Czech Republic of 26 February 2003, 25 Cdo 1862/2001; in this case, the Court decided on an issue of attorney malpractice.

59 *D Císařová et al*, Trestní právo a zdravotnictví (2nd edn 2004).

harm. According to the Biomedicine Convention,[60] the person who has suffered undue damage resulting from an intervention is entitled to fair compensation according to the conditions and procedures prescribed by the law. These quite general definitions allow the courts more flexibility in determining what is to be considered damage and what the adequate satisfaction should be in personality protection cases than in the more precisely regulated § 420 liability for damage area. For instance, in a recent personality protection case, the court found that even when accomplished harm cannot be effectively proven, it is sufficient to prove that a 'real risk of harm to personality rights' arose for the purpose of pecuniary satisfaction. Such an approach might also theoretically lead to an award of satisfaction for breach of personality rights in a loss of chance case.

13. Multiple persons involved

73 As described above, the hospital is liable according to § 420 para 2 for the actions of its employees. From the civil law point of view it is therefore not relevant which of the multiple hospital employees taking care of the patient actually caused the damage. The patient can raise a disciplinary complaint or a criminal charge against an individual staff member. Furthermore, a hospital that suffered financial loss due to the negligent behaviour of one of its employees, for instance a hospital which loses a medical malpractice case, has a remedy against such an employee. According to Act 262/2006 Coll, Labour Code, the employee is liable to the employer for damages up to 4.5 times his average monthly salary; this limit does not apply in cases where the damage was caused intentionally or under the influence of drugs or alcohol. The individual liability in cases involving more than one employee is usually judged according to the employee's position, qualification or work description. However, this typically does not influence the position of the plaintiff patient vis-à-vis the defendant hospital.[61]

60 Convention for the Protection of Human Rights and Dignity of the Human Being with regard to the Application of Biology and Medicine: Convention on Human Rights and Biomedicine, Act 96/2001 Coll Int Treaties, Art 24.

61 This can be relevant, however, in the context of professional liability insurance. A common cause of adverse events in Czech hospitals is the performance of interventions by insufficiently trained staff or a staff with improper qualification type. This is often a consequence of insufficient funding, which does not allow the hospital to have a 24/7 personnel coverage of all types of health services. Night or weekend shifts are sometimes delegated to trainee doctors, doctors indicate treatments by telephone without proper examination etc. These causes of harm, especially cases of treatment by unqualified personnel, are as a rule excluded from liability insurance.

The distribution of liabilities is more relevant in cases where more than one health care facility performs health care interventions on a patient who ultimately suffers harm. It is important to note that not only hospitals but also independent ambulatory care physicians (natural persons) are 'health care facilities' according to Czech law. These cases involve situations of wrong primary care diagnoses, belated or negligent referrals to hospitals, or negligent follow-up monitoring; other cases involve timeliness of transfers from general to specialised hospitals, general hospital follow-up care after a complicated intervention in a specialised hospital, etc. In such situations, it is vital for the plaintiff patient to correctly identify the entity which is the potential defendant and to which the cause of harm can be attributed. The patient typically sees only the adverse result, but is not usually in position to correctly evaluate the presence or absence of fault and causation on the side of different participants in the treatment process. This evaluation typically requires an expert assessment and is usually further complicated by imperfect medical records; it often happens that the discharge report of a previous provider differs significantly from the follow-up hospital admission record and only indirect evidence can show which of these records is incorrect. This situation requires the plaintiff to name all the possible defendants, despite the increased costs of proceedings. Courts very often resolve such situations with an almost complete reliance on the court-appointed expert statement. **74**

It is uncommon for 'private' health care providers, typically ambulatory care doctors, to perform surgeries in hospitals on their own account ie as a separate business entity renting space and personnel from the hospital.[62] More typically,[63] these doctors work on behalf of the hospital, usually as part-time employees.[64] In such a situation, the hospital is vicariously liable **75**

62 Czech legislation (especially Act 160/1992 Coll) does not sufficiently describe or regulate the notion of 'doctors with hospital privileges', or ambulatory doctors who 'rent' hospital rooms and personnel in order to be able to provide on their own account to their patients more complex interventions, especially surgeries which cannot be done in ambulatory settings. A 2008 legislative proposal of a new Act on Health Care Services included this possibility, but without any regulation of liability distribution between the hospital and the 'visiting' doctor.

63 In the rather rare cases when out-of-hospital doctors operate in hospitals on their own account, the organisational and liability issues are resolved in a specific contract. Their liability towards the patient would be most probably distributed according to the measure of fault, but I am not aware of any reported jurisprudence concerning such issue.

64 The main reason for this practice is that the hospitals sometimes cannot cover its 24/7 operation, especially overnight shifts, with its core personnel due to financial restraints, due to an insufficient number of doctors in some specialisations or due to recent labour law working time limitations. The hospitals therefore invite ambulatory practitioners to a part-time employment, which brings such doctors a possibility of contact with usually more advanced hospital medicine and surplus salary.

for their potential malpractice according to § 420 para 2 of the Civil Code in the same way as for their other full-time employees.[65]

14. Strict liability

76 The main exceptions from general fault-based liability are matters concerning personality protection liability described above, and liability for damage caused by circumstances originating in the nature of a tool or other item used in performing of an obligation.

77 The latter type of liability is very important in cases involving any imperfect medical device, instrument or drug. § 421a of the Civil Code states that everyone shall be liable for damage caused by circumstances originating in the nature of a tool or other item used in performing an obligation. The liable person can not relieve himself of this liability in any way. According to the Civil Code, this liability also applies to the provision of medical, social, veterinary and other biological services.

78 Categorisation of a case under this strict liability heading is very favourable for the plaintiff. The main issues of defence before the court are the proof of causal link to the harm, and the proof of whether the damage was caused by a circumstance originating in the nature of a medical item, or whether the damage was caused by an improper usage of a proper, flawless item. In the latter situation, the case falls under the general (non-strict) liability heading and negligence on the part of the acting doctor must be proven.

79 Further exceptions from the general liability heading include the liability for harm resulting from discrimination under § 10 of the new Act 198/2009 Coll on equal treatment and legal measures of protection against discrimination (Antidiscrimination Act). In future litigation the burden of proof may be borne by the defendant if the harm in the health care or social care field resulted from discrimination based on racial or ethnic origin according to the new § 133a of the Act 99/1963 Coll on Civil Procedure as amended by the Antidiscrimination Act. It is not difficult to

65 The ambulatory care doctors can thus provide their patients a benefit of 'self-referral' from their private ambulatory practice to surgeries in hospital, where they operate in employee role, thus giving their patients a benefit of automatic choice of hospital physician and possibly also a shorter waiting time. While the hospital receives the payment from the health insurance, it pays such part-time doctors a salary, provides all the equipment and bears the liability.

foresee a situation in which a plaintiff-member of a racial or ethnic minority group claims racial bias in a wrong treatment decision leading to harm.

Law also determines the liability of producers and distributors, for instance the liability of producers of pharmaceuticals for side effects of drugs in § 33 sec 5) of the Act 378/2007 Coll on Pharmaceuticals. According to this Act, the person who obtains permission to register a drug from the state drug control agency is liable for harm caused as a result of the effects of the pharmaceutical not described in the Summary of Product Characteristics (SPC); he cannot absolve himself from this liability. However, such a person is liable for the harm caused as a result of the effects of the pharmaceutical, which were described in the SPC, only if fault is proven. **80**

C. Contractual Liability

15. Basics of contracts in the health care sector

Health care in the Czech Republic is almost exclusively[66] provided in the framework of the statutory health insurance. Only a small part of the health care market involves direct contracting, especially in the areas of plastic surgeries, artificial reproduction or advanced dental treatment. There is also health care provided at non-contractual health care facilities, typically clinics which are aimed at foreign clients. Finally, it is necessary to mention services at the borderline of health care, such as life-style consulting or activities of natural healers, provided on the basis of direct payment; these are however usually declared as non-health services and thus evade both strict health care regulation and any real risk of medical malpractice liability. **81**

Concerning the majority of health care, the medical service is provided by a health care facility to the publicly insured patient and paid for by a third party health insurance fund. Legal theory has not yet clarified the exact nature of this three-sided legal relationship. The relationship between the insured citizen and the health insurance fund, involving payment of mandatory insurance and entitlement to publicly funded health services, is usually seen as a part of public, social welfare law rather than as a **82**

66 Approximately 90:10 ratio.

contractual relation.[67] Whereas the relationship between a health insurance fund and a health care facility is usually seen as a contract despite its extensive regulation concerning prices and reimbursement mechanisms. Finally, the legal relationship between a publicly insured patient and a contractual health care provider is seen basically as a contract.[68]

83 This patient-provider relation is regulated at two levels: from the viewpoint of health care provision regulation (especially Act 20/1996 Coll on Health Care of the People) and from the viewpoint of public health insurance regulation (especially Act 48/1997 Coll on Public Health Insurance). The former applies to all health care providers while the latter is only applicable to providers who act within the public health insurance system. A great majority of providers have contracts with all health insurance funds. However, for the sake of clarity, it is important to distinguish between the rights stemming from the health care provision regulation ('patient rights') and the rights stemming from the public health insurance regulation ('rights of the insured'). Patient rights involve especially the right to informed consent, to privacy and access to medical records and to 'care on the level of current available findings of medical science',[69] and professional duties of physicians include an ethical and truthful approach to patients, prohibition of economic conflict of interests in prescribing treatments and strict regulation of advertising of medical services. The rights of the insured describe the circumstances under which care is reimbursed by the third party insurer; the insured has a right to choose any contractual health care facility, doctor or other health worker and the right to receive appropriate care free of charge, but also has a duty to follow the prescribed treatment regime.

16. Differences to tort law

84 As to my knowledge, almost all medical malpractice litigation stems from general tort law and the personality protection law. The claims based on contractual bases are rare in practice, although injured patients theoretically have the possibility to sue in contract. In the context of the public health insurance system, claims arise from insured against contractual

67 The recent health reform proposal aimed at privatisation of health care funds and strengthening of the contractual nature between the insured and the health care fund. The legislative proposals were however rejected by Parliament in 2008.

68 This is not mentioned expressly in current law; however, the re-codification of the Civil Code mentions the treatment contract as a specific contractual type.

69 Act 20/1966 Coll on Health Care of the People, § 11.

providers for non-performance of covered services or waiting times, but these are handled by the public insurance funds' internal review procedures rather than by the courts. Outside of the public system, contractual claims arise concerning the pricing or quality of services provided to foreigners who pay for their care directly. Even in this context, however, cases arising from damage caused are handled under tort law.

17. Contractual claims in the absence of direct contracts?

The citizen has a constitutional right to unpaid health care on the basis of 85
public health insurance within the scope defined by the law.[70] The state delegates the fulfilment of this duty to health insurance funds and sets the scope of services covered, the amount of mandatory payments and the regulation of contracts between health insurance funds and contractual providers. Every citizen has a right to choose a public insurance fund to which he pays the mandatory insurance. The health insurance fund should guarantee the patient access to quality and safe care by establishing and sufficiently funding care in a network of contractual health care providers. Unfortunately, especially in certain specialisations such as psychiatric or long-term care, the contractual providers are not reimbursed in a way that enables them to provide care 'on the level of current available findings of medical science'.

In the case of medical error, the medical malpractice liability of a specific 86
health care facility is assessed on the grounds of the health care provision regulation regardless of the way in which the care is reimbursed. The reimbursement mechanisms can however have a significant impact on the scope and quality of care actually provided to the patients. This creates a problem in the area of public health insurance systems: the patient has a right to care in accordance with current medical knowledge, and this level of care should theoretically be properly reimbursed by the health insurance funds. But the level of actual reimbursement is implicitly limited by price limitation and quantity limits in the contracts between insurance funds and providers. The standard of care for liability purposes is therefore significantly higher than the standard of public insurance system reimbursement, namely the economic standard on which the contractual health care facilities have to operate, since they cannot legally charge the

70 Art 31 of the Constitutional Act 2/1993 Coll, Charter of Fundamental Rights and Basic Freedoms.

insured for the surplus cost of interventions that are not sufficiently covered by the public system.[71]

87 From the viewpoint of the patient who has suffered harm due to under-funding or unavailability of quality service in a contractual health care facility, it would be theoretically possible to bring an action against a health care fund. Arguably, the strict reimbursement limits and mechanisms allowing for profit-sharing[72] lead to the under-servicing of patients. Such action would thus have to claim that as a result of economic pressure and thus by implied authority over decision-making capacity of the contractual doctor or hospital, the health care fund caused the situation in which injury to the patient arose. In such situations, however, it would be much easier for the patient to lay a claim against a health care facility.

18. Informed consent

88 The doctrine of informed consent is relevant to malpractice claims. According to the Biomedicine Convention,[73] which is a directly applicable source of law in the Czech Republic, an intervention in the health field may only be carried out after the person concerned has given free and informed consent thereto. A health care intervention performed without a patient's consent or against his or her will is unlawful. Similarly, in the case of insufficient disclosure of risks and alternatives, which should always precede the consent, the informed consent itself is invalid and the intervention can be deemed as unlawful. Consent is, as a rule, necessary for every single intervention; 'general consents to treatment' which patients sometimes sign upon admission to hospital are not legally sufficient.

---

71 This was shown in the 2008 Public Defender of Rights ('ombudsman') study on psychiatric hospitals, see <http://www.ochrance.cz/zprava-z-navstev-psychiatrickych-leceben>.

72 Eg the so-called 'drug bonification-regulation mechanism', included in the recent reimbursement decrees and in contracts between insurance funds and contractual facilities. See Decree 618/2006 Coll on Framework Contracts.

73 Convention for the Protection of Human Rights and Dignity of the Human Being with regard to the Application of Biology and Medicine: Convention on Human Rights and Biomedicine, Act 96/2001 Coll Int Treaties, Art 5.

There are several major exceptions to the general consent rule:[74] 89

- Interventions based on public health needs, as described in specific Acts, especially Act 258/2000 Coll on Protection of Public Health (compulsory vaccinations, quarantine etc);
- Emergency situations. When the appropriate consent cannot be obtained because of an emergency situation any medically necessary intervention may be carried out immediately for the benefit of the health of the individual concerned: and
- Treatment of minors and persons with permanent mental disability. In the case of these patients, the necessary consent is given by a parent or a guardian. However, parents or guardians cannot refuse emergency treatment necessary for saving life or health. Furthermore, according to a Constitutional Court decision concerning a child of Jehovah Witnesses, parents need to decide according to best health interest of the child and cannot validly refuse a non-emergency lifesaving surgery, despite religious concerns.

Autopsies do not require the previous consent of the bereaved. 90

In order to be valid, consent to an intervention must be given by an 91
informed patient. The health care workers have a duty to disclose all the information relevant to the decision-making of the patient. According to the law[75], such disclosure must include:

- Purpose and nature of the intervention,
- Risks of the intervention,
- Possible treatment alternatives, including alternative of no intervention and
- Consequences, pain and necessary treatment regime.

Arguably, the provider should also disclose costs of treatment or necessary 92
co-payments, especially if the treatment is outside of the scope of publicly covered health care, and the experience of the physician, especially in the

---

74 Convention for the Protection of Human Rights and Dignity of the Human Being with regard to the Application of Biology and Medicine: Convention on Human Rights and Biomedicine, Act 96/2001 Coll Int Treaties, Arts 6, 7 and 8; Act 20/1966 Coll on Health Care of the People, § 23 (4).

75 Convention for the Protection of Human Rights and Dignity of the Human Being with regard to the Application of Biology and Medicine: Convention on Human Rights and Biomedicine, Act 96/2001 Coll Int Treaties, Art 5; Decree 385/2006 Coll on Medical Records.

case of complicated surgeries, since this information can also significantly affect the patient's decision-making. In practice, however, such an extent of disclosure is usually not given.

93 A competent patient may refuse any kind of treatment, even life-saving emergency surgery. Such a negative statement has to be made in writing. Conversely, the law does not mandate that positive consent is to be expressly given in writing, with the exception of, for example, clinical trials or assisted reproduction. In the case of major interventions, however, health care facilities usually offer patients specific consent forms which include a description of the intervention and typical associated risks.

94 The new Criminal Code, which will enter into force from 1st January 2010, expressly defines two new exceptions from criminal liability: § 30 (consent of the injured) and § 31 (acceptable risk). These two definitions will also influence the civil medical malpractice area by analogy.

95 § 30 generally states that consent of the injured precludes criminal liability. In cases of crimes against health and life, however, the consent of the injured only has this effect if given to a medical intervention compatible with findings of medical science and practice. According to § 31 (acceptable risk), criminal liability is precluded if a person who performs an activity that benefits society as a part of his profession or employment thereby endangers or violates an interest protected by the Criminal Code provided that the beneficial goal could not have been achieved any other way. This does not apply, however, if such activity endangers the life or health of another person who did not give appropriate consent thereto, or if the intended result of such activity does not manifestly correspond to the degree of risk.

96 These new statutory definitions correspond with previous findings of medico-legal theory[76] and indicate that the legality of an intervention in the field of health care requires *both* valid consent and medical acceptability of such intervention. Even valid consent given by a competent patient to a *non lege artis* intervention or to a prohibited intervention such as active euthanasia will not preclude criminal liability. Analogous rules will most probably also apply in the area of civil medical malpractice liability.

97 Despite the significant attention that is devoted to the law of informed consent by both legal theory and medical practitioners, the impact on

76 *Císařová* (fn 59).

medical malpractice litigations remains limited. Typically, plaintiffs use the lack of consent argument in a secondary role, where the primary ground for liability is a negligent performance of medical intervention. 'Pure' informed consent cases are so far typically found in immaterial harm cases and ethics complaints, and certain specific areas of medicine, such plastic surgeries, assisted reproduction, involuntary psychiatric treatment[77] and sterilisation.[78] Reasons why informed consent is less significant in malpractice litigation might include a comparatively lower emphasis on patient decision-making autonomy in general. But there are also procedural differences; Czech courts do not usually transfer the burden of proof from the plaintiff and do not require the defendant to prove conclusively the presence of valid consent and scope of disclosure. When the medical records include a note that a patient was informed, or even that a consent form was completed, and the hospital employees confirm as witnesses that sufficient disclosure was given orally, it is very hard for the plaintiff to prove that the communication was in fact absent or insufficient, or that a specific risk was not explained to him. Plaintiffs therefore only enjoy a chance of success in situations where the circumstances or indirect evidence indicate that valid informed consent could not have been given (eg laboratory findings recorded significant intoxication of the patient, or the patient did not speak Czech).

D. Public Liability

19. Key differences from cases involving private hospitals or doctors

Czech law does not treat public and private providers differently in civil liability issues. A difference can be found in the additional possibility that a patient may initiate a complaint to the public health insurance fund if improper care was provided by its contractual health care facility. This complaint procedure cannot however lead to a damage award, and its findings have little relevance to any potential civil liability proceedings. 98

77 Decision of the Constitutional Court of 30 September 1997, Pl ÚS 23/97; see also the aforementioned 2008 Ombudsman report from psychiatric hospitals.

78 Decision of the High Court in Olomouc of 17 January 2007.

E. Alternative Compensation Regimes

20. Funds and/or other alternative compensation regimes

99 So far, there is no consistent system of alternative resolution of medical malpractice cases. A patient can address complaints to the Medical Chamber, to the regional or central administrative body competent for the registration of the health care facility, or to a public health insurance fund. While these complaints do not cost the patient anything, they cannot lead to an enforceable damages award.

100 Any victim of medical injury can benefit from the system of social security, including sickness insurance, unemployment relief, disability pensions, health care insurance etc. Such benefits are awarded on a basis of statutory entitlement, thus lessening the economic loss compensable by the damages award.

101 According to the Act 209/1997 Coll on Aid for Victims of Criminal Acts, a person who suffered a health injury as a result of a crime, or a bereaved person, is entitled to a lump-sum payment to compensate for the worsened social situation resulting from the crime if the damage was not compensated otherwise. The size of these lump-sum payments is unfortunately very small; in the case of health damage, the maximum amount for one victim is CZK 150,000 (approx € 6,000) for the injured, and in case of death CZK 150,000 for the bereaved.[79]

102 According to the § 78 (2) of the Act 20/1966 Coll on Health Care of the People, the state can in exceptional cases provide financial aid to a person who suffered damage in the course of treatment, even if the duty to compensate the damage did not arise. It is however exclusively in the discretion of the state to decide whether or not to provide such aid. In practice, this article is seen as obsolete and is not applied.

103 Regional self-government authorities can in exceptional cases provide financial gifts to victims of medical malpractice from its budget, typically when the damage arose in a health care facility operated by the regional authority.

---

79 Act 209/1997 Coll on Aid for Victims of Criminal Acts, § 7.

F. Extent of Liability/Remedies

I. Pecuniary Loss

21. Introduction to indemnifying pecuniary loss

As mentioned above, according to the Czech Civil Code, two kinds of remedies for personal injury or death are available: 104

1. Liability for breach of personality protection rights (§ 11 ff Civil Code)
2. Liability for damage (§ 420 ff Civil Code).

Under the heading of personality rights, the court can provide a remedy for any violation of personal and civil rights, for instance right to family life, privacy, health or life. The remedy can be restitutory or compensatory, moral or pecuniary, whereas the appropriateness and amount of pecuniary remedy is in the discretion of the judge. 105

Concerning the damages under the liability for damage heading, the law generally states that the compensation shall include compensation of the real damages as well as of what the damaged party lost (lost profit). The Czech law does not allow punitive damages. The damages shall be compensated in cash; however, the damages shall be compensated by way of *restitutio in integrum* if the damaged party demands so and if it is possible and purposeful.[80] 106

Loss of earnings is compensated by way of a cash pension; its amount is calculated from the average earnings of the injured party before the damage arose.[81] Compensation of loss of earnings during the damaged party's incapacity to work is calculated as a difference between his or her average earnings before the injury and sickness insurance allowances.[82] Compensation for the loss of earnings after the end of incapacity to work or in the case of invalidity is calculated as a difference between the average earnings before the injury and the sum of earnings achieved after the damages and invalidity pension.[83] 107

Compensation for loss of pension allowances is calculated as the difference between the amount of pension allowances to which the injured party is 108

80 Act 40/1964 Coll, Civil Code § 442 (2).
81 Act 40/1964 Coll, Civil Code § 445.
82 Act 40/1964 Coll, Civil Code § 446.
83 Act 40/1964 Coll, Civil Code § 447.

entitled and the amount of pension allowances to which the injured would otherwise be entitled in absence of the injury.[84]

109 In the case of damage to health, compensation includes purposeful expenses connected with medical treatment.[85] These expenses are compensated to the person who paid them, which can be the injured himself or another person (eg parent). These expenses may include supplementary medical care, rehabilitation, purchase of medical or orthopedic aids, dietary meals, help with the household or care of the disabled person or expenses of close relatives connected with visiting the hospital.[86]

110 In the case of death, the survivors who were paid or entitled to maintenance by the injured are entitled to compensation in the form of a cash pension. The compensation is calculated with regard to the average earnings of the deceased.[87] In the case of death, the compensation shall also include adequate expenses connected with the burial.[88]

111 In cases requiring special consideration, the court can reduce the compensation for damage. In determining the reduction the court shall take account of how the injury arose as well as personal and property relations of the defendant and of the individual damaged party. However, the reduction is not admissible if the injury was caused intentionally.[89]

112 The abovementioned rules apply generally, without specifics for the medical malpractice area.

22. Loss of earnings vs loss of earning capacity

113 The Civil Code in the section dealing with loss of earnings[90] states that loss in earnings shall be compensated by way of a cash pension; its amount is calculated from the average earnings of the injured before the injury arose. A similar method applies in cases of death for the calculation of maintenance compensation. The plaintiff is therefore required to prove actual[91] or

---

84 Act 40/1964 Coll, Civil Code § 447a.
85 Act 40/1964 Coll, Civil Code § 449 (1).
86 *Švestka* (fn 52) 1169.
87 Act 40/1964 Coll, Civil Code § 448.
88 Act 40/1964 Coll, Civil Code § 449 (2).
89 Act 40/1964 Coll, Civil Code § 450.
90 Act 40/1964 Coll, Civil Code § 447.
91 If the value of activities of a homemaker can be evaluated, the loss of such work can be compensated under Act 40/1964 § 448 of the Civil Code.

expected[92] earnings; this might be possible in the case of some students or trainees.

Other students or trainees, who can not provide any evidence of actual or expected earnings and want to claim only general loss of earning capacity in future, must rely on the compensation of pain and loss of amenities.[93] The notion of amenities includes the work status, participation in sports or culture, or other ways of development of personality. In the area of employment it also includes choice and preparation for future work or performance of current work. It is therefore possible to assess limitations or loss of predisposition for amenities the injured enjoyed in this area, whereas actual income or its subsequent lowering as a result of injury is not decisive.[94] A similar approach would probably be applicable to a homemaker who due to injuries is no longer able to provide personal care to his or her family. **114**

In 2005 the Constitutional Court decided a case of a father whose son died by drowning at the age of 15. The father sued the river authority for negligence and claimed *inter alia* compensation of property loss, arguing that the deceased son could have in future helped him in running the family business, or could have provided maintenance to his parents in case of sickness or disability. The father, after being unsuccessful in civil proceedings, claimed that the Civil Code does not allow compensation beyond the exhaustive item list (here, pain, loss of amenities and, as of 1 May 2004, a lump-sum compensation for death, as described below). An entitlement to compensation for help of a deceased who would in future have provided maintenance to the claimant cannot be construed from or added to this exhaustive list, leading to the impossibility of obtaining fair compensation. The Constitutional Court commented that such entitlement could be applied within the framework of personality protection, which includes also protection of individual integrity and family life. Death of a close person can therefore be classified as harm significant enough to give rise to an application for financial satisfaction for infringement of personality protection rights. This is however, according to current legislation, a different entitlement to that of compensation for damage.[95] **115**

Therefore, it seems that compensation in such a situation can best be achieved via financial satisfaction for infringement of personality protec- **116**

92 Case R 10/1991: A compensable loss of earnings in the sense of § 445 may arise also in a situation when the injured did not work at the time of injury, but can prove that he should have started his employment and only due to the injury in fact did not.

93 Act 40/1964 Coll, Civil Code § 444.

94 *Švestka* (fn 52) 1147.

95 Decision of the Constitutional Court of 4 May 2005, 265/2005 Coll.

tion rights or be taken into account in deciding on the compensation of pain and loss of amenities, as described below.

23. Periodic payments or lump sum?

117 The situation is different with individual damage items. The necessary treatment costs are as a rule compensated retrospectively. Loss of earnings is compensated by way of a cash pension. Compensation of immaterial harm described below, such as damages for pain and loss of amenities, payments for causing death, and financial satisfaction for infringement of personality rights are indemnified by a lump-sum.

118 According to § 449a of the Civil Code future entitlements, especially loss of earnings payments, can also be indemnified by a lump-sum based on a written agreement between the entitled and the obliged person about their complete and final settlement.

24. Caps and thresholds

119 There are limitations on damages for pain and loss of amenities and on immaterial compensation of death. The Civil Code in its § 444 declares that in the case of death the survivors are entitled to one-time compensation, as described below. According to the same article, the Ministry of Health issues a catalogue of types of harm with point values, setting the compensation level. These limitations are not, however, considered conclusive anymore. Jurisprudence deals with the subject of these damage caps, including two recent judgments of the Constitutional Court, in which the *ratio decidendi* is that the damage caps are not unconstitutional as such, but a judge is enabled to apply his freedom of discretion when awarding higher compensation for pain and suffering than that set by the Government Regulation if so required by the exceptional conditions of the case.[96]

96 Decision of the Constitutional Court of 29 September 2005, III. ÚS 350/03: From the viewpoint of protection of constitutionality...the awarded damages for loss of amenities must be based on objective and rational reasons and...there has to be a relation of adequateness between the harm and the awarded amount; Decision of the Constitutional Court of 6 October 2007, Pl ÚS 50/05: the court may decide in case that the compensation according to the Ministerial Decree č 440/2001 Sb is not just and appropriate, not to apply this decree and decide according to its own consideration how high compensation will be just for the injured, if the court considered the application of the decree unjust and contrary to constitutional principles.

II. Non-pecuniary Loss

25. Introduction to indemnifying non-pecuniary loss

Non-pecuniary loss is indemnified primarily in two kinds of proceedings: **120**

- Liability for breach of personality protection (§ 11 ff Civil Code)
- Liability for damage (§ 420 of the Civil Code), which besides compensation of material types of harm also includes damages for pain and loss of amenities, and one-time compensation for damage caused by death.

These two kinds of cases are resolved in separate, mutually independent proceedings, before different courts and according to different set of procedural rules. **121**

Under the heading of personality protection, the court can remedy any violation of personal and civil rights, for instance right to family life, privacy, health or life. The remedy can be restitutory or compensatory, moral or pecuniary, whereas the appropriateness and amount of pecuniary remedy is in the discretion of the judge. **122**

The liability of damage heading includes two immaterial damage counts, firstly, the lump-sum compensation of pain and loss of amenities, and secondly, the lump-sum compensation for causing death. **123**

The former is provided for in terms of the Government Decree 440/2001 Coll, which includes lists of various types of injuries and diseases and awards each item a point value. Each point has the monetary equivalent of CZK 120 (approx € 4.80). The amounts of compensation for pain, suffering and future handicaps are often inadequate when calculated according to the point system. Therefore, the plaintiffs frequently request that the court to take advantage of § 7 of this decree, which allows the court in exceptional cases to raise the compensation level over the amount calculated according to the 'points'. Courts have gradually begun to use this discretionary power. According to recent Supreme Court jurisprudence young victims in particular and/or persons suffering severe, long-lasting handicaps can expect a good chance of the basic 'point' award being multiplied up to three or even five times.[97] However, this does not lend **124**

97 Eg Decision of the Supreme Court of the Czech Republic of 29 November 2005, 25 Cdo 2497/2004: Increase of compensation of aggravation of social life in case of young sportsman; Decision of the Supreme Court of the Czech Republic of 31 May 2006, 25 Cdo 2186/2004: Increase of compensation of aggravation of social life in case of 51 year old woman with quadruparesis.

itself to legal certainty for victims as it is frequently too dependent on the skills of the judge and/or the attorney involved as to whether the basic 'point' compensation will be raised and if so by how much. Due to this uncertainty and lack of predictability it is difficult to define an amount of compensation for the purpose of extrajudicial settlement.

125 In the case of death, the lump-sum compensation is paid in the amount of:

a. 240,000 CZK (approx € 9,600) to husband or wife of the deceased

b. 240,000 CZK to each child

c. 240,000 CZK to each parent

d. 175,000 CZK to each sibling

e. 240,000 CZK to any other close person living in a common household with the deceased person at the time of the event resulting in the damage.

126 Concerning this damages count, it is not necessary to prove anything except the fact of death and the personal link between the deceased and the entitled person.

127 Obviously, the indemnification of immaterial harm under the heading of liability for damage (§ 420 ff) covers a very similar scope of harm to that of financial satisfaction for infringement of personality rights under the heading of personality protection liability (§ 11 ff). Double proceedings for the immaterial harm between two different courts raise questions of violation of the principle of *ne bis in idem*, especially when the personality protection court awards financial satisfaction additional to the lump-sum compensation already awarded for pain and loss of amenities or for causing death by the damage court. Court practice however supports this possibility of double indemnification. A solution to this problem is expected from the long-awaited new Civil Code, which will unify both liability headings into one system.

128 The abovementioned rules apply generally, without specific rules in the medical malpractice area.

129 Concerning reported cases with high awards, the Supreme Court noted in its decision of 27 April 2006: '17 million CZK (€ 680,000) damages for loss of amenities of a 24 years old woman, who before the injury led a normal social, cultural, family, work and sport life, out of which she was completely excluded due to loss of mobility, cognitive and communication abilities, full dependency on care of another person in the basic personal needs, and necessity of permanent intensive rehabilitation, is not improper or unfounded.'[98]

Other recent cases with high awards include the following: 130

- 18 million CZK (approx € 750,000) in a 2008 case of a 43 years old mother of two children who suffered a violent allergic reaction to a contrast medium during angiography and fell into a permanent coma.
- 16.5 million CZK (approx € 660,000) in a 2007 case awarded to the parents of a seven year old boy who suffered irreversible severe brain damage following a belated resuscitation.
- 12 million CZK (approx € 480,000) in a 2009 case against a Prague teaching hospital awarded to the parents of a 11 year old boy who suffered permanent brain damage following hypoxia during an operation.
- 3.3 million CZK (approx € 130,000) in a recent first-instance decision, awarded to two families for breach of family and privacy rights, following an unintentional mix-up of newborns in a regional hospital, disclosed by chance after 10 months.
- 2.5 million CZK (approx € 100,000) for the family of a newborn who contracted hepatitis C during his stay in a teaching hospital in 2001.[99]

26. Who can claim compensation for non-pecuniary loss?

Both direct victim and indirect victims can claim compensation for non- 131
pecuniary loss. Whereas only the victim himself can claim the damages for pain and loss of amenities and require financial satisfaction for infringement of his personality rights, the indirect victims can claim violation of their personality rights (eg infringement of the right to family life, if their relative suffered a severe brain injury and does not interact with them, or if they suffer psychical problems and stress related to their relative's injury, etc). Indirect victims, typically parents, can also claim compensation of material expenses that they incur in connection with caring for a direct victim of medical malpractice.

98 Decision of the Supreme Court of the Czech Republic of 27 April 2006, 25 Cdo 759/2005.

99 Cases summarized at <http://www.reflex.cz/Clanek38282.html>.

132 In the case of death the relatives have a right to the § 444 lump-sum compensation for causing death, regardless of their actual affinity to the victim (theoretically, the court would have to award this compensation to a sibling or son of the deceased who did not recently have any contact with the deceased, or who even disliked and avoided the deceased). In the personality protection context, however, the court evaluates the real impact of the death on the relationship so it is possible that a loving relative could receive significantly more financial satisfaction, whereas an uninvolved relative could receive only moral satisfaction, without additional financial award.

G. Procedural Matters

27. Specific rules of jurisdiction or procedure

133 Czech law creates several specific rules for personal injury cases, which include not only medical malpractice cases, but also motor vehicle accidents or sport accidents litigation.

134 Firstly, every personal injury gives rise to liability under the heading personality protection (§ 11 ff) and at the same time under the liability for damage heading (§ 420 ff). Liability for damage cases are resolved before the district (lowest-level) court. In case of actions for personal injury, the court fee is waived. To the contrary, personality protection cases are resolved in the first instance before the Regional courts and claims for financial satisfaction are subject to a four percent court fee.

135 Secondly, the issue of limitation periods in the laws of the Czech is quite complex due to the fact that the periods of limitation are set differently for personality protection and for liability for damage. The limitation periods for tort are described in the Act No 40/1964 Coll, Civil Code, § 100 ff. The Czech law distinguishes between so-called 'objective' periods of limitations (that is, periods starting on the date of the accident) and 'subjective' periods of limitation (that is, periods starting on the date when the victim obtained knowledge of the damage and of who is liable for such damage). According to § 101, the limitation period is three years long and starts running from the day when the right could be exercised for the first time. Therefore, the default civil law period of limitation is objective and does not take into account the date of knowledge. An important exception is stated in article 106, where the Civil Code stipulates that a right to compensation of damage shall become statute-barred in two years from

the day when the damaged person learnt of the damage and of the person liable therefore. In the case of personal injury, there is no objective limitation period. This is logical because some impacts of medical injuries only become manifest after a long time. This regime does not, however, apply to the personality protection area, which falls under the general, objective three-year limitation period rule. Therefore, it might happen that a victim suffers an iatrogenic injury five years earlier yet only recently learns that this injury will have a severely adverse result; in such a case, the patient would still be able to claim compensation for personal injury. Such a plaintiff would however be unable to raise a claim for satisfaction for personality protection violation, and to take advantage of its benefits.

Finally, medical malpractice litigation is in practice highly dependant on **136** expert statements. In almost every case of medical negligence the court appoints a medical expert or an expert institution and the expert findings are typically decisive in the case – sometimes, the medical expert virtually dictates the outcome. At the same time, the quality of expert statements varies widely.[100] Obtaining expert statements takes a long time especially in the case of revision statements by expert institutions. The legal regulation of expert evidence is obsolete and does not sufficiently prevent low-quality or biased statements.[101] This creates difficulties for the plaintiff in particular who bears the burden of proof; speculative or biased expert findings can make it impossible to prove conclusively, especially concerning causation. Furthermore, medical records often tend to be insufficient and do not provide a sufficient basis for court or expert evaluation although the law mandates both health care facilities and health care workers to diligently and truthfully record relevant matters in detail.[102] Unfortunately, neither legislation nor jurisprudence have adequately responded to this problem by, for instance, transferring the burden of proof onto the defendant in cases where medical records are wholly inadequate.

---

100 A study performed in 2008 by the League for Human Rights found that a high percentage of medical expert statements does not include proper statement of relevant facts, or basis for their findings, for instance sufficient references to medical literature; and that medical experts often assess also legal questions, such as presence of fault or justification of the liability claim.
See <http://www.llp.cz/_files/file/SYSTEMOVE_DOPORUCENI_7.pdf>.

101 Both parties are free to provide to the court 'privately' obtained expert statements, and practice shows that certain medical experts cooperating routinely with either plaintiffs or defendants show a significant degree of bias.

102 Act 20/1966 Coll on Health Care of the People, § 67b; Decree 385/2006 Coll on Medical Records. Real life experience, including broadly publicised media cases, show that medical records are being even altered or falsified.

28. Special institutions handling malpractice claims

137 There is no special institution for handling medical malpractice claims out of court. Patients can raise complaints to the Czech Medical Chamber, to the administrative institution which registered the health care facility or to a public health insurance fund; resolving of these complaints is financed from the budgets of the respective institution, but cannot lead to a binding award of damages.

138 Czech medical malpractice cases normally go to trial if a negotiation with the relevant health care facility does not lead to a satisfactory settlement. The out-of-court resolution of malpractice disputes is further discouraged by the contractual conditions of professional liability insurers; in order to have the compensation award covered by liability insurance, the insured must as a rule have the case decided by the court.

H. Outlook

29. Reform plans

139 The medical malpractice litigation area has undergone significant growth in recent years, both in terms of the number of claims and the size of compensation awards. The changes are however due to interpretative activity of courts and media awareness rather than to legislative reform steps. Similar development can be expected in the future, especially with regard to burden of proof transfers and damage awards for less typical cases of harm, particularly in the context of personality protection liability.

140 A significant adverse feature of the Czech justice system is the length of the duration of the court proceedings. Theoretically, a well-prepared court case can be resolved within several months, but a typical case can take as long as one-and-a-half to two years, sometimes more. This is especially true for tort cases involving personal injury, where cases lasting three years are by no means rare and in some instances, the courts have taken more than six years to resolve the matter.[103] Recent changes in the Code of Civil Procedure[104] establish stricter rules for delivery of documents to

---

103 One of the reasons for such delays is the relatively bad accessibility of expert opinions by court-appointed experts and expert institutions.

104 Act 7/2009 Coll, amending Act 99/1963 Coll, Civil Procedure Code, in force from 1 July 2009.

parties including mandatory electronic communication, and limitations for presenting new evidence. However, the effects of these changes cannot yet be evaluated.

Finally, in 2009 the Government accepted a proposal of a long-expected re-codification of the Civil Code, inspired by German and Austrian law. This new Civil Code was not, however, accepted by the Parliament and its entry into force cannot be expected earlier than in 2012. The published text of this legislative proposal[105] includes many changes relevant to medical law in general, such as the definition of medical treatment on a contractual basis,[106] competence[107] and involuntary treatment,[108] as well as changes in the tort law pertinent to medical malpractice.[109] The new concept prioritises restitution over pecuniary compensation, integrates personality protection and liability for damage, and abolishes the pain and suffering tables defined by Ministerial decree, thus leaving more space for judicial discretion. These changes will, however, be subject to political discussion and possible amendments during the upcoming years. **141**

Cases

Applicable law. I always apply current law (2009) despite the fact that most of the cases are quite dated. The reason is that during recent years both legislation and medical malpractice jurisprudence in the Czech Republic have undergone significant development and a description of the law applicable to 1990s cases would not serve the comparative purpose of this study. This is especially so with regard to the assessment of pain and loss of amenities, because the relevant Decree (440/2001 Coll), which entered into force on 1 January 2002, significantly improved the position of the plaintiff by for instance quadrupling the amounts set by the previous Decree (32/1965 Coll). **142**

Limitation periods. Issues regarding limitation periods are not considered since, as of today, it would deprive plaintiffs in all cases *a priori* of any realistic chance of success. In practice, expired limitation periods are one of the most typical reasons for not accepting a medical malpractice litigation case. These expirations occur mainly due to relatively low awareness **143**

105 See <http://obcanskyzakonik.justice.cz/cz/uvodni-stranka.html>.
106 New Civil Code proposal §§ 2490–2505.
107 New Civil Code proposal § 16 ff.
108 New Civil Code proposal §§ 104–109.
109 New Civil Code proposal § 2755 ff.

of the lay public about the civil law remedies, poor access to medical records and to independent assessment of quality of care, and the fact that administrative and disciplinary complaint procedures do not affect the expiry of civil law limitation periods. This is especially important in the area of personality protection litigation because the limitation period for monetary satisfaction claims is three years and begins at the moment of infringement, regardless of the knowledge of the plaintiff. It thus often happens that plaintiffs must forego this otherwise very favourable litigation route because they become aware of the adverse event too late, its harmful effects materialise after more than three years, or the plaintiffs fail to take the proper legal steps in time by, for instance failing to serve the action to the court or suing the wrong defendants.

144 *Immaterial harm assessment.* Assessment of pain and loss of amenities in liability for damage cases is in the competence of medical professionals, ie the treating physician or the court-appointed expert, not in the competence of attorneys or judges. Therefore, my assessments of pain and loss of amenities point values in the cases below is only very approximate; a precise setting would require a medical professional able to examine the plaintiff and access his medical records.

Case 1

1. Passive legitimacy of defendants (ability to be sued)

145 The case presents multiple persons taking care of the plaintiffs. In order to assess the passive legitimacy (ability to be sued) in a civil liability case, it is necessary to ascertain which persons acted independently, and therefore can be liable themselves, and who, to the contrary, acted as agents of other legal entities and are thus liable for their actions under § 420 (2) Civil Code.[110]

146 Physicians A and B have a joint practice, which will be in the Czech context typically a small legal entity – health care facility with a registration pursuant to Act 160/1992 Coll valid for outpatient health care.[111] It is highly unlikely that their health care facility would also have a registration for inpatient services including complex emergency birth services and surgeries; this would require owning complex technical equipment

110 Chapter B point 11 of the general questions part.
111 Chapter A point 2 and 8 of the general questions part.

and employing a broad range of health care personnel.[112] This small ambulatory facility will be liable for all actions performed by both physicians within its registration, ie within ambulatory care. When hospital services are needed, this facility would refer the patient to another health care facility – a hospital, which has a registration for complex obstetric care. It is not uncommon that ambulatory care specialists want to do part of their work in hospital in order to follow 'their' patients also to hospital care. In such cases, however, they work for the hospital, usually as part-time employees.[113] From the legal point of view, the provider of hospital care is no longer the 'affiliated' physician, but the hospital. Therefore, when physician A acted or failed to act within hospital care, the hospital will bear the liability for his actions towards the plaintiff.

The facts do not imply any error during the ambulatory part of care provided by the joint practice of physicians A and B. It seems that all possible errors happened in the time period between 24th February and 17th March, when the plaintiff sought care in the hospital C. Since midwife D is clearly acting in a position of an employee of hospital C, and the physicians A and B would in the Czech context almost certainly provide hospital care in the position of hospital C employees, the only potential defendant will be the hospital C. **147**

2. Liability for damage (§ 420 ff)

Firstly, both plaintiffs X and Y need to prove that actions of the defendant hospital C or its employees violated law, ie that they were *non lege artis*. The facts show an omission on the part of midwife D, who obtained informa- **148**

112 The Ministry of Health sets these requirements in decrees issued according to the Act 160/1992 Coll; in our case, the requirements for an obstetric center would require at least a surgery room, ultrasound and other monitoring devices, and employing several full-time health care workers including an obstetrician, a neonatologist, a pediatrician and sufficient nursing staff. This would be economically not possible for a small joint practice. Current law does not describe the possibility of 'renting' all this equipment and support personnel from another health care facility (eg a hospital), or utilising them on the basis of contract by a visiting practitioner, so the system of 'hospital affiliation' of independent practitioners is not developed in the Czech Republic.

113 In the employee role, the physician does not and cannot guarantee 'his' ambulatory patients that he will be assigned to take the care of them while in hospital. This is a decision of their employer or direct superior, typically the head of department in the hospital, who can assign to the patient any other doctor. It is nevertheless common to let the part-time physicians treat 'their' patients whenever hospital planning allows; when emergency arises, such physician is usually informed by a phone, even if he is not on shift. Legally, however, the patient has no right to demand 'her doctor', and another physician currently on-shift might have to provide the care.

tion about pathological development on 17th March 1989 at 6.35am, but failed to contact a physician until 7.20am. The facts further show an omission on the part of physician A, who was responsible for the emergency care of plaintiff X from the moment he received the call[114] and was realistically able to get to the bedside, but failed to perform the necessary steps. The defendant can exclude itself from liability by proving that these omissions were not negligent. The defendant would have to prove that, according to the circumstances and the knowledge standard required by law[115] from a midwife or an obstetrician, midwife D, resp physician A could not and were not obliged to recognise the need to treat the plaintiff immediately. The court will assess both issues, namely, violation of the law and negligence on the basis of medical records, witness statements and (in particular) the statement of a court-appointed medical expert.

149 Secondly, the plaintiffs need to prove the scope of harm and quantify damages. Concerning plaintiff Y, the damages count will include the following:

- *Pain and loss of amenities.* According to Decree 440/2001 Coll, the evaluation of pain and loss of amenities requires a medical assessment provided by a treating physician, who subsumes the particular harm and disabilities under an item list attached to this decree. Here, the medical assessment would probably declare presence of at least the following items: 0753 – quadriplegia (3,000 points), 032 – full blindness (3,000 points), and 0643 – speech disability of central origin after an accident (1,000–2,000 points) and most probably also other items, depending on the medical examination which according to the decree is typically conducted one year after the accident. According to § 6 of this decree, the evaluating physician is entitled to increase the point value of loss of amenities in the case of severe consequences by up to 50 %; such an increase would probably be applicable in this case. Therefore, the final point count can be estimated at minimally 10,000–15,000 points.

114 The actual distribution of fault between D and A is not relevant for the plaintiff, because the only subject with passive legitimacy in a civil liability case will be the hospital C. In another type of proceedings, eg labour law or criminal law liability case, it would be very important for the court decision on individual liability to assess the contents and nature of information provided over the phone, especially concerning urgency of the case.

115 Act 95/2004 Coll, on the Conditions for Acquiring and Recognising Qualifications for the Performance of the Medical Occupations of Physician, Dentist, and Pharmacist; and Act 96/2004 Coll, on the Conditions for Acquiring and Recognising Qualifications for the Performance of Non-Medical Occupations in Health Care and for the Execution of Activities Related to the Provision of Health Care; compare Chapter A point 8 of the General questions part.

Multiplied by the point value of CZK 120, the basic amount of damages for loss of amenities can be estimated at around CZK 1.2–1.8 million (€ 48,000–72,000), depending on the medical assessment. However, in this case the judge would almost certainly also apply § 7 (3) of the decree which allows the court in 'extraordinary cases specifically worthy of attention' to 'proportionally increase' the compensation calculated according to the decree. An estimate of this 'proportional increase' can be only very rough, but the final amount would not be less than CZK 5 million (€ 200,000) and considering recent similar cases,[116] it could be in the range of CZK 15 million (€ 600,000) depending on factors such as life expectancy of the newborn.

- *Treatment costs.* In the case of damage to health, the compensation includes purposeful expenses connected with medical treatment. In the case of plaintiff Y, these include all the necessary care items – drugs, medical aids, help with the household, feeding, washing and care by a professional nurse. These expenses will however be incurred rather by her mother, plaintiff X, who will accordingly be entitled to compensation.

Concerning plaintiff X, the damages count will include the following: **150**

- *Pain and loss of amenities.* If plaintiff X suffered a grave psychic harm, a psychiatrist might assess that she fulfils the conditions of item 016 of the Decree 440/2001 Coll – serious psychic disorder caused by the impact of the shocking experience or other adverse psychological factors and depressive situations (500–1500 points). Otherwise and more probably, given the facts and likely character of psychic harm, plaintiff X will be indemnified via personality protection law, as described below.
- *Treatment costs.* Any expenses connected with the treatment of plaintiff X and the disabled child including medical aid, help with the household, salary of the professional nurse etc which the plaintiff X already paid will be compensated. It is not possible to compensate future treatment expenses, but only such expenses which were incurred by the plaintiff prior to the court decision; the plaintiff can claim further

116 Decision of the Regional Court in Brno of 12 October 2007, 44 Co 31/2007, confirming the decision of the District Court in Prostějov of 24 June 2006, 5 C 260/2003-133, awarding compensation for pain in the amount of CZK 664,800 (€ 26,592) and compensation for loss of amenities in the amount of CZK 15,885,000 (€ 635,400) against the Prostějov hospital in connection with a fatal brain damage suffered by a newborn.

compensation as soon as she pays them.[117] The plaintiff further has to prove that these expenses were necessary and connected to the injury.

- *Compensation of plaintiff X's work.* Plaintiff X claims compensation for the care she provides to Y herself, assessed according to the standard wage of a qualified nurse. If plaintiff X actually hired a qualified nurse and this would be considered necessary for the treatment of plaintiff Y, then plaintiff X would have a right to have the costs expended on the nurse duly compensated. If she however provided the care herself, she would be according to the jurisprudence[118] probably entitled only to the equivalent salary of an unqualified caregiver or a volunteer; in a similar case, the courts applied by analogy the Decree of the Ministry of Social Services, 182/1991 Coll and awarded a mother the maximum salary of a volunteer caregiver under this decree, CZK 5,500 (€ 220) per month.

151 Thirdly, plaintiffs X and Y need to prove the causal link between the negligent violation of the law on the part of hospital C and the damage. According to jurisprudence the causal link between a negligent breach of duty on the side of the defendant and damage to health on the side of the plaintiff must be proven with certainty; a mere probability is insufficient.[119] According to the facts of the case, it is possible that A and D's conduct were the sole cause of Y's impairments, but it is at the same time probable that a considerable part of Y's impairments happened before the delivery. This situation is adverse for both plaintiffs. It will be very difficult for them to bear the burden of proving the necessary certainty of causal connection between the negligent care and the damage and therefore to obtain any indemnification. The plaintiffs' chances could theoretically be higher if they attempted to split the case and find an aspect of the damage where the causal link is certain. This could be for instance an injury, which typically happens during protracted birth and which cannot be a result of a predisposition or of an adverse natural development, ie is causally linked to the negligent act with sufficient certainty. Regarding this aspect the plaintiffs would be successful and obtain at least partial

117 Compare Case R 26/1982, cited in *Švestka* (fn 52) 1170.

118 Decision of the Supreme Court of the Czech Republic of 24 October 2006, 25 Cdo 2127/2006. The situation might be different, if plaintiff Y required qualified treatment interventions and plaintiff X demonstrated skills to provide these qualified interventions herself. Alternatively, plaintiff X might also want to list the services she provides to plaintiff Y and calculate the compensation by comparison with the price lists of social service organisations.

119 Decision of the Supreme Court of the Czech Republic of 25 November 2003, 25 Cdo 168/2003; Case R 21/1992.

compensation. In practice, such a situation would be the subject of several, most probably mutually conflicting expert opinions from both parties.

3. Personality protection liability (§ 11 ff)

In the context of personality protection liability action, plaintiffs X and Y need to prove: 152

- an unlawful infringement of personality rights (especially right to health and bodily integrity),
- the scope of harm inflicted to personality rights,
- and the causal link between the above.[120]

Non lege artis omissions on the part of physician A and midwife D would be sufficient to fulfill the first condition.

Concerning the scope of harm, plaintiff Y would be able to describe a broad range of personality rights impairments, namely impossibility of any meaningful family life, work activities or social interactions. Plaintiff X would be able to demonstrate a serious harm to her physical and psychic integrity and family life, especially the distress arising from the stillbirth of her son and from the health damage suffered by her daughter. Both plaintiffs would be entitled to seek financial satisfaction for infringement of their personality rights. Setting a proportionate amount of satisfaction is in the discretion of the judge. Recently, the courts seem have abandoned the usage of analogy with the statutory CZK 240,000 (€ 9,600) one-time compensation for causing death,[121] and the financial settlements approach the millions. A recent decision in the case of death of a newborn following serious burns inflicted by a defective warming pad reached the amount of CZK 1.5 million (€ 60,000), and the aforementioned case of a newborns mix-up reached the amount of CZK 3.3 million (€ 130,000) for six defendants; the greatest proportion thereof was received by the two mothers who received CZK 1 million (€ 40,000) and CZK 700,000 (€ 28,000) respectively.[122] It is therefore possible to estimate that plaintiff Y and X would 153

120 *Švestka* (fn 52) 170.

121 Act 40/1964 Coll, Civil Code § 444 (3).

122 The two fathers received CZK 800,000 (€ 32,000) resp CZK 350,000 (€ 14,000), the two newborns received CZK 300,000 (€ 12,000) resp CZK 150,000 (€ 6,000). The differences between the amounts of financial satisfaction for the parent couples are explained by the behaviour and slight contributory negligence on the part of one of the couples. The children remained in the 'improper' families approximately for one year, before the mix-up was disclosed and the children returned to their biological parents.

each respectively receive an award of minimally CZK 1 million (€ 40,000) for violation of their personality rights since the harm is significantly more severe than in the case of a newborn mix-up; the maximum possible award cannot be estimated.

154 However, the plaintiffs would probably not succeed in proving the causation, for similar reasons as in the liability of damage action described above.

Case 2

155 Czech law does not specifically regulate the issue of 'wrongful birth'. So far, courts have dealt with similar cases in two reported judgments in the area of personality protection. In the first one the plaintiff, a young student pregnant with twins, underwent an abortion during the first trimester of her pregnancy.[123] The intervention was successful only in part and one of the fetuses survived, without knowledge of either the physicians or the woman. The continued pregnancy was detected late, only in the 16th week, when it was too late to perform another attempt of abortion. The Regional Court in Brno found liability on the part of the defendant health care facility, but awarded only CZK 80,000 (€ 3,200), rejecting the rest of the CZK 400,000 (€ 16,000) claimed by the plaintiff, reasoning that awarding the full satisfaction claim *'would ridicule the situation of parents who lose a beloved child in an accident and receive only the 240,000 CZK statutory compensation for death'*. In the second case the plaintiff, a mother of four, decided upon her fourth childbirth that she could not support another child and opted for sterilisation. However, she soon became pregnant with a fifth child. She sued the hospital which had performed the sterilisation. However, a court-appointed expert stated that the disconnected fallopian tubes can in rare cases reconnect and the sterilisation is not a 100 % effective form of birth-control. The plaintiff therefore proved only the error in the informed consent procedure, because she was not informed about the possible spontaneous restoration of fertility. The first instance court in Prague awarded the plaintiff a small satisfaction of CZK 30,000 (€ 1,200), but the appellate court rejected this and ruled for the defendant hospital, quoting that *'asking compensation for a birth of a child would be contra bonos mores'*.

---

123 According to Act 66/1986 Coll on the Artificial Termination of Pregnancy, a woman can freely choose an abortion during the first trimester of pregnancy.

Given the law as it is, plaintiff X can sue physician A under the personality protection liability heading, but with a chance of receiving a very small indemnification covering neither the real costs of bringing up the child nor the lost earnings. Furthermore, the plaintiff would have to prove that there is sufficient causation between the failure of the device Implanon and the unwanted birth; in this respect, the court would assess the failure rate of this means of birth control, and the question of whether the physician sufficiently informed the patient about the failure rate. 156

The defendant physician could probably try a defence of contributory fault. According to the Civil Code, if the damage was caused also by a fault of the injured, he bears the damage proportionally; if the damage was caused exclusively by the injured, he bears the damage himself.[124] If the physician successfully proves that he informed the patient about the contraception method, possible reasons of failure, necessity to observe the implant site or necessity to undergo regular check-ups, the patient negligently failed to observe these recommendations, and this was the cause of the negative results, the patient will have to bear the loss herself, in part or fully. From the plaintiff X's point of view, it would not be advisable to litigate such a case due to the very limited size of the possible award, possible failure on the aspects of causation and contributory negligence, lengthy proceedings, and potential infringement of privacy by negative publicity.[125] 157

It would theoretically be possible to claim compensation under liability for damage (§ 420 ff). The plaintiff would probably succeed in subsuming the situation under the special objective liability heading (§ 421a) because the harm originated in the deficiency of the Implanon device. The plaintiff might succeed in proving causation and contributory negligence. However, the definition of damages in the liability for damage law cannot be extended to new damage items such as 'wrongful birth' so the chance of success would be very low. 158

124 Act 40/1964 Coll, Civil Code § 441, Fault of the Injured.

125 In the first case, the birth took place in 2001, but the lawsuit was finally resolved only in 2009, when the 'unwanted' child was eight years old and possibly was able to understand the nature and purpose of the litigation; the court did not order *in camera* trial, so the case received close attention by media.

Case 3

1. Passive legitimacy (ability to be sued)

159 This is a similar situation as in Case 1. Here, the hospital A, the midwife B providing home care, and the hospital C are according to Czech law most probably independent health care providers. On the other hand, physician E is most probably in the position of a full-time or part-time employee of hospital C, which would be liable under § 420 (2) for any emergency treatment performed on its premises by this physician.[126]

2. Liability for damage (§ 420 ff)

160 Firstly, plaintiff X needs to prove that the actions of the defendant hospitals A and C and the midwife B violated the law – that they or their employees acted *non lege artis*, contrary to the current findings of medical science. The facts show that all three potential defendants negligently violated the law. The obstetrician in hospital A on 26th August correctly recognised the problems with hypoglycemia and diagnosed the plaintiff as a high risk newborn, but nevertheless discharged him very early after the birth, despite the fact that he knew or should have known that such action is strongly discouraged, and at the same time failed to properly inform the mother and midwife B, who was in charge of the follow-up care at home.[127] The midwife should have recognised the risks connected with hypoglycemia and reacted without a significant delay, regardless of the lack of information from the referring obstetrician. The personnel of hospital C, which admitted the plaintiff on the morning of the 28th of August failed to recognise the immediate need of intervention.

161 Each defendant can exclude himself from liability by proving that these omissions were not negligent. Each defendant would have to prove that,

126 In the Czech obstetric care settings, the midwife services would be most probably provided within hospital and by an employee midwife, not by an independent midwife at home. According to a 2005 Methodical order of the Ministry of Health, even a healthy newborn should not be discharged from the hospital sooner than 72 hours after the birth.

127 According to Czech law, patients can generally refuse hospital treatment and choose an early discharge even if it is contrary to their best medical interest, if they are competent persons, receive proper information on risks and sign an informed refusal. However, in case of an incompetent high risk child, the physician must *not* allow the discharge even if the parents order so, if the discharge would constitute an immediate and grave risk to the child. Compare § 23 (3) of the Act 20/1966 Coll on Health Care of the People.

according to the circumstances and the knowledge standard required by law from a midwife or a physician, they could not and were not obliged to recognise the necessary treatment steps. The court will assess both issues, violation of law and negligence, on the basis of medical records, witness statements, and especially the statement of an expert.

Secondly, the plaintiff X needs to prove the scope of harm and quantify damages. The damages count will include the following: **162**

- *Pain and loss of amenities.* According to Decree 440/2001 Coll, the evaluation of pain and loss of amenities requires medical assessment by a treating physician, who must subsume the particular harm and disabilities under a list of items attached to this decree. Here, the point assessment would be similar to the assessment of the child plaintiff in Case 1. Also in this case, the judge would almost certainly apply § 7 (3) of the decree, which allows the court in 'extraordinary cases specifically worthy of attention' to 'proportionally increase' the compensation calculated according to the decree. Estimate of this 'proportional increase' can only be very rough, but the final amount would be in the range of CZK 10–12 million (€ 400,000–480,000), depending on factors such as life expectancy of the newborn.
- *Treatment costs.* In the case of damages to health, the compensation includes necessary expenses connected with medical treatment. In the case of plaintiff X, these include all necessary care items – drugs, medical aid, help with the household, feeding, washing and care by a professional nurse. These expenses will however be expended rather by the parents of plaintiff X and they would thus be entitled to compensation.
- *Prospective loss of earning capacity.* Plaintiff X seeks compensation for loss of future earnings in the amount of € 2,000 per month (as of his 21st year life capitalised until his 65th year of life). Due to the fact that X is a newborn and there is no available proof as to his future earning capacity, this type of loss is not compensable under the heading of loss of earnings. It could however influence reasoning for a proportional increase in damages for the loss of amenities according to § 7 (3) of the Decree 440/2001 Coll, or in setting the amount of financial satisfaction in the area of personality protection, where the decision regarding the amount is at the discretion of the court.

Thirdly, plaintiff X needs to prove the causal link between the negligent violation of law on the part of each individual defendant, and the damage. According to jurisprudence, the causal link between the negligent breach **163** of duty on the side of the defendant and damage to health on the side of the plaintiff must be proven with certainty; a mere probability is insufficient. In this case, it seems from the facts that a correct act on the part of each of the defendants A and B, and with a very high probability also C, would have prevented the damage. If the obstetrician in hospital A had not discharged the patient and had continued to monitor (and maintain) his blood sugar level for the necessary time period, the hypoglycemia would not have occurred and the brain damage would have been prevented. If the midwife had reacted properly, eg consulted a pediatrician as soon as she had learned from the mother about the hypoglycemia on the 27th of August, the harm would have been prevented despite the mistake of the obstetrician in hospital A. If the admission nurse D and the physician E in the pediatric clinic C had reacted correctly and if plaintiff X had received proper treatment immediately after his admission on the morning of the 28th of August, the harm would, with a very high degree of probability, have been prevented, despite the mistakes in the prior treatment. Therefore, plaintiff X seems to be able to prove with reasonable certainty that the actions of each of the three defendants were the *causae sine qua non* of the damage, and can therefore succeed against each of them.

3. Joint liability

164 According to the Civil Code, if the damage is caused by more than one perpetrator they shall be liable jointly and severally.[128] This gives the plaintiff an advantage in cases with more potential defendants because he may elect to ask one of the defendants for full compensation. Even if it is shown with some probability that the damage to the plaintiff's brain might have been present before the admission to hospital C, the plaintiff will be able to succeed against the other two defendants.

165 Concerning the relations between jointly liable defendants, the Civil Code states that a person who is liable for damage jointly and severally with others shall settle with them according to the proportion in causing the

128 Act 40/1964 Coll, Civil Code § 438; In substantiated cases, the court may decide that those who caused the damage shall be liable individually according to their proportion in causing the damage.

damage.[129] In practice, the distribution of liability will be assessed according to medical records, especially the discharge and admission reports.[130]

4. Personality protection liability (§ 11 ff)

Similar to the child plaintiff in Case 1, plaintiff X would be able to describe a broad range of personality rights infringements, namely impossibility of family life, work activities or any meaningful social interactions. Setting a proportionate amount of satisfaction is in the discretion of the judge. It is possible to roughly estimate that plaintiff X would receive a satisfaction award in this regard of at least CZK 1 million (€ 40,000), probably even more. **166**

Case 4

The outcome of the case depends almost exclusively on the application of informed consent law, ie whether the plaintiff gave a valid informed consent, and if not, whether the defendant hospital will be liable for an adverse outcome of a non-negligently performed intervention. **167**

According to § 420 (2) of the Civil Code, the only potential defendant would be the hospital A, not the surgeon C, who acted on behalf of this hospital. **168**

The Czech law of informed consent has been described above in detail.[131] According to Czech law, a valid informed consent with an intervention makes the health care provider immune from liability for risks which were a part of the disclosure, if the intervention was performed *lege artis*.[132] On the other hand, if there was no consent at all, or the consent was not valid, the physician who operates on the patient without his consent acts **169**

---

129 Act 40/1964 Coll, Civil Code § 439.

130 Such situation may in practice bring some factual benefit to the plaintiff patient, because the defendants or their employees will tend to give witness statements so as to relieve themselves and assign liability to other providers instead of denying liability at all; this can be very helpful for the plaintiff in bearing the burden of proof concerning causation.

131 Supra nos 88 ff.

132 Sometimes, hospitals in the Czech Republic give patients 'informed consent' forms, in which the patient signs that he relieves the health care providers of liability in case of any adverse outcome. Such practice is not in accordance with law, because the patient cannot in advance relieve the hospital of liability for consequences of a *non lege artis* intervention, only of liability for unavoidable risks of a *lege artis* intervention.

contrary to the law, even if the operation is performed medically correctly. Theoretically, the health care facility is liable for all adverse outcomes of such intervention, even if there was no medical error.[133] In practice, however, the impact of informed consent law on liability for damage litigation is very limited, mainly due to procedural reasons such as proof of consent and proof of causation, the evidence plaintiffs and defendants are able to provide to the court, and evaluation of such evidence by the judge.

170 In this particular case, the relevant facts are:

- On 24th June, physician B signed a consent form with the plaintiff; the consent form contained statements about the nature of the operation, its risks and alternatives.
- The patient hardly speaks German[134] and arguably did not understand what physician B told him and what was written on the consent form.
- The surgery was performed medically correctly, but one of its inherent risks materialised, leading to a severe adverse outcome.
- The patient was treated for problems with his legs and spine previously. He was continuously treated and examined from the 9th of June onwards at the defendant's specialised neurosurgical clinic and surgery was recommended.
- There was an alternative to the surgery, with a lower risk of paralysis but a higher risk of death.
- The patient claims that if properly informed, he would have been in a decision-making conflict and probably would not have undergone any surgery at all. It is not known whether he would have preferred the alternative approach with the associated higher risk of death.

171 If the plaintiff claims lack of consent, the defendant will present the signed informed consent form, which is formally correct, according to Czech law.[135] From a material point of view, the plaintiff may claim that he did not understand the disclosure and therefore his consent was not a valid legal act. This is assessed according to the general provisions of the

133 *Císařová* (fn 59).

134 Here, I apply the law analogously as if a foreign patient in a Czech hospital did not speak Czech properly.

135 Especially Decree 385/2006 Coll on Medical Records, Attachment 1 section 5.

Civil Code.[136] In doing so, the plaintiff must firstly rebut the physician B's witness statement that he communicated to the plaintiff all the risks using the dictionary, before letting him sign the consent form; the plaintiff must claim and successfully prove that although he freely signed the form, he did not understand its contents, and that the physician knew or must have known that. Secondly, the plaintiff must further prove that he also did not know the necessary information about the operation from previous treatment. This would not be easy, since the facts speak to the contrary; the patient suffered from the myelopathy long time before the operation; he was referred to the neurosurgical department of hospital A specifically for this reason; he spent there over two weeks (from 9th till 24th June), during which he underwent extensive examinations and during which the surgery was proposed to him. Arguably, it would not seem very probable from the viewpoint of a judge that despite all of that, the plaintiff still knew so little about his treatment prospects when he signed the form that his consent should be regarded as an invalid expression of will.[137]

Finally, even if the plaintiff sufficiently proves that there was no valid **172**
consent, he must successfully also discharge the burden of proof of causation, to the extent of certainty or very high probability.[138] The causal link is present if the plaintiff would almost certainly have refused the consent and foregone the operation if he had received enough information. To the contrary, if the plaintiff would possibly have undergone the operation even if he had received and understood the necessary information, the causal link is not present and the violation of informed consent rule will not lead to the liability of the defendant for the adverse result of

136 A legal act is an expression of will directed in particular to create, change or abolish rights or duties connected with such expressions by legal regulations. An expression of will may be performed by an act or by an omission. It may be performed explicitly or in other way, which does not give rise to doubts on what the actor wanted to express. The legal act must be performed in a free, serious, definite and intelligible manner, otherwise it is invalid. A legal act is invalid if the acting person concluded it in an error arising from a circumstance decisive for its realisation and if the addressee of such act evoked this error or must have known about it. Act 40/1964 Coll, Civil Code §§ 34, 35, 37 and 49a.

137 In an unreported case of a patient who died from complications of a surgery, a specialised Prague hospital formulated a defence based on proof that despite no risks were disclosed to the patient by its staff, the patient was sufficiently informed by his physician in another hospital where the patient spent several weeks and which referred the patient to the specialised hospital for performing the surgery.

138 Analogously with treatment malpractice causation, similar approach to causation applies also in the informed consent malpractice; compare the decision of the Supreme Court of the Czech Republic of 25 November 2003, 25 Cdo 168/2003.

the surgery. A 'conflict of decision-making' is not sufficient for a proof of causation with certainty. Even a testimony by the plaintiff that having sufficient information he would certainly have foregone the operation may be seen as untrustworthy, expressing the hindsight of the patient now suffering from adverse effects of the surgery. In evaluating such a plaintiff's statement, the judge might also consider the fact that the plaintiff actively sought treatment of his myelopathy, willingly spending two weeks at the neurosurgery department and undergoing the necessary examinations.

173 According to Czech procedural law, a judge is empowered to freely evaluate the evidence, so the results may differ from case to case. This is illustrated by a Supreme Court and later Constitutional Court case concerning personality protection in which a Roma woman was sterilised after her second childbirth. The physicians claimed that the sterilisation was in her interest because she had already given birth by caesarean section twice and further such birth would endanger her health. According to the hospital the mother consented to the intervention, was duly informed and the medical records contain her signature. The plaintiff however succeeded with a testimony that she did not know exactly what she had signed as she was in pain during labour, that she did not want to be sterilised and that she wished to have another child.[139] Nevertheless, this case is rather an exception than a rule. The chances of a plaintiff succeeding where the only evidence is her own testimony, are generally very low, especially if the plaintiff in fact actively sought the relevant care, physicians testify that they properly informed her and the defendant presents a signed consent form.

174 If a patient in a similar position to that of plaintiff X sufficiently proves that her informed consent rights were violated, eg that she was not informed in a manner that she could understand, but fails to prove the causal link to the adverse effects of the intervention, she may still receive financial satisfaction in personality action. Such an immaterial damages

139 Decision of the Constitutional Court of 7 October 2009, IV.ÚS 1407/09; the plaintiff however failed to obtain any financial satisfaction, which was statute-barred by an expired limitation period, and therefore received only a moral satisfaction, which according to the Court cannot expire. This case related to a broader social problem of sterilisation of ethnic minority women, which was, according to patient rights activists, an unofficial policy under the past regime. Arguably, Roma women were informed that if they do not undergo sterilisation, they will be deprived of social aid funds.

award will however be comparably smaller than the indemnification of the full scope of damages to health.[140]

For the sake of completeness, if the patient managed to prove the causal link between the lack of informed consent and the adverse effects of the surgery, the damages count in a liability for damage case (§ 420 ff) would be as follows: **175**

- *Pain and loss of amenities.* According to Decree 440/2001 Coll, the evaluation of pain and loss of amenities requires a medical assessment, which would probably declare the presence of at least the following items: 0752 – paraplegia (2,800 points), 085 – disturbance of function of anal sphincters (700 points), serious disturbance of bladder function (500 points), S3403 – spinal cord lesion (400 points) and probably also other items, depending on the examination. According to § 5 (3) of the decree, the examining physician would however have to consider the previous health problems of the plaintiff. The resulting point count can be very roughly estimated at around 3,000 points. Multiplied by the point value of CZK 120, the basic amount of damages for loss of amenities would reach CZK 360,000 (€ 14,400). The plaintiff would have a fair chance that the judge would apply § 7 (3) of the decree, which allows the court in 'extraordinary cases specifically worthy of attention' to 'proportionally increase' the compensation calculated ac-cording to the decree. Estimate of this 'proportional increase' would lead to an expected amount of approximately CZK 1.5 million (€ 60,000).
- *Treatment costs.* The plaintiff seeks compensation for the conversion of his house to provide wheelchair access, for the purchase of a new car with wheelchair access and for additional increased needs arising from his paralysis. Such compensation would be justifiable only in the case that these costs had already been incurred by the plaintiff and that they were reasonably incurred in connection with the treatment. The plaintiff would further have to prove that the damage arose in causal connection with the illegal act of the defendant – in this case especially, that the adverse health result is with certainty a consequence of the medical intervention and not of an adverse development of the plaintiff's previous bad state of health.

---

140 It is possible to compare the case of unsuccessful sterilisation described above, where the patient received in the first court instance an award of CZK 30,000 (€ 1,200) as a satisfaction for the fact that the physician failed to inform her that sterilisation does not prevent pregnancy with 100 % certainty.

Case 5

176 In this case, the potential defendant is the hospital A. The plaintiff must prove that the actions of the defendant hospital responsible for its employees were not in accordance with the current findings of medical science.

177 Firstly, the plaintiff must present evidence concerning the violation of law on the side of plaintiff. The plaintiff is aware of the adverse medical outcome – damaged *nervus ulnaris* and restricted movement of his left hand. Further, the plaintiff is able to present the agreement of the national professional association of anesthetists and the professional association of surgeons concerning the responsibilities for positioning the patient on the OP-table. This agreement specifies the standard of care and that the physicians involved in the treatment are obliged to know and follow such standard. If any of the doctors, either the surgeon or the anesthetist failed to follow their duties according to such standard, the hospital would be liable if the patient consequently suffered harm to his or her health.

178 According to the facts, however, the plaintiff does not have any direct evidence that the positioning before or during the operation was improper, either from witness statements of the physicians B, C and D, or from the medical records. The plaintiff himself can give no testimony due to the fact that he was under anesthetics during the operation. Insufficient medical records do not relieve the patient-plaintiff of his duty to claim that the defendant physicians violated the law and of his duty to offer evidence to support this claim. The plaintiff could attempt to use arguments based on indirect evidence: it might be possible to successfully prove that the neural damage did not exist before the operation but that it did exist after the operation and that the cause of this adverse change must have been the wrong positioning of the arm, or another medical mistake on the part of the defendant physicians. The plaintiff will however have to rely on a medical expert statement to confirm this hypothesis. If the medical expert fails to confirm this sequence of events with a reasonable certainty, or finds a possibility of an alternative cause of the neural damage, the plaintiff will not succeed in discharging the burden of proof and will lose the case. The medical experts are usually very reluctant to authoritatively and conclusively confirm such plaintiffs' hypotheses. Typically, the court-appointed expert statements in similar situations tend to declare that the plaintiff's version is possible, but cannot be ascertained given the absence of any factual grounds in medical records, X-ray pictures or witness' statements. Any ambiguity in the medical expert statement will typically lead the court to a verdict for the defendant due to a lack of evidence, despite the fact that the plaintiff's hypothesis would prevail on a balance of probabilities.

Even if the patient successfully proves an improper positioning during the operation, he must further prove with certainty its causal link to the resulting injury. This is complicated especially in cases of acute treatment of accident victims, when the harm might have happened during the accident itself or during emergency manipulation with the patient. Typically, the defendant does not need to prove with certainty an alternative harm mechanism in order to exculpate himself. In order to prevail in the litigation, it is sufficient for the defendant that the plaintiff fails to prove with certainty the causal link between the harm and a particular treatment event. **179**

For the sake of completeness, if the patient managed to prove the negligent positioning and its causal link to the adverse results of the surgery, the damages count would include: **180**

- *Pain and loss of amenities.* According to Decree 440/2001 Coll, the medical evaluation of loss of amenities would probably include at least item 126 – paralysis of the *nervus ulnaris* (600 points), and the evaluation of pain would probably include at least item S4400 by analogy – functional loss of *nervus ulnaris* (120 points). Multiplied by the point value of CZK 120, the basic amount of compensation for pain and loss of amenities can be estimated at CZK 86,400 (€ 3,456), depending on the medical assessment. However, in this case, the judge might apply § 7 (3) of the decree, which allows the court in 'extraordinary cases specifically worthy of attention' to 'proportionally increase' the compensation calculated according to the decree. Estimate of this 'proportional increase' can be only very rough, but the final amount in such a case might be around twice or three times the basic amount. Concerning immaterial damage, plaintiff X would also be able to claim in different proceedings financial satisfaction for violation of personality rights (right to health and bodily integrity). The amount of such compensation would be in the discretion of the judge, according to § 13 of the Civil Code.
- *Loss of earnings.* Loss in earnings is compensated by way of a cash pension; its amount is calculated from the average earnings of the injured party before damages arose.[141] The assessment of the amount of compensation is based on the party's average earnings before the injury. If it is not

141 Act 40/1964 Coll, Civil Code § 445.

possible to calculate the compensation from a salary paid by an employer, the assessment must be done by other means, eg based on the tax declaration of the injured. Theoretically, earnings that are generated informally, eg by moonlighting, are not excluded from this calculation – the fact that the worker violated the law by not declaring such earnings properly for tax purposes does not mean that these earnings did not exist. However, it might be complicated for the plaintiff X to provide any verifiable evidence to the court in order to sufficiently prove such an income.[142] Plaintiff X will not be entitled to compensation for the loss of earnings arising from his refusal to consider retraining as a sales person. According to the jurisprudence, the defendant who caused the injury has the duty to compensate only those loss of earnings of the plaintiff which result from the injurious act of the defendant. If the plaintiff's inability to perform a systematic earning activity results from another cause, the liability of the defendant does not arise. This may include a situation where the plaintiff does not start working following the injury due to a lack of job offers,[143] or when the plaintiff omits to resume the earning activities without any serious reason therefor. In the latter case, the court will not award damages to the plaintiff up to the amount which the plaintiff omitted to earn.[144]

Private injuries assessment costs

181 According to the Civil Procedure Code, the proceeding costs include, *inter alia*, the costs of evidence.[145] If the decision of the court depends on assessment of issues of an expert nature, the court shall appoint an expert after hearing the participants.[146] The parties can submit to the court medical statements they commissioned themselves, but these do not fall under the formal category of 'statements by court-appointed experts' and

142 Alternatively, if the moonlighting activities had to be seen as amenities for the plaintiff (eg mutual aid within the neighbourhood) rather than means of income, the loss of an ability to perform this work would be compensable under the heading of loss of amenities.

143 Ie the cause of loss is not the injury, but the adverse situation on the labour market; compare the decision of the Supreme Court of the Czech Republic of 1 December 2000, 21 Cdo 2805/99.

144 Decision of the Supreme Court of the Czech Republic of 5 June 2008, 25 Cdo 622/2006, see also *Švestka* (fn 52) 1158.

145 Act 99/1963 Coll, Civil Procedure Code § 137.

146 Act 99/1963 Coll, Civil Procedure Code § 127.

have only the nature of documentary evidence.[147] The participant who was fully successful in the proceedings has the right to a full reimbursement of the costs of evidence necessary for the assertion or defence of rights, against the participant who was not successful.[148] The costs of court-appointed expert statements are almost always considered a part of the proceeding costs. To the contrary, the costs of privately obtained expert statements are in practice not as a rule considered reimbursable, since according to § 127 of the Civil Procedure Code the court must commission a 'formal' expertise, which the privately commissioned expertise cannot replace. The costs incurred in obtaining a private expert statement may be seen from this viewpoint as not 'purposefully' incurred. This general practice however does not exclude the possibility that in specific cases the costs of a private expert statement could also be included in the proceeding costs and reimbursed, especially when the statement suffices for the parties to reach a consensus about the reviewed issue and the court therefore does not have to commission a formal expert statement after hearing the parties. In the case of plaintiff X, who could obtain the evaluation free of charge at a medical council, any costs expended on a private assessment elsewhere would not be seen as purposeful and would therefore not be reimbursable.

Case 6

1. Passive legitimacy (ability to be sued)

The case presents multiple persons taking care of the plaintiff. All of these **182**
persons however act on behalf of the joint orthopaedic health care facility of physicians A and B. This health care facility will be liable for their actions under § 420 (2) of the Civil Code.

2. Objective liability

The case would be evaluated as a specific case of objective liability accord- **183**
ing to § 421a of the Civil Code. According to this provision, everyone shall

147 The court must evaluate all kinds of evidence, so the reasoning of the decision must include also the description how the court evaluated such documentary evidence submitted by parties. The court is bound neither by such statements commissioned by parties nor by the court-appointed expert statements; in practice, however, the persuasiveness of the court-appointed expert statements is generally regarded as higher.

148 Act 99/1963 Coll, Civil Procedure Code § 142.

be liable for damage caused by circumstances originating in the nature of a tool or other object used in performing of an obligation. The liable person cannot relieve himself of this liability in any way.[149]

184 Under this special type of liability for damage, which is based on the no-fault principle, the plaintiff X will have to claim and prove that:

- the health harm originated in the usage of the nature of the tool – here the infected syringe,
- the extent of damages, and
- there is causal connection between the usage of infected syringe and the damage to health.

185 A similar situation was resolved by the Supreme Court of the Czech Republic in a case of hepatitis C infection resulting from a non-sterile injection needle. According to the Supreme Court decisions, the scope of objective liability is not necessarily limited to substandard quality of injected substance or breakdown of an instrument or other object. The scope of objective liability extends also to cases when the object or instrument used by the defendant was not in itself faulty but had such properties which by their specific nature lent themselves to causing the damage which arose.[150]

186 To the contrary, if the infection was caused not by an object but by mere contact with an infected person, the infection would not originate in the nature of the instrument or other thing, but in the behaviour of the person, and objective liability under § 421a would not apply. Such a case would have to be assessed according to the general fault based § 420 liability. It would be necessary to examine whether the health care worker could and should have known that he is infected and that he might transmit the infection to the patient.

187 In another case, the Supreme Court decided that the absolute objective liability under § 421a does not mean liability under all conditions but only when all legal conditions are cumulatively fulfilled. In particular, the existence of the causal relation must be certain. A mere probability that the harm could arise (even if it typically arises) in a manner claimed by the plaintiff is not sufficient. If the harm did not arise from the nature of a

149 Act 40/1964 Coll, Civil Code § 421a.

150 Compare Decision of the Supreme Court of the Czech Republic of 29 May 1997, 2 Cdon 961/96.

particular instrument that was used, the prerequisites for objective liability are not present. The burden of proof is borne by the plaintiff.[151]

In the original variation of the case, plaintiff X acquired the staphylococcus infection from the contaminated syringe used during the treatment. The source of infection was the medical assistant E. If plaintiff X successfully proves that the staphylococcus infection and subsequent harm were caused by the usage of the contaminated syringe, she does not need to prove whether the doctors knew about the sickness of E or to prove any other fault on their part because the liability for use of the instrument is based on the objective, no-fault principle. Even if no hygiene shortfalls in the doctors' practice could be proved and the usual hygiene standards were observed (Variation 2), the defendant health care facility will be still liable for the harm as long as the plaintiff is able to prove that the infection originated in the contaminated syringe.[152] If, on the other hand, the plaintiff fails to prove that the syringe was contaminated, or it is shown that he contracted the infection by mere contact with the medical assistant E, the liability will be assessed according to the general fault-based rule, and the negligence issue will become critical. If the doctors did not maintain the necessary hygiene standards and the plaintiff shows that this failure is causally linked to her infection, the health care facility will be liable for violation of its general duty of prevention,[153] even under the fault-based rule. **188**

If, given the facts of Variation 1, the carrier of the bacteria cannot be identified and the plaintiff could have contracted the infection elsewhere, the plaintiff will most probably lose the case on the issue of causation. Even if it is proven that the medical assistant E actually suffered from the same infection and at the same time the hygiene standards were disregarded, the plaintiff will still have to prove that this particular contact with this health care facility led to her sickness. This will be very difficult to prove due to the fact that staphylococcus infection sources may be also found elsewhere, outside of health care facilities.[154] **189**

---

151 Decision of the Supreme Court of the Czech Republic of 27 September 2006, 25 Cdo 508/2005.

152 This proof would be probably based on the characteristics of the abscess; the medical expert will be asked to evaluate whether the fact of development of the abscess around the incision site on the neck proves that the syringe or needle must have been infected.

153 Act 40/1964 Coll, Civil Code § 415.

154 The plaintiff might want to present the proof that the particular staphylococcus line present in his organism is identical with the line cultivated from the specimens taken in the defendant health care facility.

190 The damages count will include the following:

- *Pain and loss of amenities.* According to Decree 440/2001 Coll, the medical evaluation of pain would probably include at least item T793 – post-injury infection of wound (50 points) and the evaluation of loss of amenities might by analogy apply one of the items of serious psychic harm (014–016). Otherwise, and more probably in light of the given facts and the likely character of psychic harm, plaintiff X can be indemnified via personality protection law, as described below.
- *Loss of earnings.* The compensation for loss of earnings will be calculated from the average earnings of the plaintiff X in the catering business before the damage arose.[155]
- *Treatment costs.* Any expenses connected with the treatment of plaintiff X, including cleaning assistance, can be compensated if the plaintiff sufficiently proves their connection with the injury and their necessity. The same applies to other household tasks. If such tasks are not performed by a hired worker but instead by the plaintiff X's daughter, the claim will probably only be equivalent to the salary of an unqualified caregiver or a volunteer, according to the jurisprudence quoted above.[156]

3. Personality protection liability (§ 11 ff)

191 In the context of personality protection liability action, plaintiff X needs to prove

- unlawful infringement of personality rights (especially right to health and bodily integrity),
- the scope of harm inflicted to personality rights,
- and a causal link between the above.[157]

192 Any violation on the side of the defendant, regardless of fault, is sufficient to fulfil the first condition, ie unlawful infringement of the right to health and bodily integrity. Concerning the scope of harm, plaintiff X would be able to describe to the court the depression, insomnia and pain, and further infringements of her personal and social life. If the plaintiff X

155 Act 40/1964 Coll, Civil Code § 445.

156 Decision of the Supreme Court of the Czech Republic of 24 October 2006, 25 Cdo 2127/2006; see also the analysis of Case 1.

157 *Švestka* (fn 52) 170.

proves the causation, ie that the infection arose in the defendant hospital, she will be entitled to moral and financial satisfaction. It is in the discretion of the judge to set the amount of the financial satisfaction. It is difficult to estimate the size of the satisfaction, but it might be in the range of tens of thousands CZK, depending on the duration of the health problems experienced.

Medical Liability in England

WV Horton Rogers

General Questions

A. The Health Care System Framework

I. General Introduction

1. The health care system in overview

The United Kingdom contains four law districts in public law terms: England, Scotland, Northern Ireland and Wales. This paper describes the organisation of health care solely with reference to England, which is by far the largest member, accounting for about 85 % of the population (Scotland about 8 %, Northern Ireland about 3 % and Wales about 5 %). There have always been structural differences in the organisation of public health among England, Scotland and Northern Ireland and this matter is now a 'devolved' one falling within the remit of the parliaments/assemblies for Scotland, Northern Ireland and Wales. Thus a large scale reorganisation of the system for Wales was proposed in 2009. However, the principal concern of this inquiry is legal liability for malpractice (ie private law) and here the differences are much less significant, indeed almost non-existent. The substantive and procedural law in Wales is identical to that in England. The substantive law in Northern Ireland is also the same (though sometimes contained in separate legislation) but there are procedural differences. The private law of Scotland is most recognizably distinct, certainly in respect of terminology but also to some extent conceptually. However, the substantive law of negligence which underpins malpractice liability is the same as that of England. 1

Ignoring elective matters such as cosmetic surgery, the National Health Service provides the overwhelming majority of medical treatment in England (though see no 3 below on who actually provides the treatment). Its facilities are available to anyone who is ordinarily resident here. In 2 theory there is also a general NHS dental service but in recent years many practitioners have left the service and a much larger proportion of dental work is now carried out under private contract. Generally medical treatment is free (the system being financed from general taxation), though there are charges for certain groups for drug prescriptions. The organisational structure has been changed many times since the inception of the service in 1948 but at present the basic structure is that 'secondary' (ie hospital) care is provided by NHS Trusts under ten regional Strategic Health Authorities. Since 2004 there have also been 'NHS Foundation Trusts' which have more financial freedom and are not subject to SHA direction. 'Primary' care is delivered by general practitioners via contracts (usually group ones) with Primary Care Trusts. Most general practitioners are independent contractors, though their relationship with their patients is not contractual. The name of Primary Care Trusts is somewhat misleading because although they are responsible for providing an adequate level of general practitioner service in their areas they are also in fact the main funding source for secondary care.

3 A major development in recent years has been the practice of 'commissioning' or sub-contracting NHS secondary care to private sector providers. For example, a great deal of NHS 'day surgery' is now carried out in treatment centres operated by private companies. Since mid 2009 the 'Patient Choice' policy allows referral to any 'clinically appropriate provider' for secondary treatment in consultation with the patient's general practitioner. In other words, there has been some movement away from the NHS being a 'monolithic, all service' provider to a mixed 'provider/facilitator'. However, acute and emergency care is still – and is likely to remain – all 'in house'.

4 This report was initially prepared before the change of government in 2010. The new, coalition government published a White Paper, *Equity and Excellence: Liberating the NHS*,[1] and a Health and Social Care Bill (of 281 sections, 22 schedules and 367 pages) based on this was introduced on 19 January 2011. This is still (March 2011) at Committee stage in the House of Commons so there is a long way to go and many amendments may be expected, some of the basic proposals being controversial. The Bill would abolish the Primary Care Trusts referred to in no 2 above and the 'commissioning' role of hospital treatment undertaken by those bodies would pass to consortia of general practitioners acting under the general umbrella of a NHS Commissioning Board. It is intended that all current

1 Available at <http://www.dh.gov.uk>.

NHS Trusts will become Foundation Trusts.[2] There is no suggestion that any of this will have any implications for legal liability for malpractice.[3]

II. Social Welfare Provision

2. The role of public health care

This has been largely answered in no 1 above. The essential point is that the public patient has no contractual relationship with any service provider, even if the treatment is by a private hospital on behalf of the NHS. It might also be worth pointing out that there is no real connection between the NHS and what is commonly referred to as the 'social security system'. The latter is primarily concerned with the payment of cash benefits, the former with the provision of services. Since the services are predominantly financed out of general taxation there is not the same link between the two as is found in some other systems. There is of course nothing to prevent a NHS general practitioner from referring a patient for private treatment (eg where the patient has health insurance or for treatment not covered by the NHS). In that case the patient will have a contractual relationship with the hospital and/or the surgeon. 5

3. Differences in treating patient's claims

Litigation against a health care provider is conducted in the same way whether it is a case of treatment in a NHS hospital, in a private hospital providing facilities to the NHS or treatment on a purely private basis. However, only NHS treatment will be covered by the NHS Redress Act 2006. This has not yet been implemented because of recent reorganisation of the general scheme of NHS complaints and since the Act is only a framework, enabling measure it contains no details of how the scheme will work. But when comes into force it will apply only to lower value claims (probably below £20,000). It is essentially an optional mechanism for the extra-judicial settlement of claims and in no way affects the basis of liability or the right to take conventional legal proceedings. 6

The Civil Procedure Rules contain a special pre-action Protocol for clinical negligence claims, which would be applicable whatever the nature of the 7

2 See again no 2 below.
3 As to the NHS Litigation Authority see no 12 below.

provider. Most personal injury cases are now conducted on a conditional fee basis, with the claimant's[4] liability for a successful defendant's costs being covered by insurance (for the cost of which the unsuccessful defendant is liable) and public funding has largely disappeared. However, for the moment it remains available for medical negligence cases, subject to criteria for likelihood of success and a satisfactory costs/damages ratio.[5]

4. Right of recourse

8 There is no 'dedicated' scheme for the situation described. However, the social security system has a general right of recoupment against the tortfeasor under the Social Security (Recovery of Benefits) Act 1997. Anyone satisfying a judgment or making an out of court settlement in respect of personal injuries must pay to the Compensation Recovery Unit the amount of most social security payments received by the victim in the five years after the injury or before the date of judgment/settlement, whichever is earlier, this sum being deducted from the damages. This scheme covers only cash payments to the victim and not the cost of provision of services. In *Islington London Borough Council v University College London Hospital NHS Trust*[6] the local authority was under a statutory duty to provide care for the claimant, who had suffered a stroke as a result of the defendants' negligence and although she had recovered damages, these were by way of a structured settlement and were not available for payment of the local authority's charges. A claim for recoupment against the defendants based on negligence failed. A decision in favour of the local authority would have implications which could not be fully explored for all sorts of other bodies and persons, public and private, providing services in aid of misfortune.

9 It should be noted that the NHS itself has the right to recover from the tortfeasor the cost of hospital treatment provided to accident victims up to about £41,500 under the Health and Social Care (Community Health and Standards Act 2003, replacing an earlier scheme which was confined to

---

4 In 2000 this term replaced the hallowed 'plaintiff' used by the questionnaire and by all the rest of the common law world.

5 See <http://www.legalservices.gov.uk>. However, in November 2010 the government announced proposals to remove it even in these cases. The Review of Civil Litigation Costs (2010), which is still under consideration, proposed massive changes for most litigation, including a move towards something like the American contingency fee system, whereby a successful claimant's costs would come from his damages.

6 [2005] England and Wales Court of Appeal Civil Division (EWCA Civ) 596, [2006] Personal Injury and Quantum Reports (PIQR) P3.

road accidents. The existence of this special regime was one reason in the *Islington* case, above, for concluding that the matter of recoupment of the cost of the local authority's services was a matter for Parliament.

III. Private Insurance

5. The role of private health insurance

I doubt if there are any very reliable statistics on this. I have seen suggestions that up to 12 % of the population have private health insurance but I would be very surprised if this was the figure for those having comprehensive, long-term cover and it is really only the NHS that is set up for acute or long-term care. Cover is 'duplicative', ie it does not affect the policy holder's right to NHS treatment. The CEA (European Insurance and Reinsurance Federation) estimated in 2006[7] that over 97 % of healthcare expenditure in the UK[8] came from the public sector, against a Europe-wide average of 78 %.[9] It is not merely a question of funding, however. In some European countries most hospital treatment is provided in private hospitals the charges of which are paid, in whole or in part, by the state. In England most treatment is provided in public hospitals run by the NHS or in privately owned clinics and centres acting as direct agents for the NHS on a 'block supply' basis. For example, my local day surgery centre is run by a company called Nations Healthcare on behalf of the NHS and almost all its work involves NHS patients. **10**

A policy covering medical costs would be one of indemnity and therefore in accordance with general principle the insurer would be subrogated to the rights of the insured. Hence the costs of further remedial treatment paid for by the insurer would be recoverable by it (the claim being brought in the insured's name). **11**

7 The European Health Insurance Market 2006.

8 Although this covers the whole of the UK it is unlikely that the position in England alone would be significantly different.

9 Total health care expenditure at € 152,884 million was almost precisely the same as in France but there the public sector accounted for 78.4 %, private insurance for 13.1 % and households for 8.6 % (CEA Report, fn 7 Table 8).

6. Liability insurance

12 As far as I am aware there is no law which requires doctors to carry liability insurance. One must draw a distinction here between (a) NHS hospital treatment and (b) treatment by general practitioners and in the private sector. Since 1990 the NHS has taken responsibility for the payment of damages and costs in respect of claims arising from treatment in Trust hospitals and no recourse will be taken against individuals.[10] Although the individual hospital trust, as employer of the medical staff, will be the defendant to any action, litigation is handled by the NHS Litigation Authority[11] which in effect acts as a 'pooling' agency for claims under the Clinical Negligence Scheme for Trusts.[12] It is financed by contributions from the trusts based on size, activities undertaken, claims record etc. The Authority paid £954 million in respect of damages and costs in clinical negligence claims in 2009–2010.

13 NHS 'indemnity' does not apply to most general practitioner services, nor of course to treatment in the private sector. Cover is provided by the Medical Defence Union (MDU) and the Medical Protection Society (MPS). Although these are both mutual organisations, the MDU now (though not formerly) provides indemnity cover (up to £10 million) via an insurer,[13] whereas the cover by the MPS is discretionary. However, the MPS claims that there has never been a case where a patient has failed to recover damages as a result of the exercise of this discretion.[14] Most doctors covered by the NHS indemnity will also have membership of the MDU or MPS, partly because of a perception that in any litigation (which will necessarily involve the doctor's professional reputation) the NHS will take a 'cost/benefit' approach to settlement and partly because these bodies will also cover professional disciplinary proceedings and matters which fall outside the NHS indemnity, eg 'good Samaritan' acts.

10 The text of the scheme may be found at <http://www.nhsla.com/Claims/>.

11 See generally <http://www.nhsla.com>.

12 The former 'excess' system whereby the trust paid the damages up to a variable threshold has been abolished. There are separate schemes for other types of litigation. Since the NHS has enormous property holdings and employs about 1.3 million people its role as a defendant in non-clinical claims should not be underestimated.

13 The MDU of course has power to terminate membership prospectively on risk assessment grounds. For an example (which mainly turned on the Data Protection Act 1998) see *Johnson v Medical Defence Union* [2007] EWCA Civ 262.

14 See <http://www.medicalprotection.org/uk/about-mps/insurance-versus-indemnity>.

IV. Professional Standards

7. Applicable professional standards

The right to practise medicine is dependent on registration by The General Medical Council (GMC)[15] under the Medical Act 1983 and this council has disciplinary power to remove a doctor from the register via its Fitness to Practice Rules. Such disciplinary action might be taken where, for example, there was professional misconduct, deficiency in performance or physical or mental ill-health. The civil standard of proof applies to the investigation and adjudication of complaints. The ultimate sanction is removal from the register but there is a range of lesser action which may be taken where suitable, eg restriction on area of practice, requirement of retraining or suspension from the register for a period. 'Harm' is not necessary to trigger such proceedings but they have no compensatory role. Registration is now being supplemented by a system of licensing, requiring periodic revalidation every five years. The GMC's guidelines *Good Medical Practice* run to 48 pages and are expanded by a further 19 sets of ethical guidelines on matters such as confidentiality, consent and personal beliefs and practice. Infringement of the guidelines would not of itself give rise to a civil action, though they are no doubt a good starting point on what the law would treat as proper professional standards. I suppose a fair analogy would be the Highway Code on driving. As an illustration of the level of detail, paragraphs 2 and 3 of the basic document provide as follows on clinical care: **14**

> 'Good clinical care must include:
>
> (a) adequately assessing the patient's conditions, taking account of the history (including the symptoms, and psychological and social factors), the patient's views, and where necessary examining the patient
>
> (b) providing or arranging advice, investigations or treatment where necessary
>
> (c) referring a patient to another practitioner, when this is in the patient's best interests.
>
> In providing care you must:
>
> (a) recognise and work within the limits of your competence

---

15 Detail on all these matters may be found at <http://www.gmc-uk.org/>.

(b) prescribe drugs or treatment, including repeat prescriptions, only when you have adequate knowledge of the patient's health, and are satisfied that the drugs or treatment serve the patient's needs

(c) provide effective treatments based on the best available evidence

(d) take steps to alleviate pain and distress whether or not a cure may be possible

(e) respect the patient's right to seek a second opinion

(f) keep clear, accurate and legible records, reporting the relevant clinical findings, the decisions made, the information given to patients, and any drugs prescribed or other investigation or treatment

(g) make records at the same time as the events you are recording or as soon as possible afterwards

(h) be readily accessible when you are on duty

(i) consult and take advice from colleagues, when appropriate

(j) make good use of the resources available to you.'

8. Quality and/or risk management systems

15 All NHS organisations and services are subject to a system of risk management assessment (at least once every two/three years) organised by the NHS Litigation Authority and achievement of the required standards (documentation, implementation systems and performance) leads to reductions in the contributions payable by hospital trusts etc to the Authority.[16]

B. Tort Liability

9. Fundamentals of tort liability

16 Much of tort law has no relevance or only very limited relevance to clinical claims – one might instance defamation, nuisance (neighbour disputes), trespass to land, conversion (misappropriation of goods). The core legal element of what would generally be regarded as medical malpractice is the

16 The material is enormously detailed. See <http://www.nhsla.com>.

tort of negligence[17] (though for reasons explained below contractual liability is in practice virtually identical). This has three elements, a duty of care owed by the defendant to the claimant, breach of that duty by the defendant and resulting damage to the claimant.

The duty of care is the principal control device for determining the reach or scope of liability for negligence in the light of what is considered to be sound legal policy and there is an enormous amount of modern case law on the subject. However, this largely concerns issues like pure economic loss, omissions and the position of public bodies and in practice a duty is 'taken as read' in cases of physical injury[18] so that it would never be contested that a doctor owed a duty of care to a patient with whom he came into a clinical relationship. **17**

The general standard of care is the objective one of the reasonable person in that situation. However, in the case of a profession the 'reasonable person' is not the 'man on the Clapham omnibus' as he once was (or nowadays the 'commuter on the Underground') but a competent member of the profession in question. Care for this purpose obviously includes skill. The standard of due care and skill is that of the competent practitioner occupying the post held by the defendant. Thus a general practitioner or junior hospital doctor is not expected to attain the standard of a specialist in the relevant condition but within that framework his own lack of experience is irrelevant. In other words, the standard applied to a newly qualified practitioner is the same as that applied to one of ten years' experience. The law looks primarily to the activity in which the defendant engages, so that if a doctor has a junior role in a specialist team the standard expected is that of a competent junior doctor in that team, not just that of the 'averagely competent and well informed junior houseman'.[19] Obviously a doctor should not undertake treatment which is beyond his experience or competence and should call upon expert advice when he has reason to believe that he is getting out of his depth. Only, therefore, if he has no reason to know this or some sudden emergency arises where help cannot be summoned is the 'differing standards' approach of much practical significance. Although the standard of care must take account of the task undertaken by the defendant and the expertise he professes there is one single standard – the civil law draws no distinction between 'ordinary' and 'gross' negligence. **18**

---

17 For a general overview see *WVH Rogers*, Winfield and Jolowicz on Tort (18th edn 2010).

18 Psychiatric harm not stemming from physical injury is another matter.

19 *Wilsher v Essex AHA* [1987] Queen's Bench Division Reports (QB) 730 (point not in issue on appeal, [1988] Appeal Cases (AC) 174).

19 Many medical decisions and procedures involve the exercise of judgement and of course the fact that a course was followed which with hindsight is shown to have been the 'wrong' one does not necessarily mean that the defendant is at fault. Indeed, there may be different schools of thought in the medical profession as to the most suitable treatment in particular circumstances. It is not the court's function to adjudicate upon which school of thought is correct and so long as the defendant has followed the line adopted by a respectable body of opinion in the profession he is not at fault,[20] though the court must beware of the possibility that a particular school of thought is simply the result of tradition and inertia and no longer supportable by logical analysis.[21]

20 Issues of resulting damage are likely to circle around causation, which is dealt with below.

21 A word should be said about two forms of trespass to the person, assault and battery. Technically, an assault is a threatened battery, battery being the actual physical contact. Although one might naturally think of these in the context of, say, acts by the police they are an important part of the background in medical law because they underpin the requirement of consent. A person of full age and with sufficient mental capacity to make a decision has the absolute right to determine what happens to his body and therefore any unconsented to treatment is a battery. Battery is a tort of intention, not negligence but the intention required is to do the act. Hence if a patient consents to operation A and by mistake is given operation B that is battery even if no fault is involved. Unlike negligence battery is actionable per se, ie damages may be awarded even if there is no loss in the normal legal sense. In one Canadian case the claimant recovered $20,000 damages even though the unconsented to treatment was necessary to save her life.[22]

10. Burden of proof

22 The first point to make here is that the required standard of proof is on a balance of probabilities, 'more likely than not'. It is misleading to put this in mathematical terms but if one has to, the claimant wins if he shows a

20 Commonly known as the *Bolam* approach after *Bolam v Friern Hospital Management Committee* [1957] 1 Weekly Law Reports (WLR) 582. It applies to professional negligence in general.

21 *Bolitho v City and Hackney Health Authority* [1998] AC 232.

22 *Malette v Shulman* (1990) 67 Dominion Law Reports (DLR) (4th) 321.

51/49 probability. If that threshold is reached the event or matter he has to prove is treated as being conclusively established even though in fact it may be obvious that there is some degree of uncertainty on the matter. This point is important when assessing how the law deals with 'loss of a chance'.

Loss. The burden of proof is on the claimant. Indeed it is difficult to conceive how the law could be otherwise. As to what is a loss (or damage as we would say) the matter is normally beyond dispute – any deterioration of the claimant's physical or mental condition. However, with regard to mental condition we must make a qualification. If there is a physical injury and the claimant suffers worry as a result, this will be allowed for as part of what are known as damages for pain and suffering and loss of amenity. However, if there is no physical injury, mental disturbance is not 'damage' (and hence one of the elements of a cause of action for negligence is missing) unless it amounts to a 'recognised psychiatric condition'. So in *Rothwell v Chemical and Insulating Co Ltd*[23] the claimants suffered from symptomless pleural plaques on the lung surface which indicated that their bodies had been penetrated by asbestos fibres in their employment. This did not indicate a high likelihood of an asbestos related disease but they were understandably very worried by it. The House of Lords held that they had not suffered damage and therefore had no claim.[24] **23**

Causation (of loss). The claimant has the burden of proof on a balance of probabilities that the defendant's tort caused the damage. In other words the position is the same as in any other tort claim. For qualifications see responses to questions 11 and 12 below. **24**

Fault. Again the claimant has the burden of proof on a balance of probabilities of fault by the defendant. However, this need not necessarily be by direct evidence and in a suitable case the fault of the defendant may be inferred from the happening of the accident – *res ipsa loquitur* as some still say even though Latin is now under something of a cloud in English law. This is not a special rule of law, nor does it reverse the burden of proof in the proper sense, it simply recognises that the facts shown by the claimant may have established a prima facie case which will lead to **25**

23 [2007] United Kingdom House of Lords (UKHL) 39, [2008] AC 281.

24 It is important to understand the tactical position here. The claimants wished to establish liability and obtain (no doubt modest) provisional damages. If they later developed a disease they could come back for reassessment of the damages. On the other hand, the decision that they have no claim now means that the limitation (prescription) period has not started to run and so there will be no time bar to their bringing a claim if the disease occurs. The decision has been reversed by legislation in Scotland.

judgment in his favour unless there an explanation is offered which casts doubt on the inference originally drawn. The initial inference may be strong or it may be weak, affecting the cogency of the evidence which needs to be produced to rebut it. At the end of the evidence on both sides the court must ask itself what is the effect of the rebutting evidence brought by the defendant. 'The res, which previously spoke for itself, may be silenced, or its voice, may, on the whole of the evidence, become too weak or muted.'[25] At a time when this was regarded as more of a special rule of law it was customary to say that two conditions must be satisfied: (a) the affair was under the control of the defendant or his employees and (b) the accident must be such as would not in the ordinary course of things have happened if proper care had been exercised. These 'requirements' probably remain a fair general description of the circumstances in which an inference of negligence will be drawn from the mere happening. Although this approach is obviously less likely to apply where the task being carried out is complex than where it is simple, there is no warrant for saying that it cannot be applied in a medical context.[26] If, for example, a hospital patient were to suffer symptoms consistent only with an overdose of medication and no explanation could be offered, he would probably have established simply by proving his symptoms that he had received the overdose and that this was the fault of a hospital employee. The position has been summarised as follows:

'(1) In its purest form, the maxim [*res ipsa loquitur*] applies where the plaintiff relies on the "res" (the thing itself) to raise the inference of negligence, which is supported by ordinary human experience, with no need for expert evidence.

(2) In principle, the maxim can be applied in that form in simple situations in the medical negligence field (surgeon cuts off right foot instead of left: swab left in operation site; patient wakes up in the course of surgical operation despite general anaesthetic).

(3) In practice, in contested medical negligence cases the evidence of the plaintiff, which establishes the "res", is likely to be buttressed by expert evidence to the effect that the matter complained does not ordinarily occur in the absence of negligence.

---

25 *Lloyde v West Midlands Gas Board* [1971] 1 WLR 749 at 755; *Ng v Lee* [1988] Road Traffic Reports (RTR) 298.

26 For example, it has recently been accepted that it can apply to an unexplained aircraft accident: *George v Eagle Air Services* [2009] United Kingdom Privy Council (UKPC) 21. The fact that this took so long to establish is no doubt because almost all air carriage is under international convention regimes which render general tort law irrelevant.

(4) The position may then be reached at the close of the plaintiff's case that the judge would be entitled to infer negligence on the defendant's part unless the defendant adduces evidence which discharges this inference.

(5) This evidence may be to the effect that there is a plausible explanation of what may have happened which does not connote any negligence on the defendant's part. The explanation must be a plausible one and not a theoretically or remotely possible one, but the defendant certainly does not have to prove that his explanation is more likely to be correct than any other. If the plaintiff has no other evidence of negligence to rely on, his claim will then fail.

(6) Alternatively, the defendant's evidence may satisfy the judge on the balance of probabilities that he did exercise proper care. If the untoward outcome is extremely rare, or is impossible to explain in the light of the current state of medical knowledge, the judge will be bound to exercise great care in evaluating the evidence before making such a finding, but it he does so, the prima facie inference of negligence is rebutted and the plaintiff's claim will fail. The reason why the courts are willing to adopt this approach, particularly in very complex cases, is to be found in the judgments of Stuart-Smith and Dillon LJJ in *Delaney v Southmead Health Authority*.[27]

(7) It follows from all this that, although in very simple situations the "res" may speak for itself at the end of the lay evidence adduced on behalf of the plaintiff, in practice the inference is then buttressed by expert evidence adduced on his behalf, and if the defendant were to call no evidence, the judge would be deciding the case on inferences he was entitled to draw from the whole of the evidence (including the expert evidence), and not on the application of the maxim in its purest form.'[28]

11. Uncertain causation

The paradigm case is *Wilsher v Essex Area Health Authority*.[29] The claimant, **26**
born prematurely, succumbed to RLF, a retinal condition causing serious damage to his sight. A possible cause, or contributing cause, of this was an

27 [1995] 6 Medical Law Reports (Med LR) 355.

28 *Ratcliffe v Plymouth and Torbay Health Authority* [1998] PIQR P170.

29 [1988] AC 1074.

excess of oxygen caused by a mistaken placing of a catheter but the conflicting expert evidence at the trial identified a number of other possible causes which were not attributable to the fault of the defendants and the failure of the trial judge to find that the mistake was more likely as a cause than these others[30] meant that there had to be a retrial on the causation issue.

27 To be contrasted with this is a case outside the medical context, *Fairchild v Glenhaven Funeral Services Ltd*[31] the essential facts may be summarised[32] by saying that the claimant worked for differing periods for a number of employers, each of whom exposed him, in breach of duty, to asbestos dust. He contracted a mesothelioma as a result of the exposure.[33] The case proceeded on the basis of evidence that whereas asbestosis is influenced by the total amount of dust inhaled, a mesothelioma may be produced by the inhalation of a single fibre, though the risk of contracting it is increased by constant exposure.[34] It was, therefore, scientifically impossible to identify the source of the fibre or fibres which had produced the tumour. Nevertheless, the House of Lords held that the claimant was entitled to succeed. As Lord Nicholls put it, 'Any other outcome would be deeply offensive to instinctive notions of what justice requires and fairness demands. The real difficulty lies is elucidating in sufficiently specific terms the principle being applied in reaching this conclusion. To be acceptable the law must be coherent. It must be principled. The basis on which one case, or one type of case, is distinguished from another should be transparent and capable of identification. When a decision departs from principles normally applied, the basis for doing so must be rational and justifiable if the decision is to avoid the reproach that hard cases make bad law.'[35] The decision is not confined to the liability of employers to workers but it seems that the principle only operates where each defendant whom it is sought to hold liable has exposed the claimant to the same harmful agent or at least agents which operate in a similar way. It is not, however, confined to cases of multiple defendants: hence it was applied in another mesothelioma case where some of the exposure to asbestos was

---

30 Indeed, he had placed the onus squarely onto the defendants to show that it was probably not a cause.

31 [2002] UKHL 22, [2003] 1 AC 32.

32 There were three appeals, which differed in many matters of detail.

33 There was no doubt about this since the incidence of the disease is only one in a million and those occupationally exposed have a one thousand times greater incidence than the general population.

34 The 'single fibre' theory may subsequently have become discredited in medical science: *Durham v BAI (RunOff) Ltd* [2008] England and Wales High Court (EWHC) 2692 (QB).

35 At [36].

the fault of the defendant and some of it the fault of the claimant, who had disobeyed safety regulations during periods of self-employment.[36]

The *Fairchild* case proceeded on the basis, not challenged on the appeal, that if the defendant was liable he was liable in accordance with the normal principle of joint and several liability that each defendant who contributed to the causation of an indivisible injury was liable to the claimant in full, the final accounting among defendants being made in contribution proceedings among them, a fact of considerable significance in such cases where most of the defendants who have contributed to the risk over many years are insolvent or have ceased to exist. The House of Lords reconsidered the position in *Barker v Corus (UK) Ltd*[37] *Fairchild* was not a decision holding that the claimant had proved causation by showing that the defendant had increased the risk but one which said that in limited circumstances proof of increase of risk could serve as a substitute for the proof of causation. Hence, since we are ex hypothesi saying that in these cases the defendant probably did *not* cause the harm, the application of the normal principle of solidary, joint and several liability would be unfair and instead the defendant's liability should only be proportional to the increase in risk for which he was responsible.[38] This has been reversed by statute so that joint and several liability applies again but only in respect of claims for mesothelioma.[39] So in so far as the *Fairchild* principle can be applied to other situations,[40] proportional liability is still the rule. **28**

The limits of the *Fairchild* principle are not clear but it has been emphasised that it is intended to apply to cases where conventional proof of causation is *impossible* and it is not a panacea for the judge to avoid making decisions on the evidence where proof is *difficult*.[41] Given the requirement that the agents which may have caused the damage should be similar and have operated in substantially the same way, it seems to be of limited relevance to the clinical negligence scenario, where *Wilsher* would be a much more typical case. However, it is important to remember that *Wilsher* was a case of *alternative* causes. If we are dealing with a case where the evidence is that indivisible damage is the product of more than one **29**

36 *Barker v Corus (UK) Ltd* [2006] UKHL 20, [2006] 2 AC 572; See further *Sienkiewicz v Greif* [2011] UKSC 10.

37 Ibid.

38 In the typical employment disease case presumably to be assessed by reference to length and intensity of exposure.

39 Compensation Act 2006, s 3.

40 For example, it presumably applies to the well-known 'two hunters' hypothetical where C is shot by D1 or D2 but it is impossible to determine which.

41 *Hull v Sanderson* [2008] EWCA Civ 1211.

cause and the defendant is responsible for only one of those, he is liable for the whole of the damage if 'his' cause made a material (ie more than negligible) contribution to its occurrence, even if it cannot be shown that but for 'his cause' the damage would not have occurred.[42] If the other cause is the responsibility of another solvent person, the defendant may be able to seek contribution against him; if the other cause is the fault of the claimant there may be a reduction in damages for contributory negligence; otherwise the defendant has to bear the burden in full. 'While the law does not expect tortfeasors to pay for damage that they have not caused, it regards them as having caused damage to which they have materially contributed.'[43]

30 This question finally asks what is the position where it is unclear which of the hospital's staff caused the loss. The basic principle is that if the hospital is responsible for all the people involved in the treatment it does not matter as far as liability to the patient is concerned (though it may of course be a matter of concern in a professional discipline context). If on a balance of probabilities, the injury was caused by the fault of A or B and D is vicariously liable for A and B then D is liable either way. In practice, for reasons explained in no 35 below, the position will be effectively the same if a NHS patient is treated in an outside independent facility by staff some of whom are contracted to the NHS and some to the independent provider. The problem could arise, however, – though it seems factually rather unlikely – in the case of private treatment in a private hospital where the hospital will not be vicariously liable for the surgeon. It must also be borne in mind that even if the direct cause of an injury is the negligence of A or B, it might be possible to point the finger at the hospital on the basis that whoever it was, there is some defect in the care system, a matter for which the hospital is responsible (see no 34 below).

12. Loss of a chance

31 It is not possible to give a simple, unqualified answer to the question, though if one is forced to do so it would be 'more No than Yes'. The

42 *Bailey v MoD* [2008] EWCA Civ 883, [2009] 1 WLR 1052.

43 *Dickins v O2 Plc* [2008] EWCA Civ 1144, [2009] Industrial Relations Law Reports (IRLR) 58 at [53], per Sedley LJ. In recent years there has been something of a drift, especially in asbestosis and 'work stress' cases, towards apportioning responsibility and damages between tortious and non-tortious cumulative causes even where the damage would traditionally have been regarded as indivisible. This trend has been strongly criticised in some recent Court of Appeal decisions: *Ellis v Environment Agency* [2008] EWCA Civ 1117, [2009] PIQR P5; *Dickins v O2 Plc*, above.

starting point, as has been explained in no 23 above (and leaving aside the *Fairchild* situation) is that the burden of proof is on the claimant and is on a balance of probabilities. Once this threshold is passed the disputed past event is treated as conclusively established. Hence, if the judge is satisfied that it is just more likely than not that the injury was caused by the fault of D, then the claimant recovers 100 % of his loss and not a sum discounted by the chance (45 % or whatever) that it was not caused by D's fault. Equally, if the judge considers that the position is the reverse, the claimant fails altogether. The principle is exemplified by *Hotson v East Berkshire Health Authority*.[44] The defendants failed correctly to diagnose the claimant's condition after a fall and he developed a serious disability of the hip joint. On the facts there was, statistically, a 75 % risk that this disability would have developed even if the claimant had been treated properly but the trial judge (and the Court of Appeal) held that he was entitled to damages representing 25 % of his full loss. This was reversed by the House of Lords: the judge's findings of fact amounted to a conclusion that on a balance of probabilities the disability would have occurred anyway and that the fall was therefore the sole cause of the loss. This is not of course strictly a 'loss of a chance' situation. Nothing was known about the precise degree of blood vessel damage when the claimant arrived at hospital and the figures were based on a sample of the recovery rate of persons presenting with similar conditions. In fact the claimant would have been in one of three categories: he was doomed to suffer the disability whatever was done, or he would have made a certain recovery or he fell between those groups. But it was certainly impossible to say that he would probably have recovered.[45]

The matter was looked at again in *Gregg v Scott*.[46] There was a blameworthy **32**
delay in the diagnosis of the claimant's cancer and when treatment began he had (in similar statistical terms to those in *Hotson*) only a 25 % chance of recovery, whereas if it had been diagnosed promptly his chance would have been 42 %. But even on the latter assumption it was still more likely than not that he would not have survived with treatment. The majority of the House of Lords rejected his claim that the delay in treatment had caused the damage of which he complained. The case was different from *Hotson* in that the immediate spread of the cancer would probably not have

44 [1987] AC 750.

45 Cf the argument of *A Porat/A Stein*, Tort Liability under Uncertainty (2001) who would award the *Hotson* claimant 25 % of his loss on the basis that the defendants' negligence in not examining him has deprived him of the chance of showing that they were responsible for his physical condition.

46 [2005] UKHL 2, [2005] 2 AC 176.

occurred had there been prompt diagnosis but the basis of the claim was that the claimant had been deprived of the chance of a *cure*. It also differed from *Hotson* in the fact that in that case the outcome was pre-determined by the (unknown) amount of blood vessel damage which had been caused by the fall (so that, strictly speaking, the question of loss of a chance was never before the court) whereas now the developments which reduced his life expectancy were subsequent to the negligence. Nevertheless, for Lord Hoffmann and Baroness Hale the claim was an attempt to reformulate the basis of the law in terms of lost chances rather than causal outcomes and should be rejected. 'In effect, the appellant submits that the exceptional rule in *Fairchild*'s case should be generalised and damages awarded in all cases in which the defendant may have caused an injury and has increased the likelihood of the injury being suffered.'[47] Two judges dissented, though for different reasons,[48] and the view of the third member of the majority is not on all fours with that of Lord Hoffmann and Baroness Hale.[49] The case is therefore not satisfactory but at least we can say that the law still stands on the proposition that the claimant must prove on a balance of probabilities that the outcome would have been different, not merely that there is a lesser possibility that it would have been different.

33 What has been said so far must be qualified in two respects. First, where the claimant proves to the required standard that the defendant is responsible for the injury he has suffered, the 'all or nothing' approach does not apply to the quantification of his damages for that injury. If, for example, the claim is that there may be a deterioration in the claimant's condition or that he will lose the opportunity of promotion, the court must do the best it can to assess the likelihood and award damages accordingly, even if the chance is less than 50 %.[50] Secondly, the 'all or nothing' approach does not apply to claims for economic loss where the outcome, had there been no negligence, would have depended on the action of a third party. So where defective legal advice deprived the claimant purchasers of the opportunity to bargain with the vendor for indemnity against claims in

47 At [85] per Lord Hoffmann.

48 Lord Nicholls comes closest to accepting a loss of a chance approach in clinical negligence cases (though he regarded *Hotson* as correctly decided). Lord Hope regarded it as simply a question of quantification of the damage flowing from the immediate spread of the tumour.

49 Not the least of the difficulties is the fact that the case was very long and drawn out, the appeal being heard ten years after the negligence and the claimant was still alive so that the adverse outcome, the chance of avoiding which he claimed to have lost, had not occurred. Survival for ten years was regarded as the medical criterion for 'cure'.

50 There may in some cases be other means of dealing with the first matter, eg the award of provisional damages (which may be reopened) or periodical payments.

respect of the property, they did not have to show on a balance of probabilities that the vendor would have agreed to that indemnity, but merely that there was a more than speculative chance of success. To take a simple example. a solicitor allows the limitation period on his client's claim to expire so that it can no longer be pursued. If the client would have lost the case, he has lost nothing – indeed he has gained by avoiding the costs of the unsuccessful suit. However, the outcome of the suit is likely to be to some extent a matter of uncertainty. In such a situation the claimant succeeds if he shows he had some realistic chance of success, not necessarily as much as a balance of probabilities, and recovers damages discounted accordingly. It is not clear why we depart from the 'deterministic' view in this type of case but not in others.[51]

What is certain is that a shift to a loss of a chance approach would lead to a **34**
situation which would be unpredictable in the medical negligence context. If we allow the person with a 30 % chance of recovery 30 % of his damage, it is difficult to see how we could refuse to reduce the damages of the person with a 70 % chance of recovery to 70 %.[52] Although the effect of the loss of a chance approach would mean that fewer cases would fail altogether, it does not follow that the global liability bill would be any greater, for the reduction in the claims which now succeed in full might offset (or even exceed) the amount payable to claimants whose evidence falls below the balance of probabilities threshold. But since under the present law there is no reason for a judge to put any figure on the probability of causation, whether or not it passes the point of balance, there is no way of accumulating the data from which we could know what the effect would be. In any event, it would certainly make the negotiation and adjudication of what are now regarded as straightforward claims a great deal more complicated.

---

51 Consider *Gouldsmith v Mid-Staffordshire etc NHS Trust* [2007] EWCA Civ 397. D was negligent in failing to refer C for specialist treatment and C lost fingers. The evidence was that 'most' specialists would have operated and the fingers would have been saved. The majority of the CA treated this as amounting to evidence that on a balance of probabilities the surgery would have been carried out and the claimant therefore succeeded. But Maurice Kay LJ dissented on the basis that there was no evidence of to whom the claimant would have been referred and that the evidence clearly implied that a respectable body of specialists would not have operated. He suggested that the case was essentially one of loss of a chance but this was not a route pursued by either party.

52 The unsuccessful claimant in *Gregg v Scott* accepted that any change to a 'chance-based' system would have to 'cut both ways': [2005] UKHL 2, [2005] 2 AC 176 at [225].

13. Multiple persons involved

35 A NHS hospital is vicariously liable for all its staff, who are covered by the NHS Indemnity scheme. The individual staff members remain personally liable in accordance with general principle but this is theoretical. One staff member is not liable for the negligence of fellow-staff though of course if he has a directing/supervisory role in the treatment he is liable for failure adequately to carry that out. The hospital is not vicariously liable for doctors providing private treatment on NHS premises (which is why they need their own indemnity cover) but other hospital staff assisting are treated as performing their contractual duties to the NHS, the hospital is liable for them and they are covered by NHS Indemnity. In practical terms the position is not really different in the case of private treatment in a private hospital: the surgeon would be an independent contractor and the hospital would not be vicariously liable for him but it would be liable for hospital staff assisting him. In either case it would be too narrow a focus to look at the matter solely in terms of vicarious liability for an individual's acts. The problem which has led to the claim may be what may be called an 'organisational' one (see for example case 3 below) in which case the hospital would be in breach of its 'personal' duty to provide adequate facilities and an adequate 'system' even if it is not possible to allocate blame to individuals involved in the treatment, eg because they have been forced to deal with an emergency with inadequate resources.

36 A word should be said here about the position when NHS treatment is contracted out to another provider (see no 3 above). The 'personal' duty of the hospital has affinities in historical terms with the personal duty of the employer to his workers, which grew up at a time when there were restrictions on the application of vicarious liability for the negligence of one worker causing injury to a fellow-worker. The employer's duty is non-delegable, that is to say if he chooses to discharge it via an independent contractor it is a duty to ensure that care is taken, it is not enough merely to exercise care in choosing and supervising.[53] It is in effect a form of vicarious liability contrary to the general rule for independent contractors. What is less clear is whether it merely requires the employer to ensure that the contractor has an adequate system or whether it goes further and makes him liable for casual acts of negligence in the operation of the system. If the same applies to the hospital's duty to its patients – particularly on the broader view – this has important implications wherever work

---

53 See *McDermid v Nash Dredging and Reclamation Co Ltd* [1987] AC 906.

is contracted out. The matter is considered in a rather atypical situation in *A v Ministry of Defence*.[54] The MoD had ceased to provide hospital facilities for the reduced number of British forces in Germany and contracted with an NHS Trust for the latter to procure German hospital services. The claimant was the child of a soldier and suffered brain damage during his birth at a hospital in Bielefeld. The *Gutachterkommission* investigation concluded that there had been negligence, the hospital's insurers admitted liability and it was envisaged that the damages would be no less than they would be in England. Nevertheless, the claimant brought proceedings against the MoD and the NHS Trust. The trial judge dismissed the claim against the Trust and there was no appeal against this; the Court of Appeal dismissed the appeal against a similar decision in favour of the MoD. The decision is hardly surprising as the position of the MoD, which had wholly ceased to provide medical services, was in no way analogous to a NHS Trust which has accepted a patient and then 'farmed him out' to a third party provider. Perhaps the same is true of the NHS Trust involved in the case, with which the claimant had no contact and which was really only acting as a commissioning agent for the general provision of services.[55] However, the issue is probably academic in the ordinary domestic context for two reasons. First, in very many (perhaps most) of these cases the patient will be treated on the third party's premises by a doctor who is acting under a NHS contract and in that event the NHS Indemnity scheme provides for the NHS to carry the liability.[56] Secondly, in any event although independent treatment centres cannot be members of NHS Indemnity Scheme for Trusts, the NHSLA has now given them the opportunity to gain the benefit of NHS Indemnity, via the Primary Care Trust which commissions their services, for all clinical negligence claims by NHS patients, even those involving their staff.[57] It seems therefore that the position of a NHS patient in respect of treatment errors is effectively the same whether he receives treatment 'in house' or is contracted out to an independent provider. The move away from the

54 [2004] EWCA Civ 641, [2005] QB 183.

55 One lower court decision, criticised but not overruled in *A*, makes the NHS Trust liable in the situation we are considering: *M v Calderdale and Kirklees Health Authority* [1998] 4 Lloyd's Reports Medical (Lloyd's Rep Med) 157.

56 In fact the Indemnity scheme goes further than the general law of vicarious liability in a number of respects, eg it covers medical students acting under the direction of NHS staff.

57 See the 'Claims' section at <http://www.nhsla.com>. The reason was apparently that a significant proportion of the costs of independent providers went on liability insurance cover, the details of which might vary significantly from case to case.

'monolithic' structure of health care provision within the NHS has therefore been accompanied by a move in the opposite direction as far as liability is concerned.

14. Strict liability

37 Except in relation to product liability under the Product Liability Directive there is not generally any element of strict (ie without objective fault) liability under the present tort law. The application of the Directive in a medical context is illustrated by *A v National Blood Authority*[58] where the Directive was held to have been infringed by the supply of blood products infected with hepatitis C even though at the time there was no reasonably effective method of screening for the virus – and in some cases the supply had taken place before the risk was even known. The Directive could also of course apply to drugs, subject to the availability of the so-called 'development risks' defence. Note, however, that in a typical case a hospital would not be a 'producer' of the blood or drug and would not incur liability except via the 'failure to disclose source' route.

38 As has been pointed out in no 21, above, liability is also 'strict' in the case of absence of consent to the treatment because the cause of action is trespass, not negligence. So if the wrong surgery is performed there is liability even if the surgeon is not to blame for the mistake.

C. Contractual Liability

15. Basics of contracts in the health care sector

39 As has been explained above, treatment under the NHS is not given under a contract, so contract law only applies to private treatment.[59]

---

58 [2001] 3 All England Law Reports (All ER) 289.

59 It must be remembered that the common law has the requirement of consideration for a contract. But even if payment is made it does not follow that there is a contract. Thus, drugs prescribed on the NHS are not supplied under a contract, but under a statutory scheme, even though some patients make a payment for them: *Pfizer Corpn v Ministry of Health* [1965] AC 152.

16. Differences to tort law

There is no practical difference, since the implied term in a contract for professional services is to exercise reasonable professional care and skill and the burden of proof of breach of this is still on the claimant. It is theoretically possible for a doctor to give an express warranty that treatment will be successful but it seems very unlikely that anyone would consciously do so and the court will be extremely reluctant to conclude that that is the objective interpretation of his conduct.[60] For ancillary purposes like limitation or damages, a claim for personal injury arising from private treatment[61] would also be on all fours with a tort claim. In theory a private patient has two claims, one in contract and one in tort (because he is the doctor's 'neighbour' and we have no rule of *non cumul des obligations*) and he may pursue either or both. But they will in practice amount to the same thing except for pleading and he cannot recover damages twice over. **40**

17. Contractual claims in the absence of direct contracts?

As far as the consequences of treatment are concerned this is a non-issue. **41**
At common law only a party to a contract can sue under it. Even if there is a contract between the NHS and a third party provider and (unlikely) the requirements of the Contracts (Rights of Third Parties) Act 1999 are fulfilled, this would still be irrelevant because that contract would not contain any undertaking with regard to the quality of the treatment going beyond the exercise of care and skill.

18. Informed consent

Informed consent is certainly relevant, though to our eyes the question is **42**
misplaced because it is just as relevant in tort as in contract. As has been said above, absence of consent renders treatment an assault/battery. But a consent is not generally invalidated in this sense because there is a failure

60 See eg *Thake v Maurice* [1986] QB 644.

61 This is all we are talking about. A person who undertakes only to exercise care and skill in the treatment might of course be treated as making an unqualified promise that eg he will perform it at a certain time. See *Platform Funding Ltd v Bank of Scotland Plc* [2008] EWCA Civ 930 (valuer inspecting wrong property).

to explain the risks of the procedure.[62] However, informing the patient of the unavoidable risks of the procedure is part of the doctor's general duty for the purposes of the tort of negligence and failure to fulfil this may therefore lead to a claim by a different route. If there has been a failure to carry this out and the patient would not have consented if he had been informed,[63] there will be liability for the adverse consequences even if the procedure has been carried out with all due care and skill. It is impossible to state any statistical formula for what must be disclosed, no doubt it will be affected by the nature of the procedure and the consequences of not carrying it out.[64] However, the courts have accepted that, just as in the case of treatment, the view of a respectable body of opinion within the profession is relevant in determining what should be disclosed.[65] If, on the other hand, the patient asks a specific question he is entitled to a truthful answer.

43 An interesting twist to the question of informed consent is provided by *Chester v Afshar*.[66] The defendant, in breach of duty, failed to warn the claimant of a 1 or 2 % unavoidable risk of cauda equina syndrome in surgery on her spinal column and this eventuated. The trial judge found that if the claimant had been properly warned, the operation would not have taken place when it did but he was unable to find whether if the claimant had been duly warned she would, after further medical advice, have given or refused consent to surgery at some later date. If she had so consented, the risk would have been the same because it was a random one, not related to any known feature of the method of performing the surgery. A majority of the House of Lords held that she was entitled to recover damages in respect of the worsening of her position by the adverse outcome. One might have thought that this result was a simple, straight-

---

62 *Chatterton v Gerson* [1981] QB 432. I have used the word 'generally' because there might in some cases be a failure of explanation so extreme that the patient would obviously not understand even the general nature of what was to be done.

63 Some systems ask the question of what a reasonable patient would have done but in England the focus is on the individual – though what a reasonable person would have done may of course be evidence as to what this person would have done (especially bearing in mind the inevitable risk of self-serving testimony).

64 In *Chester v Afshar* [2004] UKHL 41, [2005] 1 AC 134 it was not contested that there was a duty to inform of a 1 or 2 % risk of a serious adverse outcome in a procedure to relieve back pain. It does not seem to be the practice to disclose general risks like those of anaesthesia directly but in practice the documentation given to patients for non-urgent surgery will do so. Thus, the death rate from general anaesthesia is given (one hundred times greater than the chance of winning the National Lottery but still only about 0.007 %).

65 *Sidaway v Bethlem Royal Hospital* [1985] AC 871. Cf in Australia *Rogers v Whittaker* (1993) 175 Commonwealth Law Reports (CLR) 479.

66 [2004] UKHL 41, [2005] 1 AC 134.

forward application of the standard combination of 'but-for' causation and proof on a balance of probabilities. There was a finding of fact that if she had been informed she would not have had the surgery on that day, the adverse outcome was exactly within the risk about which the defendant had failed to warn her and even if it could have been positively shown that she would have had the procedure on another day, a random risk of 1 or 2 % would have come nowhere near establishing that the adverse outcome would have been suffered on the later occasion.[67] Nevertheless, even the majority of the court who found in the claimant's favour felt compelled to say that they were modifying the standard principles of causation, albeit in a 'narrow and modest'[68] way, in order to vindicate the claimant's autonomy, her freedom to make an informed choice about the treatment she was to receive.[69] Although there is no doubt that in a 'historical' sense the failure to warn was a cause of the injury, the reason for the failure on the traditional test seems to have been that the court regarded the defendant's breach of duty as exposing the claimant to the *risk* of the injury and that would have been in no way decreased on any later occasion when she underwent the treatment.

D. Public Liability

19. Key differences from cases involving private hospitals or doctors

I think this issue has been adequately dealt with in Section A. In practical terms there are no real differences. 44

E. Alternative Compensation Regimes

20. Funds and/or other alternative compensation regimes

There is a Vaccine Damage Payment Scheme (a lump sum of £ 120,000) for persons who are severely disabled as result of vaccination in childhood. 45

67 As the CA had held: [2002] EWCA Civ 724, [2003] QB 356 at [40].

68 Lord Steyn at [24].

69 But this right goes unvindicated where the evidence shows that she would have gone ahead there and then even if she had been informed. Cf *Rees v Darlington Memorial Hospital NHS Trust* [2003] UKHL 52, [2004] 1 AC 309 (no 65, below) where, in a different context, the award of a fixed, conventional sum was regarded as the proper way to deal with the violation of the right to autonomy.

Such persons are of course likely to be entitled to other benefits under the general social security system. There are various schemes for industrial diseases but these are not 'clinically related'. There is no automatic right to compensation in clinical trials without legal liability unless such cover is offered.

F. Extent of Liability/Remedies

I. Pecuniary Loss

21. Introduction to indemnifying pecuniary loss

46 Pecuniary loss will generally embrace (a) loss of earnings and (b) expenses consequent on the injury (nursing care, equipment, special accommodation etc). In cases of catastrophic injury, the latter often exceed the former many times over, especially bearing in mind that the claimant is entitled to claim the cost of private care and treatment even if they are available from public funds. The basic principle is that the claimant is entitled (subject to any reduction for contributory negligence – unusual in a clinical negligence situation) to be put in the position he would have been in if the tort had not been committed, insofar as a payment of damages can do that.

22. Loss of earnings vs loss of earning capacity

47 In the case of an adult with an established record or in other cases where there is an evidential basis (eg a student about to embark on a specific career), the basis of assessment would be the expected actual income (allowing for matters like career progression). In other cases, such as catastrophic injury to a young child, such evidence will not be available and we may prefer to speak in terms of loss of earning capacity but I doubt if anything really turns on the distinction (save that in the latter case the result will be more of a guess). Even in the case of a person with an established work record, he is entitled to damages for 'handicap in the labour market' if the injury will limit his capacity to find other employment. In the case of the non-earning homemaker, I doubt if we would think in terms of loss of earning capacity but he/she is certainly entitled to recover the cost of obtaining substitute services in the market.

In cases of death, the dependent family members have a claim for loss of support under the Fatal Accidents Act 1976. In the case of a surviving widow (no children) this would be based on a figure of about 66 % of the deceased's income. Damages are based on loss, not on need, so it would be irrelevant that the survivor could support herself at the same level by her own efforts. 48

23. Periodic payments or lump sum?

At common law damages can only be awarded as a lump sum. However, there is nothing to stop the parties settling – and most cases are settled – for periodical payments and the practice of making 'structured settlements' grew up in serious personal injury cases. Now under the Damages Act 2006, the court has a general discretion to award damages as periodical payments if that is suitable. They are index-linked and may be made variable for change of circumstances (up or down). Most damages are probably still awarded as lump sums and this will continue to be so because most claims are not for catastrophic injuries: periodical payments would be quite unsuitable for an award of £50,000 or £100,000. Subject to this, one may probably say the following: (1) The continuity of payments must be secure, which means in practice that they must be underwritten by an insurance market scheme or payable by a body like the National Health Service Litigation Authority. (2) If a claimant of full age and understanding wanted a lump sum, it is unlikely that the court would overrule that wish. (3) Periodical payments are peculiarly suitable for long-term, uncertain expenses such as nursing care.[70] These are common in serious clinical negligence cases and it should be noted that periodical payments are attractive on a 'cash flow' basis to the NHSLA, which pays most medical damages and is a 'self insurer'. (4) Even where periodical payments are awarded, most cases will probably still have major lump sum elements to cover pre-trial/settlement losses and expenses and non-pecuniary loss. 49

Where pecuniary loss damages are assessed on a lump sum basis and there is evidence of actual likely loss on which to proceed, damages are calculated by determining a multiplier (the length of time over which the loss is likely to last) and a multiplicand (the amount of the annual loss). For this 50

70 In effect structured settlements were 'top down', ie they were based on an assessment by the parties of what lump sum the court would be likely to award. But periodical payment orders may be 'bottom up', ie based on present needs and made variable.

purpose the tables in general use[71] assume a rate of return, set by statute,[72] on the capital fund of damages of 2.5 % net of tax. So if we take a male permanently disabled at 30 the multiplier for loss of earnings to retirement age 65 is 22.78, leading to an award of £683,400 for an assumed steady annual loss of £30,000.[73] The tables are based on general mortality so no reduction should be made for the chance of early death but the multiplier may of course have to be adjusted if there is substantial evidence of this – or any other relevant – risk.

24. Caps and thresholds

51 There are none, except in so far as in practice there are limits set by precedent on recovery for non-pecuniary loss.

II. Non-Pecuniary Loss

25. Introduction to indemnifying non-pecuniary loss

52 I confine myself here to actions for personal injury: obviously damages for non-pecuniary loss for things like libel or false arrest have strong non-pecuniary elements but they have nothing in common with personal injury. The claimant is entitled to damages for pain, suffering and loss of amenity, which are normally awarded as one lump sum and are in effect based on a flexible judicial tariff system, ranging down from about £265,000[74] for quadriplegia. Thus, total blindness is about £175,000, loss of bowel function about £95,000, loss of one arm below the elbow about £75,000, loss of thumb up to £36,000, dermatitis of hands about £10,000 and simple tibia fracture with no ongoing disability about

---

71 The so-called Ogden Tables, currently 6th edn 2007.

72 Damages Act 1996 s 1. This may have been realistic when set in 2001 but probably requires modification in view of the sharp falls in investment returns, A 1 % net table would in the example give a multiplier of 28.61.

73 Real prospects of an increase in earnings will be allowed for, but not inflation. This is because (a) inflation is wholly unpredictable except over short periods (true) and (b) it has been assumed that inflation rates above 2 % will be covered by periodic increases in the rate of return on investment. This assumption that the 'real' interest rate, shorn of the inflation element, is always about 2 % may not be true in the present unusual climate.

74 When the European Centre of Tort and Insurance law looked at this in 1999/2000 (*WVH Rogers* (ed), Damages for Non-Pecuniary Loss in a Comparative Perspective [2001]) we used a crude market rate conversion factor of € 1 = £ 0.6. I have left all figures in £ because I think that now to use a factor like € 1 = £ 0.8 would rather underestimate the true value of these damages which are, after all, likely to be spent in England.

£6,000. It must be stressed that most of these are expressed as 'ranges' or in terms of 'up to' and in some cases the ranges are necessarily rather broad (eg scarring or psychiatric trauma).[75] Although 'pain' as opposed to loss of amenity is not the major element of the award in longer-term injuries, more than usual pain will push the figure up within the bracket. These figures are kept roughly in line with inflation so all but the most recent awards must be updated for purposes of comparison.[76] I doubt if it is possible to say what the minimum is but the lowest figure I have traced is £600 for short-term food poisoning.

26. Who can claim compensation for non-pecuniary loss?

In the case of non-fatal injuries only the victim may claim damages for **53**
non-pecuniary loss.[77] Where a person with a close relationship of love and affection suffers psychiatric trauma by witnessing the injury of the victim or its immediate aftermath he may have a claim but this is his own claim, based on a duty of care to him, not one 'parasitic' on that of the victim.[78] In the case of death a very narrow range of relatives (spouses, registered same sex civil partners and parents of minor children) have an automatic statutory claim under the Fatal Accidents Act 1976 for a fixed sum of £11,800 (per death) for bereavement.[79]

---

75 The easiest source of basic information is the *Judicial Studies Board*, Guidelines for the Assessment of Damages in Personal Injury Cases (10th edn 2010).

76 In any event there was an upgrading of awards in the more serious cases as a result of *Heil v Rankin* [2001] QB 272.

77 Indeed the same is true for pecuniary loss. Any loss to the victim's family is made good by the award to the victim and in the case of more remote (eg business) relationships there is no duty of care to avoid economic loss to third parties.

78 This form of liability is, for policy reasons, more restrictive than that for physical injury. The core element is that there must be something in the nature of a 'shock' which is a reaction to a 'sudden event'. This has not proved easy to apply in some medical treatment cases, eg *Walters v North Glamorgan NHS Trust* [2002] EWCA Civ 1792, [2003] Lloyd's Rep Med 49.

79 For pecuniary loss (available to a much wider range of persons factually dependent on the deceased) see no 48, above.

G. Procedural Matters

27. Specific rules of jurisdiction or procedure

54 There is a special pre-action protocol under the Civil Procedure Rules which is to be followed in cases of claims for clinical negligence.[80] Otherwise there are no special rules, save for the fact that, as mentioned in no 6, above, some publicly-funded legal aid remains available for medical cases whereas it has disappeared for other personal injury work.

28. Special institutions handling malpractice claims

55 At the moment there are none but if and when the NHS Redress system (see no 5, above) comes into effect it will be run by the National Health Service Litigation Authority.

H. Outlook

29. Reform plans

56 Reference has been made above to the NHS Redress Act 2006 and its tardy implementation. Since the Act is no more than a framework allowing the making of subsidiary regulations it is not really possible to paint a picture of the likely end product. However, it should be noted that the scheme will not introduce any new basis of liability; that it will be capped, probably at £20,000; that it will not prevent persons with claims below the limit following the litigation route; and that it will provide for legal advice for claimants on the reasonableness of any offer made by the scheme but there will be no provision for ongoing legal advice for claimants involved in the scheme. It is likely that the legal aid currently available for clinical negligence cases will be restricted in cases which potentially fall within the scheme (it may disappear even for litigated cases – see no 7 above). There are no other current proposals and I would be very surprised if any appeared in the foreseeable future in view of the likely financial position of public services. The following propositions are truisms. (1) Medical litigation tends to be more expensive in terms of legal

80 Available at <http://www.justice.gov.uk/civil/procrules_fin/menus/protocol.htm>.

costs than other types of accident claim. (2) As with all litigation the proportion of legal costs relative to the recovery tends to be higher in smaller claims. (3) It tends to produce a higher number of 'catastrophe' cases with very high awards of damages. (4) Medical 'no fault' schemes are not a panacea since in their nature they must be limited to 'mishap' and require investigation of causation. (5) Nevertheless they are likely to produce more claims which have to be paid for and this is unlikely to be covered by the saving on legal costs.

Cases

One preliminary point. The dates in the cases are sometimes rather a long time ago. This is no doubt because they are the dates of the actual cases used so I will act on the assumption that no discussion of the law on limitation (prescription) of claims is required. 57

Case 1

From a 'structural' point of view this is perhaps a not very likely scenario in England since private maternity services are very limited outside London,[81] though some major public hospitals have 'private wings' – in effect by this means the patient obtains superior accommodation and a private consultant (though he/she will spend the great majority of practice time on NHS work). I also doubt if you would find gynaecologists practising as partners. However, I imagine that this is the standard pattern in some European countries and I doubt if the question really turns on such structural matters. I proceed therefore on the principal hypothesis that this is a 'standard' English case where the mother is receiving NHS treatment. 58

Obviously it is difficult to answer these questions without the detailed expert reports which would figure in such cases but there does not seem much difficulty in concluding that there was fault of both D and A in the failure to take prompt action on the CTG scan. The real problem lies with proof of causation of loss (see the paragraph, 'It cannot be ascertained whether …'). As has been explained above, although English law does not require 'certainty' of proof, it does require proof on a balance of probabil- 59

81 Obstetrics/gynaecology is a 'high risk' area in litigation terms and private hospitals rarely have the facilities for full scale emergency response.

ities. The case bears some resemblance to *Wilsher v Essex Area Health Authority*[82] mentioned in no 26, above. If we take the facts stated literally, then Y's claim either fails altogether or fails except insofar as the negligence exacerbated an already existing condition (though splitting that up in terms of damages might be little more than guess work). I imagine that in Germany this would be a case where the burden of proof would be eased because of 'gross treatment errors' but there is no such principle in English law. Note, however, that on such a question of fact much lies within the province of the trial judge, especially where – as is quite likely – there is a conflict of expert opinion on the likely cause of the loss. In *Wilsher* the trial judge went wrong by taking the line that if the negligence increased the risk, the burden of proof on causation was reversed, but it is expressly stated in the House of Lords that if he had directed himself correctly and found the expert evidence for the claimant more convincing, a decision in the claimant's favour would have been 'unassailable'. Hence, the result was an order for a new trial.

60 The point has been made in no 29 above that the orthodox view is that if the action of the defendants probably made a material contribution to the claimant's damage, they are liable for the whole loss even if some natural cause operated concurrently. No doubt the case would be different if the natural cause would inevitably have caused a certain degree of damage no matter what the nature of the medical intervention but my reading of the facts is that this is not the case here.

61 In order to deal with the other points it is necessary to assume that causation has been proved. Y's damages for non-pecuniary loss would be likely to be in excess of £200,000. Y's claim would also cover the reasonable commercial cost of nursing care, which in this respect would be very likely to be ordered on a periodical payment basis indexed with reference to that cost rather than the general retail price index.[83] The claimant is undoubtedly entitled to privately funded care even if state provision is available so 'reasonableness' must be assessed from that starting assumption. It is extremely unlikely that the claimant would be denied the extra cost of home care as opposed to (private) residential care unless there was a huge disparity between the figures in view of the mother's natural wish to look after the child at home. In principle, Y is also entitled to damages for future loss of earnings, though in such a case the amount can hardly be more than an educated guess. The great majority of cases are settled

---

82 [1988] AC 1074.
83 *Thompstone v Tameside and Glossop NHS Trust* [2008] EWCA Civ 5, [2008] 1 WLR 2207.

without trial and of course settlement figures are arrived at in the light of the parties' expectations of what the court might award[84] (though they can be skewed by discounts for 'litigation risk'). Every case is unique but let me give one example of cerebral palsy and epilepsy caused by failure to act on a CTG trace, life expectancy 41, where a total settlement of £4,000,000 (including £206,000 for pain, suffering and loss of amenity) appears to have been on a lump sum basis,[85] the elements of which are given by the claimant's solicitors on the following basis.

Pre-settlement pecuniary losses: Past care £108,000; Expenses £23,500; Housing costs £18,101; Interest £52,394.

Future pecuniary losses: Future care: £2,285,000; Equipment and technology £159,650; Transport £120,000; Housing £400,000; Speech therapy £19,496; Physiotherapy £20,824; Occupational therapy £11,532; Loss of earnings £275,000; Holiday costs £43,599; Case management fees £118,466; Court of Protection fees £124,641; Miscellaneous expenses £13,797.

X has no claim for damages in her own right in respect of the services she provides for Y but the value of those services is part of Y's claim, the damages then being held on trust for X: *Hunt v Severs*.[86] There is no hard and fast rule for the amount recoverable under this head. If the carer relative gives up employment, the loss of earnings would be recoverable if they did not exceed the commercial rate for those services. Where employment is not given up the amount is likely to be less than the commercial rate but should be sufficient to give proper recompense to the carer. **62**

The estate of the stillborn child has no claim because, while a duty of care is owed to the unborn child under the Congenital Disabilities (Civil Liability) Act 1976, this only applies where the child is born alive. However, X is of course also owed a duty of care. Damages have been awarded to mothers, independently of illness, for the loss of the child in such circumstances.[87] However, I can see no clear basis on which X could recover damages for the 'contemplation' of Y's distressing condition. It is true that if a person suffers a recognised psychiatric illness from witnessing the injury of a near relative by the negligence of the defendant he may **63**

---

84 And in the case of children must be approved by the court.

85 *TP v Gwent Healthcare NHS Trust*, 30 April 2007.

86 [1994] 2 AC 350. In fact Y's litigation is conducted by her 'litigation friend', who is likely to be one or both parents.

87 See eg *Bagley v North Herts Health Authority* (1986) 136 New Law Journal (NLJ) 1014.

recover damages in respect of that condition.[88] But, quite apart from the absence of any evidence that X's condition passes the 'psychiatric illness' threshold, that liability is essentially directed at sudden events, hard as that concept may be to define. This seems much more like the situation of a person who succumbs over a period of time to the strain of caring for an accident victim, and I think in that situation any English lawyer would say that there was no liability.

Case 2

64 It is likely that treatment of this type would be carried out privately in England and I propose to treat the case on that basis. However, as has been explained in no 40 above, the duty of the doctor is essentially the same whether the case is framed as contract or tort and it is inconceivable that this would be a situation where there would be an implied warranty of success. The problem here of course is the failure of a device. If the evidence is that this was probably fitted incorrectly (eg if failure of correctly fitted devices is unknown), then that no doubt would be negligence. However, that seems rather unlikely and leads to the conclusion that the claim fails anyway for lack of proof of breach of duty. Of course it is possible to argue that this is a 'mixed' contract with elements of both services and the supply of goods and in such a contract the supply of goods element generally follows the sale pattern, ie there is strict liability if the goods are not fit for their purpose and fault is irrelevant.[89] The relevance of sale of goods law to matters like medicines has not been much explored, probably because most are supplied on prescription under the NHS and that is not a contract. However, I would be very dubious about the success of this line of argument in this situation. There seems no reason why the implant should not be a 'product' within the Product Liability Directive[90] (for England see Part I of the Consumer Protection Act 1987), bringing in its manufacturer but there is no evidence that this particular item is defective (a point also relevant in seeking to pursue the doctor under quasi-sales law).

65 So there are formidable difficulties in establishing liability. As before we need to pursue the issue of damages on the basis that it can be established.

88 *Alcock v Chief Constable South Yorkshire* [1992] 1 AC 310.

89 See the Supply of Goods and Services Act 1982.

90 Blood is assumed to be: *A v National Blood Authority* [2001] 3 All ER 289.

In *McFarlane v Tayside Health Board*[91] (a failed sterilisation case) the House of Lords held, reversing nearly twenty years of case law, that damages could not be claimed in respect of the cost of the upbringing of a healthy,[92] unwanted child. The reasons were various: to award damages representing the cost of upbringing was disproportionate to the wrong committed (negligent advice to the father that his vasectomy had been successful); it would fail to take account of the real (though incalculable) countervailing benefits brought to the family by the birth of a healthy child, benefits which were still present even if the parents' intention had been to have no more children; and it would offend against the idea of distributive justice, which in suitable cases had a role to play in the mosaic of tort law alongside the more usual corrective justice. This cannot be sidestepped by basing the claim on the mother's loss of earnings in having to look after the child, for that would be the cost of upbringing under another name.[93] What may be recovered are (a) the pain, suffering and inconvenience of pregnancy and birth and for the loss of earnings and expenses immediately attendant on those processes and (b) a 'conventional' sum of £15,000 representing recognition that the mother in such a situation has suffered a legal wrong and an interference with her autonomy in being deprived of the freedom to limit her family as she wished.[94]

Case 3

Again I proceed on the far more likely assumption in a maternity case that the treatment is on the NHS. I realise of course that this puts a rather different light on what might be a live issue in the German context, namely comparative responsibility between A and C and contribution between them, since here all the damages will be paid by one, unitary source. However, it seems unrealistic to create a fantasy scenario. I shall deal with the matter briefly at the end. **66**

On the basis of my (lay) assessment of the facts, there seems to be clear negligence on the part of A, of B and of C. The question of whether E is **67**

91 [2000] 2 AC 59.

92 Though the matter is not beyond doubt, the present law is that where the child is born with a disability the parent may recover the extra costs of upbringing associated with the disability: *Parkinson v St James Hospital Trust* [2001] EWCA Civ 530, [2002] QB 266. Another view is that such costs may only be recovered where the purpose of the intervention is to avoid the known risk of a disabled child on the particular facts.

93 *Greenfield v Flather* [2001] EWCA Civ 113, [2001] 1 WLR 179.

94 *Rees v Darlington Memorial Hospital NHS Trust* [2003] UKHL 52, [2004] 1 AC 309.

personally at fault is really academic. Inexperience as such is not an excuse and the position of junior staff has been set out above in no 18. However, the issue is academic because (a) any damages due from E would be paid under the NHS indemnity scheme and (b) there also appear to be serious 'system' deficiencies in C's set up.

68 Although this is not dealt with specifically in the facts, I am proceeding on the assumption that if correct steps had been taken X would not, on a balance of probabilities, have suffered this disability.

69 I find a certain degree of ambiguity in the penultimate paragraph of the facts. On the one hand, it is said that it is not possible to establish whether any injury to X had occurred before arrival at C's clinic. However, later it is said that 'it can be assumed with a very high degree of probability that the organic damage was sustained in the C clinic'. I read the latter as amply complying with the English standard of proof on a balance of probabilities and as being enough to make C liable for the whole of the damage to X. Technically, the individual NHS Trust remains the legal defendant to a claim but in practice clinical negligence litigation is handled by the National Health Service Litigation Authority with recovery from individual trusts via their contributions to the scheme (of which the claims record is only one element). Since the claimant is assured of payment of damages awarded, there is no incentive for him to sue everyone in sight and it seems unlikely that the NHSLA would seek to involve the A trust (assuming that to be different) or the primary care trust employing B. Under the common law, if C had to pay in full it would be open to C to seek contribution from A and B's employers (this does not affect C's liability in full to X) but under the rules of the NHSLA (Rule 8.3) that body may apportion responsibility 'in whatever manner it may decide'.

70 X is therefore entitled to nursing and associated costs as outlined in no 46 above. As has been explained in no 47 above, the assessment of lost earnings in such cases is largely speculative but there are precedents for basing them on the average net wage if all else fails,[95] and I would guess that may be the basis of the claim here. There are, however, cases in which higher figures have been used where there has been evidence of prospects

95 See eg *Croke v Wiseman* [1982] 1 WLR. 71.

based on family circumstances.[96] Since more than one disability is involved it is hard to be categorical about the amount for non-pecuniary loss but the figure could well be close to £200,000.

Reverting to what was said in no 69 above, *if* this were a case involving only the private sector, it would bring in the normal principles of contribution between solidary tortfeasors. On the basis that all the damage occurred after admission to C's clinic, the liability of A and B is not necessarily excluded unless the further negligence of C breaks the chain of causation, but I think that unlikely. On that basis, C would be able to seek a contribution from A and B but I would not like to hazard a guess on the amount. I repeat that this would be a purely internal matter among the tortfeasors and does not affect X. **71**

Case 4

The duty of the doctor to explain the risks associated with the proposed procedure has been outlined at no 42 above. The issue here seems to resolve itself not so much into an issue of what ought to have been said as one of whether it was in fact said and how. If the risk has to be disclosed, the doctor must do so in a manner which is adequate, in the circumstances as they appear to him, to 'register' with the individual patient and while the consent form, with its declaration that the risks have been explained is some evidence that they have been, it is not conclusive. On the face of it (although one would wish to know something about the general state of professional opinion and practice on the matter), the risks of death and paralysis should have been explained and on the facts given it seems inevitable that a court would conclude that they were not. It seems to be accepted that no interpreter was present at the time and while it is said to be uncertain whether a dictionary was used, it is hard to see how even with a dictionary a person with no knowledge of Persian could convey the state of the weather, let alone the risks of surgery. One might also point out that **72**

96 *Taylor v Glass*, 23 May 1979; *Cassell v Riverside HA* [1992] PIQR Q1. I assume that the claimant's life expectancy has not been reduced. Where it has been there is a problem. A person whose life expectancy has been reduced may recover damages for earnings during the 'lost years' with a deduction for his living expenses during those years: *Pickett v British Rail Engineering* [1980] AC 136. This is sometimes necessary to provide for dependants since they cannot bring a claim under the Fatal Accidents Act before death. However, in *Croke v Wiseman* [1982] 1 WLR 71 the CA rejected such a lost years claim in the case of a young child. This is inconsistent with *Pickett* but under the current doctrine of precedent is binding on courts below the HL: *Whipps Cross University NHS Trust v Iqbal* [2007] EWCA Civ 1190, [2008] PIQR P9.

even if there were a difference of professional opinion on what should be disclosed, B can hardly attach himself to the 'non-disclosure' camp since his story is that he *did* disclose.

73 If, one way or the other, there is a breach of the doctor's duty, then the claimant must show on a balance of probabilities that he would not have gone ahead. On the facts stated he appears able to do this on the required balance of probabilities.

74 All of the matters adverted to in the claim for damages are in principle recoverable: nursing care, need for special equipment and so on, provided they are or will be reasonably incurred. The patient's previous condition, which would of course have continued without surgery, does not seem to have been of sufficient severity to call for such requirements.

75 Perhaps the previous condition might call for some reduction of the non-pecuniary loss damages but not, I would have thought, a very great one – confinement to a wheelchair and loss of bladder/bowel function seem to me of a different order from sometimes having to use crutches, especially bearing in mind the psychological impact.

Case 5

76 Once again we have not so much a legal as a factual issue. What happened? Was sufficient attention paid to the risk of damage by compression? Coming from a different legal culture I find the statement 'it cannot be established *whether* the anaesthetist C monitored the proper positioning of the arm' a rather unnatural one. If this case went to trial in England (still predominantly an oral process involving examination and cross-examination of witnesses), I think it is unlikely that the judge would put his conclusion this way. He would say, 'the claimant has not established that there was inadequate monitoring' or that he 'has established that there was inadequate monitoring' – in either case, I emphasise, on a balance of probabilities. He is unlikely to say, 'I do not know'. What the anaesthetist says under cross-examination and his demeanour is obviously going to have a major impact on that conclusion. So the short answer is that I cannot say without knowing much more. It is tempting – though I am now straying beyond my competence into medical matters – to suggest that it is a possible case for the application of the *res ipsa loquitur* idea. If the injury can only have been caused by prolonged compression that suggests that the responsible person failed to monitor adequately. The anaesthetist's comparative inexperience is not an excuse (though it is equally not any evidence that he was at fault).

There may be a point of general significance here. On paper at least **77**
German law insists on a level of proof higher than the English balance of probabilities but it is quite ready to formally reverse the burden of proof on a number of grounds. English law is unwilling to reverse the burden of proof but is quite ready to regard things as proved by inference to its standard. It may well be that German law overall is more generous to claimants in clinical negligence cases but the difference in practice may not be so great as it superficially appears.

As to the damages, first a claimant must act reasonably to mitigate his loss, **78**
that is to say he may not recover for loss which he could have avoided by taking reasonable steps. This is essentially a question of fact so one cannot be categorical but on the basis that continuing to work as a bricklayer is impracticable I would judge that the failure to seek alternative employment is unreasonable. 'Illegality' is often a difficult and obscure area in tort as well as in contract.[97] I am not entirely sure what is intended by the reference to 'moonlighting' at the weekend. Does it mean that there is a breach of his contract of employment, which requires him to give his whole working time to his employer? Or is it an infringement of the law, something on the lines of the 'Working Time' Directive? Alternatively, it is possible that he may have committed some criminal offence involving deception in concealing the position from his employers. If the matter is merely a breach of contract I am sure it would not attract any sanction in his tort claim. If there is active deception of his employers in concealing the matter, there is some resemblance to *Hewison v Meridian Shipping Services Pte Ltd*,[98] where the claimant had actively concealed his epilepsy (which made it illegal for him to work as a merchant seaman) from his employers and was denied damages for future loss of earnings in respect of an accident caused by his employers: that part of his claim involved an assertion by him that he would have earned the wages by continuing to commit an illegal act. That of course, is not *necessarily* the same as our case since the tort defendant and the deceived provider of the wages were one

97 For a full consideration by the HL in the very different context of an accident victim committing a crime as a result of his injuries which led to his imprisonment see *Gray v Thames Trains Ltd* [2009] UKHL 33, [2009] 3 WLR 167. See also Law Commission Consultation Paper 160, The Illegality Defence in Tort (2001) and further Consultative Report 189 (2008).

98 [2002] EWCA Civ 1821, [2003] Industrial Cases Reports (ICR) 766.

and the same.[99] Putting aside cases of criminal deception, there are plainly cases where a person may not recover damages for loss which is related to criminal activity: it hardly needs saying that a burglar injured in a road accident may not recover the lost income earned in his profession.[100] On the other hand, in *Le Bagge v Buses Ltd*[101] the New Zealand court held that a milkman was not prevented from recovering earnings attributable to days when he was contravening legislation on drivers' rest hours and the court in *Hewison* seems to have regarded it as correct on the basis that the illegality involved was 'collateral or insignificant'. The injury assessment is a matter of costs (payable by the losing party) rather than of damages. As far as I know there is no equivalent of the medical commission referred to, so the question would simply be whether the cost was reasonably incurred in the investigation and preparation of the claim.

Case 6

79 Again this is essentially a question of fact rather than of law. On the main hypothesis it seems to me that the essential question is the effectiveness of proper hygiene procedures.[102] If they would probably (not certainly) have been sufficient to prevent infection, the claimant should win and it would not matter whether or not E's infection was recognizable: after all, non-staff members attend the clinic and it would be unrealistic to suggest that they should be examined for infection before being allowed in. If, on the other hand, the evidence is that the infection could just as well have been transmitted by airborne means from a sneeze, then the question of whether the clinic should have been aware of the hazard presented by E becomes of significance. I might add that the dates make it seem unlikely that the clinic would have been on notice of any particular hazard from the earlier infection of other patients.

80 On the basis that liability is established, the claimant is clearly entitled to damages for lost earnings and non-pecuniary loss (insufficient informa-

---

99 Cases where the defendant simply fails to declare income to the tax authorities can be dealt with by awarding the net amount of the earnings as damages: *Duller v South East Lincs Engineers* [1981] Current Law Yearbook (CLY) 577.

100 *Burns v Edman* [1970] 2 QB 541 (claim by widow of deceased burglar; same result).

101 [1958] New Zealand Law Reports (NZLR) 630.

102 I do not think it is feasible on the facts given about the service providers here to say very much about the precise position of individual participants. A specialised clinic of this nature, if not run by the NHS, would be likely to be private. A and B (and/or the clinic itself if incorporated) would be responsible for the hygiene deficiencies and the fault of any staff engaged by them.

tion is given to hazard even a ball-park figure). Domestic expenses are also recoverable if reasonably necessary and the claimant may recover the 'value' of services provided to that end even if they are provided free of charge by a family member (see no 62, above).

Variation 1

If my reasoning on the main hypothesis is correct this makes no differ- **81**
ence: if the infection would probably have been prevented by correct hygiene procedures, the claimant establishes liability. If there is any substance in my airborne transmission theory, the matter may become more difficult. One might contend that the claimant was exposed to the same agent from a number of sources, it is not possible to determine which harmed him and it is therefore a *Fairchild* case (see no 27 above). However, I have some difficulty with this since it is not explained on what basis the conclusion that the infection *might* have come from another patient or a person accompanying the claimant is arrived at. If the defendant is at fault in not knowing about E's condition it seems odd to say that he can improve his position by speculating that the source might have been someone else.

Variation 2

This obviously closes off any argument based on 'system failure' at the **82**
clinic and brings the airborne transmission theory to the fore. I am afraid I do not have the medical knowledge to say more.

Medical Liability in France

Suzanne Carval/Ruth Sefton-Green

General Questions

A. The Health Care System Framework

I. General Introduction

1. The health care system in overview

The French health care system can be described with the help of certain figures published by the INSEE.[1] The most recent complete figures date from 2007.[2] 1

1) The medical profession. There are 208,191 doctors, of whom 122,103 are self-employed and 86,088 are in employment. Amongst these there are 101,549 general practitioners and 106,642 consultants. There are 41,444 dental surgeons, 17,483 midwives and 70,498 pharmacists. There are 483,380 nurses and approximately 140,000 other medical auxiliaries (physiotherapists, speech therapists, occupational therapists etc).
2) Health care establishments with a capacity for hospitalisation. There are 972 public establishments, with a total of 316,551 places and 1,800 private establishments, with 174,925 places. This makes a total (public/private) of 2,772 establishments and 491,476 places.
3) The costs of health care are financed for the most part by Social Security (76.6 %). The remaining expenses are distributed as follows: national and municipal authorities (1.4 %), mutual insurance companies (7.9 %), insurance companies (3.2 %), other insurance societies (2.5 %) and households (8.5 %).

1 Institut national de la statistique et des études économiques.
2 Drees, comptes de la santé.

II. Social Welfare Provision

2. The role of public health care

2 As the above figures indicate, the State's investment in health care is substantial. The public hospital sector is considerable and has the most specialised research teams and the most sophisticated (and therefore expensive) equipment.

3 The private sector (self-employed doctors and private hospitals) benefits substantially from public funds since a large proportion of costs paid for by patients is provided by the State (either by an initial contribution, the system of third-party payer, or by reimbursement to patients). Since 2006, a part of the doctors' insurance premiums is paid by Social Security.

3. Differences in treating patient's claims

4 The alternative dispute resolution procedures (conciliation, mediation) set up by the Law of 4 March 2002 concern accidents both in the private and public sector.

4. Right of recourse

5 The right of recourse for paying organisations is the subject of general legislative provisions (arts 28–32 of Law no°85-677 of 5 July 1985). There are no specific rules when the cause of the damage is a medical accident. However, third party payers do not have recourse when the victim of a medical accident without fault is indemnified by the ONIAM (*Office national d'indemnisation des accidents médicaux, des affections iatrogènes et des infections nosocomiales*, infra, no°27). Rights of recourse are exercised whenever possible.

III. Private Insurance

5. The role of private health insurance

6 See no 4.

6. Liability insurance

Insurance against civil liability has become obligatory by the Law of 4 March 2002 (CSP art L 1142-2). The obligation to insure concerns not only members of the medical profession and health care establishments but also manufacturers and sellers of medical and health care products. 7

If the person held liable is not insured or if the threshold level has been reached so the guarantee no longer applies, the ONIAM substitutes the liability insurer (art L 1142-15). In order to help practitioners pay their insurance premiums, which have become very expensive, the Decree n°2006-909 of 21 July 2006 provides that a part of the annual contribution of a self-employed practitioner will be paid by the *Caisse primaire d'assurance maladie* (Social Security). 8

The medical insurance market is dominated by four major organisations: the Société hospitalière d'assurance mutuelle (SHAM), the Sou Médical (MACSF), the insurance broker Branchet which distributes MIC Ltd products and the insurance broker Marsh that is the distributor of Hannover Re products. The market is worth about € 400 million. 9

IV. Professional Standards

7. Applicable professional standards

Since the *Mercier* case in 1936,[3] the *Cour de cassation* has held that a doctor must give a patient 'conscientious, attentive care in conformity with the current medical professional standards'. 10

The level of professional standards required are fixed by law (eg the duty to inform has been defined in legislation, see infra no 28), by codes of ethical conduct (although this is controversial, case-law often refers to the provisions of these codes to define a civil fault[4]) and by the medical profession itself (medical treatises, articles published in recognised jour- 11

3 Cass Civ, 20 May 1936, D 1936, p 88.

4 Cass 1st Civ 27 May 1998, no 96-19161, BC I, n° 187: 'Manque à l'obligation qu'impose au praticien l'article 18 du Code de déontologie médicale, issu du décret du 28 juin 1979, de ne pas faire courir au patient un risque injustifié et de refuser ses demandes qui l'exposeraient, sans justification thérapeutique, à un danger, le médecin gynécologue qui, malgré des contre-indications tenant à l'âge et aux antécédents de sa patiente, procède à une induction ovarienne, puis au déclenchement prématuré de l'accouchement, sans justification thérapeutique et dans des conditions obstétricales peu favorables'.

nals, publications of medical congresses, conferences by consensus). With respect to this latter source, of course the major difficulty consists in identifying a medical consensus or, in the cases where no such consensus exists, in verifying if a course of treatment used by the defendant is recognised by the medical profession.

8. Quality and/or risk management systems

12 Nowadays, public authorities implement a policy of evaluating medical practice and the management of health care costs, which results in a sort of '*normalisation technique*'. The *Haute Autorité de Santé* (HAS) has issued professional recommendations, for instance, for the use of practising members of the health care profession which describe the most appropriate treatment for a given patient, taking into account both the actual state of knowledge and medical practice.

13 It also attempts to improve the quality of treatment in health care establishments and medical care in general practices. In this respect it certifies health care establishments, approves doctors and medical teams and evaluates professional practice.

B. Tort Liability

9. Principles of tort liability

14 Medical negligence was the subject of legislative reform in the Law of 4 March 2002.[5] This law created a liability of an undefined nature, contractual or tortious, which applies to all members of the medical profession (physical persons or hospitals), including public sector hospitals. The rules are uniform and a single limitation period applies to actions: ten years running from the date at which the damage is consolidated (CSP L 1142-28).

15 The law provides that, in principle, medical negligence is only incurred in case of fault (art L 1142-1 I) but it nevertheless reserves two cases of liability without fault. The first is incurred by reason of a 'defect in a medical and health care product' (the consequence, no doubt, of the law

5 The so-called Loi Kouchner, from the name of the then Health Minister, Mr Bernard Kouchner. The law was completed by a Loi About of 31 December 2002. These two Acts have been codified into the Code of Public Health (Code de la santé publique).

transposing Directive 85/374/EEC of 25 July 1985, art 1386-1 ff of the Civil Code, C civ) and the second is incurred with respect to liability for hospital-acquired infections.

The latter liability, provided for by art L 1142-1, I, al 2 CSP, applies to the respective establishments and not to the doctors, contrary to what the *Cour de cassation* held previously. The patient must prove that the infection was acquired at the hospital; the defendant can only exonerate himself of responsibility by adducing evidence of a case of *force majeure* (an extremely limited defence). **16**

10. Burden of proof

The victim has the burden of proving the elements of liability: the fault, the damage and the chain of causation in the case of fault-based liability; the infection and the fact that it was acquired at the hospital if liability is based on strict liability. **17**

11. Uncertain causation

The ordinary rules of evidence apply. Causation can be proved by presumptions as long as they are serious, precise and concordant (art 1353 C civ). One can infer that causation does not need to be absolutely certain but it does, at least, have to be highly probable. **18**

12. Loss of a chance.

Case-law very often has recourse to loss of a chance. For example, it uses this doctrine to censure a breach of the duty to inform in relation to the risks of the envisaged treatment. It also applies when a doctor has negligently been late in giving the right diagnosis and the court expert can only testify as to the probabilities in response to the judge's questions as to whether an earlier diagnosis would have enabled the patient to be cured. In these two cases, it is deemed that the fault has deprived the patient either of a chance not to take the risk that was involved or of a chance of being cured by earlier treatment. The quantification of damages is effectuated on a 'mathematical' basis. The judge quantifies the chance lost by means of a percentage (eg 60 %), then he calculates the amount of **19** the victim's total personal injury (eg, € 100,000) and then he applies the percentage to this figure (60 % of 100,000 = € 60,000).

13. Multiple persons involved

20 In this case, the usual solution of joint and several liability is applied.

14. Strict liability

21 See infra nos 25 and 26.

C. Contractual Liability

15. Basics of contracts in the health care sector

22 Before the Law of 4 March 2002 was adopted, the *Cour de cassation* had constructed a doctrine of liability for medical negligence based on a contractual model. This had enabled them to set up a principle of fault-based liability (*obligation de moyens*) and then, in the 1990s, to add to the medical contract various obligations to achieve a certain result (*obligations de résultat*), giving rise to strict liability. The legislator put a stop to this evolution because it increased the tortfeasors' liability as well as having repercussions for medical insurance. The law set up a uniform system and whether liability is contractual or tortious is not an issue.

16. Differences from tort law

23 See no 14 ff.

17. Contractual claims in the absence of direct contracts?

24 See no 14 ff.

18. Informed consent

Before the Law of 4 March 2002 was enacted, the *Cour de cassation* and the *Conseil d'État* imposed a heavy duty to inform on doctors which even included a duty to inform of exceptional risks insofar as these were serious (Cass 1st Civ, 7 October 1998, Bull Civ I, no 87). According to article L 1111-2 CSP: **25**

> 'Every person has the right to be informed about his state of health. This information relates to different investigations, treatment or preventive action which is proposed, its utility, possible urgency, the consequences, the frequent or serious risks that are normally foreseeable as well as the other possible solutions and the foreseeable consequences in the event of refusal. Whenever new risks are identified, after the investigations, treatment or preventive actions have been carried out, the patient must be informed, except when it is impossible.
>
> The duty to inform applies to every member of the medical profession within the limit of his competence and according to applicable professional rules. Only an emergency or the impossibility of informing the patient can excuse from such duty.
>
> (...) In the event of litigation, it is up to the member of the medical profession or the health care establishment to adduce the evidence that the information was provided to the person concerned under the conditions set out in the present article. This evidence can be adduced in any manner.'

D. Public Liability

19. Key differences from cases involving private hospitals or doctors

As indicated above, the Law of 4 March 2002 unified the rules of liability for medical negligence. There are therefore no longer any specific solutions for the public sector. In contrast, the law has not modified the jurisdiction of the courts: actions can still be commenced before the administrative and judicial courts depending on whether the defendant is categorised as a person under public or private law. **26**

E. Alternative Compensation Regimes

20. Funds and/or other alternative compensation regimes

27 The Law of 4 March 2002 set up an organisation called the '*Office national d'indemnisation des accidents médicaux, des affections iatrogènes et des infections nosocomiales*' (usually called by its acronym, ONIAM). This public organisation is financed by the so-called '*dotation globale*' (being a generalised funding formula) fixed each year by a law to finance the social security system. It intervenes on behalf of national solidarity for the benefit of victims of medical acts that occurred after 5 September 2001.

28 The ONIAM indemnifies several categories of victims.

29 1) The victims of certain medical accidents and iatrogenic conditions.

According to art L 1142-1 II of the CSP:

> 'When the liability of a professional, an establishment, service or organ mentioned in I or a producer of products is not engaged, a medical accident, iatrogenic condition or hospital-acquired infection gives rise to the right to compensation in the name of national solidarity for harm suffered by the patient, and, in the event of death, his beneficiaries, when such harm is directly attributable to acts of prevention, diagnosis or care and had for the patient consequences that were abnormal having regard to his state of health as well as to the latter's foreseeable development and satisfies a test of gravity, fixed by decree, assessed in the light of the loss of functional capacity and its effects on private and professional life, measured having particular regard to the level of permanent incapacity or the length of the temporary working capacity.
>
> To open the door to compensation for harm in the name of national solidarity, there must be a level of permanent incapacity greater than a specified percentage on a schedule established by decree; this minimum percentage, at the most equal to 25 %, is to be determined by the said decree.'

Medical accidents are accidents that are 'directly imputable to preventive actions, diagnosis or treatment which have abnormal consequences for the patient with respect to his current or prospective state of health.'

They must also have caused a serious harm. This is the case when victims have died or in the following cases: permanent partial incapacity in excess of 25 %; temporary incapacity to work for at least six consecutive months or six non-consecutive months in a twelve month period; a definitive declaration of inaptitude to exercise a former professional activity; the existence of particularly serious difficulties, including those of an economic nature, in his living circumstances (Decree no 2003-314 of 4 April 2003).[6]

It is necessary that no liability is established since intervention of the ONIAM is subsidiary.

2) The victims of certain hospital-acquired infections: 30

(i) those contracted in the medical practice of a physical person provided that the double condition of gravity of harm and absence of fault are satisfied. The condition of gravity is the same as described above (criteria of the decree of 4 April 2003).

(ii) those contracted in health care establishments, with a threshold liability (death/permanent partial incapacity in excess of 25 %).

3) In exceptional cases, the victims of damage resulting from the intervention of a professional or an establishment outside its usual scope of activity. 31

4) Various other victims (victims of harm resulting from growth hormones treatment between 1973 and 1988, victims of damage directly attributable to contamination with HIV following blood transfusions or injections of blood-derived products). 32

---

6 The criterion of gravity was specified by Decree No 2003-314 of 4 April 2003, art 1 of which provides:
The percentage mentioned in the second paragraph of art L 1142-1 II of the Code of Public Health is fixed at 24 %.
A medical accident, iatrogenic condition or hospital-acquired infection also satisfies the test of gravity mentioned in art L 1142-1 II of the Code of Public Health when the duration of temporary incapacity resulting from the medical accident, iatrogenic condition or hospital-acquired infection is at least equivalent to six consecutive months or six non-consecutive months in a period of twelve months.
By way of exception, the test of gravity may be satisfied:
1. When the victim is definitively declared to be unable to pursue the occupation he pursued before the occurrence of the medical accident, iatrogenic condition or hospital-acquired infection;
2. Or when the medical accident, iatrogenic condition or hospital-acquired infection gives rise to particularly serious difficulties, including those of an economic nature, in his living circumstances.

F. Extent of Liability/Remedies

I. Pecuniary Loss

21. Introduction to indemnifying pecuniary loss

33 There is no particular approach so far as losses arising out of medical liability are concerned. The notions and ordinary principles of quantification apply. The principal heads of damage are: medical and other expenses (adapting accommodation, purchases of special vehicles, etc), assistance by a third party, loss of professional income and loss of schooling, university and training expectations.

22. Loss of earnings vs loss of earning capacity

34 The loss of earning capacity is indemnified. Students, for example, can obtain compensation for the loss of a chance to earn a salary corresponding to that expected for the professional qualification.

23. Periodic payments or lump sum?

35 Both are possible.

24. Caps and thresholds

36 None. French law upholds the principle of total indemnification of the damage. The only threshold is that of the gravity required for compensation by the ONIAM but this is in order to reserve public money for the most serious cases.

II. Non-Pecuniary Loss

25. Introduction to indemnifying non-pecuniary loss

37 Different heads of non-pecuniary damages can be distinguished, the main ones being: pain, physiological loss, sexual loss, loss of enjoyment, loss of amenities etc.

26. Who can claim compensation for non-pecuniary loss?

All persons who suffer a loss can make a claim: the primary victim, his family, heirs, even his professional partners in certain cases. The victim's action does not exclude that of other persons who may well have suffered a distinct loss (even if it is just a non-pecuniary loss). **38**

G. Procedural Matters

27. Specific rules of jurisdiction or procedure

None. **39**

28. Special institutions handling negligence claims

Victims now have the choice between litigation in court and a special procedure set up by the Law of 4 March 2002. In the latter case, the claim is filed with a CRCI (*Commission Régionale de Conciliation et d'Indemnisation*). **40**

Depending on the case, the special procedure set up by the Law of 4 March 2002 can be one of conciliation or amiable dispute resolution.

Access to one or other of these procedures depends on the gravity of the victim's damage;

1) If the damage presents the characteristics of gravity specified in the decree of 2003,[7] the victim can benefit from the procedure of amicable dispute resolution. This procedure is the most beneficial for the victim because it is binding on the ONIAM or civil liability insurers.
2) If the damage does not present these characteristics of gravity, the victim can only make a claim for conciliation, which is of a limited interest as it is not binding on civil liability insurers.

Making a claim to the CRCI must occur within a period of ten years from the time when the damage is sustained. This claim suspends the limitation period. **41**

---

7 Supra no 29.

42 The amicable dispute resolution procedure is as follows:

43 The first stage is to make a claim to the CRCI. The formalities are simple: the victim must fill in a form and attach certain documents (medical certificates, etc) enabling the CRCI to appreciate the gravity of the damage and the circumstances in which it occurred.

44 The second stage is the decision of the CRCI about its jurisdiction. It evaluates, in the light of the file, whether the gravity threshold has been reached. If this is not the case, it declares it does not have jurisdiction. If it is the case, the resolution procedure is put into motion: the CRCI designates an expert, or a board of experts, chosen from the national list of experts in case of medical accidents, for the purpose of the expert enquiry. The cost is borne by the ONIAM, which can be reimbursed in the event that someone is held liable.

The CRCI has six months to give an opinion about the circumstances and causes of the harm, the nature and scope of the damage, the rule of applicable compensation (it decides whether there is liability under the law of 2002 or whether the case relates to damage for which there is no liability and which therefore is compensable by the ONIAM).

45 The third stage is when the opinion of the CRCI is transmitted to the interested parties (victim, insurer, ONIAM).

46 The fourth stage is the compensation offer:

1) If the CRCI decides that the professional, or the establishment, is liable: the insurer of the person who is responsible must make a compensation offer to the victim under art L 1142-14.

   The offer must be made within four months after the CRCI has issued its decision. It must relate to an indemnity, which compensates the damage fully (within the limit of the threshold liability, if there is one).

   If the insurer refuses to make an offer (for example, because it contests the CRCI's analysis of the liability of its insurance-holder), the ONIAM will do this in its place and pay out an indemnity if the victim accepts such an offer. However, then the ONIAM is subrogated to the victim's rights against the insurer.

2) If the CRCI considers that the compensation is due from the ONIAM, it must make the offer according to the same conditions as those that apply for the insurer (art L 1142-17).

The amounts proposed by the ONIAM are determined by this organisation, by reference to the table entitled 'references for compensation' (which can be consulted on the ONIAM's web site).

3) If the CRCI considers that the accident was only partially the consequence of an act incurring the liability of a professional or an establishment, it determines the part of the loss attributable to this person and the part of the compensation to be paid by the ONIAM.

The fifth stage is the resolution of the proceedings. **47**

1) If the victim accepts the offer made by the insurer or the ONIAM, the agreement is a valid full and final settlement according to art 2044 C civ. The payment must be made within one month.

2) If the victim refuses the offer, he can opt for judicial adjudication. He then sues the tortfeasor, his insurer and the compensation fund before the court with jurisdiction under art L 1142-20. The opinion of the CRCI is not binding on the judge.

H. Outlook

29. Reform plans

Major reforms took place in the Laws of 4 March 2002 and 31 December 2002. It is highly unlikely that the legislator will intervene in the near future again, except on minor points. **48**

Cases

Case 1

The negligence of D and A is self-evident and does not require discussion. **49**

The most difficult question in this case relates to causation because of the uncertainty relating to Y's prior condition. A further uncertainty arises due to the lack of speed with which the delivery took place. Y may have lost the opportunity not to have suffered such severe handicaps, had X been attended to earlier on. The origin of Y's impairment is undetermined: it is possible that it is due exclusively to the negligence of D and A or due to their negligence combined with her pre-existing condition. Everything will depend on the degree of probability determined by the court expert. Art 1353 C civ requiring a high degree of probability applies. **50**

The test is of 'serious, precise and concordant presumptions' which must convince the judge. The *Cour de cassation* has indicated that this high degree must almost amount to certainty. On the facts, it is unlikely that the court would be convinced with sufficient certainty to hold A and D fully liable. The court will probably consider that causation is a combination of A and D's negligence as well as Y's pre-existing condition. In this case, the court will ask the expert to help it determine the proportion of the impairment, which is due to the pre-existing condition and that which is due to the negligence. A and D will only be liable for this part of the damage. Furthermore, if the expert determines that the likelihood of the impairment being aggravated by A and D's conduct is uncertain, then the court will use the concept of loss of chance to indemnify Y. This means that that the court will only give a percentage of the amount corresponding to the aggravated damage. This hypothesis does not seem to be excluded by the facts, as it is indicated that the CTG was already abnormal when X arrived in the delivery room.

If causation is established, who would be liable?

51 Obviously the doctor A would be liable. If he were a self-employed doctor, as is likely since it seems that he uses the premises of the hospital only for birth deliveries, then he would be personally liable.

52 It would be different if he had a double status, self-employed for his own practice outside the hospital and employed by the district hospital (it is assumed that this belongs to the public health service) for a part of his work on the hospital premises (birth delivery). This would mean he had the status of a public agent (*agent public*). The third possibility is that the hospital is a private hospital and that he has a contract of employment for part of his services. In the two latter hypotheses, he is entitled, as agent of the hospital, to immunity for his civil liability.[8]

53 Doctor B is not liable for the negligence of his associate A. In order to be held liable, it would be necessary to prove that he had committed a personal fault, ie not drawn B's attention to the particular condition of X before going on holiday.

54 It is highly unlikely that the midwife D will be held jointly liable. Either she is a public agent or an employee of the hospital, if it is a private sector hospital, and as such she will also be entitled to immunity for her civil

8 Cass 1st Civ, 12 July 2007, no 06-12624 et 06-13790, BC I, no 270.

liability. It would have been different if she had committed a fault of exceptional gravity, which does not appear to be the case here.

The hospital C, whether a public or private establishment, will be vicariously liable for the negligence committed by the midwife D. 55

If they are held liable, all these tortfeasors will be jointly and severally liable, as well as their insurers against civil liability, since the victim Y has a direct action against them, according to the Insurance Code. 56

Damages

All the harm, both material and non-economic, suffered by Y will be indemnified. The sums paid by the Social Security will be recovered by it from the defendants and their insurers. 57

The harm, both material and non-economic, suffered by X, the mother, will also be fully indemnified. The sums claimed by X for nursing care can be recovered but only insofar as they have not been allocated to Y under this head of damages. 58

Case 2

It is impossible for X to obtain damages. 59

First of all, it is not established that A was negligent (except to prove that he had put in the contraceptive implant negligently). Strict liability cannot be envisaged in this type of situation; there is no question of product liability because the doctor will not have supplied the device. In France patients buy such products directly from the chemist upon production of a doctor's prescription (and are reimbursed). 60

In any event, even if A had been negligent, the claim would fail because case-law has firmly established that the birth of a healthy child does not constitute a reparable harm. This case-law is unanimous since 1982 and 1991 (*Cour de cassation* and *Conseil d'État* respectively). 61

According to the *Cour de cassation*: 'the existence of a child cannot, of itself, constitute a legally reparable damage for the mother, even if the birth occurred after an unsuccessful abortion'. Only evidence of a 'special damage, added to the normal burdens of maternity, is of a nature to allow the mother to claim an indemnity'. 62

In a leading decision, the *Cour de cassation* indicated that the court of appeal was right to reject the claim: 'the decision appealed against notes that the 63 child was in perfect health and that Mlle X could not prove that the birth had been a cause of a moral suffering for her because she had only referred to her probable difficulties in her life and her perspectives for the future'.[9] The decision was particularly harsh because the young woman was in a difficult situation: she was a single mother aged 22, her own mother had died, she never knew her father, she had been under the care of the social services and she had already had an abortion.

64 According to the *Conseil d'État*: 'the birth of a child, even if it comes after an unsuccessful abortion requested by a pregnant woman according to the conditions contained in articles L 162-1 to L 162-6 of the Public Health Code, does not constitute a harm likely to allow the mother to make a claim against the hospital where this operation unsuccessfully took place, unless certain circumstances exist or a particular situation can be invoked by the person concerned'.[10]

Case 3

65 The negligence of the various defendants is self-evident.

66 In the case of the hospital operators A and C, there has been negligence in the organisation of the hospital structure (*faute d'organisation*)[11] which is systematically condemned by case-law.

67 As far as E is concerned, the fact that she is inexperienced is no excuse: an objective standard of negligence is applied.

68 The main problem is one of causation.

---

9 Cass 1st Civ, 25 June 1991, no 89-18617, BC I no 213.

10 *Conseil d'État*, 2 July 1982, No 23141, Publié au recueil Lebon.

11 Cass 1st Civ, 13 November 2008 no 07-15049, BC I no 255 (retard dans la prise en charge d'une femme enceinte): 'en vertu du contrat d'hospitalisation et de soins le liant à son patient, un établissement de santé privé est tenu de lui procurer des soins qualifiés en mettant notamment à son service des médecins pouvant intervenir dans les délais imposés par son état (...) la cour d'appel a constaté que les dispositions du règlement intérieur étaient insuffisamment contraignantes et trop imprécises quant aux horaires, pour que soit garantie aux malades la continuité des soins; ce manque de rigueur dans l'organisation a permis à chacun des deux médecins en cause de considérer qu'il appartenait à l'autre d'intervenir et a conduit à une vacance totale de la permanence pendant une heure et demi au moins'. La cour d'appel a donc 'pu en déduire, sans se contredire, que la clinique avait commis *dans son organisation une faute qui avait contribué au dommage*'. En outre, 'la circonstance que les médecins exercent à titre libéral et engagent leur seule responsabilité au titre du contrat de soins n'était pas de nature à exonérer l'établissement de santé privé de la responsabilité née de cette faute'.

There are two factors of uncertainty: the first is linked to the passage of time and the progressive nature of the hypoglycaemic condition (at the time when the different acts of negligence were committed, had the harm already been suffered?). The second relates to the question of whether, if treatment had been administered earlier on, would this have prevented invalidity from occurring or would it only have reduced the chance of producing such a result (loss of chance). 69

In our view, if the expert cannot determine the first point, all the defendants will be held jointly and severally liable. The award of damages will cover all the damage if it is established that an earlier treatment would have cured the child completely; it will only cover a fraction of the damage if the expert indicates that this treatment would only have created a chance of cure. The fraction will be ascertained as a percentage of the figure decided by the judge, following the indications given by the expert (for example, 30 %, 50 %, 80 %?).[12] 70

If the expert indicates, as the fact-hypotheticals suggest, that the damage was probably caused while the child was being treated at the hospital C, the solution would be the same, since the former omissions had also played a role in the causation (if they had not, then the child would not have suffered as a result of C's negligence). There is no problem of remoteness (of damage). 71

In contrast, if it seems that the child had already suffered irremediable harm by the time he was admitted to the hospital, A, C and E (except if E is immune) would either escape liability (if the harm had been suffered in its entirety before his admission) or would only be liable for the aggravation of his state of health after the admission. A decision of the *Cour de cassation*, on similar facts, indicates that the court of appeal must determine to what extent a tardy decision might have aggravated the damage and attribute the responsibility of the doctor accordingly.[13] 72

Liabilities

The liability of legal persons (hospitals A and C) is incurred when a causal link between the negligence and the damage is established. The liability of 73

12 Example (in this case for a loss of chance of survival, but the rule is the same for the loss of chance to be cured) Cass 1st Civ, 18 July 2000, no 98-20430 BC I no 224: 'Déterminée en fonction de l'état de la victime et de toutes les conséquences qui en découlent pour elle, l'indemnité de réparation de la perte de chance d'obtenir une amélioration de son état ou d'échapper à une infirmité, ne saurait présenter un caractère forfaitaire, mais correspond à une fraction des différents chefs de préjudice supportés par cette victime'.

13 Example, Cass Crim, 21 March 2006, no 05-85595.

the midwife B, and doctor E, depends on their status. If B and E are employees of A and C (or if they are public agents) they will be entitled to immunity from civil liability.

Which damage can be compensated?

74 All damage is compensated including non-economic loss. For the loss of income of very young children, French law does not have a satisfactory rule. For a long time, the judges refused to indemnify such damage on the ground that it was impossible to know what the income of the child would have been. It is thus only young victims already engaged in professional training or higher education (university or secondary professional diplomas) who have been awarded damages for loss of chance to earn income from the relevant profession. Today, there is a consensus about the need to use a method of average income scales. In the absence of legislation on this point, a change is beginning to emerge from the courts. Some judges award sums on the basis of the minimum wage.

Case 4

Negligence: breach of a duty to inform

75 The rules relating to the duty to inform are almost exactly the same before and after the Law of 4 March 2002. It is therefore not necessary to distinguish the two regimes.

76 According to art L 1111-2 CSP:

> 'Every person has the right to be informed about his state of health. This information relates to different investigations, treatment or preventive action which is proposed, its utility, possible urgency, the consequences, the frequent or serious risks that are normally foreseeable as well as the other possible solutions and the foreseeable consequences in the event of refusal. Whenever new risks are identified, after the investigations, treatment or preventive actions have been carried out, the patient must be informed, except when it is impossible.
>
> The duty to inform applies to every member of the medical profession within the limit of his competence and in respect of applicable professional rules. Only an emergency or impossibility to inform the patient can excuse him.
>
> … In the event of litigation, it is up to the member of the medical profession or the health care establishment to adduce the evidence that

the information was provided to the person concerned under the conditions set out in the present article. This evidence can be adduced in any manner.'

The information must be delivered in a comprehensible manner (except in cases of emergency or impossibility). There is no case-law about patients who do not speak French but it is obvious that it is necessary to ask for the services of a translator. Information provided to someone who does not understand it, will be considered not to have been given at all. The burden of proof lies on the doctor to establish that he has fulfilled his duty. **77**

On the facts, there appears to have been a breach of the duty to inform.

The loss

The case-law of the *Cour de cassation* is well established on this question. The patient who has not been informed can never be awarded the sum corresponding to his personal injury (physical harm). The courts have to reason in terms of a loss of chance and ask which decision the patient would have taken, if he had been informed. **78**

If it appears that he would have consented to the operation and thus accepted the related risks, he cannot obtain compensation on this ground. The chance lost is inexistent or too small to be indemnified. Can he claim damages for non-pecuniary loss? The *Cour de cassation* has recently changed its position on this point. In 2007 it had held that no compensation whatsoever could be awarded, and it had quashed a court of appeal decision that had compensated a non-pecuniary loss consisting of not being prepared psychologically for the risk that occurred.[14] This case was heavily criticised as preventing the judge from vindicating the patient's legal right to be informed in such a situation. Fortunately, the *Cour de cassation* has since changed its mind. In June 2010,[15] it held that a patient who has not been informed must be awarded *some* damages even if appears that, duly informed, he would have accepted the operation. The decision does not give any indication as to the amount of the damages to which the patient is then entitled. Some commentators are of the opinion that the amount could – and indeed should – be substantial; but others think that awards will be symbolic, especially where the risk which has not been brought to the patient's attention has not materialised. **79**

14 Cass 1st Civ, 6 December 2007, no 06-19301, BC I, no 380.
15 Cass 1st Civ, 3 June 2010, no 09-13591, BC I, no 128.

80 On the facts, as it appears that the victim would probably have refused the operation, he should only be awarded a sum for loss of chance, for example 50 % or 80 %, a percentage of the sum corresponding to the physical injury which has been suffered as a result of the risk occurring.

81 That said, another problem arises here due to the fact that the health of the victim had already deteriorated. If the principle is that any pre-existing disposition of the victim is not taken into account as diminishing the liability of the tortfeasor, it is subject to the condition that this pre-existing disposition is latent. Once the condition has been revealed, and there is a pre-existing invalidity, only the aggravation of the invalidity can be attributed to the defendant.

82 There is, therefore, a double diminution of damages here: first, the damages will be reduced by setting aside the part corresponding to the pre-existing invalidity. Secondly, a proportion of the remaining sum, representing the loss of a chance, will be granted.

83 The claims raised in this case are all reparable: purchase of wheelchair and conversion costs for wheelchair access, pain and suffering, etc.

84 If the operation were carried after 5 September 2001, the Law of 4 March 2002 would be applicable.

85 This covers medical risk, which means that the victim is entitled to compensation from the ONIAM if the harm is sufficiently serious to satisfy the threshold level and there is no link to the victim's former condition or that the evolution of the harm was unforeseeable.

86 Two hypotheses exist:

- If there is no liability at all (for example, because the court considers that the patient would have had the operation anyway and that the loss of a chance is zero): then it is possible to imagine that the ONIAM will cover the whole of the damage. But it is necessary to check that the threshold level has been exceeded and that the paralysis was not a foreseeable consequence of the victim's illness.
- If there is liability for loss of a chance, then the insurer for civil liability will be held liable to compensate a part and the ONIAM can intervene for the remainder (provided that the above two conditions are satisfied).

Case 5

If it is established – which seems to be the case, that negligence is the origin of the damage and that it was the anaesthetist C's negligence, then she will be held liable (except in the case of the immunity of a public agent or an employee of a private hospital).[16] If C had one of these statuses, then her employer will be vicariously liable for her negligence. 87

It does not seem that the surgeon B was negligent. 88

Could B be vicariously liable for C's fault?

At one time it was frequently the case that the patient had never met the anaesthetist before the operation; in these circumstances the *Cour de cassation* held in 1984 that the surgeon, as head of the medical team, would be vicariously liable for the faults of the members of his team (contractual liability for the act of another person).[17] 89

Today, legislation requires that a pre-anaesthetic consultation takes place with a doctor in this speciality, who is often the same person who administers the anaesthetic during the operation. The existence of a distinct contract between the patient and the anaesthetist means that the reasoning used in the 1984 case does not apply. The surgeon will thus not be vicariously liable for the anaesthetist's negligence and is only liable for his own faults; each person benefits from a functional independence and assumes the obligations inherent to his own speciality.[18] 90

---

16 In a case where a patient was not correctly positioned during the anaesthetic, see Cass Crim, 3 March 1993, no 92-83293, Bull crim no 96: 'le médecin anesthésiste qui a pratiqué une rachianesthésie lors d'une césarienne et n'a pas fait surélever la partie inférieure du corps de la victime dans lequel n'a pas été injecté suffisamment de sérum n'a pas donné au malade des soins conformes aux données acquises de la science'.

17 Cass 1st Civ, 9 October 1984, no 83-12287, BC I no 251: 'Le chirurgien, tenu en vertu de son contrat de faire bénéficier son malade, pour l'ensemble de l'opération, de soins consciencieux et attentifs doit, à supposer qu'il ait laissé à un tiers le soin de compter les champs utilisés, répondre des fautes des personnes qu'il se substitue en dehors du consentement de son patient pour l'accomplissement d'une partie inséparable de son obligation'.

18 Code de la santé publique: Article D. 6124-91: Pour tout patient dont l'état nécessite une anesthésie générale ou loco-régionale, les établissements de santé, y compris les structures de soins alternatives à l'hospitalisation, assurent les garanties suivantes: 1° Une consultation préanesthésique, lorsqu'il s'agit d'une intervention programmée (…). Article D. 6124-92: La consultation préanesthésique mentionnée au 1° de l'article D. 6124-91 a lieu plusieurs jours avant l'intervention. (…) Cette consultation est faite par un médecin anesthésiste-réanimateur. Ses résultats sont consignés dans un document écrit, incluant les résultats des examens complémentaires et des éventuelles consultations spécialisées. Ce document est inséré dans le dossier médical du patient. La consultation préanesthésique ne se substitue pas à la visite préanesthésique qui est effectuée par un médecin anesthésiste-réanimateur dans les heures précédant le moment prévu pour l'intervention.

91 Although this does not correspond to the fact-hypotheticals, it should be pointed out that the *Cour de cassation* does not systematically separate the surgeon's and anaesthetist's specialities, particularly during the waking-up post operative phase. The court considers that the surgeon remains liable for a general duty of care and diligence that obliges him to check that the patient is not left alone, for example.[19]

92 The chief resident D: his conduct will be assessed depending on a number of factors that are not included in the fact-hypotheticals, for example, should he have surveyed C, who was inexperienced, more carefully?

93 The question also arises of whether the quantity of work he needed to do was normal: should the hospital have had more staff? For example, perhaps there should have been two chief residents on duty rather than one. In France, it would all depend on what the law requires or on the rules of good practice.

Illicit employment during the weekend

94 The *Cour de cassation* has taken a stance on this question: it considers that these losses cannot be indemnified.[20]

Refusal to train as a sales person

95 The *Cour de cassation* has recently refused to uphold the equivalent of the English duty to 'mitigate the loss'. The case-law is very clear as far as the consequences of personal injury accidents are concerned; whatever their nature the victim does not have to submit to medical care, nor sell his or

---

19 Cass Ass plén, 30 May 1986, no 85-91432, Bull no 8: 'Si la surveillance postopératoire incombe au médecin anesthésiste pour ce qui concerne sa spécialité, le chirurgien n'en demeure pas moins tenu, à cet égard, d'une obligation générale de prudence et de diligence. Encourt dès lors la cassation l'arrêt, qui décharge un chirurgien de toute responsabilité à la suite de l'accident postopératoire survenu à son malade quelques instants après l'opération, alors que l'infirmière chargée de sa surveillance l'avait laissé seul dans sa chambre, sans rechercher si le chirurgien, en raison des conditions dans lesquelles il avait quitté la clinique, n'aurait pas dû s'assurer que le malade restait sous la surveillance d'une personne qualifiée'.

20 Cass 2nd Civ, 24 January 2002, no 99-16576, Bull civ II, no 5: 'Une victime ne peut obtenir la réparation de la perte de ses rémunérations que si celles-ci sont licites; pour évaluer comme elle l'a fait les pertes de salaire subies par Mlle X… durant la période de son incapacité temporaire totale de travail la cour d'appel a relevé qu'outre les rémunérations justifiées par la production de bulletins de salaires, il résultait d'attestations que Mlle X… percevait aussi des rémunérations non déclarées; en statuant ainsi alors que de telles rémunérations, provenant d'un travail dissimulé, n'ouvrent pas droit à indemnisation, la cour d'appel a violé l'article 1382 du code civil'.

her business at a better price, etc. As far as other situations are concerned, the case-law is not quite so well defined.

Since X's loss has arisen out of a personal injury accident, there is no room for doubt: his economic loss must be compensated, otherwise he will be penalised for his refusal to train as a sales person.[21] **96**

Private medical injuries assessment

The following information found on the website of the ONIAM may provide some kind of a response to the extent that free expertise exists in the framework of the new compensation rules: **97**

> 'The Law of 4 March 2002 installs a special procedure of compensation, given to the CRCI (*Commissions Régionales de Conciliation et d'Indemnisation des accidents médicaux*). This means of dispute resolution is optional. The judicial path can always be chosen for compensation of strict liability medical accidents. Moreover, recourse to the courts remains the only possible path when the legal conditions for the new rules have not been satisfied.

- An alternative dispute resolution procedure does not have the characteristics of judicial proceedings. There are no fees for the proceedings and the medical expertise is free of charge. However, the parties must pay for any travel expenses (of victims and persons or institutions who are involved) including those present at the commissions, as well as postal and photocopying charges.
- Representation by a lawyer is perfectly possible and left to the claimant to decide freely, as for the person from the medical profession or the establishment involved. However, the cost of representation is not covered by the framework rules.
- The claimant, person from the medical profession or the establishment involved can be accompanied throughout by any person of their choice

---

21 Cass 2nd Civ, 19 June 2003 (deux arrêts), BC II no 203: 'L'auteur d'un accident est tenu d'en réparer toutes les conséquences dommageables, et la victime n'est pas tenue de limiter son préjudice dans l'intérêt du responsable (arrêts n°s 1 et 2). Ainsi, une victime, qui exploitait un fonds de boulangerie et qui avait subi, du fait de l'accident, pendant de nombreux mois une incapacité temporaire totale et partielle de travail, puis une incapacité permanente partielle l'empêchant de reprendre son activité de boulangerie, n'était pas tenue de faire exploiter le fonds par un tiers et doit obtenir l'indemnisation de son préjudice résultant de la perte de son fonds (arrêt n° 1). De même, une victime qui demande l'indemnisation de l'aggravation de son préjudice corporel consécutif à l'accident n'a pas l'obligation de se soumettre aux actes médicaux préconisés par ses médecins (arrêt n° 2)'.

other than a lawyer: a consulting doctor, a representative of an association, the person in charge of an establishment, a member of the family or a close friend, etc. Any expenses arising as a result are not covered by the framework rules.'

Case 6

98 The Law of 4 March 2002 is not applicable, so the case falls within general private law rules.

99 The solutions are simple; self-employed doctors and establishments are strictly liable (*obligation de résultat*) for hospital-acquired infections. The rule applies to both private and public sector establishments.[22]

100 It is not necessary to prove a fault, nor even the precise origin of the infection. The only thing that must be established is its nature, ie that the infection was contracted at the defendant's medical practice or establishment. Here, the origin of the infection has been identified (the provenance of the staphylococci coming from the assistant E in the medical practice) so this should not be a problem.

Variation 1

101 It is true that if an infection is not linked to any medical activity it cannot give rise to civil liability, for example when a patient arrives in hospital already carrying an infection. It is also true that the patient must prove the nature of the infection, ie that it was acquired at the hospital. However, to do so, it suffices to establish that the infection was contracted during the course of hospitalisation.[23] Here, it should be considered that X's infection is of this nature since it was during a medical act effectuated by C and D (the injection) that a microbe penetrated into his organism. If this is the case, it does not matter that it came from a person accompanying X.

Variation 2

102 This has no bearing on liability since strict liability is in issue.

103 Note that the solution upheld by the *Cour de cassation* applies to infections of exogenous origin (the infectious agent comes from the hospital, apparatus, staff, etc). As far as endogenous infections are concerned (the agent

---

22 Cass 1st Civ, 29 June 1999, no 97-14254, BC I no 220 et 222.
23 Rapport de la *Cour de cassation* pour l'année 2007, *La Documentation française*, p 234.

was in the patient's organism but had penetrated to a sensitive zone when the operation took place, eg a microbe under the skin which penetrated into the articulation), the *Cour de cassation* applies the same rule,[24] whereas the *Conseil d'État* maintains a regime of fault-based liability.[25]

Who is liable?

The person liable for strict liability is the doctor (unless an employee) who had provided treatment which is the origin of the infection and/or the establishment where such treatment was provided. It will be difficult to know if it is C or D who is the origin of the contamination. **104**

Here, we would tend to be of the opinion that the court would condemn C and D jointly and severally, especially if the contamination came from E who was present at both injections. **105**

Apparently, A and B have not participated in the contaminating treatment and thus will not be held strictly liable as they are not under an *obligation de résultat*. **106**

However, it seems as if various faults could be imputed to them, with regard to the organisation of the medical practice and rules of hygiene. This could give rise to a fault based liability (art 1382 C civ) but it would be necessary to prove a chain of causation with the patient X. Are the negligent omissions relating to hygiene the origin of the transmission of the staphylococci by E (eg not wearing a mask)? **107**

The damage

All the consequences of the infection are reparable. If a medical expert considers that X is really incapable of looking after her household and needs a third party to look after her, she will have the right to an indemnity under this head, regardless of whether it is actually her daughter who looks after her. The case-law on this point is well established.[26] **108**

---

24 Cass 1st Civ, 4 April 2006, no 04-17491, BC I no 191; 14 June 2007, no 06-10812, BC I no 233.

25 CE, 27 11. 2002, no 211370.

26 See for example, Cass 2nd Civ, 16 November 1994, no 93-11177, BC 1994 II no 232 p 133: 'Le montant d'une indemnité allouée au titre de l'assistance d'une tierce personne ne saurait être réduit en cas d'assistance d'un membre de la famille. Encourt par suite la cassation l'arrêt qui, pour fixer l'indemnisation due au titre de l'assistance d'une tierce personne, relève que cette fonction est remplie par la mère de la victime et énonce que les charges sociales patronales ne doivent être versées que sur une justification de leur paiement'.

109 If the Laws of 4 March and 30 December 2002 apply (applicable to medical acts carried out after 5 September 2001), then the situation would be different.

110 The law retains strict liability for health care establishments (art L 1142-1) but as far as infections contracted in an establishment after 1 January 2003 are concerned (date on which the Law of 30 December 2002 came into force), infections that lead to death or an invalidity higher than 25 % are covered by the ONIAM (which can take recourse against the establishment in case of fault).

111 As for self-employed doctors, a proven fault-based liability regime applies. This 'step backwards' is partly counterbalanced by a public system of compensation put into place by the same law. In the framework of the law, if the victim of an infection contracted in a private medical practice dies or suffers from a serious harm (the criteria are laid down in the decree) and no fault was at the origin of the infection, then the victim will be indemnified by the ONIAM.

112 In this case, since physical persons are concerned, it would be necessary to prove the chain of causation between the negligent acts and the harm (which seems possible except under hypothesis 2).

113 If no fault is proven, then X can obtain compensation from the ONIAM, provided that the harm satisfies the conditions of gravity as set out in the decree.

Medical Liability in Germany

Franz Michael Petry

General Questions

A. The Health Care System Framework

I. General Introduction

1. The health care system in overview

In Germany's federal system, there is no single body that has comprehensive legislative competence for the health care system. Instead, power to legislate in this area is distributed between the federal government and the individual states. For the public health service, such powers are largely assigned to the states. The federal government holds concurrent legislative power in accordance with art 72 of the Basic Law (*Grundgesetz,* GG) relative to economic safeguarding of hospital provision and regulation of hospital and nursing charges (art 74 para 1 no 19a GG), for social security legislation (art 74 para 1 no 12 GG), and responsibility for legislation regarding registration systems for medical and other health-related professions. **1**

The health care system in Germany reflects historical developments to a special extent. Many unusual features of the health care system in Germany are based on a conception of statutory health insurance (*gesetzliche Krankenversicherung,* GKV) deriving from the social legislation enacted by Chancellor Otto von Bismarck (1815–1898) and developments following on from it. Just under 90 % of the population in Germany have statutory medical insurance. The statutory insurance system thus exercises a very strong influence on the entire health-care system. Originally initiated as a compulsory insurance system for industrial workers, its nature as an insurance scheme for employees with compulsory membership for certain parts of the population continues to have effects to the present day. For example, the GKV is still financed mainly by premiums deducted from **2** employees' earnings. Compulsory insurance for only one part of the population still exists today. Civil servants, the self-employed, and employees with an income above the income threshold for compulsory insurance (€ 49,450 per annum in 2010) are not included in the GKV.

3 In the league table for health care expenditure in the OECD nations, Germany was in fourth place in 2007, with 10.4 % of the country's GDP being spent on health care.[1]

Autonomy

4 The health-insurance companies and medical organisations entrusted with outpatient medical care (associations of statutory health insurance physicians, *Kassenärztliche Vereinigungen*) have the legal status of self-administered public bodies. This means that they are not directly part of the state administrative system and are therefore not subject to any outside directives. The state only creates the framework for these bodies and exercises supervision.

5 On the basis of legislation in the individual states regarding the medical professions, state medical boards of registration are established as professional representative bodies that also have the legal status of public bodies. Such bodies exist for dentists, veterinary medicine practitioners, pharmacists, and psychotherapists. The relevant boards have compulsory membership for all professionals working in the corresponding discipline.

6 In addition to proceedings in ordinary courts, legislation for the medical professions in the individual states also envisages disciplinary proceedings in cases in which physicians do not fulfill their professional duties. The board councils are therefore able to impose fines on or censure members.[2] Members of medical boards of registration who breach their professional duties are also subject to professional jurisdiction.[3]

7 By contrast, German hospitals are not organised in the form of public bodies.

8 Hospital trusts can voluntarily combine to form state hospital associations, whose task it is to represent the interests of the trusts or individual institutions relative to funding bodies, the state, and the public sphere. State hospital associations are assigned a number of tasks by state hospi-

1 Federal Office of Statistics, status current in August 2009.
2 Eg paras 58 and 58a of Heilberufsgesetz (HeilberG) NRW.
3 See, for example, paras 59 ff of HeilberG NRW.

tal-service legislation, particularly in connection with contractual agreements between hospitals and insurance companies, and negotiations regarding hospital daily rates. They also contribute to the states' hospital planning work.

The German Hospital Association (*Deutsche Krankenhausgesellschaft,* DKG) is an association consisting of the 16 state hospital associations, along with the 12 umbrella organisations for hospital trusts (eg German Caritas, *Diakonisches Werk,* German Red Cross, Federal Association of German Private Hospitals). The DKG represents the interests of hospital trusts at the federal level and carries out statutory duties in the context of the common self-administrative system in health care. These mainly include contributing to common self-administrative systems for physicians and health insurance companies. **9**

The most important organ for joint self-administration in the health care system is the Joint Federal Committee (*Gemeinsamer Bundesausschuss,* G-BA), in which the tasks of joint self-administration have been combined in a single body since 1 January 2004 (§ 91 para 2 SGB V). The G-BA includes representatives of the Association of Statutory Health Insurance Physicians and Association of Statutory Health Insurance Dental Practitioners, the German Hospital Association, the League of Health Insurers umbrella organisation, and three impartial members, including the chair. In addition, nine representatives of patients' organisations, who only have a consultative voice, take part in the G-BA's meetings. **10**

The task of the G-BA is to specify what outpatient or in-patient services are sufficient, suitable, and economical for the purposes of § 12 SGB V. The G-BA is intended to carry out this task by agreeing guidelines specifying what sufficient, suitable, and economical care should consist of for individual areas of health care (eg medical treatment, early detection of diseases, assessment of fitness for work; cf § 92 SGB V). The guidelines agreed by the G-BA have an extremely binding and statutory quality in the GKV and represent 'sublegal standards.' **11**

The G-BA has a particularly important task in accordance with §§ 135, 137c SGB V with regard to the structuring and further development of health care for the population. **12**

New methods of examination and treatment can only be carried out at the expense of the GKV if the G-BA has previously issued a positive recommendation on their diagnostic and therapeutic benefits, as well as their medical necessity and cost-effectiveness. The G-BA thus decides on licensing approval for new procedures used in GKV care. **13**

14 In addition, the G-BA is also intended to check methods of examination and treatment that have been introduced previously, in accordance with the criteria stated above. This means that treatment methods that have been long since introduced can be dropped from GKV care if they prove to be inadequately effective, unnecessary, or uneconomical after checking by the G-BA.

15 Decisions by the G-BA may therefore in individual cases affect the answer to the question of what a standard treatment consists of, at least for members of the statutory health insurance schemes.

16 Other important areas of responsibility for the G-BA include quality assurance and quality management in health-care institutions and the issuing of recommendations on structured treatment programs for chronic diseases (disease management programs, DMPs).

Corporatism

17 The Joint Federal Committee (G-BA) is in a sense the institutional embodiment of two characteristic features of the German health care system – ie, self-administration and corporatism. The control and further development of the health care system have to a large extent been placed under the responsibility of those directly involved by the legislature – hospitals and health care providers – who, represented by their umbrella organisations, have to agree on solutions that are binding on everyone concerned. This model of corporatist control by self-administered bodies ensures on the one hand that the state has extensive influence on the development of the overall system, while on the other it frees the state from tasks involved in direct administration.

Treatment monopoly in the outpatient field

18 During the course of historical development, registered physicians in private practice have succeeded in severely restricting the influence of the health-insurance companies, ensuring in particular that they have a monopoly on outpatient care for the population. The monopoly exercised by the Association of Statutory Health-Insurance Physicians and the associated strict separation between outpatient and in-patient medical care continue to the present day as a characteristic element of the German health care system.

19 Closely connected with the above is the generally low extent to which health care provision is integrated. The outpatient field is dominated by the small-business structure of individual physicians' offices. For a long

period, larger institutions that are better able to meet complex care tasks requiring the collaboration of several medical disciplines and also non-medical health care professions in a coordinated way, hardly developed at all. It is only in recent years that the German parliament has started to make minor changes here. Important terms in this context include 'contracts for integrated care' and 'medical care units' (*medizinische Versorgungszentren*).

In-patient treatment

In 2008, in-patient treatment was provided by 2083 acute care hospitals, 32.2 % of which were public-sector, 37.5 % charitable, and 29.5 % private.[4] In recent years, the proportion of public-sector hospitals has been continuously declining and the proportion of privately-funded hospitals has been correspondingly increasing. **20**

Financial arrangements for the hospitals are regulated by the Hospital Finance Law. Under this law, the states establish hospital plans. The inclusion or non-inclusion of a specific hospital in the plan is decided by the state authorities independently of whether the hospital is public or private. Inclusion in the hospital plan is a prerequisite for the provision of hospital services charged to the public health-insurance companies and for receiving investment support. Various levels of care are provided, with the corresponding difference in standards of service and quality. These care levels also need to be taken into account when a treatment is being assessed in relation to liability law. **21**

II. Social Welfare Provision

2. The role of public health care

As mentioned above, the majority of the population in Germany is insured under statutory health insurance (*Gesetzliche Krankenversicherung*, GKV), the premiums for which are mainly based on the insured individual's income level. In some circumstances, family members are insured jointly on a non-contributory basis. Entitlement to benefits depends on the level of the premiums paid. With a few exceptions, health-insurance premiums are paid for in equal proportions by the employee and the employer. **22**

4 Deutsche Krankenhausgesellschaft, Krankenhausstatistik, status as of 29 January 2010.

23 In addition to payments from the insurance companies, deductible payments and supplementary payments by patients represent a growing proportion of the financing of the health-care system. In addition, a substantial health-care market for 'individual health services' has developed outside of insurance payments.

Payments covered by statutory health-insurance companies

24 The extent of payments covered by the statutory health insurers is established in Book Five of the Social Security Code (*Sozialgesetzbuch,* SGB V) and is limited by the requirement of cost-effectiveness in § 12 para 1 SGB V. According to this, payments must be covered for care that is sufficient, suitable, and economic and does not exceed what is necessary.

25 Under statutory health care insurance, the principle of benefits in kind applies – ie in case of need the member of the GKV receives a benefit in kind (a visit to the doctor, operation, medication, etc). Payment is made by the health-insurance companies to the service provider – eg hospitals, pharmacies, or the Association of Statutory Health Insurance Physicians in the case of services provided by registered physicians in private practice.

26 An individual with statutory health insurance is thus not directly involved in any way in the payment of physicians' or hospitals' bills.

27 When visiting a physician, the patient presents his or her insurance card, which basically arranges everything. Since 2004, a practice fee of € 10 per quarter has had to be paid, but this has nothing to do with the actual doctor's bill. A similar regulation applies in hospitals. Each patient has to pay a supplementary charge per nursing day, but the actual hospital bill is only sent to the health-insurance company.

28 The medical treatment contract between the patient and the physician or hospital is nevertheless still a private-law contract. While the insurance relationship between the patient with statutory insurance and his or her hospital is a public-law or statutory insurance relationship, and the panel physician has a public-law membership relationship with the Association of Statutory Health-Insurance Physicians, neither of these legal relationships has any influence on the legal status of the treatment contract.[5] This arises from § 76 para 4 SGB V, according to which accepting the treatment obliges the persons or institutions named in § 76 para 1 to provide care for the insuree in accordance with the regulations applying under civil contract law.

---

5 Bundesverfassungsgericht (BVerfG) Neue Juristische Wochenschrift (NJW) 2005, 1103.

Public-law treatment relationships, by contrast, only apply to medical activities covered by public legal regulations – such as those carried out by a medical officer of health or medical referee,[6] or medical treatment provided by military physicians.[7] 29

3. Differences in treating patient's claims

As explained above under question 2, independently of the funding body or financing of the system, the contract between the patient and the physician or hospital has a private-law quality. The financing of hospitals also follows legal regulations that are independent of whether the hospital is funded by the state, privately, or by a charitable institution. 30

To this extent, there are no differences in principle that apply in the treatment of personal injury cases. 31

Systems for internal checking and management of damages are mainly found in the health-insurance and nursing insurance companies. In recent years, these have increasingly been establishing departments to support insurance holders in enforcing claims for damages. The right to do so is granted to them under § 66 SGB V. In addition, these departments of course also pursue their own claims of recourse against possible parties causing damage if any costs have accrued to themselves as a result. 32

To clarify these tasks, they use the 'Health-Insurance Companies' Medical Service' (*Medizinischer Dienst der Krankenkassen*, MDK), the responsibilities of which are described in detail in §§ 275 ff SGB V. In addition to the responsibilities described there, § 275 para 4 SGB V provides that the health-insurance companies and their associations should consult the Medical Service when carrying out tasks other than those mentioned in paras 1 to 3, particularly with regard to general medical issues in health care and advice for insurees, quality-control issues, contractual negotiations with health-care providers, and consultations with joint committees of physicians and hospitals, particularly review bodies. 33

If a suspicion of potentially incorrect treatment arises, the MDK can therefore be commissioned to carry out the relevant expert medical assessment. 34

6 Bundesgerichtshof (BGH) 9 March 2010 – VI ZR 131/09.
7 Oberlandesgericht (OLG) Stuttgart 11 December 2008 – 1 U 75/08 VersR 2010, 629.

4. Right of recourse

35 Almost the entire population of the Federal Republic is insured against the risk of suffering impaired health through the necessary compensatory systems that provide for the costs. The same also applies to damages in connection with medical malpractice.

36 Benefit providers in this sense may include statutory health care and nursing-care insurance companies, private health-insurance companies, employers' associations for regulation of indemnity insurance in connection with obligatory continuation of wage payments, public-sector employers, and social welfare agencies.

37 For this reason, a statutory transmission of claims is permitted in case of equivalence of benefit. Thus, in accordance with § 116 para 1 SGB X, claims of the injured party are transferred to the insurance fund or social welfare agency if the latter is obliged to provide welfare benefits due to the injury.

38 § 86 of the Insurance Contract Law (*Versicherungsvertragsgesetz,* VVG) represents a corresponding regulation for the transmission of claims for private insured parties and individuals eligible for benefit. § 87a of the Federal Civil Service Law (*Bundesbeamtengesetz,* BBG) contains a corresponding regulation in favour of civil servants' employers.

39 The statutory transmission of claims generally already takes place at the time of the event causing the injury, since a liability to pay is possible *a priori* due to the existing insurance relationship.[8] For welfare benefits that are not linked to the existence of an insurance relationship but require additional special preconditions, it depends on whether payments by the insurance fund can seriously already be expected at the time of the injury due to the specific circumstances in the individual case.[9]

40 Social security funds nowadays generally make use of this right of recourse in practice. Health-insurance and nursing-insurance companies have been establishing and expanding recourse claims departments in recent years, for example. Communications and thus the flow of information between payments departments and recourse claims departments have also been substantially improved in order to allow suspected cases of this type to be identified. In every case of medical malpractice, it can therefore now be assumed that claims by social security funds and other insurance funds will also be made.

---

8 BGH 27 June 2006 – VI ZR 337/04 with further references.
9 BGH VI ZR 337/04.

III. Private Insurance

5. The role of private health insurance

Approximately 10.5 % of the population have private health insurance.[10] In this case, premiums are based on the extent of coverage agreed, the patient's general state of health, gender and age at entry. Here again, health-insurance premiums are paid for in equal proportions by the employee and the employer. **41**

The fact that statutory transmission of claims also exists for private health-insurance companies in case of equivalence of benefit was already mentioned above under question 4. There are therefore no actual differences between public and private health insurance in this respect. **42**

A specific new variant is that individual private health-insurance companies are offering their policy-holders special legal insurance for claims arising from medical malpractice.[11] The special aspect here is that these insurance companies themselves provide liability insurance for hospitals, so that in case of dispute they are represented on both sides. **43**

6. Liability insurance

Compulsory insurance

In accordance with § 21 of the Model Professional Code of Conduct for Physicians in Germany (*Musterberufsordnung fur Ärztinnen und Ärzte,* MBO-Ä), physicians are obliged to have adequate insurance against liability claims associated with their professional work. A similar regulation is also included in the professional codes of conduct for each state board for dental registration.[12] However, there is no national statutory obligation to have liability insurance. Only a few of the federal states have included statutory compulsory insurance in their legislation regarding medical boards of registration.[13] In accordance with this, physicians are obliged **44**

---

10 Private health insurance data report, 2008/2009.

11 Eg, Viktoria Krankenversicherung – Patientenrechtsschutzversicherung.

12 Cf, for example, § 4 Berufsordnung (BerufsO) for the Westfalen-Lippe state dental board of registration.

13 § 30 no 4 HeilberGNRW, § 31 para 1 no 4 HeilberG Brandenburg, § 30 no 6 HeilberG Schleswig-Holstein, § 27 para 4 Hamburgisches Kammergesetz für Heilberufe, § 28 no 4 HeilberG Bremen.

to take out their own adequate liability insurance if equivalent protection is not already in place through the general liability insurance policy held by an institution's hospital trust.

45 For hospitals, by contrast, there is no obligation to take out liability insurance either under statutory law or in relation to salary agreements.

Market for liability insurance

46 The area of medical liability is in a rather paradoxical situation. As a result of increasing technological sophistication and increasing specialisation in medical science, medical risks for patients have been constantly declining. At the same time, however, medico-legal risks for the physician – ie the danger of becoming subject to claims for damages, criminal charges, and thus judicial inquiries by the public prosecutor – have been dramatically increasing.

47 All of the bodies representing expert consultants and arbitration services have thus consistently reported a sudden increase in applications, the numbers of which have doubled and in some cases even tripled during the last 15 years.

48 There has also been a strong increase in compensation payments for personal injuries. The increase is particularly affecting severe personal injury. For example, the General Association for the German Insurance Industry noted an increase in the average compensation level of nearly 6 % per annum when comparing the reporting periods 1995–1998 and 2000–2003. In absolute terms, this represents an average increase of € 1.33m to € 1.76m. In the field of obstetrics in particular, the increase reached more than 9 % per annum, from € 1.4m to approximately € 2.2m.

49 The background to this probably lies in the fact that compensation levels for the most severely injured individuals have increased dramatically in recent years. This is due on the one hand to heavy increases in nursing-care costs and the marked increase in occupational disablement damages, and on the other hand to the increased life expectancy of even severely injured individuals, due to advances in medicine.

50 These developments have of course affected the liability insurance market. In recent years, for example, a number of insurance companies have withdrawn from the liability insurance market for medical risks. Far fewer new ones have entered the market during the same period.

The average liability insurance premiums for hospitals rose by approximately 439 % in the period from 1988 to 2008.[14] 51

Similar developments have been seen in the area of professional liability insurance for physicians, particularly in the high-risk disciplines. Particularly in obstetrics and the surgical disciplines, the question is being raised in Germany of whether exercising the profession is worthwhile at all in view of the level of insurance premiums required. 52

Particularly important here is the fact that unlike other high-risk fields, the medical profession is unable to transfer increased premium costs directly to prices, as the latter are extensively regulated by law. 53

Overall, however, it is evident that thanks to market conditions, it is still possible for every hospital and every physician to take out an appropriate liability insurance policy. 54

IV. Professional Standards

7. Applicable professional standards

Art 74 no 19 of the Basic Law (GG) gives parliament the right to regulate the healing professions within the framework of concurrent legislative competence between the states and the federal government. The profession of physician is one of the healing professions thereby regulated. Requirements for entering the medical profession are definitively regulated in the Federal Medical Regulations and Regulations for the Licensing of Physicians. In addition, the following healing professions are also currently in existence: 55

- Dentists, regulated under the law on practicing dental medicine
- Veterinarians (Federal Veterinary Regulations)
- Non-medical practitioners
- Pharmacists (Federal Pharmaceutical Regulations)
- Psychological psychotherapists (Psychotherapy Law)

By contrast, physicians' right to exercise their profession, like that of the other healing professions, lies within the legislative competence of the 56

14 Evaluation by the Ecclesia Gruppe Detmold based on a representative sample of German acute care hospitals.

federal states. The framework for this is provided by the individual states' legislation on registration boards and the healing professions. Supplementary development of professional rules of conduct is the duty of the state medical boards of registration in accordance with statutory requirements. This is expressed specifically in the form of professional codes of conduct and further training codes. The former establishes what a physician is obliged to do or not do when exercising his profession, and the latter specifies the qualifications that a physician has to have in order to be entitled to use the term 'specialist.'[15]

57 The regulations for professional conduct established by the state medical boards of registration without exception require approval by the state supervisory authorities who are responsible for this under state law.[16] They have the force of statutory law and are directly binding on the members of the board.

58 Membership of the relevant medical board of registration is strictly compulsory for an individual to be able to exercise the profession of physician. One of the major implications of this is that physicians are subject to the professional supervision authority entrusted to the boards.[17]

59 The states' legislation regarding medical boards and the professional codes of conducts established by the state medical boards only describe the standard of care in general terms. For example, § 2 of the Model Professional Code of Conduct for Physicians (MBO-Ä) states that physicians must exercise their profession conscientiously and must do justice to the trust placed in them when exercising their profession. In accordance with chapter C no 2 of the MBO-Ä, accepting and undertaking treatment require conscientious execution of the medical measures required in accordance with the rules of medical art. There is no reference to national or international regulations or codes.

60 Despite this, malpractice can also be evaluated as an infringement of professional duty. For example, an emergency physician is guilty of infringing professional duty if he does not administer age-adjusted dosages of a drug to minors or only monitors a patient inadequately after treatment.[18]

61 However, proceedings of that type are extremely rare.

---

15 For details, see *A Zurstrassen/U Kosch* in: *F Wenzel* (ed), Handbuch des Fachanwalts Medizinrecht (2nd edn 2009) ch 9, no 150 ff (pp 962 ff).

16 Cf, for example, § 31 para 2 HeilberGNRW.

17 See, for example, § 6 para 1 clause 6 HeilberGNRW.

18 Landesberufungsgericht für Heilberufe Nordrhein-Westfalen, 23 September 2009 -6t A 2159/08.

8. Quality and/or risk management systems

Comprehensive regulations on the introduction of quality assurance measures in the exercise of the medical profession exist both in relation to social legislation and to professional legislation.[19] **62**

Under social legislation, panel physicians, medical care centers, approved hospitals, providers of preventive care or rehabilitation measures, and institutions with whom there is a care contract in accordance with § 111a are obliged – in accordance with § 135a clause 2 SGB V subject to §§ 137 and 137d – to participate in inter-institutional measures for quality assurance aimed particularly at improving the quality of results, on the one hand. On the other hand, they are also obliged to introduce and further develop quality management internally within their own institutions. **63**

Under professional legislation, physicians are obliged in accordance with § 5 MBO-Ä to participate in measures to assure the quality of medical work introduced by the medical boards of registration and to provide the boards with the information required for this purpose. **64**

However, health care providers are given no instructions on how to set up their quality management system, nor are there any obligatory certification procedures for quality management systems. The main certification procedure for hospitals in Germany is probably the KTQ® (*Kooperation für Transparenz und Qualität im Gesundheitswesen* – Cooperation for Transparency and Quality in Health Care) procedure, under which 533 institutions are currently certified. **65**

Certification procedures have also developed for the field of registered physicians in private practice, such as the 'Quality and Development in Doctors' Offices' (*Qualität und Entwicklung in Praxen,* QEP) procedure provided by the Association of Statutory Health-Insurance Physicians. **66**

There is as yet no direct stipulation that systems of clinical risk management need to be introduced. It is only in the context of introducing quality management systems that the topic of risk management arises. The major certification systems for hospitals have therefore now included specific requirements for this type of system in their catalogues. **67**

Many hospitals in Germany are nevertheless making efforts to establish risk management systems. The founding of the Alliance for Action on **68**

---

19 § 135 a, § 136, § 136a, § 137, § 137b SGB V, § 5 MBO-Ä.

Patient Safety (*Aktionsbündnis Patientensicherheit,* APS),[20] of which all of the main organisations involved in the health care system are members, has made this an extremely important topic in Germany.

69 The introduction of critical incident reporting systems (CIRS) in particular is being promoted in many institutions. At the end of 2009, the German Hospital Association (*Deutsche Krankenhausgesellschaft,* DKG), the Center for Quality in Medicine (*Ärztliches Zentrum für Qualität in der Medizin,* AZQ), the German Care Council (*Deutscher Pflegerat,* DPR) and the APS established a 'Hospital CIRS Network for Germany'. This makes it possible for reports of critical incidents that are relevant beyond a single hospital to be collected and analysed at the national level.

70 Quality requirements for physicians arise from § 95d SGB V. In accordance with para 1, the panel physician must undertake specialist further training as necessary in order to maintain and further develop the specialist knowledge and skills required for him to exercise his profession in panel medical care. The content of further training courses has to correspond to the current state of scientific knowledge in the fields of medicine, dental medicine, or psychotherapy. It must be free of any commercial interest.

71 Para 2 specifies that evidence of further training can be obtained through further training certificates provided by the boards of registration for medicine, dental medicine, and psychological psychotherapy, as well as for pediatric and adolescent psychotherapy.

72 Finally, para 3 obliges panel physicians to provide evidence every five years to the Association of Statutory Health Insurance Physicians to show that they have complied with their obligation under para 1 to receive further training during the previous five-year period.

73 If a panel physician does not provide evidence of further training, or fails to provide it in full, the consequence is that the Association of Statutory Health Insurance Physicians is obliged to reduce the fee paid to him in remuneration for panel-physician work by 10 % for the first four quarters following the five-year period and 25 % for the subsequent quarter. If a panel physician has not provided evidence of further training at the latest two years after the expiry of the five-year period, the Association of Statutory Health Insurance Physicians must immediately apply for his licence to be withdrawn by the accreditation board.

20 More detailed information is available at <www.aktionsbuendnis-patientensicherheit.de>.

B. Tort Liability

9. Fundamentals of tort liability

In the Federal Republic, liability law essentially involves fault-based liability. In accordance with § 823 para 1 of the Civil Code (*Bürgerliches Gesetzbuch*, BGB), a person who intentionally or through negligence illegally damages the life, body, health, liberty, property, or any other right of another person is obliged to pay the other person compensation for the resulting damage. **74**

Everyone involved in a treatment is subject to tort liability on the basis of his position as a guarantor for the treatment task undertaken, but in principle only for his own errors within his own sphere of control, not for errors caused by third parties. **75**

However, an individual's own fault can also relate to the organisation, selection, instruction, monitoring and equipment provided for his assistants. If they make mistakes, this type of fault is presumed in accordance with § 831 BGB. **76**

The Federal Court of Justice (*Bundegerichtshof*, BGH) sets very high requirements for the exonerating evidence possible under § 831 para 1 clause 2 BGB, so that in principle the differences between this and liability under § 278 BGB, according to which the guilty party is liable for his agents without any possibility of exoneration (*respondeat superior*), are cancelled out. **77**

However, agents in this sense only consist of assistants who are bound by instructions, and the decisive element is a legal rather than a factual duty to comply with instructions. The capacity of being an agent is therefore not cancelled merely because a senior physician's high level of specialisation makes it factually impossible for the chief physician to exercise specialist supervision over him.[21] **78**

The hospital trust is not capable of exoneration in the context of liability of legal persons for acts of their officers (*Organhaftung*) for mistakes made by the chief physician in his medical duties involving organisation and instruction. The BGH regards the chief physician, who is not bound by instructions from others, and also his vacation stand-ins, as being an **79**

21 BGH 10 March 2009 – VI ZR 39/08 Versicherungsrecht (VersR) 2009, 784; OLG Bamberg 14 December 1992 – 4 U 60/92 VersR 1994, 813.

'organ' of the hospital trust, whose mistakes the trust has to answer for in the same way as for its own in accordance with §§ 30, 31 BGB.[22]

80 In the field of civil liability for malpractice, the purpose of the law is to draw a distinction between injuries to health that are inevitable and based on the unpredictability of human nature, and those that occur because the physician has not observed the high quality standard in treatment that he is expected to provide. The risk of the spread of the disease present in the patient is not intended to be – and may not be – displaced by the treatment of the physician. The physician therefore has no basic legal obligation to vouch for the success of his treatment.[23]

81 Instead, he is only obliged to provide appropriate treatment without mistakes or fault. The prerequisite for liability is thus malpractice – ie culpable infringement of the specific professional duties of the physician as the cause of injury to the patient. A physician who undertakes to treat a patient places himself under an obligation to do so, thereby becoming a guarantor for the implementation of this decision and taking it upon himself to do what is medically necessary.

82 The concept of malpractice covers any medical measure in which the professionally required care in accordance with the state of knowledge in medical science is lacking; ie malpractice occurs when the physician does not properly carry out the measures objectively required in the given circumstances at the time of treatment in accordance with the findings of medical science. The physician owes the patient the standard of care of 'an experienced medical specialist' here.[24]

83 In relation to the objectified civil-law concept of negligence, the physician providing treatment is in principle also responsible under liability law for malpractice even if he might be regarded as excusable subjectively from the point of view of his own personal position. The physician's liability is thus not cancelled out only because – due to inadequate training, for example – he is not capable of managing a childbirth situation.[25]

84 If the principle of liability is established, the party causing damage must compensate the injured party for all disadvantages arising from the culpable action. In a sense, he has to restore matters to the state that would have existed if the damaging action had not taken place.

---

22 BGH 18 June 1985 – VI ZR 234/83 VersR 1985, 1043; BGH 30 June 1987 – VI ZR 257/86 VersR 1987, 1040.

23 OLG Karlsruhe 23 March 1994 – 7 U 193/82 VersR 1996, 62.

24 OLG Hamm 9 May 2001 – 3 U 259/99 VersR 2002, 857.

25 BGH 13 February 2001 – VI ZR 34/00 VersR 2001, 646.

Accordingly, the treatment costs, potential loss of income, and additional costs (eg nursing costs) caused by the damage must of course be reimbursed. Compensation is also required for immaterial injuries. 85

10. Burden of proof

This is based on the general civil law principle that the patient as claimant bears the burden of proof for all allegations of fact and law justifying a claim, while the physician bears the burden of proof for all allegations of fact and law denying it. Accordingly, the patient bears the entire burden of proof for the objective malpractice. This applies equally to incorrect acts or omissions. However, court precedents indicate a number of case groups in which facilitation of evidence in favour of the patient is possible. Examples worth mentioning include prima facie evidence and reversal of the burden of proof due to deficiencies in medical documentation. 86

The patient also bears the burden of proof for the state of affairs on which the alleged fault in treatment is based. The presumption of fault in § 282 BGB old version (replaced since 1 January 2002 by § 280 I 2 BGB new version), in accordance with which the guilty party in a contract has to prove that no guilt attaches to him, does not apply according to constant court precedents in the field of medical liability in the core area of medical activity. The physician does not owe the patient a duty to ensure successful treatment, but only a duty to make a conscientious effort to achieve a cure. The absence of success alone is thus not an indication of guilt, since the processes that take place in living organisms are not always capable of being controlled even by the best physician.[26] 87

However, the legal concept in § 282 (old version) does apply if the matter involves risks in the area of the treatment side that lie fully within the control of the hospital trust or staff.[27] This includes the area of technical preparation and patient care surrounding the medical treatment. If it is established in a specific case that the injury to the patient originates in an area in which risks can and must be completely excluded by physicians, then a presumption of fault applies. It is then a matter for the treatment side to invalidate this presumption. 88

---

26 BGH 13 February 2007 – VI ZR 174/06 VersR 2007, 1416; OLG Jena 12 July 2006 – 4 U 705/05 VersR 2007, 69.

27 BGH VersR 2007, 1416.

89 The patient in principle also bears the burden of proof for showing a causal connection between the culpable malpractice and the injury that has actually occurred.

11. Uncertain causation

90 **(a) Uncertainty with regard to causality.** In these cases, burden of proof rulings are common. As discussed under question 10, the patient in principle has to prove that there is a causal connection between the culpable mistake and the injury that has occurred. If it remains unclear whether the patient's situation has deteriorated as a result of mistakes or whether it is merely the normal course of his initial disease, then his claim will not be successful. To this extent, German law – in contrast to that of several other European countries – involves an 'all-or-nothing principle'.

91 However, court precedents in favour of patients, particularly in the Federal Court of Justice, have relieved this situation to a certain extent, particularly through the instrument of 'gross malpractice'.

92 An instance of malpractice is to be regarded as 'gross' if inappropriate medical behavior occurs which no longer appears comprehensible from an objective medical point of view because the physician simply must not make a mistake of this type.[28]

93 Evaluation of whether or not an instance of malpractice is to be regarded as gross is a legal question. However, the decision must be grounded in facts, which usually emerge from the medical evaluation of the course of treatment by the expert witness.[29]

94 In more recent court precedents, the BGH has clarified that it is sufficient for the instance of gross malpractice to be capable of causing the injury that has taken place; by contrast, the mistake need not suggest the injury or make it probable.[30]

95 Diagnostic errors have only rarely been regarded in court precedents as representing gross malpractice. This is only the case if a fundamental diagnostic error is involved.[31]

---

28 BGH 3 July 2001 – VI ZR 418/99 VersR 2001, 1116.

29 BGH 19 July 2001 – VI ZR 286/00 VersR 2001, 1115.

30 BGH 27 April 2004 – VI ZR 34/03 VersR 2004, 909; BGH 16 November 2004 – VI ZR 328/03 VersR 2005, 228.

31 BGH 9 June 2009 – VI ZR 138/08 VersR 2009, 1405.

By contrast, an improper failure to carry out a diagnostic investigation leads to a reversal of the burden of proof with regard to the causal link between malpractice and damage to health if timely and adequate clarification would have led with sufficient probability to a result requiring a response and if failure to recognise the finding or failure to respond to it would represent gross malpractice.[32] **96**

The term is more widely used in the area of treatment, however, where evaluations of malpractice as 'gross' occur fairly often in court precedents. This is mainly in cases in which there is no response to clear findings, a standard method of combatting known risks is not applied, or a therapeutic effect on a disease is not followed up.[33] **97**

The reversal of the burden of proof that can be considered in case of gross malpractice is basically related only to evidence of causality establishing liability – ie for the primary injury. By contrast, these principles are not applied in cases of causality relating to the extent of liability – ie a causal link between the malpractice and all subsequent resulting injuries. This is based on § 287 Code of Civil Procedure (*Zivilprozessordnung*, ZPO). Overwhelming probability can be regarded as sufficiently persuasive here.[34] **98**

Facilitation of evidence with regard to causality can also arise when an unsupervised physician with inadequate training or experience is employed who is not capable of providing the specialist standard for a specific procedure.[35] **99**

(b) Uncertainty in relation to the person causing the injury. According to § 830 para 1 s2 BGB if it is not possible to determine which of several persons involved caused the injury in question, it is regarded as equivalent to a case of interaction. This is a facilitation of evidence in relation to causality establishing liability for the injured party through a refutable presumption.[36] To this extent, when several medical treatments, even when temporally succeeding each other, form a factually connected consistent process together and along with the alternatively caused injury, all of the physicians involved have liability if any of the treatments is **100**

32 OLG Koblenz 10 January 2008 – 5 U 1608/07 VersR 2008, 923.
33 See *E Steffen*/*B Pauge*, Arzthaftungsrecht (10th edn 2006) no 515 ff, with a large number of example precedents.
34 BGH 21 July 1998 – VI ZR 15/98 VersR 1998, 115.
35 See *R Martis*/*M Winkhart-Martis*, Arzthaftungsrecht (3rd edn 2010) A 112 ff (pp 22 f), with many further references.
36 Palandt-*Sprau* (67th edn 2008) § 830 BGB no 7 (p 1266).

capable of having caused the injury and if it remains unclear who it was that for eg perforated the patient's bowel with the suprapubic urinary catheter.[37]

101 If it is clear in the hospital that the injury has in any case taken place due to malpractice on the part of one of the hospital physicians, the hospital trust remains liable as it is responsible for all of its agents.

12. Loss of a chance

102 In the German legal system, liability for the loss of a chance is not regarded as a separate type of injury requiring compensation.

13. Multiple persons involved

103 (a) **Liability of the persons themselves.** In the context of the increasing division of labour, the question of who is personally responsible in a specific case decisively depends on the question of the allocation of competences among the persons caring for the patient in a setting involving divided labour. Here again, this is a matter for the medical field itself, which has to establish basic responsibilities. The starting-point for legal assessment is then the fact that the patient is entitled to complete treatment in accordance with the specialist standard and that this may not be endangered as a result of the division of labour.

104 With regard to the vertical division of labour – ie the relationship between the chief physician, interns, and nursing staff – § 831 BGB sets out the evaluation. According to this, it is not only the assistant who is obliged to stave off dangers, but also the physician who is directing the treatment. The latter's liability is only cancelled for areas in which he is able to leave patient care to subordinate non-medical staff without deficiencies resulting therefrom.

105 Nursing staff are therefore generally responsible for basic and functional nursing where they carry out their own tasks and can therefore not be regarded as agents of the physician. For collaboration with the nursing field, the principle therefore applies that ensuring orderly staffing of a ward with adequately qualified personnel and adhering to the necessary mea-

---

37 OLG Koblenz 14 April 2005 – 5 U 1610/04 VersR 2006, 123.

sures are a matter for nursing management. Mistakes that occur there fall under the liability of the hospital trust, not that of the chief physician.[38]

An exception to this principle has only been made in court precedents in cases in which special nursing requirements have had to be met by the nursing staff and the measures therefore required medical instructions and checking. The BGH has regarded this type of requirement as being present in connection with decubitus prophylaxis[39] and in relation to special medical instructions to nursing staff following surgical damage to the peroneal nerve.[40] **106**

However, the physician in charge has to prevent the risk of inadequate communication and coordination among the entire subordinate staff and must establish and use the required clinical control mechanisms. **107**

In general, adequate instruction by the physicians in charge of management is required. The frequency of instruction depends on the treatment measure involved in each case. The lesser the extent to which it involves a routine measure and the greater the risk involved, the more comprehensive the instructions have to be.[41] **108**

The relevant checking of the diagnostic and therapeutic techniques used in the hospital also has to be ensured. As far as is necessary, the chief physician must ensure this through general instructions and guidelines, preferably in writing. **109**

The responsibilities associated with different areas of duty need to be taken into account in relationships between physicians. For example, in view of their lack of competence for the duty area within the framework of the vertical division of labour, interns can therefore not be held responsible for mistakes in the scheduling of surgery or for incorrectly established indications if they did not take part in those processes themselves but were only involved in the operation itself.[42] A physician undergoing further training also does not act culpably if he consults a senior physician in connection with for eg a hand injury that is difficult to assess and the senior physician endorses his diagnosis.[43] Similarly, a ward physician who **110**

---

38 BGH 10 January 1984 – VI ZR 158/82 VersR 1984, 356.

39 BGH 18 March 1986 – VI ZR 215/84 VersR 1986, 766; BGH 2 June 1987 – VI ZR 174/86 VersR 1987, 1238.

40 BGH 29 September 1998 – VI ZR 268/97 VersR 1999, 190.

41 BGH VersR 1984, 356.

42 OLG Düsseldorf 21 March 1991 – 8 U 55/89 VersR 1991, 1412 (L).

43 OLG Munich 17 June 1993 – 1 U 6626/92 VersR 1993, 1400.

only assists the gynecological chief physician in managing a birth is not liable for an injury to the child occurring during the birth.[44]

111 In the case of a horizontal division of labour – ie collaboration between physicians in various specialties – the starting-point is essentially the tasks assigned to each person involved, particularly in relation to specialty designations and professional agreements.

112 For example, decision-making regarding the type of anesthesia to be used, its administration and monitoring to prevent risks during the surgical and post-anesthetic phases until the patient recovers protective reflexes and can be transferred to the ward is the task of the anesthetist. By contrast, the subsequent postoperative treatment phase no longer lies in the area of responsibility of the anesthesiology department, but falls within the specialist competence of the surgeon managing follow-up care.[45] In the case concerned, the issue was severe hemorrhage from an indwelling catheter two days after the operation.

113 In addition, it is the sole responsibility of the anesthetist both preoperatively and postoperatively to maintain and monitor the patient's vital functions. Possible malpractice in this area therefore does not lie in the responsibility of the surgeon.[46] The same also applies to the assessment of the patient's capacity to undergo anesthesia.[47]

114 When a patient is referred by a neurologist, surgeon, or internist to a radiologist, checking of indication for a specific diagnostic measure and providing the patient with the information required is a task for the referring physicians. The radiologist can basically rely on the fact that the referring specialists have checked and approved the medical indication. Nor is it his task to provide the patient with information about the way in which the indication has been established.[48] By contrast, if an indication for surgery is wrongly approved because the radiologist has evaluated findings incorrectly in a way that is not capable of being recognised, the surgeon is not liable.[49]

115 Finally, in accordance with the principles of horizontal division of labour, liability on the part of an internist is ruled out when the internist is treating a patient with pyelonephritis and consults a urologist who fails

44 OLG Zweibrücken 20 October 1998 – 5 U 50/98 VersR 2000, 728.
45 BGH VersR 1984, 356.
46 BGH 26 February 1991 – VI ZR 344/89 VersR 1991, 694.
47 OLG Düsseldorf 1 January 1993 – 8 U 260/91 VersR 1993, 885.
48 OLG Düsseldorf 30 June 1983 – 8 U 178/80 VersR 1984, 643.
49 OLG Düsseldorf 31 July 1987 – 8 U 142/85 VersR 1989, 191.

to recognise a case of congenital reflux nephropathy, but then does not also consult a nephrologist.[50]

If the way in which a hospital is organised is such that intensive-care services in the department of surgery are entrusted to surgeons specially trained for the purpose, then it does not constitute malpractice if they attempt to carry out an urgent intubation themselves instead of immediately calling an anesthetist as an emergency.[51] **116**

In principle, the physician can rely on objective findings obtained in a different specialty, unless he has specific grounds that give rise to doubt. **117**

For example, if a neurology department initially declines the referral of a patient for a tissue biopsy procedure due to the presence of a salmonella infection, the physicians in the neurosurgical department can rely on the fact that continuing infection has previously been excluded when the patient is referred again.[52] **118**

A registered physician in private practice who has referred a patient to a hospital for further diagnosis can also use the results provided by the hospital – which is provided with staff and equipment superior to his – as the basis for further treatment if no doubts regarding their correctness necessarily arise.[53] **119**

All of the physicians involved in a treatment are obliged to counter the risks arising due to specialisation and division of labour. When several physicians are collaborating in the context of a horizontal division of labour – eg an anesthetist and an ophthalmologist during a strabismus operation – coordination of the planned measures is required in order to protect the patient and exclude any risks that might arise due to incompatibility between the methods or instruments used by the specialties concerned.[54] **120**

Particularly in hospital, it therefore has to be ensured organisationally that a physician is designated at all times to direct the treatment whose task it is to ensure coordination and communication between the physicians involved. **121**

50 OLG Hamm 5 June 2000 – 3 U 233/99 VersR 2001, 1157.
51 OLG Munich 11 June 1992 – 1 U 2395/90 VersR 1994, 684.
52 OLG Oldenburg 23 December 1997 – 5 U 75/97 VersR 1999, 452.
53 OLG Cologne 14 July 1993 – 27 U 13/93 VersR 1993, 1157.
54 BGH 26 January 1999 – VI ZR 376/97 VersR 1999, 579.

122 **(b) General liability for third-party damage.** Independently of the above, the issue of whether the hospital can be made liable for mistakes by its employees essentially depends on their contractual relationship.

123 Contractual liability only affects the parties to a contract. However, in accordance with § 278 BGB, it also covers third-party mistakes made by the assistants involved. It is immaterial here whether the hospital trust or a registered physician in private practice has authority to give such assistants instructions. However, it is a prerequisite for this that the others involved should not themselves have their own contractual relationships with the patients.[55]

124 The question of who is contractually obliged to provide compensation to the patient if applicable thus initially depends on the contractual relationship applying in the individual case. A distinction needs to be made here between outpatient and in-patient treatment.

125 **(c) In-patient treatment.** In the case of in-patient treatment, contract forms are influenced by the Hospital Financing Law (*Krankenhausfinanzierungsgesetz,* KHG), Hospital Remuneration Law (*Krankenhausentgeltgesetz,* KHEntgG) and Federal Nursing Fee Regulations (*Bundespflegesatzverordnung,* BPflV). The latter only applies to psychiatric hospitals, which are not subject to DRG. There are no major differences between patients with public or private insurance here, as § 17 para 1 clause 1 KHG envisages standard charges in a flat-rate remuneration system for DRG hospitals for all users.

126 A basic distinction is made between three types of contracts – total hospital admission contracts, split hospital admission contracts, and visiting consultant contracts.

127 **(d) Total hospital admission contract (with additional physician contract if applicable).** The total hospital admission contract is the usual type. This always applies if the parties do not make any additional agreements. The hospital trust becomes the sole contractual partner for the patient and owes the duty to provide the patient all medical and non-medical services that are necessary in the individual case, depending on the type and severity of the disease, to ensure medically appropriate and adequate treatment. This includes services by third parties arranged for by

55 BGH 29 June 1999 – VI ZR 24/98 VersR 1999, 1241.

the hospital (eg consultants). The hospital fund is liable for these as well as for its own staff in accordance with § 278 BGB.

In the case of in-patient treatment of patients with optional services, there 128 are no differences from this normal type of contract unless special contractual agreements are made. Instead, the contract between the hospital trust and the patient is supplemented by a contract between the patient and the chief physician. This has the consequence that in case of injury, the patient can make contractual claims against both the hospital and the physician, who presents the patient with his own separate bill.[56] The hospital is also liable for the chief physician as its agent.

(e) **Split hospital admission contract.** This requires a special agree- 129 ment with the patient, who must receive clear information before signing the contract that the sole provider of medical services is the physician, who will present his own bill, not the hospital, and that in case of liability only the physician will be held responsible for any potential injury.[57]

If a split hospital admission contract applies, only the physician is liable 130 for medical services; the hospital only has to provide nursing and other medical services in accordance with what is known as the minor hospital daily rate, as in the visiting consultant model.

(f) **Visiting consultant model.** In this type of contract, initial outpati- 131 ent treatment by a registered physician in private practice is continued on an in-patient basis in a hospital that provides the physician with private beds. Here again a split hospital admission contract arises, which is characterised by two separate relationships. On the one hand, the contract is between the patient and the visiting consultant and is concerned with treatment services provided by the visiting consultant; on the other, the contract is between the patient and the hospital for nursing and medical care lying outside of the medical services provided by the visiting consultant and subordinate physicians in his specialty in accordance with the designated specialty. The same also applies to visiting midwives.

In accordance with § 18 para 2 of the Hospital Remuneration Law (*Kran-* 132 *kenhausentgeltgesetz,* KHEntG), as services provided by visiting consultants

---

56 BGH 10 June 1985 – VI ZR 234/83 VersR 1985, 1043; BGH 22 December 1992 – VI ZR 341/91 VersR 1993, 481.

57 BGH 22 December 1992 – VI ZR 341/91 VersR 1993, 481; OLG Koblenz 26 June 1997 – 5 U 1825/96 VersR 1998, 1283.

or midwives do not form part of hospital services and do not represent agency services provided by the hospital, the hospital trust does not become liable to the patient alongside them.[58] Due to the provisions of § 18 para 1 no 3 KHEntgG, medical employees in the same designated specialty are also agents of the visiting consultant, not of the hospital. The same also applies to vacation stand-ins appointed by the visiting consultant. The visiting consultant is liable here in accordance with § 278 BGB, not the hospital.[59]

133 Otherwise, procuring medical and non-medical assistance, providing adequate staffing and equipment resources, and ensuring effective organisation belong to the hospital trust's treatment tasks, unless other agreements have been explicitly made with the patient.[60]

134 An independently practicing visiting midwife is also not an agent of the hospital or of the visiting gynecologist working there, provided that and as long as the gynecologist has not taken over management of the birth.[61]

135 By contrast, an employed midwife is an agent of the hospital, not of the visiting consultant, provided that the latter has not taken over management of the birth and has not claimed special competence to issue instructions.[62]

136 In both of these cases, the visiting consultant has liability from the moment at which the birth becomes his contractual task. This can be assumed if he is caring for the patient's pregnancy, is aware of the in-patient admission for delivery, and also in general for the high-risk phase.[63]

137 (g) **Outpatient treatment in hospital.** In this area, legal relationships are basically determined by the billing regulations applicable under health-insurance legislation. According to court precedent, the latter applies not only to patients with public health insurance, but largely also to private patients.[64]

58 OLG Koblenz 26 July 2000 – 1 U 1606/98 VersR 2001, 897.
59 BGH 16 May 2000 – VI ZR 321/98 VersR 2000, 1146.
60 OLG Cologne 21 August 1996 – 5 U 286/94 VersR 1997, 1404.
61 BGH 14 February 1995 – VI ZR 272/93 VersR 1995, 706.
62 BGH VersR 2000, 1146; OLG Koblenz VersR 2001, 897.
63 OLG Oldenburg 16 January 1996 – 5 U 17/95 VersR 1997, 1236.
64 BGH 20 September 1988 – VI ZR 296/87 VersR 1988, 1270; BGH 8 December 1992 – VI ZR 349/91 VersR 1993, 357.

(h) Public health-insurance patients. For outpatient treatment in hospital, patients with public health insurance also regularly enter into contractual relationships with the chief physician managing the outpatient department, rather than with the hospital trust, in accordance with panel doctor authorisation under §§ 95, 116 SGB V in conjunction with §§ 31 ff of the Accreditation Regulations for Panel Doctors (Ärzte-ZV). This is also the case if referral was to the hospital and the treatment is carried out by a subordinate hospital physician rather than by the 'authorised' chief physician holding the obligation. According to court precedent in the BGH, this has also not been altered by the health-care reform law of 21 December 1992.[65] **138**

Due to the various laws reforming the structure of the health care system, hospitals themselves now also have approval for carrying out some parts of outpatient treatment. Particularly important here is the right to carry out outpatient operations in accordance with § 115b SGB V, as well as the option for pre-admission and post-admission treatment in accordance with § 115a SGB V and in other cases in accordance with §§ 116a to 119 SGB V. **139**

- Private patient

For private patients, specific agreements with the hospital outpatient department are basically decisive in determining whether their contractual partner is the chief physician, hospital trust or both. **140**

If explicit agreements are lacking, then in the view of the Federal Court of Justice the contract with the chief physician entitled to charge for the service serves as the regulating model. In these cases, it is not the hospital trust that is liable for mistakes by physicians and non-medical assistants but the chief physician alone contractually and in tort along with the physician providing treatment. **141**

The same also applies in principle if the treatment is not carried out personally by the chief physician eg because his personal involvement is not necessary, or if the patient seeks treatment outside of his consulting hours and in the absence of the chief physician only the subordinate hospital physician who is on call is available.[66] **142**

- Outpatient treatment by a registered physician in private practice

65 BGH 20 December 2005 – VI ZR 180/04 VersR 2006, 409.
66 BGH VersR 1993, 357.

143 A patient with public health insurance, who in principle has a free choice of panel physician in the context of public health care provision in accordance with § 76 SGB V, enters into a treatment relationship with the latter that must be regarded as having a private-law quality (§§ 69, 76 para 4 SGB V). This relationship already arises at the time when the physician undertakes to carry out treatment, not only when the patient presents his health insurance certificate.

144 The duties of a panel physician towards patients with public health insurance are in principle no different from those towards patients who pay themselves.

145 When physicians in the same specialty run a joint practice that appears from the outside to be a group practice or a health clinic, not only as a result of the appearance of the offices but also because it presents itself as a specialist unit in which medical services can be provided by all of the physicians during the patient's treatment, then all of the physicians in the unit are jointly and severally liable under the contract between doctor and patient.[67]

146 A joint practice sign showing the designation 'Specialists in …,' use of the same headed correspondence paper, and joint invoicing to the Association of Statutory Health Insurance Physicians are normally sufficient to establish this fact.

147 The same also applies if the physicians work as visiting consultants in the same hospital and continue treatments started in their own joint practice there.[68] It also applies to four self-employed physicians linked in a co-operative visiting consultant system.[69]

148 The situation is different for medical services in which the patient explicitly places importance on having a specific physician. In this case, the contract is only with the physician so entrusted.

149 **(i) Liability in tort.** As discussed under question 9 above, each individual involved in the treatment is liable in tort due to his position as guarantor for the treatment task undertaken, but is in principle only liable for his own mistakes within his own area of control, not for mistakes made by third parties; his personal fault can relate to the organisation,

67 BGH VersR 1999, 1241; BGH VersR 2002, 233.
68 BGH VersR 2000, 1146.
69 BGH 8 November 2005 – VI ZR 319/04 VersR 2006, 361.

selection, instruction, monitoring and equipment provided for his assistants. If they make a mistake, then fault of this type is assumed in accordance with § 831 BGB.

The patient in hospital is thus of course also able to sue not only the hospital trust, but also the individuals directly treating him. Several persons may then be liable jointly and severally if applicable. **150**

(j) Operations carried out by a private physician in the hospital. **151** Whether a private physician who carries out operations is liable for subordinate staff in the hospital depends once again on the relevant contractual arrangements.

If he only rents operating rooms in the hospital in order to carry out surgery on patients with his own staff there, he alone is liable for his own mistakes and those of his staff, contractually and in the normal case also in tort. If he receives support from hospital staff in the process, he is also liable to the patient for their actions as his agents. **152**

If the private physician carries out only the operations in his own name, but leaves preoperative and postoperative care to the hospital, then the hospital is liable for mistakes made in those areas. **153**

If the operation is carried out under what is known as a cooperation contract – a contractual construct that is currently becoming increasingly popular in Germany – then in the normal case in a third-party relationship, the hospital is also liable for the private physician and for everyone else involved. In these cases, the patient enters exclusively into a hospital admission contract with the hospital. **154**

14. Strict liability

Under German law, there are a number of special regulations regarding strict liability. These are always concerned with liability for injuries arising from a permitted risk eg operating an institution that employs dangerous equipment. **155**

Liability of vehicle owners under § 7 para 1 of the Road Traffic Law is of special practical relevance nowadays, and another important aspect is manufacturers' liability for death or damage to health, physical injury, or damage to property due to product defects in accordance with § 1 of the Product Liability Law. In accordance with § 1 of the Law of Liability for the **156**

Environment, the owner of a building or complex is liable for death, physical injury, and damage to health or property resulting from the environmental effects of the building or complex.

157 In the field of health, strict liability may be possible in particular for damage when operating nuclear facilities, in accordance with § 26 of the Atomic Energy Act (AtG); for damage due to bringing into circulation medical products under the regulations of the Product Liability Law (*Produkthaftungsgesetz,* ProdHaftG); and in the manufacture of medicines under § 84 of the Law on the Manufacture and Distribution of Medicines (*Arzneimittelgesetz,* AMG).

C. Contractual Liability

15. Basics of contracts in the health care sector

158 As mentioned above under question 2, the contract for medical treatment between the patient and the physician or hospital has a private law character, even for members of statutory health-insurance schemes.

159 The full weight of opinion is that a contract for medical treatment represents a higher-order service contract in accordance with §§ 611 ff, 647 BGB.[70] The same also applies to dental treatment, prostheses,[71] cosmetic operations,[72] and carrying out voluntary sterilisation.[73]

16. Differences to tort law

160 For medical treatment, contractual and tort protection are in principle identical.[74] Based on court precedent in the BGH, the fact that liability is also for third-party fault on the part of assistants in accordance with § 278 BGB, but for tort only for personal fault in selection and control in accordance with § 831 BGB, is of no practical effect. Differences in the extent of liability – eg under the statutory time bar – have been largely eliminated by reforms in the law governing contractual obligations and

70 *Martis/Winkhart* (fn 35) A401 p 80.
71 OLG Düsseldorf 8 April 2004 – 1–8 U 96/03 VersR 2005, 1737.
72 OLG Cologne 21 August 1997 – 5 W 58/97 VersR 1998, 1510.
73 *Martis/Winkhart* (fn 35) A434 p 88.
74 BGH 25 June 1991 – VI ZR 320/90 VersR 1991, 1058.

the law on damages. The only real differences remaining lie in the fact that contractual liability can also protect against pure economic loss of patients.[75]

Despite this, patients are still able to choose between contractual and tort liability, or to base their claim on both. 161

17. Contractual claims in the absence of direct contracts?

This question must be answered in the affirmative. On the one hand, emergency treatment of an unconscious patient is carried out when no legal representative is able to enter into the treatment contract in accordance with regulations on permissible agency without authority (*Geschäftsführung ohne Auftrag,* GoA) on the basis of the patient's presumed volition. 162

On the other hand, third parties can enter into a treatment contract as contractual partners in their own name to the benefit of the patient. This regularly happens in the case of treatment of children, for example, where it is the parents who enter into the relevant contract. 163

18. Informed consent

The patient's agreement to undergo the treatment, and thus the problem of providing the relevant information, plays an extremely important role in practice, as patients nowadays regularly also base claims for damages on alleged errors in the informed consent procedure. This is justified by the fact that the provision of incorrect information or omission of an informed consent discussion can usually lead to a claim for damages that does not depend on an actual treatment mistake, the latter which is often difficult to prove. This is because a procedure conducted without effective consent is not permissible. If the procedure had not been carried out, as would have been correct in such a case, the patient would not have suffered any injury to his health. 164

The starting-point for court decisions on the duty to ensure informed consent is a decision in the Supreme Court of the German Reich in 1894, according to which a medically indicated procedure that is conducted in accordance with the rules of the art, is therapeutically successful, and is 165

75 See *Steffen/Pauge* (fn 33) 2 no 4 f.

carried out with an intention to cure constitutes an act of bodily harm; the illegality of this bodily harm is only relieved if there is effective consent to undergo it.[76]

166 Above all, however, the individual's right of self-determination enshrined in arts 1 and 2 of the Basic Law implies that medical treatment must be covered by effective consent in order to be legal.

167 The effective consent thus required by both of these approaches in turn is only present if the patient has previously received adequate information about what is being consented to. This is the starting point for all court decisions regarding the duty to ensure informed consent.

168 The uppermost purpose of the informed consent discussion is thus to provide the patient with a meaningful perception of his right of self-determination and to ensure that he is able to take a free decision regarding the health care measures to be undertaken and about the risks associated with them.

169 In principle, every physician has a duty to provide information about the treatment task that he is carrying out. Although the task may be delegated to another physician, who is then primarily affected by liability for inadequate provision of information,[77] this does not cancel contractual liability and only cancels liability in tort if clear organisational instructions checked by sampling procedures exist and there is no specific reason to doubt the suitability and reliability of the physician who is sent for.[78] The informed consent procedure can only be transferred to a physician who is still undergoing training if he is capable, on the basis of his state of training, of specifically assessing both the disease that the patient has and the treatment that is required.[79]

170 Effective consent by the patient also does not relieve the physician in principle of responsibility for a medically correct procedure, including observance of boundaries in medical ethics. For example, extracting 14 teeth in a 17-year-old patient, even when she has consented, is unlawful if the teeth are still worthy of being preserved.[80]

---

76 Entscheidungen des Reichsgerichts in Strafsachen (RGSt) 25, 375.

77 BGH 22 April 1980 – VI ZR 37/79 VersR 1981, 456.

78 OLG Karlsruhe 19 March 1997 – 13 U 42/96 VersR 1998, 718.

79 OLG Dresden, 11 February 2002, Gesundheitsrecht (GesR) 2003, 157.

80 OLG Oldenburg 2 March 1999 – 5 U 176/98 VersR 1999, 1499; see also OLG Cologne 25 February 1998 – 5 U 157/97 VersR 1998, 1511.

Even if the physician breaches his duty to ensure informed consent, it does not always lead to liability. He can claim that the patient would have consented to the procedure concerned even if the informed consent process had been carried out properly. This objection is in principle a substantial one. However, court precedents establish strict requirements for evidence in favour of this assertion, which the treatment side has to provide.[81] **171**

According to these, hypothetical consent must be denied if the patient can show that if a proper informed consent procedure had been observed he would have faced a 'genuine decisional conflict', might have sought a second opinion, or would have had the procedure carried out in a specialised clinic. The decisive element here is the view of the specific patient in the specific situation, not the view of a 'reasonable patient'.[82] **172**

If the trial judge still has doubts, he must assume in the patient's favour that the hypothetical consent viewpoint does not apply.[83] **173**

The objection that the patient did consent and the prerequisites there for must be proved by the treatment side. The same also applies to the assertion that the patient had already received the necessary information from another physician,[84] or did not require information due to his own medical specialist knowledge. The physician also has to prove that the patient who did not receive information, or did not receive sufficient information, would also have provided consent even if proper information had been provided. **174**

On the other hand, the patient must plausibly explain why he would have refrained from the treatment even when it was medically reasonable. **175**

The physician's burden of proof is related only to the level between inadequate information and the procedure. It does not also include the causative link between the treatment procedure and the consequential injury. If it has been established that the informed consent procedure was incorrect, therefore, it is up to the patient to prove that the unlawful treatment procedure in breach of contract caused the primary or secondary injury to him that is being claimed. **176**

---

81 BGH 5 February 1991 – VI ZR 108/90 VersR 1991, 547.

82 BGH 9 November 1993 – VI ZR 248/92 VersR 1994, 682.

83 BGH VersR 1991, 547.

84 BGH 28 February 1984 – VI ZR 70/82 VersR 1984, 538.

D. Public Liability

19. Key differences from cases involving private hospitals or doctors

177 Independently of whether the hospital is public or private, all treatment contracts involve civil law. Claims for damages are thus raised on a contract or tort basis. There are no differences between public and private institutions here.

E. Alternative Compensation Regimes

20. Funds and/or other alternative compensation regimes

178 This type of system is unknown under German law. Although there have repeatedly been demands for a compensation system free of blame in the health care field, they have never met with acceptance.

F. Extent of Liability/Remedies

I. Pecuniary Loss

21. Introduction to indemnifying pecuniary loss

179 In accordance with § 249 para 1 BGB, the party liable for compensation is obliged to restore the position that would have existed if the circumstance creating liability for compensation had not taken place. § 249 para 2 BGB states that in the case of damage to property or person, the creditor can claim the required amount of money in lieu of restoration.

180 In accordance with § 253 para 2 BGB, both pecuniary damage and immaterial damage must be compensated for. There are no differences here between the tort and contractual basis for claims. Nor are there any exceptions in cases of medical malpractice.

181 The extent of the damage is calculated in accordance with what is known as the differential hypothesis. The pecuniary damage suffered by the patient is calculated by comparing his actual financial position resulting from the damaging event and the one that would have arisen if his financial status had continued to develop without the damaging event. The difference must be compensated for by the party causing damage.

Court precedents have developed two groups of cases diverging from this in which damage can be assumed even without a reduction in the patient's financial assets. The way in which damages are calculated here is influenced by normative considerations. Normative damage is a detriment that cannot be shown in the form of a calculated difference but requires evaluative consideration. Payments from third parties (eg social insurance agencies or relatives) for the injured party that compensate him for the damage must not benefit the party causing the damage.[85] 182

In addition, usage detriments can also be compensated for in the context of the normative consideration of damages. The BGH agrees that damage has taken place here if the prevailing public understanding ascribes an independent asset value for the injured party's own use to the object concerned, and if losses to its owner have become 'appreciable' because without the damaging event he would have been able and willing to use the object.[86] For example, if a road traffic accident occurs, the injured party can claim repair costs as compensation for damage from the party causing damage, in accordance with the differential hypothesis. For the period in which he is not able to use his vehicle, he can claim the costs of a replacement vehicle, regardless of whether he actually rents one or not, because of the lost usage benefit if he did not do so.[87] The situation is different with personal injury. In this case, the injured party cannot receive compensation for notional treatment costs, but must also have the treatment for which he is claiming costs, or must seriously intend to do so.[88] 183

In addition, all further financial losses must be compensated for if they are sufficient causal consequences of the medical malpractice or unlawful treatment due to an absence of consent and were included in the specific scope of the treatment contract. 184

Eligibility for compensation for increased needs in accordance with § 843 para 1 BGB has great financial importance here. 185

Increased needs all consist of injury-related and constantly recurring additional expenses that the injured party incurs as a result of the accident in comparison with a healthy individual.[89] 186

---

85 BGH 10 July 2007 – VI ZR 192/06 VersR 2007, 1536 with further references.

86 Fundamentally BGH 9 July 1986 – GSZ 1/86 VersR 1986, 1103.

87 BGH 30 September 1963 – III ZR 137/62 VersR 1964, 225; BGH 23 November 2004 – VI ZR 357/03 VersR 2005, 284.

88 BGH 14 January 1986 – VI ZR 48/85 Monatsschrift für Deutsches Recht (MDR) 1986, 486.

89 BGH 20 January 2004 – VI ZR 46/03 VersR 2004, 482.

187 These include in particular compensation for any nursing costs for the injured party. This involves compensation for costs arising from nursing the injured party, such as costs for accommodation in a nursing home, any professional nurses employed or nursing care within the family,[90] even if the latter is free of charge to the injured party.[91] However, the costs of care provided in their free time by parents to a child whose health has been damaged are only eligible for compensation in accordance with § 843 para 1 BGB if they go so far beyond the natural and original duties of parents that paid employment for an outside nurse would not only be theoretically possible but would also be seriously considered as a practical alternative when reasonably considered.[92]

188 The injured party can also claim for professional retraining or payment of the relevant costs if he is no longer able to do his previous job as a result of the accident.[93]

189 In addition to these recurrent expenses, however, one-off costs in accordance with §§ 249, 251 BGB may be eligible for compensation. This is the case when a single purchase of an aid for the injured party is able to meet his increased needs adequately for the future.[94]

190 The concept of increased need thus also covers the following items, for example:

- Conversion or alteration of a dwelling to meet the needs of a disabled person,[95]
- Orthopedic aids,[96]
- Electronic aids for writing and reading,[97]
- Conversion of a car into a vehicle for a disabled person and
- Higher health insurance premiums.

191 In addition, costs for therapeutic treatments and housekeeping damages can also be claimed. Housekeeping, which includes child-rearing, is recognised as a distinct employment activity. It therefore involves mainte-

90 BGH 8 November 1977 – VI ZR 117/75 VersR 1978, 149.
91 BGH 10 November 1998 – VI ZR 354/97 VersR 1999, 252.
92 BGH 8 June1999 – VI ZR 244/98 VersR 1999, 1156.
93 BGH 4 May 1982 – VI ZR 175/80 VersR 1982, 767.
94 BGH VersR 2004, 482.
95 BGH 19 May 1981 – VI ZR 108/79 VersR 1982, 238.
96 BGH VersR 2004, 482.
97 BGH VersR 1982, 238.

nance costs with an independent economic value. If the household can no longer be run in whole or in part as a result of the accident, then damage eligible for compensation has taken place.[98]

22. Loss of earnings vs loss of earning capacity

In principle, loss of income can only be compensated for on the basis of income that has actually been lost. In the case of damage caused by injury to a self-employed individual, it is not the absence of the capacity to work as such, but the negative effect of the loss of work on the injured party's assets that represents damage as applicable under liability law. The damage here can only be calculated concretely, not abstractly.[99] **192**

In principle, the injured party also bears the burden of proof for the level of earnings damage. However, the injured party benefits from the facilitation of evidence provided for in §§ 252 clause 2 BGB, 287 ZPO in showing causality that meets the requirements for liability. In accordance with this, a certain degree of probability is sufficient as evidence for the level of the loss of earnings.[100] **193**

This is comparatively unproblematic in cases in which the injured parties were already in employment and regularly working before the injury. In these cases, it is often only a matter of predicting future increases in pay or salary.[101] This may be quite difficult when the injured parties are still very young and income for several decades has to be assessed, but the courts have to do it.[102] **194**

The prognosis becomes much more difficult, however, if the injured parties were still receiving education and training at the time of the injury or were not even at school yet, as is naturally the case with obstetric injuries in particular. **195**

Here again, the injured party has to present a minimum of factual links enabling the court to form a conviction regarding the overwhelming probability of the career prognosis.[103] However, excessive demands may not be made here, particularly if the injured party is still receiving **196**

---

98 BGH 25 September 1973 – VI ZR 49/72 VersR 1974, 162; BGH 3 February 2009 – VI ZR 183/08 VersR 2009, 515.
99 BGH 31 March 1992 – VI ZR 143/91 VersR 1992, 973.
100 G *Küppersbusch*, Ersatzansprüche bei Personenschäden (9th edn 2007) 18 no 46.
101 Ibid no 50 ff.
102 BGH 8 January 1981 – VI ZR 128/79 VersR 1981, 283.
103 BGH 24 January 1995 – VI ZR 354/93 VersR 1995, 469.

education or has not even started school. The opinion represented by court precedent is that the fact that the party causing the injury is responsible for the situation must not be disregarded.[104]

197 Particularly regarding children, family conditions – eg the parents' professions and siblings' educational level – are therefore taken into consideration in the assessment.

23. Periodic payments or lump sum?

198 In accordance with § 843 para 1 BGB, loss of earning capacity or a claim due to increased needs must in principle be compensated for in the form of an annuity. In accordance with § 843 para 1 BGB, lump-sum compensation can only be claimed by the injured party instead of an annuity if there are compelling reasons to do so.

199 In accordance with § 843 para 1 BGB, only the injured party can request lump-sum compensation if there are compelling reasons, not the party causing the damage. A compelling reason may lie either in the person of the injured party or that of the party causing the injury. A single capital sum may be considered rather exceptionally if the injured party wishes to become self-employed, or if the annuity claim is difficult to implement because the party causing the injury frequently changes his place of residence or lives abroad.

24. Caps and thresholds

200 German compensation law does not envisage either minimum compensation nor an upper limit for the amount of compensation.

II. Non-Pecuniary Loss

25. Introduction to indemnifying non-pecuniary loss

201 In accordance with § 253 para 1 BGB, intangible damage is only compensated for in the cases stipulated by the law. In accordance with § 254 para 2

104 BGH 17 February 1998 – VI ZR 342/96 VersR 1998, 770.

BGB, compensation money can be awarded if physical injury or damage to health is present and fairness is observed in the amount of compensation.[105]

Although it used to be the case that compensation could only be claimed in connection with claims for damages under tort law, this was changed by the second law altering compensation regulations on 1 August 2002. Since then, compensation has been awarded uniformly for both tort and contractual injuries, negligence in the course of contracting/precontractual breach of duty (*culpa in contrahendo* cic), and in all cases of strict liability. The new regulation is therefore logically assigned to the general law on contractual obligations rather than to tort law.[106] **202**

According to constant court precedent, compensation payments are intended on the one hand to represent a rectification of non-pecuniary injury, while on the other hand they should also serve as satisfaction and to make amends.[107] **203**

In the case of medical liability cases, the satisfaction and amends aspect only plays a role in exceptional cases.[108] **204**

The extent of the injury and specific impairment are decisively important for calculating the amount of compensation.[109] **205**

Factors that must be taken into account include the extent, severity, and duration of pain, suffering, disfigurement and psychological impairment.[110] The extent of pain and suffering are determined in accordance with the type of primary injury, the number and severity of operations, the duration of in-patient and outpatient treatments, the period of inability to work, and the level of permanent injury.[111] **206**

According to BGH court precedents, calculation of the type and level of the compensation amount is in principle reserved for the trial court, which is afforded particularly broad scope here by § 287 ZPO.[112] The decision only has to be commensurately justified and must therefore not be arbitrary. **207**

---

105 *L Jaeger/J Luckey* in: Wenzel (fn 15) ch 7, 765 no 547.

106 Palandt-*Heinrichs* (67th edn 2008) § 253, 301 no 2.

107 BGH 6 July 1955 – GSZ 18, 149 VersR 1955, 615; BGH 20 October 2004 – VI ZR 70/03 VersR 2004, 1334.

108 *Jaeger/Luckey* (fn 105) part I F, 152 no 610.

109 *Küppersbusch* (fn 100) 83 no 275.

110 *Jaeger/Luckey* (fn 105) no 594 p 148 f.

111 OLG Brandenburg 18 June 2009 – 12 U 213/08 VersR 2009, 1540.

112 BGH 8 June 1976 – VI ZR 216/74 VersR 1976, 967.

208 The framework of guidance for the trial judges is provided by decisions in comparable cases. On this basis, the court has to evaluate special conditions applying in the specific individual case that might lead to an increase or reduction in the amount.

209 In practice, courts are nowadays guided here by two surveys of court decisions regarding compensation payment. These compensation tables are produced by the ADAC and Beck publishing houses.[113]

210 The highest compensation amounts awarded so far have been a capital sum of € 500,000 and a monthly compensation pension of € 500.[114] These involved two cases of obstetric injury and one case of the effects of a vehicle accident. The list shows that there are no divergences of any kind for malpractice cases in comparison with other types of case.

26. Who can claim compensation for non-pecuniary loss?

211 German law does not recognise compensation for relatives or other third parties indirectly injured. Court precedents have been extremely restrictive with regard to compensation for what is known as shock injury.[115]

212 According to court precedent, compensation for shock injury due to injury or death of near relatives presupposes that objectively identifiable medical effects are present that exceed the type and severity of the symptoms normally occurring in connection with such events.[116]

213 In addition, the reason for the shock must be comprehensible. It has to be capable of triggering this type of reaction in a person of average sensitivity.[117] Finally, this type of compensation claim is only accepted for close relatives.[118]

---

113 See also the compensation payment table in *Jaeger/Luckey* (fn 105).

114 OLG Zweibrücken 22 April 2008 – 5 U 6/07 MDR 2009, 88; LG Kiel 11 June 2003 – 6 O 13/03 VersR 2006, 279.

115 Palandt-*Heinrichs* (67th edn 2008) Vorb v § 249 BGB, 272 no 71.

116 BGH 11 May 1971 – VI ZR 11/70 VersR 1971, 822.

117 BGH 5 February 1985 – VI ZR 198/1983 VersR 1985, 499.

118 Palandt-*Heinrichs*, Vorb v § 249 BGB, 272 no 71.

G. Procedural Matters

27. Specific rules of jurisdiction or procedure

There are no special rules of jurisdiction for actions for medical malpractice. Medical liability trials are basically conducted according to the regulations applying in the Civil Code Procedure. 214

However, due to the patient's inherent weakness relative to the superior expertise of the person conducting treatment, and along with the requirement for equality of opportunity to be heard and give evidence in legal proceedings, constant court precedent in the BGH has accepted the need to markedly reduce requirements for the patient's obligation to substantiate claims,[119] on the one hand, while on the other it obliges the lower courts to clarify the material medical facts on their own responsibility to a greater extent.[120] In effect, this leads to judicial investigations which are not normally known in civil law. 215

28. Special institutions handling malpractice claims

The boards of medical registration in each of the federal states have established Expertise and Arbitration Offices that offer procedures for out-of-court mediation in cases of medical liability in order to resolve disputes between patients and physicians as quickly as possible, at the request of one of the parties, by providing expert assessment of medical activity.[121] As these are bodies set up by each state board, their organisational structures and procedures vary. 216

Both patients and physicians are authorised to apply for mediation. In some cases, the hospital concerned and/or the company providing liability insurance also take part in the procedure.[122] Participation is voluntary for both parties. There are no costs risks involved in the procedure. In principle, the costs of the procedure are borne by each state medical board. However, the professional statutory insurance companies for the physicians concerned pay a flat-rate charge, independent of the result, on the 217

---

119 BGH 8 June 2004 – VI ZR 199/03 VersR 2004, 1177.

120 BGH 31 May 1988 – VI ZR 261/87 VersR 1988, 914; on this whole complex of issues, see *Rosenberger* in: Wenzel (fn 15) ch 7 nos 309 ff.

121 For a detailed description of the system and the procedure, see *H-D Laum* in: Wenzel (fn 15) ch 6, 611–631.

122 See, for example, § 2 para 2 of the Rules of Procedure for the Mediation Office for Medical Liability Issues of the North German Medical Boards.

basis of agreements between the state medical boards and the general association of German insurance companies. In some cases, costs for external expert assessments are also paid.[123]

218 The members of the Expertise and Arbitration Offices are independent. They must have many years' professional experience as physicians or members of the legal profession and work without being subject to instructions.

219 In the great majority of cases, the procedures take place in written form and end with an official notification.[124]

220 Decisions made by the Expertise and Arbitration Offices are not binding and leave open the option of going to court.[125]

H. Outlook

29. Reform plans

221 Repeated efforts have been made in recent years to reform medical liability law. On the one hand, these have been aimed at creating special legal regulations for medical liability. On the other, there have been proposals intended to lead directly or indirectly – eg by altering the burden of proof – towards strict liability. All of these initiatives have fortunately been unsuccessful. There are no plans currently in sight that have any prospect of implementation.

Cases

Old or new law?

222 The law of obligations in the Federal Republic of Germany was reformed with effect as of 1 January 2002. In accordance with § 5 of the General Transition Regulations on the Law for the Modernisation of Obligations Law of 26 November 2001, the following laws continue to apply to

123 § 6 para 3 of the Rules of Procedure for the Mediation Office for Medical Liability Issues of the North German Medical Boards.

124 § 5 para 4 of the Rules of Procedure for the Mediation Office for Medical Liability Issues of the North German Medical Boards.

125 125 § 7 para 3 of the Rules of Procedure for the Mediation Office for Medical Liability Issues of the North German Medical Boards.

obligations arising before 1 January 2002 in the versions valid up to that date, unless otherwise specified: the German Civil Code, the AGB Law (General Conditions of Business), German Commercial Code, Consumer Credit Law, the Distance Selling Act, Distance Learning Protection Law, the Law on Door-to-Door Sales and Similar Sales, the Part-Time Occupation Rights Law, the Regulation on Customer Information Duties, the Regulation on Information Duties of Travel Agents, and the Regulation on Major Faults and Guarantee Periods in the Livestock Trade.

The cases presented here therefore all need to be judged in accordance with earlier law, but there are no substantial differences that result from this. However, a claim for compensation for pain and suffering based on contractual claims might be put forward according to the new legislation, whereas under the older legislation it could only have been asserted on the basis of tort claims. **223**

Case 1

1. Contractual claims

The facts of the case show that X, a female patient of B, had already attended his joint practice with A before the incident. Admission to the hospital was thus evidently to the private department for the two physicians, where she initially received further in-patient treatment from B, before A continued the treatment as his vacation stand-in. The existence of a contract between doctor and patient between A and X can therefore be assumed. When physicians in the same specialties run a joint practice that appears from the outside to be a group practice or a health clinic, not only due to the appearance of the offices but also because it presents itself as a specialist unit in which medical services can be provided by all of the physicians during the patient's treatment, then all of the physicians in the unit are jointly and severally liable under the contract between doctor and patient.[126] The same also applies if the physicians work as visiting consultants in the same hospital and continue treatments started in their own joint practice there.[127] This was the situation according to the facts in this case. The integrity of the unborn child is protected under contractual and tort law both prenatally and during birth.[128] To this extent, both X and Y **224**

126 BGH VersR 1999, 1241; BGH VersR 2002, 233.
127 BGH VersR 2000, 1146.
128 *Steffen/Pauge* (fn 33) 50 no 122.

can both make contractual claims against A and B. In addition, liability of A and B for possible mistakes made by D is conceivable, since due to the previous in-patient admission of X, the birth was a task contractually assigned to her and D is therefore their agent.[129]

225 In the German visiting consultant system, a contract between patient and hospital only arises for nursing and medical care lying outside of the medical services provided by the visiting consultant and subordinate physicians in his designated specialty. C is therefore not liable for A and B. With regard to possible mistakes of midwife D, employed by C, D is acting as an agent of C. To this extent, contractual liability on the part of C is possible.

226 On the other hand, there are evidently no contractual relationships between D and X or Y, so that there is no basis for contractual claims.

2. Tort claims

227 Each individual involved in the treatment is liable in tort due to his position as guarantor for the treatment task undertaken, but in principle only for his own mistakes within his own area of control, not for mistakes made by third parties. X and Y can thus make claims in tort against B, but not against A.

228 The same also applies to claims in tort against C. So far as these concern possible mistakes made by the midwife, fault on the part of the hospital also arises in accordance with § 831 BGB relative to the organisation, selection, instruction, monitoring and equipment of its agent. This type of fault is presumed. No grounds for exonerating evidence are found in the facts of the case, so that the hospital would also be liable in tort for the midwife as its agent.

3. Liability on merits

229 According to the facts of the case, D incorrectly neglected to call in A in a timely fashion; independently of that, A while being aware of the situation, incorrectly initiated the required Cesarean section too late. A and B are also contractually responsible for the error made by D, as is C, who is also liable in tort for the error made by D, as no grounds for possible

129 OLG Oldenburg 16 January 1996 – 5 U 17/95 VersR 1997, 1236.

exonerating evidence are found in the facts of the case. Finally, D is also responsible in tort for her error.

However, the extent to which this error caused the injuries of Y remains an open question. In principle, the burden of proof for causality lies with the patient. It is sufficient here to show 'a degree of certainty applicable in practical life that would still any doubts, although without fully excluding them.'[130] As it is in fact highly probable, according to the facts of the case, that at least a substantial proportion of the damage had already taken place before the childbirth process, it would probably not be possible for this evidence to be shown. **230**

On the other hand, liability would be affirmable if the errors were each regarded as instances of gross malpractice. In that case, it would be sufficient for them to be capable of causing damage of the type that actually occurred. **231**

According to the facts of the case, it was evident that the cesarean section was urgently required. However, this was not seen by either A or D. Instead, A unnecessarily carried out a treatment on another patient. To this extent, there is gross malpractice, as incorrect medical conduct is present that does not appear to be comprehensible from an objective medical point of view because a physician must simply not make a mistake of this type.[131] The consequence of this is a reversal of the burden of proof in favor of Y. The defendants would have to prove that the injuries that occurred were not due to the delayed completion of the birth. According to the facts of the case, this did not happen. **232**

A, B and C are therefore contractually liable and A and C are also liable in tort for the injuries that occurred to Y. **233**

Y can therefore require A, B and C to compensate for all previous and future material injuries and damage that are attributable to the incorrect treatments and have not passed to third parties. This may involve costs for house conversion, material nursing costs, loss of earning capacity etc. Higher costs for home care in comparison with a nursing home are also subject to compensation. In principle, the injured party is free to decide how the care he requires is provided, at least as long as it is not disproportionate. The German courts do not assume this even when there are very large differences in costs between outpatient and inpatient care. When nursing care is required as a result of injuries, nursing services are also to **234**

130 BGH 26 October 1993 – VI ZR 155/92 VersR 1994, 52.
131 BGH VersR 1983, 729.

be compensated appropriately when they are provided by relatives rather than outside nurses. However, services provided by parents are only subject to compensation to the extent that by their nature they could also be comparably carried out by an outside nurse. According to the facts of the case, it can probably be assumed that Y can also claim compensation for nursing work provided by her mother. On the basis of the facts of the case as presented, it is not clear whether the standard wage rate for a qualified nurse can be assumed here.

235 In addition, she can claim damages for pain and suffering. In view of the severe injuries, an order in the magnitude of € 350,000–500,000 can be expected.

236 The claims made by X, so far as they affect nursing costs, are already taken into account with Y. With regard to her own claim for damages for pain and suffering due to stress caused by the stillbirth of her son and severe injury to her daughter, it is not clear from the facts of the case that objectively identifiable medical effects are present which with regard to their type and severity exceed the symptoms normally occurring with such experiences, so that a separate claim for damages for pain and suffering does not arise. Overall, X's claims must therefore be disallowed.

Case 2

237 The prerequisite for the contractual and tort claims is initially that liability on the part of A is generally conceivable due to the unwanted birth of a child. This question was a matter of severe controversy for a time, summed up in phrases such as 'baby as an injury', and even today it still gives rise to debate.

238 In accordance with constant court precedents in the BGH, however, the financial burdens for the parents associated with the birth of an unwanted child, and in particular costs for the child's maintenance, must be compensated for in damages if protection against such burdens was the subject of the relevant treatment contract or consultancy contract. The BGH has particularly affirmed the liability of the physician or hospital trust in this regard, based on the purpose of the contract in cases of failed sterilisation for reasons of family planning,[132] incorrect advice regarding

---

132 BGH 2 December 1980 – VI ZR 175/78 VersR 1981, 278; BGH 10 March 1981 – VI ZR 202/79 VersR 1981, 730; BGH 19 June 1984 – VI ZR 76/83 VersR 1984, 864; BGH 27 June 1995 – VI ZR 32/94 VersR 1995, 1099.

the safety of the contraceptive effects of a hormonal drug prescribed by the physician,[133] and cases of incorrect genetic advice prior to the conception of a genetically disabled child.[134] These court decisions were deemed constitutionally sound by the Federal Constitutional Court in a ruling of 12 November 1997.[135] In contrast to court decisions by the Supreme Court in Austria, the same also applies to the birth of a healthy child.

The present case belongs to this group of cases. The treatment contract entered into by A and X was clearly aimed at administering the agent Implanon to X. The only possible purpose of this measure was clearly to prevent pregnancy. To this extent, the purpose of the treatment contract entered into was certainly also to protect her against the financial burdens arising from the maintenance obligations and costs in case of the birth of a child. Liability on the part of A is therefore in principle possible. **239**

Another prerequisite is that A made an error when implanting the agent. This can be assumed in accordance with the facts of the case, as the Implanon implant was not found, nor was the active agent identified in X's blood. **240**

It can also be assumed that the treatment error was causal in X's pregnancy. **241**

The pregnant woman need not be reproached with the fact that she could have terminated the pregnancy. Neither ex post facto consent nor contributory negligence can be deduced from a pregnancy termination that was not carried out. **242**

X qualifies for compensation in her own right in relation to the childcare maintenance she has paid and will pay in the future in accordance with § 1606 para 3 clause 2 BGB. However, there is no separate claim for compensation with regard to cash maintenance provided by the child's father, as this cash maintenance is provided by Y. **243**

However, X also has claims arising from rights transferred from Y, as the latter is included in the area of protection covered by the treatment contract. **244**

In cases in which medical malpractice causally contributes to the birth of an unwanted child, court precedent of the BGH indicates that the father is **245**

133 BGH 3 June 1997 – VI ZR 133/96 VersR 1997, 1422.

134 BGH 16 November 1993 – VI ZR 105/92 VersR 1994, 425.

135 Entscheidungen des Bundesverfassungsgerichtes (BVerfGE) 12 November 1997 – 1 BvR 479/92 + 307/94 VersR 1998, 190.

included in the area protected by the contract.[136] The only questionable aspect might therefore be whether an unmarried father of a child is also included in the area protected by the contract. The BGH has affirmed that this is the case.[137]

246 In accordance with the general principles of contracts with a protective effect favoring third parties, an interest on the part of the creditor in being included is necessary, as the creditor has a special interest in the inclusion of third parties in the contract's area of protection and this is also evident to the debtor without the name or number of the third parties being protected having to be known to him.

247 The inclusion of the father in the area protected by the contract has been accepted for a non-marital – but at least quasi-marital – long-term relationship.[138]

248 The same would certainly also have to apply to other non-stable partnerships, since, particularly in a partnership that is not aimed at establishing a long-term relationship, a corresponding desire not to start a family is obvious.

249 In any case, however, it can be assumed that A in principle had an interest at least in protecting her current partner from maintenance costs in the same way as she was protecting herself, through a contract that allows a – regularly agreed – form of contraception, and that this was evident to the physician treating her. There is therefore also a claim arising from a transferred right to compensation due to the obligation to pay cash maintenance according to § 1612 a BGB.

250 Accordingly, A is liable on merit for compensation for damages caused and arising in the future to X and Y due to maintenance obligations.

251 With regard to the level of damages, it should be taken into account that – according to court precedent – the physician is only responsible for the proportion of costs required to ensure the child's life as part of the financial burdens and cash maintenance resulting from the birth of a child for which he bears responsibility.

252 For the maintenance of an under-age child, a percentage of the relevant fixed amount as established in the Standard Amounts Regulation of 6

---

136 BGH 16 June 2002 – VI ZR 136/01 VersR 2002, 1148.
137 BGH 14 November 2006 – VI ZR 48/06 VersR 2007, 109.
138 OLG Frankfurt am Main 19 May 1993 – 13 U 16/92 VersR 1994, 942.

April 1998 is set, and court precedent has regarded the subsistence level for a child as 135 % of this fixed amount.

The value of the care provided must be added to this. A supplementary amount at the level of cash maintenance – ie a further 135 % – is usually applied here. **253**

Case 3

Contractual claims exist against all three defendants. In relation to the obstetrics department A, X was included in the area protected by the contract between his mother and the hospital. With regard to B and C, it is a contract in favor of third parties that X's parents have entered into on his behalf. **254**

There are also claims in tort – directly against B, and indirectly against A and C as no grounds are evident from the facts of the case to show that the hospitals could provide exonerating evidence in accordance with § 831 BGB. **255**

According to the facts of the case, instances of malpractice must be affirmed for all three defendants. **256**

X was discharged from treatment by A although even at the time of the injury it was a confirmed pediatric fact that the blood sugar level must be monitored for at least 24 hours. In addition, a pediatrician was not consulted, nor was X's mother or his midwife informed about the need for the blood sugar to be checked. **257**

On the basis of his own training, B should have recognised the existing risk and also consulted a pediatrician. **258**

C is initially responsible for the fact that neither D nor E, as its agents and assistants, called in an experienced physician in a timely fashion, so that the treatment necessary for X was delayed by several hours. However, C is also responsible for its own mistakes. It is generally held that a hospital trust must ensure organisationally that it is able to carry out its duties with the available staff and medical equipment in accordance with the current state of medical knowledge. Among other things, it must take appropriate measures to ensure that the organisational structure and forms are effective and that the staff employed receive adequate instruction. According to the facts presented, this was evidently not the case. **259**

260 If the relevant mistakes are thus present for all three defendants, they would only be able to escape liability if it could be shown that their behavior in each case was not the cause of the brain damage that occurred.

261 As it is not clear whether or to what extent X's brain damage was already present at the time of his admission to C, it is hardly possible to present proof of causality. However, so many organisational errors are present on the part of the hospital that gross malpractice in the form of a gross organisational mistake must be affirmed. These deficiencies are also responsible for the fact that X was not examined at an early stage and that his condition was not established at the time of admission. In any case, overall examination of the individual deficiencies – even if each of them were to be regarded separately as only a simple mistake – shows that the inadequate organisation represented gross malpractice. This would be sufficient in accordance with court precedent.[139]

262 B's errors are also causative for the injury to X. If she had called in a pediatrician earlier, the hypoglycemia would have been recognised and treated at an early stage. The subsequent catastrophic course would then never have taken place.

263 The same applies to A, so that the question of whether the behavior of these physicians represents gross malpractice – which is left open in the facts of the case – is of no consequence.

264 The fact that the injury might not have occurred if C had behaved appropriately does not exonerate B or A. If incorrect treatment makes intervention by a second physician indispensable, liability for a mistake made by the second physician can also in principle be assigned to the first. This linked assignment of liability is only cancelled if the individual responsible for the second injury has infringed against all the rules of medicine to an extraordinary extent. Even gross malpractice alone is not sufficient to do this.

265 To this extent, all three are liable jointly and severally for the injuries that occurred.

266 X is entitled to claim damages for pain and suffering, which in view of the extremely severe injury and current court precedent may amount to € 500,000, as well as compensation for all material damage attributable to the incorrect treatments.

139 OLG Celle 7 May 2001 – 1 U 15/00 VersR 2002, 1558.

With regard to loss of earning capacity, however, only an application for a declaratory finding can currently be made. Due to his young age, it will only be possible to determine the level of loss of income once X has reached an appropriate age. 267

Case 4

As the facts of the case show that the operation was carried out without errors and that the paraplegia only effectuated a risk associated with the procedure, there is no liability due to malpractice. 268

However, both contractually and in tort, effective consent justifying a medical intervention presupposes that the patient has received information regarding the course of the procedure and its prospects of success and risks. 269

This was evidently not the case, as the plaintiff could not speak German and an interpreter was not present, and it is also otherwise unclear whether or in what way the physician providing the information might have been able to make himself understood to the plaintiff. 270

The consent form signed by the plaintiff is also not helpful here. Although the risk of paralysis is mentioned in it, it is questionable whether this is sufficient to suggest the risk of paraplegia appropriately. Independently of that, however, the informed consent discussion required by legal precedent is not demonstrated by the form, as it has been established that the plaintiff in any case did not understand the physician. The physician, who thus bears the burden of proof, must ensure that except in emergency cases the patient also understands the information given to him. The fact that in this case it was not C but B who carried out the informed consent discussion does not lead to a different result under German law. In principle, informed consent must be obtained by the physician carrying out the treatment, as he himself requires the patient's consent in order to justify his actions. If the task is delegated, the physician carrying out the operation is obliged to ensure for himself that appropriate specialist information has been given and that consent has been properly provided. To this extent, C is himself directly responsible for the ineffective consent. 271

It can therefore remain an open question whether a further deficiency in the consent process lies in the fact that the plaintiff was not informed about the existence of two potential access routes. The choice of treatment method is in principle at the physician's discretion. If he has selected a 272 treatment method that is indicated and customary, he is not obliged to draw attention to other methods that may also be medically indicated and customary if the method he has chosen is at least equivalent to the alternative treatments in terms of prospects of success and risk. Otherwise, legal precedent refers to these as a genuine alternative about which the patient needs to be informed, so that he himself can decide which risks he wishes to be exposed to. In the present case, it would be a matter of debate whether the fact that the mortality risk is higher with the transthoracic access route implied a duty to inform.

273 The inadequate informed consent procedure was also causative for the injuries that occurred, since according to the facts of the case the plaintiff would certainly have found himself in a decisional conflict and would probably have chosen not to undergo the operation. If the operation had not taken place, the paraplegia would certainly not have occurred at that time.

274 A is therefore liable contractually and in tort for the unlawful procedure carried out by its agent and assistant C. The latter is also liable in accordance with §§ 823, 832, 847, 249 BGB.

275 The plaintiff can require compensation for conversion of his house for wheelchair use, since although he already had limited mobility before the procedure, he was not dependent on a wheelchair. He can also claim for additional expenses caused by the injury. By contrast, costs for purchasing a new car suitable for the disabled can only be claimed to an extent equivalent to the conversion of his existing car to one for disabled use. The costs for the car itself must not be compensated for by the defendant.

276 Damages for pain and suffering can be expected to be in the order of a magnitude of € 10,000–150,000. In the present case, however, it would need to be taken into account that the plaintiff already had considerable pre-existing impairments.

Case 5

277 This case is essentially concerned with issues involving burden of proof. The plaintiff is advancing claims due to alleged malpractice. It is not clear from the facts of the case to what extent mistakes actually occurred during the operation. The only certain aspect is the outcome, an injury to the ulnar nerve. As the injury was present immediately postoperatively, there is an obvious connection with the operation.

In principle, the patient as plaintiff would have had to provide evidence that the injury is attributable to errors connected with patient positioning. 278

However, in connection with patient positioning during surgery, it is assumed in court precedent that this type of nerve injury due to positioning is basically avoidable unless any special characteristics in the patient are present that might lead to a different outcome. For this reason, technically correct positioning and the medical rules that need to be adhered to in order to protect the patient against any positioning injuries are measures which constant court precedent has assigned to the area of risk of the treatment side and which are usually completely capable of being controlled by nursing staff and the physicians carrying out the treatment. The consequence of this is that it is the treatment side that now has to prove that the injuries that have occurred are not due to an error either in initial positioning or in monitoring during the operation (which lasts several hours). 279

According to the facts of the case, this evidence cannot be provided. It is not clear from this that C adequately monitored the appropriateness of positioning throughout the whole period of the operation. It is also an open question whether, as a beginner, she was at all able to ensure the standard of a specialist physician for anesthetic monitoring during an operation lasting several hours. The hourly checks carried out by the acting senior physician were certainly not sufficient to compensate for any deficiencies that might have occurred. 280

On the basis of the agreement between the professional associations of anesthetists and surgeons, B and C are jointly responsible for patient positioning. However, it is clear that the injury did not occur immediately as a result of positioning at the start of the operation, but only developed at a later stage. As the surgeon's view of X was obstructed by the surgical drapes after the start of the operation and in addition the anesthetist is responsible for the positioning of the extremities according to the agreement, a breach of the duty of care on the part of B is not evident. 281

By contrast, a breach of the duty of care on the part of C must be affirmed, as evidence has not been provided that standard monitoring of patient positioning was carried out during the operation. As an objective standard of care based on the prevailing public understanding applies here, C is also unable to exonerate herself from the accusation of fault by claiming that as a beginner she only had subjectively inadequate specialist knowledge. 282

283 In addition, A is also responsible for C as its agent or assistant. Moreover, liability on the grounds of an organisational fault is conceivable, as A was responsible for the fact that the acting senior physician was obliged to monitor six operating rooms simultaneously and was therefore unable to effectively supervise C as a beginner.

284 As the nerve injury took place in direct connection with the operation, there are no doubts regarding causality.

285 A claim for damages for pain and suffering to the amount of approximately € 15,000 would be justified.

286 With regard to the loss of income claimed, it may initially be noted that refusal to undertake retraining as a salesperson in a building supplies store, which was clearly feasible, is likely to represent a breach of X's duty to minimise the injury, as he is in principle obliged to undertake suitable retraining in a different job that he can still do despite his disablement.[140]

287 Thus only the difference between his income as a bricklayer and a potentially lower income as a salesman would be eligible for compensation.

288 X is also not entitled to claim compensation for income from undeclared and illicit work done at weekends. Income from illicit work is not eligible for compensation if it has been obtained in violation of the Law on the Control of Illicit Employment.[141]

Case 6

1. Basis of claim

289 As discussed above under case 1, when physicians in the same specialties run a joint practice that appears from the outside to be a group practice or a health clinic, not only due to the appearance of the offices but also because it presents itself as a specialist unit in which medical services can be provided by all of the physicians during the patient's treatment, then all of the physicians in the unit are jointly and severally liable under the contract between doctor and patient.

---

140 BGH 9 September 1990 – VI ZR 291/89 VersR 1990, 437.

141 BGH 11 January 1994 – VI ZR 143/93 VersR 1994, 355 with further references; LG Oldenburg 13 June 1988 – 4 O 474/88 VersR 1988, 1246.

A and B are thus liable contractually and in tort for their own potential mistakes and also contractually for potential mistakes made by their agents – ie including stand-in physicians C and D. 290

On the other hand, liability on their part for any failures or omissions on the part of C and D in accordance with § 831 BGB does not arise, since the facts of the case do not show that any duty to comply with instructions was imposed on them. 291

By contrast, in the absence of a contractual relationship C and D are only liable in tort to X for their own faults. 292

2. Liability for infections

According to court precedent, the decisive aspect in liability for nosocomial infections is the question of whether the facts of the case can be assigned to the fully controllable area of risk – ie whether the patient's infection effectuated a risk that was created by the physician's office and could have been fully controlled if it had been organised appropriately. 293

If this question is answered in the affirmative, the plaintiff benefits from a facilitation of evidence analogous to § 282 BGB (280 para 1 clause 2 BGB new).[142] In contrast to the wording, this is less relevant to the issue of fault. Instead, in practice both the objective breach of duty and also causality for the injury are proved if it is established that a medical duty that lies in the fully controllable risk area has been breached. 294

On the other hand, the patient side has to prove the treatment error, the causal connection between the breach of duty and the primary injury that occurred, and must also prove a fault, if the issue is concerned with the core area of medical activity in which only limited control is possible – ie processes in the living organism that even the best physician cannot always control, so that a lack of success or even only a setback would suggest a fault in the treatment.[143] 295

In contrast to the decision referred to in which it remained unclear who transmitted the pathogen and it was consequently also unclear whether transmission of the pathogen was unavoidable, it is established in the present case that the cause of the infection was the fact that the physician's assistant was a carrier of the *Staphylococcus* bacterium and in addition a 296

142 BGH 8 January 1991 – VI ZR 102/90 VersR 1991, 467.
143 BGH VersR 1991, 467.

wide variety of hygienic deficiencies were present in the physician's office. To this extent, there are also no grounds for considering that transmission of the pathogen might have been unavoidable. Instead, it is clear that the transmission would have been avoidable if the physicians had observed the required hygienic precautions.

297 To this extent, the risk of pathogen transmission was fully controllable, with the consequence that the burden of proof is reversed. This proof is not provided in the facts of the case.

298 The two owners of the medical practice, as well as their stand-ins, are therefore responsible under liability law for the syringe abscess and its consequences.

3. Extent of damage

299 Damages for pain and suffering may be in the range of € 25,000. X can also claim for payment of all previous and future material damage if it is attributable to the malpractice and has not passed to third parties. As the facts of the case show that X's inability to work was due to the syringe abscess, she can claim for loss of income. The same applies to costs for a cleaner. It is of no consequence here that the cleaning was done by her daughter.

300 If assistance provided by the family is free of charge, the damage is normally calculated normatively. The starting point for damage estimation in the framework of § 287 ZPO is the net wages for a necessary and suitable temporary worker.

4. Variation 1

301 It remains unclear who transferred the pathogen. Accordingly, there is certainly no evidence that a risk has been effectuated that was created by the operation of the physician's practice. As it is already an open question what the transmission route for the infection was and who the carrier might have been, it is also not possible to prove that the hygiene deficiencies were the cause of the pathogen transmission and the resulting syringe abscess, or that a proper hygiene regime would have prevented the infection.

302 Liability for all defendants must therefore be denied.

5. Variation 2

If it has been established that the infection must have originated in a hygienically controllable area, then the physicians are responsible both contractually and in tort for the consequences of the infection unless they are able to exonerate themselves by showing that the non-observance of hygiene requirements was no fault of theirs – ie unless they can prove that all organisational and technical precautions against avoidable pathogen transmission by their medical office staff had been taken. **303**

As the facts of the case show that the usual hygiene standards were observed, this evidence could be provided by the physicians. Liability would be denied. **304**

Medical Liability in Hungary

Attila Menyhárd

General Questions

A. The Health Care System Framework

I. General Introduction

1. The health care system in overview

The health care system in Hungary presents a mixed picture. The public health care system surviving the socialist era remains the general basis of health care services. This system is maintained by the state and by the local municipalities as the part of their social tasks provided in § 70/D subpara (2) of the Constitution of the Hungarian Republic and in § 8 subpara (1) and (4) and § 63 subpara (1) of the Act no LXV of 1990 on the local municipalities. The public health care system is financed from the central state budget through the National Health Insurance Fund with a system of levies to be paid as a contribution to the central state budget by entrepreneurs, employers and employees. A great bulk of the doctors – most of them working parallel for the state and municipal medical health care providers financed from the budget as well – normally maintain a private practice too. This system creates a market for health care services exploiting the shortcomings and improper working of the public health care system. In specific areas, where there is normally no need for complex treatment (dentists, doctors providing gynaecological diagnostic services, ophthalmologists etc) or investment in expensive equipment that is slow to generate remuneration, doctors run private practices and work entirely with their own equipment. Doctors running a private practice in professional fields where services imply complex treatments and/or where there is a demand for maintaining expensive equipments which can not be a remunerative investment in a private practice (like surgical interventions, gynaecological interventions, assisting with childbirth, oncology etc) typically work as employees of state or municipal medical health care providers belonging to the centrally- 1 financed public health care system. In these areas a lot of doctors provide their services partly in their private practice and partly in the public health care system, using the facilities of the public medical health care providers (state and municipal hospitals) or sharing the tasks with these institutions, leaving the activities that they are not able to perform to these institutions. A typical scenario is where the doctor gives advice and establishes diagnoses in his private consulting hours in his own premises but performs the surgical operation and follow-up treatment in the state or municipal hospital with the hospital's equipment while the preceding laboratory tests are to be provided as a separate task of the hospital. In such mixed relationships it is often not clear how risks and responsibilities are allocated between the private doctor and the public health care provider. Sometimes it is not clear whether the doctor made a mistake as an employee working for the hospital or as a private doctor responsible for his own acts. Eg it may happen that certain risks remain undisclosed to the patient because the private doctor thought that the risks had already been disclosed by the hospital in the course of the diagnostic procedure performed there while the hospital had in fact regarded it as a task of the doctor advising the patient under a private practice.

2 There is one clearly privately owned hospital in Hungary performing a wide range of services including diagnostic procedures, advising, surgical operations and follow-up treatment of patients with or without residence. There are also institutes and hospitals providing diagnostic, treatment and one-day surgical operation services on a private (market) basis in a limited range of interventions not demanding expensive investments and not involving complex treatments.

3 Doctors working as employees for the public health care providers (hospitals) normally receive gratuity from patients. The basis of this 'custom' is the general necessity of compensating the doctors for their generally low salaries. As has been established in a Supreme Court decision,[1] such gratuities are not prohibited and shall not be deemed as illegal payments as they are paid on the basis of a personal decision of the patients. According to specific regulations, doctors are obliged to provide services to patients according to the highest possible level without demanding or receiving any extra honorary from patients. Doctors working under the Public Health Insurance Service system are not supposed to request any kind of extra payment, honorary or other material advantage as a countervalue of their services to the patient and they are prohibited from offering

1 Supreme Court, Pfv X 24.130/1997 sz – EBH 1999 no 18 (BH 1998 no 533).

their services on the condition of receiving such material advantages.[2] Doctors working as employees of hospitals are obliged to do their work on the basis of this relationship but they are not prevented from accepting such gratuities after the treatment.

The result of this mixed picture of the health care sector is that different regimes may cover the legal relationships between the patient and the various different members of the staff (medical team) performing the medical treatment. Some of the members of a team may be employees of the hospital, while others may be independent sub-contractors of the hospital or acting under an independent and separate contract with the patient and for whom the hospital can not be held liable. In such cases the different legal relationships may result in the application of different rules or regimes of liability. **4**

The number of medical malpractice cases in Hungary is relatively low (200–300 new lawsuits per year) although they are of great importance. The number of this type of cases does not appear to be increasing (the exception is Budapest). The average length of this type of cases is one to three years. Some of them, however, exceed this duration and exceptionally may take more than five years. In most of the cases the necessity of appointing judicial experts and getting their opinion prevents a settlement of the procedure in a reasonable time. Typically also the defendants do not cooperate with the courts in bringing the lawsuit quickly to an end.[3] **5**

II. Social Welfare Provision

2. The role of public health care

Under the public health care system, hospitals and other institutions providing health care services including medical advisers and doctors are medical service providers. Patients who are entitled to demand public health care services may apply for the service at the service provider whose geographic coverage includes the patient's residence. Patients have freedom in choosing the institute and the doctor but the medical service provider may refuse to provide service to persons coming from outside of its province. The financial coverage is allocated from the central budget as **6**

2 § 75 of the Act no II of 1972 on Public Health (not in force anymore).

3 Memorandum on the National Discussions of 23–25 January 2008 of high courts' civil law colleges and the Civil Law College of the Hungarian Supreme Court.

the medical health care providers and hospitals would otherwise refuse treatment to patients coming from outside their territorial scope even when they have the capacity to treat them for fear of exceeding their allocated budget.

7 Patients applying for treatment in the public health care sector do not contract in a traditional sense but rather, according to the general view – followed by the courts as well – a contract for services, of a specific character is to be construed between the patient and the health care provider (the same holds for the private health sector).[4] Thus, patients applying for the service of the public health care service provider are assumed to be individual contracting parties to the public health care service provider and the price of the services is to be covered from the central budget of the National Health Insurance Fund.

8 The administration of the National Health Insurance Fund concludes financing contracts for specific health care services with health care service providers authorised to provide the service, including contracts for dispensing medicinal products with social security subsidies, for the marketing, rental and repair of medical aids with social security subsidies, including the manufacture of custom-made devices if the manufacturer is also engaged in retail distribution and for the provision of subsidised medical care with a service provider.[5]

3. Differences in treating patient's claims

9 It seems to be a general view that a contract for services is to be construed between the patient and the medical health care service provider regardless of whether the service provider belongs to the public or to the private health care sector. Thus, claims are not to be treated in different ways depending on whether they were launched against a public or a private health care service provider. Neither the regulations nor court practice differentiates in their treatment of patient's claims between those cases launched against public or private medical health care service providers on the one hand and other personal injury cases on the other hand. As Hungarian tort law is a unified system applying the same rules for liability

4 *Á Dósa*, Az orvos kártérítési felelőssége (2004) 76 ff; *G Jobbágyi*, Orvosi jog (2005) 25 ff.

5 The system of these contractual relationships, the content of these contracts, the monitoring of performance as well as details of financing from the National Health Insurance Fund are covered by specific legislation. Act no LXXXIII of 1997 on the Services of the Compulsory Health Insurance System, § 30 ff.

in tort and for breach of contract. The contractual relationship to be construed does not lead to differences in treating patients' claims. The construed contract for services implies that doctors and employees of the medical health care provider shall act according to the required professional standards of conduct and are to be held liable for causing harm due to failure to comply with these standards.

There is no general internal review or claims management system in the **10** Hungarian national social security system.

4. Right of recourse

The right of recourse of a social welfare agency contributing to the care or **11** well-being of a patient who has suffered harm in the course of medical treatment is not covered by any specific regulation. As a general rule for the right of recourse under the publicly financed national health care insurance system, the Act no LXXXIII of 1997 on the Services of the Compulsory Health Insurance System provides for the right of recourse of services paid by the National Health Care Insurance Fund. As a general rule, the tortfeasor liable for the illness, lost working capacity, injury or death of the beneficiary of the public health care services, shall be obliged to reimburse the provision provided on this basis from the Health Care Insurance Fund where liability is established according to the general rules of liability in tort according to the Hungarian Civil Code. There are specific rules providing for the employers' obligation to provide recourse in cases of industrial accidents and occupational diseases (§§ 67, 68). This provision was presumably not designed for the right of recourse in cases where the patient has suffered harm in the course of medical treatment and another social welfare agency contributed to the care or well-being of him. If, however, the social welfare agency that provided the treatment belonged to the public health care insurance system, there is no reason to exclude the application of this rule.

If the social welfare agency contributing to the care or well-being of a **12** patient did not belong to the national health care insurance system, such rights of recourse are to be assessed under the general private law, especially the law of torts and unjust enrichment. If the services have been provided under a private insurance, the general rules for the right of recourse of private insurers provided in the Hungarian Civil Code are to be applied. There is no publicly available information on how such potential claims are managed or whether there are any attempts to exercise such rights of recourse.

III. Private Insurance

5. The role of private health insurance

13 Both first and third party insurances play an increasingly important role in the private health care sector. This tendency is a concomitant of the growing role of the private sector in the medical health care system in general. As the role of private medical health care providers grows in the medical health care system, the role of private insurance grows with it. Private health insurers may have a right of recourse against medical professionals or institutions whose services have caused harm to patients according to the general provisions of the Hungarian Civil Code covering the right of recourse of private insurers. According to the regulation of the Civil Code providing for the right of recourse of private insurers, under a first party property insurance the insurer, upon payment of compensation, shall become entitled to the rights of the insured with regard to the person responsible for damages unless this person is a relative living in the same household as the insured (§ 558 subpara (1) of Hungarian Civil Code). Thus, a general assignment (*cessio legis*) by law is provided for the insurer in cases of first party property insurance. There is no such assignment by law provided for first in party life and accident insurances. There is no publicly accessible data on how private insurance companies manage such claims.

6. Liability insurance

14 Third party insurance plays an important part in the allocation of risks of medical malpractice as there is a system of obligatory third party insurance for medical health care service providers. Medical health care service providers may practice and are allowed to provide medical services on the basis of regulatory permission which is only provided if – among other requirements – the medical health care service provider applying for the permission presents a third party insurance covering the risks of medical practice to be provided under the permission. The absence of liability insurance is also a ground for withdrawal of already-granted permission (§ 108 subpara 2 of the Act no CLIV of 1997 on Public Health Care). The system of obligatory third party insurance in the health care sector is built on a fault-based liability regime, where the basis of the insurer's obligation to provide compensation to the victim of medical malpractice is the fault (liability) of the doctor (medical health care provider). This system of

obligatory third party insurance does not change the traditional fault-based liability regime covering cases of medical malpractice.

As far as the right of recourse under a third party insurance is concerned, third party insurers shall be entitled to demand reimbursement from an insured for the amount paid in cases of wilful conduct or gross negligence defined in the contract that result in damage, unless the insured was able to prove that the conduct of the person who caused the damage was not unlawful. Thus, for third party insurances, the insurer has a right of recourse independently from the nature of the harm but only for cases of wilful or grossly negligent damage defined in the insurance contract (§ 559 subpara (3) of the Hungarian Civil Code). 15

There is only very limited information available on doctors' third party insurance but the market of professional third party insurance is in general highly concentrated (about 80 % is shared by two insurance companies). 16

IV. Professional Standards

7. Applicable professional standards

There are detailed professional standards and protocols laid down for each of the medical interventions, diagnostic procedures and indications of risks as well as for the manner of treatment in general. These protocols also normally set the standards for required duty of care. These standards or protocols do not necessarily refer to other international or national regimes but describe professional requirements in an autonomous and detailed way. There are 66 protocols issued by the Ministry of Health covering the treatments of various specific syndromes and illnesses. 17

It has never been clear in court practice whether if the defendant doctor or medical health care provider proved that they complied with the relevant professional protocols this would necessarily indicate compliance with the required duty of care in general thereby resulting in an absence of fault and thus, exoneration from liability. There are decisions declaring that compliance with the professional protocol results in compliance with the required duty of care and thus, an absence of fault.[6] In a recent decision, however, reported in 2006, the Supreme Court established that the absence of a violation of professional rules, standards and guidelines does 18

6 *Dósa* (fn 4) 91.

not preclude establishing fault.[7] This approach has been confirmed in another decision reported in 2007 where the Supreme Court concluded that compliance with professional standards and protocols itself does not prevent the court from establishing the fault of the tortfeasor and consequently, the liability of the doctor or hospital.[8] The relevant professional standards and protocols may either be established by the Ministry of Health, professional associations or implied as common general professional knowledge (eg as part of the materials taught in the universities for medical sciences,[9] issued guidelines or generally accepted professional literature[10]). Violation of these standards necessarily results in establishing fault and, thus, liability as the required duty of care necessarily involves compliance with the professional standards.[11]

8. Quality and/or risk management systems

19 There is a statutory quality management and control system established by the Act no CLIV of 1997 on Public Health Care (§§ 118–124). The pillars of this statutory quality assurance system are to lay down the quality standards, control of compliance with these standards, the evaluation of compliance, certification of quality and permanent development. Each of the medical health care providers has to maintain an internal quality management system (including assurance, development and control of quality) and the organisations supervising the medical health care providers are to maintain an external quality management system (including assurance, development, control and certification of quality). As the core of the external quality management is a voluntary certification procedure in Hungarian national health care system. Under this system the medical health care service provider may apply for a certification of compliance with the statutory and professional quality standards. The certification declares and acknowledges that the services provided by the applicant health care provider complies with the required standards of quality.

---

7 Legf Bír Pfv III 22.090/2005 sz – BH 2006 no 400.

8 Supreme Court, Legf Bír Pfv III 20.956/2006 sz – BH 2007 no 47, *A Menyhárd*, Hungary, in: H Koziol/BC Steininger (eds), European Tort Law 2007 (2008) 344 f.

9 Supreme Court, Legf Bír Pfv III 24.330/1998 sz – BH 1999 no 363.

10 § 119 subpara (3) b, of the Act no CLIV of 1997 on Public Health Care.

11 Supreme Court, Legf Bír Pfv III 20.761/2008 sz – EBH 2008 no 1867.

B. Tort Liability

9. Fundamentals of tort liability

The Hungarian tort law is based on a general clause of liability. The basic norm of fault-based liability is provided as a general clause, while specific forms of liability are covered with different forms of strict liability and liability for others (vicarious liability). The basic norm of liability (as the general rule of liability) provides that if someone causes damage unlawfully to other persons, he shall be liable for that. He is to be exonerated from liability if he proves that he acted as was generally expected under the given circumstances.[12] In the Civil Code there are specific rules for liability for damages caused by extremely hazardous activity, liability for minors, liability for employers, agents, judges, public prosecutors, animals and buildings and there are some specific forms of liability provided for in separate legislation like product liability,[13] liability for wild animals, nuclear energy, environmental damage etc. State liability is construed as a special form of vicarious liability provided in the Civil Code. The basic norm of liability is to be applied unless otherwise provided for under the regimes of these specific forms of liability. There is no special form of liability concerning the liability of doctors and health care providers or medical malpractice. **20**

Thus, medical malpractice cases, as a general rule, are to be decided according to the basic norm of fault-based liability (where fault is incompliance with the required standard of conduct) and regimes of special forms of liability are to be applied only in so far as it is established by specific relevant circumstances of the case (eg using an electric folding knife with flammable disinfectant potentially causing fire as the result of sparks).[14] **21**

10. Burden of proof

The Hungarian tort law is a system of reversed burden of proof. In this system, the victim (plaintiff) has to prove that he suffered damage (the fact of suffering compensable harm as well as the amount of damages) and that there is a causal link between the suffered damage and the tortfeasor's **22**

12 § 339 of the Act no IV of 1959 on the Civil Code of the Hungarian Republic.

13 Act no X of 1993 on Product Liability.

14 Supreme Court, Legf Bír Pfv III 25.423/2002 sz – BH 2005 no 251.

conduct. If the victim (the plaintiff) fails to prove the loss he suffered, the claim is to be rejected. The same goes for if the plaintiff proves the fact of loss but fails to prove the extent of the damage suffered if proving the extent of damage was possible. If, however, it was by the nature of the loss impossible to prove the extent of the compensable damage, the court may award – as lump sum compensation – general damages.

23 Unlawfulness is presumed. As a general principle, the conduct resulting in damages to others is unlawful and from this it follows that causing harm is always unlawful. If the tortfeasor can prove that in the given case causing harm was rendered lawful by the law, he shall not be liable.[15] The system of Hungarian tort law and the general clause of the basic norm of liability imply that causing harm shall always be deemed unlawful unless otherwise explicitly provided for by the law. Thus, the tortfeasor (defendant) has to prove that he caused the damage lawfully (that is, there is a norm permitting him to cause harm to the victim under the relevant circumstances) in order to exempt himself from liability. Fault is presumed as well: the defendant (tortfeasor) is liable unless he can prove that he acted as was generally expected under the given circumstances. That is, if the victim (the plaintiff) proves that he suffered damage and that this was the result of the tortfeasor's conduct, the defendant tortfeasor will be liable unless he proves that he acted according to the generally expected standard of conduct (or if he proves that causing harm in the given situation was lawful).

11. Uncertain causation

24 Hungarian tort law theory and court practice follow the traditional doctrine of causation with regard to natural and legal causation as well as in allocating the burden of proof. As a starting point, theory and practice use the 'but-for-test',[16] which requires that in order to establish liability, the harm must be such that it could not have occurred without the tortfeasor's conduct. As with causation, the burden of proof rests on the victim. That is, he is the one who must prove that in the absence of the tortfeasor's conduct the damage would not have occurred. According to the general liability rule of the Civil Code (§ 339), the wrongdoer shall be liable if he

15 *Gy Eörsi*, A polgári jogi kártérítési felelősség kézikönyve (1966) 221. The defences include the consent of the aggrieved person, necessity, authorised exercise of rights etc.

16 *F Petrik*, A kártérítési jog (1991) 27.

caused the harm. If a causal link cannot be established, a precondition of liability is missing. One cannot be liable for a loss that one did not cause.

The courts in Hungary, however, seem to find that the rigid application of 25
the but-for-test may result in a socially unjust and, as such, improper risk allocation. In the past few years a clear tendency can be identified for shifting the risk of uncertainty in causation to medical health care providers in medical malpractice cases. In this group of cases the courts seem to accept that the burden of proof resting on the victim concerning a causal link is discharged even if there are unclear, unrevealed facts of the case like the unknown origin of injuries or illnesses. Courts seem to accept that increasing the risk of occurrence of damage in itself may establish a causal link resulting in – at least partially – liability of medical health care service providers. A recent decision of the Hungarian Supreme Court[17] seems to fit into this trend as it reversed the burden of proof of the causal link by requiring the proof of an absence of a causal link from the defendant medical service provider in a matter where the defendant's doctors failed to comply with the required duty of care in the context of unclear facts of the case. The case was about a child born with a mental deficiency arising from an unknown cause and the plaintiffs (the child and the parents) argued that it was the fault of the doctors. The Supreme Court established that if the actual cause of the mental deficiency suffered by the plaintiff could not be clearly ascertained, all of the possible causes that may be connected to the defendant hospital's activity must be considered. In such cases the hospital may be found liable if it is unable to prove that it complied with the required standards of conduct concerning all the possible causes of the mental deficiency. If there was a significant probability that the plaintiff's brain damage resulting in mental deficiency was not of a natural origin and that it may have been a result of different unrevealed causes, the courts should consider the fault of the defendant with regard all the possible causes. If it cannot be excluded that the cause of the damage was the result of the doctors' activity, the defendant hospital has to prove either that it acted according to the required standard of conduct concerning all the possible causes or that the damage would have occurred even if it had acted according to the required duty of care.

This tendency for shifting the risk of uncertain causation to the medical 26
service provider or other potential tortfeasor seems to be clear in personal injury or medical malpractice cases but has still not been confirmed as a general rule.

17 Supreme Court, Legf Bír Pfv III 21.598/2008 sz – EBH 2009 no 1956.

12. Loss of a chance

27 Loss of a chance has not been recognised so far as a compensable loss or as being sufficient to establish a causal link and result in liability in Hungarian court practice. Courts, as a general rule, seem to insist that natural causation and actual loss or lost profit are needed to establish liability. As a general rule, they do not accept that an increased probability of the occurrence of damage may establish a causal link. However, as a result of a recent development in the context of liability for medical malpractice and liability for non-pecuniary damages, court practice now clearly accepts that increasing the risk of loss may establish liability. In a decision, reported in 2006 the Supreme Court established the liability of the doctors on the ground of failure in diagnosis that resulted in an increased risk of giving birth to children with mental deficiency and awarded pecuniary and non-pecuniary damages to the children and their parents.[18] In this case, the doctors of the defendant hospital did not act according to the proper professional duty of care in the course of the pregnancy and birth preparation as they failed to send the pregnant mother to a specialised institute which could have reduced the risk of giving birth to children with a mental deficiency. It was established that the premature birth and the brain damage of the children were probably inevitable, but that the doctors' failure to send the plaintiff to a better equipped, more specialised hospital increased the risk thereof. Since the fault of the defendant's doctors did not cause the damage in itself but only contributed to a higher risk thereof, the Court established that the defendant should be liable for 30 % of the damage. This tendency has been confirmed in another decision of the Supreme Court[19] awarding damages on the basis that the doctors, in the course of treatment of a newborn child, failed to reduce the risk of meningitis and its consequences, although they should have recognised the risk to which the child was exposed.

28 It also seems to be a tendency to handle the problem of accepting loss of a chance as compensable loss (or as being enough in order to establish a causal link) in Hungarian court practice by accepting partial causation or allocating the risk of uncertain causation. In a recent decision concerning a claim for damages for personal injury not related to medical malpractice the Supreme Court suggested that increasing the probability of the

---

18 Supreme Court, Legf Bír Pfv III 20.028/2006 – BH 2006 no 360, *A Menyhárd*, Hungary, in: H Koziol/BC Steininger (eds), European Tort Law 2006 (2007) 276 f.

19 Supreme Court, Legf Bír III 21.191/2007 – BH 2008 no 184, *A Menyhárd*, Hungary, in: H Koziol/BC Steininger (eds), European Tort Law 2008 (2009) 359.

occurrence of damage may establish a causal link between the tortfeasor's conduct and the damage. The Supreme Court indicated an inclination to see the causal link in a more flexible way and a relaxing of the traditional approach that natural causation must be proven by the plaintiff in order to establish the defendant's liability. According to the facts of the case the occupational hazard to which the plaintiff was exposed while working for the defendant might have contributed to the plaintiff's illness due to the adverse effect of the chemical materials used by the plaintiff in the course of his work. The direct causal link between the plaintiff's illness and the exposure to chemical pollution could not however be established. The Supreme Court nevertheless concluded that increasing the risk may have contributed to the damage and as such may be deemed – at least partially – as the cause establishing the causal link between the defendant's conduct and the damage occurred.[20]

Thus, although loss of a chance is still not a recognised compensable loss, **29** the recent developments present a tendency towards accepting it as establishing at least partial causation thereby permitting the courts to award partial compensation for increasing the risk of damage. In establishing fault reduction or loss of a chance to recover is taken into account in the context of causation as well as. The tendency is that the relevance of the loss of or decrease in the chance to recover has been shifted more or less to considering fault as a prerequisite of liability.[21]

13. Multiple persons involved

Multiple persons may be involved in medical malpractice cases either as **30** independent from or in a legal relationship (employment or mandate) with each other. If the doctor was the employee of a hospital, the hospital, as employer, shall be vicariously liable for the doctor, which presupposes an employment (labour law) relationship. According to § 348 of the Hungarian Civil Code, if an employee causes damage to a third person in connection with his employment, the employer shall be liable vis-à-vis the victim unless otherwise provided by the law. Under the regime of employer's vicarious liability, the victim may claim compensation only from the employer[22] and the employer may seek indemnity according to the rules of

---

20 Supreme Court, Legf Bír Mfv I 10.710/2007 – EBH 2008 no 1803, *Menyhárd* (fn 19) 350.

21 Memorandum on the National Discussions of 23–25 January 2008 of high courts' civil law colleges and the Civil Law College of the Hungarian Supreme Court.

22 *Eörsi* (fn 15) 299.

labour law, which limit the liability of employee very strictly. Thus, only the employer is liable vis-à-vis the plaintiff and the employer may in turn seek only very limited redress from the employee. In this way the Hungarian tort law provides an immunity for the employee against claims resulting from conduct falling within the scope of the employment relationship.

31 If, instead of a labour law relationship, there is a civil law relationship between the hospital and the doctor, this is normally a contract for services covered by a special form of vicarious liability. According to § 350 of the Civil Code, a principal shall be subject to joint and several liability with his agent for any damage caused to a third person by the agent in this capacity. The principal shall be relieved of liability if he is able to prove that he has not acted delinquently in choosing, instructing, and supervising his agent. In respect of a permanent contractual relationship or if the principal and the agent are economic organisations, the court may apply the regulations governing the liability for damages caused by employees in the relationship between the aggrieved person and the principal.

32 From all of this it follows that if the liability of the doctor has been established, the hospital employing him as a legal entity will be held vicariously liable for the doctor and whether the doctor is also – jointly and severally – liable will depend on the nature of the contractual relationship between the doctor and the hospital. If the doctor was an employee of the hospital, he is immune against the patient's claims. If the doctor was the agent of the hospital under a permanent contractual relationship in terms of a contract for services, he may be immune according to the decision of the court and may have to face only a very limited counterclaim by the hospital if the hospital pays the victim. If the doctor was the agent of the hospital under a temporary contractual relationship or if the court decided not to apply the employers' liability regime in a permanent relationship, the doctor is jointly and severally liable with the hospital and will furthermore not be immune to the counter-claims of the hospital (if the hospital paid the victim).

33 This also means that if a private doctor performs surgery in a hospital, he will not be liable for the hospital staff who assist in the operation (the hospital as employer or principal shall be liable for them); the same holds for others taking care of the patient before or after the operation.

34 In the absence of a contractual relationship between the hospital and the doctor, they may be held as multiple tortfeasors who are jointly and severally liable[23] resulting in them and the plaintiff being in a very similar position according to the following. If persons who contributed wrongfully to the loss acted as independent actors, they are – as multiple tortfeasors – jointly and severally liable vis-à-vis the victim. The Hungarian Civil Code provides a special regulation for damage caused by multiple tortfeasors. According to § 344 of the Civil Code, if the damage was caused jointly by two or more persons, their liability shall be joint and several towards the aggrieved person, while their liability towards one another shall be divided in proportion to their respective degree of responsibility. Liability for damages shall be divided in equal proportions among the responsible persons if the degree of their responsibility cannot be established. The court shall be entitled to declare joint and several liability and order the persons having caused the damage to pay damages in proportion to their respective contributions if so doing would not jeopardise or considerably delay the compensation for damage or if the aggrieved person has himself contributed to the occurrence of the damage or has procrastinated in enforcing his claim without any excusable reason.[24]

The regime of joint and several liability of multiple tortfeasors is to be applied to cases where the doctors contributing wrongfully to the loss are the employees of different hospitals. In such a case the vicariously liable hospitals are to be liable as multiple tortfeasors in the same manner as the doctors would be.[25] **35**

14. Strict liability

In the continental context the concept of strict liability is far from being clear and this holds in general for Hungarian tort law as well. The most general form of strict liability in Hungarian tort law is the liability for abnormally dangerous activities. § 345 of the Hungarian Civil Code pro- **36**

23 Supreme Court, Legf Bír Pfv III 21.318/2008 – BH 2010 no 65.

24 Tortfeasors shall not be jointly and severally liable if there was no causal interdependence between their harmful conduct or if the interdependency was too remote. If the integrated causal chain cannot be established, one cannot speak of a multiplicity of tortfeasors in the context of Hungarian tort law regulation but separated, independent losses with independent tortfeasors and independent claims vis-à-vis those tortfeasors. For example, if the conduct of the tortfeasors can be considered as independent acts which occurred at different times, one cannot speak of a multiplicity of tortfeasors. In such a case tortfeasors shall be liable independently (without joint and several liability) and the harm they caused shall be regarded as separate and independent losses. Supreme Court, Legf Bír Pfv VI 23.619/1998 sz – BH 2000 no 397.

25 Supreme Court, Legf Bír Pf III 20 052/1983 sz – BH 1984 no 18.

vides that a person who carries on an activity involving abnormal hazards shall be liable for damage that the activity causes. The operator (holder) of the abnormally dangerous activity shall be relieved of liability only if he proved that the damage occurred due to an unavoidable cause that fell beyond the scope of the activity involving considerable hazards or resulted from the victim's wrongful conduct. The concept of abnormally hazardous activity is an open category which gives the courts considerable discretion with regard to risk allocation. Even though there are typical activities belonging to this category, the courts sometimes use the open and abstract nature of this notion to allocate risks as they think fit through establishing strict liability. For a long time, this special, strict form of liability did not seem to be relevant in medical malpractice cases. The liability of doctors and hospitals was decided under the general, fault-based liability regime. In a decision handed down in 2005, however, the Supreme Court accepted the possibility of extending the scope of application of this form of strict liability to medical malpractice cases too,[26] although the facts of the case were very specific[27] which may indicate that this extension of strict liability is still not a general tendency. The application of a strict liability regime for abnormally dangerous activities implies two big differences from the basic norm of fault-based liability. One is that the person to be held liable under this form of strict liability regime is the one identified as the operator (holder) of the abnormally dangerous activity, which is not necessarily the actual wrongdoer. The person who is the owner, who controls the risk of the activity in general, or whose direct interest is in pursuing the activity, can be deemed as the operator of the activity and is as such liable under a strict liability regime. The operator may be liable together with the actual tortfeasor – as multi-

---

26 Supreme Court, Legf Bír Pf III 25.423/2002 sz – BH 2005 no 251, *A Menyhárd*, Hungary, in: H Koziol/BC Steininger (eds), European Tort Law 2005 (2006) 342.

27 The plaintiff's father underwent surgery in the defendant's hospital and during surgery the doctors used a special tincture containing alcohol in order to sterilise the skin of the patient. This tincture was flammable. An electrical folding knife had been used for the operation. When the doctors started the operation, this material on the skin of the plaintiff's father caught fire. The plaintiff's father died as a result of the serious injuries he suffered and the plaintiff claimed damages for the death of his father. The Court established that performing the operation in a situation like this using flammable material is deemed as an extremely hazardous activity and the liability of the hospital is thus strict. From this it follows that the hospital, in order to exculpate itself, would have had to prove that the cause of the damage fell outside the scope of the activity and was unavoidable. The proof of compliance with the required duty of care would not have been sufficient. Supreme Court, Legf Bír Pf III 25.423/2002 sz – BH 2005 no 251.

ple tortfeasors – jointly and severally.[28] The other difference is that, while according to the general rule of fault-based liability the tortfeasor may be exonerated by proving that he complied with the generally required standard of conduct, the operator of the abnormally hazardous activity may exempt himself from liability only by proving that the cause of the damage fell outside the scope of the abnormally dangerous activity and that it was unavoidable, which is a very strict standard allowing for only a very limited possibility of exoneration.

There is no distinction between holding a dangerous thing and pursuing a dangerous activity; holding a dangerous thing itself can be regarded as a dangerous activity falling within the scope of § 345 of the Hungarian Civil Code as an abnormally dangerous activity. **37**

The other strict liability regime which may be relevant in the context of medical malpractice cases is product liability for materials (medicines, blood etc) applied in the course of the treatment. Producer's liability for compensating damage caused by defective products as a subject of special regulation is the result of implementing the Council Directive 85/374/EEC of 25 July 1985 in Hungary and is not covered with any specific legislation anymore. The Act no X of 1993 on Product Liability in Hungary implemented the regime of the Product Liability Directive in Hungary. The doctor or the hospital shall be liable for equipments and pharmaceutical products produced by them and used in the course of treatment including products of blood.[29] In such cases the defences provided in the Product Liability Directive are applicable including the 'development risk defence' which has been implemented in the Hungarian product liability regime. The 'learned intermediary' or similar doctrines have not been developed in Hungarian tort law and accordingly hospitals and doctors are not held liable on the basis of product liability for equipment and pharmaceutical products sold or used but not produced by them. There is no special form of enterprise liability in Hungarian tort law. **38**

28 Eg the driver and owner of the car are, as multiple tortfeasors, jointly and severally liable if the driver was negligent in causing an accident, each of them according to the relevant liability regime – the driver according to fault-based liability and the owner of the car according to strict liability for abnormally hazardous activity.

29 Supreme Court, Legf Bír Pf III 25.894/2001 sz – EBH 2003 no 863, Supreme Court, Legf Bír Pfv III 20.146/2003 sz – BH 2005 no 250.

C. Contractual Liability

15. Basics of contracts in the health care sector

39 Medical treatment is supposed to be provided on a contractual basis, or as a *negotiorum gestio* (eg providing help in an emergency situation if the patient is not able to communicate or refuses treatment but the doctor has to act even against the patient's will) normally resulting also in the application of rules of contracts for services. That is why we can assume that the liability of doctors and hospitals is a contractual liability. The contract between patient and doctor and between the patient and the hospital is normally classified as a contract for services where the patient is the principal and the doctor or hospital is the agent for the patient. In professional legal literature it has been suggested[30] that a *sui generis* type of contract (medical contract) should be assumed between the patient and the doctor (hospital) governed by private law and specific sectoral legislation but such a specific contract has so far not been generally recognised in legislation or in court practice. The contract is concluded between the patient and the medical service provider (the private doctor or the hospital). As public hospitals and institutions are separate legal entities (legal persons) according to Hungarian law, this holds for the public health care sector too. If no contract has been explicitly concluded, the contractual relationship is to be implied or construed by indicative (concluding) conduct.

40 The social welfare regime does not seem to have any impact on the contractual relationship with medical professionals or hospitals. Hospitals and doctors are financed from this regime but this does not change the scenario of these contractual relationships neither does it have any impact on the content of these contractual relationships. Patients do not contract with the funds of the social welfare regime.

41 Contracts in the health care sector are specific in so far as they are concluded for specific services and involve the rights and duties of the patients and the medical service providers provided by the specific legislation covering the activity of medical service providers. These special features do not however result in distinguishing them substantially in court practice from ordinary private law contracts.

30 *Jobbágyi* (fn 4) 29.

16. Differences to tort law

In Hungary, the policy underlying the tort law regulation of the Civil Code in 1959 was to provide a unified system of liability. This idea included the unitary regulation of liability for torts and breach of contract. According to § 318 subpara (1) of the Hungarian Civil Code the rules of delictual (tort) liability also apply to liability for breach of contract, except where it is otherwise provided by the law. This solution resulted in a simple system which avoided borderline problems and the constant necessity of classifications. The differences are that liability for breach of contract cannot be reduced on equitable grounds (§ 318 subpara (1) of the Civil Code) which is allowed in case of delictual liability (§ 339 subpara (2) of the Civil Code) and there are differences in the preconditions of the validity of exclusion clauses and the liability for third persons as well. One obvious and significant difference has, however, been clearly developed in court practice, namely the difference in the measure for exculpation: in contractual cases courts apply stricter tests in assessing whether the tortfeasor acted according to the required standard of conduct and allow exculpation only if the defendant can prove that the harm in the given circumstances was unavoidable. Thus, the level of required standard of conduct in contractual liability is higher than in tort cases.[31] This tendency, however, has been proven only in commercial cases so far (eg contracts for sale of goods, construction contracts and contracts for work on goods). Since mandate or services contracts – the category into which contracts for medical services fall – are held as obligations binding the obligee (the hospital or doctor) to conduct themselves according to the required standards (ie not to be negligent) but not to reach a certain result, in the context of medical malpractice cases this tendency is irrelevant. As a result, it can be established that the required standard of conduct (or professional duty of care) in medical malpractice cases in the context of contractual and non-contractual liability is the same. 42

The system of the Law of Obligations of the Hungarian Civil Code allows for the concurrence of contractual and non-contractual (tort) liabilities and court practice seems also to accept this concurrence. The plaintiff is not prevented from suing in tort on the ground that the defendant's conduct causing harm also constitutes a breach of contract.[32] Moreover, since in Hungarian case-law the courts are not bound to the title indicated by the 43

31 *I Kemenes*, A gazdasági szerződések követelményei és az új polgári Törvénykönyv. Polgári Jogi Kodifikáció 2001/1, 9 ff.

32 *Gy Eörsi*, Elhatárolási problémák az anyagi felelősség körében (1962) 132 f.

plaintiff as a ground of his claim, the court would also consider – even in the absence of a request of the parties – the preconditions of tort liability even if the plaintiff had relied only on the defendant's breach of contract.[33] As the plaintiff is not prevented from relying on non-contractual liability instead of seeking remedy for breach of contract and the standard of due care for doctors and hospitals is the same in the context of non-contractual and contractual liability (ie comply with the required professional duty of care), the differences between non-contractual and contractual liability are irrelevant in medical malpractice cases. This may be the reason that courts do not emphasise the contractual nature of the legal relationship between the client and the medical service provider.

44 Thus, victims can choose between contractual and delictual liability regimes as the basis of their claims. Relying on non-contractual liability seems to be in general more favorable for them because of the system of reversed burden of proof in non-contractual liability. Under a non-contractual liability regime the fault of the tortfeasor (the doctor or the hospital's staff) is presumed and he has to prove compliance with the required standard of conduct in order to exonerate himself from liability, while in the context of contractual liability the victim has to prove that the obligee (the doctor or the hospital) breached the contract (that is, the hospital staff or the doctor failed to comply with the required duty of care and this resulted in a failure to reach the required result). These may be the grounds for the fact that in medical malpractice cases the contractual nature of the relationship between the patient and the medical service provider seems to be of secondary importance and is often pushed to the background and possibly not even referred to. The basis of liability in most of the cases is, however, liability for breach of contract.[34]

45 This tendency is supported by that the required standard of due care is of a very high level in medical malpractice cases in Hungarian courts. Courts require that the utmost care is taken.[35]

17. Contractual claims in the absence of direct contracts?

46 Even in the absence of an explicit contracting process, a contract is supposed in the context of providing medical services construed by an

33 *A Menyhárd*, A kártérítési jog egyes kérdései. Polgári Jogi Kodifikáció 2004/1-2, 47 ff.

34 Memorandum on the National Discussions of 23–25 January 2008 of the High Courts' Civil Law colleges and the Civil Law College of the Hungarian Supreme Court.

35 *Dósa* (fn 4) 89 ff.

application for services on the part of the patient and an acceptance of this request on the part of the doctor or hospital.

18. Informed consent

At the centre of regulation of medical health care services is the self-determination of the patient (§ 15 of the Public Health Care Act). The recognition and acceptance of the patient's right to decide on medical interventions is a cornerstone in the patient-doctor relationship and provides the core element thereof.[36] The recognition of the patient's self-determination implies an information model in which the medical service provider has to give all the relevant information to the patient thereby ensuring that he is in a position to make a free decision concerning the required medical service. The heart of this information model is the requirement of informed consent. The patient has the right to get all the relevant information in an individualised form. This includes the patient's right to obtain detailed information concerning his health status, including its medical evaluation; the proposed investigations and interventions; the potential risks and benefits of carrying out or not carrying out the proposed tests and interventions; the planned dates of the proposed investigations and interventions; the right of the patient to come to decisions concerning the proposed investigations and interventions; the possible alternative practices and methods; the process of services and the expected outcomes; the additional services; the likely future impacts on lifestyle and information concerning the staff treating him directly. The patient has the right to obtain the necessary information in an accessible manner that accords with his age, knowledge, experience and psychical and emotional status (§ 14 of the Public Health Care Act). **47**

The patient's right to informed consent is the basis for the duty of the medical health care provider to give all the relevant information to the patient concerning the patient's health status according to the doctor's best knowledge and as is required by the status of the patient. In this way § 134 of the Public Health Care Act imposes an onerous obligation on doctors and hospitals to provide the relevant information to the patient which gives rise to the possibility of very wide interpretation. Proving compliance with the duty to inform the patient is the part of proving compliance with the required standard of conduct in order to prove the absence of fault which could in turn result in exoneration from liability **48**

36 *J Sándor*, Gyógyítás és ítélkezés (1996) 149.

for the doctor or hospital. This wide interpretation of duty is also followed by the courts and leaves limited scope for doctors and hospitals to exempt themselves from liability by proving compliance with the duty.[37]

49 Concerning risks of surgical intervention (including its complications and its possible adverse consequences) a doctor is not at fault if the proper information was given to the patient (informed consent). Disclosure of risks is regarded as sufficient if the information was individualised, covered all the details that could be relevant[38] and took into account the intellectual abilities of the patient. High risks must always be disclosed while risks occurring only by chance do not necessarily fall under the duty of disclosure. Extremely serious risks, however, must always be disclosed even if the probability of their realisation is very slight. The consent of the patient may prevent establishing the fault of the medical service provider only if the patient had been adequately informed.[39]

D. Public Liability

19. Key differences from cases involving private hospitals or doctors

50 Public liability is not a specific form of liability in Hungarian tort law. The Civil Code provides for regulation for public liability under the vicarious liability regime,[40] but even this is irrelevant as hospitals are separate legal entities entering into normal private law relationships with patients which do not result in the application of public liability rules. Thus, in Hungarian jurisdiction, cases are not treated differently if they occur in public hospitals or in some public health care context.

---

37 *Dósa* (fn 4) 189 f.

38 The information should cover the process of treatment and the possible outcomes including negative effects. If bad health conditions or illnesses that the patient is suffering from or other individual characteristics may influence the possible outcome, this should also be noted. Regional Court of Debrecen, Debreceni Ítélőtábla Pf II 20 488/2008/4 sz – BDT 2009 no 1946.

39 Memorandum on the National Discussions of 23–25 January 2008 of the High Courts' Civil Law Colleges and the Civil Law College of the Hungarian Supreme Court.

40 This form of vicarious liability means that liability for damage caused within the jurisdiction of government administration shall be established only if common legal remedies cannot abate the damage or the aggrieved person resorts to the ordinary legal remedies in order to avoid damage (§ 349 of Hungarian Civil Code).

E. Alternative Compensation Regimes

20. Funds and/or other alternative compensation regimes

Currently there are no funds and/or other alternative compensation regimes in Hungary which offer full or partial compensation to victims of medical malpractice. **51**

F. Extent of Liability/Remedies

I. Pecuniary Loss

21. Introduction to indemnifying pecuniary loss

Compensable pecuniary loss is defined in Hungarian tort law by the concept of damages. According to § 355 subparas (1) and (4) of the Hungarian Civil Code, the tortfeasor who is responsible for the damage shall be liable for restoring the original state, or, if this is not possible or if the aggrieved party refuses restoration on a reasonable ground will be liable to compensate the aggrieved party for pecuniary and non-pecuniary damage. Compensation must provide for any depreciation in the value of the property belonging to the aggrieved person and for any pecuniary advantage lost due to the tortfeasor's conduct as well as for compensation of the costs necessary for the attenuation or elimination of the victim's pecuniary and non-pecuniary loss. Under pecuniary loss, actual damage (*damnum emergens*), lost pecuniary advantage (*lucrum cessans*) and costs necessary for the attenuation or elimination of the victim's pecuniary and non-pecuniary loss are to be understood. Actual loss is diminution in value of the victim's property (as a result of loss, destruction of or damage in a thing), the loss of value remaining in spite of repairs or the sum or value of services paid to another person as a result of the tortfeasor's act (penalty, compensation etc). Lost pecuniary advantage is the lost salary, profit or alimony (as far as the alimony has been provided as a gratuity) provided that it was legal and morally acceptable. Costs necessary for the attenuation or elimination of the pecuniary loss cover costs that were reasonably necessary in order to avoid or reduce the loss or the consequences of it including costs arising from the death (burial, tools for mourning etc) or personal injury (costs of medical care, implantations, **52** visits in the hospital, traffic costs),[41] costs of repairs and costs of enforcing one's rights. Compensable pecuniary loss is always a net value, ie the negative balance of gains and losses suffered as the result of the tortfeasor's act.[42]

53 This approach implies the principle of full compensation which is followed very strictly in Hungarian court practice and sets the limits of liability too as it supposes damages as a compensation for compensable loss. According to the prevailing theories in Hungarian tort law the main functions of liability in private law are reparation and prevention. These too are the underlying policies of the current system of tort law. A general principle of Hungarian tort law is that the victim should be prevented from making a profit on her own loss. It seems that restitutionary damages or claims for the gained benefit to be shifted from the tortfeasor to the victim (in order to deprive the tortfeasor of the profit that he gained from the wrongful conduct) are compatible with the principles and policies underlying Hungarian tort law.[43] Thus, in the course of calculating the sum of damages to be awarded, the amount of damages shall be reduced by the sum that the victim earned or saved as a result of the damage (eg payments under a national health care system[44] or an increase of value in the property of the victim as a result of the event which caused damage). In line with the principle of full compensation, the plaintiff shall be compensated for all the losses that he suffered but may not receive.[45] As damages in Hungarian tort law are of a strictly compensatory character, there are no punitive damages. The relevance of making a distinction between direct and consequential loss was abandoned in the Civil Code of 1959, which does not use these categories. The distinction between direct and indirect loss in Hungarian tort law literature covers a problem of causation.[46] Secondary categorisations like real and nominal damage,

---

41 It is still not clear whether gratuities paid to the doctor is a compensable loss but the tendency seems to be to accept that it is. In a decision, the Supreme Court rejected awarding compensation to the patient for gratuities paid by him to the doctor but declared that such payments should not be deemed illegal. Supreme Court, Pfv X 24.130/1997 sz – EBH 1999 no 18.

42 *Eörsi* (fn 16) 123 ff, esp 193.

43 *G Marton*, A polgári jogi felelősség (1993) no 117.

44 Supreme Court Legf Bír Mfv I 10.244/2002/3 sz – EBH 2002 no 695; Supreme Court Legf Bír Mfv I 10.744/2006 sz – BH 2007 no 354; Supreme Court Legf Bír Mfv I 10.697/2006 sz – BH 2007 no 274.

45 *Gy Gellért* (ed), A Polgári Törvénykönyv Magyarázata (7th edn 2007). Comments to § 355 of the Hungarian Civil Code no 4.

46 *Gy Eörsi*, A közvetett károk határai in: Emlékkönyv Beck Salamon születésének 100. évfordulójára (1985); *Á Fuglinszky/A Menyhárd*, Felelősség 'közvetett' károkozásért, Magyar Jog 2003, 283 ff.

concrete and abstract, natural and normative or subjective and objective damage[47] are not used in Hungarian tort law, neither in court practice nor in professional discussions.

As far as cases of medical malpractice are concerned, in these cases the general rules and doctrines of compensation are applied without any apparent deviations. No specific regulations or doctrines or practices are applied in medical malpractice cases in this context. 54

22. Loss of earnings vs loss of earning capacity

Damages also cover losses that will be suffered as a consequence of the wrongdoing in the future, including lost earnings. Loss of working capacity itself (without at least presumed loss of earnings) does not seem to be an accepted type of compensable loss in Hungarian tort law. It seems that even if courts speak of loss of working capacity in the context of damages, they understand presumed loss of earnings. In a recent case where the plaintiff was unemployed at the time of the accident that he suffered and claimed compensation for the losses he suffered as a result of personal injury, the Supreme Court awarded annuity as damages for the loss of his working capacity. According to the Court's arguments the fact that the plaintiff did not have a job before the accident does not prevent him claiming annuity for his lost working capacities as the possibility could not be excluded that he would have found a job had he not have suffered the accident. He was not required to prove that this would have been the case in the absence of the accident. It seems that in this case the Supreme Court did not recognise the diminution or loss of working capacity as a compensable pecuniary loss in general but rather awarded compensation for a presumed loss of salary in the future.[48] 55

The victim is to be compensated for loss of earnings resulting from the injury he suffered.[49] Loss of earning capacity is compensated by the compensation received for loss of earnings which is indemnified based on the victim's predictable income in the future. In the course of calculating the compensation for loss of earnings, however, the actual status of the victim is not necessarily decisive. The basis for calculation of damages is 56

47 *Á Fuglinszky,* Mangelfolgeschäden im deutschen und ungarischen Recht (2007) 118 ff.

48 Legf Bír Pfv IV 20.790/1996 sz – BH 1998 no 19. The principle has been confirmed in Supreme Court, Legf Bír Pfv III 22.070/2001 sz – BH 2004 no 111.

49 Guideline no PK 45 issued by the Civil Law College of the Supreme Court.

the actual (lost) earning of the victim,[50] while the reference for calculating the compensation for lost earnings in the future is the average earnings of people who have the same or a similar job to that of the victim before he lost it as the result of the injury suffered. This holds true also in the context of increasing the annuity (periodical payment) awarded earlier as damages.[51]

23. Periodic payments or lump sum?

57 The principle of full compensation requires compensating the victim for all the losses he suffered as the result of the tortfeasor's wrongful conduct. It is up to the court to decide whether compensation in one sum or in the form of periodic payments is the most appropriate way of indemnification.[52] Basically, there are two ways of providing compensation for losses that are uncertain in their amount either because they will only arise in the future or because although they have already been incurred by the victim and their existence is proven as a fact, their amount is impossible to prove.

58 One possible way of compensating losses of an uncertain amount is to award general damages. General damages (as lump sum compensation) are to be awarded if the extent of damage – at least partly – cannot be precisely calculated. In such a case the tortfeasor can be compelled by the court to pay a general indemnification that would be sufficient to provide the victim with full financial compensation. Awarding general damages is regarded as full and final compensation and there is no possibility to reclaim a general indemnification on the grounds that the extent of actual damage did not subsequently equate with the amount of the general indemnification. If, however, the obligor is paying an annuity as a general indemnification, he shall be entitled to demand a reduction in the amount of the annuity or a change in the annuity payment period in accordance with any changes in the relevant conditions (§ 359 of the Civil Code). The courts are resistant to awarding lump sum compensation. Courts seem to be reluctant to award general damages and do so only if it was impossible to prove the amount of loss although the fact of suffering compensable loss is proven (difficulties in proving the amount of the loss suffered itself is not a sufficient basis for awarding such compensation).[53]

---

50 Guidelines nos PK 45 and 46 issued by the Civil Law College of the Supreme Court.

51 Supreme Court, Legf Bír Pf III 21.218/1998 sz – BH 2001 no 15.

52 Guideline no PK 48 issued by the Civil Law College of the Supreme Court.

53 Guideline no PK 49 issued by the Civil Law College of the Supreme Court, Supreme Court, Legf Bír Gf VI 30.036/2002 sz – BH 2003 no 249.

The other possible way of compensating future losses is awarding damages as a periodical payment in the form of an annuity. As a general rule, compensation may be awarded in the form of an annuity as well. An annuity is normally awarded if indemnification is designed to support or assist in the support of the aggrieved person or those of his relatives who are entitled to be supported by him (§ 355 subpara (3) of the Civil Code). 59

A person whose capacity to work has been reduced as a result of an accident shall be entitled to claim an annuity as a compensation of lost earnings if his earnings (income) after the accident are less than his earnings were before the accident as a result of circumstances beyond his control. In the case of incapacity or a reduced capacity to work resulting from an accident, the amount of lost earnings (income) reduced[54] by the social security benefits shall be paid as an annuity. When establishing the amount of an annuity, any earnings (income) which are gained by the victim of the accident through extraordinary work performance in spite of his considerable physical disability originating from the accident shall not be taken into account in favour of the person responsible for the accident (§ 356 of the Civil Code). The loss in earnings (income) of the victim of an accident shall normally be determined on the basis of the regular monthly average earnings (income) gained in the year preceding the accident. If during this period the amount of earnings (income) changed permanently, only the average earnings (income) after this change can be taken into account. If the victim of the accident had a regular, fixed salary at the time of the accident, this shall be taken into account when determining the loss of earnings. If the loss of earnings (income) cannot be assessed according to the provisions of the Civil Code, the average monthly salary of persons performing the same or similar work on the basis of employment (membership) will govern the determination of the loss. When determining the loss of earnings (income), any future change in income that is anticipated with absolute certainty on a fixed date shall also be taken into account (§ 357 of the Civil Code). Persons dependant on a victim who dies in an accident shall be entitled to claim an annuity that will supplement any support that they receive and ensure the satisfaction of their needs in accordance with the standard of living to which they were accustomed before the accident (by considering their actual or expected earnings [income]). An annuity can also be claimed if the victim who has died in an accident had in fact failed to discharge his obligation to provide support or if the person claiming the annuity has not enforced his claim 60

54 Confirmed in court practrice with the Guidelines no PK 35 and 46 issued by the Civil Law College of the Supreme Court.

for support for an excusable reason. When establishing the amount of an annuity, it shall be considered whether the person claiming an annuity had enforced or is eligible to enforce a claim against the persons whose obligation to support him is equivalent to that of the person who died in the accident (§ 358 of the Civil Code).

24. Caps and thresholds

61 There are no statutory caps or thresholds for damages, either in general or for medical malpractice claims and caps or thresholds have not been developed in court practice either. The courts follow the principle of full compensation which implies only that they reduce the awarded compensation in accordance with damage that has already been reimbursed from other sources (payments from national health insurance, disability pensions, earnings on the loss etc).

II. Non-pecuniary Loss

25. Introduction to indemnifying non-pecuniary loss

62 § 355 of the Hungarian Civil Code provides that pecuniary as well as non-pecuniary losses of the victim suffered as the result of wrongdoing are to be compensated. The Civil Code itself does not define compensable non-pecuniary loss neither does it give guidelines for calculating the amount thereof. The prevailing view in Hungarian tort law today – followed in court practice and confirmed by theory too – is that compensable, non-pecuniary loss can be created by wrongful interference with the inherent rights of persons, that is, compensation of non-pecuniary loss is a specific sanction of wrongful interference with personality rights.[55] Although it has been argued that in the context of non-pecuniary damages the damage as a precondition of liability should be replaced by wrongful interference with the victim's personality rights and the aggrieved person should be entitled to claim non-pecuniary damages without proving any actual harm, costs or loss in the traditional sense of these words,[56] this view yet

---

55 Supreme Court, Legf Bír Pfv III 24.313/1998 sz – BH 2001 no 12; Supreme Court, Legf Bír Pf III 26.339/2001 sz – BH 2004 no 143; Supreme Court, Legf Bír Pf IX 26.426/2001 sz – BH 2004 no 235; Supreme Court, Legf Bír Pfv III 22.125/2006 sz – BH 2008 no 18, Supreme Court, Legf Bír Pf III 26.339/2001 sz – EBH 2003 no 941. *T Lábady*, A nem vagyoni kártérítés újabb bírói gyakorlata (1992) 31 and *F Petrik*, Kártérítési jog (2002) 74.

56 *Lábady*, ibid 31 and *Petrik*, ibid 74.

to be accepted in court practice. The Supreme Court seems to require a proven detriment arising from the wrongful interference with the inherent rights of the person in order to award compensation for non-pecuniary loss. As, however, the apparent reasoning behind this approach seems to be to exclude claims for compensating 'bagatelle' harms, the importance of this tension between theory and practice is not clear.[57]

The level of awarded compensation for non-pecuniary loss was very low in the socialist era but is currently a steadily increasing trend. Courts try to adjust the amounts awarded to the general ability of the society to bear such burdens (in order to not make insurance too expensive and to avoid making the price and cost of services too high through the incorporation of insurance fees). There is no catalogue for calculating the amount of non-pecuniary losses although in practice it works similarly to the calculation of compensation in insurance practice. Courts try to award similar amount of compensation for similar non-pecuniary losses taking into account also relevant personal circumstances and peculiarities.[58] Taking into account recent court practice, in cases of serious injuries depriving young persons of their social perspectives and personal capabilities, the courts are inclined to award damages for non-pecuniary loss above HUF 10,000,000 (approx € 40,000).[59] As, however, the calculation of the amounts of compensation for non-pecuniary loss is up to judicial discretion and thus depends on how the specific circumstances of the case are evaluated, the approximate sum can be predicted although it is very difficult to predict the exact amount of compensation. In medical malpractice cases the lowest sum awarded in the past two years was HUF 200,000 (approx € 700) while the highest sum awarded was HUF 14 million (approx € 46,000). The sums awarded as non-pecuniary damages still show a moderate upward tendency.[60] **63**

In medical malpractice cases personal injury, death or damage to health is normally involved; this is one of the main groups of cases where compensation for non-pecuniary loss is awarded. As the basis of awarding com- **64**

57 The Supreme Court rejected the claim for compensating non-pecuniary loss on the basis that the victim was ill for two weeks but recovered without any further complication. Supreme Court, Legf Bír Pfv III 24.313/1998 sz – BH 2001 no 12.

58 Supreme Court, Legf Bír Pfv III 20.991/1994 sz – BH 1997 no 226, Supreme Court, Legf Bír Mfv I 10.708/1998 sz – BH 2000 no 569.

59 In a recent decision the Regional Court of Pécs awarded HUF 13.000.000 (approx € 50 000) to a young victim who suffered very serious personal injury and lost his working capacity and became unable to take care of himself for the rest of his life. Regional Court of Pécs, Pécsi Ítélőtábla Pf III 20.310/2008/5 – BDT 2009 no 2006.

60 Memorandum on the National Discussions of 23–25 January 2008 of high courts' civil law colleges and the Civil Law College of the Hungarian Supreme Court.

pensation for non-pecuniary loss is the wrongful interference with the inherent rights of persons and most of the non-pecuniary damages cases belong to the category of medical malpractice, there are no peculiarities concerning compensation of non-pecuniary loss in medical malpractice cases.

26. Who can claim compensation for non-pecuniary loss?

65 The starting point of the Hungarian court practice was that grief and pain arising from the loss of a relative itself is not a sufficient basis for compensable non-pecuniary loss;[61] this approach has however been changing. Today, claims for compensation of non-pecuniary loss of close relatives of the deceased person are accepted in Hungarian court practice,[62] although their scope is limited. The ground for awarding damages to relatives for loss of the victim – ie their protected interest – is their right to live in a complete and healthy family. For this reason, in court practice parents, minor children, spouses and brothers are entitled to damages arising from the death of the victim. For such relatives the bereavement itself is the basis for claiming compensation for non-pecuniary loss.[63] Courts are however not inclined to widen this circle and have rejected claims of grandparents as well as those of an adult child who no longer lived together with the victim.[64] If the case is not about losing a relative but rather the loss suffered by the relative (eg personal injury or health damage), the relatives of the direct victim may have a claim for non-pecuniary damages as a compensation for their own personal loss (eg for giving birth to a child with mental deficiency).[65]

---

61 Directive no 16 of the Supreme Court (not in force anymore).

62 Supreme Court, Legf Bír Pfv III 21 354/1991 sz – BH 1992 no 529 (awarding non-pecuniary damages to a child for losing his parents); Supreme Court, Legf Bír Pfv III 21.795/1998 sz – BH 2001 no 14 (awarding non-pecuniary damages to parents for losing their child).

63 The claim for compensation of non-pecuniary loss on the basis of losing a brother has been explicitly accepted in court practice. Supreme Court, Legf Bír Mfv I 10.655/2007 sz – BH 2009 no 27.

64 Memorandum on the National Discussions of 23–25 January 2008 of high courts' civil law colleges and the Civil Law College of the Hungarian Supreme Court.

65 Eg Supreme Court, Legf Bír Pfv III 24.931/2002 sz – BH 2005 no 18; Supreme Court, Legf Bír Pfv III 21.212/2008 sz – BH 2009 no 208; Supreme Court, Unificatory Resolution no 1/2008, 12 March 2008.

G. Procedural Matters

27. Specific rules of jurisdiction or procedure

There are no specific rules of jurisdiction or procedure that apply to medical malpractice cases in Hungarian law. As a special form of dispute resolution, the legal framework for non-judicial mediation in the medical sector for settling patients' claims against medical service providers was established in 2000,[66] but there are still no experiences of its practical use. 66

28. Special institutions handling malpractice claims

Except for the system of mediation in the medical sector, there are no special institutions handling malpractice claims out of court. The list of mediators is maintained by the Hungarian Chamber of Judicial Medical Experts and the costs of mediation procedures are to be paid by the parties.[67] 67

H. Outlook

29. Reform plans

There are currently no published plans today in Hungary for a reform of medical liability, neither under the ongoing reform of private law for the New Civil Code nor as a separate initiation. 68

Cases

Case 1

Both having a child with mental and physical deficiencies and the loss of Y's twin brother are compensable losses according to Hungarian court practice and are the basis for a claim for pecuniary damages as well as compensation of non-pecuniary loss. Thus, X may have two separate claims for the compensation of her non-pecuniary loss for both losing Y's twin brother and for Y being born with such mental and physical defi- 69

66 Act no CXVI of 2000 on Mediation in the Medical Health Care Sector.

67 §§ 4–7 of the Act no CXVI of 2000 on Mediation in the Medical Health Care Sector.

ciencies. The amount of this compensation can not be predicted as it depends very much on peculiarities of the case (eg the age of X, her possibility of still having more children, whether they were her first and only children, how deeply X has been affected etc) which are not known. As compensation for pecuniary loss X has a claim for compensation for the costs of taking care of Y which are to be compensated with a lump sum or with a periodical payment. The standard wage of a qualified nurse may be an appropriate ground for calculating damage as these costs are necessary consequences of the loss. The fact that she personally takes care of the child should not be relevant as the tortfeasor should not benefit from this. The claim of Y for pecuniary damages already sustained and those which will be sustained in the future as a result of the alleged mistakes in treatment during the pregnancy and birth, reduced by the sum that has been paid by social insurance agencies or other third parties, is also a compensable harm. Damage that will arise in the future may either be compensated with a lump sum (general damages) or with periodical payments (annuity). As the cause of the damage (the mental and physical deficiency) suffered by Y is uncertain but is supposedly not of a genetic or teratologic origin, Y may have claim for compensation for the non-pecuniary loss she suffered.

70 The cause of the damage is uncertain but shifting the risk of uncertain causation to the medical service provider is a clear tendency in Hungarian court practice. On this ground, the necessary causal link between the conduct of D (for whom C as her employer is vicariously liable), A (the doctor treating X directly) and B (taking part in an earlier phase of treatment) must be established in so far as they can not prove that they did not contribute to the loss or that they acted in the course of treatment according to the required duty of utmost care in respect of all the possible causes of the damage.[68]

71 On this ground the Hungarian court would decide for the plaintiffs and award compensation for the pecuniary and non-pecuniary losses of both X and Y according to their claims holding A, B and C as multiple tortfeasors jointly and severally liable for damages.

---

68 A and B may be jointly and severally liable as partners in a private law partnership too (§ 568 of the Hungarian Civil Code).

Case 2

Having a healthy child has not been accepted so far as a basis for compensable damage in Hungarian court practice. In a case reported in 2004 the plaintiff (a mother giving life to a healthy child) claimed non-pecuniary damages from the defendant hospital on the ground that the doctor, as an employee of the defendant, performed an abortion improperly and after the operation she remained pregnant, finally giving life to a healthy child.[69] The Supreme Court rejected the claim on the ground that the plaintiff could not show any interference with her inherent rights which would be a precondition of establishing compensable non-pecuniary loss. The Supreme Court avoided establishing the decision upon moral assessment and arguments about the concept of damages or the moral value of birth and life and instead focused in its argument on the concept of non-pecuniary damages and wrongful interference with personality rights. The case concerned awarding non-pecuniary damages but in my opinion – assuming consequent decisions – the claim for pecuniary damages should also be rejected on the ground of absence of unlawful conduct. Thus, according to the present state of Hungarian tort law the claim should be rejected. **72**

Case 3

The deficiency of X itself and the losses suffered as consequences of his deficiency are certainly compensable harm. Although it cannot be clearly established what degree of damage had already been sustained directly after birth in hospital A and to what extent the damage was sustained during X's treatment in the clinic C, it cannot be excluded that both might have contributed to the damage or at least increased the probability of its occurrence or might have contributed to its gravity. According to Hungarian court practice both uncertain causation and increasing the risk of the occurrence of a deficiency or worsening the status of the patient are sufficient to shift the risk of damage to the hospital. The subsequent events (omissions) suggest that all of the defendants might have contributed to a single causal chain resulting in the deficiency suffered by the plaintiff X. This establishes that they caused the damage as joint tortfea- **73**

69 Legfelsőbb Bíróság (Supreme Court) Legf Bír Pf III 26.339/2001 sz – EBH 2003 no 941 and BH 2004 no 143.

sors.[70] On this ground the defendants are to be held as multiple tortfeasors being jointly and severally liable vis-à-vis the plaintiff. According to court practice which clearly tends towards shifting the risk to the hospital (doctor) in cases of uncertain causation and increased risk of worsening the patient's condition, the court would require each of the defendants to prove that they complied with the required standard of conduct (ie they acted according to the utmost professional care) concerning all the possible causes.[71] They would also be required to prove that their omissions could not have increased the risk of deficiency or the worsening of the condition of X.[72] As, according to the facts of the case, none of the defendants are able to meet any of the requirements for exoneration, the Hungarian court would likely hold them – as multiple tortfeasors – jointly and severally liable for pecuniary and non-pecuniary damages compensating the losses suffered by X and should decide for the plaintiff.

74 As far as the calculation of damages is concerned, such kind of capitalisation is not applied in Hungarian court practice as a basis for calculating the amount of an annuity. Courts do not award an annuity as compensation for lost earnings to children who were not in a position of being able to work (even if they may have reached this position in the future). The regulation of the Civil Code concerning periodic payment as damages presupposes that someone has lost his earning capacity (at least partly) and does not seem to cover cases where someone never had working capacity in the first place.[73]

75 Thus, the Hungarian court should decide for the plaintiff and establish the defendants' joint and several liability for damages. Compensation would be awarded for costs of nursing care and the expenses incurred due to his increased needs as well as compensation for his non-pecuniary loss. An annuity would also be awarded but not as compensation for lost earning capacity but in order to cover the needs of the plaintiff and would be calculated accordingly (ie according to the needs of the plaintiff and not on the basis of income or salary).

---

70 Supreme Court, Legf Bír Pfv III 21.290/2001 sz – BH 2004 no 145; Supreme Court, Legf Bír Pf VI 21.525/1993 sz – BH 1995 no 214; Supreme Court, P törv V 20 883/1979 sz – BH 1980 no 471.

71 Supreme Court, Legf Bír Pfv III 21.598/2008 sz – EBH 2009 no 1956. Supra Q 10, no 25 f.

72 Supreme Court, Legf Bír III 21.191/2007 – BH 2008 no 184. Supra no 27.

73 Supra no 60.

Case 4

Informed consent is a core element of the information model underlying the (legal) relationship of the patient and the medical service provider. The duty of the medical service provider to provide the patient with all the information legally required is a central element of risk allocation concerning the liability of the medical service provider too. This means that if the medical service provider failed to give the necessary information to the patient as required by the law, it is to be held liable for the consequences of medical intervention or treatment unless it can be proved that the consequences would have necessarily occurred even in the absence of the intervention or treatment in question.[74] **76**

The information should be regarded as sufficient and results in shifting the risk of treatment or intervention from the medical service provider to the patient if – as a minimum standard – it complied with the requirements provided in the Public Health Care Act. Among others, the Public Health Care Act[75] establishes that the patient has the right to receive the information in a way which makes the information accessible and understandable for him, taking into account his age, knowledge, psychical status, wishes and – if it was necessary and possible – with the assistance of an interpreter. In this case the information given to the patient concerning the risks of the intervention had not been given to him in an accessible and understandable way as he could not understand them, neither did an interpreter assist although it was both necessary and possible as the intervention was not urgent and seeking the assistance of an interpreter could not considerably worsen the patient's condition. A thus failed to comply with the requirement of informed consent provided by the Public Health Care Act and is to be liable for damages to compensate the loss suffered by the plaintiff as a result of surgical intervention.[76] The compensable losses may cover the costs of converting his house to provide for wheelchair access, the purchase of a new car with wheelchair access and additional increased needs arising from his paralysis,[77] as well as non-pecuniary loss. Thus A as an employer of the doctor B who failed to give the plaintiff the required information properly, should be found liable by the Hungarian court for damages according to the claim of the plaintiff. **77**

---

74 Regional Court of Szeged, Szegedi Ítélőtábla Pf III 20 527/2006 – BDT 2008 no 1884.

75 § 13 subpara (8) of the Public Health Care Act.

76 Regional Court of Debrecen, Debreceni Ítélőtábla Pf I 20 572/2007/5 sz – BDT 2008 no 1834.

77 Supreme Court, M törv II 10 019/1979/2 sz – BH 1980 no 110.

78 As both possible surgical interventions implied considerable risks of a similar nature and extent with regard to the risk of paralysis the choice made by C itself is not a basis for liability. If the obligation on C to provide the necessary information is established (ie if the information provided by B was insufficient to discharge the required duty of care) and he was an independent doctor (not the employee of A), C must also be held jointly and severally liable together with A for damages according to the plaintiff's claim. The same holds if C performed the surgical intervention with professional malpractice (which does not seem to be so). If C complied with the required duty of care (ie in so far as he was correct to rely on the adequacy of disclosure made by doctor B) he will not be liable for failing to comply with the duty to inform either.

Case 5

79 I think that although the share of responsibilities may not be clear in this case, the positioning of extremities so as to avoid damage to the patient can surely be seen as the responsibility of the staff of the medical service provider responsible for properly performing the surgical intervention. As A is the employer of B, C and D, it is not important concerning A's liability how responsibilities are to be shared amongst the doctors performing the surgical intervention, the anaesthetist and C as the intern. The positioning of the arm might have contributed to the damage suffered by the plaintiff and this uncertain causation should result in shifting the risk of such an injury to the medical service provider. I also think that A would not be able to prove that its staff complied with the required professional duty of care and would be found liable for the loss suffered by the plaintiff as the result of damage to the nervus ulnaris and the restricted movement in the hand. Thus, A shall be liable for damages.

80 The compensation to be awarded to plaintiff X should include damages for non-pecuniary loss as well as compensation for the lost legal income. I think that the fact that he refused to consider retraining as a sales person in a building supplies store is irrelevant as it could not be proven that he would have obtained the job as a sales person nor can it be proven that he could have mitigated damages by undertaking the retraining. The private medical injuries assessment that he commissioned from an 'institute for the assessment of medical injuries' in order to clarify the facts was not the necessary consequence of the damage as he needed it in order to found his claim. The assessment could also have been obtained free of charge from an assessment commission at the medical council. On these grounds, the

costs of the assessment would not be regarded as compensable damage and in this respect the claim should be rejected.

Case 6

Although it is not clear whether E was aware of his own staphylococcus infection and that he could potentially infect patients, I think that according to a Hungarian court's judgement A and B should be held liable for damages either vicariously for C, D and E on the ground that they – as the employees of A and B – were negligent in not preventing infections (if that was the case) or because they failed to maintain a proper process in order to prevent such infections (including communicating the proper hygiene standards and monitoring compliance with them). C, D and E as employees of A and B would not be held liable towards the plaintiff. Damages would be awarded for compensating the plaintiff's non-pecuniary loss as well as her pecuniary damage, including the costs for cleaning assistance and the assistance provided to her by a member of the family with household tasks if she needed this assistance and if such assistance might otherwise have been obtained via paid services (rejecting such claims would result in an unjust enrichment of the defendant).[78] **81**

Variation 1

I think that as the risk of uncertain causation is shifted to the medical service provider according to Hungarian court practice, A and B should be required to prove that the infection of the plaintiff would have occurred even if they had complied with all the required hygiene standards. As it seems that they would not be able to prove this compliance, the actual source of the infection is irrelevant and liability would lie with A and B. **82**

Variation 2

I think that if A and B complied with the required hygiene standards (including the proper conduct of C and D) their liability would depend on whether E could prevent infecting others (ie whether he was aware of his condition). If this is the case, A and B as employers of E are to be held **83**

78 Supreme Court, Legf Bír Pfv III 21.121/2008 sz – BH 2009 no 209.

vicariously liable for E's negligent conduct. If this is not the case, E, C and D would not be regarded as negligent nor would A and B have failed to comply with the required professional care in preventing infections; the claim should thus be rejected. It is remarkable, however, that compliance with the usual standards does not necessarily itself mean compliance with the required duty of care. The court may establish that the level of required professional duty of care is maintaining a system that prevents infections and as A and B surely failed to comply with this duty of care (as illustrated by the fact of the existence of the infection) they are to be held liable even if they maintained a normally acceptable system.

Medical Liability in Italy

Alessandro P Scarso/Massimo Foglia*

General Questions

A. The Health Care System Framework

I. General Introduction

1. The health care system in overview

The Italian 'National Health Service' (SSN – *Servizio sanitario nazionale*)[1] comprises the welfare activities carried out both by regional health services, bodies and institutions of national significance and by the State. The SSN's purpose is to ensure the protection of health as a fundamental right of individuals and as a collective interest, whilst respecting the dignity and freedom of the person (see art 1, *Decreto Legislativo* [Legislative Decree] 30 December 1992, no 502). The SSN was introduced by *Legge* [Statute] 23 December 1978, no 833 (the so-called *Riforma sanitaria*),[2] and is struc- 1

* Alessandro Scarso has written nos 20–40, 54–75 and 93–101, whilst Massimo Foglia is the author of nos 1–19, 41–53 and 76–92.

1 See *S Giannini/G De Cesare*, Dizionario di diritto sanitario (1988); *PL Guiducci*, Manuale di diritto sanitario (1999); *R Ferrara*, L'ordinamento della sanità (2007); *E Jorio*, Diritto sanitario (2005). See also: Libro bianco sui principi fondamentali del Servizio sanitario nazionale (2008), available at <http://www.ministerosalute.it/imgs/C_17_pubblicazioni_808_allegato.pdf>.

2 The novelty of Statute 23 December 1978, no 833 lies in the 'principle, which is not in the Constitution, of the "unity" and "universality" of interventions, which involves close interaction between all health services for prevention, care and rehabilitation, and the creation of a joint basic organisation, which is in a position to fulfil all the tasks related to health': see *Giannini/De Cesare* (fn 1) 88.

tured in so-called 'Local Health Units' – (*Azienda Sanitaria Locale* – ASL[3], formerly *Unità Sanitaria Locale*, USL) which provide medical assistance.[4]

2 It is up to the State to determine the basic level of service with reference to civil and social rights throughout the national territory (art 117, para 2, let m), Italian Constitution [Const]), which also has a concurrent legislative power (beside the Regions' legislative power – see art 117, para 3, Const) in the field of 'health protection'.[5]

3 Regions have to legislate within the fundamental principles laid down by State legislation, whilst guaranteeing the basic level of health assistance determined by the latter.[6]

II. Social Welfare Provision

2. The role of public health care

4 The SSN is a public system ensuring health care for all citizens,[7] financed by general taxation and the proceeds collected by 'Local Health Units'

---

3 The 'Local Health Units' (*Azienda Sanitaria Locale*, ASL) are legal entities with organisational autonomy, administrative, investment, accounting, managerial and technical expertise, which provide health care in their respective territories. The single ASL has the purpose 'to provide the services related to prevention, care, rehabilitation and forensic medicine, ensuring health care service levels for the entire population in conformity with art 3, paragraph 2, Statute 23 December 1978, no 833'.

4 *Giannini/De Cesare* (fn 1) 88.

5 The Amendment of the Constitution (through Constitutional Statute 18 October 2001, no 3) has extended the power attributed to Regional bodies in terms of the organisation and implementation of health assistance; they now have direct responsibility for managing the health spending and for the achievement of the health objectives of their territory. In addition, the Regions have exclusive competence in the regulation and organisation of services and activities for the protection of health and in the fixing of the criteria related to the financing of local public health authorities and hospitals.

6 According to the 'constitutional principle of subsidiarity', the SSN is structured in different levels of responsibility and government: at the central level, the State has the responsibility to ensure to all citizens the right to health; at the regional level, the Regions have the direct responsibility to direct government spending towards the achievement of predetermined health care levels. The Regions have exclusive competence in the regulation and organisation of services and activities for the protection of health and in fixing the criteria for the financing of local public health agencies and hospitals (including management control systems and the evaluation of the quality of health care provided, in conformity with the general principles established by national statutes). See <http://www.ministerosalute.it/ministero/sezMinistero.jsp?label=principi>.

7 According to art 1, para 3, Statute 23 December 1978, no 833, 'The SSN encompasses all the functions, facilities, services and activities directed at the promotion, maintenance and recovery of physical and mental health of the entire population, regardless of social or individual conditions, and in a way which ensures the equality of the citizens'. Medical assistance is also a right guaranteed to non-EU individuals (even to those not

(ASL) from prescription charges (ie the money which the majority of patients are under a duty to pay for basic health services).[8]

The SSN implements art 32 of the Constitution, which enshrines the right 5
to health of all individuals.

In Italy, similarly to other European countries, public funding covers the 6
largest share of total health expenditure (between 70 % and 80 % in recent decades).[9] The coverage by private spending, however, shows marked differences in relation to other European countries:[10] in Italy there is a much greater impact of private spending on out-of-pocket spending,[11] while private spending is irrelevant in terms of supplementary insurance (which has remained constant from 1990 to 2007 at around 3 % of expenditure).[12]

---

holding a residence permit – see art 34–36 e 41, Legislative Decree 25 July 1998, no 286 and subsequent amendments).

8 For detailed information, see <http://www.ministerosalute.it/ministero/sezMinistero.jsp?label=principi)>.

9 In 2005, public funding covered 76.6 % of the total health expenditure (which lies above the OECD average, amounting to 72.5 % – see <http://www.tesoro.it/doc-finanza-pubblica/documenti/18827/28_libro%20verde.pdf> 36). According to the Health Data 2009, published by the OECD, total health spending accounted for 8.7 % of Italy's GDP in 2007 (which is slightly below the average of 8.9 % in OECD member countries). Italy ranks below the OECD average in terms of health spending per capita, amounting to about US$ 2,686 in 2007 (the data has been adjusted to consider purchasing power parity), compared with an OECD average of US$ 2,964. Between 2000 and 2007, health spending per capita in Italy increased, in real terms, by 1.9 % per year (on average), a growth rate lower than the OECD average of 3.7 % per year. The public sector is the main source of health funding in all OECD countries, except the United States and Mexico. In Italy, 76.5 % of health spending was funded by public sources in 2007 (which lies above the average of 72.8 % in other OECD member countries). See <http://www.ordinemedicilatina.it/node/14590)>.

10 Eg <http://www.euro.who.int/document/E88550.pdf>, according to which 'out-of-pocket payments refer to cost-sharing for public services, such as co-payments for diagnostic procedures, pharmaceuticals and specialist consultations. As of 1993, users had to pay for the cost of outpatient care up to a ceiling that fixed at € 36 (since 2000). Co-payments for drugs and ambulatory specialist services have a limited impact: they reached a peak of 4.8 % of total National Health Service revenues in 1996, and have fallen to 2.9 % in 2002 (as a consequence of the abolishment of drug co-payments). Users have to directly purchase private health care services and over-the-counter drugs. About 15 % of the population has complementary private health insurance, which have been entered into either individually or have been offered by employers. In 2002, Italy's total expenditure in health services amounted to 8.5 % of the GDP, representing a per capita expenditure of US$ 2,166 (the data has been adjusted to consider purchasing power parity – see Annex. Total expenditure on health). Public sources cover 75 % of health expenditure. Private expenditure has risen since co-payment schemes were introduced, amounting to 25 % in 2002'.

11 Medical treatments paid directly by families covers almost the 83 % of the private spending: see <http://www.tesoro.it/doc-finanza-pubblica/documenti/18827/28_libro%20verde.pdf> 36.

12 *MS Caroppo/G Turati*, I sistemi sanitari regionali in Italia – Riflessioni in una prospettiva di lungo periodo (2007) 112 ff.

3. Differences in treating patient's claims

7 The same liability regime applies, regardless of whether the medical treatment is offered in a public hospital or in a private institution, and regardless of whether the treatment offered in a private medical institution is publicly funded.[13]

8 Italian jurisprudence places medical liability in the contractual field, regardless of whether a formal contract has been concluded or not, and of whether medical treatment has been received in a public or private structure.[14]

9 In terms of tortious liability, the same liability system applies both to public and private medical institutions.[15]

4. Right of recourse

10 In the event that another social welfare agency pays the costs related to the medical treatment necessary as a result of medical malpractice, it has – in the abstract – the right of recourse against the medical staff who caused the patient's injury.

11 Nevertheless, in practice, no cases of an action brought by another social welfare agency against the National Health Service for the reimbursement of such costs are known.

III. Private Insurance

5. The role of private health insurance

12 The role of private health insurance in Italy is marginal, and is considered to have an integrative function to the SSN.[16]

---

13 See Cass, Joint Chambers, 11 January 2008, no 577, [2008] Danno e responsabilità (Danno resp) 788, with a commentary by *A Nicolussi*, Sezioni sempre più unite contro la distinzione fra obbligazioni di risultato e obbligazioni di mezzi; [2008] Responsabilità civile e previdenza (Resp civ prev) 856, with a commentary by *M Gorgoni*, Dalla matrice contrattuale della responsabilità nosocomiale e professionale al superamento della distinzione tra obbligazioni di mezzi/di risultato.

14 See infra nos 41 ff.

15 See *R Simone*, La responsabilità della struttura sanitaria pubblica e privata, [2003] Danno resp 5 ff.

16 According to a survey conducted by the Italian Insurance Companies' Association (*Associazione Nazionale fra le Imprese Assicuratrici*, ANIA), the proportion of Italian families

In the case of medical malpractice, whenever medical treatment has been financed by the private health insurer, the latter has the right of recourse (within the limits of the insurance coverage)[17] against medical staff or institutions whose services have caused harm to patients pursuant to art 1916, para 1, Civil Code (CC).[18] 13

6. Liability insurance

Physicians and/or medical institutions are not required to take out liability insurance although there have been specific bills to this end proposed.[19] With reference to public medical institutions, art 28 DPR (*Decreto Presidenziale*, Presidential Decree) 20 December 1979, no 761 provides solely for the possibility for the Public Administration to conclude a tortious liability insurance policy in favour of its employees. 14

Italian legal scholars have debated the possibility of reforming liability arising from medical malpractice by introducing a new system based on risk management and insurance policies.[20] 15

IV. Professional Standards

7. Applicable professional standards

According to art 1176, para 2, CC, in carrying out a professional activity (such as the activity provided by medical staff), the standard of care ought 16

---

holding private health insurance in 2002 amounted to 7.5 %. Approximately 1 % of private spending is devoted to the purchase of private health insurance. See <http://www.ania.it/studi_statistiche/studi/lavori_svolti/articolo05.pdf>.

17 See Cass 14 November 1997, no 11262, [1997] Giust civ Mass 2169.

18 According to art 1916, para 1, Civil Code (CC), 'An insurer who has paid the indemnity is subrogated up to the extent of the amount of said indemnity, to the rights of the insured against third persons who are liable for the damage'.

19 *R Breda*, Prospettive di riforma della responsabilità in ambito sanitario: il Disegno di Legge n. 108 del 6 giugno 2001, [2003] Danno resp 431; *M Barni*, La responsabilità medica verso il difficile approdo dell'assicurazione obbligatoria, [2000] Resp civ prev 830.

20 *G Ponzanelli*, La responsabilità medica ad un bivio: assicurazione obbligatoria, sistema residuale no-fault o risk-management? [2003] Danno resp 428; *G Comandé/G Turchetti*, La responsabilità sanitaria – Valutazione del rischio e assicurazione (2004); *L Nocco*, La Responsabilità sanitaria tra Valutazione del Rischio e Assicurazione, [2005] Danno resp 805; *id*, La gestione del rischio clinico ed il monitoraggio degli errori medici: spunti di riflessione in chiave comparativa, [2003] Danno resp 444; *S Cacace*, Loi Koucher: Problemi di underdeterrence e undercompensation, [2003] Danno resp 435.

to be evaluated with reference to the nature of the activity carried out: ie the medical staff's duty of care will have to be evaluated with reference to the 'ordinary standard of care' of the professional category to which the respective professional belongs.[21]

17 Art 1176, para 2, CC has to be considered together with art 2236 CC, according to which whenever the performance to be carried out involves 'the solution of technical problems of special difficulty',[22] the debtor is not liable for damages, except in cases of intent or gross negligence.

18 Fundamental criteria to which Italian jurisprudence has recourse when assessing 'fault' by medical staff are:[23]

- the evaluation of due diligence, with reference to the specific circumstances of the case;
- the degree of difficulty of the treatment;
- the deterioration of the patient's health conditions;

---

21 Whether the conduct of the physician has been in conformity with 'professional diligence' will be evaluated with reference to the type of activity exercised: for instance, the conduct of a specialist physician will be evaluated by taking into consideration their degree of specialisation: see Cass 8 October 2008, no 24791, [2008] Giustizia civile Massimario (Giust civ Mass) 1448.

22 See, *ex multis*, Cass 28 September 2009, no 20790, [2010] I Nuova giurisprudenza civile commentata (Nuova giur civ comm) 369, with a commentary by *M Foglia*, Il prisma della prestazione medica el' 'azzeramento' dell'art. 2236 CC; Cass 29 September 2004, no 19560, [2005] Danno resp 213; Cass 20 April 2004, no 7494, [2004] Massimario della Giurisprudenza italiana (Mass Giur it); Cass 10 May 2000, no 5945, [2001] Riv it medicina legale 1137. Should the performance of particular medical treatment be considered 'easy' (from both a statistical as well as from a scientific point of view), failure to reach the expected result *de facto* supports the presumption that the physician acted negligently: see Cass 8 January 1999, no 103, [1999] Resp civ prev 683, with a commentary by *P Sanna*, I mille volti della responsabilità medica: la responsabilità della casa di cura privata. See *M Franzoni*, L'illecito, in: Trattato della responsabilità civile I (2004) 228 ff; *G Iadecola/M Bona*, La responsabilità dei medici e delle strutture sanitarie (2009) 343 ff; *R De Matteis*, La responsabilità medica. Un sottosistema della responsabilità civile (1995) 124 ff.

23 Therefore – at present – the distinction between *obligations de moyens* and *obligations de résultat* seems to be 'antiquated': see Cass, Joint Chambers, 28 July 2005, no 15781, [2006] Resp civ prev 3, with a commentary by *G Facci*, L'obbligazione di risultato del progettista al vaglio delle Sezioni unite; Cass, Joint Chambers, 11 January 2008, no 577 (fn 13). However, in the context of medical liability, the obligation to be fulfilled by the medical staff may be defined – at least from a descriptive point of view – as an *obligation de moyens*: see *L Mengoni*, Obbligazioni 'di risultato' e obbligazioni 'di mezzi', [1954] I Rivista del diritto commerciale (Riv dir comm) 185; *V De Lorenzi*, Obbligazioni di mezzi e obbligazioni di risultato, in: Digesto delle Discipline privatistiche, Sez civile, XII (1993) 397; *D Carusi*, Responsabilità del medico e obbligazioni di mezzi, [1991] Rassegna di diritto civile (Rass dir civ) 503; *A Di Majo*, Mezzi e risultato nelle prestazioni mediche: una storia infinita, [2005] Corriere giuridico (Corr giur) 38.

- the exact fulfilment of both the duty to inform – ie the patient's right to an informed consent – and of the subsequent duties to monitor the medical treatment's effects.[24]

8. Quality and/or risk management systems

No statutory provisions provide for the compulsory implementation of risk management systems for medical staff or medical institutions.[25] Nor are medical staff and medical institutions required to implement particular quality systems, though some of them adopt predetermined criteria for quality certification and have implemented internal risk management systems.[26] The topic has been hotly debated both by Italian legal scholars and by the medical community,[27] who have suggested the introduction of compulsory risk management systems.[28] 19

B. Tort Liability

9. Fundamentals of tort liability

Italian tort law is based on art 2043 CC. The rule states that 'Any deliberate or culpable act that causes unjust damage to others obliges the 20

---

24 Cass 14 February 2008, no 3520, [2008] Diritto & Giustizia; Cass 18 April 2005, no 7997, [2005] Giust civ Mass 6. See also Cass 13 April 2007, no 8826, [2007] II Nuova giur civ comm 445, with a commentary by *R Pucella*, I difficili assetti della responsabilità medica; [2007] Resp civ prev 1824, with a commentary by *M Gorgoni*, Le conseguenze di un intervento chirurgico rivelatosi inutile.

25 A bill has been presented to the Italian Parliament: see Disegno di legge no 1598 ('Disposizioni in materia di sicurezza delle strutture sanitarie e gestione del rischio clinico, nonché di attività libero-professionale intramuraria e di esclusività del rapporto di lavoro dei dirigenti di ruolo sanitario del Servizio sanitario nazionale') submitted by the Ministry of Health before the Senate of the Italian Republic on 24 May 2007.

26 The 'Italian Hospital Surgeons' Association' (*Associazione Chirurghi Ospedalieri Italiani*, ACOI) recently presented a draft-model of quality and safety certification: see <http://www.acoi.it/l-associazione/news-acoi/chirurgia-arriva-certificazione-di-qualita-e-sicurezza>.

27 See *U Genovese*, Il caso e la necessità: considerazioni sulla gestione del rischio clinico in Italia, [2008] Riv it medicina legale 1061.

28 See *Ponzanelli*, [2003] Danno resp 428 ff; *Comandé/Turchetti* (fn 20) passim; *Nocco*, fn 20 805 ff; *id* fn 20 444 ff; *Breda* fn 19 431 ff.

person who committed the act to compensate for the damage'.[29] In other words, the rule establishes the principle of *alterum non laedere*.[30]

21 In cases where medical malpractice imputable to a physician employed in a medical institution had caused personal injury to the patient, jurisprudence affirmed the existence of a contractual relationship between the patient and the medical institution. Until 1988,[31] courts stated that, due to the absence of a contract between patient and physician, the former was entitled to bring solely a tortious claim against the physician[32] (and/or the medical institution).[33] Thus, the patient could have filed both a contractual claim against the medical institution, and a tortious claim against the physician.

22 Starting from 1988, the Supreme Court has affirmed the existence of a 'special relationship' between the physician and the patient, which places the liability arising from medical malpractice within the contractual field.[34]

23 Medical institutions (public or private) and the physician (or, more generally, medical staff) are jointly and severally liable pursuant to art 2055 CC[35] both in the case: i) where the damage is caused exclusively by the physician's conduct and ii) where the damage is imputable to the physician and to the medical institution. Clearly, whoever will have to compen-

---

29 *C Salvi*, Responsabilità extracontrattuale (dir vigente), in: Enciclopedia del diritto, vol XXXIX (1988) 1186–1264; *G Ponzanelli*, La responsabilità civile. Profili di diritto comparato (1992) 105; *CM Bianca*, Diritto civile V (1994) 546 ff; *FD Busnelli*, Modelli e tecniche di indennizzo del danno alla persona. L'esperienza italiana a confronto con 'L'alternativa svedese', [1986] Jus 219; *F Galgano*, La commedia della responsabilità civile, [1987] Rivista critica del diritto privato (Riv crit dir priv) 191; *A Procida Mirabelli di Lauro*, Dalla responsabilità civile alla sicurezza sociale. A proposito dei diversi sistemi di imputazione dei danni da circolazione di veicoli (1992) 64 ff; *G Visintini*, Responsabilità contrattuale ed extracontrattuale, in: Enciclopedia giuridica Treccani (Enc giur Treccani) XXVI (1991) 1.

30 *Franzoni* (fn 22) 25 ff.

31 The *revirement* by jurisprudence dates back to Cass 1 March 1988, no 2144, [1988] I Nuova giur civ comm 604, with a commentary by *R Pucella*. See also Cass 21 December 1978, no 6141, [1979] I Foro it 4. See infra nos 41 ff and 48 f.

32 See, for instance, Cass 8 March 1979, no 1716, [1980] Resp civ prev 90.

33 Tortious liability of medical institutions for the misconduct of the medical staff working within their premises derives from art 2049 CC, according to which 'Masters and employers are liable for the damage caused by an unlawful act of their servants and employees in the exercise of the functions to which they are assigned'.

34 See infra nos 41ff and 48 f.

35 Art 2055 CC lays down the rule that 'If the act causing damage can be attributed to more than one person, all are jointly liable for the damages. The person who has compensated for the damage has recourse against each of the others in proportion to the degree of fault of each and to the consequences arising therefrom. In case of doubt, the degree of fault attributable to each is presumed to be equal'.

sate for the damage suffered by the injured patient has a right of recourse towards the other jointly liable person (or towards both of them, should a third person pay for the damages).

10. Burden of proof

In tort law, to seek compensation for damages, the injured person has to give proof of i) the damage suffered; ii) the defendant's negligent or wilful conduct; iii) the causation (see art 2697 CC). **24**

Therefore, if medical malpractice is ascribed to the field of torts,[36] the patient will have to discharge a 'significant' burden of proof. In order to mitigate the patient's burden of proof (and for policy reasons), jurisprudence has devised new criteria, based on: **25**

- the 'proximity of the evidence' (the so-called rule of *vicinanza della prova*),[37] which shifts the burden of proof to whoever is in a better position to discharge it;
- the 'evidential damage doctrine' (the so-called doctrine of *danno evidenziale*),[38] which basically states that the burden of proof will have to be discharged by the tortfeasor, so long as they are under a duty to store the data related to the damaging event.[39]

Both criteria mitigate the patient's burden of proof, especially with reference to both the medical staff's negligent conduct and causation. **26**

11. Uncertain causation

Often, in cases of medical malpractice, legal scholars are faced with the causative dilemma in its multiple profiles:[40] for instance, the onset of **27**

---

36 See supra no 21.

37 Cass 13 January 2005, no 583, [2006] Giustizia civile (Giust civ) 2186; Cass, Joint Chambers, 11 January 2008, no 577 (fn 13).

38 *U Izzo*, Il danno da contagio post-trasfusionale come 'danno evidenziale'? Regole e concetti in tema di presunzioni e responsabilità, [2001] Danno resp 255.

39 See *Iadecola/Bona* (fn 22) 362 ff.

40 See R *Pucella*, La causalità 'incerta' (2007) passim; *id*, Suicidio post-traumatico: una non facile allocazione di responsabilità, [2008] Resp civ prev 661. On this topic see also *L Caputi*, Il nesso di causalità nella responsabilità civile: un problema irrisolto o sopravvalutato? [2007] Riv crit dir priv 169; *M Franzoni*, Problemi vecchi e nuovi in tema di causalità, [2006] Res civ prev 1997; *H Koziol*, Prospettive di soluzione in tema di 'causalità alternativa' [2010] Resp civ prev 964; *P Trimarchi*, Causalità e danno (1967).

damage sometimes occurs a significant period of time after the primary harmful event; pre-existing conditions involve difficulties in determining the causal impact of individual causal factors. Similarly, the occurrence of further cases with autonomous causal force must be taken into account in order to verify disruption of the causal chain.

28 Within civil liability (as opposed to criminal liability), Italian jurisprudence has distinguished between two 'criteria'[41] of causation: ordinary causation[42] and loss of chance.[43]

29 The two criteria of causation represent different conceptual categories: ordinary causation is related to the 'probability' that the tortfeasor's misconduct caused the damage; whereas the latter is based on the assessment of whether the misconduct has deprived the injured person of the chance to prevent the harmful event.[44]

30 Ordinary causation, the prevalent and currently applied criterion in civil law litigation, is based on the more probable than not rule.[45] Indeed, the purpose of tortious liability is to compensate for the damage suffered by the victim.

31 That might well justify lesser stringency in the rules of causation as compared to criminal law, inasmuch as rules of probation (in comparison to the criminal trial) may be based on the idea of 'preponderance of evidence'.[46] For that reason, jurisprudence approaches uncertain causation in civil liability in terms of the 'probability' that a certain fact has caused a harmful event. Once the causation issue is positively solved, damage has to be compensated in its full amount, in conformity with the logic of 'all-or-nothing'.

---

41 Cass 16 October 2007, no 21619, [2008] Danno resp 43, with a commentary by *R Pucella*, Causalità civile e probabilità: spunti per una riflessione.

42 'Ordinary causation' is also applied to medical malpractice (see fn 41).

43 See infra nos 32 ff.

44 See Cass 16 October 2007, no 21619 (fn 41). See *Iadecola/Bona* (fn 22) 400 ff.

45 Cass 16 October 2007, no 21619 (fn 41); Cass, Joint Chambers, 11 January 2008, no 576, [2008] Corriere mercantile (Corr mer) 694, with a commentary by *G Travaglino*, Causalità civile e penale: modelli a confronto; Cass 15 September 2008, no 23676, [2008] Foro italiano (Foro it) 36. The more-probable-than-not-rule derives from extensive case law, which has overlapped different and alternative methods – at times more stringent, at times more permissive – to establish causation.

46 Cass 16 October 2007, no 21619 (fn 41); Cass, Joint Chambers, 11 January 2008, no 581, [2008] Resp civ prev 841, with a commentary by *F Greco*, Le Sezioni Unite ed il limite prescrizionale nel danno da emotrasfusioni infette; Cass, Joint Chambers, 11 January 2008, no 582, [2008] Giust civ Mass 34; Cass, Joint Chambers, 11 January 2008, no 584, [2008] Foro it 451.

12. Loss of a chance

Italian jurisprudence[47] awards damages for loss of chance.[48] Loss of chance is based on 'the principle of increased risk'. In the context of medical liability, loss of chance[49] consists 'in the mere possibility to achieve a different therapeutic result, and is meant as "failure" to achieve it. The patient's expectation to recover is considered a "protected interest", giving rise to an autonomous right, different from the right to health'.[50] 32

Therefore, the patient is entitled to claim damages – not for the physical injury in itself (which gives rise to so-called *danno biologico*,[51] which is intrinsic in the injury of personal integrity and, thus, is compensated according to a point system) – for the loss of the chance of recovery. 33

The amount of damages awarded depends on the degree of probability that the appropriate treatment would have allowed the patient's recovery.[52] 34

The loss of chance criterion of causation is usually adopted by the court in order to grant protection to the injured person when the criterion of ordinary causation (ie the more-probable-than-not-rule) does not allow a determination of causation beyond 'reasonable' doubt.[53] 35

47 Cass 4 March 2004, no 4400, [2005] Giust civ 2129, with a commentary by E *Giacobbe*, Brevi osservazioni sul danno da «nascita indesiderata», ovvero un bambino malformato non ha diritto di nascere.

48 See, *ex multis*, Cass 4 March 2004, no 4400 (fn 47); Cass 18 March 2003, no 3999, [2003] I Nuova giur civ comm 871; Cass 27 July 2001, no 10291, [2001] Mass Foro it; Cass 25 September 1998, no 9598, [1999] Danno resp 534.

49 See M *Franzoni*, Il danno risarcibile, in: Trattato della responsabilità civile II (2004) 76 ff; *M Bocchiola*, Perdita di una chance e risarcimento del danno, [1976] Rivista trimestrale di diritto e procedura civile (Riv trim dir proc civ) 55; *A Princigalli*, Perdita di chances e danno risarcibile, [1985] Riv crit dir priv 315; *Pucella*, (fn 40) 81 ff; *C Severi*, Perdita di chance e danno patrimoniale risarcibile, [2003] Resp civ prev 296; P *Tramarchi*, Il contratto: inadempimento e rimedi (2010), 144 ff.

50 Cass 16 October 2007, no 21619 (fn 41).

51 See infra nos 67 ff.

52 For instance, if the probability of recovery equals 35 %, and the loss suffered is 100 %, damages awarded will amount to 35 %.

53 Tribunal of Reggio Emilia, 19 October 2007, [2008] Resp civ prev 2354, the court awarded damages for the loss of the chance to survive (statistically evaluated as amounting to 40 % within 5 years from the injury and to 25 % within 10 years from the injury).

13. Multiple persons involved

36 The problem primarily involves cases of treatments provided by medical *équipes*. Where medical treatment is carried out by a plurality of individuals, Italian jurisprudence has elaborated the following principles:

- the *teoria dell'affidamento* (literally, the 'reliance/entrustment theory'), according to which every *équipe* member is liable for their own performance and may rely on the 'exactness' of the performances carried out by other *équipe* members;[54]
- the physician in charge is under a duty to supervise and manage the medical *équipe*, and their actions; *équipe* members are liable for the personal injury suffered by the patient in the event that they fail to follow instructions of the physician in charge, unless the implementation of such would have resulted in a more serious personal injury (in which case *solely* the physician in charge is liable);
- should a member of the *équipe* perceive a risk to the patient's health resulting from the conduct of other *équipe* members, they are under a duty to intervene to prevent their personal liability (unless the physician in charge takes the responsibility for the possible detrimental effects of the treatment at issue).[55]

37 In addition to the liability of (individual) *équipe* members, the medical institution is liable pursuant to art 1218 CC.[56] The medical institution's liability flows from the contractual relationship entered into with the patient.

14. Strict liability

38 There are no strict liability rules within medical liability. Medical liability is basically a 'fault-based liability', although over the last few years Italian

54 See AA VV (Autori Vari, Various authors), Profili di responsabilità nell'équipe odontoiatrica, [2008] Riv it medicina legale 1275. See, Cass 6 April 2005, no 22579, [2006] Cassazione penale (Cass pen) 2838.

55 Cass 2 March 2004, [2004] Diritto penale e processo (Dir pen proc) 1082. Therefore, the 'subordinate' physician is not a mere executor of instructions issued by the physician in charge: see *Iadecola/Bona* (fn 22) 98 ff.

56 According to art 1218 CC, which is applicable to any obligation, regardless of its source, 'The debtor who does not exactly render due performance is liable for damages, unless they prove that the non-fulfilment or the delay was caused by impossibility of performance deriving from a cause not imputable to them'.

jurisprudence has increased patients' protection by a new distribution of the burden of proof.[57]

For instance, for routine medical treatments Italian jurisprudence considers *slight* negligence as being sufficient for the liability of the medical staff; for treatments involving skills which go beyond ordinary qualifications, *gross* negligence is required, unless the physician is a specialist. **39**

An assessment of the medical staff members' behaviour in the specific case is therefore indispensable. **40**

C. Contractual Liability

15. Basics of contracts in the health care sector

Liability arising from medical malpractice is ascribed to the 'contractual field'. **41**

Basically, two scenarios can be outlined. The patient admitted to a hospital or a clinic: i) enters into a contract with the medical institution, and is treated by an internal physician who is affiliated with the medical institution; ii) concludes a contract with a physician practicing their professional activity within a medical institution. **42**

The contract concluded with the medical institution has been defined by Italian jurisprudence as the 'hospitalisation contract' or 'health assistance contract' (*contratto di spedalità* or *contratto di assistenza sanitaria*), which is an innominate and 'complex' contract, as, beyond *stricto sensu* medical treatment, services related to accommodation are provided, drugs, medicines and equipment are administered, etc. In other words, besides the *main obligation* (medical treatment), there are additional obligations which will have to be performed by the medical structure within the hospital/patient relationship.[58] **43**

In the quite common case of a patient medicated by a physician affiliated with a medical institution, there is no *formal* contractual relationship **44**

---

57 See supra no 25.

58 For instance, courts have affirmed the contractual liability of hospitals and clinics for their 'inefficiency', should the structure's deficiencies cause damage to patients (for instance, the failure of technical instruments): see Cass 16 May 2000, no 6318, [2000] Resp civ prev 940, with a commentary by *M Gorgoni*, L'incidenza delle disfunzioni della struttura ospedaliera sulla responsabilità 'sanitaria'. See also *G Iudica*, Danno alla persona da inefficienza della struttura sanitaria, [2001] Resp civ prev 3.

between patient and physician. Nevertheless, according to jurisprudence, the so-called 'social contact' (*contatto sociale*)[59] between the patient and the physician creates a special relationship giving rise to 'duties to protect' (*obblighi di protezione*, conceptually equivalent to the German *Schutzpflichten*).[60] Their non-fulfilment grounds contractual liability, ie liability for non-fulfilment of an obligation pursuant to art 1218 CC.[61] Thus, according to Italian jurisprudence, both the medical institution and the physician are contractually liable towards the patient. More specifically, the medical institution is liable for both its breach of contract and for the physician's negligence – the latter being its auxiliary in the carrying out of performance (according to art 1228 CC[62]).[63]

45 The outcome does not change in the case that the patient concludes a contract with a physician practicing their professional activity within a medical institution. Regardless of the type of labour relationship between the physician and the medical institution, in the case of medical malpractice the patient may bring an action in contract against both the physician and the medical institution. The liability of the medical institution in this case derives from the mere admission of the patient within its premises, which – according to jurisprudence – *de facto* generates a contract.[64]

---

59 See infra no 49.

60 *F Benatti*, Responsabilità precontrattuale, headword in: Enc giur Treccani, XXVII (1994) 1; *id*, La responsabilità precontrattuale (1963) passim; *CW Canaris*, Schutzgesetze – Verkehrspflichten – Schutzpflichten, in: Festschrift für Karl Larenz zum 80. Geburtstag (1983) 27 ff, which has been translated into Italian: *id*, Norme di protezione, obblighi del traffico, doveri di protezione, [1983] Riv crit dir priv 793; *C Castronovo*, Obblighi di protezione, headword in: Enc giur Treccani XXI (1991) 1; *R von Jhering*, Culpa in contrahendo, reprint (1969); *L Lambo*, Responsabilità civile e obblighi di protezione, [2008] Danno resp 129; *L Mengoni*, Sulla natura della responsabilità precontrattuale, [1956] II Riv dir comm 364; *C Scognamiglio*, Il danno al patrimonio tra contratto e torto, [2007] Resp civ prev 1255.

61 See infra Sec 17.

62 According to art 1228 CC, 'The debtor who avails themself of the services of third persons in the performance of the obligation is also liable for their deliberate or culpable non-fulfilment, unless otherwise intended by the parties'.

63 See above no 23 and no 37.

64 See infra Sec 17.

16. Differences to tort law

The main difference between contract law and tort law concern the: **46**

a) Damages awarded

Art 1223 CC[65] expressly lays down that damages must include both the actual damage as well as the lost gain. The distinction between contractual and non-contractual damages is to be found in the joint reading of art 1225 and art 2056, para 1, CC.

Indeed, art 1225 CC limits compensation for damages for non fraudulent/willful non-fulfilment to the loss that could have been predicted 'at the time the obligation arose'. Art 1225 CC is not applicable to tortious liability, as art 2056 CC (ruling – specifically – on the liquidation of damages in the case of tortious liability) does not account for the foreseeability of the loss (at the time the action originating tortious liability was committed), which therefore – as a matter of principle – does not encounter any 'cap'.[66]

b) Prescription/time limitation

In the contractual field, the ordinary term of prescription is ten years (art 2946 CC), whilst the time limitation in the case of tortious liability is five years (art 2947, para 1, CC).

c) Burden of proof

As has been stated,[67] jurisprudence considers medical malpractice as grounding contractual liability, with the consequence of imposing the burden of proof on the party in breach, ie the physician and/or the medical institution, with considerable advantages for the victim.[68]

Therefore, the injured person has to discharge the burden of allegation of the breach of contract: ie the victim will have to prove the existence of the contract[69] and the damage suffered, and will merely have to

65 According to art 1223 CC, 'The measure of damages arising from non-performance or delay shall include the loss sustained by the creditor and the lost profits insofar as they are a direct and immediate consequence of the non-performance or delay'.

66 *FD Busnelli/G Comandé*, Damages under Italian Law, in: U Magnus (ed), Unification of Tort Law: Damages (2001) 117 ff.

67 See above no 22.

68 See above Sec 10.

69 With reference to causation in contract law, the Italian Supreme Court has stated that the allegation by the creditor must be based on a 'qualified breach of contract', ie on the allegation of a breach which 'in the abstract is sufficient to produce the damage'. Conversely, the defendant has to discharge the burden of proof that there has not been

allege the (qualified) breach of contract.[70] It is up to the 'debtor' (the physician and/or the medical institution) to prove the 'exact' fulfilment of their contractual obligation (also with reference to the 'special difficulty of performance' pursuant to art 2236 CC).[71]

47 For that reason, although jurisprudence considers a cumulation (*cumulo* or *concorso di responsabilità*) of the two types of actions admissible,[72] in medical malpractice cases the victim is well-advised to bring a contractual action – given its more favorable regime. The more so as the – theoretical – limitation of damages awarded to the amount corresponding to the damage which could have been predicted at the time the obligation arose (pursuant to art 1225 CC), in cases of contractual liability, does not play any role in case of medical malpractice cases, as the full amount of the damage suffered, ie of the damage deriving from personal injury, will always have to be compensated.

17. Contractual claims in the absence of direct contracts?

48 Legal scholars have placed medical liability in the '"area of turbulence"[73] [...] between contract and tort'.[74] In this landscape, the legal paradigm loses itself within the evanescent boundary between the two liability regimes: the absence of formal contract would involve a tortious liability; the special relationship between the physician – who is neither a 'passer-by' nor a *quisque de populo*[75] – and the patient might ground an *obligation* comparable to the legal relation arising from a contract. Indeed, the patient/physician relationship is characterised by the presence of 'other duties', different from the *main* performance (which in this case is ab-

---

any breach, or that there is no link between the breach and the damage: see Cass 13 April 2007, no 8826 (fn 24); Cass 24 May 2006, no 12362, [2006] Mass Giur it 1042; Cass, Joint Chambers, 30 October 2001, no 13533, [2002] Contratti 113, with a commentary by *U Carnevali*, Inadempimento e onere della prova: see Cass, Joint Chambers, 11 January 2008, no 577 (fn 13).

70 See above fn 69.

71 See *Iadecola/Bona* (fn 22) 359 ff. See above Sec 7.

72 Cass 14 May 1979, no 2773, [1979] Giust civ Mass 5. See *PG Monateri*, La responsabilità contrattuale e precontrattuale (1998) 299 ff; *Visintini* (fn 29) 1 ff.

73 This evocative term is credited to *C Castronovo*, La nuova responsabilità civile (2006) 443.

74 *FD Busnelli*, Itinerari europei nella 'terra di nessuno' tra contratto e fatto illecito: la responsabilità da informazioni inesatte, [1991] Contratto e impresa (Contr impr) 539. The author refers to the expression used by *G Gilmore*, The Death of Contract (1995). See also *Castronovo* (fn 73) 446 ff. See also *G Alpa*, Gli incerti confini della responsabilità civile, [2006] Resp civ prev 1805.

75 See ibid.

sent),[76] referred to as *obblighi di protezione*,[77] whose non-fulfilment leads to a contractual-type liability.

This is the background against which authoritative Italian legal scholars[78] have theorised the *responsabilità da contatto sociale* (ie 'liability deriving from social contact', which in conceptual terms implies the existence of an 'obligation without the [main] performance': a so-called *obbligazione senza prestazione [primaria]*),[79] which has been implemented by jurisprudence.[80] In this context, the *contatto sociale*[81] ('social contact') between the parties is held to be a source of obligations *ex* art 1173 CC,[82] whose non-fulfilment generates a contractual-type liability pursuant to art 1218 CC.[83] Therefore, patients may base a claim on the violation of contractual duties, regardless of whether they have entered into a *formal* or *explicit* contract with a physician and/or the medical institution. **49**

18. Informed consent

The right of the patient to receive adequate information in anticipation of the treatment[84] implies, specifically, the duty on the part of the physician **50**

---

76 Ibid.

77 See above no 44.

78 *Castronovo* (fn 73). The theoretical framework on which 'liability deriving from social contact' is grounded has been developed by *Mengoni* [1956] II Riv dir comm, passim.

79 See also *Scognamiglio* [2007] Resp civ prev 1255; *S Faillace*, La responsabilità da contatto sociale (2004) passim; *A Di Majo*, Il problema del danno al patrimonio, [1984] Riv crit dir priv 322.

80 See, *ex multis*, Tribunal of Catanzaro, 18 June 2009, [2010] Resp civ prev 145, with a commentary by *M Foglia*, Duty to prevent the suicide?: I confini dell'obbligo di protezione in capo all'insegnante; Cass 22 January 1999, no 589, [1999] Corr giur 446 with a commentary by *A Di Majo*, L'obbligazione senza prestazione approda in Cassazione; Cass 13 April 2007, no 8826 (fn 24); Cass, Joint Chambers, 11 January 2008, no 577 (fn 13).

81 *F Galgano*, I fatti illeciti (2008) 251 ff; *I Sarica*, Il contatto sociale fra le fonti della responsabilità civile: recenti equivoci della giurisprudenza di merito, [2005] Contr impr 97.

82 According to art 1173 CC, 'Obligations derive from contract, from an unlawful act or from any other act or fact to produce them in conformity with the legal system'.

83 In the Italian legal system contractual liability (*responsabilità contrattuale*) does not derive exclusively from … contracts *stricto sensu*: indeed, it should be – more correctly – defined as *responsabilità da inadempimento* ('liability [deriving] from non-fulfilment'), which clearly indicates that any breach of a (pre-existent) obligation might lead to contractual liability, ie to liability ex art 1218 CC. See *L Mengoni*, Responsabilità contrattuale, headword in: Enciclopedia del Diritto XXXIX (1988) 1072 ff, who points out that a 'synecdoche' is used to define *responsabilità contrattuale*.

84 See *R Pucella*, Autodeterminazione e responsabilità nella relazione di cura (2008); *A Santosuosso*, Il consenso informato. Tra giustificazione per il medico e diritto del paziente (2006).

to provide all the information necessary in order to ensure the patient's right to self-determination.[85]

51 Indeed, save in the case of emergencies, in the Italian legal system[86] any medical or health treatment requires the prior consent of the patient without which the medical activity would be unlawful. Patients have the right to information on the consequences and risks of medical treatment (which extends to life-saving treatment),[87] and are free to decide whether to undergo or decline the specific medical treatment proposed (including terminal treatment).[88]

52 With reference to the exact content of the duty to inform,[89] jurisprudence has pointed out that it is not a mere 'bureaucratic step', as the patient's

85 With reference to the patient-medical staff relationship, see also *Pucella* (fn 84) passim; *P Zatti*, Rapporto medico-paziente e 'integrità' della persona, [2008] II Nuova giur civ comm 403; *id*, Aspetti giuridici. Il principio di correttezza nel rapporto medico-paziente, [1996] Giustizia costituzionale (Giust cost) 54.

86 The patient's rights are protected by both deontological rules and by arts 2, 13 and 32, para 2, Const. The patient's right to self-determination is also established in the Oviedo Convention and in art 3, no 2, of the Charter of Fundamental Rights of the European Union, entitled 'Right to the integrity of the person', according to which 'In the fields of medicine and biology, the following must be respected in particular: the free and informed consent of the person concerned, according to the procedures laid down by law [...]'.

87 On the delicate and sensitive topic of the right to seek the interruption of life-saving treatment and the so-called 'right to die', see: *G Oppo*, Scienza, diritto, vita umana (Lectio doctoralis di Giorgio Oppo) [2002] I Rivista di diritto civile (Riv dir civ) 11; *P Zatti*, Il diritto a scegliere la propria salute (in margine al caso S Raffaele) [2000] II Nuova giur civ comm 1; *id*, Dimensioni ed aspetti dell'identità nel diritto privato attuale, L'identità nell'orizzonte del diritto privato, [2007] 4 Nuova giur civ comm 1; *id*, Il corpo e la nebulosa dell'appartenenza, [2007] II Nuova giur civ comm 1; *G Ponzanelli*, Nancy Cruzan, la Corte suprema degli Stati uniti e il 'right to die', [1991] Foro it 72; *A Santosuosso*, La volontà oltre la coscienza: la cassazione e lo stato vegetativo, [2008] II Nuova giur civ comm 1; *id*, Il paziente non cosciente e le decisioni sulle cure: il criterio della volontà dopo il caso Cruzan, [1991] Foro it 66; *M Azzalini*, Il rifiuto di cure. Riflessioni a margine del caso Welby, [2007] Nuova giur civ comm 313; *id*, Trattamenti life-saving e consenso del paziente: i doveri del medico dinanzi al rifiuto di cure, [2008] I Nuova giur civ comm 73; *id*, Tutela dell'identità del paziente incapace e rifiuto di cure: appunti sul caso Englaro, [2008] II Nuova giur civ comm 331.

88 See, *ex multis*, Cass 16 January 2008, no 11335, [2008] Danno resp 889, with a commentary by *S Cacace*, Consenso informato: novità sul fronte giurisprudenziale. Rappresentazione in tre atti; Cass 24 June 2008, no 37077, [2009] Corr giur 182, with a commentary by *S De Flammineis*, Il consenso all'atto medico attraverso il profilo del diritto al rifiuto delle cure (e dell'eutanasia); Cass 30 July 2004, no 14638, [2005] Giur it 7, with a commentary by *M D'Auria*, Consenso informato: contenuto e nesso di causalità.

89 *G Gennari*, Il consenso informato come espressione di libertà, [2007] Resp civ prev 2133; *G Facci*, Il consenso informato all'atto medico: esercizio di un diritto costituzionalmente garantito per il paziente o una 'trappola' per il sanitario? [2006] Resp civ prev 486; *G Cassano*, Obbligo di informazione, relazione medico-paziente, difficoltà della prestazione e concorso di responsabilità, [2001] Danno resp 154; *F Introna*, Consenso informato e rifiuto ragionato. L'informazione deve essere dettagliata o sommaria? [1998] Riv it medicina

consent has to be expressed as a result of comprehensive information given by the physician, including the proposed therapy's or surgery's contraindications or potential harm and the indication of the 'seriousness' of the treatment effects.

In the case of breach of the duty to inform, it is disputed in jurisprudence whether compensation for damage should be granted on the basis of the *mere* lack of information (ie the patient was not properly informed about the consequences of the treatment) even in the absence of any personal injury deriving from the medical treatment.[90] **53**

D. Public Liability

19. Key differences from cases involving private hospitals or doctors

In terms of liability (and of compensation for damage), in the Italian legal system there currently are no differences in compensation for damage between public hospitals and private clinics or medical staff. **54**

E. Alternative Compensation Regimes

20. Funds and/or other alternative compensation regimes

There are no permanent funds or alternative compensation regimes for medical malpractice in Italy. **55**

Nevertheless, following liability for post-transfusion contagion in hospitals (infection by blood derivative/blood transfusion or damage arising from compulsory vaccination),[91] the Italian Parliament has passed a reg- **56**

---

legale 825; *G Citarella*, Obblighi di informazione e responsabilità del chirurgo plastico, [1998] Resp civ prev 677; *M Portigliatti Barbos*, Il modulo medico di consenso informato: adempimento giuridico, retorica, finzione burocratica? [1998] Dir pen proc 894.

90 Cass 9 February 2010, no 2847, [2010] Resp civ prev 2181, with a commentary by *U Carnevali*, Omessa informazione da parte del medico, danno da trattamento terapeutico e ipotetica scelta del paziente; Cass 14 March 2006, no 5444, [2007] Nuova giur civ comm 250, with a commentary by *L Gremigni Francini*, Danno extracontrattuale 'da mancato consenso informato' ed identificazione del sanitario responsabile: in contrast to the theory of contractual liability (see fn 13), the Supreme Court has held that the mere breach of informed consent grounds non-contractual liability.

91 *GM Vergallo/P Frati*, La tutela risarcitoria dei pazienti danneggiati da emotrasfusioni infette, [2009] Riv it medicina legale 39; *R Chieppa*, Giusti benefici economici a favore di

ulation (*Statute* 25 February 1992, no 210) which granted the right of indemnity to victims of contagion (such as viral hepatitis and/or HIV). The indemnity was paid for by the State, and does not prejudice any tortious claim against the tortfeasors.

F. Extent of Liability/Remedies

I. Pecuniary Loss

21. Introduction to indemnifying pecuniary loss

57 Tortious liability might be defined as a 'bipolar' system:[92] on one hand, *danno patrimoniale* ex art 2043 CC, ie pecuniary loss, which amounts to income lost and medical expenses arising from the injury; on the other hand, *danno non patrimoniale* pursuant to art 2059 CC, ie non-pecuniary loss.[93]

58 The concept of 'damage' is not established in the Italian Civil Code. For that reason, legal scholars usually refer to the traditional assessment of the difference doctrine (*Differenztheorie*).[94]

59 The plaintiff is entitled to recover only damages corresponding to the loss suffered.[95]

---

danneggiati da somministrazione di emoderivati (nella specie immunoglobulina antitetanica), ma con vantaggi per le imprese farmaceutiche, [2009] Giurisprudenza costituzionale (Giur cost) 206; *F Greco*, Le Sezioni Unite ed il limite prescrizionale nel danno da emotrasfusioni infette, [2008] Resp civ prev 841; *M Bertoncini*, Indennizzo per danni da vaccinazioni obbligatorie e possibile estensione della fattispecie alle non obbligatorie, [2007] Resp civ prev 346.

92 *C Salvi*, La responsabilità civile (2005) 34.

93 See infra no 67 ff.

94 See *Busnelli/Comandé* (fn 66) 117 ff.

95 See Cass 17 January 2007, no 1183, [2008] Hastings International & Comparative Law Review (Int'l & Comp L Rev) 753 ff, with a commentary by *F Quarta*, Recognition and Enforcement of US Punitive Damages Awards in Continental Europe; [2007] Resp civ prev 2100, with a commentary by *A De Pauli*, L'irriconoscibilità in Italia per contrasto con l'ordine pubblico di sentenze statunitensi di condanna al pagamento dei danni 'punitivi'; [2007] Resp civ prev 1890, with a commentary by *L Ciaroni*, Il paradigma della responsabilità civile tra tradizione e prospettive di riforma; [2007] I, V Foro it 1460, with a commentary by *G Ponzanelli*, Danni punitivi: no, grazie; [2007] Giur it 2724, with a commentary by *V Tomarchio*, Anche la Cassazione esclude il risarcimento dei danni punitivi; [2007] Europa e diritto privato (Europa dir priv) 1129, with a commentary by *G Spoto*, I punitive damages al vaglio della giurisprudenza italiana; [2007] I Nuova giur civ comm 981, with a commentary by *R Oliari*, I danni punitivi bussano alla porta: la Cassazione non apre. Similarly, Court of Appeal of Venice, 15 October 2002, [2002] I Nuova giur civ comm 765, with a commentary by *G Campeis/A De Pauli*, Danni punitivi,

As regards pecuniary losses, the general rule (art 2043 CC) covers any economic damage, without any (generally applicable) cap to the amount of damages awarded.[96] **60**

In terms of assessing the damages to be awarded, art 1223 CC states that damages covers both the loss suffered (*damnum emergens*) and the lost gain (*lucrum cessans*).[97] Whenever the damage cannot be demonstrated in its exact amount, damages may be 'equitably assessed' by the judge (pursuant to art 1226 CC, to which art 2056 CC refers); missed gain is determined by the judge taking into account the 'circumstances of the case' (art 2056, para 2, CC). **61**

22. Loss of earnings vs loss of earning capacity

In the case of personal injury suffered by a person not receiving any income (for instance, a student or a housewife), the injured person is nevertheless entitled to claim damages both for *danno biologico*[98] as well as for the loss of earning capacity (which therefore involves 'future damage').[99] The criteria to liquidate 'future damage' are – necessarily – based on equitable judgment, by taking into consideration the age and the social environment of the victim.[100] For instance, in a case of personal injury suffered by a housewife, damages awarded were based on income received by a maid.[101] **62**

In the liquidation of the pecuniary loss, courts will refer to the so-called 'residual earning capacity', ie they will charge up the loss of income from the profession the victim used to pursue against the income the victim earns in the 'newly' embraced profession.[102] **63**

---

ordine pubblico e sentenze straniere delibande a contenuto anfibio; [2002] I Foro padano 525, with a commentary – again – by G *Campeis/A De Pauli*, Danni punitivi, ordine pubblico e sentenze straniere delibande a contenuto anfibio; [2002] Rivista di diritto internazionale privato e processuale (Riv dir internaz priv proc) 1021 ff. For an overview, see *AP Scarso*, Punitive Damages in Italy, in: H Koziol/V Wilcox (eds), Punitive Damages: Common Law and Civil Law Perspectives (2009) 103 ff.

96 See infra Sec 24.

97 See above fn 65.

98 See infra Sec 25.

99 *Salvi* (fn 92) 258 ff.

100 Cass 15 April 1996, no 3539, [1996] Giust civ Mass 575.

101 Cass 11 December 2000, no 15580, [2001] Resp civ prev 612, with a commentary by C *Carbonaro*, La questione del risarcimento del danno patrimoniale della casalinga: la Cassazione al bivio tra azzeramento delle categorie del danno alla persona e loro reinterpretazione; Cass 3 March 2005, no 4657, [2005] Diritto & Giustizia 14, 31, with a commentary by *F Peccenini*, Incidenti stradali: danni al 'casalingo'.

102 See infra no 95, Case no 5.

64 Italian jurisprudence has also drawn a distinction between the notion of 'specific earning capacity' and that of 'generic earning capacity'.[103] The former regards the liquidation of the loss of income deriving from the impossibility of carrying on the profession the injured person used to pursue (hence, the damage suffered is qualified in terms of pecuniary loss), whereas the 'generic earning capacity' is traced to 'the value of the human being as an individual', and is compensated as *danno biologico*.[104]

23. Periodic payments or lump sum?

65 Despite the rule in art 2057 CC, according to which 'when damages to persons are permanent, damage awards can be made by the judge taking into account conditions of the involved parties and the nature of damages as a life annuity', courts usually award lump-sum damages; in practice the norm is constantly ignored by case law.

24. Caps and thresholds

66 As far as the amount of damages is concerned, except for a few exceptions,[105] the Italian legal system does not set out either a general cap or thresholds.

II. Non-Pecuniary Loss

25. Introduction to indemnifying non-pecuniary loss

67 Non-pecuniary loss can be defined *a contrario* as loss which cannot be objectively evaluated in economic terms. More precisely, according to Italian jurisprudence, non-pecuniary damages are granted by courts whenever there is 'an injury of non-economic interests – related to individuals – protected by the Constitution'.[106]

---

103 Cass 22 February 2002, no 2589, [2002] Danno resp 613, with a commentary by *A Bitetto*, La perdita o riduzione della capacità lavorativa fra danno biologico e danno patrimoniale. See also *Franzoni* (fn 49) 301 ff.

104 See infra Sec 25.

105 There are a few specific rules which provide for a liability cap, but not with reference to medical liability: see *Franzoni* (fn 49) 134 ff.

106 See Cass 31 May 2003, nos 8827 and 8828, [2003] Danno resp 816, with a commentary by *FD Busnelli/G Ponzanelli*, La Cassazione 'rimedita' l'art 2059 CC.

According to recent judgments by the Joint Session of the Supreme Court,[107] in cases of personal injury due to an unlawful act, besides pecuniary loss, the injured person is entitled to claim damages for non-pecuniary loss (*danno non patrimoniale*) as a unitary category, ie including – from a descriptive point of view – different types of non-pecuniary loss: for instance, *danno biologico*[108] (which is intrinsic in the injury of the victim's personal integrity) and *danno morale (soggettivo)*[109] (intrinsic in the pain and suffering related to the harmful event: it refers to the 'psychological suffering' of the injured person, to their 'internal sphere'). **68**

The judgments of the Joint Session of the Supreme Court at issue denied that the so-called *danno esistenziale*[110] is an autonomous type of non-pecuniary loss, different from *danno biologico* and *danno morale*.[111] **69**

---

107 The Supreme Court has rendered four so-called 'twin judgments' (nos 26972, 26973, 26974, 26975): see Cass, Joint Chambers, 11 November 2008, no 26972, [2009] Resp civ prev 38 ff with commentaries by: *PG Monateri*, Il pregiudizio esistenziale come voce del danno non patrimoniale; *E Navarretta*, Il valore della persona nei diritti inviolabili e la complessità dei danni non patrimoniali; *D Poletti*, La dualità del sistema risarcitorio e l'unicità della categoria dei danni non patrimoniali; *P Ziviz*, Il danno non patrimoniale: istruzioni per l'uso; *D Chindemi*, Una nevicata su un campo di grano; *C Scognamiglio*, Il sistema del danno non patrimoniale dopo le Sezioni Unite; *P Citarella*, Danno non patrimoniale e contratto. See also AA VV, Il danno non patrimoniale (2009).

108 The commonly accepted doctrine of *danno biologico* sets out that compensation for damages has to be awarded in the case of physical or psychological injury, regardless of the victim's ability to earn. On *danno biologico*, see – *ex multis* – *E Navarretta*, Diritti inviolabili e risarcimento del danno (1996) passim.

109 According to the Italian Supreme Court, pain and suffering constitutes a prejudice to the 'moral integrity of the person, protected by art 2 and 3 of the Constitution (with reference also to the social dignity of the person, to be jointly appraised with "health" as a fundamental value for biological and genetic identity)': see Cass 4 March 2008, no 5795, [2008] Resp civ prev 1548, with a commentary by *D Chindemi*, Danno non patrimoniale a favore della moglie per assistenza al marito.

110 The so-called *danno esistenziale* relates to the necessary change of the victim's everyday habits, as a consequence of the harmful event and therefore refers to the 'external sphere'. Both jurisprudence and legal scholars have hotly debated whether *danno esistenziale* is a distinct and autonomous (from *danno biologico* and *danno morale*) non-pecuniary loss. See, most recently, Cass, Joint Chambers, 11 November 2008, no 26972 (fn 107); Cass 20 April 2007, no 9510, [2007] Giust civ Mass 4, which have explicitly excluded its distinct and autonomous nature. Contra: Cass (Labour Section), 16 May 2007, no 11278, [2007] Giust civ Mass 5, according to which 'danno esistenziale represents an autonomous theoretical category [of damage] within art 2059 CC'. For an outline of *danno esistenziale*, see Cass 12 June 2006, no 13546, [2006] Resp civ prev 1439; Cass 24 March 2006, no 6572, [2006] I Foro it 2334; [2006] Giur it 1359; [2006] Resp civ prev 1041 and 1477; [2006] Giust civ 1443; [2006] Danno resp 852.

111 Some subsequent judgements did not follow Cass, Joint Chambers, 11 November 2008, no 26972 (fn 107): see, for instance, Cass 31 March 2009, no 7875, [2009] Danno resp 761, with a commentary by *G Ponzanelli*, Conferme ed incertezze della Cassazione dopo le Sezioni Unite. Similarly, some legal scholars still share the opinion that *danno esistenziale* should rather be considered as being a non-pecuniary loss distinct and autonomous from *danno biologico* and *danno morale*: see *P Cendon*, La giurisprudenza

70 Whilst *danno biologico* is compensated with reference to standardised economic reference values,[112] based on a point system (the so-called *calcolo a punti*),[113] the assessment of non-pecuniary loss different from *danno biologico*, ie of *danno morale*,[114] contemplates to a great degree the subjective situation of the victim.[115]

71 Recent decisions of the Supreme Court confirm the extension of the discretion of the court when setting the amount of damages for *danno morale*:[116] on one hand, in order to prevent diverging assessments of damages, *danno morale* is determined as a fraction of the compensation awarded as *danno biologico*;[117] on the other hand, the Supreme Court states

---

'esistenzialista' post 26972/08, in <http://www.personaedanno.it/cms/data/articoli/014264.aspx?catalog=0>, who has severely criticised the Supreme Court's Joint Session judgment.

112 For this reason, ie due to its objectively determinable amount, some legal scholars hold that *danno biologico* should be considered as being a pecuniary loss (instead of a non-pecuniary loss): see *FD Busnelli*, Il danno biologico – Dal 'diritto vivente' al 'diritto vigente' (2001) passim; *E Bargelli*, Danno non patrimoniale e interpretazione costituzionalmente orientata dell'Art 2059 c.c., [2003] Resp civ prev 702. The question has been explicitly addressed by the *Corte di Cassazione*, which stated in plain language that *danno biologico* constitutes a non-pecuniary loss: see Cass 4 November 2005, no 16525, [2004] I Foro it 779, with a commentary by *M Bona*, La morte del danno evento.

113 The Insurance Code (*Codice delle assicurazione private*, see Legislative Decree 7 September 2005, no 209) liquidates the *danno biologico* according to the 'seriousness' of the personal injury: for 'slight' injuries (ie injuries up to 9 %) the amount of the first point is currently € 728.16 for permanent disability (permanent *danno biologico*), and € 42.48 for every day of absolute disability in the case of temporary *danno biologico*, which increases more than proportionately by applying 'disability coefficients' which are related to the age of the victim and the seriousness of the injury (see art 139 Insurance Code). Art 139 Insurance Code applies to *danno biologico* arising from road accidents or the circulation of vessels.

114 See above fn 109.

115 Recent court decisions attest to the difficulties in the assessment of non-pecuniary loss in general, and of the different types of damage related to pain and suffering in particular. For instance, with reference to so-called 'terminal damage', ie personal injuries leading to the death of the injured person within a short time, jurisprudence holds (see Cass 14 July 2003, no 11003, [2003] Resp civ prev 1053, with a commentary by *G Facci*, La Cassazione ed il risarcimento del c.d. danno terminale) that in order to assess the so-called terminal damage it is essential 'to evaluate pain and suffering actually suffered by the victim, the seriousness of the offence and all other elements of the case submitted, in order to quantify precisely the compensation to be awarded in the case at issue'.

116 Despite providing for objective criteria to assess damages (and, thus, to limit judicial discretion), the Insurance Code does not completely cancel judicial discretion, leaving a margin for fair assessment, entrusted to the court's evaluation of the case at issue, in view of the subjective condition of the victim. Specifically, the court is allowed to increase the amount of *danno biologico* awarded within 20 % of the basic value, as long as it specifies the reasons for the increase (pursuant to art 139, para 3, Insurance Code).

117 See Cass 14 July 2003, no 11003 (fn 115); [2003] Diritto e famiglia (Dir fam) 643; Cass 16 May 2003, no 7632, [2003] Resp civ prev 1049; Cass 9 January 1998, no 1030, [1998] Danno resp 351.

that the assessment of pain and suffering cannot be reduced 'automatically to a mere fraction [of the *danno biologico*]'.[118]

Therefore, a mere mathematical assessment of damages is not permitted.[119] Courts are not allowed to state – for instance – that psychological integrity 'is worth' only half the amount of physical integrity.[120] In order to assess *danno morale*, it therefore becomes essential 'to evaluate pain and suffering actually suffered by the victim, the seriousness of the offence and all other elements of the case at issue in order to quantify precisely the compensation awarded in the concrete case'.[121] **72**

26. Who can claim compensation for non-pecuniary loss?

In the event that the unlawful act determines the death of the victim, jurisprudence grants to the relatives and to cohabitants[122] of the deceased compensation for both the pecuniary as well as the non-pecuniary losses directly suffered (so-called claims *iure proprio*). **73**

Depending on the length of the 'surviving period', ie the lapse of time between the harmful event and the death of the victim, Italian jurisprudence allows the relatives to succeed in the right to compensation for non-pecuniary loss of the victim (ie *danno biologico* and *danno morale*): a time lapse of a few days is usually considered as being sufficient to determine the acquisition by the (later deceased) victim of the right to compensation for the non-pecuniary loss suffered, which is thus passed to their relatives and to cohabitants after their death (so-called claims *iure hereditatis*);[123] on **74**

118 Cass 4 March 2008, no 5795 (fn 109); Cass 23 May 2003, no 8169, [2003] Resp civ prev 1342, with a commentary by *Facci* [2003] Resp civ prev 1053; [2004] Archivio della Circolazione 42.

119 See Cass 14 July 2003, no 11003 (fn 115).

120 See Cass 4 March 2008, no 5795 (fn 109), according to which, as *danno morale* affects the dignity of any human being, its assessment 'has to strive to grant satisfactory, and not merely symbolic compensation'. Similarly, Cass 11 January 2007, no 394, [2007] I Nuova giur civ comm 960, with a commentary by *G Sganga*, Il 'nuovo' danno biologico e la 'vecchia' personalizzazione del suo risarcimento; [2007] Guida al diritto 6, 22, with a commentary by *G Comandé*, Solo un adeguamento al caso concreto evita il rischio di risarcimenti irrisori.

121 See *Facci* [2003] Resp civ prev 1060.

122 Cass 29 April 2005, no 8976, [2006] Foro it 2448. The decision upholds the right of the cohabitant *more uxorio* to compensation for pecuniary and non-pecuniary losses suffered by the other cohabitant, provided that a 'conjugal-like relationship' – in terms of duration and intensity – is identified.

123 See Cass 14 July 2003, no 11003 (fn 115).

the contrary, the *immediate* death of the victim excludes – obviously – pain and suffering, ie any *danno morale*.[124]

75 Relatives are thus awarded damages – besides *iure proprio* (for the pecuniary loss, the *danno biologico* and *danno morale* they *directly* suffer), also – *iure hereditatis* (for the *danno biologico* and the *danno morale* the victim has suffered).

G. Procedural Matters

27. Specific rules of jurisdiction or procedure

76 No specific rules of jurisdiction or procedure apply.

28. Special institutions handling malpractice claims

77 No specific institutions handling malpractice claims exist.

H. Outlook

29. Reform plans

78 Currently no reforms plans with reference to medical liability exist.

Cases

Case 1

79 Under contract law, Hospital C can be sued because of its duty to monitor and supervise the internal medical activities. Hospital C is liable pursuant to art 1228 CC for the misconduct of both A and B and of midwife D.[125] In

124 See Cass 22 March 2007, no 6946, [2007] Repertorio del Foro italiano (Rep Foro it) headword, Danni civili no 80, according to which 'the injury to personal integrity leading to death immediately or within a short lapse of time from the harmful event does not give rise to *danno biologico*, since death does not constitute the maximal possible violation of the right to health, but affects the different "good" of life'. The Supreme Court explains that *danno biologico* suffered by the victim – for the compensation of which their heirs may sue the tortfeasor *iure hereditatis* – arises only when an 'appreciable lapse of time between the harmful event and the death due to it elapses'.

125 See above Sec 15.

addition, both A and B may be sued for breach of an *obbligo di protezione.*[126] Indeed, they perform the treatment by acting as locums for one another, even though, in practice, A seems to be the sole physician who acts negligently.[127]

With reference to the compensation for the severe damage suffered by X and Y, the issue pertains to material causation. Courts adopt two main causal rules: the more-probable-than-not rule and the loss of chance criterion. **80**

Should the court apply the more-probable-than-not rule, as a considerable part of the damage would have happened regardless of the medical misconduct (due to the pre-existing conditions of the patient), it appears likely that the plaintiff's claim would be rejected. **81**

Taking into consideration the fact that medical misconduct has occurred, the court may nevertheless award compensation for the loss of the possibility to obtain the right therapeutic result (successful birth), thereby applying the loss of chance-criterion.[128] **82**

Regardless of the applicable criteria of causation, there is a 'policy' trend in Italian jurisprudence towards the affirmation of the medical staff's liability, in such cases in order to grant to the family of the newborn (who has suffered severe damage) a *de facto* 'indemnity'.[129] **83**

It is therefore likely that Y (through her guardian) would be entitled to recover both the pecuniary damage (related to the costs of the disease) and the non-pecuniary loss.[130] Similarly, X would be entitled to seek compen- **84**

126 See above Sec/s 15 and 17, with reference to *responsabilità da contatto sociale.*

127 Subsequently, B might have right of recourse against A pursuant to art 2055, para 2, CC (see fn 35).

128 See above Sec 12.

129 Italian jurisprudence has stated that an unborn child has 'the right to be born healthy'. See Cass 11 May 2009, no 10741, [2009] Resp civ 814, with a commentary by *C Siano*, Medical malpractice e tutela del nascituro; [2009] Resp civ prev 2063, with a commentary by *M Gorgoni*, Nascituro e responsabilità sanitaria; Cass 9 May 2000, no 5881, [2001] Danno resp 169; Cass 19 May 1999, no 4852, [1999] I Foro it 2874. Moreover, once born, the newborn benefits from the 'contract with protective effects towards third persons' existing between their parents and the hospital/medical staff. See *G Varanese*, Il contratto con effetti protettivi per i terzi (2004); *M Maggiolo*, Effetti contrattuali e protezione del terzo, [2001] I Riv dir civ 58; *A Di Majo*, La protezione del terzo tra contratto e torto, [2000] Europa dir priv 20.

130 Moreover, X might claim damages for the breach of her right to 'informed consent', should she not have been informed adequately of the treatment's contraindications: Furthermore, she was deprived of the chance to interrupt pregnancy on the basis of information in reference of foetus malformations. See Cass 11 May 2009, no 10741 (fn 129).

sation for both the pecuniary damage (with reference to the care she herself provides to Y) as well as for the non-pecuniary loss she *directly* has suffered (also arising from the stillbirth of Y's twin brother).[131]

Case 2

85 The question underlying the case at issue concerns the possible recovery of 'loss' for breach of contract.

86 With reference to the pecuniary loss, X and Y might claim damages for the infringement of their 'right to conscious and responsible procreation' solely to the extent to which it implies a 'loss of income and personal consumptions due to the newborn'.[132]

87 Alternatively, the court might award damages for the expenses incurred on the occasion of delivery,[133] and for the pecuniary loss related to the future expenses for supporting the child.[134]

88 Jurisprudence awards compensation for the non-pecuniary damage suffered – *alternatively* – on either one of the two following grounds: (1) for the prejudice related primarily to the injury of psychological integrity due to the non-acceptance of the event (unwanted birth);[135] (2) for the infringement of the 'right to conscious and responsible procreation' pursuant to art 1, Statute 22 May 1978, no 194, involving the right to self-determination in deciding to procreate.[136]

---

131 According to Italian jurisprudence, the father is also entitled to claim damages inasmuch as he benefits from the 'contract with protective effects towards third persons' existing between the mother and the hospital/medical staff. See Cass 20 October 2005, no 20320, [2005] Giust civ Mass 7/8 (see fn 129).

132 Tribunal of Milan, 20 October 1997, [1999] Danno resp 82, with a commentary by *M Bona*, Filiazione indesiderata e risarcimento del 'danno da bambino non voluto'; *F Introna*, La nascita, per colpa medica, del 'figlio non desiderato': quale il danno e quale il risarcimento? [1999] Riv it medicina legale 610.

133 See Tribunal of Venice, 10 September 2002, [2003] Giust civ 2613, with a commentary by *S Baldassari*, Sterilità mancata. La nascita indesiderata e la responsabilità del medico.

134 Tribunal of Cagliari, 23 February 1995, [1995] Rivista giuridica sarda (Riv giur sarda) 669.

135 Tribunal of Venice, 10 September 2002 (fn 133).

136 It might be useful to point out that non-pecuniary loss is consequential damage and has to be alleged and proved: see Cass, Joint Chambers, 11 November 2008, no 26972 (fn 107).

Case 3

The damage is imputable to multiple tortfeasors. A, B, C and E share joint and several liability for having caused the damage.[137] In particular, A is negligent as the hospital failed to carry out controls after delivery (which could have prevented the damage, even partially); B should have recognised the risk to which X was exposed; C is liable for failing to implement an organisational structure, whilst E is liable for her inability to diagnose the disease. Each of them is contractually liable towards the plaintiff, regardless of the fact that – with a very high degree of probability – the damage occurred in clinic C. **89**

Defendants will be jointly and severally liable towards the victim, whilst in their reciprocal relations each tortfeasor will be liable for the damages according to their degree of fault and the damage deriving from it. **90**

With reference to the amount of damages awarded – similarly to case 1 – X (through his guardian) might claim damages for: (1) the pecuniary loss (in terms of both medical expenses and assistance, and the loss of earning capacity); (2) for the non-pecuniary loss (both *danno biologico* and *danno morale*).[138] **91**

Additionally, X's parents could seek compensation of the non-pecuniary loss they directly suffered as a consequence of the severe injury suffered by X. **92**

Case 4

At first glance, there is a breach of contract, specifically an infringement of the right to an informed consent. Indeed, as has been outlined above,[139] Italian jurisprudence states that the right to an informed consent is not a mere 'bureaucratic step': the patient's consent has to be expressed after full information has been given by the physician with regard to possible therapies or surgery contraindications and to potential harm, including the indication of the seriousness of the treatment's effects. As X's right to self-determination has been infringed, X is entitled to claim damages arising from the consequences of the infringement of the right to an informed consent (not for the infringement in itself).[140] **93**

137 Cass 9 November 2006, no 23918, [2006] Giust civ Mass 11.

138 See above Sec 25.

139 See above Sec 18.

140 Cass 30 July 2004, no 14638 (fn 88).

94 X is entitled to claim compensation for the pecuniary damage suffered, in relation to medical costs and to the conversion of his house and car, in order to adjust them to his handicap. Additionally, he can claim damages for non-pecuniary loss with reference to the infringement of his 'right to health'.

Case 5

95 The case involves medical *équipe* liability.[141] X can sue A, B, C and D for damages as each of them is jointly and severally liable for breach of contract. The damage is causally related to the physicians' misconduct, even though the individual 'causal share' will have to be assessed by the court in order to determine the individual shares of liability.

96 As far as the assessment of damages is concerned, X may be entitled to claim pecuniary losses, including loss of income (as a bricklayer) as well as – at least in the abstract – loss of income from moonlighting (pecuniary loss for the injury to 'specific earning capacity'). Nonetheless, X has the option to pursue a new profession (as a sales person in a building supplies store) and thus, as he has 'residual (generic) earning capacity', the damage will be reduced correspondingly.[142]

97 Additionally, X may be entitled to recover damages for the costs sustained for the assessment of his injury, even though he could have chosen other options free of charge (which, on the other hand, could have been – in the abstract – less effective).

Case 6

98 Provided that X succeeds in proving that the infection originated from E and, more generally, that it is due to the clinic's deficient hygiene practices, A and B may be sued for breach of contract, specifically for the infringement of an *obbligo di protezione* ('duty of protection') towards X[143] (ie with reference to their failure to obtain asepsis). Even though misconduct may be ascribed to C, D, and E, once again A and B are liable for them

141 See above Sec 13.
142 See above no 63.
143 See above no 41, Chap C.

pursuant to art 1228 CC.[144] A's and B's liability for C and D derives from their employment relationship.

Besides compensation for non-pecuniary loss[145], X is entitled to recover the pecuniary loss, including medical costs and assistance, as well as loss of income. As regards X's daughter's cleaning assistance, although – in the abstract – related expenses might be refundable, X must be able to prove actual *deminutio patrimonii* in order to obtain its compensation. In other words, the no-damage-no-compensation rule applies. **99**

Variation 1

Regardless of whether the carrier of the bacteria is identified or not, A and B are liable on the grounds that they have a contractual 'duty to protect' (*obbligo di protezione*) the patient and, particularly, to take any necessary measure in order to obtain asepsis. **100**

Variation 2

Once again, damage (infection) occurred inside A and B's clinic. Therefore, even if hygienic standards seem(ed) to be adequate, defendants still have to prove that the damage is not imputable to them. Practically, the burden of proof that an external event occurred and caused the damage *de facto* results in a *probatio diabolica*. **101**

144 See above no 44.
145 See above Sec 25, specifically with reference to both *danno biologico* and *danno morale*.

Medical Liability in the Netherlands

Ivo Giesen/Esther Engelhard

General Questions

A. The Health Care System Framework

I. General Introduction

1. The health care system in overview

Generally, mainstream physical and/or mental health care in the Netherlands can be divided into health care institutions and independent practitioners. Institutions are mainly hospitals, mental health institutions, psychiatric hospitals, rehabilitation clinics, homes for the elderly etc. The Quality of Health Care Institutions Act (*Kwaliteitswet zorginstellingen*) is a framework Act that serves to maintain the quality of many such institutions and that is mainly enforced by the Health Care Inspectorate. The Individual Health Care Professions Act (*Wet op de beroepen in de individuele gezondheidszorg*; hereafter: Wet Big) concerns mainly the quality of health care professionals such as general practitioners, specialists, dentists and obstetricians. For these professions, also subject to public disciplinary law, the Wet Big provides for a registration system by means of protection of the professional title. For certain paramedic professions the Wet Big sets specific educational standards. It also reserves certain medical practices for regulated (and registered) professions. Several additional national and EC rules regulate various aspects of the professions involved,[1] for example the education and training, certification, competences and free movement of these professionals, their admission to our health care system, but also impose more substantive duties of care on them. 1

1 For a more extensive discussion see *HJJ Leenen/JCJ Dute/WR Kastelein*, Handboek Gezondheidsrecht, vol 2 (2008) ch 2, and *HJJ Leenen/JKM Gevers*, Handboek Gezondheidsrecht, vol 1 (2007) ch 9.

2 Most important for the duties of care of providers of health care and for patients' rights is the Act on medical services contracts (*Wet geneeskundige behandelingsovereenkomst*, WGBO), which has been incorporated into Book 7 (Specific contracts) of the Dutch Civil Code (CC). Noteworthy for such duties and rights in cases of hospitalisation in psychiatric institutions is the Act on special hospitalisations in psychiatric hospitals (*Wet bijzondere opnemingen in psychiatrische ziekenhuizen;* hereafter: Bopz), which also includes procedural rules, for example regarding a complaints procedure. A more general application scope of the latter type of rules can be found in the so-called Act on the complaints procedure of clients of the health care sector (*Wet klachtrecht cliënten zorgsector*; hereafter: Wkcz). Based on the Wkcz for instance, health care providers must lay down procedural rules for so-called complaints procedures (*klachtenprocedures*); the Bopz and related regulations provide additional rules for the complaints procedure for patients who were hospitalised in a psychiatric institution by a court order or a similar order.[2] Additionally, there are rules based on the self-regulation of hospitals and other health care providers regarding substantive and/or procedural matters, sometimes based on the aforementioned enactments and/or on prototype regulations drafted by the Royal Dutch Medical Association (KNMG) or other (professional) organisations.

3 Patients who are not satisfied with the medical treatment that they were (or were not) given can directly approach or address the practitioner or medical institution. Psychiatric institutions and some other health care providers have an independent confidential adviser for patients (*patiëntenvertrouwenspersoon*) who may inform the patient and may intermediate in the patient's complaint and/or may offer the patient certain other forms of assistance. Patients may also opt for lodging a complaint with the practitioner or with his or her organisation or the complaint commission of the organisation. Whereas institutions such as hospitals generally have their own complaints commissions, independent individual practitioners outside such organisations will most likely work with external, regional complaints commissions.[3] Depending on the seriousness of the complaint and the legal needs of the patient, the complaints may also be lodged with the Medical Disciplinary Board (*Medisch Tuchtcollege*) or, in more exceptional cases, directly with the Healthcare Inspectorate (and/or patients may file administrative or criminal law charges against the practitioner or the health care institution).

---

2 See more in depth on this *J Legemaate*, Verantwoordingsplicht en aansprakelijkheid in de gezondheidszorg (2000) 11 ff and 18 ff.

3 Ibid 15.

If the patient, subsequent to the complaint, seeks monetary compensation (or an injunction or similar order), the latter is dealt with by civil law rules; the complaint commission cannot decide on this. Claims for compensation are mostly settled out of court between patients and the liability insurer of the practitioner or the organisation he works for. If the parties cannot reach agreement, civil litigation before a court may be in place. If the complaints commission has already given its decision with regard to the patient's complaint (which is not necessary, but may occur in practice), this will usually, also due to the informal nature of the complaints procedure, not have evidential value as such, although it may be looked at in order to establish the facts of the case.[4] **4**

II. Social Welfare Provision

2. The role of public health care

Patients can only claim compensation for that part of their damage that is not yet covered by salary arrangements, social insurance or private compensatory schemes. Under labour law, the employer (or his private insurance) needs to continue to pay at least 70 % of the victim's time-related income (subject to a maximum amount) throughout the first two years of disability to work. The exact percentage varies, based on the individual's disability to work, but in principle 70 % needs to be paid in cases of full disability (art 7:629 CC). Additionally, labour law prohibits redundancy within that period of time based on the victim's incapacity to work. **5**

After these first two years, income related payments may be made under the long-term disability scheme, the so-called Work and Income Ability Act (*Wet Werk en Inkomen naar Arbeidsvermogen*, WIA). This only offers income replacement pensions to those who are disabled to at least 35 %. It introduces two different schemes for either income related payments for those victims who are disabled permanently and for 80–100 % (*Regeling Inkomensvoorziening Volledig Arbeidsongeschikten,* IVA) or continuation to work for those partially disabled, for 35–80 % (*Regeling Werkhervatting Gedeeltelijk Arbeidsongeschikten*, WGA). **6**

The first scheme makes sure that only those who are fully (ie over 80 %) and permanently incapable of working will receive, and continue to receive, income replacement benefits equivalent to 75 % of their last **7**

---

4 *Legemaate* (fn 2) 21.

income (subject to a maximum amount). The latter scheme offers 70 % of the last income to those who – out of 39 weeks prior to their disability – had been working for at least 26 weeks (or, for victims who can find a replacement job, 70 % of the difference between their old income and the new income). These payments will, dependent on the victim's period of disability, be continued for six months up to 5 years (at the longest). Thereafter, salary related pensions will only be awarded if the victim works for at least 50 % of his remaining capacity to work; if he does not, he will be left with a certain percentage of the minimum wages. The self-employed have to take out private insurance in order to have their disability risk for lost earnings insured.

8 Private insurance may also generally cover the risk of damages which do not fall under labour law arrangements and social security benefits, and therefore would be left uncompensated. The risk of personal damages due to medical malpractice will in most cases be included in individual private sickness or invalidity insurances or in collective insurance arranged by the employer. Most notably for the Dutch health care insurance system is that it introduces a mix of general health care coverage for basic risks of medical expenses and hospitalisation combined with private administration and competition. See further below, at no 11.

3. Differences in treating patient's claims

9 Patients' claims for damage caused in the context (at least partially) of publicly funded medical treatment are in principle not handled differently from other personal injury cases. Some specific rules exist in terms of special duties that may give ground for liability and on a more detailed level some specific rules and interpretations of the rules have come up, for example in terms of causation. These will be discussed below.

4. Right of recourse

10 Based on special provisions of labour law and social security law, employers who continue salary payments and most social insurance carriers that are under the obligation to make arrangements and payments for the patient's incapacity to work and his medical expenses, have the right to reimbursement (right to recourse). This means that both these employers and social insurance carriers can use civil liability law in order to be reimbursed by the liable person for the insurance sums they had paid to the insured.[5] These labour law and social security law provisions determine that, to the extent that the employer and social insurance carriers have reimbursement claims, the victim (the patient) will lose his claim for compensation vis-à-vis the liable party. As will be seen below at no 12, private insurers that compensate damage are, to that extent, subrogated into the insured person's right to compensation.

III. Private Insurance

5. The role of private health insurance

Noteworthy is that the basic risks of medical expenses, such as the costs of medical services, hospital stay and dental care, are covered by private insurance, which is to that extent mandatory for everyone who lives or pays income tax in the Netherlands. Health insurance companies are under the legal obligation to offer this basic health care insurance and cannot reject individuals on other grounds than those provided for by law. A less fortunate side-effect is that the new system has left a number of people uninsured.[6] Additional insurance can be purchased and offered on a voluntary basis. All these arrangements are no different for the risk of suffering medical expenses (and other damage) due to malpractice than they are for other risks of damage. **11**

Based on the rules of insurance law that are laid down in Book 7 (Specific contracts) of the Civil Code, private first-party insurers, such as the victim's medical insurer, who have compensated the victim's damage, are to that same extent subrogated into the victim's right to compensation under tort and/or contract law (art 7:962 CC). This right to subrogation is primarily intended for the patient's own private insurers; it does not protect insurance parties that cover the risk of salary continuation of the patient's employer in case of work disability as the latter has no right to compensation, only to reimbursement. But this rigid and rather technical approach seems to lose support with the increasing financial burdens of employers in terms of salary continuation: the Amsterdam court of appeal allowed an employer's insurance carrier to be subrogated into the employer's right to reimbursement for salary continuation payments (art 6:107a **12**

5 For an extensive overview and discussions *EFD Engelhard*, Regres (2003) 73 ff.

6 *EH Hondius* (ed), The Development of Medical Liability (2010), mentions in the introduction to this volume that 240,000 people were left uninsured.

CC), by analogy to art 7:962 CC.[7] To be clear: these rules are principally no different in cases of medical liability than they are in other cases of contractual or non-contractual liability.

6. Liability insurance

13 As in most European countries, the risk of claims for negligence and malpractice is seen as an occupational hazard and practitioners and health care organisations generally chose to limit this risk by taking out liability insurance. It is often said that insurances for medical risks are hardly, if ever, profitable and this is also seen as an explanation for the relatively small number of insurers that offer these insurances, especially where hospital and other health care institutions are concerned.[8] The medical liability insurance is, however, not mandatory. As in other personal injury claims it seems possible that the amount of compensation to be awarded to the claimant exceeds the amount covered by liability insurance, in which case the mitigation rule of art 6:109 CC may be relevant, see no 76.

14 More generally over the last 15 to 20 years there has been a shift from 'occurrence' to 'claims made' systems, which means that the insurance only covers cases that were reported during the duration of the insurance and not just any damage that has occurred in that period (but was only reported later in time). It has been noted that this may make it expensive for practitioners to change liability insurance carriers (as they may then have to take out additional coverage for the risk of damage caused during the running-time of the previous liability insurance).[9]

15 Much debated are special clauses in the insurance contract that do not allow the practitioner or the institution to make any statements as to admitting to fault or civil liability and that require them to abstain from any acts that might harm the liability insurer. The main idea behind this is that doctors may admit to having been at fault, when legally there is no wrong and this admission to wrongs may establish liability more easily. The aforementioned clauses have however been heavily criticised by people who claim that it is part and parcel of professional responsibility to prevent the possible deterioration of the patient's state by not telling

7 Hof Amsterdam 10 February 2009, not published but cited and discussed by *M Snel-De Kroon*, PIV-Bulletin 9 (2009).

8 See *inter alia* the (Belgian) thesis of *J ter Heerdt*, Het experiment beproefd. Een juridische analyse van experimenten met mensen (2000) 631.

9 *Legemaate* (fn 2) 59.

them what has happened.[10] For this they see support in the information duty of art 7:448 CC, which we will discuss below (see no 70). Since 2006 Dutch insurance law determines that the violation of such prohibition clauses has no effect if the information admitted is actually correct. Also this rule determines that clauses that prohibit acknowledging facts have no legal effect (art 7:453 CC).[11] Disciplinary boards have held doctors accountable under (public) disciplinary law for not having reported incidents properly or fast enough.[12]

IV. Professional Standards

7. Applicable professional standards

The prevention of harmful incidents caused by or through medical treatment has become an important goal within the policy to improve patients' safety and the quality of our health care. Over the last few years several special prevention and safety programs were set up.[13] In February 2009, the Healthcare Inspectorate even proclaimed a prize for the best initiative to promote the prevention of incidents. Also many professional rules, protocols and other regulations were put in force, for the sake of the quality of patient care and for the organisation, administration, registration and sanctioning of incidents. Hereafter we will highlight the most common and basic regimes, some of which – mainly governmental enactments – were mentioned already. **16**

Of course one of the drawbacks of enactments by the legislator is its lack of expertise in the medico-professional area.[14] Self-regulated protocols and guidelines as to medical practices, albeit not directly legally enforceable, have therefore an important function in health law.[15] Such 'rules', where applicable, are considered to be important guidelines for determining whether the health care provider incurs civil liability.[16] Vice versa, by taking the violation of such rules as an indication, albeit not necessarily a **17**

---

10 See *RWM Giard*, Aansprakelijkheid van artsen: juridische theorie en medische praktijk (2005) 144 and *Legemaate* (fn 2) 13.

11 Though on drawbacks of this ruling: *EFD Engelhard*,Verzekeringsrecht Praktisch Belicht (2008) 349–375.

12 See *Legemaate* (fn 2) 6.

13 See *Leenen/Dute/Kastelein* (fn 1) ch 2 and para 8.1.

14 Ibid para 1.3.

15 I *Giesen*, Alternatieve regelgeving in privaatrechtelijke verhoudingen, in: WJ Witteveen/ I Giesen/JL de Wijkerslooth, Alternatieve regelgeving (2007) 84.

16 Ibid 106.

decisive pointer, that the practitioner has, according to his own professional standards, acted wrongfully, civil liability rules in effect make non-binding protocols 'binding'.[17]

8. Quality and/or risk management systems

18 Alongside these forms of self-regulation are national enactments that were briefly discussed above, the Quality of Health Care Institutions Act (*Kwaliteitswet zorginstellingen*), which we mentioned in no 1, is a framework law that imposes the obligation on health care institutions to deliver acceptable health care and, *inter alia*, the duty to systematically safeguard, control and improve its quality. The Act on medical services contracts (*Wet Geneeskundige Behandelingsovereenkomst;* WGBO), incorporated in the Civil Code, regulates the legal position of patients (see no 2). The aforementioned Individual Healthcare Professions Act (*Wet op de beroepen in de individuele gezondheidszorg;* Wet Big, at no 1 above) seeks to protect patients against unprofessional practices *inter alia* by means of registration. It also determines which professionals are qualified to practice certain treatments and which requirements must be met in order to use certain professional titles. Also the Wet Big extends disciplinary law to various health care professions.

19 The enforcement of all of the aforementioned rules is left to different sanctioning mechanisms that may be called upon by patients or others prior to or as an alternative to the rules on civil liability law. We have mentioned most of these above, viz: complaints commissions of care providers (*Klachtencommissies*), regional disciplinary boards (*Regionale tuchtcolleges*) and the Central disciplinary board (*Centraal tuchtcollege*), the Healthcare Inspectorate (*Inspectie voor de Gezondheidszorg*), which not only handles certain complaints but also promotes the quality of the health care system through working visits, and lastly the dispute settlement board of hospitals (*Geschillencommissie voor ziekenhuizen*). In addition to these sanctioning systems we note that medical liability insurers in their engagements with health care institutions and/or in the insurance contracts as well as patients' boards and quality and certification boards or committees of hospitals and alike may, to some degree, contribute to the quality of the health care system.

---

17 Ibid 107.

Civil liability law is also generally seen as a sanctioning system although this system has many drawbacks, such as the burden of proof in terms of fault, relativity and causation and its relatively long procedures and high transaction costs.[18] But as in other European jurisdictions,[19] Dutch lawyers, quite generally,[20] seem to agree that liability law aims at more than mere compensation: the threat of an action for damages, and the subsequent law suit, must give health care providers proper incentives to take the appropriate measures to prevent harm. 20

B. Tort Liability

9. Fundamentals of tort liability

Tort and contract liability rules for medical practice offer patients the right to compensation from the care-provider or its liability insurer in cases of negligence or the use of dangerous equipment (see no 62). In tort law, somewhat differently from contractual liability law (which is *inter alia* dealt with by art 7:453 CC, see below), there are no separate rules whatsoever for medical malpractice. For both, the standard of care and other requirements of liability law are given true meaning in case law. Tort liability can either be based on fault or on risk based (strict) liability. Fault liability (art 6:162 CC) requires wrongful behavior for which the defendant can be held accountable. 21

In the Dutch Civil Code, title 6.3 deals with tort law. The main provision is article 162 of Book 6 of the Civil Code (hereafter: art 6:162 CC). This is a very general clause and an open rule on tortious liability, which basically reads as follows (paragraph 1) in our own translation: 'A person who commits an unlawful act towards another which can be imputed to him, must rectify the damage which the other person suffers as a consequence thereof'. Note that an act could also be an omission to act. The conditions that need to be fulfilled are, first, that there should be '*een onrechtmatige daad*' (an unlawful act, in a strict sense, wrongfulness), and, second, that 22

18 *EFD Engelhard/GE van Maanen*, Aansprakelijkheid voor schade: contractueel en buitencontractueel (2008) 11.

19 See eg *H Bocken/I Boone et al*, Nieuwe wettelijke regelingen voor vergoeding van gezondheidsschade (2008) 83 f.

20 *J Dute/MG Faure/H Koziol* (eds), No-fault compensation in the health care sector (2004) 7; *RMPP Cascão*, Prevention and Compensation of Treatment Injury: A Roadmap for Reform (2005) 121; *Giard* (fn 10) 85 ff; *WH van Boom*, Compensatie voor geboorteschade – van aansprakelijkheid naar "no fault"? Aansprakelijkheid, Verzekering & Schade (AV&S) 1 (2006) 8–24, para 4.3.

this act should be accountable to the actor in question ('*toerekening*'). Next to that, damage and causation (*conditio sine qua non* link and legal causation, based on art 6:98 CC, which deals with the issue of remoteness) are required, and the so-called relativity question of art 6:163 CC needs to be resolved.

23 The first requirement, wrongfulness, is further elaborated on in art 6:162 para 2 CC: 'Except where there is a ground of justification, the following acts are deemed to be unlawful: the violation of a right, an act or omission violating a statutory duty or a rule of unwritten law pertaining to proper social conduct'. What this comes down to is that there are three categories of unlawful acts: breaching a (subjective) right, violating a statutory rule and violating a norm of good conduct. Each category can lose its unlawful character if there is a ground for justification. The third and last category is the most important one; this is what most case law is built upon and where the tort law system is expanded. This is where one asks whether there was a duty of care (*zorgplicht*) and whether this was breached (negligence). The determination usually depends on certain factors identified in the Dutch Supreme Court's judgment in the so-called Cellar Hatch (*Kelderluik*) case, ie foreseeability, the degree of blame, the likelihood of harm, the nature and seriousness of the harm).[21] The yardstick (standard of care) as to whether or not the duty was upheld by the defendant is objective: what would a reasonable man in these circumstances have done? What kind of behaviour is appropriate?

24 The second condition concerns the accountability of the act to the actor. It deals with the culpability, the subjective element, of the actor but adds something thereto. Again, three possibilities exist: an unlawful act can be imputed to its author if it results from his fault or from a cause for which he is answerable according to the law or common opinion within society. Fault, culpa, is the most important of the three; this is the classic case in which one asks whether the actor was culpable, ie was to blame. *De facto* this condition is covered by the concept of '*zorgplicht*' (negligence) explained earlier, which means that the defendant generally has to rebut a presumption as to his blameworthiness once the wrongfulness is given. Unlawfulness is in theory a judgment of the act, and the question as to fault is to be determined by judging the actor, but both elements can be found in the negligence test. Under Dutch law, the actor can be held liable even if personal fault is not present, however. This is the case if he is answerable for the act anyway, because the law or common opinion state

21 Hoge Raad (HR) 5 November 1965, Nederlandse Jurisprudentie (NJ) 1966, 136.

so. For instance, handicapped persons may not be at fault with regard to active acts that cause damage to others, but nevertheless they are liable because the law says so (art 6: 165(1) in conjunction with art 6:162 para 3 CC). Equally, based on common opinion, the state will be held accountable regardless of personal fault for wrongful administrative decisions made by its organs or state officials. Accountability (*toerekening*) is thus a wider concept than fault. Through this device of accountability, legal persons which could not otherwise be said to have been subjectively at fault can also be held liable for wrongful acts committed by them as such. It should be noted that this is not a form of strict liability in the usual sense as wrongful behaviour is still be required.[22]

Once liability has been established, the medical practitioner or hospital **25** may seek to limit the amount of compensation based on the defense of contributory negligence (*eigen schuld*) of the plaintiff. This means that not only fault but also risks for which the plaintiff can be held accountable may cause a reduction of damages. The defendant needs to raise this defense (art 6:101 CC). Contributory negligence also entails the plaintiff's duty to mitigate his losses.

In cases of medical negligence either art 6:162 CC as explained above or **26** art 6:74 CC, in conjunction with art 7:453 CC (see below at nos 65–67), will be applied.

10. Burden of proof

In principle, the plaintiff will have the burden of proving that his health **27** status had deteriorated (a loss), causation, and someone's fault. However, these rules are not without exception.[23] For claims based on fault liability the asserted wrong may in rare cases (partly) be characterised as the omission to achieve a given result (*obligation de résultat, resultaatsverbintenis*). Some examples are omissions in respect of laboratory research or the refusal to give patients access to their medical status.[24] If the poor result in such instances has been shown by the patient it is for the defendant to show that he or she cannot be held accountable for the omission. In general though, practitioners will be bound by the obligation to perform

22 Next to this general rule on tort law, there are several specific clauses on specific related topics (mostly cases of strict liability), see art 6:164-191 CC.

23 See also *I Giesen*, The Burden of Proof and other Procedural Devices in Tort Law, in: H Koziol/BC Steininger (eds), European Tort Law 2008 (2009) 49 ff, especially no. 6 ff.

24 *Legemaate* (fn 2) 42.

to the best of their abilities (*obligation de moyens, inspanningsverbintenis*),[25] and it is then for the patient (the plaintiff) to prove fault as well as causation.

28 Another general exception is the use of presumptions (of fact). A presumption, be it in the form of '*res ipsa loquitur*', '*Anscheinsbeweis*' or otherwise, is in essence a mode of reasoning which leads to certain inferences being drawn, ie to the acceptance of certain facts or legal consequences from other proven facts.[26] To do so, use is made of rules of thumb and facts that are common knowledge. A presumption thus provides the judge with the opportunity to base the existence of a certain factual element on the presence of another fact which has been proven. So, in essence, the object of proof (the fact that needs to be proven) is changed.

29 It is important to note also that accepting such a presumption does not change the burden of proof. It only denotes that for the time being that burden has been discharged. It is then for the opposite side to come forward with evidence to rebut that provisional judgment. In order to do so, the presumption must be countered to such an extent that the judge remains in doubt again as to the existence of the fact in question; going further and actually providing proof to the contrary is not needed. So, in essence, only the 'evidential' burden of proof shifts when a presumption is accepted, but not the 'legal' burden.[27] As stated, a presumption does not alter the division of the burden of proof. It just makes it easier to come up with the proof needed because an additional way of 'gathering' evidence is used, alongside the usual modes of providing evidence. The function a presumption thus fulfils is that it might alleviate the evidential needs one may encounter (it is a *Beweiserleichterung*) and it provides for the possibility of using probabilities when deciding a case.[28]

30 As regards the specific element of causation, the possibility of using an exception to the fundamental rule that the burden of proof rests on the plaintiff is an important way of dealing with uncertain causation, which will be dealt with below (at no 36 ff).

31 As regards fault, the burden of proof will remain on the plaintiff but the plaintiff is then helped out to some extent by the use of a devise known in the Netherlands as the '*gemotiveerde betwisting*' or '*aanvullende stelplicht*'.

---

25 See also Rb Alkmaar 11 February 2004, LJN AO3453, r ov 5.5.

26 Cf *I. Giesen*, Bewijs en aansprakelijkheid (2001) 65. See also on presumptions *WDH Asser*, Bewijslastverdeling (2004) 87 ff.

27 *Giesen* (fn 26) 65 f.

28 Ibid.

This is also known, in Germany, as the *'sekundäre Behauptungslast'*, which could also be named (even though it is non-existent in English law) as 'the duty to provide an extra motivated pleading'. This instrument is part of the law of evidence and warrants our attention because of its relevance for tort cases and its potential to solve the evidential needs of (usually) plaintiffs. What we are dealing with here is the obligation of one litigant, usually the defendant, to not only deny the plaintiff's statement of claim and the facts asserted therein, but to go one step further and to underpin and motivate that denial by bringing in factual details and relevant sources. It comes down to this: according to case law, the defendant is charged with a duty to substantiate his defense or claim that he has not acted wrongfully. He has to do so by supplying information on all the factual aspects of the claim. What is thus needed is that the defendant takes an extra step when denying the asserted facts and supplies a certain degree of extra information (which is typically not available to the plaintiff).[29] Think of a doctor who is obliged to hand over the medical file, with his notes, to the patient claiming damages.

Since a breach of the medical standard of care is usually hard to prove for a **32** patient, the courts tend to 'lower' the burden of proof a bit and give it a different content when duties of care are supposedly breached. By using this instrument the substantiation of a claim thus rests partly on the defendant. This is done however without reversing the (legal) burden of proof, which is of course important.[30] Only the (evidential) burden of producing (pieces of) evidence is shifted.[31]

Even if the defendant complies with this procedural duty to provide **33** information, the plaintiff still needs to prove his or her claim, using the extra information provided by the defendant. If the defendant has not provided the information, the existence of the fact at stake is considered to have been established by law (on the basis of art 149 of the Civil Procedure Code (CPC) in the Netherlands).[32] In Germany this legal notion, based on

---

29 See *Giesen* (fn 23) no 21; *G Baumgärtel*, Beweislastpraxis im Privatrecht (1996) nos 307 ff, 347 ff, as well as the references below.

30 See *D Magnus*, Beweislast und Kausalität bei ärztlichen Behandlungsfehlers, Zeitschrift für Zivilprozeß (ZZP) 120 (2007) 353.

31 On these two notions, see *Baumgärtel* (fn 29) nos 9, 14; *P Murphy*, Murphy on evidence (2007) 71 ff, *Giesen* (fn 23) no 12 ff.

32 Cf *Saenger*, ZZP 121 (2008) 145; *Giesen* (fn 23) nos 41 and 43–47, although the range of possible sanctions is, wrongly as far as we are concerned, considered to be somewhat wider in the Netherlands, see HR 15 December 2006, NJ 2007, 203 (*Noord-Nederlands Effektenkantoor/Mourik*).

the notion of *'Treu und Glauben'*, can be invoked if three conditions have been met. First, the party which carries the burden of invoking and stating facts to support its claim has no further knowledge concerning the determining facts because that party has been outside of the realm in which the facts in question occurred, while second, the opposing litigant knows or is supposed to know these facts, and, thirdly, the obligation can be attributed to that opposing party to introduce those facts into the dispute at hand.[33] In the Netherlands case law has not come up with a specific (similar) list of conditions to be met, but in essence the same principles seem to apply there as well.[34]

34 This *'sekundäre Behauptungslast'* is meant and used as an instrument to alleviate the plaintiff's burden of proof in cases in which it is obvious that such burden cannot be met without some external assistance. The burden of proof is not shifted onto the defendant but lessened in the sense that one is given certain factual information that is needed to build one's claim and which was not available before. An important question is of course why someone would be obliged to help out his opponent this way. Basically, this duty is accepted because without the duty to supply information the burden of proof would become too burdensome. Since it would be an illusion to think that the plaintiff could provide the evidence needed without this duty bestowed on the opponent, the protection that substantive law aims to offer a party would become illusionary as well.[35] It is thus the desire to safeguard the protection offered by substantive law that ignites this procedural protective measure.

35 In principle the use and applicability of the *'sekundäre Behauptungslast'* is not confined to certain cases, although its use has not yet become 'universal'. Of course the conditions that need to be met in order to be able to use the instrument do in fact shape the extent to which it can be invoked in practice. This duty has however already proven to be useful in liability cases, most notably, at least in the Netherlands, in cases of medical negli-

---

33 See, for example, BGH 18 May 1999, Neue Juristische Wochenschrift (NJW) 1999, 2887 ff; *Saenger*, ZZP 121 (2008) 144; *Magnus*, ZZP 120 (2007) 353; *Giesen* (fn 23) no 41. Cf also *Baumgärtel* (fn 29) 307.

34 *Giesen* (fn 23) no 42.

35 See the preliminary advise to the Supreme Court by Asser in the case of HR 10 January 1997, NJ 1999, 286 (*Notary W*) at no 2.9, and *Giesen* (fn 23) no 42.

gence and other forms of professional negligence.[36] The information deficit a patient usually encounters when suing a medical practitioner can be balanced by imposing on the doctor the duty to come forward with certain information at his disposal, thus leveling the 'playing field' between the parties to some extent.

11. Uncertain causation

As elsewhere, Dutch law requires the presence of causation to establish liability in tort. This is expressed in art 6:162 s 1 CC, by using the term '*dientengevolge*' (translation: as a consequence thereof) and reinforced by art 6:98 CC. **36**

A first test as to the existence of causation concerns the *conditio sine qua non*:[37] would the damage have occurred if the act under consideration had not taken place? This requirement is the first (and in principal also a minimal) hurdle that needs to be tackled when dealing with causation.[38] An additional test, laid down in art 6:98 CC, then seeks to further delineate the scope of protection. Art 6:98 CC holds that these consequences must also be legally attributed to the defendant given the nature of the liability involved and the type of harm. **37**

There is not a lot of case law in the Netherlands that deals explicitly with the question of whether a *conditio sine qua non* link is needed or required to establish liability because this is accepted in general as one of the cornerstones of liability law. It is as such simply not disputed.[39] Of course, many unlawful acts are in fact omissions to act, but in the Netherlands, it is generally accepted that such an omission can be the cause of the damage **38**

---

36 *Giesen* (fn 23) no 39 ff. Especially in medical liability cases, this is standing case law since HR 20 November 1987, NJ 1988, 500 (*Timmer/Deutman*). See also HR 18 February 1994, NJ 1994, 368 (*Schepers/De Bruijn*); HR 13 January 1997, NJ 1997, 175 (*De Heel/Korver*); HR 7 September 2001, NJ 2001, 615 (*anesthesia*); HR 23 November 2001, NJ 2002, 386 (*Ingenhut*) and HR 15 December 2006, NJ 2007, 203 (*Noord-Nederlands Effectenkantoor/Mourik*). To be sure, in the Netherlands such cases are either rooted in contract law or in tort law, without this distinction being relevant for the duty of care.

37 In the Netherlands '*conditio*' is used instead of '*condicio*' (on the use of these terms, see *JH Nieuwenhuis*, Eurocausaliteit, Agenda voor het Europese debat over toerekening van schuld, Tijdschrift voor Privaatrecht (TPR) 4 (2002) 1698).

38 *RJB Boonekamp* in: AR Bloembergen (ed), Schadevergoeding (losbl) Art 98, note 9.

39 See *Boonekamp* (fn 38) Art 98, note 9.

and thus lead to liability.[40] There is not a lot of theoretical debate about the question of whether an omission can as such be a cause of anything because in practice both acts and omissions are treated alike.[41]

39 One way of dealing with uncertain factual causation is by the use of the *'gemotiveerde betwisting'* as explained above. A second is the use of presumptions, as explained earlier. A third option is to accept a reversal of the burden of proof. This is particularly relevant where traffic rules or safety regulations or other protective measures have not been followed, for instance in cases of traffic accidents or work related accidents.[42] Think also of cases of omissions to inform or warn someone else against the potential dangers of a certain act.[43] The question arises in such situations also whether the person who should have been given the information or should have been warned, would have acted differently if he had received the information or warning. Would he not have acted differently, the omission to warn that person did not cause the damage.

40 This is of course a difficult (factual) question to answer because it inquires about someone's state of mind in the past, which is something that cannot be easily proven. Ever since the famous 1996 judgment in the case of *Dicky Trading II*,[44] there have been cases in which the rule on the division of the burden of proof, given by the Supreme Court, is contrary to the general rule as laid down in art 150 CPC. This burden of proof does not rest on the claimant as usual, but on the defendant. Therefore, if the facts needed for constituting or denying the claim that causation is present or not, are not clarified (or actually proven), the defendant will lose.

41 The precise extent and ambit of this rule (now known as the reversal rule or *'omkeringsregel'*) are still not exactly settled but it has gained a lot of importance and has triggered a lot of litigation. The Supreme Court has limited the instances in which this burden of proof rule might be applicable. Nowadays, it needs to be made clear, before the rule can be applied,

---

40 See *A Wolfbergen*, Onrechtmatige daad (1946) 19; *J van Schellen*, Juridische causaliteit (1972) 175; *CC van Dam*, Aansprakelijkheid voor nalaten (1995) 41; *Boonekamp* (fn 38) Art 98, note 11.

41 See however *Wolfsbergen* (fn 40) 19–21; *GHA Schut*, Rechterlijke verantwoordelijkheid en wettelijke aansprakelijkheid (1963) 73–75; *Van Schellen* (fn 40) 167–179.

42 See *Boonekamp* (fn 38) Art 98, note 11, for further case law.

43 There is a vast amount of literature on this, see eg: *I Giesen*, Bewijslastverdeling bij beroepsaansprakelijkheid (1999) 66 ff; *Giesen* (fn 26) 116 ff; *AJ Akkermans*, De omkeringsregel bij het bewijs van causaal verband (2002); *DT Boks*, Notariële aansprakelijkheid (2002) 211 ff.

44 HR 26 January 1996, NJ 1996, 607 (*Dicky Trading II*).

that a certain specific risk of damage was created or enlarged and that this specific risk has in fact materialised.[45]

As for the application of the reversal rule in cases of medical negligence, special attention should be focused on two judgments of the Supreme Court dated 23 November 2001.[46] The two cases were handed down on the same day and both involved a doctor failing to inform the patient properly about the medical procedure to be undertaken and especially on the risks thereof. The doctor's negligence in not performing their duties was no longer an issue; the debate focused on whether the necessary causal connection was present. The claimants both alleged that the courts of first instance should have applied the reversal rule mentioned above (the '*omkeringsregel*'). **42**

The Supreme Court, in two identical judgments, first stated the rule known in the Netherlands as the reversal rule. The court then continued: this case concerns a failure by a doctor in fulfilling his duty to inform his patient about the risks of the proposed medical treatment. This duty is meant to enable the patient to make a well-informed decision as to whether or not to agree with the proposed treatment. This duty is rooted in the protection that art 10 of the Constitution grants the right to privacy and that art 11 grants a persons' bodily integrity. It is enshrined in Book 7 of the Civil Code, in art 7:448 and art 7:450 CC. The duty to inform the patient about the risks of a treatment is thus not meant to protect against these risks as such, but is meant to enable the patient to decide well-informed whether or not to consent to the treatment and the risks. Not fulfilling this duty creates the risk of a patient not being able to use his right to self-determination as he wishes; the risk thus of making a choice which would not have been made if the patient had been well informed. The damaging facts in these cases then cannot be seen as a materialisation of the risk that was created by the defendant by not fulfilling his duty to inform. The reversal rule therefore cannot be applied. **43**

With regard to the specific non-application of the reversal rule in these cases, one can say that the cases in this respect fit into the pattern laid down in the last years by the Supreme Court. This pattern is clearly **44**

---

45 HR 29 November 2002, NJ 2004, 304 (*TFS/NS*) and HR 29 November 2002, NJ 2004, 305 (*Kastelijn/Achterkarspelen*) and on these important cases *GE van Maanen*, Nederlands Tijdschrift voor Burgerlijk Recht (NTBR) 2003, 111–116; *C Van Dijk*, Tijdschrift voor Vergoeding Personenschade (TVP) 2003, 7–15; *T Hartlief*, Ars Aequi (AA) 2003, 298–306; *GR Rutgers*, AA 2003, 307–313.

46 HR 23 November 2001, NJ 2002, 386 (*I/Stichting Gezondheidszorg*) and NJ 2002, 387, note *JBM Vranken* (N/P).

designed to limit the application of this rule and its consequences. The Courts' statement that the duty to inform is designed to prevent someone from deciding without the necessary information and that it is not meant to prevent the medical risks as such, has been criticised however.[47] It has been challenged in lower courts, for example in a case where the claimant had undergone an experimental treatment without being properly informed after which he claimed that the reversal rule should apply in experimental treatments because of their special associated risks (compared to regular treatments);[48] this argument failed.

45 In other medical cases not dealing with the failure to supply the judgment of the Dutch Supreme Court of 2 March 2001 is also important.[49] A patient, H, went into surgery to undergo an arthroscopy on his left knee. A part of the meniscus was removed. During a check up shortly after the surgery, the surgeon and another doctor diagnosed thrombosis in the left leg. Almost two years later, the same occurred in the patient's right leg. It was undisputed that the protocol of the hospital required the doctor to apply an anti-coagulation or anti-clot treatment after the kind of surgery that the patient had undergone. This treatment was in fact never administered. H then instituted a claim against the doctor and the hospital for damages.

46 The Supreme Court first concluded that the appellate courts' judgment on the non-fulfillment of the doctor's duty of care towards the patient (the hospital failed to provide him with an anti-clot treatment) was correct. The court then considered the defendant's claim that the necessary causal connection between not providing the anti-clot treatment and the thrombosis was missing and that the lower court has considered that the reversal-rule should be applied in this instance. This judgment was wrong according to the hospital because the court made the mistake of regarding the violated protocol as a safety rule (which if correct, would have warranted the application of the *'omkeringsregel'*). The Supreme Court upheld the judgment because the court of first instance had already ruled that the connection between the surgery and the thrombosis was likely enough – a judgment that was not contested later on in the proceedings. Given that state of affairs, applying the *'omkeringsregel'* was correct. The *'omkeringsregel'* has also been applied in other instances of failures during operations or treatment.[50]

---

47 See the case note by *Vranken*, NJ 2002, 387, and *I Giesen* in: WR Kastelein (ed), Medische aansprakelijkheid (2003) 21–22, as well as 22–24 for additional critical remarks.

48 Hof Den Haag 19 December 2007, LJN BC1632, paras 12–13.

49 HR 2 March 2001, NJ 2001, 649, note *FCB van Wijmen* and *JBM Vranken* (MCL/H).

50 See eg Hof Den Bosch 10 March 2009, LJN BH5919 (*Speetjens/Jeroen Bosch Ziekenhuis*).

One point should be added to the discussion above. In 2006,[51] proportionate liability (damages awarded in accordance with the degree of possibility or chance, in percentage terms, that the defendant had in fact caused the disease) has been introduced by the Supreme Court. In the case of *Karamus/Nefalit* an employee suffered from lung cancer after having worked with asbestos due to the fault of his employer, while at the same having been a heavy smoker. The Supreme Court stated that it would be more just to accept proportionate liability in such a case. This new development in the case law[52] might also be of influence in the future also in medical negligence cases, as an additional fourth mechanism to deal with uncertain causation, but there is still no certainty in that respect.[53] **47**

In a small number of instances in lower court decisions this proportionality judgment of the Supreme Court has been invoked for other situations. In a medical negligence case it was employed in an attempt to solve the uncertainty as to the causal link between an experimental treatment and damage,[54] but with no result.[55] However, if all the above mentioned means of aid have failed and it still remains unclear which staff member of a hospital caused the loss, the so-called central liability of the hospital can be invoked. This will be dealt with more extensively below (see nos 61–62). **48**

As was said above, once the *conditio sine qua non* link has been established, an additional ruling, art 6:98 CC, is used, to further delineate the amount of liability. This rule was used in the case *Hospital De Heel/Korver*, which was decided by the Supreme Court and involved a medical malpractice claim. In this case a man underwent jaw-surgery. In the hospital, he accidentally fell out of his bed, since safety-ropes were missing, and lost his eye. Though this was a highly improbable consequence of the negligent act of the hospital, the Supreme Court established liability, since safety instructions where neglected and physical harm was suffered.[56] **49**

51 HR 31 March 2006, Rechtspraak van de Week (RvdW) 2006, 328 (*Karamus/Nefalit*).

52 See also *I Giesen* in: I Giesen/TFE Tjong Tjin Tai, Proportionele tendensen in het verbintenissenrecht, Preadvies VBR (2008) 57.

53 Articles 7:400–413 CC also apply, since these contain general rules on the service contract as such (*'overeenkomst van opdracht'*). See for an introduction to the WGBO: *B Sluijters/MCIH Biesaart*, De geneeskundige behandelingsovereenkomst (2005).

54 Hof Den Haag 19 December 2007, LJN BC1632, para 17.

55 Also prior to the Supreme Court's judgement of 31 March 2006, the proportional liability as a way to circumvent causality problems was tried in vain for medical liability cases, see eg Hof Leeuwarden 22 February 2006, LJN AV2474, para 4.1 (concerning the first court's judgment) and Hof Den Haag 26 March 2003, LJN AF6263 (*Baby Kelly*) paras 13 and 15, where the defendants invoked proportionality to be only partially liable (here too in vain).

56 HR 13 January 1995, NJ 1997, 175 (*De Heel/Korver*); third parties who exercise subrogated or recourse rights also benefit from his judgment, see *Engelhard* (fn 5) 273 f.

Based on this (the nature of the harm and the kind of liability), the causal link was extended to cover even an unlikely course of events. There is a long-standing line of decisions in which this extensive interpretation of causation under the scope of art 6:98 CC has been applied with regard to other facts. The defendant's liability is also not limited by the fact that the individual patient may have responded more severely than other persons would have due to pre-existing vulnerabilities or other predispositions.[57]

12. Loss of a chance

50 There have been cases where recovery has been allowed despite the fact that the patient had not suffered actual damage (yet), but had lost his chance to recovery. A first important step in the gradual acceptance in the Netherlands of the loss of a chance doctrine, at least in some parts of liability law, was the judgment of the District Court of Amsterdam of 15 December 1993, and the following judgment, on appeal, of the Amsterdam Court of Appeal dated 4 January 1996.[58]

51 The plaintiff's one-month-old daughter Ruth was referred to the hospital by the family physician after several small spontaneous bleedings were discovered. The doctor consulted there, defendant De Kraker, examined her but did not find conclusive signs of a brain hemorrhage, as was feared. He decided that Ruth could go home and should come back the next morning for an extensive examination. The same evening, around 20:00, the claimant went back to the hospital again. The doctor on duty concluded there was no need for further examinations at that point in time. The next morning Ruth was examined again. A large brain hemorrhage on the left side was discovered; Ruth was placed on the intensive care ward immediately and underwent brain surgery that same day. Ruth parents' started a civil procedure claiming medical faults were made (they claimed that a more extensive examination should have been undertaken immediately; Ruth should not have been sent home) and these faults caused or at least contributed to the disabilities that Ruth subsequently suffered from. The doctors claimed that Ruth's late admission into the hospital did not cause the damage. Since the bleeding had already been going on for some time,

57 See inter alia HR 9 June 1972, NJ 1972, 360 (*neurotic depression*); HR 21 March 1975, NJ 1975, 372 (*coronary thrombosis*); HR 8 February 1985, NJ 1986, 137 (*Henderson/Gibbs*); HR 4 November 1988, NJ 1989, 751 (*ABP/Van Stuyvenberg*).

58 Hof Amsterdam 4 January 1996, NJ 1997, 213 (*Wever/De Kraker*).

there would have been residual damage in any case, even if there had been an early diagnosis. Experts had concluded this as well.

The District Court concluded that not admitting Ruth when she visited the hospital the second time, at 20:00 in the evening, was a medical error. With regard to the question of whether this fault lead to more residual damage for Ruth than would have occurred if she had been admitted sooner, the court concluded the following, based on the report by the medical experts: the fault had led to the loss of a chance for Ruth at a better end result, given adequate medical treatment. That this chance was nil or negligibly small was not decided by the experts, nor raised by defendants. The court did not however agree with the plaintiff's claim that the chance of complete recovery was lost as well. Considering the above, the court found that the damage, being the lost chance of reaching a better result of treatment, was 25 %. For this percentage, the defendants are liable for Ruth's damage. The Court of Appeal had to consider, inter alia, objections raised against the decision by the District Court that the chance of complete recovery had not been lost. It decided that although the chance of a complete recovery could not be excluded with 100 % certainty, the chance was extremely large that even with an early diagnosis residual damage would have remained. It also ruled that the District Court was right in holding that the percentage of damage due to the late admittance into the hospital had to be put at 25 %. **52**

The importance of the case sketched above is simple: this was basically the first case, at least in modern times,[59] in which a Dutch court used the loss of a chance theory to decide a case in which the *conditio sine qua non* link was doubtful.[60] It involved an issue of medical negligence. Later on, the approach as such was approved by the Dutch Supreme Court in a case against a lawyer (see below). Ever since, the lower courts have increasingly used the loss of a chance approach to decide cases and several of those have been published.[61] One can thus safely say that the loss of a chance approach has been accepted in the Netherlands. **53**

59 See however Rb Utrecht, 28 October 1942, NJ 1943, 231, where the chance of winning in court was set at fifty percent.

60 See on that theory in general *AJ Akkermans*, Proportionele aansprakelijkheid bij onzeker causaal verband (1997) 107 ff; *AJ Akkermans* (ed), Proportionele aansprakelijkheid (2000), and *Nieuwenhuis*, TPR 4 (2002) 1710–1717.

61 See eg Hof Arnhem 14 December 1999 and Rb Den Haag 12 July 2000, TVP 4 (2000) 94 ff (note *Giesen*) and the cases mentioned by C Van Dijk in *C van Dijk*, Toepassing van de theorie van verlies van een kans bij medische aansprakelijkheid, in: Kastelein (fn 47) 27 ff.

54 This does not mean however, that the loss of a chance theory has become predominant or the only approach that might be taken. For instance, the reversal of the burden of proof is also still used. Several approaches are thus at hand to decide a case.[62] Sometimes these two approaches are even combined, or at least, it is suggested that a combination of the two might work.[63]

55 Another important step was the Dutch Supreme Court's decision of 24 October 1997,[64] which dealt with the professional liability of a lawyer. A former employee, Baijings, of the Sara Lee/DE company claimed damages for not having been able to cash in on a set of stock options after the termination of his employment contract. Through a fault made by his attorney, his appeal against the negative verdict was never filed. Baijings thus claimed damages from his (by then former) attorney. The main issue in the second case was whether an appeal in the previous proceedings could and would have been successful if the appeal had been filed on time.

56 The Court of Appeal decided that given the rules of Dutch labour law the claim of Baijings against Sara Lee/DE would not have succeeded. The claim against the attorney was therefore also dismissed. The Supreme Court first dealt rather extensively with the labour law aspects of the original case and overruled the decision of the Appellate court in this respect. The Court continued as follows: the question in this case is whether, and to what extend, the client of the attorney has suffered damage as a consequence of his failure to file an appeal against the verdict in first instance. To find the answer to this question the court needs to determine how the Court of Appeal would have decided the original case, or alternatively, to estimate the amount of recoverable damage on the basis of the good and bad chances that the party would have had on appeal. In order to enable the judge to do so, it is desirable that the plaintiff and the defendant (the former attorney) provide the judge with all the information that would have been brought to the attention of the judge had the appeal been filed. The client, Baijings, should be given the opportunity to be as well-equipped as he would have been in the appeal. The attorney should have the freedom to take the position that the party who had won the original case in first instance would have taken.

57 In cases dealing with damage resulting from the fact that the appeal, contrary to what was intended, had not been filed or had been filed too

---

62 On the cumulative use of several techniques in this respect, see *Giesen* (fn 43).

63 *Akkermans* (fn 60) (1997) 393 ff; *Giesen* (fn 43) 72 ff and 122 ff and *Giesen* (fn 26) 474 f.

64 HR 24 October 1997, NJ 1998, 257 (*Baijings/mr H*).

late, the relevant *conditio sine qua non* question is whether the original proceedings would have led to success in appeal. If that is not the case, the plaintiff has suffered no damage by the negligent act. The plaintiff's claim should then be struck down. Determining what would have been the outcome of an appeal if it had been filed properly is of course difficult, if only because one of the parties that would have been present at that appeal, the original defendant, is no longer present. Furthermore, a ruling on what someone else 'would have done if', is always difficult.

The Dutch Supreme Court allows the courts to use either one of two methods in determining this issue. Courts can decide what would have been decided in the original case and determine the damages based on that outcome (leading to an 'all or nothing' result), or they can determine by an estimate the chances of success in appeal and base the amount of damages on that estimate. In essence, the Supreme Court decides here that a court is allowed to use the theory of the loss of a chance (the chance lost here is of course the chance at a better result on appeal), leading to a percentage of the claim being awarded. Courts are not obliged to use this method, but they may do so as an alternative to the more classic approach of deciding what (another) court would have decided in the original case (a trial within a trial).[65] In general, the loss of a chance approach is seen as a subsidiary option.[66] By now, this is standing case law.[67] **58**

The dogmatic features of this theory and its place within the system of Dutch liability law are not entirely clear yet. The wording by the Supreme Court suggests that this loss of a chance doctrine can be based on art 6:97 CC in conjunction with art 6:105 CC. The former article basically states that if the amount of damage cannot be determined precisely, it will be estimated. This estimate could then of course be the percentage of chance that the claim would have had on appeal. The second article states that the determination of future loss can be postponed or undertaken immediately, after weighing the good and the bad chances.[68] In the literature the search is not so much focused on finding a suitable place within the system for this loss of a chance theory but more on fitting in the concept of 'proportional liability' in general. In essence, this theory of the loss of a **59**

---

65 See also the preliminary advice ('*Conclusie*') of the Advocate-General before the decision of the Dutch Supreme Court, under no 3.3 ff, who also deals with the pros and cons of both methods.

66 See *Akkermans* (fn 60) (2000) 108; *C Van Dijk*, Onzeker causaal veband in de rechtspraak, in: Akkermans (fn 60) (2000) 39.

67 See HR 19 January 2007, NJ 2007, 63 (*Kranendonk Holding BV en De Vries/A*).

68 See *T Hartlief*, Proportionele aansprakelijkheid: een introductie, in: Akkermans (fn 60) (2000) 15.

chance is then seen as a way of 'implementing' proportional liability,[69] for which the case of *Karamus/Nefalit* is another example, see no 47.

60 Since this approach has been approved by the Supreme Court more and more lower courts have used the loss of a chance approach to decide cases (of professional liability) and several of those have been published.[70] One can thus safely say that the loss of a chance approach has been accepted in the Netherlands. This does not mean however, that the loss of a chance theory has become predominant or the only approach that might be taken, as was demonstrated earlier.

13. Multiple persons involved

61 Due to the so-called central liability approach, if the patient received treatment based on a specific 'contract of medical treatment' as laid down in the arts 7:446–468 CC (see no 65), he can not only sue his professional caregiver in person, but also the hospital (or institution).[71] The relevant ruling is art 7:462 para 1 CC, which states that when a medical services contract is executed in a hospital and the hospital is not a party to this contract, it is nonetheless to the same extent liable in case of non-performance. In addition to this central liability approach the treatment provider remains liable too, jointly and severally (cf art 6:102 CC). Central liability in this context thus means that 'if in the process of performance of the treatment contract activities take place in a hospital that is not a party to the contract, the hospital is jointly and severally liable for a failure in the performance of the contract as if the hospital were a party to the contract'.[72] The idea behind this is not to create liability in a larger number of cases, but to identify the defendant to enable the patient to claim damages.[73] As many professional caregivers may not be under a contract of services and/or organisations may be complex, the patient

---

69 See *Akkermans* (fn 60) (1997) 431 ff and 444–446 on this specific aspect, and *Hartlief* (fn 68) 16–18.

70 See for example Hof Arnhem 14 December 1999 and Rb Den Haag 12 July 2000, TVP 4 (2000) 94 ff (note *Giesen*) and the cases mentioned by *Van Dijk* (fn 61) 27 ff. See also *Akkermans* (fn 43) 102 ff.

71 Ie all hospitals, nursing homes or mental institutions that are acknowledged by the so-called Act on the admission of health care institutions (*Wet toelating zorginstellingen*).

72 See for this translation of art 7:462 CC, see: PEL SC, Chapter VII, Article 7:111, Comp notes 1, p 900.

73 See the Parliamentary Reports of the Second Chamber of Parliament (TK) 1989/1990, no 21 561, no 3 (Explanatory Memorandum) 23; *CJJM Stolker*, WGBO en aansprakelijkheid, in: De WGBO: van tekst naar toepassing (1995) 114.

must be relieved of the burden of finding out who can be held accountable. Miscommunication between persons working at the hospital should thus not result in a situation where the patient has to find out who did something wrong. Also, it is no longer relevant on what legal basis a treatment provider was active at the hospital.

To clarify, central liability refers only to claims for damages, and not to the exercise of other patient rights such as the right to be informed and the right to inspect medical records. But if the patient's doctor violates these rights, the hospital can be held liable for the consequences. If the claimant chooses to address the hospital, the latter will then in some cases have recourse against the physician. **62**

14. Strict liability

Health care institutions can be held liable regardless of fault for the malpractices of their own staff (ie persons they give orders to, such as their doctors and operation room staff; see art 6:170 CC) and independent contractors to whom they assign tasks in the course of the hospital's performance (eg doctors who have their own practice but who work on an independent basis for the hospital or an external lab that analyses blood samples of the hospital's patients, art 6:171 CC).[74] As for the independent contractors, there needs to be a functional link between the independent contractor's malpractice and the assigned tasks (analysing the blood sample). Also Dutch law has a ground for strict liability for anyone who can be regarded as the keeper of movable objects such as needles, catheters etc, that cause damage, provided that the object was defective. The hospital can then only free itself from liability if, in the hypothetical scenario where the hospital would have had control over the defective object, there would not have been fault liability on the part of the hospital (art 6:173 CC). **63**

Contract law has comparable but slightly less rigid grounds for strict liability. Art 6:76 CC states that if the debtor to an obligation (which may include health care providers that act upon medical services contracts) uses other persons in order to fulfil his obligation, he shall be liable for their acts or omissions in a similar manner as for his own behaviour. It is not clear how far the scope of this article reaches in the medical sphere: does it **64**

---

74 Provided the hospital can be regarded as an enterprise (*bedrijf*), see art 6:171 CC and in the affirmative *RD Lubach*, Aansprakelijkheid voor zelfstandige hulppersonen (2005) 310 (and 363).

mean that the physician can be held liable for the faulty analysis of a pathologist?[75] Art 6:77 CC holds parties to a contract (which may include medical services contracts) liable for damage caused by objects that they use to perform their actions but that are unfit 'unless this is thought to be unreasonable, given the content and purpose of the legal act in question, societal views and other circumstances.' Examples of situations where such an 'unreasonable' result can be assumed are if the defectiveness is extremely rare and/or could not even have been traced by professional experts.[76] The legislation does not hold the physician (or other contracting parties) liable in cases where the producer of the defective material was liable but that view is generally rejected: the patient may sue each party and they may in turn then have recourse against the other liable person or entity.[77] At no 65 below, we will discuss whether liability based on each of both contractual grounds may be exonerated.

C. Contractual Liability

15. Basics of contracts in the health care sector

65 Next to the general rules of contract law in Book 6 of the Dutch Civil Code which include the general rule for liability based on a breach of contract (art 6:74 CC), there are special rules laid down in Book 7 CC, which deals with several specific contracts such as Sales, Rent, Employment, Insurance *et cetera*. The specific 'contract of medical treatment' (*geneeskundige behandelingsovereenkomst*) is dealt with by articles 7:446–468 CC and is based on the '*Wet op de geneeskundige behandelingsovereenkomst*' (WGBO), which is a separate law, in force since 1 April 1995, that has been incorporated in Book 7 CC. The liability of health care providers that conclude such contracts with their patients (as well as the consequential central liability of the hospital, see no 61) may not be contractually limited or excluded (art 7:463 CC). This ruling is based on the unequal position between professional practitioners compared to their patients and the high value of the interests that are involved with their practices such as life and health. Other health care providers however, who fall outside the scope of the aforementioned

75 In the affirmative: *EH Hondius,* Medical Liability in Dutch Law, in: EH Hondius (ed), Modern Trends in Tort Law, Dutch and Japanese Law Compared (1999) 9 (though with mention of many contrasting views).

76 *Parlementaire Geschiedenis van het Nieuwe Burgerlijk Wetboek,* Boek 6 (1981) 273 (MvA II).

77 *Hondius* (fn 75) 9 and *idem* in: Leenen/Dute/Kastelein (fn 1) (2008) 168.

articles of the Civil Code, such as physiotherapists and speech therapists, may still exonerate their (risk of) liability.[78]

66 The basis of the WGBO is formed by the principle of self-determination (patient autonomy) and – as a part of that – the right to physical integrity, together with the awareness of the dependence of the patient who needs medical treatment. These ideas are concretised in several patients' rights. Usually four rights are distinguished: the right to information (art 7:448 CC), the requirement of consent for every/any medical treatment (art 7:450 CC; together they form the requirement of 'informed consent'), the right to inspect the medical records (art 7:454 and art 7:456 CC) and the protection of 'privacy' (arts 7:457–459 CC). There is also a provision dealing with the duty of care that practitioners have to live up to: art 7:453 CC determines that practitioners can be expected to act as 'competent and reasonable' caretakers would have acted when performing the medical services contract.[79]

67 This standard of care is similar to the standard of care under tort liability (art 6:162 CC).[80] What the open norm of art 7:453 CC entails in practice will depend on the circumstances of the case as they were at the time (and given the state of the art) that the medical treatment took place, similar to the negligence test that we discussed above. If a (written or judge-made) safety rule has been violated, the standard of care with regard to the liability test will generally be higher: more care is expected.[81] But the mere fact that 'competence and reasonable behaviour' of the practitioner are expected, also indicates that a lack of experience should generally, in terms of legal attribution, not be to the patient's detriment. Lastly, we reiterate that in these cases there may also be central liability of the hospital, see above no 61 f.

16. Differences to tort law

68 Whether a claim is founded on contract law or tort law is hardly of any consequence under Dutch law. As was seen above (no 67), the standard of care remains the same ('competent and reasonable caretaker'), the burden of proof is also the same. The only difference is that the accountability of

78 *Sluijters/Biesaart* (fn 53) 136.
79 Cf likewise HR 9 November 1990, NJ 1991, 26.
80 *Legemaate* (fn 2) 43.
81 HR 13 January 1995, NJ 1997, 175.

an act is presumed present in a contract case (art 6:75 CC: unless...) and not in a tort case. In practice however, also in tort cases the accountability is presumed.

17. Contractual claims in the absence of direct contracts?

69 The question as to whether contractual claims can be possible when there is no direct contract is left to the general rules of contract law under Dutch law: it is a matter of interpretation of the contract. This is confirmed by the Supreme Court in its so-called *Baby Joost* judgment, which deals with a claim for damages of parents for their emotional distress caused by medical malpractice in the treatment of their minor son.[82] In their appeal before the Supreme Court, the parents argued that the Court of Appeal had no right in holding that the parents were not a contracting party alongside the child in respect of the contract for medical treatment. The Supreme Court however upheld the Court of Appeal's decision in this respect. According to the Supreme Court the Appellate Court had not gone so far as to conclude from the mere fact that the parents had not asked the doctor for any particular performance owed directly to themselves, that the parents were 'thus' just acting as legal representatives. By this the Supreme Court seems to indicate that the mere fact that the contract did not contain any duty directly owed to the parents is not necessarily conclusive; the court must in its assessment of the parties' intentions also look at any statements made and other relevant circumstances to the case. Here however, nothing else was said or done with regard to the parent's capacity in this respect. Therefore, it was fair for the doctor to assume that the parents were only acting as legal representatives. The fact that the parents had a substantive, personal interest in the medical treatment of their son is not sufficient reason to assume that they intended to enter the contract themselves, as contracting parties. This judgment has been rejected in the literature for its highly technical character: parents who are discussing the medical treatment of their son, will generally not be aware of the exact statements that they need to put forward in order to safeguard their own, personal legal position in case there is later malpractice.[83] Also the fact that the Supreme Court did not hold the (high) moral

82 HR 8 September 2000, NJ 2000, 734.

83 *CC van Dam*, De ouders van Joost, Verkeersrecht (VR) 2001, 1–7 and also *Aansprakelijkheidsrecht* http://www.aansprakelijkheidsrecht.com/oudersvanjoost.htm_ftnref1 (with further references).

and material interests of the parents to be sufficient reason to justify them as direct parties to the contract, has been highly criticised.[84]

18. Informed consent

Prior to any medical service based on their contract, the health care provider needs the patient's consent (art 7:450 CC), which must be so-called informed consent. Art 7:448 CC imposes the contractual obligation on health care providers to inform their patients in a clear and reasonable manner, written if requested, about (proposed) medical examinations, the proposed treatment and developments concerning the medical tests, the treatment itself and the patient's health and condition.[85] The WGBO imposes the obligation on the practitioner to inform his patient in a clear way (*'op duidelijke wijze'*), if requested in writing, about the intended tests and the intended treatment (art 7:448 para 1 CC). In doing so, the practitioner needs to communicate to the patient all that the latter 'reasonably' needs to know with respect to the nature and the purpose of the medical exams or treatment and the medical operations (*'verrichtingen'*) that in the practitioner's view need to be undertaken as well as the expected consequences and risks thereof and the alternative methods of examination or treatment that may be used (art 7:448 para 2 CC). Clearly not all the possible risks need mentioning, but the common, foreseeable risks must be explained to the patient. Generally more information needs to be given if the surgery is less urgent.[86] The fact that 'clarity' is required is generally understood to mean that the information must be sufficiently understandable for the patient. This right does not extend to the patient's relatives. The right to information is of particular relevance to the requirement of the patient's permission, which is dealt with by art 7:450 of the WGBO (in order to give his permission, the patient needs to be sufficiently informed), but the information duty also covers information that is not needed to give permission but that the patient should nevertheless have, such as information concerning possible side-effects of the prescribed medication etc. However, if the information may seriously harm the patient (ie it may have risks in terms of psychological crisis or suicide attempts or similar such effects), it can be withheld from him and, if it is in the patient's best interest, be given to someone other than the patient (art 7:448 para 3 CC). The patient also **70**

84 *Van Dam*, (fn 83) para 3.
85 *J Legemaate*, Patiëntveiligheid en patiëntenrechten (2006).
86 *Sluijters/Biesaart* (fn 53) 24.

carries an information duty. He needs 'to the best of his knowledge' to inform the practitioner and cooperate with him in as far as is reasonably needed for his treatment (art 7:452 CC).

D. Public Liability

19. Key differences from cases involving private hospitals or doctors

71 As both private and public hospitals risk liability on the same grounds, the private-public dichotomy makes hardly any difference in principle. On more specific aspects there may be differences however, such as the fact that art 6:171 of the Dutch Civil Code imposes strict liability for the acts of independent contracts on 'enterprises' but, as was seen above, this term is not interpreted too strictly (and even seems to cover public hospitals).

E. Alternative Compensation Regimes

20. Funds and/or other alternative compensation regimes

72 Currently there are no particular funds or alternative compensation schemes for victims of medical malpractices in general. For victims of medical experiments there are special legislative arrangements that require insurance coverage. The so-called Act on medico-scientific research involving humans *(Wet medisch-wetenschappelijk onderzoek met mensen)* determines that such research can only take place if the risk of (liability for the) injury or death of the experimental subjects (the persons whom are used for testing) is covered by insurance. Additional mandatory rules for this insurance coverage are laid down in a special Ministerial Decree of 23 June 2003 *(Besluit verplichte verzekering bij medisch-wetenschappelijk onderzoek met mensen)*, which has set the insured sum in principle at € 450,000 per testing person and at € 3,5 million per research, which is further specified in the sense that it gives caps (maximum awards) for the various heads of damage per person, such as income loss (max € 60,000 per year), household costs (max hourly rate of € 7.5), etc. The institution and its staff that conduct the research cannot exonerate their liability risk for the aforementioned damage.[87]

---

87 Art 7 (secs 1, 6 and 8) of the Act. See on this *Ter Heerdt* (fn 8) 343 ff and for Dutch law *EFD Engelhard*, Schade door medische experimenten, AV&S (2004), 89–97.

F. Extent of Liability/Remedies

I. Pecuniary Loss

21. Introduction to indemnifying pecuniary loss

Under general tort law, and contact law for that matter, the rules on compensation for damage[88] are laid down in art 6:95-110 of the Civil Code (CC). These same rules apply to cases of medical negligence as well. Damage that should be compensated (whenever it has been determined according to tort law that there is a right to damages) includes physical and economic loss (loss suffered as well as profits not gained), and other disadvantages, such as immaterial losses.[89] In principle, all losses suffered should be fully reimbursed, irrespective of the type of injury that occurred. There are thus no specific rules limiting compensation according to the type of injury in certain types of tort cases. This means that not only physical harm (personal injury) and damage to property is recoverable under Dutch law, but also pure economic loss.[90] **73**

All kinds of damages that are recognised under Dutch law are thus theoretically available in any sort of case. A more general limitation is that damages for non-pecuniary loss are only recoverable if the law explicitly so specifies (see art 6:95 CC) as stated in rather general terms in art 6:106 CC. This does however exclude punitive damages since Dutch law does not (yet) recognise this form of damages.[91] **74**

Under the Dutch law on damages the principle of full reparation applies (although it has not as such been codified), albeit that contributory negligence (*eigen schuld*) may reduce the amount of compensation (and in **75**

---

88 See also *I Giesen/MBM Loos,* Liability for Defective Products and Services; The Netherlands, in: EH Hondius/C Joustra (eds), Netherlands Reports to the Sixteenth International Congress of Comparative Law (2002), and in general on that part of the Dutch Civil Code: *SD Lindenbergh*, Schadevergoeding: algemeen, vol 1 (2008).

89 See arts 6:95, 96 and 106 CC.

90 Since arts 6:95–110 CC apply to both contractual and tortuous claims in similar ways, the same would apply if a claim were to be based on contract law. See on pure economic loss in general *WH van Boom et al* (eds), Pure Economic Loss (2004). It is believed, however, that the compensation of loss due to personal injury will be granted more readily than loss due to property damage, see *J Spier*, De uitdijende reikwijdte van de aansprakelijkheid uit onrechtmatige daad (1996) 242 f.

91 Although the question whether punitive damages should be accepted under Dutch law is discussed in doctrinal works, the general view has so far been that this should not be the case, although the balance seems to be shifting to some extent. See eg *L Dommering-Van Rongen*, Productaansprakelijkheid, Een rechtsvergelijkend overzicht (2000), and *AJ Verheij,* Onrechtmatige daad (2005) nos 57 and 58.

serious cases of contributory negligence, eg intentional behaviour, the victim may even lose his/her claim). This principle deserves further attention because of its importance. An important aim of liability law in general is that of doing justice to the individual. In the law of damages this is reflected in the principle that the defendant should compensate the total amount of the loss that was suffered by the individual victim. The plaintiff should be made 'whole'. We will refer to this principle as 'the principle of full (individual total) reparation' (*restitutio in integrum*).[92]

76 However, also important is that many individuals entitled to full reparation of their damage in theory, may have difficulties in obtaining it in practice. The costs of taking legal action may be high. A major problem for most plaintiffs is the stronger negotiation position of liability insurers in situations of factual or legal uncertainty, which results from their ability to spread the risks of the trial over thousands of cases. Furthermore, the principle of individual total reparation is not without exceptions. Calculating damages in an abstract manner, as the Dutch call it, using general measures of damages instead of individual assessments, is not an uncommon phenomenon in the law of damages. This kind of damages calculation is already a deviation from the principle of full reparation, at least in those instances where the victim cannot choose between individual damages assessment and relying on the general, abstract approach prescribed.[93] A second exception to the principle lies in the authority given to the judge to mitigate damages. Art 6:109 CC allows the court to mitigate the damages if it decides that awarding the full amount of compensation would be 'unacceptable' given the circumstances of the case, such as 'the nature of the liability, the legal relation between the parties and the financial strength of each of both parties' (art 6:109 para 1 CC), be it no less than the maximum sum for which the defendant has liability insurance coverage (para 2; cf no 13 and no 81). Some authors claim that individual practitioners and health care organisations will have better chances to see the amount of their liability mitigated than commercial businesses such as pharmaceutical companies.[94]

77 The plaintiff may seek damages, ie compensation – either in the form of natural restitution *(herstel in natura)*, which aims to restore the status quo ante, or in the form of monetary reimbursement, which provides for an equivalent. As stated monetary compensation covers losses *(damnum emer-*

---

92 See eg *Lindenbergh* (fn 88) nos 10–12; *J Spier/T Hartlief*, Verbintenissen uit de wet en Schadevergoeding (2006) no 196.

93 On this, see *Spier/Hartlief* (fn 92) nos 207–208; *Lindenbergh* (fn 88) no 36 ff.

94 *Legemaate* (fn 2) 59.

gens), as well as lost profits and other lost gains *(gederfde winst)*. Based on art 6:97 CC the court must calculate damages in the way that is best suited to the nature of the harm and if the amount of damage cannot be calculated in exact numbers, it must be estimated.

22. Loss of earnings vs loss of earning capacity

Both the loss of earnings and the loss of earning capacity are to be compensated under the principle of full reparation explained above. If needed the measure of damages can be assessed by making an estimate (art 6:97 CC). **78**

As regards the loss of non-declared income, this will of course not be fully compensated if the violated interest for which compensation is awarded is (partly) illegal. For the situation in which the income gained from legal activities was not declared, the Supreme Court has ruled that the loss of income can then be awarded but with a deduction of the amount of taxes and social insurance premiums (and similar payments) that would have been deducted if the income had been declared to the tax inspector. Based on decisions by the Supervisory Board of insurers *(Raad van Toezicht van de schadeverzekeringsmaatschappijen)*, insurance companies may not report income for which compensation was claimed to the tax authorities. Illegally-earned wages are therefore not to be compensated it seems; the lost earnings can still be recovered however, but only up to the amount that would in fact have been received if the necessary taxes would have been paid.[95] **79**

23. Periodic payments or lump sum?

Based on the Dutch law of damages the claimant has the choice to opt for compensation in the form of periodical payments or to ask for a lump sum. In practice claimants prefer a lump-sum payment. **80**

24. Caps and thresholds

With regard to the amount of damages that may be claimed, things such as generally applied caps or limitations do not as yet exist in the Nether- **81**

95 HR 24 November 2000, NJ 2001, 195 (M/G).

lands.[96] Art 6:110 CC does recognise the possibility of imposing, by means of a Royal Decree, a limit on the amount of damages that can be recovered, but that possibility has only been used once so far, recently in a case dealing with (a limit on) liability for security companies working at airports.[97] One should realise, however, that the court does have the discretionary power to limit an award in a specific case on the basis of equity and reasonableness (see art 6:109 CC) if it feels that granting the full amount of damages that would normally be recoverable would lead to unacceptable consequences, given the nature of the liability, the legal relationship between the parties, and their mutual financial capacities. The court can only lower the award to the level at which insurance is or should have been available.[98] The Dutch Supreme Court has warned the lower courts to be very cautious when using this power,[99] and it has thus not (yet) gained much popularity.

II. Non-pecuniary Loss

25. Introduction to indemnifying non-pecuniary loss

82 The application of the principle of total individual reparation is difficult in the area of damages for pain and suffering (art 6:106 CC). In general, and also for medical negligence cases, art 6:106 CC provides that if a victim has sustained physical harm he is also entitled to be compensated for non-pecuniary loss (damages for pain and suffering; *smartengeld*).[100] The amount thereof is to be established by the (lower) courts on the basis of equity.[101] In determining what amount is to be awarded, all circumstances need to be taken into account.[102] In a case decided in 1992, the Dutch Supreme Court stated that the following are especially relevant

96 Leaving aside the *de minimis* of € 500 in product liability cases based on the European Directive for damage to property used in a private setting. See art 6:190 CC.

97 See Staatsblad van het Koninkrijk der Nederlanden (Stb) 2004, 358.

98 See *Dommering-Van Rongen* (fn 91) 146.

99 HR 28 May 1999, NJ 1999, 510 (*G/H*).

100 For the compensation of other forms of non-pecuniary damages, see *Lindenbergh* (fn 88) 17 ff.

101 The Supreme Court does not touch upon the amount of compensation that is awarded for non-pecuniary losses by the lower courts, see HR 8 July 1992, NJ 1992, 770 (*AMC/O*) and HR 17 November 2000, NJ 2001, 215 (*Druijff/BCE Bouw*).

102 Cf HR 17 November 2000, NJ 2001, 215 (*Druijff/BCE Bouw*). See also *Lindenbergh* (fn 88) 65 ff.

here: on the one hand, the nature of the liability,[103] and on the other hand, the nature, duration and intensity of the pain, suffering and loss of amenity sustained by the victim which arose following the act on which the liability is based.[104] Courts must further take note of the amount awarded by other courts in comparable cases, including the highest amounts awarded, taking into account the inflation rate since these cases were decided. Courts may also take into account developments regarding the amounts of compensation in other countries, although such a development may not be decisive for determining the amounts to be awarded in the Netherlands.[105]

In practice, courts, lawyers, and insurance companies use the so-called *Smartengeldbundel*[106] as their point of reference. This *Smartengeldbundel* is published every three years and contains a listing of amounts of compensation for non-pecuniary damages awarded by the courts over the years.[107] Generally, the level of compensation for non-pecuniary loss awarded is not all that high,[108] with claims not exceeding (back then) DFL 250,000 (€ 113,445 without inflation) for the more severe cases.[109] The highest amount was awarded in 1992 in a case of (wrongful) contamination with the HIV virus; the amount awarded was (then) DFL 300,000 (€ 136,134).[110] There is not a detectable trend towards higher amounts being awarded,[111] even though claims as such demand higher amounts, at least if one makes allowance for the fact that awards increase to compensate for inflation.[112] **83**

Of course for the calculation of these non-pecuniary damages, there is no easily applicable yardstick. If the willingness to pay, to accept the damage or the willingness to pay the costs of avoidance of the damage is taken as the benchmark, the damages awarded by European courts are generally **84**

---

103 Eg: tortuous or contractual liability, fault based or strict liability, or the specific types of liability (employer's liability, traffic liability, product liability or services liability etc).

104 Cf HR 8 July 1992, NJ 1992, 770 (*AMC/O.*). To that extent also HR 17 November 2000, NJ 2001, 215 (*Druijff/BCE Bouw*), a case in which the liability of a building company towards its injured employee was invoked. See also *SD Lindenbergh*, De hoogte van het smartengeld in Nederland, Een verkenning van de top, VR 1999, 129 ff.

105 Cf HR 17 November 2000, NJ 2001, 215 (*Druijff/BCE Bouw*).

106 See the latest (17th) edition, *M Jansen* (ed), Smartengeldbundel (2009).

107 Cf *WCT Weterings*, Vergoeding van letselschade en transactiekosten (1999) 93.

108 Cf ibid 92.

109 Cf *Lindenbergh*, VR 1999, 129 ff.

110 HR 8 July 1992, NJ 1992, 770 (*AMC/O*). Cf *Lindenbergh*, VR 1999, 129 and 133.

111 *Lindenbergh* (fn 88) 78.

112 From HR 17 November 2000, NJ 2001, 215 (*Druijff/BCE Bouw*), it becomes clear that the court must take the inflation rate into account when comparing an earlier case with the present claim.

set at levels so low that the principle of full reparation is not observed.[113] However in the Netherlands, as elsewhere in Europe, these damages are generally seen as offering some form of comfort with regard to the grief suffered, especially in cases of severe disabilities, not as full reparation of the damage.[114]

26. Who can claim compensation for non-pecuniary loss?

85 Dutch personal injury law holds the principle that only the primary or the direct victim (ie the person whose physical or mental injury was caused directly by the accident or malpractice itself and not through his confrontation with another person's injury, as is the case with secondary nervous shock victims or similar) can claim compensation for non pecuniary loss.[115] Subsequently a claim for bereavement damages is not possible. A legislative proposal to change the law in this respect, by allowing a claim for '*affectieschade*' for the remaining relatives (emotional loss, bereavement damage, *préjudice d'affection*), was rejected by the first Senate of the Dutch Parliament in March of 2010. It was proposed that certain categories of close relatives, such as the spouse or parents of a seriously injured or deceased person would be able to claim a standardised amount of money (€ 10,000). The arguments of the small majority (36 against 30) of Members of Parliament who objected against this legislative proposal felt either that the latter might contribute to the threat of a 'claim culture' and/or that the fixed amounts paid by insurers was not the right way to do justice or to acknowledge the wrong.[116]

86 However, it is possible to claim pecuniary and non pecuniary damages for nervous shock, not only for primary accident victims but also for the so-called secondary victims: those confronted with serious injury or death of others caused by the violation of safety or traffic rule.[117] These claims are,

---

113 Which is generally the case, see *Spier/Hartlief* (fn 92) no 196. With regard to non-pecuniary losses, the principle of full reparation does not apply as such, since no amount will by itself fully compensate the immaterial damage that was suffered.

114 See *CJJM Stolker/FH Poletiek*, Smartengeld – Wat zijn we eigenlijk aan het doen? in: Bewijs en letselschade (1998) 78–80.

115 *EFD Engelhard*, Third party losses in a comparative perspective (triptych with CC van Dam and I Giesen), Utrecht Law Review (ULR) 3 (2007) 82 ff.

116 On this enactment, see the Parliamentary Proceedings of the Second Chamber of Parliament (TK) 2004/2005, no 28 781, nos 1–3 ff.

117 HR 22 February 2002, NJ 2002, 240 (*Nervous shock*), recently affirmed HR 9 October 2009, LJN BI8583 (*Reaal Schadeverzekeringen NV*).

as of yet, quite rare though in the field of medical negligence,[118] and will accordingly not be further discussed.

G. Procedural Matters

27. Specific rules of jurisdiction or procedure

87 Until now there are no specific rules of civil procedure for medical negligence cases. Quite recently however, legislation involving the so-called '*deelgeschillen*' has been enacted. This legislation allows future claimants in personal injury claims, and thus also in cases of medical negligence, to put (only) a specific part of his dispute with the wrongdoer before a judge (eg a dispute over the compensation of a certain loss). The judge will rule on that part of the dispute, without touching upon the rest of the possible issues, thereby giving parties legal certainty on that point and thus allowing them to continue negotiating the out of court settlement of the claim between them, thus without further involving a judge. This system is supposed to enhance negotiations because certain insurmountable problems between the parties are taken away, thus clearing the path for a successful settlement.

28. Special institutions handling malpractice claims

88 The so-called Hospital Dispute Settlement Commission (*Geschillencommissie Ziekenhuizen*) handles claims for damages of patients who have suffered damage caused by an affiliated health care institution, after they have first addressed the institution itself and/or its liability insurer. The Dispute Settlement Commission only allows claims that do not exceed € 5,000 and that are not pending as a civil court procedure. Clearly this alternative dispute settlement system enables the victim or his relatives to claim damages via a means that entails less costs and fewer procedural barriers than public (civil law) court procedures. However, if one or both of the parties do not agree with the decision of the Dispute Settlement Commission, they may still subsequently start legal proceedings before the civil court.

---

118 The few examples are mainly from prior to the principal nervous shock case of 2002, mentioned in the previous footnote and deal with parents that suffer from mental distress caused by malpractice concerning their child (of which most notably HR 8 September 2000, NJ 2000, 734, *Baby Joost*) and women in labour experiencing severe distress from difficulties at child birth, particularly Rb Maastricht 22 March 2003, LJN AV7273 (*omission concerning Caesarean section*).

H. Outlook

29. Reform plans

89 Although several authors and practitioners have suggested a move away from liability law and a shift towards an alternative insurance plan or something similar, no consensus has ever been reached on this.[119] Currently, the Dutch legislature has not presented any plans to reform medical liability.

Cases

Case 1

90 Under Dutch medical liability law it is generally assumed that the unborn child can have rights to compensation in case of malpractice, and such a claim has in the so-called *Baby Kelly* case been proven to be successful in a case of wrongful life.[120] This claim can be either contractual, as Y is to be regarded as a contractual party to the treatment contract (art 7:453 CC; cf the *Kelly* case) or in tort, based on the violation of a duty of care owed by the defendant(s) towards her directly (art 6:162 CC; see no 21 ff). To be clear, in the present case the claim does not seem to include that Y, given the seriousness of her impairments, would not have wished to be born, nor do the facts exhibit that Y's impairments were (partly) caused by a heritable genetic defect within her family for which she was wrongfully not tested (as in the *Kelly* case). Rather, Y's claim seems to be based on the argument that based on the results of the cardiotocograph (CTG) both the midwife D and gynecologist A (acting *ad interim*) omitted to take the medical action that was required, in the absence of a good justification ground. Particularly A, after having seen the results of the CTG, should have carried out further investigations and ordered a caesarean section. If A's contractual and/or non contractual liability based on one of these grounds can be established, the hospital and/or A and B's practice will also be liable (either based on the hospital's central liability in medical

119 See on this *Giard* (fn 10) and further *Cascão* (fn 20) (both with further references).

120 HR 8 March 2005, NJ 2006, 606 (*Baby Kelly*).On that case also *EH Hondius*, The Kelly Case – Compensation for undue damage for wrongful treatment, in: JKM Gevers et al (eds), Health Law, Human Rights and the Biomedicine Convention. Essays in Honour of Henriette Roscam Abbing (2005) 105 ff; *I Giesen*, Of Wrongful Birth, Wrongful Life, Comparative Law and the Politics of Tort Law Systems, Tydskrift vir Hedendaags Roomsch-Hollandsch Recht (THRHR) 72 (2009) 257 ff.

contract law, which we discussed at no 61 above, or vicariously, see nos 63–64). Given the fault-based foundation of the liability of the practicing physicians themselves, we do not think a claim vis-à-vis B *personally* will succeed given that B was on holiday at the time that X's condition worsened and A stood in for him at the time.

The problem here seems not to be with the question of wrongfulness or breach of contract (which both seem to be given), but rather with causation. It is probable that Y's impairments existed to a certain extent before the delivery and it is also possible that A and D's conduct were the sole cause of the impairments. But from the facts of the case as presented here, it seems also possible that Y already had a pre-existing problem which could 'at least' partially – which means: or fully – have contributed to her present condition. Clearly the defendants cannot be held liable for impairments that would in any case have occurred.[121] If it can be ascertained that Y's pre-existing condition has contributed to her present condition, that fact will not stand in the way of the defendants' liability as defendants in Dutch law must 'take the victim as they find him' (see above, no 49). What is needed, is that Y produces evidence that there is a *conditio sine qua non* connection between A's malpractice and her impairments. This seems uncertain from the facts as presented, even more so because (as in many medical negligence cases) it seems far from clear what Y's condition would have been like if A (and D) would have taken proper action (and thus complied with the professional standards). However, it seems likely that Y's claim can be made successful either through the so-called reversal rule (*omkeringsregel*, see no 40 ff), by awarding damages for the loss of a chance (to be born unharmed, see no 50 ff) or by means of proportional liability (in proportion to the percentage of likelihood that Y's impairments may have been caused or worsened by A's omissions, see no 47). Which one of these options can and/or will be applied will depend on the information that can be discerned from statements of professional experts. **91**

Under Dutch law, the claimant (here Y) is under the duty to mitigate his loss as far as it seems possible, in all reasonableness; if he violates this rule this is usually treated as a form of contributory negligence.[122] However, it seems most unlikely that this duty would give the hospital a successful defence here as this would mean that civil law would, indirectly, intervene in the decision of Y's (and her parents) right to family life (cf art 8 of the **92**

121 Likewise: HR 2 February 1990, NJ 1991, 292 (*Vermaat/Staat*) and on this *Engelhard* (fn 5) 273.

122 *ALM Keirse*, Schadebeperkingsplicht, over eigen schuld aan de omvang van de schade (2003).

European Convention of Human Rights). At the utmost, the fact that the associated costs of Y's care (by day in the form of professional care and exclusively by her mother during nights and weekends) are greater than if Y lived in a care home, could be considered to be a reason to mitigate the amount of liability, albeit not below the sum covered by liability insurance (art 6:109 CC; see nos 76 and 81). Y will also be entitled to non-pecuniary damages, of course (again) provided that the *conditio sine qua non* connection between her impairments and the malpractice can be shown based on one of the aforementioned theories.

93 As for X's claim for the special care costs that she incurs for Y, a special rule for personal injury cases is applicable which is based on the so-called 'transferred loss theory' (*leer van de verplaatste schade*).[123] Based on this ruling, the defendants' liability vis-à-vis Y is extended to any concrete pecuniary damage (eg expenses, lost income and alike) that X incurs for the care that Y needs. Based on relevant jurisprudence on this matter, X may, given the seriousness of Y's condition, even claim damages if she has incurred no concrete loss of income but has had to take leave days (or similar) in order to look after Y.[124] The time spent on this special care will be calculated on the basis of (no more than) the professional costs that X saved by taking on this care herself, albeit only to the extent that it would have been 'normal and common' (*normaal en gebruikelijk*) to get professional help in the given situation.[125] As far as X's claim for non pecuniary damages is concerned, she can be seen as the contracting party to the contract for medical services with hospital C, which means that *mutatis mutandis* similar to the arguments discussed for Y's claim above (nos 90–91) X too will have a contractual claim against A and C (cf the aforementioned *Baby Kelly* case) for her mental distress. Affectionate damages (no 85 above) are not recoverable.

---

123 *Engelhard* (fn 5) 142 ff.

124 There is currently a preliminary proposal for a special ruling in respect of such costs, see *EFD Engelhard*, Naar een nieuw criterium voor de vergoeding van derden: het Voorontwerp Inkomensschade en het wetsvoorstel Reïntegratiekosten, VR 2008, 1–9.

125 HR 28 May 1999, NJ 1999, 564 (*Kruithof*) and HR 6 June 2003, NJ 2003, 504 (*Krüter/Wilton*); on these cases *Engelhard*, ULR 3 (2007) 82 ff. Cf as to fatal injury cases, HR 5 December 2008, RvdW 2009, 1 (*Stichting Ziekenhuis Rijnstate/R*) and on this *R Rijnhout*, Vergoeding voor huishoudelijke hulp door naasten: een overkoepelende analyse van art. 6:107 en 108 BW, AV&S 2009, and *SD Lindenbergh/I van der Zalm*, Vergoeding ter zake van verzorging en huishoudelijke hulp bij letsel en overlijden, Maandblad voor Vermogensrecht (MvV) 2009, 146–151.

Case 2

The mother's claim has a good chance of succeeding under Dutch law, but the father's chances of success are doubtful. Cases like this dealing with a wrongful birth claim of X and Y, the parents of Z, who was born as a result of the failure of the contraceptive implant 'Implanon', are increasingly brought before Dutch courts.[126] We note that claimants may also opt for a product liability (and/or wrongful advertisement, art 6:194 CC) claim against (most likely) Organon, the type of claim which has also led to many cases in practice.[127] The case at hand, against the practitioner, will generally be based on art 7:453 in conjunction with art 6:74 CC (breach of contract) and alternatively fault liability. The facts as presented in the case are not completely clear regarding the (alleged) negligence of the gynecologist. First we need to decide if the medical intervention to place the implant can be construed as the practitioner's obligation to achieve a given result, which in Dutch law is a matter of interpretation of the parties' mutual expressions (cf no 27). If this was the case, then it will usually be assumed, with hindsight, that he has violated this obligation if the patient got pregnant quite soon (within a year or so) and if the implant could no longer be traced on an echo.[128] However, it is often not so much the (apparent) failure in placing the implant, but rather the violation of having informed the patient of the risk that the implant may fail, that will be the breach of contract.[129] That may then relieve the court of the difficult decision of having to interpret the contractual obligation of placing the implant as an obligation to exercise with due care (trying to properly place the implant) or to guarantee a particular result (proper placement of the implant).[130] The answer to this question, also for the case at hand, will depend on whether the practitioner had sufficiently warned his patient of the risk of failure, which will be for the claimant to prove (helped in that **94**

126 Inter alia: Rb Arnhem 11 June 2003, LJN AG0130; Rb Alkmaar 11 February 2004, LJN AO3453; Rb Den Bosch 15 June 2005, LJN AT7382; Rb Alkmaar 24 May 2006, LJN AX4831; Hof Den Bosch 28 August 2007, LJN BB2385; Hof Amsterdam 24 January 2008, LJN BC9815 and Rb Den Bosch 26 March 2008, LJN BC7489.

127 See esp the 27 cases of 15 women before Hof Den Bosch 15 June 2005, LJN AT7353 (*Claimants/Organon*) and the joined decision: LJN AT7382 (*X/Organon*). In the prior case (LJN AT7353 at para 4.20) the District Court has shifted, on grounds of reasonableness, the burden of proof with regard to the defectiveness of the Organon implant to the manufacturer.

128 Hof Alkmaar 11 February 2004, LJN AO3453, para 5.14.

129 Rb Arnhem 11 June 2003, LJN AG0130 (*Implanon implant*) at para 14.

130 Cf HR 1 December 2000, LJN AA8724 (*Wrongful birth II*), where the wrongful birth claim of a mother whose pregnancy had resulted from a failing sterilisation procedure by Falope rings, was rejected because she had not shown this was caused through negligence.

respect by the so-called *'aanvullende stelplicht'*, dealt with above at no 31 ff, to the detriment of the defendant who will then have to rely on his charts) as the practitioner has agreed to no more than making his best effort, with no results guaranteed (*inspanningsverbintenis*).[131]

95 If there *has* been malpractice, the practitioner will be held liable for the woman's damage to the extent that it can be attributed to him based on art 6:98 CC (see nos 37 and 49); her choice not to terminate her pregnancy is in any case no causal defense. The woman will however have to convince the court of the fact that if it had not been for the malpractice she would have chosen not to have children. For this, witnesses, particularly loved ones, may be heard.[132] In a recent decision of the Appellate court The Hague a gynaecologist was held liable for not having properly informed a 37 year old woman, who had consulted him regarding her infrequent menses. The court's decision was based on the fact that he had told her that her blood test results were similar to those of a fifty to sixty year old woman without warning her that using birth control was still needed in order to prevent a pregnancy. He was held liable for the costs of her pregnancy (of twins). The fact that the woman had decided not to have the pregnancy terminated did not break the chain of causation (as was argued by the gynecologist), given the personal nature of that decision.[133]

96 In a wrongful birth case where the gynecologist had *forgotten* to re-insert the woman's intra-uterine device (thus no Organon implant) after she had undergone medical surgery, the Dutch Supreme Court held that for the legal causation (art 6:98 CC) it suffices in principle that a risk was created due to the malpractice, which has materialised. If that can be said then 'in principle' all kinds of pecuniary damage will be attributed to the defendant (the gynecologist), including the costs for maintenance of the child. The court rejected fundamental objections against the compensation of these maintenance costs, namely that making these costs recoverable would suggests that the child is seen as damage or as unwanted. It turned these objections around: compensating the maintenance costs is needed to enable the parents to realise their choice to continue the pregnancy and to raise their child.[134] However, in an *obiter dictum* the court noted that to the

131 Rb Alkmaar 11 February 2004, LJN AO3453 (*Implanon implant II*) para 5.9.

132 See the extensive witness testimonies in this respect that were taken into account by the Rb Alkmaar 24 May 2006, LJN AX4831 (*Implanon implant III*).

133 Hof Den Haag 10 July 2007, NJ 2007, 656 (*Gynecologist/Claimant*).

134 HR 21 February 1997, NJ 1999, 145 (*Wrongful Birth I*) at para 3.8 of the judgment. Other contra-arguments are given at paras 3.9–3.10. Advocate-General Vranken had, in his advice, elucidated the position of other law systems, particularly German law.

extent that maintenance costs *exceed* the average costs that are calculated objectively (by the so-called National Institute for Budget Consultancy, NIBUD), it is left to the discretion of the court in question to see if that part of the claim must be rejected as it is then based on personal preferences of the parents (and thus their own responsibility). The Supreme Court also pointed to the possibility of mitigating the compensation if the gynecologist has no liability insurance (art 6:109 CC, see no 76).[135]

Another relevant aspect of the Supreme Court's case for present purposes is related to the part of the mother's claim that dealt with her income loss as a result of her pregnancy and the child's birth. She was at the time married to the father and they already had two children but lived on unemployment benefits. According to the Supreme Court her income loss was 'in principle' recoverable, but it was necessary to determine whether the mother's choice to temporarily stop working could be regarded as a 'reasonable' decision in the concrete circumstances of the case.[136] The claimant would have had to convince the court of this. On the one hand, regard should be had to her right to arrange her life (as well as her child's) in such a way as she thinks fit, while on the other hand she should mitigate her damage in so far as possible and can reasonably be expected of her. The particular circumstances of her family, such as the number and ages of the other children, whether she has a husband and if so, whether he is employed or not and the financial means of the family would have to be considered here.[137] **97**

As for the non pecuniary damage, it is generally left to the discretion of the courts-of-fact, as was explained above (see no 82 ff), to determine whether there are good grounds to award compensation. The court needs to take all the relevant circumstances into account such as, inter alia, the kind of liability in question (eg intent or mere negligence, fault or risk-based).[138] The Supreme Court even seemed to suggest in its 1997 case that a deduction could be madefor the joy that even unplanned children will (also) bring, but in the literature this has met with some criticism.[139] This **98**

135 HR 21 February 1997, NJ 1999, 145 (*Wrongful Birth I*) at para 3.11. In his case note Brunner criticised the court's strong emphasis on an objective calculation of the maintenance costs (based on NIBUD standards).

136 HR 21 February 1997, NJ 1999, 145 (*Wrongful Birth I*) para 3.13.2.

137 HR 21 February 1997, NJ 1999, 145 (*Wrongful Birth I*) para 3.13.2.

138 HR 9 August 2002, LJN AE2117 (*St KUN/Applicant*) para 5.3.

139 In these words Advocate-General *Spier* in his advice preceding HR 9 August 2002, LJN AE2117 (*St KUN/Applicant*) at para 4.25.1–4.26.2 of his advice (with references), but Spier concludes that the non pecuniary advantages outweigh the disadvantages and non pecuniary damages should thus not be awarded here (para 4.41). In this last sense also for an *Implanon* case as the one at hand: Rb Alkmaar 24 May 2006, LJN AX4831 (*Implanon implant III*).

has in some cases actually led to the rejection of the part of the parents' (the woman's) claim related to non pecuniary damages.[140]

99 It must be noted that so far as cases that have reached Dutch courts are concerned, the father's right to compensation has received much less attention as claims in almost all of these cases came from the mother and are centred around her damage. His position is very different from hers in the sense that generally he will not be regarded as a contracting party, with respect to the contract for medical services concerning her pregnancy.[141] Exceptions can be made if there are special indications that the parties were intending to include the father, for example because the mother has told the practitioner that she also acts on the father's behalf (which is of course rare).[142] In most cases so far, however, the father's claim has been rejected for lack of grounds for liability (also in tort).[143] Some courts, however, will consider the malpractice which constituted a breach of contract towards the mother, almost intrinsically as tortuous against the father.[144] In wrongful life claims the Supreme Court has ruled that the violation of the right to self-determination may equally affect the father. He does not have the final say in the decision regarding the possible termination of the pregnancy, but his interests are so closely involved that the contractual malpractice towards the mother constitutes a wrongful act (or rather omission) towards the father. If he can prove that this has resulted in mental injury, then he too is entitled to non pecuniary damages.[145] In our view the latter should also apply to wrongful birth claims, such as the present one.

Case 3

100 Under Dutch law X's claim for damages against the defendants seems quite likely to succeed. The case presents several serious omissions by

---

140 Rb Alkmaar 24 May 2006, LJN AX4831 (*Implanon implant III*).

141 Art 7:446 para 1 CC allows specific thirds (*'bepaalde derden'*) to be included in the contractual scope of protection only if they are the one receiving the treatment. Since the father does not receive any pregnancy treatment, he is by no means party to the contract (ibid Rb Arnhem 11 June 2003, LJN AG0130, at para 5 and Rb Alkmaar 11 February 2004, LJN AO3453, para 5.3).

142 Rb Alkmaar 11 February 2004, LJN AO3453 (*Implanon implant*) para 5.3.

143 Rb Arnhem 11 June 2003, LJN AG0130, at para 9; Rb Alkmaar 11 February 2004, LJN AO3453, para 5.19 (the claim for tort liability against the father needs further proof), Rb Alkmaar 24 May 2006, LJN AX4831.

144 Cf for instance the Court of Appeal's judgment in the wrongful life (!) claim that led to HR 8 March 2005, NJ 2006, 606 (*Baby Kelly*).

145 HR 8 March 2005, NJ 2006, 606 (*Baby Kelly*).

several involved practitioners. Firstly, three omissions by the obstetrician of hospital A: X, a newborn diagnosed with hypoglycaemia (which should have made him a 'high-risk' newborn), was not monitored as was medically indicated, the paediatrician was not consulted and X's mother and the midwife were not informed about the need to monitor his blood sugar level. Secondly the case presents two omissions by the midwife B: she should have recognised the risk posed to X and did not consult the paediatrician. Thirdly the case presents omissions in the organisational sphere by C's paediatric clinic due to which valuable time was wasted. Fourthly, nurse D did not take the proper measures. The crucial question lies of course with the *conditio sine qua non link* between these respective malpractices and the (ultimate) damage: X's severe disability: for X's claim to succeed, it must be established that his severe disability has been or, at least may have been (art 6:99 CC, see no 102 below) caused by any of these failures, and if so, by which one(s). The facts of this case are unclear with regard to the exact *conditio sine qua non* for each of the malpractices seen individually. However, it does seem likely that the sequence of events has caused the damage. This could point to concurrent liability, which means that all defendants are jointly and severally liable for X's damage (art 6:102 CC). There is a high(er) probability that the organic damage was sustained in C's clinic, but that of course tells us nothing about X's serious deterioration process that led to his final state of health (meaning that not just C, but also A and B may be equally, or even more, to blame). It also seems to be unclear at what point in time (and by which of the actions that should have been taken) X's deterioration could have been prevented.

Under Dutch law this issue will probably be treated as one of cumulative **101**
causality, meaning that each of the defendants will be held to have contributed to X's deterioration, which ultimately led to his organic damage. The damage may then be attributed to each (art 6:98 CC). The reversal rule as discussed above (no 40 ff) may be used in this regard against any defendant brought to court: the specific risk caused, for instance, by A's omission to monitor X for 24 hours is then taken to have materialised unless the defendant shows that his or her omission did not cause X's deterioration. A similar line of reasoning may be used for the specific risk entailed in not consulting the paediatrician and for the other wrongful acts as well. All defendants can then be held jointly and severally liable and the paying party may seek reimbursement (which will then, in that subsequent procedure amongst the defendants themselves, beg the question as to who caused what). As was said above, in personal injury cases the legal attribution (in terms of causation, art 6:98 CC) of the series of events goes quite far under Dutch law: the defendants liability will

extend also to an unlikely matter of events (eg if the victim of a minor traffic accident suffers from a long-lasting disability because of a cumulative wrong caused after he had been admitted to the hospital).

102 Of course it is not apparent that the first series of malpractices already caused X's condition to worsen, although to us this does appear to have been likely. Other options might then be to use the rules on proportional liability or loss of a chance, as explained above (no 47 and no 50 ff), or (more claimant-friendly perhaps) to invoke the rule on alternative liability as laid down in art 6:99 CC and applied in the famous *DES* case.[146] In the 1950s and 60s a pregnancy enhancing drug was marketed by a number of pharmaceutical companies. Later it was discovered that both mothers and daughters suffered considerable physical damage as a result of the use of this drug by the mother. A number of injured daughters claimed compensation from a number of manufacturers, without presenting specific evidence of the identity of the origin of the tablets that their mothers had used. The manufacturers asserted that they could not be held liable in full. The Supreme Court decided that the interests of the injured DES-daughters should prevail over the interests of the manufacturers. As a result, an injured daughter could claim in full from any of the manufacturers, even though no specific causation by that manufacturer was proved. Wrongful marketing of the unreasonable unsafe drug was held to be sufficient.

103 The DES case was decided under the old 1838 Dutch Civil Code, which did not yet have any provision on alternative causation. The Hoge Raad decided that the material rule contained in art 6:99 CC was already substantive law before enactment in 1992. According to the standard of art 6:99 CC, if two or more wrongful acts may have caused the damage, but it is unclear which of these alternative causes did in fact cause the damage, then each responsible actor is liable in full unless he can prove that his act certainly did not cause the damage. In the DES case, the wrongful acts were the distribution by several manufacturers of an unreasonable unsafe drug. Any victim of the drug could claim in full from any of the manufacturers, which in effect may cause serious problems in administrating and settling mass injuries such as the DES-related injuries. In Case 3 as spelled out here, the same reasoning seems to be possible, since all possible wrongful acts have or could have caused the same damage.

104 This option seems to be strengthened by a subsequent Supreme Court case.[147] In that case a (believe it or not) 'second group' of arsonists claimed

146 HR 9 October 1992, NJ 1994, 535 (*DES daughters*).
147 See HR 31 January 2003, NJ 2003, 346 (*Multiple arsonists*).

that the acts of 'their group' had not caused the entire damage to a certain building. The building they had set fire to must have been already damaged beyond repair by a previous fire by other arsonists, or so they alleged. The Court of Appeal however considered that, based on an evaluation of the facts, the second group's acts in fact could well have caused the entire damage, and concluded therefore that art 6:99 CC should be applied. The Hoge Raad concurred in the sense that the arsonists were held liable in full (art 6:99 CC) unless they could prove that they had not caused the entire damage (which they could not). It seems to us, that this line of reasoning with regard to art 6:99 CC could be followed in the medical case at hand as the facts of that case seem to leave the possibility open that each defendant may have caused the entire damage.

Case 4

This claim may succeed under Dutch law, if X's paralysis has in fact resulted **105**
from the surgery and if, this is of course the crucial point, the paralysis would not have occurred in any case (which remains unclear). The case deals with a core issue of 'informed consent', to which we refer in our previous discussion, at no 70. The information duty (as was discussed there) that the Act on medical services contracts (*Wet geneeskundige behandelingsovereenkomst,* WGBO) imposes on practitioners clearly includes the surgery suggested for X in the case at hand, all the more since this particular surgery had such serious risks was attached and was, according to the facts presented, not absolutely necessary. As was explained above, the WGBO imposes the obligation on the practitioner to inform his patient in a clear way (*'op duidelijke wijze'*) about the intended tests and treatment and that this means the information must be sufficiently understandable for the latter. In the explanatory memorandum the legislature indicates that if the patient has language difficulties, the practitioner needs to bring the information across by using somebody who may assist him, if needed through a centre for translators.[148] In the Netherlands medical practitioners can turn to the Centre for Translators to request the services of a translator on relatively short notice (within days) or even immediately (in case of an emergency or if telephone services will suffice). The Dutch Ministries of National Health, Welfare and Sports and of Justice subsidise the costs of professional translators in the sectors of health care and social affairs.

---

148 See the Parliamentary Reports of the Second Chamber of Parliament (TK) 1989/1990, no 21 561, no 3 (Explanatory Memorandum), 11.

106 The burden of proof with regard to the violation of the duty to inform the patient is on the latter. As was explained in no 35, practitioners are expected to come forward with factual information to motivate their defences, at the risks that the burden of proof of the plaintiff will be changed or alleviated to the disadvantage of the defendant.[149] Much can be said for that in the present case. The kinds of damage claimed by X are all recoverable under Dutch law, possibly with a deduction for social benefits that already cover part of X's expenses for the adjustments made in his house and/or his car if X did not deduct these already.

Case 5

107 There may be a chance that this claim will succeed under Dutch law, despite the high level of uncertainty as to what has happened. The facts of this case state that it is certain that the damage to the patient can only have been caused by the positioning of the patient's arm at the beginning of the surgery (for which the surgeon was responsible) combined with the compression during the operation (which was foremost the anaesthetist's responsibility). This could result in joint liability, but for the fact that it cannot be proven that the way that the patient's arm was positioned was in any way incorrect or that the anaesthetist, who was an intern at the time, acted negligently. The court may assist the plaintiff in proving this (using the '*aanvullende stelplicht*', no 31 ff) if it is certain that his complaints can be related to the operation (the fact that his complaints started directly following the surgery may be indicative of this). This may be particularly so, as the fact that both matters cannot be proven is due to the lack of documentation with regard to the operations during surgery (which might perhaps even give rise to a substantive claim, based on art 7:454 CC, in which case the lost chance theory could be invoked, see no 50 ff above, although for the case at hand this seems somewhat farfetched).

108 Dutch courts use an objective standard of care for professionals, which means that generally a lack of experience (as for C) and lack of time (as for D) will not relieve them from their duty to act as 'good' practitioners (in terms of art 7:453 CC, see nos 67 and 23 above). If several persons can be held liable for the same damage, they will each be jointly and severally liable (art 6:102 CC) and after having paid the plaintiff they are entitled to reimbursement from one another (art 6:6ff CC). Using the article on central liability of the institution is also an option of course (see no 61).

149 HR 20 November 1988, NJ 1988, 500 and HR 18 February 1994, NJ 1994, 368.

As for the rules for compensation, provided that there is sufficient ground for compensation, X will, subsequent to his physical disability, be entitled to non-pecuniary damages (art 6:106 section b CC) and compensation for his loss of earnings. If his weekend job was not declared, the loss of income can be awarded but with a deduction of the amount of taxes and social insurance premiums (and alike) that would have been deducted if declared to the tax inspector (see no 79). The fact that he refuses retraining may give problems under social security law, but will probably have no effect under the law of damages (notwithstanding the fact that X is under a duty to mitigate his damage, but only within the boundaries of what can be 'reasonably' expected of him). As for the assessment costs, these are recoverable under Dutch law (art 6:96 CC), but there is a so-called double test for reasonableness: was it, given his duty to mitigate his damage, reasonable to incur these costs in the first place (in our view it may well be), but secondly: was it in all reasonableness necessary to incur high costs or could it also have been done for less costs or even free of charge. Given that the free of charge method was available to the defendants it will be for X to convince the court that it was reasonable by explaining, for example, the (possible) differences as to the quality of each of both alternatives (was the one assessment more extensive than the other and was this necessary for his claim, etc). **109**

Case 6

It is doubtful whether this claim will succeed. Household costs are recoverable under Dutch law, even if they are made by people other than professionals (cf no 93) and can be calculated objectively, but the problem in the present case rests with the grounds for liability. There was a contract between the patient and C and/or D (as the legal representatives of the orthopaedic practice). The patient can file a claim vis-à-vis the practice as such and against C and/or D in person. There are at least two major questions that may cause difficulties in succeeding with the claim: firstly the question of whether the practitioners' duty was breached and secondly the causal link issue. As regards the duty of care, the Health Authorities' Report seems to indicate that (unwritten) standards of hygiene were not respected; whether this gives rise to sufficient arguments to establish liability depends in part on the hygiene rules that are common in this area. It seems to us that the practice was not sufficiently hygienic. **110**

Variation 1

111 If the carrier of the bacteria cannot be identified, the claim will generally fail as it is, in principle, for the victim to prove the causal link between the defendant's lack of hygiene and the infection. If she can prove that the infection was caused by someone from the staff, but cannot prove which one, she may be helped by the ruling for alternative causation (art 6:99 CC), which may shift the burden of proof. Here however, it could have been anyone, and for this (general) causation problem there is no special ruling in the Civil Code. She can probably not be helped by the court on the ground that 'the facts speak for themselves' either, as this seems not to be the case here, nor may the reversal rule (*omkeringsregel*) work; given the Supreme Court's restrictive approach it seems very doubtful that the creation of a specific risk which relates to the infection may be derived from the Health Authority's report (in terms of the violated rules of hygiene). See no 41 ff. The solution of proportionate liability, which was introduced in an asbestos case, will not easily be extended to what we suspect to be more common cases like the one at hand. Although in HR 24 December 2010, LJN BO1799 the Supreme Court has accepted the possibility (under strict conditions) of using proportionate liability outside asbestos cases. Accordingly, the claim will probably not be awarded.

Variation 2

112 From what we have discussed above, it will come as no surprise that in the absence of fault, there will be no liability under Dutch law, as the rules for strict liability (see nos 63–64) are not applicable here and the mere fact that the patient acquired the infection will not in itself constitute fault.

Medical Liability in Poland

Ewa Bagińska

General Questions

A. The Health Care System Framework

I. General Introduction

1. The health care system in overview

In 1997 the Act on Universal Health Insurance[1] introduced a system of universal health insurance, compulsory for the whole population.[2] On 1 January 1999 17 regional health insurance funds (similar to the German *Krankenkassen*) were created,[3] which on 1 January 2003 were transformed into one National Health Fund. Currently, the system of public health care and the right of the insured to treatment abroad, including in the EU countries,[4] is regulated by the Act of 27 August 2004 on health care services financed from public sources (hereafter Public Healthcare Act).[5] 1

Under the universal health insurance scheme almost all health care services are paid from the National Fund, which receives premiums. The 2

---

1 Dziennik Ustaw (Official Journal, Dz U) 1997, no 28, at 153.

2 It was later replaced by the Act of 23 January 2003 on the universal health insurance in the National Health Fund (Dz U no 45, item 391), which was held unconstitutional by the Constitutional Tribunal in the judgment of 7 January 2004, K 14/03 (OTK ZU 2004, no 1A, item 1). The Constitutional Tribunal held that the most parts of the Act (chapters 1, 4, 5, 6, 7, 8, 9, 13) are unconstitutional because they have created a public institution structured in a way that it is impossible for it to act diligently and efficiently. Therefore, the act breached the rule of law and the right to equal access to health care financed from public resources (art 68 and art 2 – the rule of law). Consequently, the latter Act was repealed as of 31 December 2004.

3 See *E Baginska/M Nesterowicz*, The Polish solution to the problem of realising the right to health care in view of the changes in the political and social system, in: A den Exter/ H Hermans (eds), The right to health care in several European countries (1998) 115 ff.

4 According to the community law, and in particular the Regulation no 1408/71/EC.

5 Dz U no 210, at 2135 as amended.

compulsory premium is set as a percentage (7.5 %) of income and independent from the actual health risk. The benefits are unconnected from the premium and are intended to be equally available to all eligible. Some services are still financed from the state budget. The system covers almost the entire population, including categories such as family dependants. Currently, the health insurance benefit package embraces a wide range of services: medical examination and advice, diagnostics, treatment (both in and out-patient care), rehabilitation, maternity care, pharmaceuticals, vaccinations and other preventative activities. Certain types of dental care, extra-standard services, high technology care, and medical treatment abroad (the so-called negative package) are excluded from the coverage. In some cases co-payments are required (eg in long term day care establishments or in connection with rehabilitation services).

3 In addition to the fundamental systematic change, substantial amendments to a number of statutory regulations pertaining to the realisation of the constitutional right to health care (art 68 of the Constitution) were also introduced in the nineties. One of the most important was the 1997 amendment of the Act of 30 August 1991 on Medical Care Establishments (hereafter MCE Act).[6] Already in 1991 the MCE Act officially repealed the former state health care system and opened a way for establishing private activities, including the provision of health care services, the pharmaceutical industry, medical supplies, ambulatory diagnostic services and a wide range of hospital services that could be contracted out. The Act also introduced control and supervision of the public regulators (the Health and Social Welfare Ministry and of other bodies). The pre-existing private health care providers (mainly individual practices as well as laboratories) that had been operating in Poland before the late eighties were afforded the possibility of contracting with the State in 1997.

II. Social Welfare Provision

2. The role of public health care

4 Under the MCE Act the category of medical care establishments embraces hospitals, dispensaries and other health care institutions (eg emergency departments, clinics or laboratories and rehabilitation centres). These institutions can have a private or public character; in the latter case, they are established by governmental bodies and are publicly funded.

6 The consolidated text Dz U 2007, no 14, at 89 as amended.

Both private and public medical establishments, as well as private individual or group practices of physicians or nurses (and midwives) may contract with the National Health Fund (or the relevant regional office) for the provision of health care services financed by public money. These contracts determine the type and scope of services provided, the terms and conditions of the provision of the services, the (maximum) health service cost settlement, principles of service quality, quality monitoring and control mechanisms, as well as the principles of supervision, documentation and complaint procedures. **5**

Public health care providers may also sub-contract with a private health care institution for the provision of health care services 'within the scope of their public tasks' (this refers *inter alia* to contracts commissioned by local authorities – see art 35 of the MCE Act). In the latter case both contracting parties are jointly and severally liable for injuries stemming from the services (art 35 sec 5 of the MCE Act). **6**

However, highly specialised services (such as specific operations, diagnostic tests and rare, costly pharmaceuticals) may not contract with the Fund, but with the Ministry of Health. The Ministry also oversees the waiting lists for these services (which must be accessible through the Internet). **7**

Within this framework patients are free to choose both the health care provider and the relevant health fund. **8**

3. Differences in treating patient's claims

There are no major differences between the treatment of personal injury cases in the context of publicly funded medical treatment and other personal injury cases, with the exception of the mandatory insurance coverage of the former (see below at III 6). There are no internal review management systems in place. **9**

4. Right of recourse

The welfare agency (*Zakład Ubezpieczeń Społecznych*, ZUS) provides compensation to those who are insured in the case of sickness. It covers the diagnoses of major diseases and disabilities as well as disabilities resulting from accidents. Under this social insurance scheme in neither instances is the costs of treatment important. ZUS has a right of recourse against perpetrators who intentionally cause injury, which, at least theoretically, **10** includes health care providers. In practice, however, this recourse is not exercised.

11 With respect to the National Health Fund, there is a right of recourse available on general grounds. Naturally, the Fund provides for contractual claims against its contractors. However, this presupposes that the victim's claim was brought directly against the Fund and that the latter has actually repaired the damage. Potential direct liability of the Fund, is covered by the regime of public authorities' liability. See no 72.

III. Private Insurance

5. The role of private health insurance

12 In Poland patients receive treatment through public insurance but spend considerable amounts of money on private health care. This is mostly via direct contracting with medical professionals or private establishments.

13 The organised schemes which are contracted for by the networks of private medical establishments usually constitute 'fee-for-service' expenses of patients seeking better care. The contracts are typically signed and the respective premiums paid for by employers who provide additional benefits to their employees. Strictly speaking, these beneficiaries do not have a pure commercial health insurance coverage. An illustrative example is Medicover, which offers customers health plan packages that guarantee treatment in private clinics in return for regular payments. Comprehensive medical services are covered by such health plans, including home visits by general practitioners and specialists, a wide range of diagnostic and laboratory tests and other advanced examinations. Medicover also handles rescue and medical transportation services as well as a wide range of hospitalisation and physiotherapy procedures.

14 Private health insurance is still of little importance in Poland. Where it exists, the general conditions of such insurance usually exclude liability of the insurer for medical malpractice.

6. Liability insurance

15 By virtue of art 4 of the MCE Act medical establishments or individual persons who hold appropriate professional qualifications may provide health care services. Both the individual doctors and the establishments

must have compulsory civil liability insurance if they provide services financed from public sources. This duty applies to:

- contracts concluded by providers with the National Health Fund (the legal basis for taking out the insurance policy is art 136b of the Public Healthcare Act, see the Regulation of the Minister of Finance of 28 February 2007),[7] and
- contracts concluded by both private and public providers with a public health care establishment concerning services financed from public resources (the legal basis for taking out the insurance policy is art 35 secs 5 and 6 of the MCE Act; see the Regulation of the Minister of Finance of 23 December 2004).[8]

The general conditions of the third party insurance are partially contained in the regulations cited above. The 2004 Regulation also provides for minimum guaranteed sums. These sums appear extremely low if one takes into account the extent of potential personal injuries: a minimum of € 46,500 per incident in a medical care establishment and of € 25,000 per incident in an individual practice. In addition, the Regulation of 28 February 2007 sets minimum overall guaranteed sums (for all events in which consequences are covered by the policy): € 275,000 (a medical care establishment) and € 140,000 (an individual practice). Regarding health care professionals other than doctors and nurses, the respective sums are € 12,000 per incident and € 67,500 per contract coverage. **16**

A new bill was passed on 2 December 2009[9] which replaced the Act on the Chamber of Physicians of 17 May 1989 and inserted arts 48 a and 48 b into the Law on the Professions of Physicians and Dentists of 1996.[10] The new provisions impose a compulsory civil liability insurance for doctors practicing individually or in a medical care establishment. The minimum guaranteed sums have been set by the Minister of Finance in the Regulation of 26 April 2010[11] (€ 100,000 for selected major specialisations, € 25,000 for other doctors, and € 50,000 for dentists). **17**

7 Dz U 2008, no 3, at 10.
8 Dz U 2008, no 283, at 2825.
9 Dz U 2009, no 219, at 1708.
10 The Act of 5 December 1996, Dz U 2002, no 21, at 204.
11 Dz U 2010, no 78, at 515.

IV. Professional Standards

7. Applicable professional standards

18 The standard of care is generally addressed in art 355 of *Kodeks cywilny* (the Civil Code, KC): 'a person is obliged to display the diligence generally required in relations of a given type' (subsec 1). However, the Civil Code also provides that the due diligence of the debtor within the scope of his economic activity shall be assessed with consideration to the professional nature of that activity (in subsec 2 of art 355 of KC). This means that the duty of care required of a person engaged in a business or a free profession is higher than the duty required of an ordinary person outside her profession.[12]

19 More specifically, the Law on the Professions of Physicians and Dentists defines the rights and duties pertaining to the practice of physicians, the code of professional conduct as well as detailed rules regarding the recognition of qualifications, the practice of medicine, admissibility and conditions for medical experiments, and criminal sanctions imposed for the provision of health services without the necessary competence. The Act's greatest achievement is the detailed regulation of the exercise of the physicians' profession with respect to patients' rights. The provisions on medical experiments are in conformity with the Helsinki Declaration of the World Medical Association of 1964 and CE Recommendation No 90/3 regarding medical experiments on human beings.

20 The binding rules of professional ethics are contained in the Code of Medical Ethics, proclaimed by the National Medical Congress (1993). The Code has a normative character. It defines the physician's conduct towards the patient, the principle of conduct in medical practice, the duties of the physician towards the public, mutual relations between physicians, as well as the principles of scientific research and medical experiments. Any infringement of the principles of vocational ethics may lead to disciplinary action against a physician.

21 The EC Directive 2001/20/EC relating to good clinical practice was implemented by the Regulation of the Minister of Health of 10 March 2002.[13] In addition, the Minister of Finance issued a regulation relating

12 See *T Wiśniewski*, Commentary to Civil Code Obligations, vol I (2002) 32, Sąd Najwyższy (Polish Supreme Court, SN) judgment 20 May 1986, CRN III 82/86, Orzecznictwo Sądu Najwyższego (OSN) 8/1987, at 125.

13 Dz U no 221, at 1864.

to the compulsory civil liability insurance of physicians conducting medical research and persons (corporations) mandating such examinations (Regulation of 30 April 2004).[14]

Violations of medical standards may lead to disciplinary liability. Under civil law the violations are regarded as wrongful, which in Polish law equates with the objective element of negligence. Wrongfulness includes conduct contrary to the legal order, ie to statutory law and principles of community life (principles of justice). Under the old regime of vicarious liability of the State for doctors' negligence Polish courts assumed that the concept of due care should set a special, higher standard of care expected from a good doctor. In the contemporary jurisprudence and doctrine there is a strong trend to place high expectations upon physicians on account of their long period of professional education and because of the particularly significant character of the patients' legal interests. The model of due care must not be limited to care expected of an 'average physician'.[15] The Supreme Court ruled that the principles of justice contain a duty to perform medical interventions in conformity with the latest medical knowledge and with the highest diligence required from professionals (SN judgment of 29 October 2003, III CK 34/02, OSP 4/2005, item 54).[16] 22

8. Quality and/or risk management systems

One should first mention the MCE Act which deals with administrative, 23 financial and contractual matters concerning health care institutions. A health care institution comes into being via a standard procedure. It may be created by anyone who fulfils the requirements defined in the MCE Act and the regulations of the Minister of Health regarding rooms, equipment and the employment of staff.[17] There is no need for license or approval to be obtained. It must be entered in a register kept by the *voivode* (the head of the provincial authorities) or another competent body. If a person who sets

14 Dz U no 101, at 1034.

15 See *S Kalus*, Liability for Medical damages in Polish law, in: B Heiderhoff/G Żmij (eds), Tort law in Poland, Germany and Europe (2009) 70; *M Nesterowicz*, Prawo medyczne [Medical law] (8th edn 2007) 45 ff; *M Sośniak*, Cywilna odpowiedzialność lekarza (2nd edn 1977) 152 ff.

16 Note by *E Bagińska*, Orzecznictwo Sądów Polskich (OSP) 4/2005, item 54, reported in *E Bagińska*, Poland, in: H Koziol/BC Steininger (eds), European Tort Law 2005 (2006) no 27 ff.

17 These institutions can be established by various legal persons, including the State and local authorities, non-profit and for-profit private entities (churches, foundations, associations and insurance companies).

up a health care institution fulfils all the requirements, the *voivode* may not refuse to register the institution. The creation of public hospitals together with their rules of operation, management and budget strategies are heavily regulated.[18]

24 The establishment of a supervisory board in every health care institution is required by the MCE Act. Art 65 ff of the MCE Act provides detailed competencies of the Minister of Health with respect to control, supervision, and inspection of health care institutions. Moreover, pursuant to art 66 sec 1, the Minister and local authorities are empowered to order professional inspections to be performed by various bodies, including the professional chambers of physicians.

25 The Health Fund imposes further conditions regarding the qualifications of physicians and other medical staff, proper premises, medical devices and equipment, etc, when contracting for health care services. It also carries out regular inspections of the implementation of current contracts and specifically monitors the use of services by the insured, their availability, quality and organisation, the quality of diagnostic and therapeutic procedures and their compatibility with the adopted standards, the manner of using specialised services and medical technologies, and the justification of the choice of medicines and medical materials, including orthopaedic devices. It also monitors auxiliary measures applied in diagnostics, treatment and rehabilitation, and the principles of issuing prescriptions. Failure to meet the requirements entitles the Fund to terminate the current contract or/and to refuse to conclude another one. Violations of the organisational, hygiene or sanitation standards indicate wrongful conduct of the hospital or doctor concerned.

26 As regards physicians, the right to practise medicine is granted by the Regional Physicians' Council to a person who is a Polish national or a national of any Member State of the EU, has full capacity for legal acts and possesses one of the following:

a) a degree in medicine gained at a Polish academy or university,

b) a certificate or any other document which certifies that the person is qualified to practise medicine, issued by an EU Member State, or

c) a physician's certificate issued by a state from outside the EU, on the condition that this type of certificate is recognised in Poland as an equivalent document to those described in a) and b).

---

18 Ie hospitals originating from the transformation of the former national health service and which are still supported by the State or self-government bodies.

A physician-candidate should also be in good health allowing her to practise the physician's profession, and have a flawless ethical attitude. Polish physicians must also complete post-graduate training, which lasts for 12 months and ends with a state exam.[19] A physician who is granted the right to practise his profession is placed on a register held by the Regional Physicians' Council in the region where she practises her profession. **27**

A physician possessing adequately high qualifications who is not licensed to practise on the Polish territory, but who is licensed in another country, may participate in a counsel of physicians and perform procedures arising therefrom. She may do this provided that she has been invited by: a licensed practitioner acting with prior consent of the competent Regional Physicians' Chamber, a practitioner practising in a health care establishment acting with prior consent of the competent Regional Physicians' Chamber, or a clinical hospital or medical scientific and research institute that informs the competent Regional Physicians' Chamber thereof. **28**

A physician or dentist physician who is an EU Member State national and temporarily resides in Poland may temporarily practise medicine without having to obtain the right to practise the respective profession (medicine or dentistry) and without registration in the register of individual practices or the register of individual specialised practices, provided that each time prior to practising she: **29**

a) notifies the competent Regional Physicians' Chamber in writing of her intention to practise, the place of practise and its duration,

b) presents certification from the competent authorities or bodies of an EU Member State confirming her license in that country, and

c) presents a certificate issued by the competent authorities or bodies of an EU Member State confirming her diploma or other documents confirming her formal qualifications for general, specialised or dental practice.

A physician is obliged to continually improve her knowledge. Pursuant to art 11 of the Law on the Professions of Physicians and Dentists, if the Regional Medical Council ascertains that there is reasonable evidence to suggest that a physician is not professionally prepared, it may appoint a commission composed of physicians with appropriate medical qualifications which will issue its opinion on the vocational preparation of the relevant physician. The Regional Medical Council, acting upon the opi- **30**

---

19 Art 15 of the Law on the Professions of a Physician and a Dentist Physician.

nion of the commission, may compel the physician to take supplementary training. The latter has a right to participate in the session of the Regional Medical Council when her case is heard.

B. Tort Liability

9. Fundamentals of tort liability

31 In Poland, the general provisions of Book 3 of the Civil Code of 1964 (Obligations) apply to contracts, torts and other types of obligations. These common rules concern: causation, scope of damages, assessment of damages, reparation for damages other than personal injury, and contributory negligence. Torts are regulated in Chapter VI of the Code.[20] The law of tort, established primarily by the 1933 Code of Obligations, underwent minimal change under the socialist regime. After 1990, the main revisions concerned the liability of public authorities, strict product liability, and the rules governing recovery for non-pecuniary loss in non-personal injury cases. The first mentioned modification has had the greatest impact on the grounds of liability for medical malpractice (see D72).

32 In general, the Polish system of civil liability is based on three principles: fault, risk and equity. A specific norm must be met for strict liability causes of action, whereas the general requirement of liability is fault. Equity (fairness) is provided for in three cases only and is regarded as subsidiary. The division between liability for one's own acts and liability for those of others is of course recognised in the jurisprudence, but there is no such formal division in the Code.

33 The factual elements of the cause of action in tort are the same as (or similar to) those laid down in other systems of codified law, namely:

a) the victim must have suffered damage,

b) there must have been a factual occurrence on which the law bases the right to recover, and

c) there must be a causal connection between the first two elements (established according to the adequate causation theory).

---

20 The literal translation of the Polish term *czyny niedozwolone* is 'prohibited conduct' (in plural) and it corresponds to the German *unerlaubte Handlung*. It is a technical term only, ie it extends to all cases of liability based on fault, on risk and equity.

Pursuant to art 361 § 2 of the KC the scope of reparable damage comprises *damnum emergens* and *lucrum cessans*, both of which must be established in accordance with the theory of differentiation and the adequate causation test (art 361 § 1 of KC). Pecuniary loss is to be compensated in every case, while non-pecuniary loss is compensable only when it is permitted by the law. As in other legal systems, damages are to restore the victim to the position in which she would have been if the wrong complained of had not been committed. At the same time, the amount of damages may not exceed the scope of damage or enrich the injured party. Personal injury is regulated in more detail in the chapter on torts (arts 444–449 of KC). **34**

In Poland, the general clause of liability for one's act (fault) is expressed in art 415 of the KC which provides that 'whoever by his fault caused a damage to another person shall be obliged to redress it'. As used in art 415 of the KC, the term 'fault' refers to a deviation from the required standard of care. The departure from the required standard of care does not need to be egregious in order for liability to be imposed. Any degree of departure – even *culpa levissima* – is enough for liability to be found and damages assessed.[21] The standard against which a professional tortfeasor's conduct is measured is objective, ie the comparison is with the conduct that would be expected of a professional of the given type, not with that of the individual tortfeasor herself. As to vicarious liability see no 50. **35**

Art 361 § 1 of the KC stipulates that 'the person obliged to pay compensation is liable only for the normal effects of the act or omission from which the damage resulted (...)'.This is known as the principle of 'adequate causation'. Adequate causation plays two roles in the Polish civil law: the role of establishing the premise of liability (causal link between the damage and the harmful event) and the role of limiting damages. The latter becomes particularly important for the redress of lost profits. The courts use objective criteria flowing from life experience and science for the establishment of adequate causation. **36**

10. Burden of proof

The burden of proof of a loss and causation is principally on the claimant (patient), pursuant to the rule of art 6 of the KC. **37**

21 See G *Bieniek*, Commentary of the Civil Code, vol I (Warsaw 2002) 226; SN 10 October 1975, ICR 656/75 (unpublished).

38 Many cases show that harm suffered by a patient may be a result of medical malpractice or of a proper treatment for which the patient did not express her consent.[22] In particular, non-pecuniary loss may occur without the accompanying pecuniary damage, for instance when an operation was carried out on a patient's deteriorated organ without the patient's consent. In a case of 20 March 2002 (V CKN 909/00),[23] the Supreme Court ruled that mental and emotional trauma and distress caused to the plaintiff by the disclosure of contradicting information, due to diagnostic errors, followed by irreconcilable methods of treatment, may be regarded as a disturbance of health and justify the award of non-pecuniary damages. On the other hand, deterioration in health caused by a physician is not always considered as reparable damage. If it occurred despite a *lege artis* performance of a medical procedure which was necessary to rescue the patient's life (for instance an amputation of a leg), the decline in health will not be regarded as the patient's loss.

39 The rule in art 322 of the Code of Civil Procedure (*kodeks postępowania cywilnego*, CCP) provides: 'if in the case of a claim for damages a court deems that it is impossible or extremely difficult to prove accurately the amount of the claim, it may adjudicate a relevant amount of money in accordance with its evaluation based on the consideration of all circumstances of the case'. This rule may be viewed as the relaxation of the burden of proof concerning damage and is often applied to medical malpractice cases.

40 The causal relation between the physician's conduct and the patient's harm may be direct or indirect. Therefore, it makes no difference whether the cause is close or intermediate provided that the effect is within the limits of 'normal' results. Jurisprudence emphasises that the certainty of causation in medical malpractice cases is not required. It is possible to use 'probability of high degree' as the gauge of causation. Hence, it is necessary to determine to which degree the negligence of a physician is a probable cause of the harm sustained when compared to other factors (eg independent development of a disease). If there is a high degree of probability that the action or omission of a physician was the reason for the injury, the causation is established.

41 The answer to the question who bears the burden of proof of fault depends on the ground of liability (see C.16.61). In general, the injured patient

22 SN 14 October 2005 III CK 99/05 (unpublished), SN 21 September 1967, ICR 188/67, Przeglad Ustawodawstwa Gospodarczego 6/1968.

23 Przegląd Sądowy 4/2003.

must prove the physician's fault. This is done with reference to the facts which are essential for the adjudication of the claim. As this proof is frequently very difficult for the patient, it is particularly important to have a thorough evidential proceeding and a versatile consideration of all evidence gathered by the court. Medical documentation is a crucial exhibit. Jurisprudence holds that possible defects in the medical documentation that cannot be removed may not be used in the process to the disadvantage of the patient. Although it is up to the parties to indicate the means of evidence, a court may also admit evidence that was not offered (art 232 of the CCP). A court shall comprehensively consider the whole collected evidence (art 233 § 1 of the CCP), not limiting itself to a passive rephrasing of experts' opinions, and adjudicate in accordance with the principle of free assessment of evidence.

The Court may avail itself of any evidence, both direct and certain as well **42** as indirect, which has a significant degree of probability. It can recognise as established the facts which have crucial importance for the adjudication of the case, if such a conclusion may be drawn from other established facts (art 231 of CCP). Hence, the physician may be presumed culpable based on the presumption of facts if no contradictory evidence exists. A number of cases illustrate this approach. For example, a court may deem that leaving foreign objects in the patient's body (*res ipsa loquitur*) or the damage inflicted as the result of lack of the safety of treatment (for instance infecting a patient with a contagious disease) is a presumed negligence of the physician. The exculpatory proof burdens the physician or the health care institution.

11. Uncertain causation

As mentioned above, the certainty of causation in medical malpractice **43** cases is not required in order to establish liability. In order to determine the scope of damage, it is necessary to compare the condition the patient would have enjoyed had the physician not failed to deliver appropriate treatment with the condition which arose as a result of this malpractice.

The independent development of a patient's disease which has a negative **44** impact on her health shall also be taken into account when establishing the scope of liability. Nevertheless, the so called 'egg-shell scull' theory is disputed in Polish legal academic writing. There are many supporters of the theory that a special susceptibility of a victim's psyche or body to an injury is not to be taken into account as a factor exempting the tortfeasor from liability. Hence, such a unique feature of a victim does not exclude the possibility of accepting the adequate causation between the damaging event and the loss.

45 A few rules regarding uncertain causation have been developed in jurisprudence. Firstly, the evidence that some other reasons (apart from the physician's negligence) could, but not necessarily did, cause the patient's injury does not release the physician from liability. Secondly, the increased risk of treatment (ie the risk dependent on the patient's condition) does not exempt the physician from liability if at least one of the reasons behind the occurrence of the injury was his negligent conduct. In a case of 11 January 1972, the Supreme Court held: 'If the fatal result of an operation was preceded by negligence of the surgeon or of any other functionary of the health care institution, the court may deem, on the grounds of factual assumption, that there is a normal causal connection between these neglects and the patient's death, unless there were reasons to conclude that the principles of medicine excluded such a connection'.[24]

12. Loss of a chance

46 In Polish law compensation covers actual harm, future harm which is certain to occur as well as harm which can be foreseen at the moment of adjudication. If at the time the damage cannot be assessed precisely, the court may issue a declaratory judgment proclaiming the defendant's liability for future damage.[25] This is particularly justified in the case of minors.

47 A claim for a loss of chance has not yet been approved of by Polish academic opinion. Courts, on the other hand, often award damages for a lost chance under the head of an annuity (eg in a case of the loss of future prospects) or in the form of compensation of non-pecuniary loss. For example in the case where a patient lost capacity to have more children as a result of medical malpractice during the first child's delivery, the court awarded compensation for a 'loss of a chance to give birth to a child'.[26] In the judgment of 17 June 2009,[27] the Supreme Court ruled that negligent omissions of the health care providers can lead to damages that take the form of lost or reduced changes for healing or improvement of the health

---

24 SN I CR 516/71, OSN 1972, at 159.

25 SN 7 August 1969, OSN 1970, at 217.

26 SN 1 September 1978, CR 510/77, OSN 11/1978, at 210.

27 IV CSK 37/09, Orzecznictwo Sądów Polskich (Decisions of the Polish Courts, OSP) 9/2010, item 93, Cmt by *M Nesterowicz*, OSP 9/2010, 657.

condition. The standard of proof in such cases is a sufficient degree of probability. In this case a minor lost his chance to reduce the disability for which no-one was to blame. He was diagnosed with cerebral palsy and epilepsy in December 1999. The early signs of the disease, reported by the mother shortly after his birth in 1998, were either ignored or misdiagnosed by the attending doctors. If cerebral palsy had been diagnosed at an early stage, the effectiveness of rehabilitation could have been 20 % higher. The adequate causation between the negligent delay in discovering the cause of the disability and the lost chance of improvement through rehabilitation was established. The minor plaintiff was entitled to both compensation for non-pecuniary loss and an annuity.

13. Multiple persons involved

Art 441 § 1 of the KC lays down a general rule of joint and several liability in all cases where more than one person is liable for the damage arising from a tort. The basic requirements of the article are: the tortious infliction of damage, the sameness of the damage for which all the persons are liable, and the causal relation between the damage and the tortious event, for which each of the joint tortfeasors bears liability. The notion of 'the same damage' refers both to pecuniary and non-pecuniary loss. It means damage that is one and indivisible. Damage is still 'the same' even if it has occurred at different consecutive times and in different forms (for example personal injury that causes several losses, eg a loss of the capacity to work justifying a claim for an annuity, costs of treatment and non-pecuniary loss). Where multiple parties are responsible for the damage, it does not matter whether the actions of one party were direct or indirect or whether one party is more responsible or blameworthy than the other. As a principle, in cases where more than one person caused the damage, the degree of liability of individual persons is not to be identified or differentiated in the main lawsuit.[28] **48**

In order to determine all the persons who should be allocated joint and several liability, it is critical that the law imposes tort liability on all of them, whether as a direct tortfeasor or through vicarious liability or for aiding, abetting or consciously taking benefit from the damage caused to other persons. **49**

28 See M *Nesterowicz/E Bagińska*, Multiple Tortfeasors under Polish Law, in: WVH Rogers (ed), Unification of Tort Law: Multiple Tortfeasors (2004) 153, 156.

50 A hospital is liable both for its own fault and for the fault of its medical staff. If damage was the result of acts or omissions by a physician or other medical staff, the health care institution in question is vicariously liable for a 'subordinate' in accordance with art 430 of the KC (the liability is based on risk, but the fault of the physician is the condition of liability). A physician may be deemed a subordinate for this purpose because she is subject to the organisational management of a health care institution where she performs her services for the institution, even if she has her own interest therein. The professional independence of a physician with reference to the medical arts is not incompatible with the organisational subordination status arising from her employment in a health care institution.

51 In reality, however, a medical care entity is the only party that bears civil liability for the loss inflicted by an employed physician who commits medical malpractice or other negligence. Pursuant to the provisions of the Labour Code (*kodeks pracy*, 1974) if an employee causes damage to a third party while performing her duties, the employer is solely obliged to redress the damage (art 120 §1). This provision applies to a hospital regardless of whether it is a public health care institution, a physicians' co-operative or a private clinic. This means that the victim cannot file her claims in court against the physician, but exclusively against the health care institution which is obliged to redress the damage in accordance with the provisions of the Civil Code.

52 According to case law the above rule contained in art 120 of the Labour Code abrogates the direct liability of an employee unless one of the following three exceptions applies: (i) the damage was caused by an intentional fault, (ii) the employer is insolvent or under-insured, or (iii) the damage was not inflicted in the course of employment, but 'on the occasion' of employment.

53 A medical institution (employer) has the right of recourse against the physician. The recourse in the labour relations is limited to the equivalent of three months earnings of an employee unless the latter inflicted the damage intentionally, in which case the employer, after having paid the damages, may claim full recourse.

54 The limited employee liability does not relate to physicians who are not employed pursuant to an employment contract, but on the basis of a civil law contract (similar to mandate). Such physicians incur full tortious liability for damage inflicted while treating patients (art 415 of KC), which is joint and several with the health care institution (art 441 of KC).

A physician who only 'rents' a surgery theatre from a hospital for a given procedure is fully liable for her conduct and the conduct of her assistants. That said, however, the hospital may still be held liable for the 'organisational' and sanitary part of the service. 55

14. Strict liability

No-fault liability is only applicable to public hospitals under exceptional circumstances. It may be applicable in the context of public authorities' liability. Health care institutions, however, rarely exercise *imperium*. They do so when they, for example, refuse a special procedure such as prenatal examinations guaranteed by law or a legally justified abortion. Other examples include the failure to provide first aid services to patients calling at a hospital, ordering the isolation and quarantine of patients suspected of contagious disease and obligatory vaccinations as well as compelling admission to public psychiatric hospitals and the treatment of accused and convicts (including prisoners in prison health establishments). In all of these cases liability may be based on unlawfulness of the conduct or on fairness (see D). 56

The liability for pharmaceuticals is subject to the regime of product liability (art 449^{1-11} of KC). The liability for blood transfers and the use of technical equipment is subject to general rules (hence, fault liability). 57

C. Contractual Liability

15. Basics of contracts in the health care sector

We should begin with the rule that an insured patient does not conclude a contract with a public health care institution as he has a right to be treated on the grounds of his health insurance (and within its scope). 58

A patient may contract for private health care with a physician having a private practice, a physicians' co-operative or a medical care establishment (hospital, laboratory, etc). It is typically a contract for the provision of medical services (art 750 of KC) to which the corresponding provisions on the contract of mandate (art 734 of KC) apply. The physician is obliged to treat the patient on the terms defined in the contract. She is subject to the general obligations applicable to all physicians because of her profession as well as additional, contractual obligations (for instance the duty to care for the patient, home visits etc). There are no specific common features of 59 contracts between patients and service providers. Privately financed health care is usually aimed at a better care, more modern medical tests and painless diagnostics. The highly specialised procedures, however, are presently available only through a public system (usually at medical universities) or contracted abroad.

60 Contracts concluded by service providers with the Health Fund or with the public health care establishments are heavily regulated with the view to provide transparency and undistorted competition. The most problematic issue is the cap payment for the services contracted for a given year (especially when hospitals are under a statutory duty to not refuse the admission of patients coming to hospital in life-threatening situations).

16. Differences to tort law

61 The liability of a privately contracted physician or a medical care institution is contractual (art 471 of KC) in conjunction with tortious liability (art 415 of KC). Courts have long established that inflicting bodily injury on a person always constitutes a tort. If failure to perform or the improper performance of an existing obligation constitutes at the same time a tort, the debtor may be liable either *ex contractu* or *ex delicto*. This is a consequence of the concurrence of contractual and tortious liability (art 443 of KC). The victim has a choice between the contractual or delictual basis of their claim. Hence, the source of civil liability of a physician may be either a tort or a contractual obligation between a physician in private practice and the patient (or between a patient and a medical care establishment).

62 In the contractual regime the debtor's fault is presumed (art 471 of KC). A hospital is liable both for its own fault and for the negligent or intentional conduct of its medical staff. In the latter case, a health care institution is strictly liable for the people that it uses to perform its obligations (art 474 of KC – a contractual action). The major difference with a tort action (for a subordinate in accordance with art 430 of KC) lies in the burden of proof of the physician's fault, which is shifted to the defendant in an action *ex contractu*, whereas the standard of care is the same, unless explicitly agreed otherwise.

63 A contractual exclusion of the physician's liability or its limitation to a certain degree of fault is deemed invalid. All clauses aimed at the exclusion or reduction of liability for personal injury violate the principles of fairness (art 58 § 2 of KC) and/or are deemed unfair (art 385 point 1 of KC).

Finally, it should be underlined that a claim for non-pecuniary loss damages is not available under the contractual regime (see no 91). There are also significant differences in respect of prescription periods. **64**

17. Contractual claims in the absence of direct contracts?

In the absence of a direct contract with a patient, a medical care institution employing medical staff is liable for any damage caused by its staff on the tort basis arising from liability for subcontractors (art 429 of KC) or for a subordinate (art 430 of KC). In the latter case the negligence of a member of staff may be based on violations of contractual duties. However, Polish case law accepts the concept of 'anonymous fault' of an unidentified worker or public servant. It has been developed and applied regularly in medical malpractice cases.[29] Accordingly, it is irrelevant which of the physicians or nurses caused damage as long as the damage is causally linked with a breach of professional duties and occurs in the course of the performance of a health care service. **65**

Correspondingly, a health care institution also bears liability in tort when damage results from an improper organisation of the services, lack of qualified staff, insufficient skills of staff, inappropriate conditions for surgeries or other treatment, as well as in other cases related to a flawed organisation of the process of treatment (ie violations of the contract with the Health Fund). This is a 'fault in organisation' which should be attributed to the relevant health care institution. This is regarded as a legal person's own fault (art 416 of KC). **66**

18. Informed consent

The Law on the Professions of Physicians and Dentists deals with the obligation of informed consent in arts 31–34. The Act imposes a duty on physicians to furnish a patient (or his statutory representative) with clear information regarding the state of her health, suggested or possible diagnoses and treatment, foreseeable consequences of their application or non-application and prognosis (informed consent). This obligation, not included in the former Physicians' Profession Act of 1950, was largely neglected by physicians in previous years. Since 2009, the regulation of informed consent is also contained in arts 15 -19 of the Act of 6 November **67**

---

29 See *Nesterowicz* (fn 15) 338–347.

2008 on Patients' Rights and the Patient Ombudsman, hereafter the Patients' Rights Act.[30] The rules are further developed by the Code of Medical Ethics.

68 Generally, a patient's consent may be given orally or in any other way that indicates the patient's will without a doubt to submit to the proposed medical acts. However, according to art 34 of the Law on the Professions of Physicians and Dentists, a physician may only perform an operation or apply treatment or a diagnostic method that creates an increased risk for the patient after having obtained the latter's written consent. The positive law is not precise as to the consequences of the lack of written consent. Courts have adhered to the view that a patient's consent is a declaration of will similar to a juridical act, the effect of which is the elimination of unlawfulness of a physician's medical intervention. The Civil Code provisions relating to juridical acts, in particular with respect to defects and form, are applicable. Accordingly, the fact that the patient's consent to an operation was not given in writing does not give any grounds for the invalidation of the consent, but causes only evidential restrictions.

69 The physician is bound by the patient's declaration of will and cannot change the direction of acts, established methods or the object of the intervention beyond it. He can neither change nor widen the operating field. The Law on the Professions of Physicians regulates the complex issue of broadening the scope of surgery, that is the right of a physician to transgress the consent given by a patient. The physician's duty to comply with the scope of the patient's consent is a rule when a physician makes the right diagnosis and there are no unforeseen complications during the intervention. Nevertheless, there are medical cases when the proper diagnosis can only be made during the operation, or when unforeseen circumstances arise.

70 The Supreme Court has shaped the essence and scope of informed consent in numerous verdicts. It has held *inter alia* that supplying the patient with adequate information about the medical intervention risk and methods of treatment is the prerequisite for legitimacy of her informed consent to carry out a medical procedure. A physician cannot be required to warn a patient of all complications, in particular those which arise very rarely. The manner of informing the patient should correspond to the type of intervention.[31]

---

30 Dz U 2009, no 52, at 417 and no 76, at 641.

31 SN 28 August 1973, I CR 441/73, Orzecznictwo Sądów Polskich i Komisji Arbitrazowych (OSPiKA) 1974, at 123.

In general, a patient's consent does not mean consenting to any complications or negative results of the intervention, especially when the patient is not aware of the possibility of such complications. The operational risk which is taken by a patient when he expresses his consent to the intervention includes typical post-operational complications. Courts have consistently held that a physician should perform a surgery in compliance with medical art and the highest professional diligence. The patient's consent to the surgical procedure does not include complications arising from the physician's error.[32] 71

D. Public Liability

19. Key differences from cases involving private hospitals or doctors

Since 17 October 1997 (entry into force of art 77 sec 1 of the Constitution)[33] 72
the liability of public authorities is based on unlawfulness of their conduct. Art 417 § 1 of the KC expresses the general rule of liability for damage resulting from an unlawful exercise of public authority. New articles 417–417^2 of the KC came into force on 1 September 2004.[34] This change brought about the problem of classifying medical services as either acts of *imperium* or, alternatively, as *dominium*. Under the old law Polish courts avoided the troubling governmental/proprietary distinction,[35] and held public (state) hospitals liable on the basis of state liability, which was more favourable to the victim than the ordinary vicarious liability rules.[36] Under the present law the question arises whether and when a public health care establishment could be liable on the basis of the new rule that is, for the unlawful act of public authority. Most legal writers have accepted the view that a functional criteria should be applied in order to determine the nature of the conduct in question. This brings us to the conclusion that treatment and

32 SN 29 October 2003, III CK 34/02, Orzecznictwo Sądów Polskich (OSP) 4/2005, at 54.

33 According to art 77 'everyone shall have the right to compensation for any harm done to him by any action of an organ of public authority contrary to law'.

34 The Act of 17 June 2004 (Dz U no 162, at 1692).

35 In a judgment of 8 January 1965 II CR 2/65 (OSPiKA 1967, at 220) the Supreme Court adopted the concept of full liability of a health care institution (ie that of the State Treasury) for damage inflicted by a physician who is a public functionary while carrying out the act entrusted to him, and even so when the damage is the consequence of a culpable error in medical art.

36 Former arts 417–420 KC provided for the liability of the State for the fault of its functionaries, whereas medical professionals were regarded as functionaries.

diagnosis are not 'an exercise of public authority' and should be subjected to the general principles of civil liability.[37] Hence, 'common' torts of physicians employed by public hospitals trigger liability which is based on the same grounds as the liability of private hospitals in similar cases, ie on fault or risk, but not on fairness.[38]

73 No-fault liability, based on either art 417 of the KC (the main rule of strict public liability) or art 417[2] of the KC (the subsidiary principle of fairness), applies only exceptionally to public hospitals (see no 56). The requirement of unlawfulness encapsulates civil wrongfulness, which refers to a conduct contrary to the legal order, that is to statutory law and the principles of community life (fairness). The courts adopt the widest possible approach to wrongfulness, in particular in violations of patient rights cases.[39]

E. Alternative Compensation Regimes

20. Funds and/or other alternative compensation regimes

74 Such funds or alternative compensation regimes do not presently exist in Poland.

F. Extent of Liability/Remedies

I. Pecuniary Loss

21. Introduction to indemnifying pecuniary loss

75 Medical malpractice cases show no difference in the treatment of remedies. Various general rules apply.

76 According to doctrine and case law, art 361 § 2 of the KC establishes the principle of full compensation. The rule reads: 'In the absence of contrary provisions of a contract or law, redressing of the damage includes losses which the injured incurred (*damnum emergens*) and lost profits (*lucrum cessans*)'. The notion of pecuniary damage is based on the theory of

37 See E *Bagińska*, Odpowiedzialność odszkodowawcza za wykonywanie władzy publicznej [Liability for damage caused by exercise of public authority] (2006) 204.

38 See eg Regional Court in Lublin 4 April 2002, I C 656/99, Prawo i Medycyna (PiM) 3/2004.

39 See eg SN 29 October 2003, III CK 34/02, OSP 4/2005, at 54.

difference: damage is the difference between what the victim would have had at her disposal (with respect to the values affected by the damage) if the event which caused the damage had not occurred, and what she actually has at her disposal in consequence of this event.

In accordance with art 363 § 2 of the KC the scope of the damages will be assessed with reference to the prices current on the day of their determination, unless particular circumstances demand that prices in force on another day be adopted as the basis. As mentioned earlier, compensation should also cover future harm which is certain to occur as well as harm which can be foreseen at the moment of adjudication. **77**

With reference to personal injury, there is a list of heads of damage eligible for compensation that can be drawn from arts 444–446 of the KC: **78**

(a) Claims of the directly injured: 1) A general rule: in the case of bodily injury or a disturbance of health, the redress of damage covers all resulting costs (art 444 § 1 of the KC). This includes all necessary and suitable expenses causally linked to the injury (cost of treatment, special diet etc). **79**

2) A claim for annuity: Pursuant to art 444 § 2 of the KC, if a victim completely or partially loses her ability to work or if her needs have increased or her future prospects have been diminished, she may demand an appropriate annuity from the person obliged to redress the damage. Any of the above conditions, whether alone or concurrent with others, constitutes a sufficient ground for the claim. However, according to case law, annuity based on the loss of earning capacity or on the loss of future prospects may not be awarded to a minor. **80**

(b) Claims of the close persons (family members) in the case of the victim's death (victims *par ricochet*) – art 446 of the KC: 1) Refund of the costs of treatment and the funeral to the person who has incurred them (art 446 § 1 of KC). This claim does not belong to the estate of the deceased, but is an autonomous claim of the person who incurred the expenses, unless the costs were paid by the injured herself. **81**

2) A mandatory annuity may be demanded by a person to whom the deceased had the statutory maintenance duty (provided for in the Code of Family Law of 1964) computed in relation to the needs of the injured and to the earning and financial capacities of the deceased for the time of the likely duration of the said duty (art 446 § 2 sentence 1 of KC). **82**

83 3) An optional annuity may be claimed by other related persons (eg a life partner or a family member to whom the deceased owed no duty of support) to whom the deceased voluntarily and permanently supplied maintenance if it follows from the circumstances that this is required by the principles of community life (art 446 § 2 sentence 2 of KC). The nature of claims for an annuity is compensatory; they are not a type of maintenance claim. The persons are entitled to enforce those claims *sui generis*, thus the cause of action is independent of the rights of the directly injured and of the pecuniary and non-pecuniary loss compensation that she receives. If the directly injured person, while still alive, relinquishes or settles the claims, these acts will have no legal effect after her death.

84 4) A court may award the closest members of the family of the deceased an appropriate indemnity (a lump sum) if her death resulted in a considerable worsening of their standard of living (art 446 § 3 of KC). This compensation covers those elements of pecuniary damage that are not taken into account in the award of an annuity.

22. Loss of earnings vs loss of earning capacity

85 When awarding an annuity to the victim of a personal injury (art 444 § 2 of KC) a court usually makes an overall assessment of different elements of pecuniary damage, including loss of earnings and loss of earning capacity. Polish courts emphasise that in a case of the diminution of working capacity the damage may not be purely theoretical. Some pecuniary consequences of the loss must be proven. Accordingly, this damage should be understood as the difference between what the victim could have received from her work if the damaging event had not occurred and what she will actually receive after this occurrence. The income of a victim after a damaging event is not to be compared to the pre-accident earnings or the lack of it, but to these she would have earned if there had been no accident. It is sufficient that the victim proves a high probability of receiving this income.[40]

86 An annuity must be 'appropriate'; the court enjoys a margin of discretion in the assessment of its extent. If at the moment of adjudication the damage cannot be accurately assessed, the injured person may be awarded a temporary annuity.

40 SN 30 January 2004, I CK 131/03, OSNC 2/2005, at 40.

23. Periodic payments or lump sum?

The payment of expenses, costs of treatment, damage to property, as well as non-pecuniary loss damages are awarded in a lump sum, but listed individually in the judgment. In particular, damages for pecuniary and non-pecuniary losses must always be listed as separate elements of an award. A court may not grant these two components of damage in one all-inclusive sum. **87**

Claims embracing reparation of the loss of future earnings and loss of working capacity or increased needs, based on arts 444 § 2 and 446 § 2 of the KC, are awarded in periodic payments. By way of exception, pursuant to art 447 of the KC, a court may for important reasons and upon the victim's request award a lump sum instead of an annuity or a part thereof. In particular, this applies to a case where the injured person became disabled and the award of a lump sum would help her to engage in another profession. The victim carries the burden of establishing the existence of 'important reasons'. The assessment of a lump sum is based on the annuity to which the plaintiff would be entitled. The payment of a lump sum must equate with the obligation to pay an annuity (hence, as long as the victim is entitled to an annuity he may request a lump sum). **88**

24. Caps and thresholds

In general, Polish tort law does not provide for liability caps. Any present limitation in respect of personal injury claims does not arise from national legislation, but originates in binding international conventions or EU directives. **89**

In Polish tort law there are no thresholds except for the € 500 threshold for product liability. **90**

II. Non-pecuniary Loss

25. Introduction to indemnifying non-pecuniary loss

In Polish law pecuniary loss is to be compensated in every case, while non-pecuniary loss is compensable only when it is permitted by the law. Apart from personal injury cases (where the victim may claim compensation for pain and suffering), other non-financial wrongs are also reparable (such as the violation of patients' rights or copyright infringements). Pursuant to **91** art 448 of the KC, in the case of infringement of personal interests the court may award an injured person an adequate sum as compensation for non-pecuniary loss or, if she so demands, award an appropriate sum for a designated social purpose, irrespective of other means necessary to eliminate the effects of the damage caused. However, non-pecuniary loss may not be compensated in the contractual regime unless the violation of a contract constitutes concurrently a tort (concurrence of liabilities).[41]

92 Damages for non-pecuniary loss play firstly a compensatory role as they purport to make good for the moral harm. Courts have recently rejected the criterion developed in the sixties and seventies, according to which the size of the award should reflect 'the current living conditions of an average member of society'. The present jurisprudence and legal scholars underline that this factor is only secondary and may not lead to the frustration of the compensatory function of damages for moral harm.[42] Courts award compensation for non-pecuniary loss according to its evaluation in the light of all circumstances of the case.[43]

93 One should note that in medical cases there may be two distinct basis for awarding non-pecuniary loss damages: (i) medical malpractice which inflicted pain and suffering (art 445 of the KC) and (ii) the infringement of a patient's right (art 4 of the Patients' Rights Act, in conjunction with art 448 of KC).[44] There has been some litigation recently regarding the relationship between these two bases of a claim. It has been held that art 445 of the KC aims at compensation for pain and suffering due to personal injury and that art 4 of the Patients' Rights Act protects dignity, privacy and the autonomy of a patient, regardless of the diligence and effectiveness of a medical intervention.[45]

94 The following are illustrative examples. A comatose victim (resulting from malpractice at birth, where the mother is the victim) who has no contact with the outside world and does not feel pain was awarded € 125,000 in

41 SN 17 December 2004, OSP 2/2006, at 20.

42 SN 30 January 2004, I CK 131/03, OSN 2/2005, at 40, SN 10 March 2006, IV CSK 80/05, OSP 1/2007, at 11.

43 See *E Bagińska/M Nesterowicz*, Non-Pecuniary Loss under Polish Law, in: WVH Rogers (ed), Damages for Non-Pecuniary Loss in a Comparative Perspective (2001) 176 ff.

44 Formerly art 19a of the MCE Act (in conj with art 448 KC). The Patients' Rights Act has not changed the main contents of the rules. It has simply collected the patient rights stated in MCE and other acts and confirmed a claim for compensation in art 4.

45 SN 29 May 2007, V CSK 76/07, OSN 7-8/2008, item 91, reported in *E Bagińska*, Poland, in: H Koziol/BC Steininger (eds), European Tort Law 2008 (2009) no 53 ff.

2008.[46] A 51-year old man who suffered serious injuries in a car accident and was declared 77 % disabled, with a complete, irreversible loss of working capacity and the loss of sexual functions, was awarded € 50,000 by the Court of Appeals (€ 100,000 by the court of first instance). The verdict was however reversed by the Supreme Court in 2008. A young girl who, after several months of inadequate treatment, suffered necrosis of parts of her skin and permanent scarring (50 % disability), was awarded (at the age of eleven) € 62,500 for non-pecuniary loss.[47]

26. Who can claim compensation for non-pecuniary loss?

The directly injured party has a pecuniary claim for non-pecuniary loss **95** stemming from bodily injury, ie for pain and suffering or from a breach of patient rights. The close persons (victims *par ricochet*) are entitled to compensation of the moral damage arising from the victim's death (art 446 § 4 of KC). The bereavement claim was introduced by the revision of the Civil Code on 30 May 2008.[48]

If the direct victim has survived there is no claim for non-pecuniary loss of **96** the close persons (such as one that is permitted in the Swiss law of obligations). They may demand damages only when their stress and other effects of the direct victim's injuries causes them personal injury (such as depression or other similar medically recognised conditions). It is sufficient to prove that the causative factor simply exacerbated an existing health disorder or increased physical suffering. However, although permanent health changes are not required, a slight and brief disorder will not support the claim.[49] As concerns psychiatric injury, Polish law does not set any special threshold for a qualifying claim.

46 The same amount of compensation was granted to a widow for the deterioration of her life due to the death of her husband in a car accident. See SN of 14 March 2007 I CSK 465/06, OSP 11/2008, item 123, cmt by M *Wałachowska*. On demand the Court of Appeals awarded PLN 500,000 (€ 125,000) with interest, which made a total of PLN 1 million (€ 250,000). The average awards in similar cases hover around PLN 200,000 (€ 40,000).

47 The Court of Appeal in Poznan, 23 November 2006, I ACa 561/06, PiM 2/2008, 140 cmt by *Nesterowicz*.

48 Dz U 2008, no 116, at 731. Compensation for the breach of a patient right to die in dignity is actually awarded to a social cause/charity (art 4.2 of the Patients' Rights Act).

49 SN 24 February 1969, ICR 438/69 (unpublished).

G. Procedural Matters

27. Specific rules of jurisdiction or procedure

97 With regard to procedural issues, one should note that there is no jury in the Polish system. The court will evaluate the evidence and decide both the issues of facts and the questions of law. No specific rules exist in respect of medical malpractice cases.

98 However, a class actions law was enacted in 2009[50] and became effective on 18 July 2010. The first Polish class action was filed in a case with over 400 patients infected with the hepatitis C virus via the administration of a drug. The class seeks approximately PLN 75 million (€ 18.7 million) in damages.

99 A class action may be brought only with respect to claims of consumer protection, claims based on product liability and claims based on tort law[51] (except for claims for the protection of personal rights). Hence, claims related to health care services may fall within the scope of this regime. A class action is allowed where single-type claims are asserted by at least 10 persons and are based on the same facts or on the same legal bases provided that material circumstances that substantiate the claim are common for all the claims. There is no maximum limit of claimants. However, with regard to claims for payment of money, all the group's members have to agree on the unified amount per person being claimed. Diversified amounts are still possible, provided that they are settled within subgroups of at least two persons. If claims are pecuniary, instead of demands for payment, the plaintiffs may demand that the court establishes the liability of the defendant (art 2). It is an opt-in procedure. The claimants must be defined (not anonymous) and they have to make a declaration of willingness to participate in the class action before the court. The regime of a class action does not exclude the right to pursue individual claims under the general rules of civil procedure.

---

50 The Act of December 17, 2009 on Pursuing Claims in Group Proceedings (Dz U 2010, no 7, item 44).

51 The distinction of product liability claims from tort claims is fake. Product liability claim is a tort claim under Polish law. Perhaps it is due to the fact that torts are regulated in Chapter VI and the product liability regime in Chapter VI prim of the Book Three of the Civil Code. Chapter VI prim implemented the EU Directive 374/85 (it was technically more convenient to create an additional chapter in the code).

28. Special institutions handling malpractice claims

There are no specific institutions designed to handle malpractice cases. **100**

H. Outlook

29. Reform plans

Opinio juris has strongly supported the introduction of alternative, compensatory schemes, in particular with respect to hospital infections, infections stemming from blood transfers, medical accidents and vaccinations.[52] The Swedish No-Fault Patient Insurance and the French model are regarded as the most suitable for Polish juridical, economic and social conditions. Finally, in November 2010, a governmental proposal for an alternative system of compensating patients' injuries – the Bill on the Revision of Act on Patients' Rights and Patient Ombudsman – was brought before the parliament (Bill no 3488). The draft has already met with strong criticism due to its general poor quality, several errors and inconsistencies with the Civil Code, very low compensation caps and an unreasonably limited scope of application. The government alleges to have been inspired by the Nordic (in particular Swedish) legislature and experience. However, as it stands, the draft Act is especially unfit to incorporate the system into the existing Act on Patients' Rights and Patient Ombudsman (2008), as the former has little to do with remedying patients' rights.[53] **101**

For the foregoing reasons only a brief layout of the proposed system should be given at this stage of the parliamentary process: **102**

It is an administrative system based on regional commissions consisting of lawyers and physicians in equal numbers (with a very low remuneration for the public service). The procedure is a hybrid form of mediation and arbitration; its maximum duration is three months. The costs are to be borne by a hospital or its insurer and in cases where the medical error is not established by the claimant. A patient has the choice to pursue the **103**

---

52 See *Nesterowicz* (fn 15) 377 ff; *K Bączyk-Rozwadowska*, Odpowiedzialność cywilna za szkody wyrządzone przy leczeniu [Liability for Medical Malpractice] (2007) 350 ff.

53 See *E Kowalewski/M Śliwka/M Wałachowska*, Kompensacja szkód wynikłych z błędów medycznych. Ocena projektowanych rozwiązań prawnych, Prawo i Medycyna 4 (2010) 22, *M Tenenbaum-Kulig*, Mechanizm pozasądowego uzyskiwania odszkodowania lub zadośćuczynienia za błąd medyczny w ujęciu projektu nowelizacji ustawy o prawach pacjenta i Rzeczniku Praw Pacjenta, Prawo i Medycyna 4 (2010) 40.

claims in court. A patient, his statutory representative or heirs, are entitled to file a claim (within a one year limitation period, maximum three years);

104 The alternative regime is only applicable to 'medical errors' as defined below, which are the result of the provision of medical services in a hospital (sole respondent). The scope of the regime is hence very limited and raises serious constitutional doubts. Hospitals have to take out compulsory insurance (it is not, however, clear, whether the Bill talks about third party insurance or first party insurance);

105 'Medical error' is narrowly defined, and, moreover, this definition is very specific. It includes:

a) contracting a contagious disease, or

b) inflicting personal injury or death as a result of the following conduct not complying with the current state of medical knowledge:

   i) improper or delayed diagnosis,

   ii) treatment,

   iii) application of a pharmaceutical or a medical product.

106 Fault (or subjective fault) as a condition of the liability of hospitals is eliminated (which is a clear advantage of the system);

107 A regional commission establishes whether the damaging event was a 'medical error' in the above meaning. The commission will not determine damage and causation;

108 Based on the positive decision of the commission the insurer has to make an offer of compensation to the claimant. The insurer is bound by the decision as to the determination of the medical error. The offer of compensation may not exceed the maximum sums provided in the draft, ie PLN 100,000 (€ 25,000) for personal injury or contracting a contagious disease, and PLN 300,000 (€ 75,000) in the case of death. It is not clear whether it is a maximum aggregate sum, or the caps apply separately to pecuniary and non-pecuniary losses. If the patient rejects the offer, he may still pursue the case in regular court proceedings. However, if he accepts it, then he has to renounce any further claims concerning the losses that have occurred until the filing of the motion to the commission;

109 If the insurer fails to make an offer, the patient is entitled to the sums sought, but not exceeding the caps. The decision of the commission has the force of a court judgment and can be enforced in the execution proceedings.

Cases

Case 1

Cases concerning delay in ordering a caesarean section at birth are a common subject of litigation in Poland. In the given scenario, where Y's damage is one and indivisible loss, a Polish court would hold doctor A jointly and severally liable with hospital C (which answers for D). See no 48. **110**

Both A and D were negligent in treating X. C is strictly liable for D's fault (art 430 of KC). The plaintiff did not establish that B's failure to diagnose a pre-existing condition could have been one of the causes of X's injury. Therefore, B should be exempted from liability. **111**

The Polish Supreme Court accepts indirect causation as sufficient to establish liability for medical malpractice. If negligence in medical treatment was a factor which contributed to the damage to a considerable degree, the case should be decided in the plaintiff's favour. A high degree of probability of a certain cause of the damage is necessary to determine the causal connection (see no 45). However, the Supreme Court in the recent judgment of 19 March 2008 (V CSK 491/07, not published) required proof of an unambiguous causation between the different impairments of the child borne through a delayed caesarean section and the conduct of the doctors. In that case, the plaintiff suffered from at least two ailments, one of which (nanocephaly) could have been a pre-birth condition (the pre-existence of which it is not possible to prove). **112**

All of Y's claims for pecuniary losses are valid under Polish law. **113**

X may not demand compensation for herself for the personal care that she has provided to Y. Pursuant to art 444 § 2 of the KC, if the victim's needs have increased (eg permanent expenses for treatment or care or assistance by third persons), she may demand an appropriate annuity from the person obliged to redress the damage. An annuity for increased needs is generally to cover future expenses. The defendant must pay compensation in the form of an annuity regardless of any other person's existing commitment to supply the victim with means of maintenance. However, if the care and assistance by third persons have already been given, the court must award this compensation as outstanding annuity. The claim should be awarded *to the victim* on the basis of art 444 § 1 of the KC as this loss (although suffered directly by the family members) is considered to be causally linked with her personal injury. **114**

115 As regards non-pecuniary loss, Y's damage is reparable on the ground of art 445 § 1 of the KC. Presently, a birth-related injury may trigger successful non-pecuniary claims as high as PLN 500,000 = (€ 125,000) (compared to PLN 150,000 = € 37,500 at most in the previous decade). X may only claim compensation for the distress arising from the still birth of her son (art 446 § 4 of the KC), but not for the distress stemming from the serious injury suffered by her daughter. In the first situation X could successfully claim between PLN 30,000 and 70,000 (€ 7,500 – €17,500).

Case 2

116 No similar case can be found in Polish case law. I believe that the doctor would not be liable for X's losses unless his negligence was established.

117 In general, a physician is not liable for the harmful effects of pharmaceutical treatments. However, if she prescribes a medicine to a patient without knowing its properties or side effects in a case where she could and should have been aware of them, she will be liable for any interaction that causes damage. The liability also arises in the case where a highly toxic medicine, unnecessary for the patient, was prescribed by a doctor who should have known that this could cause undesirable side effects.

Case 3

118 The defendants A and C should be held jointly and severally liable for the entire loss. A's fault in an early discharge of X, despite his high risk condition, is patent. This conduct was in clear breach of established knowledge and therefore wrongful and negligent. Several Polish decisions show examples of wrongfulness arising from the negligence of a hospital regarding the duty to perform complex tests on newborn children during the first week of their lives. The duty is imposed on the hospital where the delivery took place. Failure to fulfil this obligation and to reveal the results of the tests, as well as to inform the parent(s) of the test results, giving rise to the occurrence and development of a disease, merit compensation.[54]

119 The organisational fault of clinic C has been established. X's damage is one and indivisible and there is a high probability that this damage was

54 See Court of Appeals in Katowice, I AC 562/05 (unpublished) – concerning screening examination towards phenulketonuria (Folling's disease), cited by *Kalus* (fn 15) 67.

sustained in the clinic. C is also vicariously liable for B's, D's and E's fault. B's conduct was objectively incorrect and fell below the standards of medical practice. Failure to provide assistance to a patient or a delay in performing a medical procedure is a doctor's negligence. The Law on the Profession of Physicians and Dentists states that a physician is obliged to provide medical aid in any case where a delay in its provision could result in a threat of a loss of life, severe bodily injury or a severe health disorder, and in all urgent cases (art 30).

The defendants B, C and E are liable in recourse towards their employer C **120**
(see no 51).

As regards the claim for loss of capacity to earn, it is not relevant at this **121**
stage, as X is a small child. In such cases Polish courts award an annuity on the basis of increased needs and establish liability for the future damage. When the victim reaches maturity, he/she may claim compensation for the loss of capacity to earn.

Case 4

The facts demonstrate the violation of the patient's right to informed **122**
consent.

In this case the risk of complications was linked with the procedure, but in **123**
the absence of fault, the doctor/hospital are not answerable for the effects of the realisation of this risk (see no 71).

However, there is a direct relation between the lack of informed consent **124**
and the creation of liability of physicians and hospitals. The culpable character of a physician's conduct does not have to consist of a medical error. Liability in informed consent cases may arise regardless of whether a physician acted in accordance with the latest medical developments.[55] In such cases a patient may demand compensation for non-pecuniary loss arising from the culpable violation of his right to informed consent based on art 4 of the Patients' Rights Act and art 448 of the KC (see no 93).

The core question here is whether X's consent was valid. I am inclined to **125**
say that it was not. There are two elements: 'consent' and 'informed', which together form a necessary condition for the lawfulness of a physician's act. Nesterowicz emphasises that a patient has a right to 'know the

55 See *M Nesterowicz/E Baginska/A den Exter*, Poland, Medical law, in: International Encyclopaedia of Laws (2002) 62 ff.

truth' as befits her intelligence, mental condition, sensitivity, as well as the necessity and urgency of the relevant medical procedure.[56] As mentioned above in no 68, the statutory provisions are not explicit as to the burden of proving that a duty to inform a patient was fulfilled. First, the general rule in art 6 of the KC applies: 'the burden of proof relating to a fact rests on the person who attributes legal consequences to that fact'.[57] Both Polish jurisprudence and doctrine dictate that since it is the doctor who has the duty to provide information to a patient, she thus also has the burden of proving that she has fulfilled her obligation. The illegality of a medical intervention is lacking only when a physician provides convincing evidence of sufficient and full instructions to her patient.[58] In my opinion, X has proven that before the operations were performed he had not been informed in a proper manner of the scope and degree of the risks. Hence without this awareness, he could not have given an informed consent (see no 70).

126 The plaintiff seeking damages in a tort regime bears the burden of proving that her damage was caused by the negligent conduct of the doctor acting as a servant in the meaning of art 430 of the KC. The latter's negligence, imputable to the defendant hospital, is a breach of the duty to undertake a medical intervention after a patient's informed consent has been properly obtained. This condition of liability has been met in this case, hence X is entitled only to damages for non-pecuniary loss due to the fact that he was ill-informed. The ground for his claim is art 4 of the Patients' Rights Act and art 448 of the KC. As to the amount of compensation, reference can be made to a similar case decided by the Court of Appeals in Warsaw.[59] The court established the hospital's liability for the lack of informed consent to a cardiac surgery, during which the patient suffered a stroke. The information of the risk of the stroke was not communicated to the patient. No medical error was established. The patient, who became disabled due to the neurological damage, claimed PLN 250,000 (€ 62,000), the Regional Court awarded PLN 50,000 as damages for moral harm, but the sum was doubled on appeal (final award € 25,000). In the assessment of the damage the Court took account of the

56 See *Nesterowicz* (fn 15) 146 ff.

57 SN 17 December 2004, II CK 303/04, OSP 11/2005, item 131, reported in *Bagińska* (fn 16) no 38 ff.

58 Note by *M Świderska*, OSP 11/2005, 13.

59 13 June 2007, VI ACa 1246/06, Orzecznictwo Sądów Apelacyjnych [Decisions of the Courts of Appeal] 12/2009, item 64, noted by M Świderska, Przegląd Sądowy 11 (2010) 201.

extent of the permanent injuries that the plaintiff suffered, in particular the deterioration of his mental condition.

In other cases that involved a breach of a patient's right, the awards of a non-pecuniary loss are typically lower: 127

- PLN 10,000 (€ 2,500) for the violation of the duty of medical confidentiality;[60]
- PLN 60,000 (€ 15,000) was awarded to the mother as compensation for the violation of her right to information and to prenatal tests and PLN 30,000 (€ 7,500) to the father as compensation for the infringement of his right to plan a family and for burdening him with the obligation to raise a second handicapped child – wrongful birth case.[61]

Case 5

In this case negligence is a condition of the hospital's liability. However, 128 the impossibility in determining the direct wrongdoer, or which of the medical staff in question committed the error, does not release the hospital from liability if it is proved that there was negligence and that consequently the patient incurred damage. In such a case, the Polish courts assign 'anonymous fault' to the hospital.[62] Moreover, A should also bear liability for fault in organisation of services because it permitted a situation in terms of which only one chief resident was available to supervise numerous surgeries simultaneously. It is established case law that a health care institution is liable for entrusting an operation to a physician who has either insufficient experience or who acts without any supervision or to a physician not specialised in a given field. A hospital is also liable for restraining physicians in their choice of medical or technical measures when these could have an impact on the effects of a medical procedure, as well as for failing to appoint sufficient medical staff to assist a physician.

I believe none of the doctors involved was individually negligent and the 129 right of recourse will thus not arise.

---

60 SN 12 June 2008, III CSK 16/08, OSNC 3/2009, item 48, reported in E *Bagińska*, Poland, in: H Koziol/BC Steininger (eds), European Tort Law 2009 (2010) no 51 ff.

61 Court of Appeals in Białystok 4 July 2008, I ACa 278/08, PiM 2/2009, noted by M *Nesterowicz*, 126.

62 SN 26 May 1994, II CRN 244/94, SN 17 April 1974 II CR 133/74, OSPiKA 1974, item 207, the Regional Court in Lublin 4 April 2002, IC 656/99, PiM 3/2004, 122, reported in *Bagińska* (fn 16) no 55.

130 As to the burden of proof see no 42.

131 X's claims embrace pecuniary loss including the loss of income and the cost of the medical opinion (as there was no duty to commission the opinion from the medical council).

132 As regards the method of calculating an annuity for X:

133 a) A partial loss of working capacity due to a personal injury raises a claim for an annuity. In a case of the diminution of working capacity damage consists of the difference between what X could have received from his work if the accident had not occurred and what he will actually be able to receive after the accident using his diminished working capacity (in addition to the social benefits). Any further damage resulting from the inability to find employment (provided that the victim wishes to make use of his limited working capacity) may be regarded as consequential damage. However, the Supreme Court has denied compensation of this damage. It held that the lack of employment opportunities arising from the state of the job market is not in an adequate causal relation with the tortfeasor's conduct.[63] An annuity is not to compensate the income lost because of inability to find a suitable job. In the cited case, the court of first instance awarded a partial annuity compensating the income that was not gained due to the lack of job opportunities; the Court of Appeals, however, changed the verdict in this respect and dismissed the claim (the Supreme Court confirmed).

134 b) Polish case law requires that one takes into account only income from legal sources and not income that is received in violation of the law, is corrupt (*lucrum illicitum vel inhonestum*) or that contravenes the principles of justice. It is not always clear, however, what kinds of income fall within these categories. There is no doubt, for example, that profits received from criminal acts, ie acts in violation of penal law (such as drug trafficking, dealing in stolen property, pandering, and corruption) fall into this category.[64] Opinions are divided, however, as to income obtained in violation of administrative, taxation or social security law, and in particular as to earnings received in the 'grey' labour market. In the case of 20 January 2004 the Supreme Court included the latter in the annuity.[65]

---

63 SN 4 June 2003, II UK 296/02 (unpublished).

64 A commercial court (GKA) in the judgment of 28 January 1986 (DO-9139/85, OSPiKA 1987, at 102) held that if a fishing company did not have an administrative license to use waters for fishing activities for a certain period it cannot demand compensation of lost profits caused by the pollution of its ponds and inability to breed fish in that period.

65 II CK 360/02 unpublished.

However, on similar facts, the Court of Appeals in Białystok in the judgment of 18 September 2002 ruled to the contrary.[66] It held that the regular illicit earnings which the deceased victim received in 'the grey zone' may not increase the quantum of damages. The Court stated that failure to pay a personal income tax is a fiscal criminal offence.[67]

Case 6

Assuming that the joint practice is a private practice and provides services on a contractual basis, both A and B are jointly and severally liable for E, C and D on the basis of art 474 of the KC. The claims for personal injury may also be based on tort, in which case the grounds of joint and several liability are arts 430 and 441 of the KC. **135**

E should have known that when suffering from hay fever he should have no contact with patients. Even though the doctors C and D could not have recognized the bacteria infection of their assistant, they should have observed his hay fever and taken necessary precautions. Hence, their negligence appears to be established. **136**

Since X's needs have increased (*inter alia* she now has to employ a cleaning assistant), she is entitled to an annuity (art 444 § 2 of the KC). This part of the damage is described as the emergence of a need to bear expenses (eg the cost of a special diet, of an additional nursing aid). The tortfeasor must pay compensation in the form of an annuity regardless of any other person's existing commitment to supply the victim with care, assistance or means of maintenance. In the cases where a family member renders care personally the courts limit the damages to the cost of nursing and care that would have to be paid if the care could have been rendered by a professional third party.[68] If we apply this rule to cleaning assistance, X should be entitled to an annuity as long as the said expenses stem from her personal injury and are justified in a given situation, regardless of whether they have actually been incurred by X. Hence, the value of the daughter's cleaning (household) services, assuming that they can be regarded as additional personal care to her mother, will be compensated **137**

66 I ACa 399/02, OSAB 2003, at 7.

67 Accordingly, in earlier case law the Supreme Court held that if legal provisions prohibited a pensioner from earning money in excess of certain amount (resulting in the suspension of the social pension), this element if his income would not be compensated. See SN 6 June 1968, I CR 148/68, OSNC 11/1969, at 199.

68 SN judgment of 4 October 1973, II CR 365/73, OSNC 9/1974, item 147.

under Polish law. The need for future cleaning assistance should be assessed as an element of an annuity and the assistance that has already been given by X's daughter since X's infection is an outstanding annuity. X also has a claim for compensation of non-pecuniary loss resulting from the mere infection (which is deemed damage without the necessity of its developing into a disease). However, the cost of personal care provided to X's mother is not a compensable damage as long as it is not linked to additional expenses (the causation is too remote). X has a claim for compensation of non-pecuniary loss resulting from the mere infection (which is deemed damage without the necessity of its developing into a disease).

Variation 1

138 In principle, liability of medical institutions arises in cases of bad sanitary conditions, improper distribution of infected patients or violations of the principles of antiseptics. These circumstances are considered a fault in organisation. According to case law, a health care institution is obliged to exercise due diligence aimed at the protection of patients from the danger of infecting them with a contagious disease. If an infringement of this duty causes increased risk of infection, and the patient's contagious disease is related thereto, the health care institution bears liability for the damage incurred by the patient unless it presents evidence that the damage is a consequence of other circumstances.

Variation 2

139 In the reported 'infection cases' the courts ruled that in a situation where a patient was infected with a contagious disease or a virus (HBV, HCV, HIV or staphylococcus) in a hospital,[69] the latter may be exempted from liability only if it proves that there is a high probability of a different source of that damage.[70] Hence, a proof of a high probability of infection is sufficient where, given the lack of indication of the infection's sources, it is usually impossible to state with absolute certainty that the infection should be associated with a particular event.[71]

69 In Poland, more than 60 % of all persons infected with Hepatitis B virus (about 80 % of children under two years old), have been infected in a health care institution.

70 The Provincial Court in Bydgoszcz 29 December 1993, IC 298/92 (unpublished).

71 The Court of Appeals in Katowice I ACa 252/06 (unpublished), cited by *Kalus* (fn 15) 65.

Polish courts hold that requiring the injured person to prove a direct causality between the conduct which increased the risk of infection and the infection with the contagious disease would result in insurmountable evidential difficulties for the injured person.[72] Accordingly, the Court of Appeals in Wroclaw held that a plaintiff has proven causation by showing that when entering the hospital he was not infected with any virus and that he could not have contracted it anywhere else because of the poor quality of his personal life.[73] Doctrine is in accordance with this and emphasises the significance of the judicial practice.[74] Nesterowicz also encourages the use of the presumption of fact (art 231 of the CCP) that an infection was acquired in the hospital. This in turn creates a presumption of negligence and causation which are sufficient to establish liability in the face of a lack of evidence to the contrary (see no 40). **140**

72 The Court of Appeals in Cracow 14 October 1992, I ACr 374/92, OSA Kr r II, at 44.

73 SN 28 April 1998, I Aca 308/98, PiM 2002/12, 147.

74 See *Nesterowicz* (fn 15) 355.

Medical Liability in Spain

Miquel Martín-Casals/Josep Solé

General Questions

A. The Health Care System Framework

I. General Introduction

1. The health care system in overview

One of the main characteristics of the Spanish health care system is the preponderance of the public health sector over the private one. According to data published by the Spanish Ministry of Health corresponding to 2007, the network of public hospitals in Spain runs 71.2 % of the total 158,306 beds installed (ie 112,775 beds installed in public centres), while the remaining 28.8 % (ie 45,531 beds) are in private hospitals.[1] In terms of centres and hospitals, the Spanish National Health System integrates 2,913 public health centres, 10,178 local consulting rooms, and 331 public hospitals.[2] With respect to equipment, the public sector accounts for 64 % of the operating theatres, 70 % of maternity wards and 84 % of incubators. Regarding staff, in 2007 there were 489,960 professionals working in hospitals and centres of health specialisation. Among them, 10 out of 11 physicians and 8 out 9 nurses were attached to the public health sector.[3] Finally, 5,255,314 patients were admitted to Spanish hospitals in 2007. From among these patients, 3,925,332 were admitted to public hospitals 1

1 *Agencia de Calidad del Sistema Nacional de Salud. Instituto de Información Sanitaria*, Estadística de Establecimientos Sanitarios con Régimen de Internado (Indicadores Hospitalarios). Año 2007 (Madrid, Ministerio de Sanidad y Política Social 2007), 4–12 (the statistics are available on the Internet: <http://www.msc.es/estadEstudios/estadisticas/docs/EESCRI_2007.pdf>)(Date 17.09.2009).

2 According to data provided by the *Agencia de Calidad del Sistema Nacional de Salud Instituto de Información Sanitaria* (fn 1) 49.

3 Ibid.

and 1,329,982 to private hospitals, which means that 74.6 % of the admissions were to public hospitals, as opposed to 25.4 % in private hospitals.[4] In terms of financing, 78.3 % of hospital discharges and 77.1 % of emergency services were borne by the Spanish National Health System.[5]

2 The origins of public health care cover in Spain are to be found in the creation, of the so-called '*Seguro Obligatorio de Enfermedad*' (SOE) [Illness Compulsory Insurance], established by Act 14 of December 1942 aimed at protecting specifically vulnerable workers whose income was under the legally established minimum amounts. The SOE was managed by the '*Instituto Nacional de Previsión*' (INS) and covered health care assistance in cases of illness and maternity as well as compensation for the loss of income caused by these situations. Later, in 1963, the Act of 28 of December created the general system of Social Security, whose benefits in the field of health care were increased by Decree 2065/1974 of 30 May. When the Spanish Constitution was passed in 1978 (CE 1978), the right to health care assistance was enshrined in Art 43 CE-1978 and developed by Act 14/1986 of 14 April, *General de Sanidad*. Among others, the following principles were established: public financing, universality and cost-free status of health care benefits; decentralisation of health care policy in favour of Autonomous Communities; provision for all-inclusive health care at a high level of quality, duly evaluated and supervised and the integration of the different public health care structures and services under the '*Sistema Nacional de Salud*' (National Health Care System). Accordingly, public health care services in Spain are currently provided by the Health Care Services of each Autonomous Community under the coordination of the Spanish Government through the '*Consejo Interterritorial del Sistema Nacional de Salud*' (CISNS) ('Interterritorial Council for the National Health Care System').[6] The Spanish Government only provides direct health care services in the autonomous cities of Ceuta and Melilla, in the north of Africa ('*Instituto de Gestión Sanitaria*', attached to the Spanish Ministry of Health).

3 As regards private health care services, some recent surveys state that private health care providers own about 22 % of the overall health care

4 Ibid.
5 Ibid.
6 This body was created in 1986 by the General Health Care Act and its powers were expanded by the Act 16/2003, of 28 May, *for the cohesion and quality of the National Health System.*

market share.[7] This represents 349 private non-charitable hospitals[8] and 120 private charitable hospitals.[9] Most of the cost of the services provided by private health care institutions is financed by private health care insurances (60 %), while 20 % corresponds to services financed by public Social Security with whom private hospitals have signed cooperation agreements (the so-called *centros concertados*).[10] The remaining 20 % comes from private patients who pay for the services directly.[11] This is the main reason why it has been said that 'the sector's growth is limited since underwriting health insurance amounts to a double payment for the citizen who already pays to Social Security for the provision of these services'.[12] Ownership of most of the private health care hospitals and centres is divided among health care insurers, foundations or other non-profit making institutions and private companies. In this latter case, some companies are owned by the doctors and professionals providing their services in the corresponding hospitals, while in other cases, doctors are only auxiliaries of the company owned by private shareholders.

In terms of applicable norms and procedures, these different ways of **4**
providing health care services have two main legal consequences. As regards applicable rules, when health care is provided by a private institution, rules applicable to liability are those related to breach of contract (Arts 1101 ff Civil Code [CC]), liability in tort (Arts 1902 ff CC) or Art 148 of the Royal Legislative Decree 1/2007 of 16 November, passing the Recasted Text of the General Act for the Protection of Consumers and Users and other complementary statutes [LGDCU][13], which applies regardless of the existence of a contract. The first two sets of rules contained in the Civil Code provide for a fault-based liability system (see infra nos 27–32), while

7 In this sense, see *M Claramunt/A Felipe*, Informe sobre la práctica actuarial en seguros de salud en Cataluña (España), Barcelona, Col·legi d'Actuaris de Catalunya, 4 <http://www.actuaries.org/events/congresses/Cancun/associations_reports/health_reports/hr_spain.pdf> (Date 24.09.2009).

8 *Agencia de Calidad del Sistema Nacional de Salud. Instituto de Información Sanitaria* (fn 1) 49; *A Mars*, El hospital privado ya es un producto de masas, El País, 22.05.2008, 1 <http://www.elpais.com/articulo/sociedad/hospital/privado/producto/masas/elpepuso/20080522elpepisoc_1/Tes> (Date 24.09.2009).

9 *Agencia de Calidad del Sistema Nacional de Salud. Instituto de Información Sanitaria* (fn 1) 49.

10 *Mars* (fn 8) 2.

11 Ibid 2–4.

12 *Claramunt/Felipe* (fn 7) 4 <http://www.actuaries.org/events/congresses/Cancun/associations_reports/health_reports/hr_spain.pdf> (Date 24.09.2009) *Mars* (fn 8) <http://www.elpais.com/articulo/sociedad/hospital/privado/producto/masas/elpepusoc/20080522elpepisoc_1/Tes> (Date 24.09.2009).

13 Real Decreto Legislativo 1/2007, de 16 de noviembre, *por el que se aprueba el texto refundido de la Ley General para la Defensa de los Consumidores y Usuarios y otras leyes complementarias* (Boletin Oficial del Estado [BOE] no 287, of 30.11.2007, 49181–49215).

the provision aiming at protecting Consumers and Users burdens the provider of health care services with a regime of strict liability (see infra nos 51–53). By contrast, when harm occurs in the field of public health care treatment, the applicable rules are those provided for in Arts 139 ff of Act 30/1992 of 26 November Legal Regime of Public Administrations and General Administrative Procedure [LRJAP].[14] These provisions establish a vicarious liability regime in which liability is channelled through public administration bodies performing health care services and prevents the victim from bringing claims against the specific civil servant or other health care professional who directly caused the harm (see infra nos 66–73).

5 The same dichotomy appears in the field of procedure. When the action is brought against a private health provider, it is tried by civil courts according to Art 9.2 LOPJ[15] and Arts 45 ff Civil Procedural Act (LEC). By contrast, when the victim brings the claim against public administration bodies, proceedings must be followed in the administrative courts in terms of Art 9.4 of the Organic Act of Judicial Power (LOPJ), Art 2 of the Act of the Administrative Jurisdiction (LJCA)[16] and the Additional Disposition of LRJAP, as amended by Ley 4/1999.

6 When the damaging event also amounts to a crime or a minor offence, regardless whether it occurred within the framework of public or private health care provision, the rules on tort liability included in the Penal Code [CP] apply (see Arts 109 ff CP) and, if the plaintiff does not reserve his or her claim for damages for a further suit before a Civil Court the Penal Court will also have the final word on the tort liability of the physician or the health care institution (Art 109.2 CP and Arts 111, 112 and 114 Criminal Procedural Act [Lecrim]). Tort law provisions set out in the Penal Code provide rules regulating liability in tort for the tortfeasor's own conduct and for a plurality of tortfeasors (Art 116 CP), as well as rules regarding the liability of the insurer 'for liabilities arising from the use or operation of any good, enterprise, industry or activity when, as a consequence of an act provided for in this Code, the event determining the insured risk takes place'. Moreover, Art 120.4 of the Penal Code deals with tort liability of the employer for the crimes and minor offences committed

---

14 Ley 30/1992, de 26 de noviembre, *de régimen jurídico de las Administraciones Públicas y del Procedimiento Administrativo Común* (BOE no 285, of 27.1.1992), amended by the Act 4/1999, of 23 January 1999, *de modificación de la Ley 30/1992, de 26 de noviembre, de Régimen Jurídico de las Administraciones Públicas y del Procedimiento Administrativo Común* (BOE no 12, of 14.1.1999).

15 Ley Orgánica 6/1985, de 1 de julio, *del Poder Judicial* (Organic Act of Judicial System).

16 Ley 29/1998, de 13 de julio, *de la Jurisdicción Contencioso-Administrativa.*

by his employees. In contrast to Art 1903 IV CC, this provision of the Penal Code establishes on the one hand that the employer's liability for the acts of his employees is vicarious, ie independent of his/her own fault, and on the other hand, that the employer's liability is not direct but subsidiary to the liability of the employee (cf Art 120.1 CP).[17] With regard to public administration bodies, Art 121 CP establishes that they will be held liable in tort when a person working in their service commits a crime or a minor offence if the damage 'is a direct consequence of the provision of public services'. Liability of public administration bodies is also vicarious and subsidiary to that of the civil servant or person acting for the public body.

II. Welfare Provision

2. The role of public health care

Public health care is provided in Spain to all Spanish citizens and to foreigners staying in the Spanish territory. In practical terms, this means that public health care is potentially provided to 45,200,736 Spanish citizens and to 4,519,554 foreigners.[18] Public health care in Spain is a non-contributory benefit which is financed through taxes. As has been said above, provision of public health care in Spain is decentralised in favour of Autonomous Communities, each of them having its own health care service and receiving the corresponding share of funds from the State every year.[19] According to data from 2006, public health care costs amount to 71.2 % of the overall health care costs in Spain, the remaining 28.8 % corresponding to the cost of private health care services. The Spanish Health Care System is organised on two basic levels: 'Primary Care' ('*Atención Primaria*') and 'Specialised Care' ('*Atención Especializada*'). 'Primary Care' is the basic structure which aims at promoting health and preventing illness. It is provided in the so-called '*Centros de Salud*' (Health Centres), which must be no further than 15 minutes drive from one's place of residence. The centres are staffed by family doctors, paediatricians, nursing personnel, and other professionals, such as midwives, psychothera- 7

17 Instead of many, *VL Montés Penadés* in: T Vives Antón (ed), Comentarios al Código Penal de 1995, vol I, Art 120 (1996) 641.

18 According to data from 2007 (Real Decreto 1683/2007, de 14 de diciembre, *por el que se declaran oficiales las cifras de población resultantes de la revisión del padrón municipal referidas al 1 de enero de 2007*).

19 *Ministerio de Sanidad y Consumo*, Sistema Nacional de Salud. España (Madrid, Ministerio de Sanidad y Consumo 2008) 23–27.

pists and social workers. On a second level, 'Specialised Care' is provided in the so-called '*Centros de Especialidades y Hospitales*' (Speciality Centres and Hospitals). They provide diagnostic, therapeutic and rehabilitation activities and offer specialised health care once the possibilities of the primary care have been surpassed. Specialised care is provided according to the characteristics of each patient and the course of his/her disease, whether in outpatients departments (*consultas externas*), day hospitals (*hospitales de día*) or in a hospital admissions regime (*regimen de internamiento hospitalario*).[20] Access to Specialised Care services is only possible after referral by a primary care or specialised doctor, or for emergency reasons or danger to life.[21] However, it is important to bear in mind that patients receive their medical treatment by means of referral through the social security carrier, not by means of an individual contract with the professional or the hospital providing him/her with the relevant health care services. This is not in contradiction to the fact that the patients can choose, if possible, the professional they would like to treat them from among the range of professionals included in the health care public system. Recent case-law has confirmed that the relationship between patients and social security providing health care assistance cannot be considered as being contractual and liability arising from medical activities is not based in contract but in tort (SSTS 12.2.2000 [Repertorio de Jurisprudencia Aranzadi (RJ) 2000\820], 11.6.2001 [RJ 2001\5674] and 26.3.2009 [RJ 2009\2803]).[22] The reason for this is that public bodies are obliged to provide public health care services in terms of Art 41 of the Spanish Constitution (right of citizens to receive sufficient social assistance and benefits). Providing health care services is a duty that, according to the Constitution, lies with the State, the origin and structure of which have a statutory nature (STS 26.3.2009 [RJ 2009\2803]).

3. Differences in treating patient's claims

8 As has been said before in response to question 1, and will be developed in further detail below in question 19, when injuries suffered by patients are caused within the framework of the public health care system, the rules

20 Ibid 39–41.

21 Ibid.

22 Against this position, arguing that relationships between patients and the Social Security are based on contract, see *J Plaza Penadés*, El Nuevo Marco de la Responsabilidad Médica y Hospitalaria (2002) 50.

regulating the liability of public bodies and those guiding the courts which will try the claim, are different (regarding these regimes see infra nos 66–73).

4. Right of recourse

According to Art 140.1 LRJAP, 'when management arising from joint formulas of action between public authorities gives rise to liability as provided in this Act, the authorities involved will be held solidarily liable'. The victim will thus be allowed to claim against any of the public bodies participating in the join action for the whole amount of compensation.[23] Once one of these public bodies has made the payment, it can seek a contribution thereto from the others according to the internal distribution of liability mechanisms dictated by the legal instrument regulating joint action (Art 140.1 *in fine* LRJAP). If nothing had been agreed on, liability will be allocated between participants in the joint action in equal parts.[24] This solution is applicable to public administration bodies providing health care services. When several public administration bodies acting independently concur in causing damage, 'each public administration will be held liable according to the powers that each one has been conferred,[25] according to the public interest which is protected and according to the intensity of the participation. If this delimitation cannot be marked out, they will be held solidarily liable' (Art 140.2 LRJAP). In this latter case, then, each public administration body providing health care services will be held liable for the harm that has been caused, and only in a case where its participation cannot be established, will solidarity arise. If this is the case, the public administration body will have a right of recourse against all the others once compensation has been paid.[26] The reporters have no information on whether Spanish social welfare agencies do really exercise this right of recourse in practice. 9

23 See, among others, *O Mir Puigpelat*, La reforma del sistema de responsabilidad patrimonial de las Administraciones públicas operada por la Ley 4/1999, de 13 de enero, de modificación de la LRJ-PAC, Revista Jurídica de Catalunya (RJC) 1999/IV, 1002 f.

24 *JM Busto Lago*, La responsabilidad civil de las Administraciones Públicas, in: LF Reglero Campos (ed), Tratado de responsabilidad civil III, (2008) 899 and note 53.

25 For instance, if the conflict arises between the State and a specific Autonomous Community, it will be useful for the judge to determine which health care powers correspond to the State and which have been transferred to the corresponding Autonomous Community. *Busto Lago* (fn 24) 900.

26 *Busto Lago* (fn 24) 900.

III. Private Insurance

5. The role of private health insurance

10 As has been said above, in the field of private health care private health insurance has a very important role since 60 % of the costs of private health care institutions are provided by private insurance.[27] It has also been said that, in comparison with public health care, the private sector still has a very small share of the market given that public health care has a universal character in Spain.[28]

11 As a rule, damage arising from medical malpractice can be covered either by first or third party insurance. Insurance contracts are governed by the provisions of the Insurance Contract Act 1980 (LCS).[29] Specifically, the types of insurance that can cover damage caused by medical and health care assistance are:

12 ▪ Liability insurance (third party insurance), governed by Art 73–76 LCS, which may have been bought individually by the physician or the health care personnel or by the hospital or centre that renders health care services.

13 ▪ Life insurance (Arts 80, 83 LCS)

14 ▪ Accident insurance (Art 100–104 LCS). According to Art 100 LCS, it covers 'all bodily injuries resulting from a cause which is violent, sudden, external and alien to the intention of the insured and which produce temporary or permanent disability or death'. By 'external cause' the provision refers to bodily injuries that do not result from an illness that the insured suffers. This sort of insurance basically covers health care expenses if this has been agreed in the policy (Art 103 LCS) and sums or rents agreed upon in the event of impairment resulting from the accident, the level of which will be mechanically assessed (Art 104 LCS).

15 ▪ Another relevant insurance contract is so-called medical insurance (Art 105, 106 LCS), which covers medical and medicinal expenses and the payment of certain sums when sickness has been medically certified. In its form of 'health care assistance insurance', the insurer under-

---

27 *Mars* (fn 8) 2.

28 Recent surveys consider that private health care services represent 22 % of the market (*Claramunt/Felipe* [fn 7] 4 <http://www.actuaries.org/events/congresses/Cancun/associations_reports/health_reports/hr_spain.pdf> [Date: 24.09.2009]).

29 Ley 50/1980, de 8 de octubre, *del Contrato de Seguro* (BOE no 250, 17.10.1980).

takes the obligation to provide health care and surgical services, either directly or by means of health care professionals and centres included in its 'medical panel' ('*cuadro medico*') to the extent demarcated in the insurance policy. According to Art 106 LCS, provisions of the LCS referring to accident insurance also apply to these types of insurance. Indeed, over the last few years, health care assistance insurances have given rise to several decisions of the Supreme Court holding insurers liable for the medical malpractice of doctors included on their 'medical panel' ('*cuadro medico*'). The grounds for liability of insurance companies for the damage caused by doctors or health professionals included on their 'medical panel' vary. Some decisions have held insurers liable on the grounds of the link of dependence or subordination existing between the insurer company (as employer) and the doctor (as employee or auxiliary). In this case the legal grounds are to be found in Art 1903 IV CC (see for instance STS 12.2.1990 [RJ 1990\677] and 27.9.1994 [RJ 1994\7307]).[30] Some other exceptional decisions apply the former Art 28 LGDCU (current Art 148 LGDCU) establishing a strict liability regime for those providing health care services (STS 19.6.2001 [RJ 2001\4974]). Recently, most decisions base the liability of insurers on contractual grounds, considering either that the insurers obliged themselves to provide health care by means of their auxiliaries, or that they created the 'appearance' that health care services were directly provided. 'Legal appearance' is thus an element that is integrated into the contract, as required by good faith (Cf Art 1258 CC) (see for instance STS 4.10.2004 [RJ 2004\6066] and among many others, see SSTS 4.12.2007 [RJ 2008\251], 4.6.2009 [La Ley 92018/2009]).

Once private health insurers have paid compensation for the harm caused **16**
by their medical professionals or institutions, they have a right of recourse against them. If liability of insurers rests upon Art 1903 IV CC (liability for others), Art 1904 CC confers a right of recourse to the employer against his/her auxiliary causing the harm. In the specific field of the insurance regulation, Art 43. I of the Insurance Contract Act 1980 (LCS),[31] applying to both first-party and third-party insurances, states that 'once the insurer

30 Some decisions have held insurers liable on the grounds of Art 1903.IV CC even when it was doubtful that the insurer intervened or controlled the conduct of the health professional in any way (see, for instance, SSTS 10.11.1999 [RJ 1999\8057] and 17.11.2004 [RJ 2004\7238]). Critical against this position is *M Martín-Casals/J Ribot/J Solé*, La responsabilidad de las entidades de seguros de salud en las reclamaciones judiciales por errores o negligencias médicas (2006) 32 ff.

31 Ley 50/1980, de 8 de octubre, *del contrato de seguro*.

has paid compensation, he will be entitled to exercise the rights and actions that the insured person has as a result of the accident, against all those persons who are responsible for it, up to the amount that he has paid as compensation'.

6. Liability insurance

17 Spanish law obliges health care professionals and institutions acting in the field of private health care to take out liability insurance or other guarantees covering the consequences of their potential liability. Thus, according to the Art 46 of the Act organising health care professions (Ley 44/2003, de 21 de noviembre, *de ordenación de las profesiones sanitarias*),[32] 'health care professionals exercising in the field of private health care provision, as well as legal persons or other bodies of private ownership providing whatever sort of health care services, are obliged to underwrite the corresponding insurance contract covering their liability, a reference ('*aval*') or other financial guarantee covering compensations arising from a possible harm to persons caused while providing this assistance or services'. This regulation does not provide the minimum amounts to be covered, nor any other sorts of conditions. On the other hand, the Act regulating Professional Societies (Ley 2/2007, of 15 march, *sobre Sociedades Profesionales* [LSP]), obliges those societies that consist of several professionals exercising their profession in a group to take out a liability insurance covering tort liability that the society in question could incur while exercising its activity (Art 11.3 LSP).[33] This provision will also apply to those professional societies providing health care services.

18 In practice, doctors usually do underwrite liability insurance from insurance companies selling 'collective liability insurance' to all members of a specific medical association. These policies contain some basic conditions which are applicable to all the members and, at the same time, leave open the possibility of increasing coverage when taking out the individual policy open. Some of these policies extend the possibility of covering liability both in the private field as well as in public health activity. Liability insurance policies usually cover – within the limits agreed –

32 BOE no 280, of 22.11.2003.

33 Moreover, Art 11.2 LSP sets down that the society and the professionals, whether they are associated or not, will be held solidary liable for the debts arising from professional acts. In such a case, rules regulating contractual and non-contractual liability will apply.

compensation for the damage caused by the insured amounting to liability in tort; they also cover criminal bail and the costs of legal defence of the insured, in both tort law and criminal law proceedings. Most policies cover compensation for damage caused by the insured him/herself, as well as damage caused by members of his/her staff. Specifically, policies usually mention, among other events covered by the insurance, liability for errors, excesses and deviations from treatment, errors in the development of surgical interventions, errors in the organisation of the working centre or office committed by the physician or by other persons (assistants, nurses and other health care personnel), errors committed while informing patients or third persons about the complications or consequences of a treatment or of a disease, etc.[34] By contrast, they usually exclude, among others, damage caused by the malfunctioning of X-ray or similar machines, by the use of radioactive substances; by clinical trials governed by Royal Decree 223/2004 of 6th February, by the production and selling of pharmaceutical products, by intentional acts or acts breaching legal, ethical or professional rules in a deliberate manner and claims for aesthetic damage and for not attaining the result that the treatment or the operation intended.[35] With regard to amounts covered, policies offer several possibilities. For instance, in 2009 the *Agrupación Mutual Aseguradora (AMA)* commercialised policies which offered physicians the possibility of choosing between two options: € 150,253 or € 601,012 per harmful event covered. Premiums vary according to the option chosen as well as to other cover voluntarily included by the insured person.[36] As regards the geographical area, policies usually cover damage caused by acts performed in any country in the world except the United States, Canada and associated territories.[37]

34 See, for instance, the insurance policy commercialised in 2009 by *Agrupación Mutual Aseguradora (AMA)* for odontologists and dentists through the Odontologists and Dentists' Association (<http://www.coem.org.es/index.php?option=com_content&task=view&id=28&Itemid=63> [Date 5.10.2009]).

35 See, for instance, the information available on the website of the Medical Association of Sevilla (<http://www.comsevilla.es/publicacion.php?id_pub=1388&id_area=26&id_ar=2 6&id_suba=0> [Date 5.10.2009]).

36 See <http://www.coem.org.es/index.php?option=com_content&task=view&id=28&Itemi d =63> (Date 5.10.2009).

37 Ibid.

IV. Professional Standards

7. Applicable professional standards

19 According to legal writing and case law, the standard of care applicable to medical professionals and providers of health care services is higher than the general standard of the reasonable person (*buen padre de familia*) that Art 1104 CC imposes on non-professionals.[38] As skilled professionals, their standard of care must conform to the *lex artis ad hoc*, ie the standard of conduct corresponding to a skilled professional in medicine who acts in accordance with the state of art of knowledge of medical science in the specific field of expertise to which the professional belongs.[39] As SSTS 11.3.1991 (RJ 1991\2209) and 25.4.1994 (RJ 1994\3073) hold, the *lex artis ad hoc* standard means that the medical performance will be evaluated by 'taking the specific case in which the medical performance takes place and the circumstances under which it develops into account, as well as the usual incidences that cannot be separated from normal professional performance'. This includes bearing in mind 'the specific characteristics of the actor, of the profession, of the complexity of the patient and the importance of the performance for the life of the patient and, eventually, the influence of other internal factors, such as the estate of the patient, of his or her relatives, or of the health care organisation itself'.[40] In the field of health care, the standard of care does not confine itself to the specific health care act or performance (for instance, surgical operations) but extends to other different activities taking place prior or subsequent to the intervention. This, for example, includes the case where the information that must be provided to the patient in order to obtain informed consent or the monitoring of his or her progress.[41]

20 Several decisions state that in order to evaluate the standard of care of health professionals courts must pay attention to the performance of technical protocols in conformity with the state-of-the-art practices[42] and also to their application with the care and accuracy required by the

38 In this sense, see STS 5.12.2006 (RJ 2007\232).

39 Among many others, *JM Fernández Hierro*, Sistema de responsabilidad médica (1998) 214 ff; *CI Asúa González*, Responsabilidad civil médica, in: Reglero (fn 24) vol II, 736 ff.

40 Other decisions, in the same sense, are SSTS 26.9.2000 (RJ 2000\8126); 30.9.2000 (RJ 2000\8130) and 26.3.2004 (RJ 2004\1668).

41 This emerges from the Basic Act 41/2002, on the Autonomy of the Patient and his or her Rights to Clinical Information and Documentation (*Ley 41/2002, de 14 de noviembre, básica reguladora de la autonomía del paciente y de derechos y obligaciones en material de información y de documentación clínica* [BOE no 274, 15.11.2002]).

42 In this sense, explicitly, STS 5.12.2006 (RJ 2007\232).

circumstances and the inherent risks arising from the intervention. Consequently, it is not sufficient to perform to the standards of conduct set up by technical protocols; it is also required that health care professionals take into account all the circumstances of each case in order to adapt their conduct to all relevant specific characteristics of the case (characteristics of the patient, risks involved by the intervention, etc).[43] These technical protocols, even when adopted by Spanish institutions (ie medical associations, associations of experts in specific fields of medical knowledge, such as for instance, gynaecology,[44] etc, Spanish Ministry of Health, etc) do not have an exclusively national scope since they commonly take into account the scientific knowledge existing at international level.[45]

Moreover, in order to define the content of professional duties of health **21**
care professionals, case law takes into account several sets of rules. As STS 5.12.2006 (RJ 2007\232) has declared courts shall bear in mind, on the one hand, the legal framework within which health professionals exercise their activity. This includes various provisions of the Spanish Constitution (in particular Art 10.1: dignity, Art 43: right to health, Art 51.1: right of consumers and users to be protected) and provisions of the Spanish Civil Code dealing with liability in contractual and in tort (Arts 1101 ff and Arts 1902 ff CC), as well as those other specific statutes regulating health care issues: Act 14/1986 of 25 April General Health Act, Act 44/2003 of 12 November Organizing Health Professions, and various other statutes regulating specific matters in the field of biomedicine, biotechnology or bioethics.[46] On the other hand, the standard of care of health professionals also incorporates 'the set of moral rules making up the Deontological Code or the professional conduct' (STS 5.12.2006 [RJ 2007\232]). According to

43 SSTS 23.5.2006 (RJ 2006\3535); 19.10.2007 (RJ 2007\7309) and 24.10.2008 (RJ 2008\5793).

44 Thus, STS 23.10.2008 (RJ 2008\5789) and STSJ of Galicia 9.4.2008 (RJCA 2008\558) mention protocols adopted by the Spanish Society of Gynaecology.

45 See <http://www.msc.es/organizacion/sns/planCalidadSNS/ec02-2.htm> (Date 29.09.2009) and documentation on standards and recommendations mentioned therein.

46 Among others, Ley 45/2003, de 12 de noviembre, *sobre técnicas de reproducción asistida* (Act 45/2003, of 12 November, on Assisted Reproduction Techniques); Ley 42/1998, de 28 de diciembre, *sobre Donación y Utilización de Embriones y Fetos Humanos o de sus Células, Tejidos y Órganos* (Act 42/1998, of 28 December, on the Donation and Use of Human Embryos and Foetus, their Cells, Tissues and Organs); Ley 9/2003, de 25 de abril, *por la que se establece el régimen jurídico de la utilización confinada, liberación voluntaria y comercialización de organismos modificados genéticamente* (Act 9/2003, of 25 April, on the Legal Regime for the Limited Use, Voluntary Liberalisation and Commercialisation of Genetically Modified Organisms); Ley 41/2002, de 14 de noviembre, *básica reguladora de la autonomía del paciente y de derechos y obligaciones en materia de información y documentación clínica* (Act 41/2002, of 14 November, Basic Act on the Autonomy of the Patient and his or her Rights to Clinical Information and Documentation).

this decision, 'these rules, due to their ethical or moral character, do not have by themselves coercive force', but this 'does not mean that they are not useful in the shaping of legal principles resting on certain ethical values or conceptions'. By contrast, these ethical rules affect medical practice and are useful for defining the content of professional duties that are to be observed during the course of health care activity. So, 'rules on professional deontology and statutes of professional associations guide, in a decisive manner, not only medical protocols, but more specifically the evaluation of the conduct of physicians and their adaptation to the level of care of a good professional, ie to the *lex artis ad hoc*' (STS 5.12.2006 [RJ 2007\232]).[47]

22 In legal writing it is also unanimously agreed that rules on professional deontology are an 'indirect source of a key value, embodied in the legal system' in order to evaluate whether the individual conduct of a physician conformed to the standard of care applicable to a skilled health professional.[48] The same can be said with regard to hospital and health regulations, as well as other health care guidelines.[49] The Spanish Medical Ethics and Deontology Code 1999, passed by the Spanish Medical Association on 10 September 1999, obliges Spanish physicians to provide their patients with 'health care of a scientific human quality' (Art 18.1). This means that 'the physician is responsible for providing health care (…) and that this obliges him/her to use the means offered by medical science in a suitable manner to his/her patient, according to the state-of-the-art practice, the scientific knowledge in force and the available possibilities' (Art 18.1). However, according to the Code of Deontology itself, the breach of its provisions has no effect in the field of tort liability but is only an administrative infringement giving rise to administrative sanctions provided for in the General Statutes of the Medical Association[50]: a private warning, suspension from professional activity or expulsion from the Association (cf Art 2.2 Deontological Code and Art 65.1 General Statutes).

23 In conclusion, it can be said that in some decisions compliance with health care standards and medical protocols is considered to be evidence of the fact that the conduct of the health care professional was in accordance with

---

47 In the same vein, see for instance, SSTS 7.2.1990 (RJ 1990\668) and 12.7.1994 (RJ 1994\6730).

48 In this sense, see *J Fernández Costales*, Estado actual de la casuística de la responsabilidad sanitaria, in: JA Moreno Martínez (ed), La responsabilidad civil y su problemática actual (2007) 267.

49 See, *Fernández Costales* (fn 48) 267; *Fernández Hierro* (fn 39) 214 ff.

50 Real Decreto 1018/1980, de 19 de mayo, *por el que se aprueban los Estatutos generales de la Organización Médica Colegial y del Consejo General de los Colegios Oficiales de Médicos* (Royal Decree 1018/1980, of 19 May, passing the General Statutes of the Medical Association).

the *lex artis*.[51] However, this evidence is not sufficient since the standard of care required for the *lex artis ad hoc* goes beyond mere compliance with these standards. This means that the mere compliance with health care regulations, medical protocols, deontological codes and other standards and recommendations is not decisive in evaluating whether the physician conformed to due care or not. In spite of compliance with these rules, judges and courts may nevertheless consider that a skilled health care professional would have taken other additional circumstances into account and would have adopted other complementary measures in order to heal the patient (see for instance 4.2.1999 [RJ 1999\748]).[52]

8. Quality and/or risk management systems

Spanish hospitals and health care centres are advised to comply with 24
standards of quality. The Spanish Ministry of Health publishes standards and recommendations regarding different fields of activities of hospitals concerning, for example, hospital deliveries, surgical performances, hospital day units, surgical day units, multi pathological patients etc.[53] These standards are crafted by an Expertise Group appointed by the Ministry of Health, which takes into account not only the Spanish experience – including the social and economic context, as well as human resources existing in Spanish hospitals – but also standards imposed in the European and International context (for instance those of the US Department of Health & Human Services, the NHS Healthcare Commission in the UK, the International Association for Ambulatory Surgery (IAAS) and others). However, as the Spanish Ministry of Health declares, 'these standards and recommendations are not a required condition in order to obtain an opening or operating authorisation.[54] Their main goal consists in providing public bodies as well as private managers and health care professionals with guidelines which guarantee safety and quality conditions in health care centres'.[55]

---

51 See, for instance, STSJ Madrid 14.10.2008 (Westlaw-Aranzadi Jurisprudencia [JUR] 2009\37283); STSJ Murcia 10.3.2007 (JUR 2007\4366).

52 *L Aguilar/JA de Andrés/O de León/A Gómez-Luque/A Montero*, Tratado de Anestesia y Reanimación (2001) 72.

53 The documents regarding these standards can be found in <http://www.msc.es/organizacion/sns/planCalidadSNS/ec02-2.htm> (Date 5.11.2010). Some of them are published in English.

54 See *Ministerio de Sanidad y Consumo* at <http://www.msc.es/organizacion/sns/plan CalidadSNS/ec02-2.htm> (Date 5.11.2010).

55 <http://www.msc.es/organizacion/sns/planCalidadSNS/ec02-2.htm> (Date 5.11.2010).

25 Both the State and several Autonomous Communities have passed legislation on standards of safety and quality applicable to health care centres.[56] Some of them refer to standards for authorisation and registration with which centres must comply before coming into operation.[57] Others refer to standards for accreditation concerning the evaluation of operational centres. According to Royal Decree 1277/2003 the Autonomous Communities have powers to authorise the establishment, operation, modification or shutdown of health care centres in their own territory (Art 3.1). This authorisation is mandatory and must be first obtained before the centre comes into operation once the autonomous health care authority has verified that the centre meets all the conditions required by the regulations (Art 3.2). With regard to the accreditation of health care centres and services, only four Autonomous Communities[58] have legislation and official programs for accreditation of health care centres, which are based on non-compulsory external assessment. Some other Autonomous Communities[59] have accreditation programs only for specific types of centres, services or activities for example organ transplants, assisted reproduction, haemotherapy.[60]

B. Tort Liability

9. Fundamentals of tort liability

26 The fundamentals of tort liability for medical malpractice depend on the legal provisions grounding the claim. Thus, whereas claims filed on the

---

56 See, for instance, Ley 14/1986, de 25 de abril, *General de Sanidad* (Act 14/1986, of 25 April, General Health); Ley 16/2003, de 28 de mayo, *de cohesión y calidad del Sistema Nacional de Salud* (Act 16/2003, of 28 May, on the Cohesion and Quality of the National Health System); Real Decreto 1277/2003, de 10 de octubre, *por el que se establecen las bases generals sobre autorización de centros, servicios y establecimientos sanitarios* (Royal Decree 1277/2003, of 10 October, establishing the general basis for authorisation of health care centres, services and institutions).

57 See Annex II of the Orden del Departamento de Salud y Consumo de Aragón, de 8 de marzo de 2006, *por la que se regulan los requisites mínimos para la autorización de centros quirúrgicos en la Comunidad Autónoma de Aragón* (Aragonese Health Authority Order of 8 March 2006 [Official Regional Gazette no 36, dated 27/03/06]); Orden de la Consejería de Sanidad Castilla La Mancha, de 29 de Junio de 2007, *sobre autorizaciones administrativas de centros y servicios de cirugía* (Health Authority Order of 29 June 2007 on administrative authorisation of surgery centres and services [Official Regional Gazette of 12 July 2007]).

58 Catalonia, Andalusia, Galicia and Extremadura.

59 As is the case of Madrid and the Basque Country.

60 See, *Spanish Ministry of Health and Consumer Affairs*, Day Surgery Guide (Madrid, 2008) 17–19.

grounds of Arts 1902 ff CC require fault (in addition to other general requirements for liability), when proceedings are brought according to Art 148 LGDCU – 2007 a strict liability regime applies.

a) Liability based on fault. As STS 19.12.2008 [RJ 2009\536] declares, tort liability for medical malpractice requires that the three requirements provided in Art 1902 CC be met namely fault, damage and a causal link between them. In order for the claim be accepted it is also required that the claim be brought within the time limitation period established in Art 1968.2 CC.[61] When tort liability arises out of the conduct of others (ie hospitals for acts of their auxiliaries) Art 1903 CC also requires fault, although in this case fault is presumed and the burden of proof is reversed against the defendant. 27

Regarding fault, as will be seen infra nos 58–59, the Spanish courts do not differentiate between whether liability is in contract or in tort. Health care professionals are considered to be bound to act with the necessary care so as to attain a result of the patient being healed (*obligation of means*, obligación de medios) but are not obliged to attain the result itself (*obligation of result*, obligación de resultado).[62] This is true irrespective of whether there is a contract binding the patient and the physician or not. Consequently, the standard of care applicable to health care professionals will not vary from contract to tort and the proof of a breach of contract of medical services overlaps with the proof of fault in the area of tort law.[63] In this sense 'there is no conduct that is negligent in tort which is not negligent in contract and vice versa'.[64] 28

'The standard of care of health care professionals is higher than the general standard of the reasonable person established in Art 1104 CC. As skilled professionals, their liability is measured according to the yardstick of the so-called *lex artis ad hoc*, ie, the standard of care that must be met by a skilled professional in medicine who acts in accordance with state-of-the-art knowledge of medical science'.[65] As STS 11.3.1991 (RJ 1991\2209) sets forth, the *lex artis* standard means that the medical performance will be evaluated by 'taking into account the specific case in which it takes place 29

---

61 Among many others, *Asúa González* (fn 39) 731 ff; *D Bello Janeiro*, Responsabilidad civil del médico y responsabilidad patrimonial de la Administración sanitaria (2009) 30 ff.

62 STS 10.11.1999 (RJ 1999\8057).

63 *M Martín-Casals/J Solé Feliu/JC Seuba Torreblanca*, Spain, in: J Dute/MG Faure/H Koziol (eds), No-Fault Compensation in the Health Care Sector (2004) 339.

64 *Asúa González* (fn 39) 734.

65 *L González Morán*, La responsabilidad civil del médico (1990) 79; *Fernández Hierro* (fn 39) (3rd edn 2000) 218 ff.

and the circumstances under which it develops, as well as the usual incidences that cannot be separated from normal professional performance'. This means taking into account 'the specific characteristics of the agent, of the profession, of the complexity of the patient and the importance of the performance for his or her life and, eventually, the influence of other internal factors, such as the condition of the patient, of his or her relatives, or of the health care organisation itself'. According to STS 5.12.2006 (RJ 2007\232), the duties that conform the medical standard of care 'merge with technical rules in order to shape the *lex artis ad hoc*, guiding medical activity and establishing the parameters to evaluate it in accordance with the state-of-the-art techniques of the profession'. Specifically, due care in the field of health care does not confine itself to the specific health care act or performance (for instance, surgical operations) but it also encompasses the performance of different activities, whether prior to the intervention or subsequent to it. This includes, among others, the duties (a) to use all remedies and techniques known to medical science and required by the *lex artis* in order to heal the patient, (b) to inform patients or, where appropriate, their relatives, of the diagnosis of the illness, the treatments and the risks inherent to them – in particular whenever the treatment involves surgical interventions, in order to obtain informed consent, a prediction on the evolution of the illness etc, (c) to continue the treatment until the patient is discharged from the hospital and at the same time to warn him about the risks of abandoning it and (d) in the case of chronic or evolving illnesses or diseases, to inform the patient of the need to undergo analysis, preventive care and other tests and to monitor his or her progress.[66]

30 Causation is the second requirement for establishing liability. Case law and legal scholarship currently agree that the issue of causation must be tackled in a two-step analysis, ie causation in fact (*conditio sine qua non*) and causation in law (*imputación objetiva*).[67] This is also the current method for dealing with causal issues in the field of medical malpractice as noted in for instance, SSTS 21.10.2005 (RJ 2005\8547) or 7.5.2007 (RJ 2007\3553). Specifically, STS 29.6.2007 (RJ 2007\3871), dealing with a case of wrongful conception, declares that causation in fact, due to its factual nature, can

66 SSTS 25.4.1994 (RJ 1994\3073); 11.2.1997 (RJ 1997\940); 7.5.1997 (RJ 1997\3874) and 20.11.2000 (RJ 2000\9310).

67 Among others, see *A Dominguez Luelmo*, Derecho sanitario y responsabilidad médica. (Comentario a la Ley 41/2002, de 14 de noviembre, sobre derechos del paciente, información y documentación clínica) (2003) 58; *C Díaz-Regañón García-Alcalá*, Relación de causalidad e imputación objetiva en la responsabilidad civil sanitaria, Indret. Revista para el Análisis del Derecho 1/2004, Working Paper no 180, 4 ff.

only be revised by the court of instance, whereas causation in law is a matter that can be dealt with in cassation. Among the different tests of causation in law the most common one in Spanish case law is the test of adequacy. In the area of health care liability, STS 6.2.1999 (RJ 1999\1052) defines this test as that which 'requires the result to be a natural, adequate and a sufficient consequence of the determination of will. It must be understood that a natural consequence is one that favours, between the initial act and the damaging event, a relationship of necessity according to the accepted knowledge'. According to this understanding, 'in every single case it must be assessed whether the preceding act that is presented as a cause has the potentiality of bringing about, as a necessary consequence, the harming effect that has been produced'. By contrast, causality shall be discarded when 'the harm appears to be as extraordinarily unlikely to an experienced observer with the specific knowledge of the tortfeasor and who has examined the issue at the time immediately prior to the conduct' (STS 21.10.2005 [RJ 2005\8547]).[68] Spanish courts have also made recourse to other tests of causation in law, as for instance, in STS 4.11.2010 (RJ 2010\411012), with regard to a wrongful birth case. This decision expressly mentions the so-called test of the 'causalidad alternativa conforme a derecho' (*rechtmäßiges Alternativverhalten*) in the sense that 'damage cannot be attributed to the person who caused it whenever, had he acted according to law, the same type of damage and with the same extension would have taken place' and this 'shifts the burden of proof to the person who acted negligently in order to verify whether his conduct, when compared with its diligent alternative conduct, did increase the risk of occurrence of the damage at stake'. Other decisions also mention other tests as the general risk of life, the test of the increased risk or the protective purpose of the norm violated (STS 21.10.2005 [RJ 2005\8547]) although, for the moment, they are very rarely applied. With regard to causation specific problems arise in cases where causation remains uncertain. These issues will be tackled with *infra* in questions number 11 (uncertain causation) and 12 (loss of a chance).

Thirdly, medical liability also requires the claimant to suffer damage. As **31**
regards damage, the same general tort liability rule applies to medical and health care liability. Art 1902 CC does not even mention the distinction between pecuniary and non-pecuniary losses and it is accordingly understood by both legal scholarship and case law to include both heads of

68 See also, among many others, STS 6.2.1999 (RJ 1999\1052) and STS 10.6.2008 (RJ 2008\4246).

damages.[69] In the area of health care liability, this means that both pecuniary and non-pecuniary losses (which include psycho-physical damage as well as pain and suffering) resulting from personal injury are recoverable.[70] In agreement with this, case law compensates regularly for 'pecuniary losses, physical injury and pain and suffering'[71] or, in a wrongful birth case according to STS 21.12.2005 (RJ 2005\10149) courts compensate the parents of a handicapped child for the 'pain and suffering associated with the birth and further growth of a disabled child' and the 'economic losses arising from the cost of diagnostic tests, of an unnecessary pregnancy and birth, and the need for parents to adapt to the new social, family and economic situation, and of specific care, coming out of an unforeseeable and extraordinary event'. These issues are discussed in more detail infra questions nos 21–26.

32 Finally, the claimant must bring his or her action within the limitation period provided by the law. In the case of liability in tort this period is of 1 year, running from the moment the victim knew of the damage and could have brought the claim (Art 1968.2 CC) (see for instance SSTS 15.10.2008 [RJ 2008\7125] and 19.12.2008 [RJ 2009\536]). For torts committed in Catalonia the Catalan Civil Code (CCC) establishes a three year period of prescription (Art 121-21 CCCat).

33 **b) Strict liability in private health care.** See answer to question 14.

10. Burden of proof

34 In medical malpractice case law and legal scholarship, it is agreed that the burden of proof of the conditions for liability rests upon the claimant. This rule, on the basis of Art 217 LEC, is the general rule of proof applicable in tort law trials and applies not only to damage and to the causal link, but also to fault. However, courts tend to apply it more severely to health care services than they do in other tort law areas.[72] As STS 17.9.2008 (RJ 2008\5517) declares, in medical liability 'there is no room for the reversal of the burden of proof which courts accept in cases of

69 *F Rivero Hernández*, Responsabilidad por hecho a jeno, in: JL Lacruz Berdejo, Elementos de Derecho Civil II. Derecho de obligaciones, vol 2 (2009) 458.

70 *Martín-Casals/Solé Feliu/Seuba Torreblanca* (fn 63) 340.

71 See, among many others, SSTS 26.9.2000 (RJ 2000\8126) and STS 29.5.2003 (RJ 2003\3916) compensating both for pecuniary and non-pecuniary losses.

72 In this sense, *G Ormázábal Sánchez*, Carga de la prueba y sociedad de riesgo (2004) 77; *A Luna Yerga*, La prueba de la responsabilidad civil médico-sanitaria (2004) 128 ff; *Dominguez Luelmo* (fn 67) 50.

losses arising from other sources, the patient being in charge of the proof of the causal link and the proof of fault (…)'.[73]

As regards losses, this rule does not pose specific difficulties in case law. Regarding causation, the main problem arises in cases where the causal relationship remains uncertain, ie when it is uncertain which cause from among a plurality of potential causes has actually caused the harm. These difficulties will be discussed under question number 11 (see infra), but it can now be said that in the health care area courts are stricter when evaluating the proof of causation than in other tort law areas. In that sense STS 8.2.2000 (RJ 2000\1235) declared that 'there is no room, in the sphere of the causal relationship, for mere deductions, guesswork or probabilities and evidential certainty is required'. Even if facts are established on the grounds of a judicial presumption ('presunción judicial', accepted by Art 386 LEC) courts declare that the judge must attain 'subjective certainty'; the test of probabilities (ie 'more probable than not') that prevails in other legal systems is not regarded as sufficient.[74] Notwithstanding, in the last few years some changes seem to suggest making proving causation easier for the plaintiff. So, for instance, the extension of the so-called doctrine of the 'disproportionate damage' (see the following nos 36 ff) to the field of causation; or the exceptional use of judicial presumptions in the field of infections for hepatitis C and HIV viruses after a blood transfusion (cf SSTS 15.11.2004 [RJ 2004\7233]; 25.4.2007 [RJ 2007\3687]; 4.12.2007 [RJ 2008\251]). **35**

With regard to fault, case law follows the general rule in tort law which (according to Art 217 LEC) places the burden of proof on the claimant. However, over the last few years some legal developments have taken place specifically in the area of medical malpractice cases, making the proof of fault easier for the claimant. On the one hand, Spanish courts have developed the so-called doctrine of the 'daño desproporcionado' (disproportionate damage) with regard to cases where the seriousness of the damage suffered by the patient is out of all proportion to the diagnosis that has been made or to the operation that has been performed, so that the fault stems from the existing circumstances (SSTS 29.6.1999 [RJ 1999\4895], 15.9.2003 [RJ 2003\6418] and 26.6.2006 [RJ 2006\6127]). This doctrine appeared for the first time in the Supreme Court decision STS 2.12.1996 (RJ 1996\8938), dealing with the case of a woman who after an apparently normal labour suffered haemorrhaging which was so serious that she required several blood transfusions and it could only be finally stopped by **36**

73 See also, among many others, STS 11.1.2008 (RJ 2008\585).

74 See, *Luna Yerga* (fn 72) 514 ff.

a full extirpation of her uterus. The great quantity of blood lost was the cause of a brain anoxia which she suffered, giving rise to serious injuries (spastic tetraparesia). Here the Supreme Court states that in cases of medical liability it is possible to presume the physician's negligence when the outcome resulting from his action 'on account of its disproportion in comparison to what, according to the rules of experience and to common sense is usual, presents signs that reveal the negligent insufficiency of the means employed, with regard to the state of science and the circumstances of time and place, or oversight in its duly and timely use'.[75] The application of the 'disproportionate damage' doctrine is discarded when the harm is one of the consequences of the typical risks associated with the treatment.[76] Following this first decision, many other courts have applied the doctrine repeating its *dictum* verbatim in an extensive variety of cases, such as the case where a woman underwent an operation in order to have a maxillary cyst removed and suffered hypotension under anaesthesia which prevented oxygen from reaching her brain with the result of irreparable brain damage (permanent vegetative life) (STS 12.12.1998 [RJ 1998\9431]). See also the case of a patient who underwent a cataract operation in her left eye and who, several days later and after a some complications, had to have her eye removed (STS 9.12.1999 [RJ 1999\8173]) or the case of the death by cardio-respiratory arrest of a woman who underwent an operation to have her gallbladder removed (STS 29.6.1999 [RJ 1999\4895]), the case of a child suffering burns in his abdomen and scrotum as the result of the defective iodine that was applied to him during an operation of appendicitis (STS 17.5.2002 [RJ 2002\6748]), and the case of a man who underwent an operation under anaesthesia in order to correct a deviation of his nasal septum and who as a consequence of some complications, entered into coma and died a few days later (STS 23.5.2007 [RJ 2007\3273]).[77]

75 A sector of the legal scholaship has critised this doctrine – see for instance *L Díez-Picazo*, La culpa en la responsabilidad civil extracontractual, Anuario de Derecho Civil (ADC) (2002), 1009–1027, p 1015.

76 See for instance, the important dissenting opinion ('Voto Particular') of the Supreme Court Judge Francisco Marín Castan in STS 31.1.2003 (RJ 2003\646).

77 There are other decisions putting this doctrine into practice such as, for instance, SSTS 18.2.1997 (RJ 1997\1240); 19.2.1998 (RJ 1998\877); STS 11.4.2000 (RJ 2000\2359); 14.5.2001 (RJ 2001\6204); 19.7.2001 (RJ 2001\5561); 31.1.2003 (RJ 2003\646); 19.7.2007 (RJ 2007\4692) and 23.10.2008 (RJ 2008\5789). To a certain extent, it can even be said that some decisions go too far with this doctrine, applying it to cases where the ensuing damage is one of the typical risks of the medical intervention the patient has undergone, as in STS 31.1.2003 (RJ 2003\646), where a dissenting opinion of one of the judges declares that an unwanted and unsatisfactory damage 'cannot be described as a "disproportioned outcome" when, it is framed within the typical risks of the operation, that is, within the probable complications that can happen even when the surgeon acts according to due care'.

In some of these decisions the courts have expressly connected the doctrine of disproportionate damage as a device that aims at easing the proof of fault for the claimant to other devices such as the Common Law doctrine of *res ipsa loquitur*, the German '*Anscheinsbeweis*' or the French '*faute virtuelle*'.[78] Until 2008, it could be said that the doctrine of 'disproportionate damage' did not correspond well to any of these other doctrines since it gave rise to a presumption of fault only – as with the Anglo-American *res ipsa loquitur* and the French *faute virtuelle* –, whereas the German *Anscheinsbeweis* applies both as a presumption of fault and of causation. However, since the decision STS 23.10.2008 (RJ 2008\5789) the Spanish Supreme Court has extended – at least *obiter dicta* – the doctrine of the 'disproportionate damage' to the field of causation. In this decision, as well is the SSTS 8.7.2009 (RJ 2009\4459) and 20.7.2009 (RJ 2009\3161), the Supreme Court declares that 'the existence of a disproportioned damage affects the attribution of causation and of culpability, shifting, thereby, the general rules regarding the '*onus probandi*' of causation and fault in the area of medical malpractice liability'. Currently, it can thus be said that under the new approach taken by the Supreme Court the doctrine of 'disproportionate damage' plays a role both as a presumption of fault and a presumption of causation. **37**

A second device aimed at easing the proof of fault for the claimant concerns the distribution of the burden of proof in cases where the defendant, due to the particular circumstances of the case, is in a better position than the claimant to furnish proof. In these cases, the burden of proof of fault is shifted from the claimant to the defendant. This rule, which was first developed in case law, is currently laid down by Arts 217.6 and 7 LEC-2000. Although this provision is a general rule of procedure and is not restricted to health care liability, it is most commonly applied in this area. According to these two subsections, when applying the general rules of proof provided in the prior subsections of Art 217 LEC-2000, 'the court will have to take into account the availability and the facility of proof that corresponds to each of the parties in the proceedings', so that circumstances may allow the court to shift the burden of proof of fault to the defendant when he has easier access to evidence. This happens, for instance, when the physician or the health care centre is in the 'proximity of the sources of proof' and, they are therefore in a 'better position to **38**

78 These sort of dicta can be found, among many others, in SSTS 9.12.1998 (RJ 1998\9427); 29.6.1999 (RJ 1999\4895); 9.12.1999 (RJ 1999\8173); 17.11.2004 (RJ 1002\7238); STS 26.6.2006 (RJ 2006\5554) and 23.5.2007 (RJ 2007\3273).

obtain access to them.'[79] Case law has also acknowledged the possibility of shifting the burden of proof of fault 'when the court has been able to establish obstruction or lack of cooperation from the physician' or the hospital.[80] The idea behind this rule is that 'when there is no *bona fidei* cooperation by the parties – whether on the part of the claimant or the defendant – proof can be facilitated' for the other party.[81] In the area of health care liability this second device has become rather important in cases of informed consent, which will be analysed below under question 18 (see infra nos 62–66).

11. Uncertain causation

39 Leaving aside the previous case of the doctrine of the 'disproportionate damage', which has been recently extended to the field of causation in Spanish law, there are no specific rules on causation in the area of medical malpractice. Consequently, courts apply the general rules governing causation in tort law. Moreover, it must be stressed that in Spanish health care liability the requirement of causation is very strict, not only in the sense that it is an indispensable condition of liability, but also in the sense that it must be proven with certainty by the claimant according to general rules set up in Art 217 LEC-2000. As STS 6.2.1999 (RJ 1999\1052) has stated, in a case of health care liability, 'categorical proof with regard to the link between the agent and the damage ensued is necessary' so that 'in every single case it must be assessed whether the preceding act that is presented as a cause has the potential to bring about, as a necessary consequence, the harming effect that has been produced. Pure conjecture, or the existence of some facts that by coincidence lead to thinking of a possible interrelation between these events, is not sufficient'. Along the same lines, STS 23.10.2000 (RJ 2000\9197) states that 'vagueness on the cause of the death does not allow a causal relationship between the death and the conduct of the physicians co-defendants to be established'.[82] SSTS 24.11.2005 (RJ 2005\7855) and 10.6.2008 (RJ 2008\4246) have also stated that 'in the

79 In this sense, see SSTS 28.7.1997 (RJ 1997\5954); 6.2.2001 (RJ 2001\2233); 29.11.2002 (RJ 2002\10404) and 15.9.2003 (RJ 2003\6418).

80 See SSTS 2.12.1996 (RJ 1996\8938); 17.5.2002 (RJ 2002\6748); 23.12.2003 (RJ 2003\914); 26.6.2006 (RJ 2006\5554) and 19.7.2007 (RJ 2007\4692).

81 SSTS 2.12.1996 (RJ 1996\8938); 30.10.2007 (RJ 2007\7334) and 8.11.2007 (RJ 2007\8253).

82 See also STS 22.6.2000 (RJ 2000\4431), declaring that 'if it is not possible to establish a link of causation based on fault, liability of the health care professional cannot be declared'. The same opinion can be found in STS 29.3.1994 (RJ 1994\2305).

area of liability for health professionals a strict liability regime and a reversal of the burden of proof are to be discarded (...) except in those exceptions specifically established by law (Art 217.5 LEC). Liability of Art 1902 CC is based on fault and requires the patient to prove the causal link and the fault'; 'in the absence of this proof, no health liability arises' (STS 17.9.2008 [RJ 2008\5517]).

This specific rigidity with the proof of causation also becomes evident in connection with judicial presumptions, acknowledged in Art 386 LEC-2000. Here the Spanish Supreme Court makes the admissibility of these presumptions conditional not only on the circumstance that the basic fact from which the presumption stems is clear and proven – 'mere suppositions or subjective appreciations' not being sufficient (STS 7.2.1990 [RJ 1990\668]) – but specifically on the circumstance that the damaging event cannot be attributed to another cause or to several different causes other than the action of the health care personnel.[83] Decision STS 7.2.1990 (RJ 1990\668) also explains the reason for this rigor in the area of medical liability: 'when direct proof is lacking, the use of the proof by presumptions will require a relationship that brings the damaging effect and the prior [medical] treatment into agreement, so that this effect cannot be attributed to several circumstances, since precisely with regard to medical acts (...) the resulting consequences can be attributed to unforeseeable complications which, with more or less risk, depending on the sort of intervention, are always possible'.[84] As a result of these criteria a high percentage of decisions in the area of medical liability which, when confronted with several facts that may potentially have caused the damage, solve the uncertainty ensuing from the lack of direct proof of causation by dismissing the claim, especially if there is no hospital or public administrative institution among the defendants. Outside the area of medical liability the tendency is precisely the opposite and Spanish courts usually establish the causal link[85] and declare joint and several liability of all potential tortfeasors.[86] **40**

STS 22.6.2000 (RJ 2000\4431) illustrates this strictness in the proof of causation in health care liability cases. In the decision, the son of the **41**

83 In this sense see SSTS 8.9.1998 (RJ 1998\7548) and 20.7.2000 (RJ 2000\6754).

84 Along the same lines see SSTS 26.5.1986 (RJ 1986\2824); 13.7.1987 (RJ 1987\5488); 12.2.1990 (RJ 1990\677) and 9.6.1997 (RJ 1997\4731).

85 As, for instance STS 21.5.2001 (RJ 2001\6464). This is a frequent solution in cases regarding fires, whose specific cause does not appear to be clear (SSTS 27.2.2003 [RJ 2003\2152] and 9.6.2005 [RJ 2005\4431]).

86 See, for instance, STS 29.12.1998 (RJ 1998\9980).

claimants died as the result of gangrene which he developed after three male nurses, on several consecutive days, had given him three injections. The parents of the deceased brought a claim against the male nurse who gave him the first injection, arguing that the fatal result was attributable to his conduct since he had used a syringe that had been sterilised by boiling instead of using safer material such as chemically disinfected or throwaway syringes. The Supreme Court dismissed the claim on the grounds that on the next days the patient had received two other injections that had been given by two different male nurses and at least one of them had also used material that had been disinfected by boiling. According to the Supreme Court 'the proof of the causal link rested upon the claimants and in the case under decision there was a complete lack of any evidence, even by the means of the proof by presumptions' permitting them to decide the case in favour of the claimants. More precisely, the court held that 'since different professionals delivered three injections in subsequent periods, there is a possibility in three directions, which the means of proof that have been used have not clarified'. In the same vein, in STS 6.2.1999 (RJ 1999\1052) the claimant had bought a health care insurance policy from the company 'Sanitas' whose cover also extended to his wife. In December 1989 he requested the emergency services of 'Sanitas' as his wife was having breathing difficulties. The emergency physician diagnosed a bronchoconstriction and the existence of some mucosity, but did not consider that the condition of the patient required admittance into hospital. Instead, he maintained the treatment that the patient was already receiving and prescribed her an intake of oxygen. Accordingly, the claimant repeatedly requested the urgent delivery of a cylinder of oxygen from 'Sanitas' but the oxygen was never supplied. The patient died on the same day due to a cardiorespiratory arrest. The husband brought a claim for compensation against 'Sanitas' for the damage caused by the death of his wife. 'Sanitas' objected to the claim arguing that liability should fall upon the company with which it had contracted to supply the oxygen ('Oxifar'). The Court of First Instance and the Court of Appeal of Madrid recognised the causal link and ordered 'Sanitas' to compensate for damage arising from the death of his wife. However, the Supreme Court reversed the prior judgments, ruling in favour of the defendant, and dismissed the case. It rejected the possibility of establishing a causal link, charged the Court of Appeal with taking some facts as proven when they started from mere speculation and declared that 'there is no proof at all which gives rise to state, in the categorical form that the doctrine of the courts so requires … that the death was the result of the lack of supply of oxygen.' In addition, the Supreme Court affirmed that there was no proof that 'permits us to establish what the cause of the cardiorespiratory arrest was (...), and this can result from a variety of different causes'. It stated further that 'neither is there proof that permits us to assert what the cause of such a sudden worsening of the patient was which, in only a few hours, led to her death, nor proof that such worsening was the direct result of the lack of a supply of oxygen to the patient'. In another decision from 1995, STS 20.2.1995 (RJ 1995\886), a claim was brought by the parents of a boy who suffered a cardiorespiratory arrest while being operated on for a deviation of his nasal ridge and from which irreversible brain damage resulted. The claimants argued that the most usual cause of a heart attack during surgical procedures is ventricular fibrillation and that when the cardiac arrest came about the physicians had not adopted the measures required in order to obtain the patient's recovery. However, the Supreme Court rejected this reasoning and declared that 'even when putting the statistics aside, the evidence shown in the proceedings does not prove what caused the heart attack'. It is worth noting that although the Court resorts to a probabilistic yardstick as a criteria to solve the uncertainty surrounding causation, it concludes that a direct proof of the cause of the cardiac arrest was lacking.

The latter does not necessarily mean that judicial presumptions are not **42** admitted in medical malpractice claims in Spain. However, their admission is restricted and courts make recourse to presumptions very exceptionally. This happens, for instance, with regard to cases where the damage consists of being infected with the hepatitis C or HIV viruses after receiving a blood transfusion. Although the causal link between the transfusion and the infection cannot be established with absolute certainty, the Spanish Supreme Court acknowledges that it is possible to presume that the infection is causally connected with the transfusion under certain conditions, ie that the grounds upon which the presumption is based give sufficient certainty to the court and that no other circumstances exist that can raise a different conclusion. Accordingly, courts presume that a transfusion has caused the infection when it is proven that the victim did not belong to a group at risk, or that the infection did not exist before the transfusion, or that a brief period of time elapsed between the transfusion and the diagnosis of the infection, etc. (SSTS 11.4.2002 [RJ 2002\3382]; 15.11.2004 [RJ 2004\7233]; 25.4.2007 [RJ 2007\3687]; 4.12.2007 [RJ 2008\251]). By contrast, many other decisions reject the presumption arguing that the existing circumstances do not offer the court sufficient certainty in order to discern a causal connection between the transfusion and the infection (Cf STS 21.10.2002 [RJ 2003\1113]; 5.12.2007 [RJ 2008\469]; 9.12.2008 [RJ 2009\67]).

12. Loss of a chance

43 In Spanish case law, loss of a chance was originally recognised as a separate compensable head of non-pecuniary loss. In the field of health care liability, the Spanish Supreme Court acknowledged the doctrine of the loss of a chance for the first time in 1998.[87] In the STS 10.10.1998 (RJ 1998\8371), a worker in an ice cream factory suffered an accident while repairing a machine, which caused his right hand to be amputated. The nurse attending him in the factory gave instructions to put the hand in a box with normal ice in order to prevent it from deteriorating. However, a colleague of the victim thought that the hand would be better conserved if it was put in a specific box used for frozen tart, adding dry or synthetic ice to it. All this was done without the nurse's knowledge. When the ambulance came and she accompanied the victim to the hospital, she observed that the container had changed. Nevertheless, she did not open the box and she delivered it to the hospital. There, they realised that it was not possible to re-connect the hand, since it had frozen as a result of being in contact with synthetic ice. The worker brought an action against the nurse. The Supreme Court considered the nurse had been negligent since she had not taken any measures when she realised that the box had been changed, especially as she knew how important it was for the amputated member not to be preserved in synthetic ice. Nevertheless, the Court stated that the nurse could not be responsible for the failure of the operation of reattachment, but 'only for the claimant's lost opportunity to undergo an operation to replace the hand, whether or not it would have finally succeeded being unknown.' Although the claimant asked for more than € 120,000, the Spanish Supreme Court awarded € 9,000, without any further justification.[88]

44 Other decisions in the field of medical malpractice award compensation for the loss of a chance to heal or to survive. Almost all of them take the approach that considers the doctrine of the loss of a chance as a matter of damage, not as a causal issue.[89] Thus, Spanish courts do usually recognise causation without any further analysis and compensate for a specific head

87 Some time earlier the Supreme Court had received the doctrine of the loss of a chance for claims against negligent attorneys and '*procuradores*' (which we inaccurately translate as 'solicitors' *faute de mieux*) for the 'loss of procedural chances' (SSTS, 1ª, 16.12.1996 [RJ 1996\8971] and 28.1.1998 [RJ 1998\357]).

88 *J Ribot/A Ruda*, Loss of a Chance. Spain, in: B Winiger/H Koziol/BA Koch/R Zimmermann (eds), Digest of European Tort Law, vol 1: Essential Cases on Natural Causation (2007) 567, no 1–4.

89 *C Asúa González*, Pérdida de oportunidad en la responsabilidad sanitaria (2008) 54.

of damages – mostly qualified as 'non-pecuniary losses' – called 'loss of a chance' (*pérdida de oportunidad or pérdida de expectativas*).[90] In STS 12.7.2007 (RJ 2007\4993) a patient with a history of a duodenal ulcer, diabetes and blood pressure came to a hospital where the physician attending him diagnosed a blood pressure crisis and the intensification of the ulcer. Some hours later, the patient felt worse and returned to the hospital where the casualty department diagnosed an acute heart attack. As a consequence, the patient died shortly afterwards. His widow brought an action against the public hospital claiming compensation. The trial court did not admit the action. However, the Spanish Supreme Court awarded compensation considering that the erroneous diagnosis amounted to medical negligence. This negligence, 'irrespective of what the final outcome of the treatment would have been, produced a loss of a chance to be treated correctly according to the actual illness and, therefore, a compensable harm was caused, which is not the death that was caused, with respect to which it cannot be ascertained whether it could be avoided or not, but the loss of a chance to be treated adequately from a medical point of view'. Again, STS 4.7.2007 (RJ 2007\6617) established that 'the damage was limited to compensation for the loss of a chance to heal within a suitable time' and STS 17.4.2007 (RJ 2007\2322) declared that 'deprivation of the expectancy is a compensable harmful outcome'. More specifically, this later decision confirms the decision of the trial court when it qualified the so-called 'deprivation of the expectancy' as a 'non-pecuniary loss'. Similarly, see STSJ Madrid 23.10.2007 (JUR 2007\166246), which compensated for the 'non-pecuniary losses arising from the loss of the opportunity to receive treatment before the illness got worse'.

STS 7.7.2008 (RJ 2008, 6872) awarded the percentage of the chance lost, **45**
although this percentage finally had no effect on the quantification of the compensation award. In this decision Mr. Valentín suffered an accident of decompression while he was diving in Cullera (Valencia) and was promptly transferred to a public hospital, first in Cullera and then to another hospital in Valencia. Since the hospital in Valencia lacked a hyperbaric chamber which was required for his treatment, he had to be transferred to another hospital in Barcelona. Health authorities could have transported the patient in a medicalised helicopter, but they chose to transport him by ambulance. When it was finally possible to treat him at the hospital in Barcelona, more than ten hours had passed since the time of the accident After 37 days in hospital he was discharged, suffering,

90 Critically *idem*, 20; *E Vicente Domingo*, in: Reglero Campos (fn 24) (3rd edn 2006) 278.

among other sequelae, paraplegia which meant that he was prostrated in a wheelchair. The Supreme Court considered that the undue delay in the transfer deprived the claimant of the opportunity to obtain treatment under the best possible conditions and, consequently, this prevented him from avoiding the sequelae that he now suffered. According to the Court, 'the deprivation of these expectations, known in our case law as a *pérdida de oportunidad* (loss of chance) amounts to wrongful damage since, although uncertainty about result is something inseparable from the practice of medicine (a characteristic that explains why a right to be cured does not exist), citizens must have the guarantee that, at least, they are going to be treated with due care by applying all the means and instruments that medical science makes available to health care authorities'. The Court declared that 'it doesn't matter that recompression in a hyperbaric chamber does not guarantee a 100 per cent recovery for those who suffer disbaric accidents, given that 28.5 per cent of those treated within the first six hours nevertheless suffer permanent impairments. In any case Mr. Valentín was deprived of the opportunity of joining the 71.5 per cent of those who suffer injuries but, when treated in time, recover in full'. Accordingly, 'compensation is not awarded for the injury that he has in fact suffered ... but only for the mere possibility that if such delay had not occurred he could have obtained a more favourable result'. However, in establishing the amount of the compensation, the Court did not take into account those specific percentages. It only mentioned the age of the victim when the accident happened, his profession, and the nature of the sequels resulting from this loss of chance, all this amounting to € 90,000 compensation.

46 The doctrine of the 'loss of a chance' has also been received in decisions dealing with 'loss of procedural chances' due to an attorney's or solicitor's negligence. In this area, however, case law has undergone some evolution. At the beginning, courts awarded compensation for 'the frustration for the victims arising out of the loss of the possibility of winning the process' (STS 26.1.1999 [RJ 1999\323]), what was considered to be a 'non-pecuniary loss' (SSTS 25.6.998 [RJ 1998\5013]; 14.5.1999 [RJ 1999\3106] and 30.12.2002 [RJ 2002\333]). Notwithstanding this, in recent years, the Supreme Court recognises that the chance lost by the victims in these cases is of an economic nature. For this reason 'it shall be considered that there is an economic loss if the object of the frustrated claim was aimed at obtaining an economic advantage, something which involves calculating the chances that the frustrated claim would have been successful' (SSTS 27.7.2006 [RJ 2006\6548]; 21.6.2007 [RJ 2007\3781] and 15.2.2008 [RJ 2008\2670]).

Reasoning like this should also be extended to medical liability cases since the loss of a chance to heal does not only cause pain and suffering, but also pecuniary losses (cost of future medical treatments, loss of future earnings due to the sequels etc) which should be compensated according to the proportion that corresponds thereto.[91] However, the Spanish Supreme Court has not yet reached this point. **47**

13. Multiple persons involved

a) Multiple persons involved. In cases where more than one individual has been involved in the provision of medical services to the patient, all of them will be held solidarily liable for the damage caused, provided that each defendant has met the required conditions for liability. Although Arts 1137 and 1138 CC establish that in cases of concurrence of several debtors in a single obligation solidarity is not presumed and it will only apply when 'the obligation expressly so provides', the prevailing legal doctrine as well as case law hold the opposing view. Accordingly, it is a general rule in the area of tort law that the causation of damage by multiple tortfeasors must give rise to solidary liability for all the participants. In this sense, it is considered that the presumption of non-solidarity as provided in Arts 1137 and 1138 CC only applies to obligations arising from contract and not to those arising from tort (STS 14.4.2001 [RJ 2001\3640]). Solidary liability favours foremost the compensation of victims not only in cases of the insolvency of one of the debtors but also when it could be extremely burdensome for the victim to have to prove which part of the damage caused would be attributed to each tortfeasor.[92] Moreover, solidarity is the solution favoured in most specific provisions dealing particularly with tort liability.[93] In the area of health care liability, there **48**

91 *M Martín-Casals/J Solé Feliu*, Comentario al Art 1902 del Código Civil, in: A Dominguez Luelmo (ed), Comentario del Código Civil (2010) 2049.

92 In this sense, see SSTS 25.11.1993 (RJ 1993\9134); 21.12.1999 (RJ 1999\9747); 15.2.2001 (RJ 2001\1449); 14.4.2001 (RJ 2001\3640); 7.3.2002 (RJ 2002\4151) and 8.11.2007 (RJ 2007\8253). For a synthesis of the different arguments, see *R de Ángel*, Tratado de responsabilidad civil (1992) 847; *F Pantaleón*, Comentarios del Código Civil, II (CMJ) (2001); *CI Asúa González*, La responsabilidad, in: Ll Puig Ferriol et al, Manual de Derecho Civil, II. Derecho de obligaciones. Responsabilidad civil. Teoría general del contrato (3rd edn 2000) 476.

93 In that sense, see for instance, Art 123 of the Act of 21 July, 1960, *de Navegación Aérea* (Air Navigation Act, LNA); Art 52 of the Act of 29 April, 1964, *de Energía Nuclear* (Nuclear Energy Act, LEN); Art 65 of the Act of 18 March, 1966, *de Prensa e Imprenta* (Press and Printing Act); Art 132 of the LGDCU–2007, etc.

are plenty of decisions establishing solidary liability among a plurality of tortfeasors such as SSTS 24.3.2001 (RJ 2001\3986) and 8.11.2007 (RJ 2007\8253), between the doctor and the insurance company covering the cost of health care assistance; STS 13.4.1999 (RJ 1999\2583) between the doctor and the private hospital where the intervention took place; STS 25.11.1993 (RJ 1993\9134) among the doctors whose negligent conduct caused the damage; SSTS 25.11.1993 (RJ 1993\9134), 11.6.2001 (RJ 2001\5674) and 17.9.2008 (RJ 2008\5517) between the doctor and the public administration body owning the hospital or among several public administrations responsible for health care services (in claims brought before legal reforms introduced in 1999).

49 **b) Liability for others.** As a rule, hospitals and private doctors are held liable for the acts of their auxiliaries. In these cases, liability is established pursuant to Art 1903 IV CC, which requires that the following conditions are met: (1) The existence of a relationship of dependence between the owner of the establishment or company and the person who causes the damage. This relationship requires that the principal (the hospital or the doctor) has a power of supervision, control or direction over the acts of the auxiliary.[94] (2) There must be a causal link between the damage and the act of the auxiliary, this act being within the scope of his or her employment.[95] (3) The employee must have been negligent.[96] Case law has however been quite flexible with regard to this latter condition and courts have occasionally held the employer liable under the presumption of fault of an unidentified employee (STS 9.6.1998 [RJ 1998\3717]).[97] (4) Liability of the employer is based on a *iuris tantum* presumption of his or her fault, which can be rebutted by proving that he/she acted diligently (Art 1903 VI CC). (5) Finally, once the principal has paid the compensation, Art 1904 CC allows him/her to recoup the damages that he or she has already paid from

---

94 SSTS 2.11.1999 (RJ 1999\7998) and 16.1.2003 (RJ 2003\6). In legal doctrine, see *F Pantaleón*, Enciclopedia Jurídica Básica (EJB), vol II (1995) 5957; *J Barceló Doménech*, Responsabilidad extracontractual del empresario por actividades de sus dependientes (1995) 216.

95 STS 2.7.1990 (RJ 1990\5766). *Barceló Doménech* (fn 94) 311.

96 SSTS 20.9.1997 (RJ 1997\6706); 15.9.1998 (RJ 1998\6742) and 5.12.2006 (RJ 2007\269). *Rivero Hernández* (fn 69) 504.

97 This flexibility has led courts to hold employers liable pursuant to Art 1903 IV CC without requiring the employee to have been held liable as well. Or it has even been accepted that the claim be brought against the employer only and not against the specific employee who caused the damage, although the court has to deal subsequently with the question referring to whether the employee (who is not a part in the proceedings) acted negligently or not (see, among others, SSTS 16.4.1993 [RJ 1993\2886]; 24.2.1992 [RJ 1992\1427] and 10.11.1990 [RJ 1990\8538]).

the auxiliary.[98] Under these conditions the liability of hospitals and doctors for the acts of their staff must be evaluated. So in sum: hospitals will be held liable for the acts of their staff if they supervised, controlled or guided the activity of the staff, if the auxiliary who acted was at fault and caused the damage acting within the scope of his/her employment (Art 1903 IV CC). In this case, fault of the hospital will be presumed unless it can be proven that it acted with due care (Art 1903 VI CC). Doctors' liability for acts of the hospital's staff will depend upon whether the doctor supervised, controlled or directed the activity of the staff and the staff acted within the scope of the activity entrusted to them by the doctor. If these conditions are met, doctors will be held liable according to Art 1903 IV CC, without detriment to the liability of the staff themselves pursuant to Art 1902 CC (in which case, case law establishes that the principal and the auxiliary are held solidarily liable).[99] At the same time, it also will depend on the obligations assumed by the doctor regarding the patient. As a rule, the doctor will be held liable for the acts of the hospital staff who assist him during the operation (case a), because in this case the staff will act under the direction of the doctor. By contrast, acts of nurses or other professionals taking care of the patient before or after the operation will usually lead to liability of the hospital not the doctor, since they will have acted on instructions from the hospital (case b), with the exception of any specific instructions that were given by the doctor.

Additionally, it should be borne in mind that hospitals can also be held **50**
strictly liable according to Art 148.2 LGDCU–2007 (on this issue, see infra nos 51 f).

14. Strict liability

Art 148.2 LGDCU–2007 establishes a strict liability regime for the provider **51**
of health care services which applies regardless of whether liability is in contract or in tort.[100] Recoverable damages are pecuniary loss, including

98 Although this provision seems contradictory to a system of liability of the employer for his or her 'own acts', a sector of legal scholarship tries to overcome the problem pointing out that, in fact, Art 1904 CC does not allow the employer to recoup all he has paid but only the part that is related to the employee's fault. See, in that sense, *R de Ángel Yágüez* in: C Paz Ares/R Bercovitz/L Díez-Picazo/P Salvador (eds), Comentario del Código Civil II (1991) 2035; *Rivero Hernández* (fn 69) 507.

99 *J Solé Feliu*, La pluralidad de causantes del daño y solidaridad, Revista de Derecho Privado (RDP) January-February 2008, 3–42, at 40.

100 For the former see Art 28.2 LGDCU–1984, *R Bercovitz*, in: R Bercovitz/I Salas, Comentarios a la Ley General para la Defensa de los Consumidores y Usuarios (1992), Art. 28, 715.

both actual losses – provided that they arise from damage to property mainly intended for private use (Art 129.1 LGDCU–2007) – and loss of earnings arising from personal injury. According to some scholars, non-pecuniary losses (both psycho-physical harm, which can be medically assessed, and pain and suffering or *daño moral* strictly speaking)[101] are also recoverable. However, for certain specific cases the Act sets a cap of € 3,005,060.52 (cf Art 148.3 LGDCU–2007), which means that for the damage exceeding this amount the victim will have to resort to the general rules of fault liability provided by Art 1902 ff CC.[102] It has been questioned whether development risks are also a defence or not. Whereas some scholars consider that the fact that the Act does not mention the defence should be taken to exclude such a defence,[103] others consider that this is a valid defence,[104] while still others contend that the question should be resolved on a case-by-case basis taking into account the circumstances of the case.[105]

52 The broad scope of the expression 'health care services' contained in Art 28.2 LGDCU–1984, current Art 148.2 LGDCU–2007, has led a sector of legal scholars to assume that the strict liability regime established by this provision could apply not only to liability of hospitals but also to liability of physicians and to health care personnel in general.[106] However,

---

101 Compensation for non-pecuniary losses was generally admitted under the text of the old Art 28 LGDCU–1984. However, the new text of Arts 128.II and 129 LGDCU–2007, extending rules stemming from the Directive 85/374/EEC referring to products to services and giveing rise to many doubts, also in this respect. Thus, according to some legal scholars, the new wording of Art 129 LGDCU–2007 can be understood in the sense of recognizing compensation for non-pecuniary losses caused, both by defective products as well as by services (including 'health care services') (*M Martín-Casals/J Solé Feliu*, ¿Refundir o legislar? Algunos problemas de la regulación de la responsabilidad por productos y servicios defectuosos en el texto refundido de la LGDCU, Revista de Derecho Privado (RDP) September/October 2008, 98 f). By contrast, what seems to be the prevailing position holds that new Art 129 LGDCU–2008 reduces precisely the scope of protection for damage caused by services with regard to the regulation provided in the LGDCU–1984. So, it has to be interpreted as excluding the compensation for non-pecuniary losses caused by services (among others, by *A Cavanillas Múgica*, El Real Decreto Legislativo 1/2007, por el que se aprueba el texto refundido de la Ley General para la Defensa de los Consumidores y Usuarios y otras leyes complementarias, Aranzadi Civil 1/2008, 15 ff; *Asúa González* (fn 39) 785.

102 For the former Art 28.2 LGDCU – 1984, see *Bercovitz* (fn 100) 727.

103 *I Díaz de Lezcano Sevillano*, La responsabilidad del productor: referencia a la directiva comunitaria y a las leyes y proyectos de actuación, ADC 1990, 764; *MA Domínguez García*, Responsabilidad civil por productos defectuosos en el marco de la legislación especial en materia de consumo. Perspectivas de adaptación y reforma, in: Estudios de derecho mercantil en homenaje al profesor M. Broseta Pont, vol I (1995) 894.

104 *Bercovitz* (fn 100) 718.

105 *MA Parra Lucán*, Daños por productos y protección del consumidor (1990) 399.

106 *R Bercovitz*, Comentario a la STS 2 de julio de 1997, Cuadernos Civitas de Jurisprudencia Civil (CCJC) 1997, no 35, 1219; *E Gómez Calle*, El fundamento de la responsabilidad civil en el ámbito médico-sanitario, ADC 1998, 1755.

the practice of the courts refutes this assumption. Although initially courts expressly refused to apply this provision to health care services,[107] since 1997 several decisions of the Spanish Supreme Court have begun to apply the strict liability regime established by the former Art 28 LGDCU–1984 (current Art 148 LGDCU–2007) to owners of private hospitals and health care centres, but have continued to apply a fault liability regime (Arts 1902 or 1903 CC) to physicians and other health care personnel.[108] As STS 4.12.2007 (RJ 2007\251) has recently declared, the strict liability regime provided in the LGDCU 'according to the most recent case law … does not affect the medical practitioner's acts strictly speaking, given that the application of liability based on negligence arising from the breach of the *lex artis ad hoc* is inherent to them …'. Consequently, the liability regime established by the consumer protection provisions is only applicable to the organisational aspects or to the provision of health care services outside the medical practitioner's activity in the strict sense. Besides that, it must be added that not all 'health care services' are submitted to a strict liability regime, but only those services that, according to Art 148.1 LGDCU–2007 (former Art 28.1 LGDCU–1984) 'necessarily include the guarantee of certain levels of purity, efficacy or safety, under objective conditions of ascertainment, and that purport technical, professional or systematic controls of quality' (in that sense, STS 28.11.2007 [RJ 20078427]). For this reason, Spanish courts usually restrict the application of this provision to cases related to infections contracted in the hospital (nosocomial infections) and damage caused on hospital premises by surgical tools and in general by other hospital services which are required to meet specific conditions of safety.[109]

Strict liability is also established with regard to liability of public administration bodies, as has been explained in more detail infra in question 19. 53

C. Contractual Liability

15. Basics of contracts in the health care sector

In private health care patients may receive medical services on contractual basis. Whether this contractual relationship is established with the doctor, 54

107 SSTS 22.7.1994 (RJ 1994\6581); 29.7.1994 (RJ 1994\6937); 11.2.1997 (RJ 1997\940) and 27.6.1997 (RJ 1997\5758).

108 See SSTS 1.7.1997 (RJ 1997\5471); 21.7.1997 (RJ 1997\5523); 11.2.1998 (RJ 1998\707); 6.5.1998 (RJ 1998\2934) and 9.6.1998 (RJ 1998\3717).

109 So, in case law, STS 5.2.2001 (RJ 2001\541). In legal writing, *Asúa González* (fn 39) 795.

the hospital or with other health professionals depends upon the circumstances of each case. Thus, if the patient contracts with a hospital acting through its auxiliaries, the hospital will be held liable in contract whereas the auxiliaries could only be held liable in tort by the patient.[110] If, by contrast, the patient enters into a contractual relationship with the doctor or simultaneously with the hospital and the doctor [or other health professionals], proceedings will be brought against all of them on a contractual basis (STS 12.3.2004 [RJ 2004\2146]).

55 Case law and legal scholarship agree that the contract between the patient and the doctor is generally a contract of services in which the doctor commits him/herself to do his or her best to cure the patient (the so-called 'obligation of means'). According to this, his liability is fault based, since the doctor binds him/herself to act with the care required by the specific medical standard of care (*lex artis*) and to take all the available measures (according to current scientific knowledge) necessary to attain the result (see for instance STS 30.6.2009 [RJ 2009\339880]).[111] On the other hand, the contract between the patient and the hospital, the 'hospitalisation contract' (*contrato de hospitalización*), 'clinic contract' (*contrato de clínica*) or 'contract for hospital services' (*contrato de servicios hospitalarios*), has no specific legal regulation. In practice it includes a different sets of services – sometimes only some of them – such as (a) extra-medical services (accommodation, use of hospital facilities etc) and paramedical or assistance services (administration of medicines, temperature control, analysis and tests etc), (b) medical services strictly-speaking, such as a surgical operations, the prescription of medicines and post-operative control. In the latter case, the hospital provides diagnosis, prognosis and medical treatment through its own health care personnel.[112] Contractual liability of hospitals is usually based on fault and in practice the courts deal with their liability either in contract (Art 1101 ff CC) or in tort (Art 1902 ff CC). Sometimes courts also base their decisions on Art 148 of the General Act for the Protection of Consumers and Users, which considers hospitals to be strictly liable as providers of health care services to consumers and users. Finally, in the private sector, it is also common in Spain for health care assistance to be provided by means of a 'contrato de seguro de asistencia sanitaria' ('health care assistance insurance contract') (see supra

110 *Asúa González* (fn 39) 712.

111 Among others, *A Sánchez Gómez*, Contrato de servicios médicos y contrato de servicios hospitalarios (1998) 31 ff. In case law, STS 14.4.1999 (RJ 1999\2615).

112 SSTS 11.11.1991 (RJ 1991\8720) and 12.3.2004 (RJ 2004\2146). See also *Sánchez Gómez* (fn 111) 309–327; *J Ataz López*, Los médicos y la responsabilidad civil (1985) 207–212.

nos 10–18). Theoretically, this contract stands on a three-sided relationship: on the one side, there is an 'insurance contract' between the patient and the insurer covering the risk for the patient who needs medical services; on another side, there is the contract between the insurer and the doctor or the hospital, in which the latter undertakes the obligation to provide medical services to the insured, at no cost to him if the services are covered by the policy. At the appropriate time, the insurer undertakes the obligation to pay the agreed amount to the doctor or to the hospital, either for each medical activity separately, or as a lump-sum. Finally, there is the relationship between the patient and the doctor or the hospital, which should be treated independently from the other two provided that the health professional or the hospital have acted independently and not under the direction or the control of the insurer[113] (see for instance STS 4.10.2004 [RJ 2004\7238]). However, the Spanish Supreme Court does not share this view and in cases of medical malpractice has systematically held health care insurers liable by considering that (1) their obligations 'do not only consist of running with the financial cost of medical services, but also to render them through doctors or centres acting as contractual auxiliaries', (2) even when a 'dependence relationship' does not exist, the insurer creates a 'contractual appearance' to ensure that the health care services will be provided under safe conditions (SSTS 4.12.2007 [RJ 2008\251]; 19.6.2001 [RJ 2001\4974] and 2.11.1999 [RJ 1999\7998]). Beyond their specific content, none of these contracts have relevant specific features that allow them to be distinguished from general ordinary private law contracts.

Regarding the influence of the social welfare system on the relationships **56**
of the patients with doctors and hospitals, it must be taken into account that in Spain the majority of health care services are provided by the public health care system. In practice, this means that in a vast number of cases damage suffered by patients will be governed by the liability rules applicable to public bodies ie Arts 139 ff LRJAP. Consequently, on the one hand claims will be dealt with by administrative courts (Arts 9.4 LOPJ and 2 Ley 29/1998)[114] and on the other, tortfeasors will be held strictly liable for the 'normal or abnormal functioning of public services' (see in more detail infra nos 66–73).[115] These consequences apply even when the medical service has been provided by a private hospital acting under an agreement with the Social Security (*centro privado concertado*) (Additional Provision

113 On this matter, see *Martín Casals/Ribot Igualada/Solé Feliu* (fn 30) 78 ff.
114 *Dominguez Luelmo* (fn 67) 72.
115 Ibid 74.

12th of Act 4/1999, amending LRJAP). Basically, this regime favours medical doctors and other professionals since, as set out infra no 66, Arts 139 ff LRJAP channel liability through the public body, preventing the victim from claiming against the civil servant or, in this case, the medical doctor or other health care personnel working for the Administration.

16. Differences to tort law

57 Legal scholarship generally agrees that when there is a contractual relationship between the patient and the doctor/hospital/health professional, claims should be brought in contract (Arts 1101 ff CC), whereas when there is no contract between the tortfeasor and the victim the claim should be brought in tort (Arts 1902 ff CC).[116] However, in a substantial number of judgments – if not in the majority of them – courts overcome this division by declaring that the harm caused in cases of health care assistance can give rise to liability in tort as well as to liability in contract. The consequence of this conclusion is that the claimant is allowed to choose between bringing his claim in contract or in tort.[117] In fact, the differences in practice between these two regimes are not substantial, except in a few aspects. Following the French model, the Spanish Civil Code devotes few provisions to tort liability, which leads courts and legal scholars to apply most of the general provisions primarily applicable to liability in contract to liability in tort by analogy (cf Art 1101 ff CC). These provisions include those related to *ad hoc* mitigation by the courts (Art 1103 CC), standard of care (Art 1104 CC) or scope of the recoverable damage (Art 1107 CC).[118] Probably the most important difference between contract and tort liability is to be found in the limitation periods, there being 15 years for actions in contract (Art 1964 CC) and only one year for actions in tort, running from the moment from which the victim became aware of the damage (Art 1968.2 CC). Another important difference can be found in the case of plurality of tortfeasors. Whereas Art 1137 CC – a provision that should apply theoretically to all obligations regardless of their source – establishes the principle that in the case of a plurality of debtors they are not held solidarily liable, the Supreme Court has long established that tortfea-

116 Among many others, see *Asúa González* (fn 39) 712.

117 SSTS 9.12.1998 (RJ 1998\9427) and STS 26.9.2000 (RJ 2000\8126).

118 Although some legal writers and certain decisions consider that Art 1107 CC applies to tort liability (SSTS 20.6.1989 [RJ 1989\4702] and 24.11.1995 [RJ 1995\6352]), another part of legal doctrine – correctly, in our opinion – rejects extending its application to tort law (thus, *F Pantaleón*, El sistema de responsabilidad contractual [Materiales para un debate], ADC 1991, 1031).

sors are always held solidarily liable whenever the court cannot individualise the conduct or establish the degree of participation of each potential tortfeasor in causing the harm.[119]

However, as legal writing emphasises, most conditions for establishing liability, such as those regarding fault, causation in fact or causation in law (*imputación objetiva*), damage and proof of fault, causation or damage 'do not change their roles depending on whether liability is in contract or in tort'.[120] Indeed, health care liability is one of the areas where Spanish case law applies the so-called 'principle of the unity of civil fault' (SSTS 6.5.1998 [RJ 1998\2934] and 12.2.2000 [RJ 2000\820]) or the idea of 'juxtaposition of contractual and non-contractual aspects' (STS 26.9.2000 [RJ 2000\8126], which means that the existence of a contract between the parties will not suffice for contract liability to exclude tort liability. For this to occur, it is required for the damaging act to happen 'within the rigorous scope of the agreement and as a normal development of its contractual content' (SSTS 6.5.1998 [RJ 1998\2934] and 10.6.2004 [RJ 2004\3605]). However, when the act that causes damage is at the same time a breach of contract and an infringement of the general duty not to harm others, the claimant can choose between a claim in contract or in tort. The Supreme Court also states that the accumulation of liability in contract and liability in tort gives rise to actions that can be brought to court alternatively or subsidiarily in contract or in tort. The Supreme Court even allows the claimant to present the facts to the judge as they stand, so that the judge may choose to frame the action on the grounds that are most suitable to the case, and that may be more favourable to the victim, in order to offer him or her the most complete compensation for the damage sustained.[121] Accordingly, if the 'causa petendi' of the claim is clear, and there is no doubt that the parties are clearly asking for compensation for damage, the judge cannot dismiss the claim because the specific legal provisions that serve as the grounds for the claim were mistaken (ie contractual liability provisions instead of tort liability provisions, or vice versa), since it is for the judge to decide – or to correct – the legal provision **58**

---

119 So, for instance, in the health care liability area see among many others SSTS 23.10.2000 (RJ 2000\9197); 12.3.2004 (RJ 2004\2146); 10.5.2006 (RJ 2006\2399); 19.7.2007 (RJ 2007\4692) and 17.9.2008 (RJ 2008\5517).

120 *Asúa González* (fn 116) 728, 733. With regard to the specific issue of the burden of proof, see *Luna Yerga* (fn 72) 134.

121 Legal scholarship has severely critised this doctrine, considering that whenever a contract exists between the victim and the tortfeasor contract rules should take precedence. See *L Díez-Picazo*, Derecho de daños (1999) 263 ff; *Asúa González* (fn 116). 723 ff.

applicable to the case at stake, by means of the 'iura novit curia' principle[122] (Art 218.1.II Civil Procedural Act [LEC]).[123]

17. Contractual claims in the absence of direct contracts?

59 As a rule, there are no contractual claims in the absence of direct contracts in Spanish law. Although one exception can probably be found in the area of 'health care insurance contracts', where persons other than the contractual parties can be covered by the health care policy such as certain relatives (eg spouses, children and parents).[124]

18. Informed consent

60 Over the last few years, the doctrine of informed consent has acquired a great deal of importance in Spanish case law. As STS 10.5.2006 (RJ 2006\2399) states, informed consent 'aims at allowing the patient to participate in decision making with regard to his/her health and that, by means of the information the patient is given, he/she can evaluate the possibility of not undergoing surgery, to check the prognosis with other physicians and to decide whether to entrust surgery to other medical centres or specialists'. This duty exists irrespective of whether surgery has been performed according to the *lex artis* or not (SSTS 23.5.2007 [RJ 2007\4667] and 4.10.2007 [RJ 2007\5352]). For this reason, several decisions have declared that the duty to inform – as a pre-condition for the patient giving his/her consent – conforms the content of the obligation of means assumed by health care professionals, so that it is an essential element of the *lex artis*, infringement of which leads to liability.[125]

61 Until 2002, informed consent was regulated generally by Art 10 of the General Healthcare Act (Ley 14/1986, de 25 de abril, *General de Sanidad*,

---

122 SSTS 23.12.2004 (RJ 2005\82) and 4.3.2009 (JUR 2009\153728).

123 Ley 1/2000, de 7 de enero, *de Enjuiciamiento Civil* (BOE no 7, de 8 de enero de 2000). Corrección de errores BOE no 90, de 14 de abril de 2000 y no 180, de 28 de julio de 2001.

124 *Asúa González* (fn 39) 715.

125 Among others, see SSTS 2.10.1997 (RJ 1997\7405); 24.5.1999 (RJ 1999\3925) and 29.5.2003 (RJ 2003, 3916). In legal scholarship, see for instance, *J Ribot Igualada,* Comentario a la Sentencia del Tribunal Supremo de 2.7.2002, CCJC, vol 60, Oct/Dec 2002, 1159–1183; *JC Seuba Torreblanca/S Ramos González,* Derechos y obligaciones en materia de autonomía privada, información y documentación clínica, Indret, April 2003, 1–17 [www.Indret.com]; *J Ribot Igualada,* Comentario de la sentencia de 10 de mayo de 2006, CCJC, vol 74, May/August 2007, 773–800.

hereafter LGS).[126]. According to paragraph 5 of this provision the patient and his/her relatives were entitled 'to receive in understandable terms, complete, continuing and written information about his/her process, including diagnosis, prognosis and alternatives to treatment'. Paragraph 6 of Art 10 LGS established that written informed consent of the patient is required in order to freely choose whether to undergo an operation, except in the following cases: a) when no intervention entails a risk for public health, b) when the person has no legal competence to give his or her consent, in which case, consent will be given by relatives or close persons and c) when the urgency of the situation does not permit any delay as it could cause irreversible injuries or there could be the risk of death (Art 10.6 LGS). Although this provision dealt only with informed consent with regard to patients treated by 'the different public administrations', case law extended its application to private health care services'.[127]

As of November 2002, informed consent is regulated by the Basic Act on **62**
self-determination of patients and rights and duties regarding clinical information and documentation (Ley 41/2002, de 14 de noviembre, *básica reguladora de la autonomía del paciente y de derechos y obligaciones en materia de información y de documentación clínica,* hereafter LBAPIC).[128] Art 4.1 LBAPIC acknowledges that patients have the right to know all the information available regarding the health care intervention; this must at least include the aims, nature of associated risks and the consequences of the intervention. Art 10.1 specifies that the information will include 'a) the relevant or

126 BOE no 101, 29.04.1986.

127 See, M *Martín-Casals/J Solé Feliu/JC Seuba Torreblanca,* Liability for and Insurability of Biomedical Research Involving Human Subjects under Spanish Law, in: J Dute/MG Faure/H Koziol (eds), Liability for and Insurability of Biomedical Research with Human Subjects in a Comparative Perspective (2004) 288 ff and references quoted therein.

128 This Act entered into force on 16 May 2003. It should also be noted that almost all Autonomous Communities have already passed statutes on informed consent. Thus, for instance, in Catalonia, see Ley 21/2000, de 29 de diciembre, *sobre los derechos de información concernientes a la salud y la autonomía del paciente, y la documentación clínica* (DOGC, no 3303, 11.1.2001, p 464, correction of mistakes in DOGC no 3353, 22.3.2001; BOE no 29, 2.2.2001, p 4121); Galicia, Ley 3/2001, de 28 de mayo, *reguladora del consentimiento informado y de la historia clínica de los pacientes* (DOG no 111, 8.6.2001, p 7593; BOE no 158, 3.7.2001, p 23537); Extremadura, Ley 10/2001, de 28 de junio, *de Salud de Extremadura* (DOE no 76, 3.7.2001; BOE no 177, 26.7.2001, p 27021); Madrid, Ley 12/2001, de 21 de diciembre, *de Ordenación Sanitaria de la Comunidad de Madrid* (BOCM no 306, 26.12.2001; BOE no 55, 5.3.2002, p 8846); Aragon, Ley 6/2002, de 15 de abril, *de Salud de Aragón* (BOA no 46, 19.4.2002, p 3741; BOE no 121, 21.5.2002, p 18061); La Rioja, Ley 2/2002, de 17 de abril, *de Salud* (BOR no 49, 23.4.2002; BOE no 106, 3.5.2002, p 16210); Navarre, Ley Foral 11/2002, de 6 de mayo, *sobre los derechos del paciente a las voluntades anticipadas, a la información y a la documentación clínica* (BON no 58, 13.5.2002, p 4225; BOE no 129, 30.5.2002, p 19249).

important consequences that the intervention brings about with certainty; b) the risks related to the personal and professional circumstances of the patient; c) the probable risks under normal conditions, according to the experience and to state-of-the-art medical practice or directly associated to the kind of intervention and d) counter-indications of the intervention'. The physician 'will also have to evaluate in each case that, the more doubtful the outcome of an intervention is, the more necessary it becomes to obtain the previous written consent of the patient' (Art 10.2 LBAPIC). However, case law agrees that the duty to inform does not have an 'absolute or all-inclusive character' (see for instance STS 2.7.2002 [RJ 2002\5514]). In this sense, Spanish case law makes a specific distinction between so-called 'healing medicine' (*medicina curativa*, ie medicine aiming at healing) and 'satisfactive medicine' (*medicina satisfactiva*, ie interventions that the patient has no medical need to undergo but which he aims to achieve a successful transformation of his body as is the case in aesthetic or sterilisation interventions). In the area of 'healing medicine' 'it is not necessary to inform about those risks which are not frequent or which are not characteristics of the specific treatment (ie non-typical risks), provided that they are exceptional and of no extraordinary seriousness' (SSTS 17.4.2007 [RJ 2007\2322] and 4.10.2007 [RJ 2007\5352]). By contrast, in the area of so-called 'satisfactive medicine' the duty to inform is more detailed since, in most cases, there is no a specific need for the patient to undergo the intervention. For this reason case-law requires the duty to include providing 'objective, truthful, complete and affordable information, embracing the possibilities of the failure of the intervention, the probabilities of success, any sequelae, risks, complications or adverse outcomes that may occur, whether permanent or temporary, irrespective of their frequency' (see for eg STS 23.5.2007 [RJ 2007\4667]).

63 According to Art 4.3 LBAPIC, the person who has the duty to inform is 'the physician in charge of the patient'. In spite of this, other professionals taking care of the patient during the health care process or undertaking a technique or procedure will also be obliged to inform him/her (Art 4.3 LBAPIC). Beyond the statutory text, case law also extends the duty to inform to hospitals and centres where the operation or the treatment is performed (see for instance SSTS 19.6.2007 [RJ 2007\5572] and 4.10.2007 [RJ 2007\5352]).[129] As regards the persons who receive the information and must give their consent, Art 5.1 LBAPIC clarifies that these are the patients. Relatives and close persons can however also receive information

---

129 With regard to hospitals and centres, this duty is frequently based on Arts 1902 and 1903 CC (*Seuba Torreblanca/Ramos González*, Indret April 2003, 7).

as far as the patient expressly or implicitly allows it. Patients must also be informed when they are not fully competent, according to their possibilities of understanding, and information shall also be given to their legal representatives (Art 5.2 LBAPIC). If the patient does not have any capacity to understand the information due to his/her condition, the physician or hospital must directly inform his/her relatives or close persons (Art 5.3 LBAPIC).

Information must be given in an understandable and adequate manner, according to the needs of the patient in order that he/she can be made aware of the consequences and risks of the treatment and can decide whether to reject or delay the treatment, or even to choose a different specialist or centre. For this reason, case law declares that 'information shall be given in a basic and a personalised way, not being a mere administrative step' (SSTS 15.11.2006 [RJ 2006\8059] and 4.10.2007 [RJ 2007\5352]). With regard to formal requirements, the general rule is that no specific form is required either to give information to the patient (Art 4.1 LBAPIC) or to give consent (Art 8.2 LBAPIC). Consequently, both verbal and written forms are, generally, valid and sufficient.[130] However, written consent is required for surgical interventions, invasive diagnosis and treatment procedures and, generally, for the application of procedures that entail risks and inconveniences with a noticeable and foreseeable negative impact on the patient's health (Art 8.2 LBAPIC). **64**

Art 9.2 LBAPIC provides for situations where consent from the patient or from other persons who have to give it will not be needed. Basically, these exceptions refer to the case where no intervention could entail a risk to public health and where an emergency requires intervention and a delay could cause irreversible injuries or the death of the patient. Finally, Art 9.3 LBAPIC establishes cases where consent can be validly given by means of a representative. These cases are: a) when the patient is not able to take decisions, according to the physician's opinion, b) when the patient has been legally incapacitated or c) when the underage patient is not intellectually and emotionally capable of understanding the scope of the intervention, in which case the consent must be given by the minor's legal representative, after listening to the opinion of the minor if he/she is over twelve years of age. If the minor is emancipated and over sixteen years old, there is no need for the representative's consent. However, in this case, if the treatment is according to the physician's opinion high risk, the **65**

130 *Martín-Casals/Solé Feliu/Seuba Torreblanca* (fn 127) 291, no 114.

parents are to be informed and their opinion must be taken into account in order to make the appropriate decision.

D. Public Liability

19. Key differences from cases involving private hospitals or doctors

66 As has been pointed out, most health care services are provided in Spain by professionals working in hospitals or centres run by public authorities, whether national, regionally autonomic or local. This panorama has an important consequence with regard to the regime of liability, since public health care services are governed by rules concerning tort liability of public administration bodies.[131] These rules provide for a strict liability regime for damage that 'results from the normal or abnormal operation of public services' (Art 139.1 LRJAP). Public bodies will be held strictly liable for the damage caused by their personnel working for them in the performance of their duties, regardless of whether the tortfeasor is a civil servant or not. They will also be held liable for damage caused by concessionaires of a public service or by private contractors performing public works.[132] Pursuant to Arts 145 and 146 LRJAP, claimants can bring their claims against public bodies only, not against the specific civil servant or contracted member of the personnel who caused the harm. Notwithstanding, once compensation has been paid, whenever the tortfeasor who caused the damage acted with intent or gross negligence, the relevant public administrative body has the duty to bring a claim for recoupment against him/her (Art 145.2 LRJAP).

67 In accordance with these rules (Arts 139 ff LRJAP), the conditions that must be met in order to hold public bodies liable for providing health care services (STS 26.6.2008 [RJ 2008\6525]), are:

68 1) As regards damage, pursuant to Art 139.2 LRJAP, it must be 'actual'; it must be possible for it 'to be evaluated in money' and also 'to be individualised with regard to a person or to a certain group of persons'. The first requirement excludes harm that can be deemed doubtful and that which, although unavoidable, has not yet occurred when the claim is made. Legal doctrine considers that the individualisation of damage for harm that is

131 Cf Art 106.2 CE; Arts 139 to 146 LRJAP, as amended by Ley 4/1999.

132 SSTS 10.11.1990 (RAJ 1990\8538); 26.9.1991 (RAJ 1991\6869) and 11.2.1997 (RAJ 1997\898).

inherent to life in society is not recoverable (STS 20.5.1992 [RJ 1992\4165]).

2) Damage must also be subsequent to the normal or abnormal operation of public services (Art 139.1 LRJAP). 'Abnormal operation' is usually related to the infringement of a legal rule (unlawful act) or to the disregard of technical standards that apply to the situation.[133] 'Normal' operation may make public bodies liable for harm caused by acts that are perfectly lawful but in which the harm occurs as a result of the risk created by the mere fact of the existence of certain public services or of their organisation and accordingly, liability is only excluded in cases of *force majeure*.[134] The inclusion of the normal operation of public services as a source of liability has been severely criticised by legal scholars.[135] As case law has clearly established however, this regime of liability does not necessarily mean that public administration bodies can be held automatically liable by the mere fact of providing health care services. By contrast, they are bound to provide all the care that the *lex artis* requires in order to attain the result, but they are not obliged to attain the result itself: 'liability in public health care services does not arise from the result but from the provision of the required reasonable means… That is, liability can only be claimed once it has been proven that a health care centre has breached statutory rules, or when the claimant proves that there is an arbitrary organisation of the resources it uses to provide its health care service', ie, an organisational defect or a '*défaut de service*'.[136] **69**

3) The third condition for liability of public administration bodies that must be established is that damage will only be compensated for when it amounts to harm that 'the individual does not have the duty to endure according to the law' (Art 141 LRJAP). This is a requirement that legal **70**

133 See *G García-Álvarez* in: J Bermejo Vera (ed), Derecho Administrativo. Parte Especial (1999) 1067–1217, at 1137.

134 See STS 27.5.1987 (RAJ 1987\3488) and also *E García de Enterría/TR Fernández*, Curso de Derecho Administrativo II (1999) 370.

135 For the different opinions see *S Muñoz Machado*, Responsabilidad de los médicos y responsabilidad de la Administración sanitaria (con algunas reflexiones sobre las funciones actuales de la responsabilidad civil), in: La responsabilidad civil concurrente de las Administraciones Públicas (Y otros estudios sobre responsabilidad) (1998) 286; *L Martín Rebollo*, Ayer y hoy de la responsabilidad patrimonial de la Administración: un balance y tres reflexiones, Revista de Administración Pública (RAP) 150 (1999) 317–371, 367 f; *Oriol Mir Puigpelat*, La responsabilidad patrimonial de la Administración sanitaria. Organización, imputación y causalidad (2000) 248 f.

136 Among many others, see SSTS 29.6.2007 (RJ 2007\3747); 11.7.2007 (RJ 2007\6698); STS 26.6.2008 (RJ 2008\6525); 7.7.2008 (RJ 2009\6872) and 25.2.2009 (RJ 2009\2094).

doctrine has identified with the idea of wrongfulness, in the sense that damage must be unlawful.[137] The idea behind this condition is that citizens must endure general burdens (nuisances, detriments etc) arising from the general operation of public services while attaining communal or public interest;[138] harm is considered wrongful when the risk inherent to the operation of the service has exceeded the limits established by the standards of safety that society considers to be required.

71 An important number of decisions connect wrongfulness with the only two defences that are expressly accepted in the case of liability of public administration bodies: *force majeure* (Art 139.1 LRJAP) and development risks (Art 141.1 LRJAP) (SSTS 24.1.2006 [RJ 2006\733] and 10.5.2007 [RJ 2007\3403]). These decisions have frequently arisen in the context of damage caused by infections with HIV and HCV before state-of-the-art practice made it possible for these viruses to be detected (among other decisions, see SSTS 22.12.1997 [RJ 1998\737], 31.5.1999 [RJ 1999\6154], 3.12.1999 [RJ 1999\9349], 9.10.2000 [RJ 2000\9420], 10.2.2001 [RJ 2001\2629] and 20.9.2001 [RJ 2001\8038]).[139] Following a period in which the Spanish Supreme Court held public administration bodies liable for damage caused by blood infections, thereby rejecting the defence of *force majeure* (see for instance, STS 5.6.1991 [RJ 1991\5131]), in the second half of the nineties, it started to admit the defence, considering that the impossibility of the state-of-the-art practice to be able to detect the viruses amounted to *force majeure* (as, for instance, SSTS 22.12.1997 [RJ 1998\737] and 5.4.2000 [RJ 2000\3284]). In 1999, an amendment to the LRJAP introduced new wording in Art 141.1 LRJAP which now provides that public bodies can be exonerated for development risks if they prove that the damage resulted 'from facts or circumstances that could not have been foreseen or avoided, according to the state of scientific and technical knowledge existing at the time damage was caused'. After this amendment came into force several decisions applied this provision to exonerate public administration bodies providing health care for damage caused by contaminated blood (among many others, see SSTS 25.11.2000 [RJ 2000\550] and 10.2.2001 [RJ 2001\2629]). However, it must be stressed that these decisions refer to transfusions which took place before the

137 *JM Busto Lago*, La responsabilidad civil de las Administraciones Públicas, in: Reglero Campos (fn 24) (2008) 909 ff.

138 Dictamen del Consejo de Estado no 464/1995, of 16 March.

139 On these issues, see *JC Seuba Torreblanca*, Sangre contaminada, responsabilidad civil y ayudas públicas (2002) 316 ff.

detection of these viruses was possible. Currently, public administration bodies are strictly liable for damage resulting from HIV and HCV and such a defence is not available.[140]

4) Finally, case law as well as legal doctrine require a causal link to be established between the 'normal' or 'abnormal' operation of public services and the damage (SSTS 26.6.2008 [RJ 2008\6525] and 7.7.2008 [RJ 2008\6872]).[141] 72

The prescribed time period for bringing the claim against public health care providers is one year from the time the event causing the damage took place or from the time the damages became apparent. In the case of physical or psychical damages, this runs from the time that the sequels either occurred or their scope could be established (Art 142.5 LRJAP). As has been said previously, after the reforms carried out in 1998 and 1999, tort claims for damage caused by public bodies or by their personnel are only dealt with by administrative courts (Arts 9.4 LOPJ[142] and Art 2 LJCA). More explicitly, the Twelfth Additional Disposition LRJAP[143] states that claims against Social Security and health care services of the national health care system will be tried by administrative courts. These rules will also apply to private hospitals or health centres providing health care services under an agreement with Social Security or Health Care Public administration (the so-called 'centros privados concertados').[144] 73

E. Alternative Compensation Regimes

20. Funds and/or other alternative compensation regimes

Compensation funds related to health care liability have only been established for infections with HIV and HCV resulting from blood transfusion or treatment with blood products which were carried out within the 74

140 On these issues, see *Seuba Torreblanca* (fn 139) 312 ff, holding that, in the case of HIV, the development risk defense can be raised for infections before July 1982. In the case of VHC the borderline must be established in 1975.

141 *D Bello Janeiro*, Responsabilidad civil del médico y responsabilidad patrimonial de la Administración sanitaria (2009) 167 ff.

142 The new wording was introduced by the amendment made by LO 6/1998, of 13th of July (BOE no 167, 14.07.1998).

143 As amended by Act 41/1999.

144 See *J Fernández Costales*, Estado actual de la casuística de la responsabilidad sanitaria, a la luz de los Consejos Consultivos, del Consejo de Estado y de la Jurisprudencia, in: JA Moreno Martínez (ed), La responsabilidad civil y su problemática actual (2007) 265.

framework of public medical health care. See Royal Decree 9/1993 of 28th May on benefits in favour of persons affected by HIV as a consequence of actions within the framework of the public health care system.[145] With regard to HCV, the Spanish Government passed the Act 14/2002 of 5th June, establishing social benefits in favour of persons with haemophilia and other congenital diseases related to blood who have developed hepatitis C as the result of receiving medical treatment with blood products within the public health care system.[146] This Act was developed by Royal Decree 377/2003 of 28 March.[147]

75 **Beneficiaries and requirements for compensation.** Royal Decree 9/1993 and Royal Decree 377/2003 establish different sorts of beneficiaries as well as several requirements that must be met in order to receive compensation.

76 With regard to HIV, persons entitled to obtain benefits are haemophiliacs and persons suffering blood coagulation diseases who have become infected with HIV through blood products and blood transfusions administered or performed within the public health care system before proofs detecting HIV were compulsory. Other persons entitled to these benefits are (a) the spouse or other persons with whom the main beneficiary had established a duly proven family union and who had become infected with HIV due to the relationship with this person, (b) children of the aforementioned persons infected with HIV, as long as the infection had been diagnosed after pregnancy occurred, (c) children dependent on the aforementioned persons, as long as they are under 24 years of age and (d) persons older than 75 years dependent on the aforementioned beneficiaries (Art 1 Royal Decree Law 9/1993).

77 As regards hepatitis C (HVC), Royal Decree 377/2003 considers beneficiaries of the social benefits to be persons who are haemophiliacs and persons suffering blood coagulation diseases having developed HVC as a consequence of receiving medical treatment within the public health care system. The Royal Decree provides that in order to receive compensation these persons must be registered in a specific census. If such persons pass away, the persons entitled to the benefits are their underage and disabled adult children. In the absence of these persons, the beneficiaries will be the spouse who is not legally separated from the deceased or the person

---

145 BOE no 130, of 1.06.1993.

146 BOE no 135, of 6.06.2000.

147 BOE no 76, of 29.03.2003 (correction of mistakes BOE no 99, of 25.04.2003).

with whom the deceased was living for a period of at least two years before the time of death. In the absence of both categories of persons, those entitled to receive the benefits will be the parents of the deceased (Art 1 Royal Decree 377/2003).

Heads of damages, incompatibility with compensation awards in tort and assessment of the benefits. Since these benefits are based on social solidarity, they only provide for the payment of a lump sum, without specification of the heads of damages that they cover. These benefits can accumulate with other social benefits that the beneficiary may obtain (Art 3.1 Royal Decree 9/1993 and Art 2.1 Royal Decree 377/2003), but they cannot accumulate with damages awards resulting from tort liability. Thus, according to Art 3.2 Royal Decree 9/1993 and Art 2.1 Royal Decree 377/2003, before receiving the benefit the beneficiary must waive his/her legal claims against public administration bodies for the damage caused by infection. In addition, those persons who have already obtained a court order in his/her favour against public administration bodies in a proceeding related to tort liability resulting from an infection with HIV or HVC are excluded from the application of benefits (Arts 3.3 Royal Decree Law 9/1993and 2.4 Royal Decree 377/2003). **78**

In the case of HVC, the benefit will consist of the payment of a single lump sum of € 18,030.36 (Art 2.1 Royal Decree 377/2003). In the case of HIV, the assessment becomes more complicated, since the beneficiary will obtain a lump sum of 10 MPTA (Millones de Peseta, approx € 60,100) and a monthly payment which will be established by taking the minimum wage as a reference and which will vary according to the personal circumstances of the beneficiary (age, impairment, dependency etc) (Art 2.1 Royal Decree Law 9/1993). **79**

Finally, it must be taken into account that several Autonomous Communities have also passed regulations establishing social benefits in favour of persons infected with HCV. This is the case of Catalonia,[148] Castilla-La Mancha,[149] the Basque Country,[150] Aragón[151] and the Canary Islands.[152] **80**

148 Additional Provision 37th of the Act of the Catalan Parliament 3/2000, of 19 May, on the budget of the Generalitat de Catalunya for the year 2000 (DOGC no 3144, of 22.05.2000) and Order of 14 June 2000 (DOGC no 3164, of 20.06.2000).

149 Order 22 April 2008 (DOCastilla La Mancha, no 94, of 7 May 2008).

150 Order of 15 May 2007 (BO Basque Country no 110, of 8 June 2007; correction of mistakes BO Basque Country no 117, of 19 June 2007).

151 Order of 13 March 2008 (BO Aragón no 40, of 7 April 2008).

152 Order 13 June 2005 (BO Canary Islands, no 141, of 20 June 2005; correction of mistakes BO Canary Islands num. 164, of 22 August 2005).

81 To the reporters' knowledge, there are no other no-fault compensation systems or other alternative compensation schemes covering damages suffered by patients as a consequence of health care assistance in Spain.

F. Extent of Liability/Remedies

I. Pecuniary Loss

21. Introduction to indemnifying pecuniary loss

82 With regard to pecuniary losses, the starting-point is that Spanish tort law is governed by a principle of *restitutio in integrum* or full compensation of the damage sustained by the victim. This means that compensation must take into account both the harm actually sustained (*damnum emergens*) and the loss of profits (*lucrum cessans*) (Cf Art 1106 CC). In the case of personal injury, full compensation would consist of: (1) reimbursement of the expenses already incurred and of those which are foreseeable (medical treatment and health care, medicines, ambulance and transport, rehabilitative treatment, and continued care after discharging the victim) and (2) compensation for the loss of earnings due to the temporary or continuing lack of earning capacity. This second head of damages would take account of a) the temporary loss of earnings due to the personal injury and b) the continuing or permanent lack of earning capacity due to permanent impairment. As a rule, for pecuniary losses to be compensated it is required that their existence and amount are certain and proven.[153]

83 With regard to *lucrum cessans,* Spanish courts are cautious and only award compensation when the existence and amount of loss of earnings 'arise from a prospective assessment based on the reasonable foresight of future events' (STS 27.7.2006 [RJ 2006\6548]) or when losses 'are proved with a reasonable probability' (SSTS 4.2.2005 [RJ 2005\945]; 31.10.2007 [RJ 2007\8515] and 21.4.2008 [RJ 2008\4606]). By contrast, compensation for future losses must be rejected in all those cases where they appear to be merely hypothetical, when there are doubts about their future materialisation, or when their future production is not probable according to the

153 Thus, among many others, see *E Vicente Domingo,* El daño, in: LF Reglero Campos (ed), Tratado de responsabilidad civil I (2008) 316 ff; *Rivero Hernández* (fn 69) 458; *Maita Mª Naveira Zarra,* El evento dañoso, in: JMª Pena López, Derecho de responsabilidad civil extracontractual (2004) 45.

way circumstances would have developed (SSTS 29.7.2009 [RJ 2009\3161]; 31.10.2007 [RJ 2007\8515] and 21.4.2008 [RJ 2008\4606]).[154]

22. Loss of earnings vs loss of earning capacity

The most common practice in Spain compensates for loss of earning capacity of victims, whether they were carrying out paid or unpaid activities, or whether they actually had employment or not. The legal tariffication scheme for personal injuries caused by traffic accidents (LRCSCVM) refers expressly to compensation for pecuniary loss in a variable rate of up to 10 % from € 26,209.38 (as a correction factor increasing the amount of the basic compensation) for 'any victim of working age although revenues are not justified'.[155] This occurs in cases of compensation for death[156] and permanent disability.[157] **84**

Paradoxically, this possibility is not mentioned with regard to compensation for temporary disability,[158] which has led to opposing opinions in case law. According to one trend, the percentage of correction for any victim of working age shall be applied to harm producing temporary disability even when income is not justified. This is the prevailing position among courts of appeal, some of which base their reasoning on the application by analogy of the rules referring to death and permanent disability, considering that if this were not possible, persons such as housewives, who are working for the benefit of the family without obtaining income therefore, would be excluded from compensation.[159] By contrast, there is the view that temporary disability is different when compared with death or permanent disabilities. Accordingly, analogy is inappropriate and temporarily disabled victims can receive compensation for pecuniary losses only when they prove them.[160] **85**

---

154 *Martín-Casals/Solé Feliu* (fn 91); *Vicente Domingo* (fn 153) 332–336.

155 See, *LF Reglero Campos*, Valoración de daños corporales. El sistema valorativo de la Ley de Responsabilidad Civil y Seguro de Vehículos a Motor, in: Reglero Campos (ed), Tratado de Responsabilidad Civil, 648.

156 Section B), Table II, Annex LRCSCVM.

157 Section B), Table IV, Annex LRCSCVM.

158 Section A), Table V, Annex LRCSCVM.

159 So, for instance, SAP Madrid 10.1.2003 (JUR 2003\114150); SAP Madrid 14.6.2004 (AC 2004\1851); SAP La Rioja 29.6.2006 (JUR 2006\240362). Other references in *Reglero Campos* (fn 155) 706.

160 Many other decisions of the Courts of Appeal, such as, for instance, SAP Barcelona 10.1.2000 (AC 2000\55); Alicante 8.6.2006 (JUR 2006\270560) and Almería 11.7.2007 (JUR 2008\24820) follow this second approach and it also seems to be endorsed by the Civil Chamber of the Spanish Civil Court in STS 18.6.2009 (RJ 2009\4318).

86 In the area of medical malpractice, as in areas other than traffic liability, the tariffication scheme for traffic accidents has been used only as a guide for the courts and not as a statute with a gap filling function. According to this, and aside from the above-mentioned difference of opinion, some decisions award compensation for pecuniary losses to victims who do not prove income but who are of working age. This was the case, for instance, in SAP Alicante 30.4.2008 (AC 2008\1428) concerning a 31 year-old victim suffering sequelae resulting from medical negligence in plastic surgery. Similarly, SAP Madrid 14.6.2004 (AC 2004\1851), in a case of negligence during surgery, expressly established that the application of the corrective factor for economic losses 'will proceed even when the victim did not have a job and was 54 years old at the time of the accident'.

23. Periodic payments or lump sums?

87 As a general rule, Spanish case law awards compensation in the form of lump sums. However, over the last few years it has become more and more frequent to indemnify victims with periodic payments. This latter system is considered to be an adequate tool in compensating for cases of 'serious disabilities' ('*grandes invalideces*'), as well as for care and maintenance expenses.[161] According to legal scholarship, periodic payments best protect victims and prevent fraud on the part of their relatives.[162] Thus, they avoid lump sums which being out of the control of the victim, might be spent by their relatives on matters other than the victim's care. Besides that, periodical payments also avoid the personal enrichment of victim's heirs in cases where the victim dies before the time that was taken as a '*dies ad quem*' in calculating the amount of the lump sum.[163]

88 In legislation, the possibility of fixing periodical payments is set out in the legal tariffication scheme for personal injuries caused by traffic accidents. Thus, in Royal Decree 8/2004 of 29th October recasting the Traffic Liability Act (LRCSCVM), the Annex providing for a 'System to evaluate personal injuries in traffic accidents' sets out that 'at any time, the parties may agree, or the Judge may give the order, to replace compensation totally or partially by endowing an annuity in favour of the victim' (rule

161 *Reglero Campos* (fn 155) 539.

162 *F Soto Nieto*, La reparación de los daños personales. Criterios y métodos de valoración de los perjuicios no económicos y de los perjuicios futuros, Revista Española de Seguros (RES) 101 (2000) 44 ff.

163 *Reglero Campos* (fn 155) 539 f.

no 8).[164] And it adds that 'compensation or the annuity can only be modified when there are substantial changes in the circumstances which were taken into account in establishing those amounts or when supervening losses arise' (rule no 9).[165] According to these provisions, it is not necessary for periodic payments to be established at the time of awarding the compensation, but they can be agreed upon or ordered subsequently ('at any time'). It is also possible for the judge to grant a mixed award which combines a lump sum and periodic payments.[166]

Spanish case law does not limit the award of periodical payments to the area of traffic accidents, but extends it to other fields such as medical malpractice (see SSTS 24.9.2005 [RJ 2005\416] and 18.5.2006 [RJ 2006\4724]).[167] **89**

24. Caps and thresholds

As a rule, Spanish law does not provide for general caps and thresholds limiting compensation for pecuniary loss. The only caps and thresholds existing in Spain are to be found in specific Acts establishing strict liability regimes, which do not necessarily restrict their scope to pecuniary losses. **90**

With regard to thresholds, the Act implementing the Product Liability Directive provides that 'from the amount of compensation for pecuniary losses, a threshold of 390.66 € shall be deduced' (Art 141a) TRLGDCU. **91**

As for caps, fixed maximum amounts are found in several Acts: **92**

(a) The Spanish Act implementing the Product Liability Directive also establishes a cap of € 63,106,270.96 applied to a producer's total liability for damage resulting from death or personal injury which is caused by identical items with the same defect. **93**

---

164 '8. En cualquier momento podrá convenirse o acordarse judicialmente la sustitución total o parcial de la indemnización fijada por la constitución de una renta vitalicia en favor del perjudicado'.

165 '9. La indemnización o la renta vitalicia sólo podrán ser modificadas por alteraciones sustanciales en las circunstancias que determinaron la fijación de aquellas o por la aparición de daños sobrevenidos'.

166 *Reglero Campos* (fn 155) 540; *Mª Fernández Martín*, Indemnización en forma de renta vitalicia. Paper presented at the VII Curso de Valoración de Daños Personales. Los grandes inválidos, organised by SEAIDA, Madrid, 10–17 May 2007, p 7 <www.iurapraxis.com/datos/f_IFRV.pdf> (Date: 27.11.2009).

167 Other decisions awarding periodical payments in cases of serious disabilities are, for instance, SSTS 17.3.1998 (RJ 1998\1122); 29.7.1998 (RJ 1998\6453) and 18.12.2002 (RJ 2003\47).

94 (b) In the area of air accidents, Art 3.2 of the Council Regulation (EC) No 2027/97 of 9 October 1997 on air carrier liability in the event of accidents (which has superseded Art 117 Air Navigation Act-1960 [LNA]) sets out that the air carrier cannot limit his liability for bodily injuries to passengers below the amount of 100,000 SDR (approx € 118,874).[168] With respect to injuries not included in the scope of this Council Regulation, several caps apply as established in Art 118 for luggage lost or damaged and in Art 119 LNA (amended by Arts 3 and 4 of Royal Decree 37/2001 of 19th January) for damage caused to persons and things by aircraft action, either flying or on the ground, or for things falling off or being thrown from the aircraft.[169]

95 (c) Finally, as regards nuclear accidents, Art 16 Decree 2177/1967 of 22nd of July, on the coverage of nuclear risks (RRN), sets out that the operator of a nuclear plant will be liable to the maximum amount of 300 MPTA (approx € 600,000) per accident and per plant in operation, regardless of the number of persons injured and of the type of nuclear damage that they sustain.

II. Non-Pecuniary Loss

25. Introduction to indemnifying non-pecuniary loss

96 The prevailing legal scholarship classifies non-pecuniary loss arising from personal injuries according to the following criteria:

97 a) psycho-physical or biological damage, consisting of the temporary or permanent functional impairment suffered by the victim, either physiological or psychophysical, whose compensation should be the same for all persons, and which is characterised by the fact that it can be evaluated medically. This is an autonomous category of damage which can be assessed medically and which has been understood as an 'im-

168 *MT Álvarez Moreno*, La responsabilidad de las compañíías aéreas en caso de accidente: régimen instaurado por el Reglamento comunitario 2027/97 de 17 de octubre, Actualidad Civil 22 (2000) 813–833. In the case of air carriers to which Council Regulation (EC) No 2027/97 does not apply, Royal Decree 37/2001, of 19th of January (BOE no 29, 2.2.2001), prescribes the amounts applicable to their liability for death and for personal injuries.

169 So, for instance, a cap of 500 SDR (€ 594) for each item of luggage lost or damaged. For damage to property or injuries to persons other than passengers the caps for the total amount of damages are established according to the weight of the aircraft (for instance, 13,580,000 SDR [€ 16,143,218] plus 130 SDR [€ 154] for each kilogram that exceeds 50,000 kilograms for aircrafts that weight more than 50 tones.

pairment in the health or in the bodily or mental integrity of the human being, which is certain and real and independent from the pecuniary and non-pecuniary results that it produces'.[170] For this reason, Spanish case law awards compensation to comatose victims, as was the case in the SSTS 30.1.1990 (RJ 1990\74)[171] and 24.9.2005 (RJ 2005\416).[172]

b) specific personal detriments, which include all those heads of damages that cannot be evaluated medically, but that can be verified in medical terms such as aesthetic damage, sexual damage, loss of amenities or exceptional pain. In the case of aesthetic damage ('*perjuicio estético*'), the existence of which can be proved more easily than other types of non-pecuniary losses,[173] its assessment is therefore not left to the discretion of judges but undergoes medical evaluation, and the amount of damages is quantified and regulated by the legislator.[174] **98**

c) pain and suffering, pure *daño moral* strictly speaking, which refers to the physical and psychical pain that the victim has sustained as a result of the personal injury. Pain and suffering must be broadly construed and is not confined to those situations where a physical or mental illness has arisen.[175] Courts tend to refer here to feelings such as anxiety, restlessness, grief, uncertainty[176] and sorrow.[177] **99**

---

170 *R de Ángel Yágüez*, Tratado de responsabilidad civil (1993) 698.

171 The decision awarded 10 MPTA (€ 60,101) to a person who remained 'clinically dead' as a result of medical malpractice.

172 This decision confirmed the prior decision of the Audiencia Nacional, to award 20 MPTA (€ 120,000 approx) to a child in a 'vegetative state' for the 'injuries suffered'.

173 *Vicente Domingo* (fn 153) 367.

174 *M Martín-Casals/J Ribot/J Solé*, Non-Pecuniary Loss Under Spanish Law, in: WV Horton Rogers (ed), Damages for Non-Pecuniary Loss in a Comparative Perspective (2001) 194. Indeed, the legal tariff scheme evaluating damages caused by traffic accidents includes aesthetic damages such as an autonomous type of damages, independent from the physical prejudice, based on a specific system of gradual evaluation (see 8th Additional Provision of the Ley 30/1995, of 8th November, *de Ordenación y Supervisión de los Seguros Privados* [BOE no 268, 9.11.1995] (Act about ordering and supervision of private insurance, modifying the Act 122/1962, of 24th December, of the Use and Circulation of Motor Vehicles). Act 30/1995 has been reformed several times, the last one being the reform to Act 26/2006, of 17th July, *on Mediation of Private Insurances and Reinsurances* (BOE no 170, of 18 July 2006).

175 As the STS 16.5.1998 (RJ 1998\4878) declares, compensation for non-pecuniary loss does not need the harm to have 'become more definite with regard to specific pathological or psychological upsets'.

176 Instead of many, see STS 27.1.1998 (RJ 1998\551).

177 See STS 31.5.2000 (RJ 2000\5089), referring to the grief produced by delay in a trip by plane, but which sums up the current state of opinion of the courts with regard to non-pecuniary loss.

100 As regards the award for damages, as a rule, Spanish courts do not assess separate amounts to compensate for the different heads of damages but award a lump sum. Although it is now becoming common for decisions to differentiate between pecuniary and non-pecuniary losses, it is quite rare for courts to go beyond this and to specify the particular heads of damages referring to non-pecuniary losses which make up the award. Even when the decisions specify some types of non-pecuniary losses in conclusion they award a lump sum for all losses. Legal scholarship has criticised this approach since it leads to the misuse of non-pecuniary losses, using it as a device that allows the victim to obtain compensation for damages that have not been proven in the proceedings.[178]

101 It is difficult to establish what the maximum amounts awarded for non-pecuniary losses are since courts have not until recently begun to separate pecuniary and non-pecuniary losses and they usually follow the tariffication scheme established for traffic accidents which does not clearly separate these types of losses. However, with this caveat, it can be pointed out that for instance the decision STS 24.9.2005 (RJ 2005\416) awarded € 120,000 as 'non-pecuniary losses' to the parents of a child who was in a 'vegetative state' after medical malpractice.[179] STS 31.5.2004 (RJ 2004\3895) awarded 25 MPTA (approx € 150,600) to the parents of a child who died as a consequence of hepatitis C contracted after receiving a blood transfusion. STS 3rd Ch, 20.4.2005 (RJ 2005\4312), awarded 50 MPT (approx € 301,204) for non-pecuniary losses to a woman aged 39 who suffered an abortion and lost her child after an amniocentesis. The physician did not inform her about the risks of the treatment and she was accordingly unable to consent in an informed way. After losing the child, the woman entered a depression, suffering distress and serious agoraphobia, which led the Social Security to give her permanent sick leave. To our knowledge, there are no specific differences departing from the general rules in medical malpractice cases.

26. Who can claim compensation for non-pecuniary loss?

102 Spanish law takes a generous approach with regard to who can claim compensation for non-pecuniary losses arising from medical malpractice.

---

178 For a critical analysis on this point see *F Gómez Pomar*, Daño moral, Indret. Revista para el Análisis del Derecho, 12.11.2001.

179 The decision also awarded other amounts to the parents in order to cover pecuniary losses (the cost of moving house: 10 MPTA (approx € 60,240) and future medical expenses: 7 MPTA per year (approx € 42,168 per year). It also awarded approx € 120,000 to the child 'for personal injuries'.

Spanish case law awards non-pecuniary losses not only to the victim him/herself but also to close relatives. This compensation is awarded to indirect victims *iure proprio*, ie for their own bereavement, and not *iure hereditatis*. Moreover, compensation to indirect victims is granted not only when the primary victim dies (STS 22.2.2001 [RJ 2001\2242]) but also in certain cases where the primary victim survives (STS 2.11.2007 [RJ 2007\463]).

As STS 13.12.1996 (RJ 1996\8970) states, in a case where the primary victim died, 'frequently/in general the persons entitled to recover damages in case of death are the closest relatives of the victim, although *iure proprio* and not by succession'. Moreover, this decision sets out that compensation also extends to other persons related to the victim 'by ties of affection'. According to this, many decisions compensate for non-pecuniary losses suffered by the parents of the primary victim,[180] the spouse,[181] the spouse and children of the primary victim[182] or the spouse, child and pupil of the deceased.[183] The Spanish Supreme Court has also compensated for non-pecuniary losses of a *de facto* partner of the deceased (STS 19.12.1997 [RJ 1997\8799). Very few decisions compensate brothers of the primary victim, as was the case in STS 24.11.1970 (RJ 1970\4889), where damages were awarded to the brothers of the deceased, as the closest relatives of the victim who was single and whose parents had died long before. Spanish case-law also compensates relatives of primary victims who live; see for instance STS, 3rd Ch, 2.3.2004 (RJ 2004\2641), where non-pecuniary losses suffered by the parents and the sister of a child who contracted HIV and HCV after a blood transfusion, deteriorating his quality of life, were compensated. **103**

G. Procedural Matters

27. Specific rules of jurisdiction or procedure

There are no specific rules of jurisdiction or procedure which apply to medical malpractice cases only. The specificities that exist only refer to more general conditions, depending on whether the claim is brought against public health care providers or against a private health care centre, **104**

---

180 SSTS 20.7.1995 (RJ 1995\5728); 24.9.2004 (RJ 2004\416); 23.11.2004 (RJ 2004\7384) and 31.5.2004 (RJ 2004\3895).

181 STS 12.9.2007 (RJ 2007\4984).

182 SSTS 1.6.1981 (RJ 1981\3037); 15.4.2004 (RJ 2004\3566) and 7.3.2007 (RJ 2007\953)).

183 STS 23.9.2004 (RJ 2004\5890).

institution or the physician. As has been said supra nos 66 ff, regarding the former the claim is tried by administrative courts and the rules governing liability are those contained in Arts 139 ff LRJAP. In the latter case, claims are brought in ordinary courts and the applicable rules are to be found in Arts 1101 ff (contractual liability), Arts 1902 ff (tort liability) of the Civil Code, or in Art 148 LGDCU establishing strict liability for the provision of health care services to consumers and users (see *supra* nos 27 ff).

28. Special institutions handling malpractice claims

105 The only recognised possibility for handling medical malpractice claims out of the court is arbitration. Arbitration is regulated in Spain by Act 60/ 2003 of 23 December of Arbitration (LA)[184], which allows arbitration in all those disputes relating to matters within the free disposition of the parties according to law (Art 2.1 LA). Arbitration is entrusted not only to natural persons, but also to public corporations empowered to exercise arbitral functions according to their governing rulings, as well as to non-profit associations and societies whose rules envisage arbitral functions (Art 14 LA). Within the frame of this provision, some Bar Associations have created courts of arbitration,[185] as is the case, for instance, with the Bar Association of Madrid, which has a specific section aimed at arbitrating disputes related to medical malpractice claims. According to the Statute organising the Court of Arbitration of the Bar Association of Madrid,[186] the 'Section of Medical Malpractice of the Court of Arbitration' is entrusted to handle claims 'regarding liability of physicians, dentists, veterinarians and pharmaceuticals', as well as claims on 'liability arising from the wrong or defective use of products and services' (Art 9 Statutes). The Medical Malpractice Section of the Court of Arbitration is composed of (a) three lawyers belonging to the Bar with reputed prestige and knowledge in health care law, (b) three members appointed by different Medical Associations in Madrid, (c) two members appointed by the consumers and users organisations, (d) two members appointed by public authorities and (e) two members appointed by insurance companies insuring medical malpractice (Art 10 Statutes). The Section meets at least twice a year and

184 BOE no 309, of 26.12.2003.

185 Art 4.m) of the General Statute for Legal Profession (Real Decreto 658/2001, de 22 de junio, *Estatuto General de la Abogacía*) confers the power to arbitrate and to create courts of arbitration to bar associations.

186 *Estatutos de Funcionamiento de la Corte Arbitral de Madrid*, passed by the governing body the 17th February of 2004.

every time that its president so decides. Parties are obliged to pay costs of arbitration, including arbitrators' fees, according to a scale approved by the bar association. This scale awards fees in proportion to the amount of the matter submitted and provides for the possibility of raising or lowering them, up to 50 %, according to the complexity of the matter, the time needed by the arbitration and the effort – in terms of work and professional study – spent on it.[187]

In legal scholarship, some writers hold the opinion that 'mediation' and **106** 'conciliation' should be promoted as options prior to arbitration. The reason for this is that these means of dispute resolution try to bring the conflicting positions of the parties closer before transferring the decision into the hands of a third neutral party ie the arbitrator or the judge.[188] However, these systems have not yet been widely received in practice and currently most claims on medical malpractice are tried in legal proceedings before courts.

H. Outlook

29. Reform plans

To the reporters' knowledge, there are no plans in Spain aimed at intro- **107** ducing strict liability, no-fault or other alternative regimes covering damage caused by medical malpractice.

Cases

Case 1

In the case under analysis, fault of the gynaecologist seems to be proven **108** since he delayed in assisting X and did not adopt some of the measures required by the *lex artis* to prevent damage. His liability could be based on the general clause of fault liability in tort pursuant to Art 1902 CC. Fault of the midwife D also seems proven, since she failed to immediately notify the physician of the abnormal test results, something which due care

187 All these documents can be found on the website of the Bar Association of Madrid: <http://www.icam.es/web3/cache/NS_CA_cfa_cortearbitraje.html> (Date 7.10.2009).

188 So, for instance, *J Hernández Moreno/ML Hernández Gil/A Hernández Gil*, Responsabilidad por malpraxis médica: la vía extrajudicial, Cuadernos de Medicina Forense, no 28, April 2002, 7–24.

required. This circumstance would establish the grounds for her liability according to Art 1902 CC and, to the extent that she was acting as an auxiliary of C (the hospital), C could also be held liable on the grounds of Art CC 1903 IV, which establishes a presumption of fault of the principal for negligent conduct of its auxiliaries (see supra nos 49 f).[189] According to recent case law, a hospital's liability could also be based on Art 148 TRLGDCU, which establishes a strict liability regime for the provider of health services when they 'necessarily include the guarantee of certain levels of purity, efficacy or safety, under objective conditions of ascertainment, and that purport technical, professional or systematic controls of quality'. As described above in nos 51–53, case law of the Civil Chamber of the Supreme Court applies this regime to holders of private clinics and hospitals, 'with regard to the organisational aspects of the provision of health care services' (cf SSTS 5.1.2007 [RJ 2007\552]; 26.4.2007 [RJ 2007\3176] and 4.12.2007 [RJ 2007\251]). By contrast, we think that B, the gynaecologist who held a joint practice with A, should not be held liable, since he did not behave negligently, unless he consented to the replacement of A with the knowledge that he was not prepared to pursue his medical profession or to take care of his patients.[190]

109 However, what is crucial is whether the cause of the damage suffered by Y and presumably also the fact that her twin brother was stillborn was a pre-existing problem or arose from the negligent conduct of A and D. Both scenarios could have given rise to the same damage. If causation by A and D cannot be proven they will not be held liable. In this regard, as noted above in nos 39–42, the Spanish Supreme Court has consistently declared that in the area of medical malpractice 'when it is not possible to establish the causal link with negligence, there is no health care liability' (STS 29.3.1994 [RJ 1994\2305]) and that 'as regards liability of the medical professional, both strict liability and the regular application of the reversal of the burden of proof must be excluded...except when specifically provided by law (Art 217.5 LEC)' (SSTS 24.11.2005 [RJ 2005\7855] and 10.6.2008 [RJ 2008\4246]). It also contends that 'Article 1902 is based on

---

189 Art 1903 IV CC has also been used to hold clinics and hospitals liable for injuries caused as a result of a lack of adequate infrastructure or technical machinery or for the 'poor organisation of the technical and human resources' (so, for instance, STS 31.7.2002 [RJ 2002\7741]).

190 If A and B practice medicine jointly under the the form of a professional society (civil or commercial), Article 11 of the Ley 2/2007, de 15 de marzo, *de sociedades profesionales* (Professional Societies Act, BOE no 65 of 16.03.2007) provides for solidary liability of 'the society and professionals, either members of the society or not, who have acted.' In the case under analysis, the professional society established between A and B would be held solidarily liable, but it does not seem possible to hold B personally liable.

fault and requires from the patient the proof of a causal connection or link and of fault' (SSTS 24.11.2005 [RJ 2005\7855] and 10.6.2008 [RJ 2008\4246]) and that in the area of medical liability the burden of proof of causation rests upon the claimant 'without operating the reversal of the burden of proof accepted by this Chamber [Civil] for damage stemming from other sources and it is for the patient to prove the causal connection or link and fault (...) without this there is no health care liability' (STS 17.9.2008 [RJ 2008\5517]).

Given the circumstances, this difficulty could be overcome by resorting to **110** the doctrine of loss of chance which, as explained above in nos 43–47, is accepted by Spanish case law in the area of health care liability (SSTS 10.10.1998 [RJ 1998\8371], 10.5.2006 [RJ 2006\2399] and 12.7.2007 [RJ 2007\4993]). In our view, this would lead to compensating X in proportion to the likelihood that the negligence of the defendants (B and C) may have caused the damage for both the pecuniary and non-pecuniary loss resulting there from. Compensable also are pecuniary and non-pecuniary losses resulting from the impairments of Y and from the death of her twin brother. Damage caused to Y is not a case of wrongful life (the SSTS 18.5.2006 [RJ 2006\4724] and 16.6.2010 [JUR 2010\248618] granted compensation for wrongful life. With the exception of these cases, all other decisions of the Spanish Supreme Court after STS 23.11.2007 [RJ 2008\24] have rejected compensation). It is damage directly caused by medical negligence at the time of delivery (at least in a certain probability) and should therefore be compensated for in the corresponding proportion. However, as noted above in no 43, Spanish case law on medical malpractice still seems to consider loss of chance as an independent harm, a moral or non-pecuniary damage, which is different from injury to the physical integrity and the pecuniary and non-pecuniary losses arising from it (see for instance STS 17.4.2007 [RJ 2007\2322] or STSJ Madrid 23.10.2007 [RJ 2007\166246], compensating the 'non-pecuniary losses arising from the loss of chance to receive treatment').[191]

191 As explained above in nos 43–47, this understanding of the loss of chance as an autonomous non-pecuniary damage has been taken over by case law referring to the so-called 'procedural chance' which provides that, when the proceedings that have been frustrated by the legal professional's negligence dealt with assets having pecuniary value, the amount of compensation for the lost chance will be determined 'from a prospective calculation of the chances of success of the claim' (see SSTS 27.7. 2006 [RJ 2006\6548]; 21.6.2007 [RJ 2007\3781] and 15.2.2008 [RJ 2008\2670]).

Case 2

111 In cases of wrongful conception both Spanish legal doctrine and case law unanimously reject that damage consists in the conception and subsequent birth of the unexpected child.[192] In this sense STS 5.6.1998 (RJ 1998\4275) stated that 'human life is a precious asset in any civilised society and its legal system protects it first of all and above all. It cannot be accepted that the birth of unforeseen children could entail an evil for their parents'.

112 There is also general agreement to compensate for the positive damage and loss of earnings stemming from pregnancy and the subsequent birth of the child. Thus legal doctrine and case law allow compensation for the expenses resulting from pregnancy and childbirth, such as medical costs and other additional costs.[193] They also endorse compensation for loss of profit resulting from pregnancy and childbirth when the mother 'needed to rest in bed because of pregnancy and, therefore, failed to properly run the business she owned with a consequent slowdown in production'[194] or when she had to temporarily or permanently give up her usual job with subsequent pecuniary damage.[195] Accordingly, it seems that X should be compensated for the loss of earnings resulting from the impossibility of taking on the position she had been offered because of her pregnancy and for having to care for the child.

113 Spanish courts tend not to object neither to compensation for non-pecuniary damage stemming from pregnancy nor the subsequent birth of the unexpected healthy child. Thus, it is common for damages awards to include compensation for distress, feelings of frustration and anxiety caused by the unexpected conception of the child,[196] as in the case of STS 24.9.1999,[197] which compensated for non-pecuniary damage of a mother

---

192 See, amongst many *R de Ángel Yágüez*, Diagnósticos Genéticos Prenatales y Responsabilidad (II), Revista de Derecho y Genoma Humano 5/1996, 152; *Mª P García Rubio* Comentario a la STS de 20 de mayo de 1998, CCJC 48/1998, 1218; *M Martín-Casals/J Solé Feliu*, Responsabilidad civil por anticoncepción fallida (wrongful conception), La Ley 2001/5249, 1–6 at 3.

193 STS 5.6.1998 (RJ 1998\4275) and STS (Administrative Chamber) 3.10.2000 (RJ 2000\7799). See also SAP Álava 18.5.1998 (AC 1998\5514).

194 As in STS 24.9.1999 (RJ 1999\7272).

195 STS 5.6.1998 (RJ 1998\4275); SAP Barcelona 30.7.1990 (RJC 1990/4). In legal scholarship see *García Rubio*, CCJC 48/1998, 1220.

196 See *García Rubio*, CCJC 48/1998, 1220 and *M Ureña Martínez*, Comentario a la STS 6 de junio de 1997, CCJC 45/1997, 1112.

197 RJ 1999\7272.

for whom pregnancy caused 'a situation of depression that altered her psychic harmony and gave rise to an unavoidable state of worry detrimental to her freedom'.

As regards compensation for maintenance of the unexpected healthy child, although some scholars are in favour thereof,[198] others consider that maintenance is a legal obligation that rests upon the parents, is linked to the principle of family solidarity, and is part of an institutional framework of rights and duties (such as the right to maintenance and rights to legitimate portion and intestate succession in the estate of the parents) that cannot be separated from the parent-child relationship and which is disturbed by third party compensation.[199] Using similar arguments, the Spanish Supreme Court has usually rejected compensation for the maintenance of the unexpected healthy child.[200] For these reasons neither X nor would Y be entitled to receive an award on the grounds of maintenance for the child. **114**

However, in isolated decisions some lower courts have employed a more conciliatory approach and held that in extreme situations and in light of the circumstances of the case (eg parents who undergo sterilisation because they cannot maintain the children that they already have), the maintenance of a further child can be too heavy a burden to carry and it can thus be compensated for by way of exception (see STSJ Castilla-León (Valladolid) 13.6.2006 [JUR 2006\248717]). This also seems to be the position of STSJ Madrid 25.3.2008 (JUR 2008\163551) in which the court held that in 'this case there is no evidence showing what the financial situation of the family, constituted by the claimants and their three children, was in order to obtain any conclusion as regards the impact of **115**

198 See F *Pantaleón Prieto*, Procreación artificial y responsabilidad civil, in: II Congreso Mundial Vasco, La filiación a finales del siglo XX (1988) 251 and *García Rubio*, CCJC 48/1998, 1219.

199 See, with further details, *M Martín-Casals/J Solé Feliu*, Comentario a la sentencia de 29 de mayo de 2003, CCJC 64/2004, 193–218 at 212–214.

200 Thus, for instance STS 29.5.2003 (RJ 20003\3916) reduced the amount of 30 million PTA (approx € 180,000) initially requested by the parents to 10 million PTA (approx € 60,000). This 10 million PTA was granted in compensation for 'pecuniary and non-pecuniary damage' and the Court rejected awarding a sum that the applicant sought as 'maintenance and other charges involving economic assistance to the said minors'. Other judgments, such as STS (Administrative Chamber) 3.10.2000 (RJ 2000\7799), refused to compensate for the child's maintenance, and described the inclusion in the compensation for pecuniary damage 'amounts for the maintenance of the unexpected child' as a 'serious mistake', since this is an obligation for his parents imposed by law within the order of family relationships, so that the damage suffered would not be wrongful, because there is an obligation on them to bear it.

the birth of the new child on the family's economy or on the expectations of the other members' and concluded, reaffirming the traditional reluctance to compensate for maintenance of the child, that 'finally, the base for calculation of pecuniary losses used by the claimant, which consists of a report on the costs of a child from birth to 18 years, is unacceptable'.

Case 3

116 In this case, fault of the obstetrician who was taking care of the new born and his mother seems clear, since he should have sought advice from a paediatrician and he did not do so. The claim was not brought against the obstetrician but against the director of the hospital where the delivery took place. If we understand that the obstetrician acted as an auxiliary of the hospital or as part of its organisation, we think that A (the hospital) could be held liable, either pursuant to Art 1903 IV CC (rebuttable presumption of fault of the principal for the acts of its auxiliaries) or Art 148 TRLGDCU (strict liability of the hospital for providing health care services that must meet 'certain levels of purity, efficacy or safety, under objective conditions of ascertainment, and that purport technical, professional or systematic controls of quality'). Nevertheless, the fact that the case states that 'it can be assumed with a very high degree of probability that the organic damage was sustained in clinic C' seems to indicate that despite the existence of fault of the obstetrician A should be absolved from liability on the grounds of lack of proof of causation between the negligent conduct and the injury suffered by X.

117 As regards the conduct of midwife B, it can be established that she was at fault to the extent that she should have noticed the risk to which X was exposed and taken the necessary measures without delay including seeking expert advice from a paediatrician. However, considering that 'it can be assumed with a very high degree of probability that the organic damage was sustained in clinic C', once again causation fails to the extent that B's fault does not appear to have been causally relevant in producing the final result.

118 Finally, the liability of clinic C and the physician must be analysed, since both took care of the new born child during his second stay at hospital. From the facts stated in the case, it appears that clinic C was at fault either for its own acts (Art 1902 CC) or for the acts of its auxiliaries, pursuant to Art 1903 IV CC. In the first case, fault would have led to the defective organisation of the services the clinic provided. The facts of the case set out

that 'even in the year 1997, such an organisational structure fell below the medical standards for a full-service hospital, such as clinic C'. In the second case, vicarious liability, ie liability of the principal for the negligent acts of its auxiliaries would arise, particularly for doctor E who neither had enough experience nor reacted quickly enough when faced with the serious condition of the new born. See for instance STS 31.7.2002 [RJ 2002\7741] which held a hospital liable pursuant to Art 1903 IV CC on the grounds of the 'poor organisation with regard to technical and human means'. Organisational defects could also lead to strict liability pursuant to Art 148 TRLGDCU for the defective provision of 'health care services' which, by their nature or according to specific regulations, must meet 'certain levels of purity, efficacy or safety, under objective conditions of ascertainment, and that purport technical, professional or systematic controls of quality'. It also seems clear to us that doctor E was at fault, since she should have been aware of her lack of experience in assisting the new born with the required professional care (*lex artis*) and should have taken appropriate action more quickly and sought the assistance of an experienced physician.

All of the above however raise an important causal problem namely that 'in **119** retrospect it is no longer possible to establish what degree of damage had already been sustained and to what extent more damage was sustained during X's treatment in the C clinic'. Taking as a starting point the assertion that 'on the basis of how things continued it can be assumed with a very high degree of probability that the organic damage was sustained in clinic C', liability of doctor E and clinic C could be established provided that this 'very high degree of probability' is sufficient to meet the required legal degree of certainty for the existence of a causal connection between their conduct and the harm suffered by X to be recognised. In this regard we should note that unlike other jurisdictions, where proof of the causation is satisfied when it is 'more probable than not' (ie at least 51 % of probability) that the defendant's conduct caused the damage, Spanish law requires a higher standard of proof which is normally described as close to 'certainty'. As a general rule, Spanish courts hold that there is no need for 'absolute certainty' (although some isolated decisions such as STS 2.3.2000 [RJ 2000\1204] do) and that it is sufficient to reach 'reasonable certainty regarding the facts that are being proven' (SSTS 23.12.2002 [RJ 2003\914] and 30.3.2006 [RJ 2006\2129]). However, no lower standards of proof are accepted. In this sense, for instance, STS 8.2.2000 [RJ 2000\1235] declared that 'there is no place, in the area of causal relationship, for mere deductions, guesswork or probabilities, but evidential certainty is required' (see also STS 16.1.2002 [RJ 2002\8]).[201]

120 If E and C are declared liable according to what has been explained above the most probable outcome is that Spanish courts would hold them solidarily liable (see supra no 48) and order them to compensate both for pecuniary and non-pecuniary losses resulting from the personal injury suffered by the patient. Actual damage is compensated if duly proven and future damage will also be compensated provided that its occurrence is certain and proven.[202] In this respect, Spanish law would not object to compensating for personal care costs and increased costs arising from the condition of the victim resulting from the damaging event. It would not object either to compensating for non-pecuniary loss arising from bodily injury and its sequelae. However, we think that the courts would not compensate for his 'prospective loss of capacity to earn in the amount of € 2,000 per month (from his 21st year of life capitalised until his 65th year of life)', since they might consider this damage very distant and merely possible.[203]

Case 4

121 As far as we know, there is no decision dealing with the way foreign patients or patients with language difficulties should be informed to enable them to understand the information. In accordance with Art 4.2 LBAPIC, information 'shall be communicated to the patient in a manner which is understandable and appropriate to his/her needs and will help him/her to make decisions in accordance with his/her own free will'.[204] In the view of legal scholarship, this means that the medical doctor must give the patient

---

201 Legal scholarship requires a high standard of proof, close to certainty (see, *Francisco Rivero* in: Lacruz Berdejo et al (fn 69) 469; *Encarna Roca Trías*, Derecho de daños, [4th edn 2003] 159). In legal writing, some authors have proposed that it should be around 80 % (see for instance, *Luis Medina Alcoz*, La teoría de la pérdida de oportunidad. Estudio doctrina y jurisprudencial del Derecho de daños público y privado, 316 f). This is, however, the opinion of a single scholar which so far has not found any support in case law. As another scholar rightly notes, case law is characterised by a lack of clarity on this point (see *Asúa González* [fn 89] 87 f).

202 See, in this sense, *Vicente Domingo* (fn 153) 318.

203 At this point it should be borne in mind that the Tables applicable to cases of traffic liability apply the correction factor related to the loss of income from personal work, even if he/she does not justify income, as long as the victim is of working age.

204 In the case of disabled patients, the principle followed by LBAPIC is also directed to inform them 'in a manner suited to their ability to understand' (Art 5.2 LBAPIC).

'information tailored to his/her individual circumstances' taking into account his/her age, mood, cultural level, training or maturity.[205]

In the case STS 20.5.2003 [RJ 2003\3916] the court declared that information given to patients 'must be timely, correct, truthful, loyal, continuous, accurate and comprehensive, that is, that for the understanding of the recipient it is integrated with the knowledge within his reach so that he can properly understand it'. In addition, some regional Acts on the subject, such as Art 11.1.a) of La Rioja Act 2/2002 on Health, explicitly mention the need for information to be understandable considering the 'linguistic features' of the patient. Accordingly, we can conclude that in Spanish law there is a duty to tailor the information to the subjective characteristics of the patient in order to make it understandable and that these characteristics include the patient's language difficulties regarding any of the official languages in Spain. Moreover, from the data given in the case under discussion, it seems that the risk of paralysis was one of the 'probable risks under normal conditions, according to experience and the state of science or directly related to the type of intervention' (Art 10.1.c) LBAPIC) and the doctors involved in the process should thus have informed the patient X. We therefore think that a Spanish court, in a case similar to the one decided by the German court, would consider that physicians B and C were at fault. In the case of B, because it seems that he was the doctor who coordinated the information and medical care of the patient, and on whom Art 4.3 LBAPIC imposes the duty to inform. In the case of surgeon C, for not providing sufficient information regarding the two alternatives of the operation particularly in light of the risks that they entailed. In this sense, Arts 4.2 and 3 LBAPIC also imposes a duty on professionals other than the doctor coordinating medical care (as in the case of C) who treat the patient 'during the process of care or apply a technique or a specific procedure to him' to inform him or her understandably. Additionally, B's liability (in the case of C it is not known whether he was acting independently or as an auxiliary of clinic A) could also give rise to liability of clinic A in accordance with the regime of vicarious liability for the acts of others pursuant to Art 1903 IV CC. **122**

Once liability of the defendants A and C has been established, Spanish law would not object to compensation under all heads of damage sought in **123**

205 Amongst many, see *Domínguez Luelmo* (fn 67) (2nd edn 2007) 212; *Ana I Berrocal Lanzarot*, La autonomía del individuo en el ámbito sanitario. El deber de información y el consentimiento informado como derechos del paciente en la nueva Ley 41/2002, de 14 de noviembre, Foro. Revista de Ciencias Jurídicas y Sociales, no 0/2004, Facultad de Derecho. Universidad Complutense de Madrid, 227–298, p 255.

the claim, whether pecuniary (such as adjustments to the house, the purchase of a new vehicle to adapt it to the need a wheelchair, and increased care costs resulting from the paralysis) or non-pecuniary, including anatomic-functional loss, as well as pain and suffering resulting there from.

Case 5

124 SAP 20.4.2002 Las Palmas (AC 2002\1074) resolved a similar case and upheld the judgment of the Court of First Instance which had established solidary liability for the surgeon, the anaesthetist and the clinic where the claimant had undergone surgery. As a result of the bad position in which the victim's arm had been placed during surgery, she suffered permanent injury that prevented her from using the arm 'from the shoulder to the hand, giving rise to permanent disability regarding her usual activities for the rest of her life'. According to the decision, it was for the surgeon to ensure a proper arm position at the start of the operation, while the position of the limb during the intervention was the joint responsibility of the surgeon and the anaesthetist, as well as of the support staff of the clinic. The court held that both professionals had been at fault and ordered them, solidarily with the clinic employing the support staff, to compensate for a) 1,802,381 PTA (approx € 10,857.71) for temporary disability while the claimant was undergoing rehabilitation and b) 9,830,500 PTA (approx € 59,219.88) for permanent sequelae and disability such as the development of her life and work routine, including non-pecuniary loss.

125 Another decision, SAP Guipúzcoa 4.5.2005 (AC 2005\1206) also dealt with a case of liability for damage suffered by the claimant (loss of vision in the left eye) as a result of the poor position in which his head was placed during an operation for an herniated disc which caused arterial embolism. The claim was brought against the surgeon, the clinic where the intervention occurred and the insurance company of the latter. The Court of Appeal confirmed the lower court's judgment and ordered the three defendants to compensate the victim with the sum of € 70,000. In appeal, the surgeon claimed that the responsibility for patient's positioning on the operating table was for the anaesthetist (who had not been brought to proceedings). However, the judgment concludes that the correct patient positioning on the operating table was a matter concerning all members of the medical team involved in the surgical operation. Therefore, the decision states that the surgeon cannot be exonerated from liability, since

'the lex artis requires of the professional the technical knowledge of his intervention, and in this case, he must make sure, together with the rest of the health care personnel, that the patient has been correctly positioned in order to prevent a greater harm (...)'. Consequently, 'this is an operation carried out jointly by a medical and health care team, where none of them can take on full responsibility or pass it on the other members, since everyone knows his profession and must ensure that surgery takes place under the right conditions'. Thus, the surgeon's liability is based on the violation of the *lex artis* (Art 1902 CC), while the court establishes the liability of the clinic on the grounds of liability for the auxiliaries (in the persons of 'its doctors or auxiliary staff'), pursuant to Art 1903 IV CC. As regards the damages award, the decision does not distinguish the different heads of damage that it includes, although it emphasises that it does include 'psychological damage'.

In short, in situations similar to the case under discussion, Spanish courts **126** often hold the surgeon, the anaesthetist and the hospital or clinic where surgery has taken place solidarily liable although the reasoning is usually very generic and the courts do not specifically analyse the corresponding professional duties of each defendant. In our opinion, a detailed analysis of the data referred to in the questionnaire might lead to a partially different solution. Thus, as explained in the case under analysis, it appears that damage to the *nervus ulnaris* could only occur during the operation and not before it. If it is correct that due care of the surgeon only required him to have taken care of the position of the patient before surgery, while it was for the anaesthetist to take control of the position of the patient during surgery especially of those limbs necessary to monitor and administer anaesthesia, including the arm we can then conclude that while surgeon B was not at fault, anaesthetist C was. Her liability could be based on fault for her own acts pursuant to Art 1902 CC. Probably D could also be held liable since C had the status of resident physician and was under the supervision of chief of residents D. It seems to be clear that having to oversee six operations simultaneously, with an average presence of D in the operating theatre once every hour, is not what was required to constitute professional care and D could therefore be held liable for fault pursuant to Article 1902 CC. The agreement between the national professional associations of anaesthetists and surgeons concerning the allocation of responsibility for positioning of patients on the operating table both during and after the intervention, would probably have an impact on a possible internal liability claim between both professionals, but we do not think that it would effect the other parties since it seems to be an agreement between two national professional associations which does not reflect (at least, the contrary does not result from the described facts) standards of professional conduct, technical standards or action protocols.

127 As regards hospital A, there are two possible grounds for liability of the hospital. On the one hand, the anaesthetist was acting as an employee of the hospital and accordingly, the employee's fault would be the basis for A's liability pursuant to Art 1903 IV CC which provides for liability of the principal for the acts of its auxiliaries. On the other hand, its liability could also result from the poor or inadequate resources used to monitor all the residents of the hospital in an appropriate manner. D was the sole supervisor and, according to the facts set out, it seems that he could not cope with all interventions and all residents acting simultaneously at the hospital. Also, this might determine the responsibility of hospital A pursuant to Art 1903 IV CC or, according to the strict liability regime established for the provision of health services which by their nature or as required by regulations must meet 'certain levels of purity, efficacy or safety' (Art 148 TRLGDCU).

128 In terms of the compensable damage, X could claim both pecuniary and non-pecuniary loss. As regards the latter, this means compensating for damage corresponding to the anatomic-functional damage and other non-pecuniary losses arising from such damage. As regards pecuniary losses, compensation would include X's loss of earnings resulting from the injury, and there would be no objection to compensating for loss of income from the moonlighting that X carried out on the weekends if the existence of the loss of such earnings is proven. We think that the fact that the claimant rejected retraining as a business agent in a warehouse supplying building materials is not relevant for the purpose of reducing the compensation for loss of earnings, since we think that the Spanish courts would not consider there to be a duty to mitigate which includes retraining into a job that the victim does not want.

129 As regards the cost of private medical injuries, the assessment of which the claimant commissioned from an 'institute for the assessment of medical injuries', this is one of the expenses included in court proceedings in Spain and must in principle be paid by the party who incurs them. In this sense, this cost is not encompassed in the damage for which the defendant must compensate. According to Art 241 LEC-2000 'except otherwise provided for in the Legal Aid Act, each party shall bear the costs and expenses caused in the proceedings on the request of each of them as they arise. Proceedings expenses will be those expenditures that have direct and immediate origin in the existence of such proceedings, and those costs relating to the payment of the following: … 4th fees of the experts and other payments that must be made to persons who have participated in the proceedings.' However, the final judgment may contain a statement concerning the allocation of costs to either party. Thus, the general rule of Art 394 LEC-2000 states that: '1. in declarative proceedings, the costs of the first instance will be imposed on the party whose petitions in the claim have been rejected in full, unless the court considers, and so argues it, that the case presented serious doubts of fact or of law'. If the acceptance or rejection of the petitions included in the claim is partial, 'each party shall pay the costs incurred on his/her request and those incurred on common request in half, unless there are reasons for imposing them on one of the parties on grounds of reckless litigation' (Art 394.2 LEC-2000). Finally, if costs are imposed on the party who has lost in the proceedings 'he may be ordered to pay, from the part corresponding to lawyers and other professionals who are not subject to a tariff rate, a total amount not exceeding a third of the amount in dispute, this rule referring to each of the litigants who have been ordered to pay; for this purpose solely, claims that do not have an estimated amount are valued at 18,000 euros, unless the court provides otherwise on the grounds of the complexity of the case'. (Art 394.3).

Case 6

In our view, it is not clear from the description of the case that C and D **130**
were at fault. Despite the fact that the injections were the cause of the abscess developed by the victim X, it is not shown that C and D infringed any professional standard of care when administering them. As regards the infection with staphylococcus caused by E, E will be at fault and will be held liable pursuant to Art 1902 CC if she had known she was carrying the bacteria and should have taken measures to avoid infecting patients in the office (such as washing her hands before and after attending a patient, or using other mechanisms to prevent transmission, or even not attending the workplace). For the same reason, we consider that A and B, the holders of the orthopaedic office, are also liable for not taking the necessary hygiene measures designed to provide services that meet the required health care conditions for their patients. Although the case under discussion states that 'it is not possible to establish whether it would have been possible for the doctors to recognise the staphylococcus infection of the medical assistant E', the truth is that the next paragraph of the case actually explains the various breaches detected by the health authority regarding hygiene of the premises and the staff working in the office (including, for instance, that 'it was not usual for the medical assistants to

disinfect their hands before drawing up a syringe and working surfaces were not disinfected every day as required but only once a week'). According to this we think that a Spanish judge would consider that A and B's conduct amounted to fault and probably also E's if it appears that he did not meet the hygiene standards required by professional care and this may have been one of the potential causes of transmission. This conduct is also causally linked to the damage suffered by X, both from the viewpoint of factual and legal causation. Accordingly, if E is considered to be at fault she will be held liable pursuant to Art 1902 CC. A and B will be held liable either vicariously for the acts of others, as provided by Art 1903 IV CC, or for their own fault, pursuant to Art 1902 CC, for their failure to adopt the hygienic and sanitary measures required in order to keep the office free of sources of infection if it can be proven that such measures would have prevented the damage from happening. In this case, A, B and E could be considered solidarily liable as regards X.

131 A Spanish court would not object to compensating most of the heads of damage sought in the claim, except for the head of damage claimed by the daughter who is helping with household chores, to the extent that she is already being compensated by the mother. Thus, X would receive compensation for non-pecuniary loss resulting from the ailments she suffers. She would also be compensated for pecuniary loss resulting from loss of earnings for having to interrupt her working activity. A Spanish court would also compensate for the costs of home help, either by awarding a specific amount for this head of damages (eg STS 18.4.2000 [RJ 2000\2672],)[206] or by including it in a general award of compensation for loss of the ability to continue carrying out these activities in person.[207]

Variation 1

132 The fact that the person carrying the bacteria can be identified would only affect the potential liability of E, but not the liability of the holders of the office, A and B. First, if liability of both was based on their own fault for

206 This decision acknowledged the distinction between cost for the personal care services of the victim, on the one hand, and 'family domestic help', on the other, and awarded 20,000,000 PTA (approx € 120,000) for this second head of damages, which was added to the 77,754,600 PTA (€ 470,314,56) awarded on the grounds of the first.

207 As noted above (supra nos 86 ff), this practice has its legislative recognitions in Tables IV and V of the Annex to LRCSCVMN, regarding damage resulting from death and permanent disability. On these issues, see (*M Martín-Casals/J Ribot Igualada* in: Koch/Koziol/Winiger/Zimmermann (fn 88) vol 2: Essential Cases on Damage (2011) forthcoming.

failing to adopt health and hygiene safety measures according to Art 1902 CC, it is irrelevant whether the particular auxiliary causing harm has been identified or not. Second, if liability was based on the presumption of A and B's fault in their capacity as employers for the wrongful acts of their auxiliaries (Art 1903 IV CC), Spanish court practice does not require specific identification of the auxiliary who caused the damage. As stated inter alia by STS 9.6.1998 [RJ 1998\3717], this article is applicable 'when the results of the proofs show that the harmful event occurred by negligent act or omission within the circle of the company's activity and for circumstances which, with criteria of normality and under the rules of the experience, can be attributed to employees or members thereof, without it being a necessary condition to identify the specific individuals.' Finally, A and B's liability could also be based on the strict liability regime established by Art 148 TRLGDCU for providing 'health services' in breach of 'certain levels of purity, efficacy or safety'. In this case, the identification of E was not relevant either, since liability arises here for organisational defects or for the provision of health care services by the holders of the orthopaedic office.

Variation 2

If 'no health shortfalls in the doctor's practice can be proved', and if 'the usual standards were observed', then one would probably have to reject A, B and E's liability. Whether liability is fault based (Arts 1902 or 1903 IV CC) or strict for the defective provision of certain health services (Art 148 TRLGDCU), it nevertheless requires the infringement of hygiene and health care rules and standards that must be met to provide the service safely. Compliance means that one of the indispensable requirements for triggering liability in either case is missing. **133**

Medical Liability in Sweden

Philip Mielnicki*/Mårten Schultz**

General Questions

A. The Health Care System Framework

I. General Introduction

1. The health care system in overview

The following presentation of the Swedish health care system is taken from the official home page of the Swedish Institute (www.sweden.se): 1

'In Sweden the responsibility for providing health care is decentralised to the county councils and, in some cases, the municipalities. A county council is a political body whose representatives are elected by the public every four years on the same day as the national general election. According to the Swedish health and medical care policy, every county council must provide residents with good-quality health services and medical care and work toward promoting good health in the entire population. 2

[...] The role of central government is to establish principles and guidelines for care and to set the political agenda for health and medical care. This is achieved by means of laws and ordinances or by reaching agreements with the Swedish Association of Local Authorities and Regions (*Sveriges Kommuner och Landsting, SKL*), which represents the county councils and municipalities. 3

At national level there are a number of authorities within the area of health care. The National Board of Health and Welfare (*Socialstyrelsen*) plays a fundamental role as the central government's expert and supervisory authority. The others are The Medical Responsibility Board (*Hälso-* 4

* Doctoral Candidate, Stockholm Centre for Commercial Law, Stockholm University
** Full Professor of Civil Law, Uppsala University.

och sjukvårdens ansvarsnämnd, HAS), The Swedish Council on Technology Assessment in Health Care (*Statens beredning för medicinsk utvärdering, SBU*), The Pharmaceutical Benefits Board (*Läkemedelsförmånsnämnden, LFN*), The Medical Products Agency (*Läkemedelsverket*) and state-owned Apoteket AB, a national chain of pharmacies.

5 Organisation: Primary care has traditionally played a less important role in Sweden than in many other European countries. However, the aim is now to make it the basis of the health and medical care system. Today most health care is provided in health centers where a variety of health professionals – doctors, nurses, midwives, physiotherapists and others – work. This should simplify things for patients and foster teamwork. Patients should be able to choose their own doctor. Around 25 percent of health centers are privately run by enterprises commissioned by county councils. There are special clinics for children and expectant mothers as well as family planning clinics for teenagers.

6 Sixty hospitals provide specialist care with emergency room services 24 hours a day. Eight are regional hospitals where highly specialised care is offered and where most teaching and research is located. Since many county councils have small service areas, six health care regions have been set up for more advanced care. Furthermore, as Sweden only has nine million inhabitants, the entire country must serve as one service area for the most advanced specialist care. This is coordinated by a newly formed committee, *Rikssjukvårdsnämnden*, within the National Board of Health and Welfare: The county councils own all emergency hospitals, but health care services can be outsourced to contractors. For pre-planned care there are several private clinics from which county councils can purchase certain services to complement care offered within their own units. This is an important element of the effort to increase accessibility.

7 Financing: Costs for health and medical care amount to approximately 9 percent of Sweden's gross domestic product (GDP), a figure that has remained fairly stable since the early 1980s. In 2005, care and services provided by the county councils, including the subsidisation of pharmaceuticals, cost SEK 175 billion (USD 25.4 billion). Seventy-one percent of health care is funded through local taxation, and county councils have the right to collect income tax, the average level being 11 percent. Contributions from the state are another source of funding, representing 16 percent, while patient fees only account for 3 percent. The remaining 10 percent come from other contributions, sales and other sources.

8 Most county councils use some form of purchaser–provider system, in which a council negotiates compensation agreements with health care units – for example, performance-based compensation determined by diagnosis-related group (DRG), that is, a system to classify hospital cases into one of approximately 500 groups expected to have similar hospital resource use. This allows hospitals to become more independent of political bodies. In some cases hospitals have become corporations owned by the council. It is now more common for county councils to buy health care services – 10 percent of health care is financed by county councils but carried out by private health care providers.

Patient fees: The fee for staying in a hospital is SEK 80 per day (approx 9
€ 9 Euro in September, 2009). Fees for outpatient care are decided by each county council. Fees to consult a primary care physician range from SEK 100 to 150. An appointment with a specialist will cost more. To limit costs for the individual there is a high-cost ceiling, which means that after a patient has paid a total of SEK 900, medical consultations in the twelve months following the date of the first consultation are free of charge. A similar ceiling exists for prescribed medication, so no one pays more than SEK 1,800 per twelve-month period.'[1]

II. Social Security

2. The role of public health care

Social security is financed through the tax system, whereby the county 10
councils organise medical services by assigning them to both public and private health care providers. Thus, the patient does not contract medical services with the individual health care provider. (See further question 1 above.)

3. Differences in treating patient's claims

In general, claims for damages associated with a perceived wrong in the 11
course of medical treatment will be dealt with under the no-fault patient insurance scheme. The patient insurance scheme covers private and public health providers alike, who all are obliged by law to have such insurance. This insurance scheme and the right to insurance compensation for the patient are regulated under the Patient Injury Act.

1 <http://www.sweden.se/eng/Home/Society/Health-care-in-sweden> accessed November 2009.

12 Compensation of a patient injury is calculated in accordance with the general principle concerning the law of torts. This means that you get the same compensation that a public court would have awarded. A 'fee' is deducted from the compensation, under the Patient Injury Act this is 5 % of the base amount defined by law (SEK 2,050 in 2008). Claims for compensation are handled by a panel.[2]

4. Right of recourse

13 As mentioned above, harm caused in the course of medical treatment is covered by a compulsory no-fault insurance under which an injured patient can seek compensation. Concurrence of action nevertheless remains – the injured patient may choose to seek redress under the general rules of tort law, although this is very rare because of the insurance scheme.

14 As far as the right of recourse is concerned, the following applies. If insurance compensation is awarded, the insurance provider has a right of recourse against the health care provider if intent or gross negligence can be attributed to the latter (sec 20 Patient Injury Act). This is the general standard for the right of recourse under Swedish insurance law. If the health care provider (usually financed by the social security scheme) pays damages to the injured patient, the health care provider has a right of recourse against the insurance provider for patient injury compensation which may be awarded from the insurance (sec 19 Patient Injury Act). However, this does not apply if the health care provider was grossly negligent or acted with intent.

15 Hence, the two possibilities of recourse mentioned above are mirrored by each other. Unless gross negligence or intent can be attributed to the health care provider, liability is channelled to the insurance provider.

III. Private Insurance

5. The role of private health insurance

16 Private health insurance used to be quite uncommon in Sweden but is now on the increase. It is sometimes purchased by companies for the benefit of their employees and the purpose is, for instance, that key persons within

2 See further question 26.

the company should be able to receive health care immediately (instead of having to go on a waiting list for an operation).

Private health insurance in Sweden is not a form of liability insurance. **17** Patient injuries will always be covered by the patient injury insurance scheme (if they are covered by the protection of the law or responsibility).

6. Liability insurance

Liability insurance in Sweden is mandatory and regulated in the Patient **18** Insurance Act. Patient insurance is supplied by a company called *Landstingens Ömsesidiga Försäkringsbolag* (LÖF). LÖF has in its turn contracted a company called *Patientskadereglering AB* (PSR) to handle the individual claims for compensation.

All county council districts (*landsting*), which are the chief suppliers of **19** health care in Sweden, have taken up insurance with LÖF. Private health care providers also fall under the insurance scheme as regulated by their contracts with the county council districts.

IV. Professional Standards

7. Applicable professional standards

The Health Care Act (SFS 1982:763) regulates the general organisation and **20** standards of health care providers in Sweden. The Act on Professional Conduct in the Health Care Sector (SFS 1998:531) lays down the professional obligations of health care personnel, which entails an obligation to exercise the profession in accordance with scientific and generally acknowledged professional standards. Also, other rules stipulate more specific obligations, for the purpose of eg giving the patient sufficient information on the treatment provided, and protecting the integrity of the patient. The Act furthermore regulates disciplinary measures which may be taken against medical staff, regardless of whether harm has been inflicted on a patient.

8. Quality and/or risk management systems

The Health Care Act and regulations from the National Board of Health **21** and Welfare, which also exercises oversight of all health care providers, provide that the quality of the health care shall continuously be developed and safeguarded. Each health care provider shall establish routines for the systematic evaluation of the quality and risks within the organisation. However, the methods for evaluating and managing the risks of each health provider or medical practitioner are not specifically regulated on a national level; instead they are suggested in handbooks.

B. Tort Liability

9. Fundamentals of tort liability

22 Tort law is a legal discipline that has gone from being perceived as part of criminal law, to a 'pure' civil law subject in Swedish law. There are still remnants of the idea that tort law is connected to criminal law, noticeable for instance in the fact that the rules on defences in the Criminal Code are thought to apply in tort law too, without it even being mentioned in any tort law legislation.[3] Also, tort law has developed from the time when there were very few statutory rules that directly (that is, without being applied by analogy) dealt with tort liability. This changed in the 19th century. The most important legislative input in the development of the current understanding of fault liability is undoubtedly the introduction of the Tort Liability Act.

23 In 1972, the Tort Liability Act (*skadeståndslag*, 1972:207) came into force. This act was the first overarching legislation on tort liability in Swedish law. Previously the main source of tort principles in legislation was the sixth chapter of the Penal Act (*straffslagen*), a predecessor of today's Criminal Code. The Tort Liability Act was never intended to be a full codification of tort law. Many basic criteria for liability were left out of the statute. For instance, the general requirement of causation is not mentioned at all in the act. Still, it is clear from the preparatory works that causation was still to be considered a requirement of liability.[4] Many other basic liability requirements, as well as other tort principles, were also left uncodified.

24 This general overview of Swedish tort law has implications for the understanding of fault liability in Swedish law. It is traditionally held that the main rule in Swedish tort law is the 'culpa rule', which is the expression

---

3 See *J Hellner*/*M Radetzki*, Skadeståndsrätt (7th edn 2006) 119 ff.
4 Proposition 1972:5, 21 f.

for a general rule that liability presumes negligence. This rule has a long history in Swedish law, albeit perhaps a shorter history than in other jurisdictions, and was the main liability rule long before Sweden had any general legislation on liability.[5] There is (now) statutory support for this assumption, but it is generally thought that the scope of the *culpa* rule goes beyond the area covered by legislation. For instance, it is generally held that the culpa rule applies also in contractual relationships. To put it in other terms: the culpa rule is more important than the legislation from which it partly follows.

Medical liability will in practice seldom be handled under the rules of tort law. Instead it will be dealt with under the special patient insurance compensation scheme. However, the patient still has the option of claiming compensation under tort rules instead if she would prefer. The patient insurance then works as liability insurance. **25**

10. Burden of proof

Very few medical malpractice cases will be dealt with directly under the rules of tort law. If such a case went to court, however, the plaintiff would bear the burden of proving the circumstances on which she bases her claim. That means that the burden of proof for loss, causation and fault falls on the plaintiff. **26**

11. Uncertain causation

The question of how Swedish law deals with uncertain causation in medical malpractice cases is difficult to answer for several reasons. The concept of causation is vaguer in Swedish law than in many other legal orders. Sweden does not have the firm basis of a *conditio sine qua non* view of causation that most other Western countries share, instead Swedish tort law often operates with a more open, pragmatic approach to the causal requirement.[6] This entails also that courts are open to finding ways around the difficult problems of uncertain causation using flexible variations of the concept of causation. **27**

---

5 Cf *J Hellner*, Compensation for Personal Injuries in Sweden – a Reconsidered View, 41 Scandinavian Studies in Law (2001) 249, 251 ff.

6 See, generally, *M Schultz*, Kausalitet (2007).

12. Loss of a chance

28 Loss of chance is not recognised as a special type of loss in Swedish tort law (yet).

13. Multiple persons involved

29 Vicarious liability is at hand. The Tort Liability Act, chap 3 sec 1, provides for strict liability of the employer. Thus, the hospital will generally be liable for patients harmed by malpractice. A hospital is also liable for eg a senior consultant, even if the administrative management of the hospital cannot instruct the doctor as to how to conduct his work with patients. The management is still deemed to have the economic control of the hospital, and thus shall assume the economic risk for it. A claim against an employee, such as a medical staff member, may only be made in exceptional cases where special circumstances are at hand – otherwise such a claim is barred. This is based on the idea that the risk is to be assumed by the employer, who should arrange for sufficient insurance coverage.

30 If a private doctor performs surgery in a hospital together with its staff, one has to establish who the employer is, within the meaning of the rule on vicarious liability. This should be decided with regard to which person most closely exercises the supervision and control of the employee and the work that such person carries out.[7] Thus, persons assisting a private surgeon in an operation would be subsumed under his supervision and also liability. Persons who take care of a patient before or after such an operation are not necessarily considered to be under the supervision of the private surgeon, which would generate vicarious liability of the surgeon. Furthermore, it is possible that the hospital and the surgeon could be jointly liable for harm inflicted on a third party (the patient).

14. Strict liability

31 The patient injury insurance scheme, which already has been mentioned, is the major framework for compensating patient injuries in Sweden. It is regulated under the Patient Injury Act. Accountability does not depend on negligence (*culpa*). Instead, the Act stipulates six different categories of

7 See Nytt Juridiskt Arkiv (NJA) 1979, 773 and NJA 1992, 92 concerning non-employees carrying out work for a certain project and period of time.

injuries caused in the course of health care which may render a right to insurance compensation (sec 6). The injury must have been caused:

1. in the course of examination, care, treatment or similar procedure, under the condition that the injury could have been avoided either by performing the chosen treatment in a different manner or by choosing a different treatment which according to a subsequent medical assessment would have provided the necessary care with a smaller risk involved; or,
2. by faulty technical medical product or health care apparatus used for examination, care, treatment or similar procedure, or the wrongful use thereof; or,
3. by wrongful diagnostic procedure; or,
4. by the transfer of infectious matter, which has caused an infection, in the course of examination, care, treatment or similar procedure; or,
5. by an accident in the course of examination, care, treatment or similar procedure or transport or in connection with a fire or other damage to the health care facilities or equipment; or,
6. by prescribing or giving medicine in violation of rules and recommendations.

The Act furthermore provides for a relaxed burden of proof: the injury **32** must have been caused by one of the enumerated types of acts or omissions on a balance of probability [*überwiegende Wahrscheinlichkeit*].

Liability under this insurance scheme is excluded by the Act (sec 7) with **33** regard to: (1) a necessary procedure for diagnosing or treating a medical condition or injury which without treatment is directly life-threatening or leads to severe disability; and, (2) if the injury has been caused by medicine in any other way than referred to under sub-paragraph 6 above.

The first exception – referring to 'necessary' treatment – can also be **34** interpreted in sec 6, which requires that a different treatment could not have been chosen. The second exception excludes injuries caused by the medication itself, whereas pharmaceutical injuries are covered by a separate no-fault insurance scheme.

C. Contractual Liability

15. Basics of contracts in the health care sector

35 A patient does not enter into a contract with the health care provider which is financed by the social security system, notwithstanding that the provider is a private association that has been contracted by a public institution responsible for organising public health care. However, if a person chooses to use medical services from a private health care provider, without being referred to that provider or otherwise on the basis of social security, a contractual relationship arises between the patient and the private health care provider.

16. Differences to tort law

36 The previously mentioned remedies under the insurance scheme or the otherwise applicable rules on extra-contractual liability remain available, regardless of how medical services are offered. The former will almost always be most advantageous for the patient.

17. Contractual claims in the absence of direct contracts?

37 The general rule for extra-contractual liability is that a person is not liable for independent sub-contractors. Thus, if the injured person cannot establish vicarious liability for another person who has inflicted harm, that other person is liable for himself. A patient can thus not usually rely on contractual obligations that the health care provider has towards another party.

18. Informed consent

38 The notion of informed consent is recognised under Swedish tort law with regard to medical malpractice that leads to a tort claim, and is relevant for the purposes of assessing whether negligence can be attributed to the medical practitioner who has caused the patient an injury. It is clear that the patient must be given sufficient information about his or her condition and the available procedures which may be undertaken and that a consent must be asked for as far as is possible. This follows from the obligations of medical practitioners regulated in the Act on Professional Conduct In The Health Care Sector (SFS 1998:531).

The question as to what constitutes an informed consent and whether liability may be exempted in certain cases where a relevant consent has not been given, arose in a Supreme Court case of 1990.[8] A person suffering pain in the hip was operated on. The patient was informed that the purpose of the operation was to loosen up a nerve. However, during the operation the surgeons deemed it necessary to cut the nerve. This caused the patient pain after the operation, which was a complication due to the operation for which there was a probability of 20 %. The patient made a damages claim against the municipal council, which had the vicarious liability for the surgeons. The defendant argued that the general consent which the patient had given for the operation, also encompassed the procedure carried out during the operation. The Court did not accept that position – the patient should have received information about the cutting of the nerve in order to give an informed consent. However, the lack of such consent did not necessarily engender liability. In the present case the Court denied liability, having regard to the fact that the cutting of the nerve was medically the correct course of action since the source of the patient's pain had not been found, and it would not have been possible to cut the nerve on another occasion since it would be almost impossible to find it again. It was thus deemed defensible that the surgeons at that point cut off the nerve without the patient's consent. **39**

The judgment has been criticised for not establishing in what regard the informed consent is relevant for the tort law assessment and it is unclear how such consent should be weighed against the risks of the procedure carried put. However, the general contention is that informed consent is part of the assessment of negligence.[9] Its been argued that had there been a graver risk for actual outcome – had there been a higher probability for the necessity of cutting of the nerve in the aforementioned case – negligence would have been at hand if relevant information and consent therefore has not been given.[10] **40**

Under the Patient Injury Act, concerning the right to compensation under the insurance scheme, the lack of informed consent does not have a particular relevance for the right to such compensation. Instead, an objective assessment of the causation of the injury and the available alternative means of treatment is conducted.[11] **41**

---

8 NJA 1990, 442.

9 *J Hellner/M Radetzki* (fn 3) 304 ff; *H Andersson*, Skyddsändamål och adekvans (1993) 429 ff.

10 *H Andersson* (fn 9) 434.

11 See question 13.

D. Public Liability

19. Key differences from cases involving private hospitals or doctors

42 There is no difference.

E. Fund and other alternative compensation regimes

20. Funds and/or other alternative compensation regimes

43 As described throughout this report,[12] the most relevant remedy for an injured patient in Sweden is the no-fault insurance scheme, which is compulsory for all health care providers – public and private. Thus, those parties finance the insurance. Patients can first submit their claims to a company, which has been contracted to handle claims,[13] and secondly a claim can be made to an expert panel which adjudicates the claim.[14] There is free concurrence with damages liability – a tort claim remains open to the injured person.

F. Extent of Liability/Remedy

I. Pecuniary loss

21. Introduction to indemnifying pecuniary loss

44 Compensation for material harm is regulated in chapter 5 of the Tort Liability Act. Compensation from patient insurance is calculated in accordance with the tort law rules. Compensation for medical malpractice will therefore be dealt with under the rules of the Tort Liability Act, whether it is compensation in tort law or under the patient insurance scheme.

45 In the first section of the chapter, the general rules on compensation for personal injury are laid down. This states that damages for personal injury are awarded, inter alia, for hospital costs and other costs, loss of income, and pain and suffering. The second section deals with the right to

---

12 See questions 3 and 26.
13 See question 6.
14 See question 26.

compensation for the heirs of a deceased. The third, fourth and fifth sections deal with some special questions on the relation between insurance compensation and damages, etc.

22. Loss of earnings vs loss of earning capacity

Compensation is awarded for the loss of actual earnings (past time) or estimated earnings (future time). If the patient claims that she would in the future have had a higher income than at the time of the injury, she needs to prove that she would have received a higher income in the future. The Supreme Court has stated that the burden of proof in these situations is lower than in general, thus enabling the victim to claim higher compensation if she can show it probable that she would have received the higher income in the future.[15] This will often enable a student whose future was destroyed to be compensated in accordance with an estimation of the earnings she would have had if she had been able to finish her studies and start a career. If on the other hand, the victim was, for instance, a homemaker without any plans to pursue a career she would be unable to claim compensation for future loss of earnings. **46**

23. Periodic payments or lump sum?

Compensation under the Patient Injury Act is compensated in accordance with the rules in chapter 5 of the Tort Liability Act. Compensation for material harm may be awarded as a lump sum but may also be specifically calculated. **47**

24. Caps and thresholds

In general tort law there is no cap on damages. Under the patient insurance scheme there is a cap. Sec 10 of the Patient Injury Act states: 'Patient injury compensation is for each event limited to at most 1,000 times the base amount [currently approx € 4,000] under the National Insurance Act (1962:381) applicable when the compensation is determined. However, for each injury event the patient injury compensation is limited for each injured patient to at most 200 times this base amount. **48**

15 Cf NJA 2007, 461.

The amounts stated in the first paragraph do not include interest or compensation for litigation costs.'

II. Non-pecuniary loss

25. Introduction to indemnifying non-pecuniary loss

49 Compensation for immaterial harm under the patient insurance scheme, which will generally handle compensation claims for medical malpractice, is calculated in accordance with general tort law principles. The rules in chapter 5 of the Tort Liability Act will thus provide the support for compensation for both material and immaterial loss under the patient insurance scheme as well as under traditional tort law rules.

50 In accordance with the rule in the Tort Liability Act, chap 5, sect 1, the victim has a right to compensation for non-pecuniary loss for pain and suffering, loss of amenities and duress. In practice, compensation for immaterial loss will be calculated in accordance with standardised formulas. The most important of these standardised formulas are special charts developed for dealing with claims against the traffic insurance (*trafikskadenämndens tabeller*). These charts are often used as a starting point for the calculation of compensation for non-pecuniary loss in tort law as well as under special compensation schemes.

51 Compensation for medical malpractice would in general be dealt with under the above-stated principles. There are, however, some further possibilities.

52 A special compensation rule on non-material loss applies for criminal offences; this allows a victim to claim compensation for the violation against her personal integrity. This kind of compensation lies outside the scope of traditional compensation for non-pecuniary loss: It is in fact not intended to 'compensate' the loss but rather to reflect a violation of the 'value' of the victim's humanity.[16] If in a case of medical malpractice it is established that a doctor or a nurse acted criminally, there is a possibility also to claim compensation in tort law for the integrity violation, *kränkning*, thereby incurred.

53 Compensation for '*kränkning*' has also been discussed in cases in which the patient had not been given the possibility to give an informed consent to a

16 Cf *M Schultz*, Kränkning (2008) ch 2.

procedure. There is an explicit rule in the Health Care Act that requires, for instance, hospital staff (primarily doctors) to inform a patient so that she can understand what kind of treatment she can receive and its implications. The patient also has a right to consent to or refuse treatment. The implications of these requirements from the perspective of responsibility are not clear. In one case the Swedish Supreme Court found that the lack of informed consent did not as such entail a right to compensation when the procedure was medically justified. There are different arguments for this, but one argument is that the lack of consent will often not be perceived to be a cause of the injuries that a procedure can lead to if the procedure is considered necessary or reasonable from a medical perspective.[17] This argument focuses on the relationship between consent/information and a physical injury. However, the concept of '*kränkning*', integrity violation, is now considered to be completely detached from the issue of physical or psychological injury.[18] The question then is if compensation for '*kränkning*' can be awarded for not respecting a patient's right to be accorded the possibility to give informed consent. The rule in the Tort Liability Act deals only with criminal offences and does not support such an approach. Traditionally it has been held that compensation for these kinds of 'pure ideological injuries' requires an explicit statutory support. In the discussion on the Supreme Court decision of 1990 just mentioned it was generally held that compensation for '*kränkning*' was not an option since there was no statutory provision that made room for such compensation in these cases. However, the possibility to claim compensation for non-criminal '*kränkning*' has recently been substantially increased since the Supreme Court has opened up the option of claiming '*kränkning*'-compensation for violations against the rights protected by the European Convention of Human Rights.[19] As a result it seems that the question of compensation for '*kränkning*' in cases of medical malpractice consisting of a failure to inform the patient sufficiently and/or to provide her with the possibility to consent to a procedure is still open.

17 NJA 1990, 442. A similar case is RH 1999:15 where compensation for lack of informed consent was denied on the basis that it was not a cause of the injury that occurred after the procedure.

18 This was made clear, if not before, by the Supreme Court in NJA 2007, 540.

19 NJA 2005, 462. The development is sketched in *M Schultz*, Rights Through Torts, European Review of Private Law (ERPL) 2009, 305–333.

26. Who can claim compensation for non-pecuniary loss?

54 A rather new rule in the Tort Liability Act, which is also used in dealing with claims under the patient insurance scheme, stipulates that if someone is responsible for the death of another person, she is also obliged to compensate the close relatives of the deceased person for their injuries.[20] Compensation in these cases is awarded for the psychological injury suffered by the relatives. The Supreme Court has in these cases laid down a particular rule on the burden of proof, which holds that the close relatives of a person that was killed by a behaviour that makes someone responsible in tort law will be presumed psychologically injured as a result.[21] In practice, the amount of compensation will often follow standards laid down by the Supreme Court.

55 Mere bereavement is not compensable in Swedish law. In practice, however, compensation for presumed psychological injuries for the relatives is awarded under 'objective standards' (ie without regard to the individual circumstances) to such an extent that it resembles a right to compensation for bereavement.

56 The rule in the Tort Liability Act only deals with compensation to relatives of a deceased person. In court practice, the same kind of compensation has been awarded to a close relative of a person that was severely injured but survived.[22]

G. Procedural Matters

27. Specific rules of jurisdiction or procedure

57 The patient injury insurance scheme, regulated under the Patient Injury Act, involves a special expert panel which adjudicates insurance claims.[23] Tort claims do not involve any special rules on jurisdiction or procedure.

---

20 Tort Liability Act, chapter 5, section 2, sub-section 3. In NJA 2003, 9 this rule was discussed in connection with a medical malpractice case where the patient died. However, the event occurred before the rule had entered into force and the claim was therefore unsuccessful in that case. Today the decision would have been the opposite.

21 Cf NJA 2000, 521.

22 NJA 2006, 181.

23 See the next paragraph.

28. Special institutions handling malpractice claims

In 1975, a special Patient Claims Panel was established.[24] As from 1997, the Panel has been part of the organisation of the Patient Insurance Association (which also finances it). The Panel consists of a chairperson and six other members. The members are chosen for terms of three years. The Chairman is a regular judge, or a retired judge. Three of the other members represent the interests of the patients, one must be a medical expert, one must be familiar with the personal injury settlement process of the insurers, and one must have special knowledge of health care activities. The Panel issues advisory opinions in compensation cases under the Patient Injury Act that are referred to the Panel by a patient or other claimant, a care provider, an insurer or a court. As the Panel is an advisory body, its opinions are recommendations. However, these have always been followed by the insurer. Bringing a matter before the Panel is free of charge for the patient, who benefits from being able to have his or her patient injury compensation matter heard by an expert body before the case might be brought to court. The patient is entitled to choose whether to go before the Patient Claims Panel, or to proceed directly to court with his or her compensation claim. **58**

H. Outlook

29. Reform plans

There are currently no plans to reform medical liability. **59**

Cases

Case 1

Under tort law, it is unclear how cases of wrongful birth and wrongful life shall be assessed. It has just barely been dealt with in academic literature. The reason for this is probably that the costs resulting from a child born with a disability are covered by the social security system. **60**

---

24 This section is based on and partly cites the report The Patient Insurance Act, by *Carl Espersson* from the Swedish Patient Insurance Association, available at <http://www.patientforsakring.se/resurser/dokument/engelska_artiklar/Comments_on_the_Patient_Injury_Act.pdf >.

61 Turning to Y's tort claim, based on negligence, such a claim might be recognised when the injury was inflicted during the pregnancy and delivery of the child.[25] The causation of Y's condition, however, is unclear; it seems that the conduct of the medical staff is a probable cause on the balance. The case-law indicates that a relaxed burden of proof may be applied when dealing with several probable causes in complicated cases. The relevant threshold has been stated as requiring that the cause referred to by the claimant must be 'clearly more probable' than any other cause.[26] This may place Y in the difficult position of having to prove that the conduct of the medical staff was the cause of her disability. Nevertheless, if successful on this point, Y's heads of damages for pecuniary and non-pecuniary damages are recognised under Swedish tort law. As far as the placement of liability, the hospital is vicariously liable for all the medical staff members who cannot individually be sued.

62 The alternative remedy for Y would be under the patient injury insurance scheme, as regulated by the Patient Injury Act. A child that is born with a disability caused by treatment during the mother's pregnancy is considered to be a patient within the meaning of the Act. Thus, Y may seek insurance compensation. Here one may note that a relaxed burden of proof is provided for in the Patient Injury Act, whereby the claimant must show that the relevant cause was more probable on the balance of probabilities (at least more than 50 %) than any other cause. Furthermore, accountability does not require negligence, but instead it has to be ascertained that the care and treatment given by the medical staff was incorrect and that the injury could have been avoided by acting differently. The insurance compensation is calculated in accordance with tort law rules.

63 As far as the mother X's tort claim is concerned, one cannot establish that compensable damage has been caused to X within the meaning of Swedish tort law, since a personal injury cannot be established. It would instead be considered a pure economic loss, which generally is not recoverable unless a criminal offence has been committed. Damages for distress – so-called shock-damages – may be awarded to a person who has a close relationship to another person who has had serious, life threatening harm inflicted by the tortfeasor.[27]

---

25 Cf H *Andersson* (fn 9) 559 f.

26 Inter alia NJA 1977, 176; NJA 1982, 421.

27 NJA 2006, 181, where the Court broadened the scope of liability from previously only applying to cases where the other person died; this case involved a life threatening personal injury caused by intent which in turn caused the mother of the harmed man distress; the Court held that caution should be applied concerning the scope of liability, but that an intentional act causing the resultant personal injury was not necessarily pre-requisite.

The mother X has not suffered a compensable damage (besides distress perhaps) which could render a right to patient injury insurance compensation. 64

Case 2

The notion of wrongful pregnancy has not been dealt with in Swedish tort law (see the previous question for the related issues of wrongful birth/life). However, it is seems unlikely that X has suffered damage which is compensable, under Swedish tort law as it presently stands. On the other hand, this is an area in which developments will probably take place in the near future so the result of a case such as this in a Swedish court is difficult to assess. 65

Case 3

Under tort law, X may seek damages for his personal injury based on negligence. 66

The potentially liable persons in this case are only A, B, and C, based on vicarious liability and based on the assumption that these persons are independent health care providers and not employees of another. Joint and several liability may apply, if the injury and damage inflicted cannot be divided in relation to each defendant. Claims towards employees are generally barred. 67

As to the causation, A, B and C may have joint and several liability if they each contributed to a damage which cannot be apportioned. The same would also apply if they separately contributed with a sufficient cause for the damage inflicted in the end to X. In both scenarios, each of them are accountable for a cause to the damage, notwithstanding that it was not the [most relevant] cause. However, in the present case there is some uncertainty as to how each agent contributed to the damage and how risky each cause was. Nevertheless, it has been established that C's treatment of X with a very high degree of probability was the cause of his organic damage. Using the alleviated standard of proof – requiring a 'clearly more probable' cause – C could be held liable for that damage. 68

The heads of damages X is claiming are within the scope of Swedish tort law. Damages for income loss, concerning a substantial part of the injured person's income in the future, are generally capitalised in the form of periodical payments. 69

70 X may, instead of seeking damages, seek insurance compensation under the patient injury insurance scheme. This involves less costs, procedure and burden of proof. The Patient Injury Panel would from an objective point of view assess whether the parties involved deviated from medical practice and rules and whether the injury inflicted upon X could have been avoided had those standards been followed and another course of action had been chosen. The standard of proof in that connection is on the balance of probabilities. The compensation would be calculated according to the same standards as under tort law.

71 The insurer's right of recourse (towards A, B or C) may be triggered if gross negligence can be attributed to any of the liable persons.

Case 4

72 To begin with, X can only seek compensation from A (the clinic), assuming that A has vicarious liability for the surgeon C. As far as the lack of informed consent is concerned, a general consent to the operation is not sufficient. X cannot be considered to have been informed about (and consented to) the risks and alternatives at hand. However, under Swedish tort law this is part of the negligence assessment. A procedure can nevertheless be defensible. But in the present case, an operation was not absolutely necessary. Under those circumstances, it may be argued that X was subject to a high risk of injury without having the opportunity to consent to that possibility. However, the exact relevance of informed consent is still unclear under Swedish tort law, ie whether it has an independent importance for the basis of liability. In one debated case the lack of informed consent prior to an operation (that went wrong) did not establish liability.[28]

73 X may choose to seek patient injury insurance compensation instead of damages. However, under this insurance scheme, governed by the Patient Injury Act, informed consent is not given any particular legal relevance. The Patient Injury Panel only assesses whether the medical staff chose the wrong medical procedure when operating on X or otherwise deviated from medical practice during the operation. Hence, X may have to make a tort law claim instead.

74 If liability is established, X would be compensated for all the claims stated in the case. Pain and suffering would probably be awarded with reference

---

28 NJA 1990, 442.

to the standardised charts prepared by the Motor Traffic Injury Board (*trafikskadenämnden*) that is often used as a starting point in these assessments. However, it should be noted that X would only receive compensation for costs that were necessitated by the injuries related to the operation. That is, he would not receive compensation if the costs relating to his invalidity would have been necessitated already by his previous condition. In reality, it seems likely that a court that has established liability would look favorably on the plaintiff's argument in dealing with the causal issue. That X might have been especially sensitive due to his previous condition does not affect his right to compensation; Swedish law generally adheres to a thin skull rule in causal evaluations of this type.

Case 5

X can only claim damages, based on negligence, from the hospital A as the employer who is vicariously liable for the other persons involved. Any claim against B, C and D is thus barred as a general rule. The causation of the injury of X is somewhat unclear. The medical staff did deviate from normal procedure, but that does not trigger a reversed burden of proof. X would at least have to show that the medical staff's conduct was a clearly more probable cause of his condition than any other explanations. **75**

If liability is established, one must note that X has a duty to mitigate his damage. In the present case he refuses to seek alternative employment which would be more fitted for his new condition. The damages for his future income loss are based on his past earnings and possible increases in the future. Thus, the degree of rehabilitation is assessed, often much later, in order to ascertain to what extent the injured person would be able to work. If only partially disabled, X cannot expect to receive damages for future income loss to the full amount of his former earnings. He will have to seek alternative employment. **76**

X also seeks damages for costs he incurred for an assessment of his injuries made by a private institute. Costs relating to inquiry into the causation of damage are not recoverable in damages as a consequential loss, but may in some instances be recoverable as trial expenses with regard to technical evidence or expenses for calling an expert witness if the costs are deemed reasonable and necessary for the plaintiff to protect his rights.[29] **77**

29 Code of Judicial Procedure (*rättegångsbalken*) ch 18 sec 8.

78 Instead of seeking damages, X may find it more practical and effective to seek compensation under the patient injury insurance scheme, with an alleviated burden of proof for causation and an objective assessment as to whether the misconduct of the medical staff caused his condition. The calculation of damages follows the general rules of tort law.

Case 6

79 Only the persons responsible for the practice in the capacity of employers (A and B, or rather their company perhaps) can be held liable – based on vicarious liability for all persons involved.

80 It is unclear whether the negligence of the medical staff members can be established as the cause of the infection to X, since it was difficult to establish that E had the infection. *Variation 1* complicates the issue of causation even more, since several potential agents for which the practice is not liable are involved. X may instead seek patient injury insurance compensation, governed by the Patient Injury Act, which offers a possibility for compensation caused by infectious matter. The infection must have occurred in connection with an examination, care, treatment or similar procedure. Thus, if infected by someone who accompanied X, it has not been caused in that connection. If X was infected by another patient, the infection may be deemed as caused in connection with the care provided.

81 With regard to *Variation 2*, no negligence can be attributed to any of the medical staff, so that a damages claim would be fruitless. However, the patient injury insurance scheme, governed by the Patient Injury Act, provides compensation regardless of negligence. Compensation for infections are only exempted when the infection is an inherent risk of the patient's condition.

Medical Liability in Switzerland

Corinne Widmer Lüchinger

General Questions

A. The Health Care System Framework

I. General Introduction

1. The health care system in overview

Under the Swiss Federal Constitution, both the Cantons (*Kantone/Cantons/ Cantoni*) and the Federal State (*Bund/Confédération/Confederazione*) are committed to ensuring that all persons are secured against the economic risks of sickness and accidents.[1] An important role in this respect is played by the different branches of social insurance, in particular by social health insurance,[2] social accident insurance[3] and invalidity insurance.[4] 1

The costs of medical care in Switzerland are covered by social health insurance (*Krankenversicherung/assurance-maladie/assicurazione malattie*) and, to a lesser extent, by social accident insurance (*Unfallversicherung/assurance-accidents/assicurazione contro gli infortuni*) and invalidity insurance (*Invalidenversicherung/assurance-invalidité/assicurazione per l'invalidità*).[5] 2

Social health insurance is, as a rule, compulsory for all individuals domiciled in Switzerland, regardless of nationality, age, occupation, sex, or 3

---

1 Art 41(2) of the Swiss Constitution (*Bundesverfassung der Schweizerischen Eidgenossenschaft*) of 18 April 1999, SR 101. The official German, French and Italian language versions of Swiss Federal Acts are available online at <http://www.admin.ch/ch/d/sr/sr.html>.

2 See infra, nos 10 ff.

3 See infra, nos 18 ff.

4 See infra, nos 22 f.

5 See *A Maurer/G Scartazzini/M Hürzeler*, Bundessozialversicherungsrecht (3rd edn 2009) § 12 no 42 ff; *T Gächter/I Vollenweider*, Gesundheitsrecht (2nd edn 2010) paras 829 ff, 840 ff.

financial means.[6] However, as the term 'insurance' implies, social health insurance does not actually provide health care, but only bears the costs for (certain) health care services required by the insured. Switzerland does not have a national health care provider. Rather, health care is provided by public and private hospitals, by doctors or other health care professionals. Persons wishing to benefit from social health insurance are generally free to choose their own health care provider.[7]

4 As a rule, compulsory social health insurance only covers the costs for medical care in case of illness.[8] It does not provide any entitlement to pensions (*Rente/rentes/rendite*) or daily benefits (*Taggeld/indemnités journalières/indennità giornaliere*).[9] However, if a person's capacity to work is reduced due to a health impairment, entitlements to daily benefits or pensions may arise under other branches of Swiss social security law, in particular under the laws of social accident insurance and invalidity insurance.

5 Entitlements under social accident insurance law only arise in cases of 'accidents' (ie a sudden, involuntary injury caused by an extraordinary and extraneous event), not, however, in cases of mere 'illness', except if the illness is work-related.[10] If a patient is harmed by a medical procedure, it is therefore of central importance whether the medical procedure can be classified as an 'accident', a question which is often hotly debated.[11] Social accident insurance law is compulsory for persons who are employed in Switzerland, although it is also available on a voluntary basis for self-employed individuals.[12]

---

6 Art 3(1) of the Federal Health Insurance Act (HIA) (*Bundesgesetz über die Krankenversicherung [KVG]*) of 18 March 1994, SR 832.10.

7 See infra, no 13.

8 See infra, no 10.

9 However, the Federal Health Insurance Act (fn 6) does provide for an optional daily benefit insurance (art 67 HIA); see *U Kieser*, Schweizerisches Sozialversicherungsrecht (2008) 278 f; *Maurer/Scartazzini/Hürzeler* (fn 5) § 15a.

10 Art 6(1) of the Federal Accident Insurance Act (AIA) (*Bundesgesetz über die Unfallversicherung [UVG]*) of 20 March 1981, SR 832.20, in conjunction with art 4 of the Federal Act on the General Principles of Social Security Law (GPSS) (*Bundesgesetz über den Allgemeinen Teil des Sozialversicherungsrechts [ATSG]*) of 6 October 2000, SR 830.1. See generally *Kieser* (fn 9) 155 f.

11 See *A Largier*, Schädigende medizinische Behandlung als Unfall (2002) *passim*; *Maurer/Scartazzini/Hürzeler* (fn 5) § 16 no 71; for an overview of the decisions of the Swiss Federal Court, see *A Rumo-Jungo*, Bundesgesetz über die Unfallversicherung (3rd edn 2003) 23–25, 30, 33 f. Cf also infra, no 26.

12 See arts 1a and 4 AIA (fn 10).

Entitlements under invalidity insurance law may arise in cases of 'invalidity', ie in cases of reduction or loss of earning capacity due to a health impairment.[13] The cause of invalidity (ie accident, sickness or birth defect) is irrelevant. Like social health insurance, invalidity insurance is compulsory for all individuals domiciled in Switzerland.[14] **6**

In principle, the availability of insurance coverage has no impact on the legal relationship between the patient and the health care provider.[15] Rather, it is the law under which the health care provider is organised which is, as a rule, decisive. Thus, if the health care provider is a private person, eg a private practitioner or a private hospital, the relationship between the patient and the health care provider will be governed first and foremost by federal private law. In contrast, if the health care provider is a public hospital, the relationship with the patient will generally be governed by cantonal public law.[16] **7**

In medical malpractice cases, the distinction between private federal law and cantonal public law can become relevant in several ways.[17] Firstly, requirements for liability and statutes of limitation under cantonal public law may differ from those under federal private law. Secondly, cantonal public law may exclude the liability of certain persons, in particular by providing that claims may only be brought directly against the Canton, not, however, against the responsible individual. Thirdly, courts with jurisdiction to hear cases governed by federal private law do not necessarily have jurisdiction over cases governed by cantonal public law. And finally, different procedural rules may apply. Thus, each of the 26 Swiss cantons has its own distinct laws governing public procedure, whereas civil procedure is governed by the new Federal Act on Civil Procedure, which entered into force on 1 January 2011.[18] **8**

---

13 See *Maurer/Scartazzini/Hürzeler* (fn 5) § 12 no 15 ff.

14 And also for other persons; see art 1b of the Federal Invalidity Insurance Act (IIA) (*Bundesgesetz über die Invalidenversicherung* [IVG]) of 19 June 1959, SR 831.20, in conjunction with arts 1a and 2 of the Federal Old-Age and Survivors' Insurance Act (*Bundesgesetz über die Alters- und Hinterlassenenversicherung* [AHVG]) of 20 December 1946, SR 831.10.

15 See also infra, nos 24 and 81.

16 See infra, nos 45 and 95 ff.

17 See infra, nos 95 ff.

18 Federal Act on Civil Procedure (*Schweizerische Zivilprozessordnung* [ZPO]) of 19 December 2008, SR 272. See also infra, no 103.

II. Social Welfare Provision

2. The role of public health care

9 As pointed out above,[19] Switzerland does not have a national health care provider. However, several different branches of social insurance play an important role in public health care. These are, in particular, social health insurance,[20] social accident insurance[21] and invalidity insurance.[22]

10 Social health insurance covers the costs of medical care in case of illness and is, as a rule, compulsory for all individuals domiciled in Switzerland.[23] Pensions or daily benefits are not available under compulsory social health insurance.[24] Compulsory social health insurance only provides coverage in case of illness; in contrast, accidents are not covered. An exception is made for accidents which are not covered by accident insurance.[25] Insurance premiums are owed and paid for by the insured individuals.

11 Although Swiss social health insurance is a state responsibility, there is no monopoly with regard to its administration.[26] Thus, social health insurance can generally be administered by health insurance funds (*Krankenkassen/caisses-maladie/casse malati*) organised under private or public law, or by private insurance companies subject to insurance control,[27] on condition that they have been approved by the federal administration.[28] There is no statutory restriction on the admitted number of insurers.[29] Insured persons are free to choose and change their social health insurer provided they observe the statutory termination periods.[30]

12 Social health insurance coverage is not automatic; rather, each person domiciled in Switzerland is under a statutory obligation to take out social

---

19 Supra, no 3.
20 See infra, nos 10 ff.
21 See infra, nos 18 ff.
22 See infra, nos 22 f. On the coordination of the different branches of social security, see *Kieser* (fn 9) 351 ff.
23 See supra, no 3.
24 On the optional daily benefit scheme, see fn 9.
25 Art 1(2)(b) HIA (fn 6).
26 See *Gächter/Vollenweider* (fn 5) para 689.
27 Federal Insurance Control Act (*Bundesgesetz betreffend die Aufsicht über Versicherungsunternehmen [Versicherungsaufsichtsgesetz, VAG]*) of 17 December 2004, SR 961.01.
28 See arts 11–13 HIA (fn 6).
29 See *Gächter/Vollenweider* (fn 5) para 690. Regularly updated official lists of admitted social health insurers are available online, see <http://www.bag.admin.ch/themen/krankenversicherung/00295/index.html?lang=de> (12.01.11).
30 Arts 4(1), 7(1) and (2) HIA (fn 6).

health insurance within three months.[31] Social health insurers are not allowed to refuse any person applying for insurance within their local area of activity.[32]

In general, insured persons wishing to benefit from social health insurance coverage are free to choose any health care provider admitted under Swiss social health insurance law,[33] although they may agree to restrict this freedom of choice in order to benefit from lower insurance premiums.[34] **13**

The requirements for admission as a health care provider under Swiss social health insurance law vary. In principle, medical doctors with a federal (or equivalent) diploma and certificate of advanced vocational training are automatically admitted as health care providers under Swiss law.[35] In consequence, social health insurers cannot choose which private practitioners they (do not) wish to cooperate with, but must bear the costs regardless, as long as the medical service itself is covered by social health insurance. **14**

In contrast, hospitals must be formally admitted if their services are to be paid for by social health insurance. Besides having to meet general requirements regarding infrastructure, personnel and medical attendance, hospitals must correspond to an actual medical 'need' of the population.[36] Only services provided by those hospitals which are included in the so-called 'hospital list' (*Spitalliste*) of a Swiss Canton are covered by social health insurance.[37] However, if the statutory requirements are met, both **15**

---

31 See art 3(1) HIA (fn 6).

32 Art 4(2) HIA (fn 6).

33 Art 41(1), (1bis) and (1ter) HIA (fn 6). On the different categories of admitted health care providers, see *Maurer/Scartazzini/Hürzeler* (fn 5) § 15 nos 152 ff.

34 Arts 41(4) and 62 HIA (fn 6).

35 Art 36 HIA (fn 6); arts 38, 39 of the Federal Health Insurance Regulation (HIR) (*Verordnung über die Krankenversicherung* [KVV]) of 27 June 1995, SR 832.102. See *T Poledna*, Arzt und Krankenversicherung, in: MW Kuhn/T Poledna (eds), Arztrecht in der Praxis (2nd edn 2007) 393, 395 f. With a view to preventing further increases in social health insurance premiums, a maximum cap on admitting new private practitioners was introduced as a temporary (and highly controversial) federal measure in 2002. Its validity was recently extended for certain categories of private practitioners and doctors in ambulatory medical care institutions (until 31 December 2011). See art 55a(1)(d) HIA (fn 6) in conjunction with arts 1 and 1a of the Federal Regulation on the Restriction of the Admission of Health Care Providers under Compulsory Social Health Insurance (*Verordnung über die Einschränkung der Zulassung von Leistungserbringern zur Tätigkeit zu Lasten der obligatorischen Krankenpflegeversicherung* [VEZL]) of 3 July 2002, SR 832.103.

36 Art 39(1) HIA (fn 6).

37 Art 39(1)(e) HIA (fn 6).

public and private hospitals can be admitted as health care providers for the purposes of social health insurance.

16 Not all medical services are covered by social health insurance, although coverage is very broad. In general terms, social health insurance covers the costs for all medical services which aim to diagnose or treat an illness (or, by way of exception, an accident)[38] and its consequences, such as physical examinations, treatment or patient care by doctors, and hospitalisation in the general ward of admitted hospitals.[39] Maternity-related medical services are also covered.[40] All medical services must satisfy the requirements of efficacy, utility and cost effectiveness.[41]

17 If coverage is available under social health insurance, health care providers must charge their patients on the basis of standard rates (*Tarife/tarifs/tariffe*).[42] Standard rates are generally agreed on between doctors' professional associations on the one hand and social health insurers on the other; such agreements (*Tarifvertrag/convention tarifaire/convenzione tariffale*) require approval by the authorities.[43] All standard agreements regarding ambulant medical services are based on a nationwide framework agreement[44] (TARMED)[45] approved by the Federal Council (*Bundesrat/Conseil fédéral/Consiglio federale*).

18 If an individual is insured under social accident insurance law, the costs of medical care in case of an accident (as opposed to mere illness) will not be covered by social health insurance, but by social accident insurance.[46] Insurance covers both work-related and non-work-related accidents, and also work-related illnesses.[47] If a person's capacity to work is reduced, social accident insurance law also provides entitlements to pensions or

38 See supra, no 10.

39 See art 25 HIA (fn 6).

40 See art 29 HIA (fn 6).

41 Art 32 HIA (fn 6). See *A Büchler/T Gächter*, Medical Law: Switzerland, in: H Nys (ed), Medical Law, International Encyclopedia of Laws (2010) paras 133 ff.

42 Art 44(1) HIA (fn 6). For details, see *Maurer/Scartazzini/Hürzeler* (fn 5) § 15 no 182 ff; *Poledna* (fn 35) 393, 408 ff.

43 Art 46(4) HIA (fn 6).

44 Art 43(5) HIA (fn 6).

45 See *Poledna* (fn 35) 393, 408 ff; for the current versions of TARMED, see <http://www.tarmedsuisse.ch> (12.01.11).

46 See supra, nos 5 and 10.

47 Art 6(1) AIA (fn 10); *Maurer/Scartazzini/Hürzeler* (fn 5) § 16 no 51 ff. Part-time employees are only insured against the risk of non-work-related accidents if they are employed for more than eight hours per week by any one employer; see art 7(2) AIA (fn 10) in conjunction with art 13 of the Federal Accident Insurance Regulation (AIR) (*Verordnung über die Unfallversicherung [UVV]*) of 20 December 1982, SR 832.202.

daily benefits. Persons for whom social accident insurance law is compulsory, ie employees, must be insured through their employers. Insurance premiums for work-related accidents and illnesses are paid for by the employers, whereas insurance premiums for non-work-related accidents are paid for by the insured.[48]

For approximately a third of all employees,[49] compulsory social accident insurance is administered through the Swiss Accident Insurance Fund (SUVA), an independent, non-profit company organised under federal public law.[50] Other employees may be insured with either a private insurance company subject to insurance control, or an accident insurance fund organised under public law, or an approved health insurance fund, although in the latter case, pension entitlements are not insured.[51] There is no statutory restriction on the admitted number of insurers.[52] Except for those categories of employees for whom insurance with SUVA is compulsory, employers are generally free to choose the social accident insurer for their employees.[53] **19**

In principle, insured persons wishing to benefit from social accident insurance coverage are free to choose any health care provider recognised under social accident insurance law.[54] Doctors with a federal (or equivalent) diploma are automatically recognised as health care providers.[55] However, social accident insurers may limit the patients' freedom of choice by entering into nation-wide cooperation agreements with health care providers and entrusting such providers exclusively with the medical treatment of the insured.[56] Stationary institutions, such as hospitals and convalescent homes, must meet certain statutory requirements[57] and also be party to a cooperation agreement with an insurer.[58] **20**

48 Art 91 AIA (fn 10).

49 *Maurer/Scartazzini/Hürzeler* (fn 5) § 16 no 14.

50 Art 61 AIA (fn 10).

51 Art 70(2) AIA (fn 10); see *Maurer/Scartazzini/Hürzeler* (fn 5) § 16 no 16.

52 *Gächter/Vollenweider* (fn 5) para 725. Regularly updated official lists of admitted social accident insurers are available online; see <http://www.bag.admin.ch/themen/versicherung/00321/index.html?lang=de> (12.01.11).

53 Art 69 AIA (fn 10).

54 Art 10(2) AIA (fn 10).

55 Art 53(1) AIA (fn 10).

56 Art 56 AIA (fn 10) in conjunction with art 70(1) AIR (fn 47). See *Gächter/Vollenweider* (fn 5) para 732.

57 See art 68(1) and (2) AIR (fn 47).

58 See arts 15 and 68(3) AIR (fn 47).

21 Social accident insurance coverage for medical services is generally the same as under social health insurance.[59] In particular, medical services must satisfy the requirements of efficacy, utility and cost effectiveness.[60] Unlike social health insurance, however, social accident insurance law also provides entitlements to pensions or daily benefits.[61]

22 In case of invalidity,[62] costs for certain types of medical care for insured persons up to the age of 20 are covered by invalidity insurance, which is compulsory for all individuals domiciled in Switzerland.[63] However, except in case of birth defects, only costs for medical care aimed directly at integrating the patient into the work (or similar) environment are covered.[64] Other entitlements may also arise, such as to daily benefits or pensions.[65] Invalidity insurance is administered by cantonal public invalidity insurance funds (*IV-Stelle/Offices AI/Uffici AI*) together with the institutions that administer Old-Age and Survivors' Insurance (*AHV/AVS/AVS*).[66]

23 In principle, insured persons wishing to benefit from social invalidity insurance coverage are free to choose any health care provider recognised under Swiss social invalidity insurance law.[67] Doctors with a federal (or equivalent) diploma are automatically recognised as health care providers.[68]

24 As pointed out above,[69] the availability of social insurance coverage generally has no effect on the legal relationship between patient and health care provider.[70] If the health care provider is, eg a private practitioner or a private hospital, the patient will receive medical treatment by way of an individual contract with the practitioner or hospital.[71] In contrast, if the health care provider is a public hospital, cantonal public law will deter-

---

59 See *Maurer/Scartazzini/Hürzeler* (fn 5) § 16 no 98.

60 See arts 10(1) and 54 AIA (fn 10); BGE 123 V 53, 59 (Federal Court decision of 20 February 1997); *Gächter/Vollenweider* (fn 5) paras 727 ff. Published and, from 2000 onwards, also unpublished Federal Court decisions are available at <http://www.bger.ch>.

61 Cf *Kieser* (fn 9) 279 ff, 337 ff; *Maurer/Scartazzini/Hürzeler* (fn 5) § 16 no 113 ff, 116 ff.

62 On the meaning of invalidity, see supra, no 6.

63 See supra, no 6.

64 Art 12(1) IIA (fn 14); see *Maurer/Scartazzini/Hürzeler* (fn 5) § 12 no 42 ff.

65 Cf *Kieser* (fn 9) 276 ff, 328 ff; *Maurer/Scartazzini/Hürzeler* (fn 5) § 12 no 30 ff.

66 On the organisation of Swiss invalidity insurance, see *Maurer/Scartazzini/Hürzeler* (fn 5) § 12 no 3 ff.

67 Arts 26 ff IIA (fn 14); *Maurer/Scartazzini/Hürzeler* (fn 5) § 12 no 79.

68 Art 26(1), (2) IIA (fn 14).

69 Supra, no 7.

70 See also infra, no 81.

71 See infra, nos 77 ff; see also infra, no 45.

mine the nature of the legal relationship between hospital and patient.[72] Both under social health, accident and invalidity insurance, patients are generally free to choose their health care provider.[73] Accordingly, it is their choice, rather than the question of insurance coverage, which will influence whether potential damages claims for medical malpractice will be subject to private or public law. However, it has been suggested that cantonal public law should also apply where patients are treated in a private hospital, insofar as such treatment is covered by social health insurance.[74]

3. Differences in treating patient's claims

If a patient is harmed during the course of medical treatment provided by a **25** private practitioner or hospital, his claims for compensation, if any, will be directed against the health care provider itself and/or (where applicable) its employees.[75] If the patient was treated in a public hospital, cantonal law may provide that claims shall be brought exclusively against the Canton where such hospital is located.[76] In both instances it is in principle irrelevant whether the harmful medical treatment was (wholly or partially) covered by social health insurance or not. Social health insurance coverage has no impact on the liability of the health care provider. The same applies if the medical treatment in question was covered by social accident insurance[77] or invalidity insurance. However, social security coverage does have an impact on the amount of damages owed directly to the patient by the liable health care provider, as the insurers' contributions will be deducted from the patient's damages claim.[78]

With respect to a patient's social security claims it is in principle irrelevant **26** whether the medical procedure which harmed the patient was already covered by social insurance. However, an exception applies to social accident insurance claims. As pointed out above, social accident insurance

72 See infra, nos 95 ff; see also infra, no 45.

73 See supra, nos 13, 20, 23.

74 See *T Eichenberger*, Arzt am Spital, in: Kuhn/Poledna (fn 35) 351, 353; *P Jäger/A Schweiter*, Rechtsprechung des Bundesgerichts zum Arzthaftpflicht- und Arztstrafrecht (2nd edn 2006) 19.

75 Cf infra, nos 45 ff, 77 ff.

76 See infra, nos 95 ff.

77 See *TA Bühlmann*, Die rechtliche Stellung der Medizinalpersonen im Bundesgesetz über die Unfallversicherung vom 20. März 1981 (1985) 155 f, 196 f.

78 Cf infra, nos 27 ff.

claims only arise in case of an 'accident'.[79] If, however, a patient is harmed during medical treatment for an injury which in itself constitutes an 'accident' (eg during medical treatment for an injury suffered in a car accident), such harm will be sufficient to give rise to social accident insurance claims. It will not be necessary for the harmful event to also qualify as an 'accident'.[80]

4. Right of recourse

27 To the extent that a patient who has suffered harm in the course of medical treatment is legally entitled to contributions from social health, accident or invalidity insurers, such insurers subrogate in all claims of the insured and the insured's survivors against those providing the treatment, regardless of the basis of such claims (ie tort or contract).[81] Subrogation takes place at the moment of the event.[82]

28 This right of recourse is also exercised in practice primarily by those insurers whose contributions are long-term, such as social accident insurance and, in particular, invalidity insurance. Both the Swiss Accident Insurance Fund (SUVA)[83] and the Federal Social Insurance Office (FSIO) operate a division dedicated solely to recourse against liable third parties.[84] In the case of medical malpractice, the practice of SUVA is to exercise its right of recourse if its own doctors consider the case to be clear-cut. SUVA will then endeavour to reach an agreement with the health care provider's liability insurer, if necessary based on an expert opinion jointly commissioned by both insurers.[85] In practice, however, subrogation by invalidity insurance is more important, and in case of

---

79 See supra, no 5.

80 Art 6(3) AIA (fn 10); art 10 AIR (fn 47). See, eg, BGE 128 V 169, 171 (Federal Court decision of 2 May 2002).

81 Art 72 GPSS (fn 10).

82 See *U Kieser*, ATSG-Kommentar (2nd edn 2009) art 72 para 12.

83 See supra, no 19.

84 Cf art 14 of the Federal Regulation on the General Principles of Social Security Law (*Verordnung über den Allgemeinen Teil des Sozialversicherungsrechts [ATSV]*) of 11 September 2002, SR 830.11. See also the official site of the FSIO, <http://www.regress.admin.ch/regress/organisation/d/index.htm> (12.01.11).

85 Information obtained with thanks from lic.iur. Sylvia Läubli Ziegler, head of the recourse division of SUVA, in January 2010.

dispute, such claims are also brought before court.[86] Social health insurers only rarely exercise their right of recourse.[87]

29 As pointed out above,[88] any social insurance contributions to which the patient is entitled will be deducted from any claim brought by the patient against the liable party.[89] However, the insured patient is entitled to the so-called preferential quota of damages (*Quotenvorrecht/droit préférentiel/diritto preferenziale*).[90]

III. Private Insurance

5. The role of private health insurance

30 In addition to compulsory social health insurance, persons may take out supplementary private health insurance (*Zusatzversicherungen/assurances complémentaires/assicurazioni complementari*). Private health insurance complements social health insurance in that it offers benefits beyond those provided under social health insurance, for example by granting access to the private or semi-private ward of a hospital. For persons unable to benefit from social accident insurance law or wishing to take out complementary accident insurance, private accident insurance is also available.[91]

31 Contracts for private health or accident insurance are governed primarily by private law.[92] The contents of such contracts can be determined more or less freely by the insured and the insurer; in the case of private health insurance, relatively few restrictions apply.[93]

32 To the extent that a patient who has suffered harm in the course of medical treatment has actually received indemnification from his private

86 For a recent example, see BGE 134 III 636 (Federal Court decision of 23 September 2008).

87 See *O Guillod*, Compensation in the Swiss Health Care Sector, in: J Dute/MG Faure/H Koziol (eds), No-Fault Compensation in the Health Care Sector (2004) 392, 411 (at no 78).

88 Supra, no 25.

89 Art 73(3) GPSS (fn 10).

90 Art 73 GPSS (fn 10). See *Kieser* (fn 82) art 73 paras 1 ff; *G Frésard-Fellay*, Le recours subrogatoire de l'assurance-accidents sociale contre le tiers responsable ou son assureur (2007) paras 968 ff.

91 See *Maurer/Scartazzini/Hürzeler* (fn 5) § 16 no 94; *R Nebel*, in: H Honsell (ed), Bundesgesetz über den Versicherungsvertrag (VVG) (2001) art 101 no 54.

92 In particular by the Federal Act on Insurance Contracts (AIC) (*Bundesgesetz über den Versicherungsvertrag [Versicherungsvertragsgesetz, VVG]*) of 2 April 1908, SR 221.229.1.

93 See *Maurer/Scartazzini/Hürzeler* (fn 5) § 15 no 217 ff.

health or accident insurer,[94] such insurer subrogates in the claims of the insured against the person providing the treatment.[95] However, under federal insurance contract law, subrogation only takes place with respect to claims in tort, as opposed to claims in contract.[96] Moreover, subrogation under federal insurance contract law requires that the tortfeasor acted intentionally or negligently; strict liability is not sufficient.[97] If the third party is liable only in contract, it is controversial whether a private insurer may nonetheless take recourse against such party based on the general provisions of the Code of Obligations.[98] In any case, the insured patient is entitled to the preferential quota of damages.[99]

6. Liability insurance

33 Where a patient alleges medical malpractice, claims will often be considered by the health care provider's liability insurer before the claim is brought before a court. Until September 2007, liability insurance for medical activities was only compulsory under federal law in a few specific areas.[100] Outside these areas, it was for the Cantons to decide whether to introduce compulsory liability insurance for medical practitioners. However, the new Federal Act on Academic Medical Professions now provides that all persons who practice an academic medical profession independently must take out professional liability insurance or provide other, equivalent security, regardless of the type of medical activity involved.[101]

34 Whether or not health care providers which fall outside the scope of this Act (such as hospitals, academic medical professionals conducting their

94 Contrast art 72 GPSS (fn 10), pursuant to which the mere fact of entitlement already triggers subrogation by social insurers; see supra, no 27.

95 Art 72(1) AIC (fn 92).

96 Art 72(1) AIC (fn 92). See *AK Schnyder* in: H Honsell et al (eds), Basler Kommentar: Obligationenrecht I (art 1–529 OR) (4th edn 2007) art 51 no 22; *C Graber* in: Honsell (fn 91) Art 72 no 7.

97 BGE 120 II 191, 196 (Federal Court decision of 23 June 1994); *R Brehm*, Berner Kommentar zum schweizerischen Privatrecht, Bd VI, 1. Abt, 3. Teilbd, 1. Unterteilbd: Kommentar zu Art 41–61 OR (1998) art 51 no 61; *Schnyder* (fn 96) art 51 no 22; *Graber* (fn 96) art 72 no 7, 9; *H Hausheer*, Unsorgfältige ärztliche Behandlung, in: P Münch/T Geiser (eds), Schaden – Haftung – Versicherung (1999) para 15.124.

98 Namely arts 50 and 51 of the Code of Obligations (CO) (*Bundesgesetz betreffend die Ergänzung des Schweizerischen Zivilgesetzbuches [Fünfter Teil: Obligationenrecht]*) of 30 March 1911, SR 220; see *Brehm* (fn 97) art 51 no 111 ff; *Graber* (fn 96) art 72 no 8.

99 Cf *Hausheer* (fn 97) para 15.124; *Graber* (fn 96) art 72 no 36 ff. Cf also supra, no 29.

100 See infra, no 34.

101 Art 40 lit h of the Federal Act on Academic Medical Professions (AAMP) (*Bundesgesetz über die universitären Medizinalberufe [MedBG]*) of 23 June 2006, SR 811.11.

practice in the form of a company by whom they are employed, or non-academic medical professionals) must take out professional liability insurance remains a matter for cantonal law,[102] except with respect to a few specific areas as mentioned above. Thus, liability insurance must be taken out under federal law where ionizing radiation or radioactive substances are applied to the human body.[103] Where clinical drug trials are conducted on humans, the person or institution managing or financing the trial must take out liability insurance or provide other, equivalent security.[104] Liability insurance for an amount of CHF 20 million or equivalent security is also required for xenotransplantation procedures.[105]

According to a report of the Federal Health Office from the year 2005,[106] **35**
the following annual liability insurance premiums can be considered typical for doctors practicing in Switzerland (calculated on the basis of an insured amount of CHF 5 million and a franchise of CHF 200):[107]

- general medicine: approx CHF 1,000;
- surgery (excluding cosmetic and plastic surgery): approx CHF 6,500;
- internal medicine, including gastroenterology and endoscopy: approx CHF 4,000;
- otorhinolaryngology: approx CHF 6,500;

---

102 *C Müller*, Medizinische Berufshaftpflichtversicherung, Aktuelle Juristische Praxis (AJP) 2007, 329, 336; see generally *W Fellmann*, in: A Ayer/U Kieser/T Poledna/D Sprumont (eds), Medizinalberufegesetz (MedBG): Kommentar (2009) art 40 no 16 f.

103 Art 28 in conjunction with art 31 lit d of the Federal Act on Radioprotection (*Strahlenschutzgesetz [StSG]*) of 22 March 1991, SR 814.50.

104 Art 54(1)(b) of the Federal Act on Drugs and Medical Products (DMPA) (*Bundesgesetz über Arzneimittel und Medizinprodukte [Heilmittelgesetz, HMG]*) of 15 December 2000, SR 812.21, in conjunction with art 7(2) of the Federal Regulation on Clinical Trials with Drugs and Medical Products (CTR) (*Verordnung über klinische Versuche mit Heilmitteln [VKlin]*) of 17 October 2001, SR 812.214.2.

105 Art 46 lit a of the Federal Act on Transplantation of Organs, Tissue and Cells (TA) (*Bundesgesetz über die Transplantation von Organen, Geweben und Zellen [Transplantationsgesetz]*) of 8 October 2004, SR 810.21, in conjunction with art 26(1), (2) of the Federal Regulation on Transplantation of Animal Organs, Tissue and Cells (*Verordnung über die Transplantation von tierischen Organen, Geweben und Zellen [Xenotransplantationsverordnung]*) of 16 March 2007, SR 810.213.

106 Bundesamt für Gesundheit (BAG), Bericht zu Handen der SGK-S, Auftrag SGK-N vom 28.4.2005: Abklärungen zum Obligatorium der Berufshaftpflichtversicherung/Berufshaftpflicht der Ärztinnen und Ärzte, accessible at <http://www.bag.admin.ch/themen/berufe/00993/01238/01268/index.html> (12.01.11); see also *Müller*, AJP 2007, 329, 333.

107 On the liability insurance market in Switzerland, see also *M Pergolis*, Die Haftpflichtversicherung für Ärzte und Spitäler, in: W Fellmann/T Poledna (eds), Die Haftung des Arztes und des Spitals (2003) 167 ff; *Guillod* (fn 87) 392, 410 f (at para 74).

- urology: approx CHF 6,000;
- paediatrics: approx CHF 1,200;
- plastic surgery (pure cosmetic surgery): approx CHF 20,000–60,000.

36 According to unofficial estimates, the total amount of insurance premiums paid by all Swiss public hospitals lies somewhere between CHF 50–100 million per year.[108]

IV. Professional Standards

7. Applicable professional standards

37 All persons practicing an academic medical profession independently must comply with the general professional rules set out in federal law. In particular, such persons are required to 'practice their profession carefully and conscientiously and to respect the limits of the skills acquired through university education, postgraduate training and advanced vocational training.'[109] Violations of these rules may entail disciplinary sanctions.[110] More specific rules are set out in federal acts relating to particularly sensitive areas, such as organ transplantation.[111] Professional rules for those health care providers to whom federal law does not apply,[112] remain a matter of cantonal law.[113]

38 Members of the Swiss Medical Association (FMH) are also subject to the association's rules of professional conduct (*Standesordnung/Code de déontologie/codice deontologico*),[114] which provide that doctors must practice their profession 'carefully and conscientiously'.[115] A violation of these rules can be

---

108 *PJ Meier/M Klee*, Ärztehaftpflicht: Versicherer sahnen ab, Beobachter 24/2008.

109 Art 40 lit a AAMP (fn 101).

110 Art 43 AAMP (fn 101). See *M Marti/P Straub*, Arzt und Berufsrecht, in: Kuhn/Poledna (fn 35) 233, 258 f.

111 See art 4 TA (fn 105), pursuant to which persons handling organs, tissue or cells are required to take all measures necessary according to the latest findings of science and technology in order to prevent health risks. See also *W Fellmann*, Arzt und das Rechtsverhältnis zum Patienten, in: Kuhn/Poledna (fn 35) 103, 124 ff.

112 See MedBG/*Fellmann* (fn 102) art 40 no 15 ff.

113 See, eg, § 19(1) of the Health Act of the Canton of Zurich (*Gesundheitsgesetz*) of 2 April 2007, accessible at <http://www.zhlex.zh.ch> (12.01.11).

114 Available at <http://www.fmh.ch/fmh/rechtliche_grundlagen/standesordnung.html> (12.01.11).

115 Art 3(1) (fn 114).

sanctioned by the FMH professional conduct committee. However, as the FMH is a private organisation, its rules are only binding on its members.

39 The various guidelines of the Swiss Academy of Medical Sciences,[116] such as guidelines on reanimation, palliative care or coercive measures, also lack binding authority as the Academy does not have law-making power.[117]

40 Where a patient has suffered harm in the course of medical treatment, the test applied by the courts is generally whether the doctor acted *lege artis*, ie in accordance with the 'generally recognised rules of the medical profession'.[118] The nature and scope of these 'generally recognised rules' are determined in the instant case on the basis of expert advice.[119] According to the Federal Court, the requirements 'cannot be fixed once and for all. Rather, they depend on the particularities of the instant case, such as the nature of the intervention or the treatment and the associated risks, the scope for discretion, the time and means available, and the training and capacity of the doctor.'[120]

41 Violations of the *leges artis* constitute a breach of contract and, if the further requirements are met, may lead to contractual liability for pecuniary and non-pecuniary loss.[121] In tort, a violation of the *leges artis* may lead to unlawfulness.[122] Moreover, both in contract and in tort claims, the act of departing from professional standards constitutes fault.[123]

8. Quality and/or risk management systems

42 The Federal Council has the power to introduce systematic quality controls with regard to those medical services which are covered by social health insurance. It may entrust professional or other associations with these controls.[124]

43 To date, the Federal Council has merely introduced a legal obligation on all health care providers admitted under social health insurance law (or

---

116 See <http://www.samw.ch> (12.01.11).
117 Cf D *Rüetschi*, Die Medizinisch-ethischen Richtlinien der SAMW aus juristischer Sicht, Schweizerische Ärztezeitung (SÄZ) No 23/2004, 1222 ff.
118 See, eg, BGE 133 III 121, 124 (Federal Court decision of 9 February 2007).
119 See *Fellmann* (fn 111) 103, 120 ff.
120 See, eg, BGE 133 III 121, 124 (Federal Court decision of 9 February 2007).
121 Cf infra, nos 82 and 86.
122 See infra, nos 51 f. For an overview of the decisions of the Swiss Federal Court relating to doctors' professional standards, *see Jäger/Schweiter* (fn 74) 31 ff, 37 ff.
123 Cf *Guillod* (fn 87) 392, 394 (at para 8).
124 Art 58(1) and (2) HIA (fn 6).

their professional associations) to develop concepts of, and programmes on, quality standards and quality advancement.[125] However, the modalities of quality control and the consequences of failure to comply with quality standards are not set out in federal law; rather, these must be developed and agreed on by health care providers and insurers (or their respective associations). Currently, there are no such agreements in place.[126] However, several hospitals and managed care networks of general practitioners have introduced quality management systems on a voluntary basis, or are considering doing so.[127]

44 As far as risk management is concerned, health care professionals are under an obligation to inform the authorities in certain statutorily defined situations, in particular in case of uncertain cause of death.[128] However, there is no legal obligation to introduce actual risk management systems. Nonetheless, several hospitals have introduced such systems on a voluntary basis.[129]

B. Tort Liability

9. Fundamentals of tort liability

45 In the context of medical malpractice in Switzerland, it is essential to distinguish between liability under federal private law on the one hand, and liability under cantonal public law on the other. In general, federal private law will apply if the health care provider is a private person (eg a private hospital or a private practitioner). However, there are exceptions. Thus, where a Canton has delegated the exercise of State power (*imperium*) to a private hospital, the relationship between patient and hospital may be subject to cantonal public law.[130] Moreover, where a public hospital has been privatised, the majority opinion in Switzerland is that the liability of

---

125 Art 77 HIR (fn 35).

126 See *Maurer/Scartazzini/Hürzeler* (fn 5) § 15 no 210.

127 Cf, eg, the website of the EQUAM association: <http://www.equam.org> (12.01.11).

128 For an overview, see *U Zollinger/K Hartmann*, Ärztliche Melderechte und Meldepflichten gegenüber Justiz und Polizei, SÄZ No 26/2001, 1384 ff.

129 On the current situation with regard to clinical risk management systems, see *M Briner et al*, Erste Schweizer Erhebung zum klinischen Risikomanagement im Spital, SÄZ No 15–16/2009, 635 ff. Several hospitals have also introduced Critical Incident Reporting Systems (CIRS); see *U Haller et al*, Von der Schuldfrage zur Fehlerkultur in der Medizin, SÄZ No 27/2005, 1665 ff; *H Kuhn*, It is forbidden to crash this airplane, in: Fellmann/Poledna (fn 107) 181, 210, 211.

130 See the references to case law in *Jäger/Schweiter* (fn 74) 20 ff.

such hospital will remain subject to cantonal public law.[131] It is controversial whether a private hospital's liability should also be subject to cantonal public law where a patient's treatment is covered by social health insurance.[132] Finally, where the liability of public hospital doctors toward their private patients is concerned, the Cantons are free to preempt federal private law.[133]

The following paragraphs on tort liability are confined to liability under federal private law. Liability under cantonal public law will be discussed separately,[134] as will liability in contract.[135] **46**

Under the general clause of art 41(1) of the Code of Obligations (CO),[136] four requirements must be met for liability in tort. Firstly, a person must have suffered damage, ie a pecuniary loss (*Schaden/dommage/danno*). Secondly, such damage must be wrongful (*widerrechtlich/illicite/illecito*). Thirdly, there must be a causal link between the wrongful conduct and the damage suffered, ie the conduct must be a *conditio sine qua non* of the damage suffered (so-called 'natural causation'; *natürliche Kausalität/causalité naturelle/causalità naturale*), and such damage must not be too remote (so-called 'adequate causation'; *adäquate Kausalität/causalité adéquate/causalità adeguata*). Finally, it is required that the tortfeasor was at fault, ie that he was of sufficient mental capacity (*Urteilsfähigkeit/capacité de discernement/capacità di discernimento*) and that he acted either intentionally or negligently.[137] It is undisputed in today's case law that a doctor is liable for any fault, regardless of the degree.[138] **47**

A person may also be held responsible for the wrongful conduct of third parties under art 55(1) CO (vicarious liability). Other than the general requirements of damage, wrongfulness and causation, liability under art 55(1) CO requires that the person who actually caused the damage (the 'servant') must be subordinated to the party who is to be held liable (the **48**

131 See *J Gross*, Haftung des Spitalarztes und des Spitals, in: Fellmann/Poledna (fn 107) 35, 44 f; *Fellmann* (fn 111) 103, 109 f. On the liability of privatised hospitals, see generally *M Hofer/S Schmid-Geene*, Die Haftung privatisierter Spitäler – ein Überblick, Haftung und Versicherung (HAVE) 2002, 196 ff.

132 See supra, no 24 and the references in fn 74.

133 See infra, nos 80 and 97 and the references in fn 280.

134 See infra, nos 95 ff.

135 See infra, nos 77 ff.

136 See fn 98.

137 See *H Rey*, Ausservertragliches Haftpflichtrecht (4th edn 2008) paras 805 ff, 834 ff; *Brehm* (fn 97) art 41 no 1 ff.

138 See, eg, BGE 133 III 121, 124 (Federal Court decision of 9 February 2007); BGE 113 II 429, 432 f (Federal Court decision of 3 November 1987); *Guillod* (fn 87) 392, 394 f (at para 11). For an overview of the development in case law, see *id* (fn 87) at paras 8 ff.

'master'). A person is 'subordinated' for the purposes of art 55(1) CO if he is subject to another's supervision and authority to issue directives.[139] The legal nature of the relationship between 'master' and 'servant' is irrelevant. Rather, it is the *de facto* subordination of one person to another which is decisive.[140] Both natural persons (eg a private practitioner) and legal persons (eg a hospital with independent legal personality) can be 'master' for the purposes of art 55(1) CO.

49 Liability under art 55(1) CO also requires that the damage must have been caused in the course of the subordinated person's work or duties (*in Ausübung der geschäftlichen oder dienstlichen Verrichtung/dans l'accomplissement de son travail/nell'esercizio delle incombenze di servizio o d'affari*). A merely accidental connection to the subordinated person's work or duties will not suffice.[141]

50 A party may avoid liability under art 55(1) CO by proving that he took all precautions necessary to prevent damage of the kind suffered, namely that he exercised all due diligence in selecting, instructing and overseeing the 'servant' (*curae in eligendo, instruendo et custodiendo*), and also that all work processes were organised diligently. If this proof fails, he may still avoid liability if he can show that damage would have occurred even if all due diligence had been exercised.[142]

51 In the context of medical malpractice, particular importance lies with the requirement of wrongfulness under art 41(1) and art 55(1) CO. Under the majority opinion, each and any interference with a person's physical integrity constitutes wrongfulness for the purposes of tort law, unless the tortfeasor can invoke grounds for justification. The Swiss Federal Court has constantly held that this also applies in the medical context, so that prima facie, any interference with a patient's physical integrity constitutes wrongfulness, even if the intervention was made by a doctor with the purpose of healing the patient, and even if there was no mistake in treatment.[143] The doctor can avoid liability by showing that such intervention was justified, in particular by proving that the patient gave his

---

139 See, eg, *Brehm* (fn 97) art 55 no 7 ff, 11 ff; *Rey* (fn 137) paras 903 ff.

140 See, eg, *Rey* (fn 137) para 904; *Brehm* (fn 97) art 55 no 7.

141 See, eg, *Rey* (fn 137) paras 912 ff.

142 See generally *Brehm* (fn 97) art 55 no 45 ff. On liability for organisational deficiencies, see infra, nos 61 f.

143 See, eg, BGE 108 II 59, 62 (Federal Court decision of 12 January 1982); unpublished Federal Court decision 4C.378/1999 of 23 November 2004, at para 3.1; for further references, see *Jäger/Schweiter* (fn 74) 65 ff. For a critique of this development, see *V Roberto*, Schweizerisches Haftpflichtrecht (2002) paras 93 ff.

informed consent.[144] If he succeeds in proving this, the intervention will only be considered wrongful if the patient can show that the intervention was not *lege artis*, which is often very difficult to prove.

If a medical intervention which interferes with a patient's physical integrity is not *lege artis*, the requirement of wrongfulness will always be met. Informed consent does not cover mistakes in treatment.[145] **52**

A characteristic of Swiss tort law is its comparatively short statute of limitations. The general limitation period for pecuniary and non-pecuniary loss claims in tort is one year from the day that the harmed person acquired knowledge of the damage and the liable party's identity. In any event, the maximum limitation period is ten years from the day of the harmful conduct.[146] The short one-year period is one of the reasons why claimants generally prefer to sue in contract rather than in tort.[147] The extension of the general limitation period for tort claims is currently on the political agenda.[148] Longer time periods are already provided for in other federal acts, such as the Federal Act on Radioprotection[149] or the Product Liability Act,[150] and may also apply where the injury was caused by an act which constitutes a criminal offence.[151] Claims brought under cantonal public law are subject to the respective Canton's statute of limitations.[152] **53**

10. Burden of proof

The burden of proof is allocated by federal law. In general, the person seeking compensation from another must prove that he has suffered damage, that such damage was caused by the alleged tortfeasor, and that such tortfeasor was at fault.[153] These rules also apply in the area of medical **54**

---

144 On the consequences of failure to prove informed consent, see infra, nos 89 ff.

145 See, eg, Federal Court decision 4C.378/1999 of 23 November 2004, at para 3.1; BGE 123 II 577, 583 (Federal Court decision of 12 September 1997).

146 Art 60 CO (fn 98).

147 See infra, no 83.

148 See the Federal Council's press release of 21 January 2009, available at <http://www.ejpd.admin.ch/ejpd/de/home/dokumentation/mi/2009/2009-01-21.html> (12.01.11).

149 See *Guillod* (fn 87) 392, 409 (at para 67).

150 See infra, no 74.

151 Art 60(2) CO (fn 98); see *Guillod* (fn 87) 392, 409 (at para 66).

152 See infra, no 102.

153 Art 8 of the Swiss Civil Code (CC) (*Schweizerisches Zivilgesetzbuch*) of 10 December 1907, SR 210.

malpractice.[154] Moreover, the damaged party must prove the facts on which he bases his allegation of wrongfulness, eg the doctor's alleged mistake in treatment.

55 In a much-criticised decision,[155] the Federal Court held that in certain circumstances, the mere fact of a negative outcome may lead to a 'natural presumption' of medical malpractice.[156] In this case, a patient had received peri- and intraarticular injections of cortisone preparations which ultimately and irreversibly destroyed her humeral head and shoulder socket. According to the Federal Court, 'if a doctor could and should recognise that the proposed medical treatment might have adverse effects, he is required to take all necessary precautions to avoid such effects. If such effects occur, there will be a natural presumption that the doctor failed to take the necessary precautions.'[157] The doctor may rebut this presumption, for example by showing which precautions he took in order to avoid the adverse outcome and that even with the utmost care, a remaining risk could not be avoided.[158] However, the Federal Court later clarified that not every adverse outcome might establish such a 'natural presumption', and that its decision had been inseparably linked to the particular facts of that case.[159]

56 The burden of proof with regard to causation (*conditio sine qua non*-test) has hitherto not been shifted to the tortfeasor in medical malpractice cases, not even in cases of grave mistake. However, the standard of proof of causation is at least relaxed in medical malpractice cases.[160] Thus, it is sufficient that the mistake more likely than not caused the damage

---

154 See, eg, unpublished Federal Court decision 4C.378/1999 of 23 November 2004, at para 3.2; *Hausheer* (fn 97) paras 15.79 ff; *MW Kuhn*, Arzt und Haftung aus Kunst- bzw. Behandlungsfehlern, in: Kuhn/Poledna (fn 35) 601, 613; *T Sutter-Somm/B Spitz*, Beweisfragen im Arzthaftungsprozess, in: Fellmann/Poledna (fn 107) 143, 150 ff; *O Guillod*, Responsabilité médicale: de la faute objectivée à l'absence de faute, in: C Chappuis/B Winiger, Responsabilités objectives (2003) 155, 159 f.

155 See *H Hausheer*, Country Report: Switzerland, in: M Faure/H Koziol (eds), Cases on Medical Malpractice in a Comparative Perspective (2001) 201, 216 f; *idem* (fn 97) para 15.83; for further references, see *Sutter-Somm/Spitz* (fn 154) 143, 152 f.

156 BGE 120 II 248, 250 (Federal Court decision of 29 July 1994).

157 BGE 120 II 248, 250 (Federal Court decision of 29 July 1994).

158 BGE 120 II 248, 250 (Federal Court decision of 29 July 1994).

159 Unpublished Federal Court decision 4C.53/2000 of 13 June 2000, at para 2.b.

160 On the regular standard of proof and its exceptions, see *R Brehm*, Schadenersatz für Körperschäden in der Schweiz, in: BA Koch/H Koziol (eds), Compensation for Personal Injury in a Comparative Perspective (2003) 325, 334 f (at paras 41–48).

suffered.[161] Also, where an omission (rather than an act) is at issue, the Federal Court has held that a doctor is required to cooperate in the evidentiary proceedings before the court.[162] Although the burden of proof is not shifted to the doctor, the court may take a failure to cooperate into account when appreciating the evidence.[163] The mere possibility of causation is, however, never sufficient.[164]

Thus, the patient seeking compensation for medical malpractice faces two hurdles. Firstly, he must prove that a mistake in treatment actually occurred, and secondly, he must prove that such mistake was a *conditio sine qua non* of the damage suffered. Because of these difficulties of proof, it is generally easier for a patient to allege that he was not properly advised of the risks of an intervention.[165] **57**

In its published case law, the Federal Court has left open the question of whether the burden of proof of causation may exceptionally be shifted to the doctor (or other health care provider) if evidence has been destroyed or concealed, be it intentionally or negligently, or if the clinical records are incomplete. However, in such situations, the court may relax the standard of proof.[166] **58**

11. Uncertain causation

As pointed out above,[167] a patient bringing a claim for medical malpractice must at least be able to prove that the treatment more likely than not caused the damage suffered. If this standard of proof is not satisfied, ie if the existence of a causal link between treatment and damage is uncertain, the patient's claim will fail.[168] Thus, if it is unclear whether the patient's situation deteriorated because of the treatment or in the ordinary course of his pre-existing condition, and neither can be said to be the more likely cause of deterioration, liability for medical malpractice will be denied. **59**

---

161 See, eg, unpublished Federal Court decision 4C.378/1999 of 23 November 2004, at para 3.2; BGE 133 III 462, 470 f (Federal Court decision of 13 June 2007); further references to case law in *Jäger/Schweiter* (fn 74) 105 ff.

162 Unpublished Federal Court decision 4C.53/2000 of 13 June 2000, at para 2.c. See *Hausheer* (fn 155) 201, 217.

163 Cf BGE 119 II 305 f (Federal Court decision of 17 August 1993).

164 See, eg, *Sutter-Somm/Spitz* (fn 154) 143, 155. For references to case law, see *Jäger/Schweiter* (fn 74) 106 ff.

165 See supra, no 51 and infra, no 90.

166 See *Jäger/Schweiter* (fn 74) 108 ff.

167 Supra, no 56.

168 On the doctrine of loss of a chance, see infra, no 63.

60 Under orthodox rules of causation, a person who has suffered damage must also prove the identity of the person who caused such damage.[169] If a person is unable to prove the identity of the tortfeasor, liability will fail. This also holds true in case of alternative causation, ie where it is established that the damage must have been caused by one of several tortfeasors, but it is impossible to prove which one.[170] However, if such tortfeasors acted in concert within the meaning of art 50(1) CO, an exception is made and they will be jointly and severally liable.[171]

61 A further exception may apply where the requirements of art 55(1) CO[172] are met, although the Federal Court has not yet been called on to decide this issue in a medical context. Thus, if it is established that a member of a certain group of persons must have caused the damage in the course of their work, and all of the group members are subordinated to one and the same 'master', such master should be held liable if he is unable to prove that he took all precautions necessary to prevent the damage.[173] In this situation, the damaged party should not be required to establish the identity of the person who actually caused the damage.[174] Rather, liability should turn on the issue of subordination and on the master's (in-)ability to prove that he took all necessary precautions to prevent such harm, in particular with respect to an appropriate organisation.[175] Nonetheless, the patient will need to prove that his damage was caused by a member of the group (and not by a third person). If the patient alleges that his harm was caused by a mistake in treatment, he will also need to prove such mistake, and that such mistake caused his damage.[176]

62 Accordingly, if it is established that the harm was caused eg by a member of a hospital's staff, without the identity of such staff member being known, the patient may bring a claim against the hospital under art 55(1)

---

169 See *Kuhn* (fn 154) 601, 653 f.

170 This is probably still the majority opinion in Swiss law (see, eg, *Brehm* [fn 97] art 41 no 124 ff), although there is an increasing number of critics (see, eg, *Rey* [fn 137] paras 623, 624; for further references, see *Schnyder* [fn 96] art 41 no 25).

171 See *Rey* (fn 137) paras 625 ff; *Brehm* (fn 97) art 50 no 6 ff. On joint and several liability, see infra, no 66.

172 See supra, nos 48 ff.

173 Cf supra, no 50.

174 Opinion shared by *Rey* (fn 137) para 898; *H Honsell*, Schweizerisches Haftpflichtrecht (4th edn 2005) § 13 no 21. See also *Werro*, La responsabilité civile (2005) para 456.

175 The only published federal case discussing (and accepting) liability for organisational deficiencies in a medical context is concerned with cantonal public law: see BGE 112 Ib 322 (Federal Court decision of 30 September 1986); see also infra, no 100. However, the Federal Court has applied similar reasoning in product liability cases: see BGE 110 II 456 (Federal Court decision of 9 October 1984).

176 See supra, nos 54, 56, and 57.

CO. In such a case, the hospital should be held liable unless it is able to prove that it took all necessary precautions to prevent such harm, in particular with respect to an appropriate organisation. The patient should only be required to prove the identity of the individual who actually caused the harm if he wishes to bring a claim against such individual.[177]

12. Loss of a chance

In 2007, the Swiss Federal Court was called upon for the first time to decide whether a cantonal court's refusal to impose liability for loss of a chance was arbitrary.[178] The scope of the Federal Court's review was limited to the question of arbitrariness as the cantonal court's decision was based on cantonal public law, and not on federal private law, where the scope of review would have been broader. Cantonal public law was at issue as the patient had been treated in a cantonal public hospital.[179] Although the situation under federal private law has not yet been decided by the Federal Court, the Court did indicate that it considered the loss of chance theory to be problematic.[180] As such, it is unlikely to recognise this theory under federal private law in the near future.[181] **63**

13. Multiple persons involved

Where more than one individual is involved in the provision of medical services to the patient, several different situations must be distinguished with regard to liability in tort: **64**

In the first scenario, all individuals involved in the provision of medical services are employed by one and the same 'master'. As pointed out above, **65**

177 This view was also taken by the Amtsgericht Luzern-Stadt, decision of 26 June 1993, SG N 895, at para 7.2. Opinion shared by *TM Mannsdorfer*, Haftung für perinatale Schädigung im medizinischen Bereich, HAVE 2003, 101, 110; *J Gross*, Haftung für medizinische Behandlung im Privatrecht und im öffentlichen Recht der Schweiz (1987) 251 f; cf also *Kuhn* (fn 154) 601, 654, who is, however, more reserved in his analysis of the situation *de lege lata*.

178 BGE 133 III 462 (Federal Court decision of 13 June 2007). See *C Widmer*, A Civil Lawyer's Introduction to Anglo-American Law: Torts (2008) 266 ff.

179 See infra, no 96.

180 This sceptical attitude was confirmed in the unpublished Federal Court decision 4A.227/2007 of 26 September 2007.

181 For a discussion of this case, see *C Müller*, Hat die perte d'une chance in der Schweiz noch eine Chance? – BGE 133 III 462, ZBJV 2007, 862 ff.

a 'master' may be liable in tort for its 'servants' under art 55(1) CO.[182] The master-servant relationship turns on the requirement of subordination.[183] Employees are generally considered to be subordinated to their employers for the purposes of art 55(1) CO.[184] Thus, a hospital is 'master' in relation to its employees, be they chief physicians, senior physicians, interns, nurses, members of the internal legal department, accountants, or cleaning staff. Although persons lower down in the hospital hierarchy will receive their instructions from, and be supervised by, intermediate staff members, it is always the person at the top of the hierarchy, ie the hospital itself that will qualify as 'master' in relation to lower staff members, not the intermediate staff.[185]

66 If something goes wrong in this comparatively straightforward scenario, the hospital will be liable in tort toward the patient under art 55(1) CO, unless it can show that it took all necessary precautions to avoid the damage, in particular with respect to an appropriate organisation.[186] If the patient is able to identify the individual staff member(s) who actually caused the harm,[187] he may also choose to sue such individual(s) instead under art 41(1) CO,[188] although this will generally be the less attractive route for the patient due to the hospital's 'deeper pockets'. Liability of the hospital and the responsible staff member(s) is joint and several (*Solidarität/solidarité/solidarietà*),[189] so that the patient may choose whether to bring a claim in an individual action against one of the responsible parties, for all or only part of his damages, or against all liable parties in a joint action.[190]

67 In the second, more complex scenario, one or more affiliated doctors (*Belegarzt/médecin agréé*) are involved in the provision of medical services to the patient, together with hospital staff members. As before, if the patient is able to identify the individual(s) who actually caused the harm, he may bring a claim against such individual under art 41(1) CO. However, it may be difficult to establish the identity of such individual, or such individual's pockets may not be 'deep' enough. The question then arises whether the

182 Supra, nos 48 ff.
183 See supra, no 48.
184 But see infra, nos 67 ff, on the situation with respect to hospital staff assisting an affiliated doctor.
185 See generally *K Oftinger/EW Stark*, Schweizerisches Haftpflichtrecht, Band II/1 (4th edn 1987) § 20 no 73, 79; *Rey* (fn 137) para 905; *Werro* (fn 174) para 450.
186 See supra, nos 50 and 61 f.
187 On this condition, see supra, nos 60 ff.
188 On the requirements under art 41(1) CO, see supra, no 47.
189 Art 51 CO (fn 98).
190 Art 144(1) CO (fn 98). See also *Mannsdorfer*, HAVE 2003, 101, 117.

individuals involved in the provision of medical services to the patient are subordinated to a 'master' for the purposes of art 55(1) CO, and if so, who that 'master' is.

First of all, the affiliated physician himself is not subordinated to the hospital, and accordingly, the hospital cannot be held liable for any of the affiliated doctor's mistakes.[191] However, the situation is less clear if a mistake is made by a member of the hospital staff. Although staff members are employed by the hospital, there are situations where the affiliated doctor, and not the hospital, will be classified as 'master' under art 55(1) CO. Thus, the affiliated doctor will qualify as 'master' if the mistake occurred in a phase where the responsible staff member was subject to the affiliated doctor's supervision and authority to issue directives, for example whilst assisting during an operation under the affiliated doctor's guidance. In contrast, the hospital will qualify as 'master' if a mistake is made by a staff member in an area where such member is subject to the hospital's supervision and authority to issue directives, for example whilst taking care of the patient prior to the affiliated doctor's arrival.[192] **68**

Once the 'master' is identified in this second scenario, he will be liable toward the patient under art 55(1) CO unless he can show that he took all necessary precautions to avoid the damage.[193] If the patient is able to identify the individual(s) who actually caused the harm, he may also choose to sue such individual(s) under art 41(1) CO. Liability of the master and the responsible individual(s) is joint and several.[194] **69**

Where several specialist doctors are on an operating team together, they will generally not be subordinated to one another for the purposes of art 55(1) CO. However, this will depend on the structure and organisation of the specific team.[195] If all of the specialists are employed by one and the same hospital, such hospital will qualify as the 'master' under art 55(1) CO.[196] **70**

---

191 *Mannsdorfer*, HAVE 2003, 101, 117.

192 See ibid, 101, 117; cf also *C Götz Staehelin*, Teamarbeit und geteilte Verantwortung in Spital, Arztpraxis und Belegarztverhältnis, HAVE 2007, 226, 233.

193 See supra, no 50.

194 Cf already supra, no 66.

195 See *Götz Staehelin*, HAVE 2007, 226, 233.

196 On this straightforward scenario, see supra, no 65.

14. Strict liability

71 Under federal private law, strict liability of private hospitals, private practitioners or other health care providers is available only in very restricted situations. Strict liability under cantonal public law will be dealt with separately.[197]

72 If a patient is harmed by a defective product, such as a drug, medical device or technical equipment,[198] the producer of such product may become liable toward the patient under the federal Product Liability Act.[199] A health care provider may qualify as a 'producer' in case of activities such as the preparation of medical products (eg sterilisation of unsterile medical products).[200] Moreover, any health care provider who imports a product for commercial distribution in Switzerland is considered a 'producer' under the Act.[201] The Act is based on the EC directive of 5 July 1985. Liability under the Act is strict. Accordingly, the producer may be held liable regardless of fault.[202]

73 Any moveable thing, including those things which form a component part of another moveable thing or of an immoveable thing, constitutes a 'product' under the Act.[203] Other than drugs, medical devices and technical equipment, blood and human organs also constitute products once they have been separated from the body and prepared.[204]

74 Other than the fact that liability under the Act is strict, product liability law also deviates from general tort rules with regard to the statute of limitations. Thus, claims brought under the Act are time-barred three years from the day the harmed person acquired – or should have acquired – knowledge of the damage, the defect and the producer's identity.[205] Moreover, liability under the Act cannot be limited or excluded.[206]

---

197 See infra, nos 95 ff.

198 On the meaning of 'defective' in the medical context, see *M Gattiker*, Arzt und Medizinprodukt, in: Fellmann/Poledna (fn 107) 495, 526 ff.

199 See art 2 of the Federal Product Liability Act (PLA) (*Bundesgesetz über die Produktehaftpflicht [Produktehaftpflichtgesetz, PrHG]*) of 18 June 1993, SR 221.112.944.

200 See *Gattiker* (fn 198) 495, 525 ff.

201 Cf art 2(1)(c) PLA (fn 199); see *Gattiker* (fn 198) 495, 526.

202 See, eg, *Rey* (fn 137) paras 1167 ff.

203 Art 3 PLA (fn 199).

204 *W Fellmann* in: Honsell et al (fn 96) art 3 PrHG no 4; *Honsell* (fn 174) § 21 no 29. Special rules apply to liability for harm caused by xenotransplants; see arts 3(2)(b) and 5(1bis) PLA (fn 199).

205 Art 9 PLA (fn 199). On the one-year period under the general statute of limitations (art 60 CO), which only starts to run in case of actual knowledge, see supra, no 53.

206 Art 8 PLA (fn 199).

Strict liability may also be available in the case of clinical drug trials. Under federal law, clinical drug trials may only be conducted if it is ensured that test persons will be fully compensated for any damage suffered in the course of the trial.[207] Although the wording of federal law is not unequivocal and its meaning has not yet been clarified by the Federal Court, such liability is generally considered to be strict.[208] It has also been suggested that the standard of proof with regard to causation is relaxed as the test person is only required to show that harm was suffered 'in the course of the clinical trial'.[209] As under the Product Liability Act, it is argued that liability in case of clinical drug trials cannot be limited or excluded.[210] However, many questions remain open.[211] **75**

In a certain sense, liability for failure to obtain informed consent as developed by the Federal Court can also be considered strict,[212] as the doctor who proceeds without such consent will become liable for all damage suffered in consequence of the medical intervention, including damage which was caused simply by chance, as long as such damage is not too remote.[213] **76**

C. Contractual Liability

15. Basics of contracts in the health care sector

If a patient with the capacity to act seeks medical advice or treatment from a private practitioner, a private hospital or other private health care provider, such patient will, as a rule,[214] enter into a private law contract with such provider. Private law contracts for provision of medical services are traditionally classified as a mandate (*Auftrag/mandat/mandato*).[215] This **77**

---

207 Art 54(1)(a)(5) and (1)(b) DMPA (fn 104) in conjunction with art 7(2) CTR (fn 104).

208 See *D Sprumont/M-L Béguin*, La nouvelle réglementation des essais cliniques de médicaments, SÄZ No 18/2002, 894, 900; *O Guillod/P Schweizer*, Expérimentation de nouveaux médicaments et responsabilité civile, in: P Tercier (ed), Aspects de droit médical (1987) 93; *J Gross*, Staatshaftung und Heilmittelrecht, leges 1/2003, 137, 138; *D Sprumont/S Boillat/H Amstad*, Essais cliniques, responsabilité civile et contrats d'assurance, SÄZ No. 40/2002, 2092, 2093; *Gattiker* (fn 198) 495, 519.

209 *Sprumont/Béguin*, SÄZ No 18/2002, 894, 900.

210 Ibid, 894, 899, 900.

211 See *Gattiker* (fn 198) 495, 519 f, with further references.

212 See *Guillod* (fn 87) 392, 399 (at para 26).

213 See infra, no 90.

214 For the exceptions to this rule, see supra, no 45.

215 Arts 394 ff CO (fn 98). See, eg, BGE 132 III 359, 362 f (Federal Court decision of 20 December 2005); *W Fellmann*, Die Haftung des Privatarztes und des Privatspitals, in: Fellmann/Poledna (fn 107) 47, 49 ff; *id* (fn 111) 103, 106; *Guillod* (fn 87) 392, 393 (at para 3).

also applies to contracts between patients and private hospitals, at least insofar as the provision of care and medical services (and not, eg, catering) is concerned.[216]

78 In the case of stationary medical care in a private hospital, two different scenarios must be distinguished.[217] In the first, the patient enters into only one contract, namely with the hospital. Under this so-called 'comprehensive hospital contract' (*totaler Spitalaufnahmevertrag/contrat global d'hospitalisation*), the hospital is contractually bound to provide the patient with accommodation, catering, care and medical treatment, and the patient is contractually bound to remunerate such services. Accordingly, if something goes wrong in the course of medical treatment, a contractual claim for medical malpractice can only be brought directly against the hospital. The responsible doctor will be considered an auxiliary of the hospital under art 101(1) CO, so that his acts or omissions will be imputed to the hospital for the purposes of liability.[218] If the patient wishes to sue the responsible doctor, he may do so; in this case, hospital and doctor will be jointly and severally liable.[219] However, as the patient only has a contract with the hospital and not with the doctor, any claim against the doctor will of necessity be a tort claim.[220]

79 In the second scenario, the patient also enters into a contract with the hospital. However, the hospital is only contractually bound to provide the patient with accommodation, catering, and care (so-called 'fractioned hospital contract'; *gespaltener Spitalaufnahmevertrag/contrat partiel d'hospitalisation*). In contrast, medical treatment is provided on the basis of a separate contract between the patient and the doctor who is treating the patient in the hospital.[221] Accordingly, if something goes wrong in the course of treatment, the question will arise whether the measure which caused the harm was within the remit of the hospital or the doctor. Whether or not a contractual claim can be brought against the hospital or the doctor in this second scenario will depend on the outcome of this assessment.[222] The doctor's acts and

---

216 *Fellmann* (fn 111) 103, 106, 107.

217 See *Guillod* (fn 87) 392, 393 (at para 5); *Fellmann* (fn 111) 103, 106 f; *M Amstutz/W Schluep* in: Honsell et al (fn 96) Einl vor art 184 ff no 343 ff.

218 See infra, no 85.

219 Art 51 CO (fn 98). On the consequences of joint and several liability, see supra, no 66.

220 *Fellmann* (fn 215) 47, 51; *Amstutz/Schluep* (fn 217) Einleitung vor art 184 ff no 355.

221 *Fellmann* (fn 215) 47, 51.

222 See Amtsgericht Luzern-Stadt, decision of 26 June 1993, SG N 895, at para 7.2; *Gross* (fn 177) 249 f, 254 ff; see also *Amstutz/Schluep* (fn 217) Einl vor art 184 ff no 356; *Fellmann* (fn 111) 103, 107.

omissions cannot be imputed to the hospital under art 101(1) CO,[223] as the hospital is not contractually bound to provide medical treatment.

80 If a patient is treated in a public hospital, the relationship between hospital and patient will be subject to public law.[224] If the patient is a private patient of one of the hospital's doctors, such patient will also enter into a private law contract with such doctor.[225] Nonetheless, it does not necessarily follow that hospital doctors will become personally liable toward their private patients if something goes wrong during treatment, as the Cantons have the power to preempt federal private law with regard to the liability of their employees.[226]

81 In general, the social health system has no impact on the relationship between patients and health care providers.[227] However, an exception applies with regard to the question of who is bound to pay the health care provider's fees. In the case of social health insurance coverage, the rule is that the patient will pay the health care provider's fees directly. The patient will then be entitled to reimbursement from the insurer (so-called *tiers garant*-system). Nonetheless, insurers and health care providers may deviate from this rule by agreeing that the insurer, and not the patient, will be the health care provider's debtor (so-called *tiers payant*-system).[228] Also, where a patient requires stationary care, the rule is reversed under federal law, so that the health care insurer will always be the health care provider's debtor.[229] In the case of social accident insurance coverage, the health care provider's debtor is generally the insurer, and not the patient.[230]

16. Differences to tort law

82 Under art 97(1) of the Code of Obligations (CO),[231] four requirements must be met for liability in contract. Firstly, a person must have suffered damage, ie a pecuniary loss. Secondly, there must be a breach of contract. Thirdly, there must be a causal link between the breach and the damage

223 Cf infra, no 85.
224 See infra, no 96.
225 The same apples if the public hospital allows for medical treatment by affiliated doctors; see *Fellmann* (fn 111) 103, 110 ff.
226 See infra, no 97 and the references in fn 280.
227 See supra, no 24.
228 See art 42 HIA (fn 6).
229 Art 42(2) HIA (fn 6).
230 *Gächter/Vollenweider* (fn 5) para 732.
231 See supra, fn 98.

suffered, ie the breach must be a *conditio sine qua non* of the damage, and such damage must not be too remote.[232] Finally, the potentially liable party must be at fault, ie he must be of sufficient mental capacity and must have acted either intentionally or negligently. These requirements also apply to contracts for the provision of medical treatment.[233]

83 If the requirements for both contractual and tort liability are met, patients who are harmed in the course of medical treatment are free to choose whether to bring their claim in contract or in tort.[234] However, contractual claims are generally more advantageous.[235] Thus, the statute of limitations for contractual claims is ten years from the date on which the claim was due,[236] whereas in tort, the regular limitation period is one year from the day the harmed person acquired knowledge of the damage and the tortfeasor's identity.[237]

84 A further distinction between claims in contract and tort relates to the burden of proof with regard to fault. In tort claims, it is the harmed party who must prove that the alleged tortfeasor acted intentionally or negligently, whereas in contract claims, the burden of proof is shifted to the party in breach under art 97(1) CO. Unless such party succeeds in showing that he bears no fault, such fault will be presumed for the purposes of liability. However, where medical malpractice is concerned, this advantage has little practical impact.[238] In a contractual claim for medical malpractice, the patient must prove that the health care provider breached the contract by violating professional standards, ie by not acting *lege artis*.[239] If the patient succeeds in proving such breach, it will be practically impossible for the health care provider to free himself from liability by showing that he was not at fault. Accordingly, the central question is whether the health care provider breached the contract, and that is for the patient to prove.[240] In tort claims, an alleged violation of professional standards must also be proved by the patient, namely in the context of wrongfulness.[241] Both in tort and in contract claims, the requisite stand-

---

232 For the corresponding requirements in tort law, see supra, no 47.
233 See, eg, BGE 133 III 121, 123 ff (Federal Court decision of 9 February 2007).
234 See, eg, *I Schwenzer*, Schweizerisches Obligationenrecht Allgemeiner Teil (5th edn 2009) para 5.03.
235 See, eg, *Schwenzer* (fn 234) para 5.04.
236 Art 127 in conjunction with art 130(1) CO (fn 98).
237 See supra, no 53.
238 See generally *Werro* (fn 174) para 1481.
239 See, eg, BGE 133 III 121, 124 (Federal Court decision of 9 February 2007).
240 See, eg, BGE 133 III 121, 126–127 (Federal Court decision of 9 February 2007).
241 See supra, no 54.

ard of care is the same.[242] As in tort, a doctor is also liable in contract for any fault, regardless of the degree.[243]

Another difference between contractual and tort liability is that a debtor's contractual responsibility for auxiliaries is more far-reaching than in tort law, and thus more advantageous to the claimant. Unlike in tort, where a relationship of 'subordination' is required,[244] acts and omissions of an auxiliary are generally imputed to the debtor under art 101(1) CO, as long as the auxiliary's conduct can be classified as a breach of contract.[245] Any person acting with a view to executing the debtor's contractual obligations with the debtor's consent and knowledge qualifies as an auxiliary for the purposes of liability, including independent third parties.[246] Moreover, the debtor cannot escape liability by showing that he exercised all due diligence.[247] Neither the debtor's nor the auxiliary's fault is required for liability; rather, it is sufficient that the debtor would have been at fault had he acted in the same way as the auxiliary (so-called 'hypothetical fault').[248] It is for the debtor to prove that the auxiliary complied with the standard of care owed by the debtor.[249] **85**

Insofar as the patient's claims are concerned, the same types of damages are compensable both in tort and in contract. Claims for non-pecuniary loss are also available both in tort and in contract.[250] However, damages claims by the victim's relatives for wrongful death can only be based in tort, not in contract.[251] In principle,[252] this also applies to claims for non-pecuniary loss brought by a disabled victim's relatives, as well as to independent claims for non-pecuniary loss brought by a deceased victim's relatives.[253] **86**

---

242 BGE 115 Ib 175, 810 (Federal Court decision of 17 May 1989).

243 See BGE 133 III 121, 124 (Federal Court decision of 9 February 2007); cf also supra, no 47 *in fine*.

244 Art 55(1) CO; see supra, no 48.

245 See *Schwenzer* (fn 234) paras 23.07 ff.

246 See, eg, ibid, para 23.04.

247 Contrast art 55(1) CO; see supra no 50.

248 See, eg, *Schwenzer* (fn 234) para 23.10; for an example from case law, see Amtsgericht Luzern-Stadt, decision of 26 June 1993, SG N 895, at paras 6.2 ff (liability of a hospital for acts of its auxiliaries).

249 See *P Gauch/W Schluep/S Emmenegger*, Schweizerisches Obligationenrecht vol 2 (9th edn 2008) para 3049; unpublished Federal Court decision 4C.307/2003 of 19 February 2004, at para 5.2; BGE 119 II 337, 338 (Federal Court decision of 22 June 1993).

250 Cf BGE 123 III 204, 206–207 (Federal Court decision of 9 June 1997).

251 BGE 123 III 204, 207 (Federal Court decision of 9 June 1997).

252 See infra, no 137.

253 BGE 123 III 204, 213 (Federal Court decision of 9 June 1997). On the practical consequences, see infra, no 137.

17. Contractual claims in the absence of direct contracts?

87 In certain limited circumstances, a patient who has not entered into a contract with a health care provider may nonetheless be able to base a claim on the violation of contractual duties. If, for example, a patient lacks the capacity to act, he cannot conclude a contract for the provision of medical services on his own behalf. Rather, his legal guardian must act for him. Depending on the circumstances of the case,[254] the legal guardian will either act as the patient's agent, so that the contract will be concluded directly between the health care provider and the patient, or the contract will be concluded between the health care provider and the legal guardian. In the latter case, the patient is not a party to the contract. Nonetheless, if something goes wrong in the course of medical treatment, the patient will have a contractual claim against the health care provider, as the contract was entered into for the patient's benefit.[255]

88 In contrast, the concept of contracts with protective effect for third parties (*Vertrag mit Schutzwirkung zugunsten Dritter/contrat avec effet protecteur envers des tiers/contratto con effetto di protezione a favore di terzi*) has not hitherto been adopted by the Federal Court[256] and remains controversial in Swiss law.[257] Accordingly, it is doubtful whether a patient basing his claim on a violation of the contract between (eg) the hospital and the doctor would be successful.

18. Informed consent

89 The doctrine of informed consent can become relevant both in tort and in contract claims for medical malpractice. As pointed out above,[258] a patient alleging medical malpractice must prove that the medical treatment was not *lege artis,* which can be difficult. Both in contract and in tort, however, it is the doctor (or, if the hospital's liability is at issue, the hospital) who must prove that the patient gave informed consent.[259]

---

254 See *Schwenzer* (fn 234) paras 86.11 f.

255 See art 112(2) CO (fn 98). Cf BGE 116 II 519, 520 (Federal Court decision of 23 October 1990); *Schwenzer* (fn 234) para 86.11.

256 Question left open in BGE 130 III 345, 347–348 (Federal Court decision of 23 December 2003).

257 See *Schwenzer* (fn 234) paras 87.01 ff.

258 Supra, nos 51 (for tort claims) and 84 (for contract claims).

259 For tort claims, see supra, para 51; for contract claims, see BGE 133 III 121, 129 (Federal Court decision of 9 February 2007).

Swiss law not only recognises medical malpractice in its narrower sense, but also a distinct cause of action for failure to obtain informed consent.[260] If something goes wrong during a medical intervention and it cannot be shown that the patient gave his informed consent, the consequences are drastic. The doctor will be held liable for all damage suffered in consequence of the intervention, regardless of whether such damage was caused by a mistake in treatment or simply by chance, as long as such damage is not too remote.[261] He may only avoid liability if he can show that the individual patient would have consented to the intervention even if he had been properly informed (so-called 'hypothetical consent').[262] If he fails, the patient will only be required to show that he suffered damage as a consequence of the intervention (eg surgery) as such.[263] This will generally be an easy task. Accordingly, questions surrounding informed consent are of great practical importance, and it is the rule, rather than the exception, that a patient will allege lack of informed consent in medical malpractice cases.[264] **90**

The legal requirements of informed consent have been developed in case law, although there are statutory rules in particularly sensitive areas, such as reproductive medicine, organ transplantation or genetic testing.[265] Informed consent also forms one of the cornerstones of the Oviedo Convention on Human Rights and Biomedicine.[266] Cantonal law may provide additional statutory rules on the scope of the duty to inform.[267] The Swiss Medical Association's rules of professional conduct[268] also provide that doctors must inform their patients,[269] as do various guidelines of the Swiss Academy of Medical Sciences (SAMW).[270] **91**

---

260 See, eg, *Hausheer* (fn 155) 201, 212.

261 See, eg, BGE 108 II 59, 62 (Federal Court decision of 12 January 1982); BGE 133 III 121, 128 (Federal Court decision of 9 February 2007). See also *Guillod* (fn 87) 392, 398 (at para 23). On the test of remoteness in contract and tort claims, see supra, nos 47 and 82.

262 See, eg, BGE 133 III 121, 130 (Federal Court decision of 9 February 2007); unpublished Federal Court decision 4.C.66/2007 of 9 January 2008, at para 5; *Hausheer* (fn 155) 201, 209 f; *Fellmann* (fn 111) 103, 227 ff. For further references to case law, see *Jäger/Schweiter* (fn 74) 86 ff.

263 See, eg, BGE 108 II 59, 62–63 (Federal Court decision of 12 January 1982).

264 See, eg, *Guillod* (fn 87) 392, 399 (at para 26). For a critique of this development, see *Roberto* (fn 143) paras 93 ff; *Honsell* (fn 174) § 5 no 22.

265 See *Guillod* (fn 87) 392, 398 (at para 24); *Fellmann* (fn 111) 103, 182 ff.

266 See arts 5–9 of the Oviedo Convention (*Übereinkommen zum Schutz der Menschenrechte und der Menschenwürde im Hinblick auf die Anwendung von Biologie und Medizin [Übereinkommen über Menschenrechte und Biomedizin]*) of 4 April 1997, SR 0.810.2.

267 See *Jäger/Schweiter* (fn 74) 68, 69.

268 See supra, no 38.

269 See art 10 (fn 114).

270 On the guidelines of the SAMW, see supra, no 39.

92 The purpose of informed consent is to provide adequate information to the patient so that he can make an intelligent decision about a given diagnostic or therapeutic procedure. The scope of the duty to inform patients depends on the nature and the possible consequences of the medical treatment involved.[271] In broad terms, the patient should receive all the information necessary for him to be able to decide whether or not to agree to the proposed intervention. The individual patient's information needs are decisive, not those of a 'reasonable' patient.[272] Information must be given early enough for the patient to be able to reach a decision without pressure. In the case of heavy surgery or if grave risks are involved, a patient must be informed at least three days beforehand, unless there is an emergency. Otherwise, one day beforehand is sufficient.[273]

93 In particular,[274] doctors are under a duty to inform their patients of the nature of the proposed treatment and the risks involved, except in case of commonplace measures which neither pose a serious threat to the patient's health nor may lead to irrevocable harm or long-term impairment. There is no duty to inform of risks which are generally involved with all larger interventions, such as bleeding, infections, thrombosis or embolisms. In contrast, the patient must be informed of specific risks of the proposed intervention, as well as of rare risks with serious consequences. In general, statistical risk percentages are not used for determining the scope of the duty to inform.[275]

94 The doctrine of informed consent is limited by the so-called 'therapeutic privilege', meaning that a doctor need not (and indeed must not) give information which might induce a state of anxiety in the patient such as to injure the patient's health.[276]

---

271 See *Fellmann* (fn 111) 103, 167 ff; *Hausheer* (fn 155) 201, 203 ff.

272 See *W Wiegand*, Die Aufklärungspflicht und die Folgen ihrer Verletzung, in: H Honsell (ed), Handbuch des Arztrechts (1994) 119, 136 ff; *Fellmann* (fn 111) 103, 179.

273 See unpublished Federal Court decision 4P.265/2002 of 28 April 2003, at para 5.2; *Guillod* (fn 87) 392, 399 (at para 25).

274 For references to pertinent case law, see *Jäger/Schweiter* (fn 74) 76 ff; see also *Fellmann* (fn 111) 103, 173 ff, 178 ff; *Wiegand* (fn 272) 119, 127 ff, 134 ff; *Hausheer* (fn 155) 201, 205 ff; *Guillod* (fn 87) 392, 397 (at paras 19 ff).

275 On this latter issue, see *Wiegand* (fn 272) 119, 134 f; *Fellmann* (fn 111) 103, 180, 181.

276 For references to case law, see *Jäger/Schweiter* (fn 74) 76.

D. Public Liability

19. Key differences from cases involving private hospitals or doctors

Where a patient is injured in a public hospital, the first question which arises relates to the law governing (1) the relationship between the patient and the hospital (or, where the hospital does not have an independent legal personality, with the hospital proprietor), and (2) the relationship between the patient and the hospital's employees, in particular its doctors. **95**

The liability of public legal entities in Switzerland is not governed by federal private law, but by federal public law (in the case of federal entities) or cantonal public law (in the case of cantonal entities).[277] With a very few exceptions,[278] public hospitals in Switzerland are either cantonal or municipal. Accordingly, the liability of such hospitals (or, where applicable, the hospital proprietor) is governed by the respective Canton's public law. According to the majority opinion, this also applies in cases of privatisation.[279] **96**

As far as the relationship between a patient and the public hospital's employees, including hospital doctors, is concerned, the Cantons are free to deviate from the liability regime under federal private law by subjecting such persons' liability to cantonal public law. This power to preempt federal private law also extends to a doctor's relationship with his private patients.[280] **97**

If the Cantons do not make use of this power, the provisions of federal private law will apply by default, so that a hospital doctor may become liable toward a patient under the provisions of the Swiss Code of Obligations.[281] Accordingly, the liability of doctors employed by a public hospital may be governed by federal private law or by cantonal public law, depending on the legislation of the Canton where the hospital is located.[282] To date, **98**

---

277 Art 59 CC (fn 153).

278 See *Guillod* (fn 87) 392, 402 (at para 38).

279 On this and on other instances where cantonal public law might apply, see supra, no 45.

280 See, eg, BGE 122 III 101, 104–105 (Federal Court decision of 11 March 1996); *Guillod* (fn 87) 392, 408 (at paras 62 ff); *Gross* (fn 131) 35, 36 f; *Fellmann* (fn 111) 103, 111. For further references to case law, see *Jäger/Schweiter* (fn 74) 12 ff.

281 See fn 98.

282 See, eg, *Fellmann* (fn 111) 103, 112 ff; *Eichenberger* (fn 74) 351, 359. For an overview of the pertinent decisions of the Swiss Federal Court, see *Jäger/Schweiter* (fn 74) 4 ff. On liability under federal private law, see supra, nos 45 ff and nos 77 ff.

all Cantons have made use of their power to legislate in this area.[283] Although each of the 26 Swiss Cantons has its own distinct public law, most cantonal liability regimes are similar.

99 Liability under cantonal public law may differ in several ways from the liability regime under federal private law. The majority of Cantons provide for the exclusive liability of the State, meaning that any claims for pecuniary or non-pecuniary loss may only be brought against the State, and not against the responsible State employee. The Canton may have a right of recourse against the responsible employee, but this is generally restricted to cases where such employee caused the damage intentionally or through gross negligence.[284]

100 In most Swiss cantons, fault is not a requirement for State liability.[285] In particular, this means that the Canton cannot avoid liability by showing that it exercised all due diligence in selecting, instructing and overseeing its employees and that all work processes were organised diligently.[286] Accordingly, a patient will not have to identify the actual tortfeasor in claims against the Canton.[287] The Federal Court has also accepted liability for organisational deficiencies under cantonal public law.[288]

101 However, the Canton will only be liable for acts which are wrongful (*widerrechtlich/illicite/illecito*). The notion of 'wrongfulness' corresponds to that which is used in federal private law. Accordingly, any interference with a patient's physical integrity constitutes wrongfulness, so that the Canton will have to prove that the patient gave his informed consent.[289] If this can be proved, the intervention will only be considered wrongful if the patient can show that the intervention was not *lege artis*.[290] As far as the

---

283 *Gross* (fn 131) 35 f.

284 See, eg, §§ 6(1), 6(4) and 15(1) of the Public Liability Act of the Canton of Zurich (*Haftungsgesetz*) of 14 September 1969, accessible at <http://www.zhlex.zh.ch> (12.01.11); §§ 3(1), 3(2) and 9 of the Public Liability Act of the Canton of Basel-Stadt (*Gesetz über die Haftung des Staates und seines Personals [Haftungsgesetz, HG]*) of 17 November 1999, accessible at <http://www.gesetzessammlung.bs.ch> (12.01.11); see also *Gross* (fn 131) 35, 37; *Guillod* (fn 87) 392, 404 (at para 44).

285 See *Guillod* (fn 87) 392, 404 (at paras 47 ff) for references to cantonal law.

286 Contrast art 55(1) CO (see supra, no 50).

287 Cf *Gross* (fn 131) 35, 39 ff; *Kuhn* (fn 154) 601, 654; see also the references in fn 177, supra.

288 BGE 112 Ib 322 (Federal Court decision of 30 September 1986). On the unclear situation in federal tort law, see supra, nos 61 f.

289 See supra, no 51.

290 See, eg, BGE 123 II 577, 583 (Federal Court decision of 12 September 1997) with further references.

burden of proof is concerned, the situation of the patient is no different from that under (federal) tort and contract law.

Claims brought under cantonal public law are subject to the respective Canton's statute of limitations, which may differ from the limitation periods provided under federal private law.[291] **102**

Finally, the nature of the law governing liability (ie federal private law or cantonal public law) can also have an impact on jurisdiction and procedural rules. Cantonal courts with jurisdiction to hear civil cases do not necessarily have jurisdiction over cases governed by public law, and different procedural rules apply to civil law and public law cases. However, most cantonal laws provide that public liability claims fall within the jurisdiction of civil law courts, and accordingly, the laws on civil procedure will apply.[292] Until recently, each Canton had its own distinct laws on civil procedure. However, on 1 January 2011, the different cantonal laws were replaced by the new Federal Act on Civil Procedure.[293] **103**

E. Alternative compensation regimes

20. Funds and/or other alternative compensation regimes

There are currently no funds or alternative compensation regimes offering compensation (in whole or in part) to victims of medical malpractice. A proposal to introduce a private compensation fund was made in 2002[294] but has not been implemented to date. **104**

291 See *Guillod* (fn 87) 392, 409 (at para 68). On the general limitation period in federal tort law, see supra, no 53.

292 See, eg, § 19 of the Public Liability Act of the Canton of Zurich (fn 284); § 6(1) of the Public Liability Act of the Canton of Basel-Stadt (fn 284); see also *J Gross*, Schweizerisches Staatshaftungsrecht (2nd edn 2001) 143, 361; *Guillod* (fn 87) 392, 413 (at para 84); *T Jaag*, Öffentliches Entschädigungsrecht: Gemeinsamkeiten und Unterschiede zwischen verschiedenen Formen öffentlichrechtlicher Entschädigungen, Schweizerisches Zentralblatt für Staats- und Verwaltungsrecht (ZBL) 1997, 145, 166 f.

293 See supra, no 8.

294 Joint proposal by the Swiss Society for Health Care Policy (SGGP/SSPS), the Swiss Medical Association (FMH), the Red Cross and the journal 'Beobachter'; see *Guillod* (fn 154) 155, 169.

F. Extent of Liability/Remedies

I. Pecuniary loss

21. Introduction to indemnifying pecuniary loss

105 The general principle in Swiss law is that the tortfeasor is liable for all pecuniary loss caused by the tortious act, as long as such damage is not too remote.[295] The aim of compensation for pecuniary loss is to place the injured person in the position in which he would have been had the tortious event not occurred.[296] Punitive damages are not available.[297]

106 The person claiming compensation must prove that he has suffered pecuniary loss, and quantify such loss.[298] If it is impossible to prove or quantify the loss, the court may use its discretion to determine the loss, giving due consideration to the 'ordinary course of things' (*gewöhnlicher Lauf der Dinge/cours ordinaire des choses/ordinario andamento delle cose*) and the measures taken by the injured person.[299] Such difficulties of proof are typical of claims for future pecuniary loss.

107 It is in the court's discretion to decide whether the pecuniary loss suffered by a claimant shall be compensated in kind (*Naturalrestitution/réparation en nature/risarcimento in natura*) or through a monetary award (art 43 CO). The Code of Obligations[300] does not give preference to one or the other type of compensation. In practice, however, monetary relief is the rule.

108 Compensation is calculated on the basis of the loss actually suffered by the individual claimant ('subjective-concrete' method, as opposed to the 'objective-abstract' method),[301] although certain exceptions have been recognised by the Federal Court. Thus, no actual loss is required in case of so-called 'household damage'[302] or where an injured person is taken care of at home by friends or relatives.[303]

---

295 See, eg, *Schwenzer* (fn 234) para 15.07. On the test of remoteness in tort claims, see supra, no 47.
296 See, eg, *Brehm* (fn 97) art 41 no 70.
297 See *Widmer* (fn 178) 300.
298 Art 41(1) CO (fn 98).
299 Art 42(2) CO (fn 98). For details, see *Brehm* (fn 97) art 42 no 1 ff.
300 Supra fn 98.
301 See, eg, BGE 129 III 135, 141 (Federal Court decision of 19 December 2002); *Schnyder* (fn 96) art 42 no 2–3; *Werro* (fn 174) paras 928 ff.
302 See infra, no 117.
303 See infra, no 111.

Compensation should not lead to an enrichment of the injured person.[304] Accordingly, if the injured person receives any monetary benefits owing to the tortious conduct, such benefits will be taken into account when determining the loss (*Vorteilsanrechnung/imputation des avantages/imputazione dei vantaggi*). This also applies if a third party is statutorily or contractually obligated to make a contribution because of the injury (eg statutory sick pay by the injured person's employer), although such party may be entitled to take recourse against the tortfeasor.[305] Benefits are not deducted if such deduction is excluded by statutory provisions (eg in the case of fixed-benefit insurance)[306] or by the intention of the parties (eg in the case of voluntary contributions by the injured person's employer).[307] **109**

If tortious conduct leads to bodily injury, the injured party is entitled to compensation for all costs incurred as a result of the injury (*damnum emergens*), eg first aid costs, transportation costs, hospital fees, expenditure for medical drugs and devices, as well as to compensation for loss of earnings (*lucrum cessans*) (art 46 CO).[308] If the injured person will receive less social retirement benefits as a result of his reduced income, the tortfeasor will also be liable for such 'retirement damage' (*Rentenschaden/dommage de rente/danno di rendita*).[309] **110**

Compensation is also owed for costs and losses suffered by relatives when visiting the injured person in hospital (ie costs of the trip and loss of earnings). If the injured person is cared for at home by friends or relatives at no charge, compensation is available on the basis of the average cost of home care, even if no actual loss has been suffered.[310] In such cases, compensation is due to the injured party himself. The (rather far–fetched) dogmatic construction is that such relatives would be entitled to claim remuneration from the injured party for their visiting costs or the provision of care, so that their claims against the injured party (even if they never actually arise) constitute additional items of damage.[311] **111**

---

304 See, eg, *Werro* (fn 174) paras 942 ff; *Brehm* (fn 97) art 42 no 27 ff; *Schnyder* (fn 96) art 42 no 7.

305 On the right of recourse of social insurers, see supra, nos 27 ff.

306 See art 96 AIC (fn 92).

307 See, eg, *Brehm* (fn 97) art 46 no 38 f; *Rey* (fn 137) para 215.

308 For details, see *Brehm* (fn 97) art 46 no 7 ff.

309 See, in particular, BGE 129 III 135, 141 (Federal Court decision of 19 December 2002).

310 See unpublished Federal Court decision 4C.276/2001 of 26 March 2002, at paras 6.b.aa and 6.b.bb; BGE 97 II 259, 266 (Federal Court decision of 12 October 1971). For details, see *Brehm* (fn 160) 325, 340 (at paras 72 f).

311 See *Brehm* (fn 97) art 46 no 14, 17; *V Roberto*, Schadensrecht (1997) 153 f.

112 If tortious conduct leads to a person's death, the deceased's heirs are entitled to compensation for funeral expenses. If death was not immediate, the tortfeasor will also be liable for medical expenses and loss of earnings. Persons to whom the deceased provided support are entitled to compensation for loss of that support (*Versorgerschaden/perte de soutien/perdita del sostegno*) (art 45 CO).[312]

113 These general rules also apply in case of medical malpractice.

22. Loss of earnings vs loss of earning capacity

114 Compensation for temporary or permanent loss of earning capacity (*Arbeitsunfähigkeit/incapacité de travail/impedimento al lavoro*) is calculated on the basis of the injured person's actual or expected loss of income. A merely abstract loss of earning power is not indemnified.[313]

115 In the case of a permanent loss of earning capacity, the court may not simply consider the injured person's current income. Rather, it must make a projection as to how the injured person's career path and income would have developed if such person had not suffered any injury. This is especially difficult where the injured person is a young adult who has not yet embarked on a career, and even more so where children are concerned.[314]

116 The Federal Court recently changed its case law by holding that compensation for loss of earnings must be calculated on the basis of the injured person's net (and not gross) income.[315] The injured person's 'retirement damage'[316] is indemnified on the basis of such person's actual loss. Such loss is calculated by deducting the social insurance benefits that will actually be paid out to the injured person upon reaching old age from the hypothetical old-age benefits that such person would have received if he had not been injured.[317]

117 Where a homemaker has been injured, the Federal Court recognises an exception to the rule that only an actual or expected loss of income may be compensated. If the homemaker is unable to take care of the household

312 See, eg, *Brehm* (fn 160) 325, 346 ff (at paras 95 ff).
313 See *Brehm* (fn 160) 325, 342 (at para 80); *id* (fn 97) art 46 no 35; *Honsell* (fn 174) § 8 no 67.
314 For details, see *Brehm* (fn 160) 325, 342–343 (at paras 81–84); see also *Roberto* (fn 143) paras 660 ff.
315 BGE 129 III 135, 141 ff (Federal Court decision of 19 December 2002).
316 See supra, no 110.
317 BGE 129 III 135, 150–151 (Federal Court decision of 19 December 2002).

because of an injury, he will be entitled to compensation calculated on the basis of the average cost of home help, regardless of whether home help is actually employed or not (so-called 'household damage'; *Haushaltschaden/ dommage ménager/danno della casalinga*).[318] Similarly, where the injured person worked gratuitously, eg in an effort to assist a spouse to establish or maintain a business venture, such person will also be entitled to compensation.[319]

23. Periodic payments or lump sum?

Pecuniary losses caused by bodily injury can be indemnified on a periodic basis or by lump sum. In general, it is in the court's discretion to decide whether indemnification shall be paid on a periodic basis or by capitalised (lump) sum.[320] **118**

Until fairly recently, the constant practice of the Federal Court was that in the case of permanent damage, lump sum payment should be the rule rather than the exception. In 1999, however, it changed its position and decided that in principle, the injured person may choose between a lump sum or periodic payment.[321] **119**

Costs incurred as a result of the tortious conduct are generally indemnified by a lump sum.[322] **120**

24. Caps and thresholds

As a rule, there are no caps on the amounts available as compensation in Swiss law. An exception applies with respect to aviation liability under the Warsaw Convention.[323] Likewise, there is no general minimum damage requirement. **121**

---

318 See, eg, BGE 129 III 135, 151 ff (Federal Court decision of 19 December 2002); BGE 127 III 403, 405 ff (Federal Court decision of 21 June 2001); BGE 132 III 321, 332 (Federal Court decision of 17 January 2006); *Schwenzer* (fn 234) para 14.10; *Brehm* (fn 160) 325, 341 (at para 79); *Roberto* (fn 143) para 732.

319 BGE 99 II 221, 224 (Federal Court decision of 26 June 1973).

320 Art 43(2) CO (fn 98). See BGE 125 III 312, 320 (Federal Court decision of 11 May 1999); *Brehm* (fn 97) art 43 no 7.

321 BGE 125 III 312, 320–321 (Federal Court decision of 11 May 1999). For details on capitalisation, see *Brehm* (fn 160) 325, 344 f (at paras 90 f).

322 See, eg, *Schnyder* (fn 96) art 46 no 12.

323 See *Brehm* (fn 160) 325, 350 (at para 117).

122 Both a cap and a minimum damage requirement are included in the Federal Act on Crime Victims Support.[324] However, this Act does not establish or limit civil liability; rather, it aims to fill the gap where a crime victim and/or his relatives cannot otherwise receive compensation (eg because the offender is unknown or insolvent)[325] by providing an entitlement against the Canton where the crime was perpetrated. Under the Act, compensation for pecuniary loss is capped at CHF 120,000, and the minimum required damage is CHF 500.[326] Moreover, such compensation is only available to persons with modest income.[327] Compensation for the victim's non-pecuniary loss is capped at CHF 70,000, whereas the maximum compensation available to his relatives for their non-pecuniary loss is CHF 35,000.[328]

123 Under the Swiss Product Liability Act,[329] the claimant must bear his own pecuniary loss up to an amount of CHF 900. This sum will be deducted from his damages claim. At the same time, this provision works as a minimum damage requirement. However, it does not apply to losses sustained as a result of bodily injury.[330]

II. Non-pecuniary loss

25. Introduction to indemnifying non-pecuniary loss

124 The main provisions on non-pecuniary loss are set forth in the Swiss Code of Obligations (CO).[331] Compensation for non-pecuniary loss may also be available in the case of public liability; however, that is a matter of cantonal law.[332] The following paragraphs are confined to non-pecuniary loss under federal private law.

125 If a person has suffered bodily injury, the court may award him an appropriate sum for emotional distress (*Genugtuung/réparation morale/ripa-*

324 Federal Act on Crime Victims Support (CVSA) (*Bundesgesetz über die Hilfe an Opfer von Straftaten [Opferhilfegesetz, OHG]*) of 23 March 2007, SR 312.5.
325 Art 4(1) CVSA (fn 324).
326 Art 20(3) CVSA (fn 324).
327 Art 6(1) CVSA (fn 324).
328 Art 23(2) CVSA (fn 324).
329 See supra, no 72.
330 Art 6(1) PLA (fn 199).
331 Supra, fn 98.
332 On cantonal public law, see supra, nos 95 ff.

razione), 'giving due consideration to the circumstances of the case' (art 47 CO).[333] Compensation will usually be awarded if the claimant has suffered permanent damage which will cause physical discomfort or emotional distress for the rest of his life, although lesser injuries (such as an injury necessitating a long stay in hospital) may also qualify.[334] Compensation is also available even if the victim is no longer able to appreciate his situation due to the injury, such as in the case of severe brain damage.[335]

If a person is killed, the court can award the victim's relatives an appropriate sum for emotional distress, again giving due consideration to the circumstances of the case (art 47 CO).[336] **126**

Compensation for non-pecuniary loss is also available if a person's personality rights are otherwise wrongfully infringed, on condition that such infringement is sufficiently serious to merit compensation and cannot otherwise be made good (art 49 CO). In particular, a victim's relatives may be entitled to compensation for the emotional distress caused them by the victim's injury.[337] **127**

Both under art 47 and art 49 CO, compensation for non-pecuniary loss is only available if the claimant has a cause of action in tort or in contract.[338] However, contractual claims are generally only available to the direct victim. As a rule, indirectly affected persons can only sue in tort.[339] **128**

If more than one person owes the injured party compensation for non-pecuniary loss, the Federal Court has held that such persons will be jointly and severally liable.[340] **129**

Compensation for non-pecuniary loss is determined on a case-to-case basis; there are no fixed standard rates. Rather, the court may determine the amount of compensation at its discretion. However, courts tend to follow the amounts awarded by other courts in previous decisions with **130**

---

333 On the relevant criteria, see infra, no 130.

334 See, eg, *Brehm* (fn 160) 325, 349 (at para 110).

335 BGE 108 II 422, 431 ff (Federal Court decision of 6 July 1982); for further references and a critique of the Federal Court's decisions, see *Brehm* (fn 97) art 47 no 21 ff.

336 See infra, no 135.

337 See infra, no 136.

338 See *Schwenzer* (fn 234) para 17.06; cf also BGE 123 III 204, 206–207 (Federal Court decision of 9 June 1997).

339 See infra, no 137.

340 See, eg, BGE 116 II 645, 650–651 (Federal Court decision of 9 October 1990). For a detailed discussion of this issue and further references to case law, see *Brehm* (fn 97) art 47 no 97 ff.

similar facts.[341] Criteria for assessing compensation are, in particular, the nature of the injury, the gravity, intensity and duration of its effects on the victim, the degree of the liable person's fault, whether the victim is partially at fault, and the chances that the award will alleviate the victim's emotional distress.[342]

131 The Federal Court recently held that non-pecuniary losses can also be indemnified on a periodic basis, although payment by lump sum is the rule.[343]

132 Swiss Courts are traditionally reluctant to award large sums for pain and suffering, although awards are getting larger. In recent years, the following sums have been awarded:

- in the case of severe disability: up to CHF 200,000;[344]
- in the case of death of a close relative: CHF 10,000–50,000 (depending on the closeness of the bond between victim and relative);[345]
- in the case of severe disability of a close relative: CHF 20,000–50,000; the Federal Court has indicated that close relatives should receive approximately half of the amount awarded to the injured person himself.[346]

133 These general rules on non-pecuniary loss also apply in case of medical malpractice.

26. Who can claim compensation for non-pecuniary loss?

134 In the case of bodily injury, the direct victim may claim compensation for non-pecuniary loss under art 47 CO.[347]

135 If the direct victim dies, the court may award the victim's 'relatives' compensation for emotional distress (art 47 CO). The term 'relatives' is

---

341 Courts often consult the table of court decisions provided by *K Hütte/P Ducksch/K Guerrero*, Die Genugtuung: eine tabellarische Übersicht über Gerichtsentscheide aus den Jahren 1990–2005 (3rd edn 2006).

342 BGE 132 II 117, 119 (Federal Court decision of 19 January 2006).

343 BGE 134 III 97, 99 f (Federal Court decision of 8 January 2008).

344 See *M Sidler*, Die Genugtuung und ihre Bemessung, in: Münch/Geiser (fn 97) 445, 468 ff (at paras 10.54–55); *Schwenzer* (fn 234) para 17.14; *Rey* (fn 137) para 504; *Brehm* (fn 160) 325, 354 (at para 132).

345 See *Sidler* (fn 344) 445, 476 ff (at para 10.66); *Schwenzer* (fn 234) para 17.14; *Rey* (fn 137) para 505.

346 See *Sidler* (fn 344) 445, 480 (at para 10.69); *Schwenzer* (fn 234) para 17.14 with further references.

347 On the requirements under art 47 CO, see supra, nos 125 and 130.

misleading, as it is neither sufficient nor necessary for the claimant to be a member of the victim's family. Rather, the closeness of the bond between victim and claimant is decisive. Spouses, registered partners, parents and children of the victim will usually be entitled to compensation; fiancé(e)s and non-married partners may also qualify, as may brothers and sisters, grandparents and grandchildren etc as long as their bond with the deceased was sufficiently close.[348] It is not necessary for these persons to have lived in the same household as the deceased.

If the victim is severely disabled, the victim's close relatives, such as **136** parents, spouses and children,[349] may also claim compensation in their own right on the basis of art 49 CO. However, such compensation is only granted if the victim's injury affects them at least as much as the victim's death would have.[350] Although art 49 CO could also serve as a basis for compensating other persons whose personality rights are infringed as a result of the victim's injuries, such claims have not yet been brought before the Federal Court.

As a rule, claims brought by a disabled victim's relatives under art 49 CO **137** or by a deceased victim's relatives under art 47 CO can only be based in tort, not in contract.[351] The practical consequence is that such claims will be subject to the shorter statute of limitations for tort suits.[352] The only exception is where the victim's relative himself contracted with the liable party, for example where the victim's legal guardian entered into a contract for the provision of medical services.[353]

G. Procedural Matters

27. Specific rules of jurisdiction or procedure

As pointed out above, procedural laws relating to public liability in **138** Switzerland are not federal, but cantonal, and until recently, the same

---

348 See *Schwenzer* (fn 234) para 17.09; *Brehm* (fn 97) art 47 no 133 ff.

349 See BGE 116 II 519, 520–521 (Federal Court decision of 23 October 1990). For further references to case law, see *Brehm* (fn 97) art 49 no 67 f.

350 BGE 123 III 204, 206 (Federal Court decision of 9 June 1997).

351 See supra, no 86.

352 Cf supra, no 83. For an example from case law, see BGE 123 III 204, 206 ff (Federal Court decision of 9 June 1997).

353 Cf supra, no 87. For an example from case law, see BGE 116 II 519, 520–521 (Federal Court decision of 23 October 1990). See also Case 1, infra, nos 151 ff.

was also true with respect to civil procedure.[354] It is beyond the scope of this report to give details on the procedural laws of each of the 26 Cantons. Generally, however, medical malpractice cases will not be treated differently to other cases under cantonal procedural laws, and the same applies under the Federal Act on Civil Procedure.

139 If claims are brought under federal private law, jurisdiction will lie with the ordinary civil courts of the Cantons.[355] The place of jurisdiction is determined by federal law,[356] which does not set forth any special rules regarding medical malpractice.

140 If public liability is at issue, claims will often also fall within the jurisdiction of the ordinary civil law courts; however, this is a matter of cantonal law.[357]

28. Special institutions handling malpractice claims

141 If a patient suffers injury in the course of medical treatment and suspects that he is a victim of medical malpractice, he (or his successor) may contact the Swiss Medical Association (FMH) before going to court. The FMH operates a special 'Out-of-Court Expert Report Office' (*aussergerichtliche Gutachterstelle/Bureau d'expertises extra-judiciaires*).

142 The proceedings before the Office are governed by a regulation passed by the FMH.[358] All FMH-members must submit to, and cooperate in, proceedings before the Office.[359] If a member refuses to cooperate, he will be subject to the disciplinary sanctions under the FMH's rules of professional conduct.[360]

143 As the FMH is a private organisation, its regulations are only binding on its members. As soon as other persons (eg non-members, hospitals, or a Canton) might be liable, be it exclusively or together with a member of the FMH, the Office will not act unless such persons agree to submit to the proceedings.[361]

---

354 See supra, nos 8 and 103.

355 See *Guillod* (fn 87) 392, 413 (at para 83).

356 See the Federal Act on Civil Procedure (fn 18), which includes jurisdictional rules in its arts 9 ff.

357 See supra, no 103.

358 Regulation on the FMH-Office for Out-of-Court Expert Reports on Medical Liability (*Reglement für die FMH-Gutachterstelle zur aussergerichtlichen Begutachtung von Ärztehaftpflichtfällen*) of 1 February 2002, available at <http://www.fmh.ch/files/pdf1/Reglement_D.pdf> (12.01.11).

359 Art 2 of the Regulation (fn 358).

360 On these rules, see supra, no 38.

361 Art 3 of the Regulation (fn 358).

The Office will only commission an expert report on the patient's case if certain requirements are met.[362] In particular, the alleged mistake must have caused considerable injury to the applicant. The Office will not accept a patient's application for an expert report if a court case is pending. **144**

The subject-matter of the expert reports commissioned by the Office is limited. The designated expert(s) must first assess whether the doctor breached any duty of care with respect to diagnosis or treatment. If this is answered in the affirmative, the expert(s) must also assess the consequences of the breach for the patient's health (issue of causation).[363] The parties are not legally bound to accept the expert's conclusions,[364] although the doctor concerned (and the liability insurer, who is also involved in the proceedings) usually does so.[365] **145**

In all cases, the applicant must pay administrative charges of CHF 600 (plus VAT). In certain circumstances, the Office may request an additional CHF 2,000 as security from the applicant, in particular if there is only a small likelihood of a mistake in diagnosis or treatment.[366] **146**

From 1982 to 2009, 3233 expert reports were made under the Office's supervision.[367] A mistake in treatment or diagnosis was confirmed in 1065 cases (32.9 %), denied in 2075 cases (64.2 %), and left undecided in the remaining 93 cases (2.9 %). The majority of alleged mistakes occurred in surgery (804 reports made, 278 mistakes confirmed), orthopaedic surgery (596 reports made, 211 mistakes confirmed), and gynaecology/obstetrics (395 reports made, 151 mistakes confirmed).[368] **147**

H. Outlook

29. Reform plans

There are currently no comprehensive reform plans relating to medical liability in Switzerland. Although the preliminary draft law on tort reform **148**

362 See art 5 of the Regulation (fn 358).
363 Art 13(1) of the Regulation (fn 358).
364 Art 14(2) of the Regulation (fn 358).
365 See *Guillod* (fn 87) 392, 414 (at para 87 *in fine*).
366 Art 9 of the Regulation (fn 358).
367 The Office's annual reports are available at <http://www.fmh.ch/service/gutachterstelle/jahresberichte.html> (12.01.11).
368 *L Rabia/N Favre*, Annual Report of the FMH-Office 2009 (*Aussergerichtliche FMH-Gutachterstelle – Jahresbericht 2009*), SÄZ No 30–31/2010, 1131 ff.

included several provisions which would have had an impact on various aspects of medical liability,[369] this project has now been abandoned by the Federal Council.[370] The only remaining item on the tort reform agenda is the extension of the general limitation period for tort claims.[371]

149 Nonetheless, issues relating to selected areas of medical activity are being discussed. Thus, the draft Federal Act on Human Research[372] provides that persons or institutions that have initiated human research projects shall be strictly liable for any damage suffered by human research subjects, although the Federal Council may provide for exceptions.[373] Strict liability under the draft covers compensation for bodily injury, property damage, and harm caused to the subject's personality rights. Both pecuniary and non-pecuniary losses are covered.[374] Claims are subject to a limitation period of three years from the day the harmed person acquired knowledge of the damage and the liable party's identity. In any event, the maximum limitation period is ten years from the day the research project was completed. The Federal Council may provide longer limitation periods for particular research areas.[375] The potentially liable party must take out liability insurance or provide other, equivalent security.[376]

150 Another item on the political agenda relating to health issues is the draft Federal Act on Prevention and Health Promotion.[377] However, this draft does not include any provisions on medical liability.

---

369 See *P Wessner*, La révision totale du droit de la responsabilité civile: quelques orientations nouvelles susceptibles d'influencer le domaine des soins médicaux et hospitaliers, Le responsabilité médicale (1996) 57 ff.

370 See the Federal Council's press release of 21 January 2009, supra fn 148.

371 See supra, no 53.

372 *Entwurf eines Bundesgesetzes über die Forschung am Menschen (Humanforschungsgesetz, HFG)* of 21 October 2009, available at <http://www.admin.ch/ch/d/ff/2009/8163.pdf> (12.01.11).

373 Art 19(1) of the draft (fn 372).

374 Message of the Federal Council concerning the Federal Act on Human Research *(Botschaft zum Bundesgesetz über die Forschung am Menschen)* of 21 October 2009, *Bundesblatt* 2009, 8045, 8109, available at <http://www.admin.ch/ch/d/ff/2009/8045.pdf> (12.01.11).

375 Art 19(2) of the draft (fn 372).

376 Art 20 of the draft (fn 372).

377 *Entwurf eines Bundesgesetzes über Prävention und Gesundheitsförderung (Präventionsgesetz, PrävG)* of 30 September 2009, available at <http://www.admin.ch/ch/d/ff/2009/7189.pdf> (12.01.11). The Message of the Federal Council is available at <http://www.admin.ch/ch/d/ff/2009/7071.pdf> (12.01.11).

Cases

Case 1

The following analysis is based on the assumption that the hospital run by C is a private hospital, subject to federal private law.[378] From the facts of the case, one can assume that both A and D made a mistake during treatment. **151**

As the newborn Y does not have a contract with either A, B, or C, she will not be able to sue any of them in contract – at least not under traditional rules.[379] Y might sue in tort instead, but will in any case face several difficulties. **152**

A might be liable for Y's pecuniary loss under art 41(1) CO[380] and for Y's non-pecuniary loss under art 47 CO.[381] However, Y's claims will only succeed if she can prove that A's conduct was a *conditio sine qua non* of her condition. The burden of proof with regard to causation lies with Y, even if A's conduct qualifies as a grave mistake. Y will have to show that A's mistake more likely than not caused, in whole or in part, the damage suffered. A will not be liable if it is merely possible that his conduct caused Y's injury in whole or in part.[382] **153**

The issue of causation will also arise if Y sues B or C in tort. Moreover, as B himself did not make any mistake, he might only be liable for Y's pecuniary and non-pecuniary loss if either A or D's conduct could be imputed to him under art 55(1) CO.[383] However, neither A (with whom B shares a joint practice) nor D (who is employed by C) is subject to B's supervision and authority to issue directives.[384] Accordingly, B cannot be held responsible toward Y for either A or D's conduct. **154**

Likewise, A's conduct cannot be imputed to C under art 55(1) CO, as A is an affiliated doctor and therefore not subordinate to C.[385] In contrast, as midwife D is employed by C, her conduct will generally be imputed to C **155**

378 Cf supra, no 45.
379 The concept of contracts with protective effect for third parties has not hitherto been recognised in Swiss law (see supra, no 88). However, a lawyer representing Y might argue that the contracts entered into by Y's mother were also concluded for the benefit of her unborn child, so that Y, once she was born, could base her claim in contract (see supra, no 87). This line of argument has not yet been brought before the Federal Court.
380 On the requirements under art 41(1) CO, cf supra, no 47.
381 On liability for non-pecuniary loss, cf supra, nos 124 ff.
382 Cf supra, no 56.
383 On the requirements under art 55(1) CO, see supra, nos 48 ff.
384 On the requirement of subordination, see supra, no 48.
385 Cf supra, no 68.

(and not to A), unless her mistake occurred whilst she was *de facto* subject to A's supervision and authority to issue directives.[386] Accordingly, C might be liable for Y's pecuniary and non-pecuniary loss if the further requirements of art 55(1) CO are met. C could avoid liability by proving that he took all precautions necessary to prevent damage of the kind suffered.[387] However, the central issue in a claim against C will be that of causation: Y will have to prove that her injury was caused, in whole or in part, by D's tortious conduct.[388]

156 If Y succeeds in proving causation both with respect to A and D, and if C is unable to prove that all necessary precautionary measures were taken, A and C will be jointly and severally liable toward Y for any pecuniary loss suffered by Y which is not too remote (art 51 CO).[389] Such compensation would also, in principle, cover the costs of day care by professional nursing staff, even if the associated costs are greater than if Y lived in a nursing home. Although the injured party must take all reasonable steps to mitigate the loss, he is not required to take the least expensive option. Rather, if a certain measure is necessary or at least beneficial to the injured party and also appropriate from a medical standpoint, the ensuing costs should be compensated.[390] However, this issue has not hitherto been raised before the Federal Court.

157 If Y succeeds in proving causation, she will also be entitled to claim compensation for the care provided by X, on the basis of the average cost of home care.[391] Due to the gravity of the injury,[392] Y would also receive compensation for non-pecuniary loss under art 47 CO. If a cause of action is maintainable against both A and C, they will again be jointly and severally liable.[393]

158 Unlike Y, X entered into a contract with B and, once she was admitted to C's hospital, also into a contract with C. X's contract with C will be classified as a 'fractioned hospital contract'.[394] Accordingly, both B and C may be liable toward X in contract under art 97(1) CO.[395]

---

386 Cf supra, nos 68 and 48.
387 Cf supra, no 50.
388 Cf already supra, no 153. On the standard of proof, see supra, no 56.
389 On joint and several liability, see supra, no 66.
390 Cf *Roberto* (fn 311) 152 f.
391 See supra, no 111.
392 Cf supra, no 130.
393 Cf supra, no 129.
394 See supra, no 79.
395 On the requirements under art 97(1) CO, see supra, no 82.

As B's locum, A will be considered B's auxiliary under art 101(1) CO,[396] so that A's acts or omissions will be imputed to B for the purposes of liability. Midwife D will be considered either C's or B's auxiliary, depending on whether the taking of a CTG fell within C's or B's contractual responsibilities.[397] In any case, however, the central problem for X will also be the issue of causation, which she must prove. With respect to B's liability, X must show that A's mistake more likely than not caused, in whole or in part, her pecuniary loss. Likewise, if D is qualified as C's auxiliary, C will only be liable for X's pecuniary loss if D's mistake more likely than not caused such loss, in whole or in part.[398] **159**

If X succeeded in proving causation both with respect to A and D's conduct, B and C would be jointly and severally liable toward X for her pecuniary loss (art 51 CO).[399] It is probable that Swiss Courts would award X compensation for the care that she herself is providing to Y on the basis of the average cost of home care. It would not be necessary for X to suffer actual pecuniary loss (eg by giving up her job). However, the Federal Court has hitherto only had occasion to discuss such claims brought by the injured party himself.[400] **160**

Due to the gravity of the injury, X would also be entitled to compensation for non-pecuniary loss under art 49 CO.[401] If a cause of action were maintainable against both B and C, they would be jointly and severally liable for such loss.[402] This would also apply with respect to the stillbirth of X's son, if X were able to prove that such stillbirth was caused by A and D's mistakes. **161**

As X did not enter into a contract with A, any claims against A would be in tort (art 41[1] CO). Here, as before, the main issue will be that of causation. Additionally, the question will arise as to whether A's conduct toward X can be classified as wrongful under art 41(1) CO. X seeks an award of compensation for the care that she herself is providing to Y. Such damage constitutes pure economic loss, for which compensation is only available if a 'protective norm' (*Schutznorm/norme de protection/norma protettiva*) has been breached. The same problem would also arise if X were to sue B and/or C **162**

396 On art 101(1) CO, see supra, no 85.
397 Cf supra, no 79.
398 On the burden of proof with regard to causation, see supra, no 56.
399 On joint and several liability, see supra, no 66.
400 Cf supra, nos 111 and 157.
401 Cf supra, no 136.
402 See supra, no 129.

in tort rather than in contract, although given the advantages of contract claims,[403] she would be unlikely to do so.

Case 2

163 The Federal Court decided the controversial issue of 'wrongful conception' in favour of the child's parents in 2005.[404] In that case, the claimant was to undergo a Caesarean section with her second child and had requested that she be sterilised at the same time. The claimant and her husband had decided on sterilisation for economic reasons. However, the hospital negligently omitted to perform the sterilisation. Unaware of the mistake, the claimant soon after became pregnant and subsequently gave birth to her third child. The claimant's husband assigned his contractual rights to the claimant, who then successfully sued the hospital. She was granted compensation for pecuniary loss, including child maintenance costs, by the cantonal courts, as well as compensation for non-pecuniary loss. The cantonal decision was confirmed by the Federal Court.

164 As a result of the Federal Court's decision, it is safe to assume that in principle, A will be liable in contract toward X for any pecuniary loss sustained as a result of the birth of her son Z, including child maintenance costs throughout the child's minority and loss of earnings, on condition that A breached his contractual obligations toward X (art 97[1] CO).[405] However, one important difference between the Federal Court decision and Case 2 is that in Case 2, it is not clear whether X had decided against having children once and for all, or only for the time-being. This issue of 'timing' was not raised before the Federal Court, and even if it had been, it would probably not have made any difference as the claimant and her husband already had two children. The situation is different with respect to X; although her choice of contraception indicates that she had no wish to become pregnant in the near future, it is not clear whether she had decided against having children once and for all. It has been suggested that where a woman has only decided against having children at a certain moment in time, only the pecuniary loss resulting from the premature birth of a child may be compensated.[406] However, one might object that it will usually be impossible to prove whether the woman in question has

---

403 See supra, nos 83 ff.
404 BGE 132 III 359 ff (Federal Court decision of 20 December 2005).
405 On the requirements under art 97(1) CO, see supra, no 82.
406 See *Roberto* (fn 143) para 768.

reached a final decision or not, nor can anyone (including the woman herself) know whether she might have changed her mind in the future. It remains to be seen how the Federal Court would decide this issue.

It might also be possible for X to bring a claim in tort under art 41(1) CO,[407] although this issue has not yet been raised before the Federal Court (and is unlikely to be, unless the claimant is unable to sue in contract).[408] In a tort claim against A, the central issue would be whether A's conduct qualifies as wrongful for the purposes of art 41(1) CO. This would probably be answered in the affirmative, as X's personality rights (namely her autonomy of decision) have been infringed.[409] **165**

The matter is more complex with respect to Z's father, Y. As the concept of contracts with protective effect for third parties has not hitherto been recognised in Swiss law,[410] Y would only be able to sue in contract if he was also a party to the contract between A and X. However, it might be possible for Y to bring a claim against A in tort under art 41(1) CO. The central issue in such a claim would be whether A's conduct can be considered wrongful with regard to Y. This issue has not yet been raised before the Federal Court, but might be answered in the affirmative based on Y's personality rights.[411] **166**

Case 3

The following analysis is based on the assumption that both the hospital run by A and the clinic run by C are private hospitals, subject to federal private law.[412] **167**

As X himself did not enter into a contract with A, any claims by X against A would be be based in tort, at least under traditional rules.[413] It is probable that such a claim would succeed, both with respect to X's pecuniary loss under art 55(1) CO[414] and his non-pecuniary loss under art 47 CO.[415] The obstetrician's failure to seek the advice of a paediatrician and the failure to **168**

407 On the requirements under art 41(1) CO, cf supra, no 47.
408 See also *Roberto* (fn 143) para 486. On the advantages of contract claims over tort claims, see supra, nos 83 ff.
409 Cf *Roberto* (fn 143) para 486.
410 See supra, no 88.
411 Cf supra, no 165, with regard to X.
412 Cf supra, no 45.
413 Cf supra, no 152 with fn 379.
414 On the requirements under art 55(1) CO, see supra, nos 48 ff.
415 On liability for non-pecuniary loss, cf supra, nos 124 ff.

inform X's mother and the midwife of the necessity to monitor X's blood sugar levels would be imputed to A under art 55(1) CO. Although it is recognised in Swiss law that the link between original cause and effect may be interrupted by subsequent events (*Unterbrechnung des Kausalzusammenhangs/interruption de la causalité/interruzione della causalità*)[416] with the result that the original cause will be considered too remote, it is unlikely that this would help A to avoid liability. Such an 'interruption' is admitted only rarely by Swiss courts, as it means taking an 'all or nothing' approach to liability.[417] Moreover, had X been treated properly in A's hospital, midwife B and the clinic C would not actually have had the 'opportunity' to contribute to X's injuries. It is also unlikely that A would succeed in showing that it exercised all due diligence in selecting, instructing and overseeing the obstetrician.

169 With respect to midwife B, it is probable that she would be held liable toward X not only in tort under art 41(1) CO,[418] but also in contract under art 97(1) CO,[419] as X's mother entered into the contract with B for X's benefit.[420] However, midwife B will in any case only be liable toward X if her conduct was a *conditio sine qua non* of X's injuries, which X will have to prove. It is sufficient, but also necessary, that X's injuries would probably have been avoided if B had sought the advice of a paediatrician.[421] If such proof is provided, B will also be liable for X's non-pecuniary loss, on the basis of art 47 CO in conjunction with art 41(1) and art 97(1) CO, respectively.

170 C will likely also be held liable toward X in contract under art 97(1) CO, as X's parents entered into a contract with C for X's benefit.[422] The failure to provide X with adequate care on time due to organisational deficiencies qualifies as a breach of C's contractual duties toward X, and as C will be considered responsible for ensuring that the clinic is organised satisfactorily, C will not succeed in showing that it bore no fault. Also, E's conduct will be imputed to C on the basis of art 101(1) CO.[423] As it can be assumed with a very high degree of probability that X's injuries were sustained in C's clinic, the requirement of causation is also fulfilled. Accordingly, C

416 See, eg, *Rey* (fn 137) paras 551 ff.
417 See, eg, *Werro* (fn 174) para 223.
418 On the requirements under art 41(1) CO, cf supra, no 47.
419 On the requirements under art 97(1) CO, see supra, no 82.
420 Cf supra, no 87.
421 Cf supra, no 56.
422 Cf supra, no 87.
423 On art 101(1) CO, see supra, no 85.

will be liable for X's pecuniary loss, as well as for X's non-pecuniary loss under art 97(1) in conjunction with art 47 CO.

C could also be held liable for X's pecuniary and non-pecuniary loss on the basis of art 55(1) CO. Although a contractual claim will be more advantageous,[424] X is free to choose whether to sue C in contract or in tort. As E is subordinated to C, her conduct would be imputed to C under art 55(1) CO. C would not succeed in showing that it had exercised all due diligence in selecting, instructing and overseeing her, as E had not been instructed to take and record a detailed case history, nor to call an experienced doctor within a reasonable period of time. **171**

On condition that E's conduct constituted a *conditio sine qua non* of X's damage (which X has to prove), E will be liable toward X in tort under art 41(1) CO. Her lack of experience will not serve to exonerate her, as she should at least have recognised that she lacked the experience to correctly assess X's state and called on an experienced doctor when she saw the alarming results of the first test. She will also be held liable for X's non-pecuniary loss under art 41(1) in conjunction with art 47 CO. **172**

Liability of A, B, C, and E will be joint and several (art 51 CO).[425] Compensation for X's pecuniary loss will cover the costs of nursing care and the expenses caused by X's increased needs (art 46 CO).[426] With respect to X's loss of earning capacity, the court will make a projection as to how X's career path and income would have developed without the sustained injuries. Swiss courts tend to base such projections on the careers chosen by the victim's family members. In case of very young victims, courts tend to be conservative when assessing loss of future earnings.[427] X may choose between compensation by lump sum and periodic payment.[428] Damages will be calculated on the basis of X's estimated future net income. In addition, X will be entitled to compensation for his 'retirement damage'.[429] Given the grave nature of X's injuries, A, B, C, and E will also liable for X's non-pecuniary loss (art 47 CO). Such liability will be joint and several.[430] **173**

424 On the advantages of contract claims over tort claims, see supra, nos 83 ff.

425 Cf supra, nos 66, 78.

426 For details on calculating such costs, see the case discussion by *Brehm* (fn 160) 325, 359 (at paras 158 ff).

427 See *Brehm* (fn 160) 325, 342 f (at paras 83, 84).

428 See supra, no 119.

429 See supra, nos 110 and 116.

430 See supra, no 129.

Case 4

174 The following analysis is based on the assumption that the A clinic is a private hospital, subject to federal private law,[431] and that X had a contract only with the A clinic ('comprehensive hospital contract').[432]

175 X was not properly informed of the risks involved with the proposed operation. Firstly, there was no interpreter present during the consultation, although X could only speak Persian (and B could not). Accordingly, B's information did not put X in a position to reach a well-considered decision about the suggested procedure.[433] Secondly, X was not informed of the different types of procedure available (transthoracic opening versus dorsal approach) and the different risks involved. And finally, X was informed only one day prior to the operation. Given the nature of the operation and the risks involved, this was too late.[434] It is for the A clinic to prove that X gave his informed consent to the proposed operation.[435]

176 As the A clinic has not satisfied the legal requirements of informed consent, it will be liable in contract under art 97(1) CO[436] for all damage suffered by X as a result of the operation, regardless of whether such damage was caused by a mistake in treatment or simply by chance, as long as such damage is not too remote.[437] B's failure to properly inform X will be imputed to the A clinic under art 101(1) CO.[438] The A clinic will not succeed in showing that X would have consented to the intervention even if he had been properly informed. The test for such 'hypothetical consent'[439] is not whether a 'reasonable' patient, but whether the individual patient would have consented to the intervention. According to the facts of the case, X would probably not have had surgery at all if he had been properly informed, and his condition would not necessarily have deteriorated without the operation.

177 Accordingly, the A clinic will be liable in contract toward X for the pecuniary loss caused by the operation, as long as such loss is not too remote. Compensation will include the costs of converting X's house to

431 Cf supra, no 45.
432 On comprehensive hospital contracts, see supra, no 78.
433 Cf *Fellmann* (fn 111) 103, 196.
434 Cf supra, no 92.
435 Cf supra, no 89.
436 On the requirements under art 97(1) CO, see supra, no 82.
437 Cf supra, no 90.
438 Cf supra, no 85.
439 See supra, no 90.

provide wheelchair access. In contrast, the costs of a new car with wheelchair access will only be compensated if X is still able to work and needs an automobile for that purpose.[440] X will also be entitled to compensation for non-pecuniary loss under art 47 CO, given the grave consequences of the intervention.[441]

X could also claim compensation for pecuniary and non-pecuniary loss from the A clinic in tort (art 55[1] CO), as B, the doctor who (inadequately) informed X, is subordinated to A.[442] It is unlikely that A would succeed in showing that it exercised all due diligence in selecting, instructing and overseeing B. As in contract, it would be for the A clinic to prove that X gave his informed consent to the operation.[443] However, contractual liability is more advantageous for X.[444] **178**

As X did not enter into a contract with surgeon C,[445] C might only be liable toward X in tort (art 41[1] CO),[446] which is less attractive for X than suing the A clinic in contract. C will be liable in tort if he was under an individual duty to inform X prior to the operation. The Federal Court has not hitherto had to determine with whom precisely the duty to inform lies in the case of hospitalisation, as injured patients generally sue the hospital itself (and not the individual doctor). In general, the doctor who is to perform the procedure is under a duty to inform the patient of the risks involved. The prevailing opinion in Switzerland is that a doctor may delegate his duty to inform to another doctor, except where such other doctor does not have sufficient knowledge of the case or is not sufficiently qualified. In any case, the delegating doctor must ascertain whether the patient has been sufficiently informed before he carries out the procedure.[447] It follows that in Case 4, surgeon C was at the very least under a duty to make sure that X had been properly informed by B before the operation. It is for C to prove that he complied with this duty,[448] but as the facts of the case show that X was not properly informed, C will not succeed. Accordingly, C will be liable toward X in tort for the same items of damage as the A clinic and also for non-pecuniary loss under art 47 **179**

440 Cf *Brehm* (fn 97) art 46 no 24, with references to case law.
441 On liability for non-pecuniary loss, cf supra, nos 124 ff.
442 On the requirements under art 55(1) CO, cf supra, nos 48 ff.
443 Cf supra, no 89.
444 Cf supra, nos 83 ff.
445 Cf supra, no 174.
446 On the requirements under art 41(1) CO, cf supra, no 47.
447 See *Fellmann* (fn 111) 103, 194; *Wiegand* (fn 272) 119, 149 f.
448 Cf supra, no 89.

CO.[449] Liability of C and the A clinic will be joint and several, both with regard to compensation for pecuniary and non-pecuniary loss.[450]

180 A and C might object that sooner or later, X would have suffered the same damage anyway, as X was already suffering from myelopathy with paralysis symptoms when he was operated on. It is not clear to what extent such an objection might be heard in Swiss law.[451] In any case, the success of such an objection would depend on the likelihood that damage would have occurred regardless of the operation at a later point in time.

Case 5

181 As before, the following analysis is based on the assumption that the hospital run by A is a private hospital, subject to federal private law,[452] and that X had a contract only with A ('comprehensive hospital contract').[453]

182 A might be liable toward X in contract under art 97(1) CO.[454] In principle, the acts and omissions of A's employees B, C, and D during the operation will be imputed to A under art 101(1) CO.[455] However, X will have to prove that B, C, and/or D made a mistake which constitutes a breach of the contract between A and X, and that such a breach caused his damage. The mere fact that X suffered injury is not sufficient to infer medical malpractice. Nor is it recognised in Swiss law that the hospital and responsible doctors bear the burden of proof with regard to the correct positioning of a patient during an operation.[456]

183 With respect to A's liability, two hypotheses are imaginable. Under the first hypothesis, not even the slightest risk of damage to the nervus ulnaris is inherent in this type of operation. If this hypothesis is correct, the damage suffered by X will necessarily imply that his injury was caused by a mistake made during the operation, so that A will be liable in contract.

---

449 Cf supra, no 177.
450 Cf supra, nos 78 and 129.
451 See, eg, *Schwenzer* (fn 234) para 21.05 with further references.
452 Cf supra, no 45.
453 On comprehensive hospital contracts, see supra, no 78.
454 On the requirements under art 97(1) CO, see supra, no 82.
455 Cf supra, no 78.
456 The Federal Court has not yet been called on to decide this issue. See also *Kuhn* (fn 154) 601, 653 ff.

Under the second hypothesis, damage to the nervus ulnaris is an inherent risk of this type of operation. If this hypothesis is correct, X will be well-advised to allege that he was not properly informed of this risk, as A will have to prove that X gave informed consent. If the legal requirements of informed consent are not satisfied, A will be liable in contract for all damage suffered by X as a result of the operation, as long as such damage is not too remote. A may only avoid liability if A can show that X would have consented to the operation even if he had been properly informed (hypothetical consent).[457] **184**

If A succeeds in proving that X was sufficiently informed of the risks, or that X would have consented anyway, X will be required to prove that a mistake was made during the operation. According to the facts of the case, it cannot be ascertained whether surgeon B positioned X's arm improperly, as the clinical records are incomplete. Nor can it be ascertained whether anaesthetist C monitored the proper positioning of X's arm during the operation. It is uncertain in Swiss law whether the burden of proof might be shifted to A because the records are incomplete, although at the very least, the standard of proof might be relaxed.[458] With respect to the issue of monitoring, C will be required to cooperate in the evidentiary proceedings before the court. Whether or not a court will be satisfied that B and/or C made a mistake during the operation cannot be said in the abstract; rather, this will depend on the court's appreciation of the evidence. If the court is satisfied that B and/or C made a mistake, it will suffice for X to show that such mistake more likely than not caused his injury.[459] Whether or not he is successful will depend on how large the inherent risk of damage to the nervus ulnaris is. **185**

By itself, the fact that C was not supervised more closely by D is not sufficient to hold A liable toward X. If C was not supervised sufficiently under current professional standards, this will constitute a breach of contract by A. However, X will still have to prove that such breach more likely than not caused his damage.[460] This will be difficult to prove unless the court is satisfied that C did not monitor the position of X's arm correctly. **186**

---

457 Cf supra, no 90.
458 Cf supra, no 58.
459 Cf supra, no 56.
460 Cf supra, no 56.

187 X might also choose to sue A in tort on the basis of art 55(1) CO,[461] as B, C, and D are all subordinated to A. However, apart from the fact that tort claims are less advantageous to the claimant,[462] X will still be faced with the problem of proving that a mistake was made which caused his damage. As in contract, the situation will change for X's benefit if he was not properly informed of the risks inherent in the operation,[463] or if no risk at all of damage to the nervus ulnaris is inherent in this type of operation.[464]

188 As far as the liability of B, C, and D is concerned, the same problems of proof arise as with respect to A, ie as to the questions of mistake and causation. Again, the situation will change if X did not give his informed consent or the risk of damage to the nervus ulnaris is not inherent in this type of operation. In any case, B, C, and D might only be liable toward X in tort (art 41[1] CO).[465]

189 If liability of A, B, C, or D were accepted, X would receive compensation for loss of earnings, as he is no longer able to work as a bricklayer. X would also be entitled to compensation for loss of earnings from his weekend job. However, if X can reasonably be expected to retrain, for example as a sales person in a building supplies store, the wages X would earn in such a position would be deducted from X's compensation. Whether or not such retraining can reasonably be expected will depend on X's age; the older an injured person is, the less he can be expected to change his occupation.[466] Damages for loss of earnings would be calculated on the basis of X's net income. X's 'retirement damage' would also be indemnified.[467]

190 In contrast, it is unlikely that the costs of the private medical injuries assessment commissioned by X would be compensated, as such assessment would not have been necessary in the instant case. However, this might depend on whether X had legal representation or not, for although a lawyer would be expected to know that the facts could be evaluated free of charge by a specific assessment commission, this might not necessarily apply to laypersons.

---

461 On the requirements for liability under art 55(1) CO, see supra, nos 48 ff.
462 See supra, nos 83 ff.
463 Cf supra, no 184 and (generally) no 90.
464 Cf supra, no 183.
465 On the requirements under art 41(1) CO, cf supra, no 47.
466 Cf *Brehm* (fn 97) art 44 no 51 with further references.
467 See supra, nos 110 and 116.

Liability of A, B, C, and D would be joint and several (art 51 CO),[468] both with respect to X's pecuniary and non-pecuniary loss.[469] Compensation for non-pecuniary loss would be available under art 47 CO.[470] **191**

Case 6

The following analysis is based on the assumption that A and B do not conduct their joint practice in the form of a company (with independent legal personality) by whom they are employed. **192**

A and B might be liable toward X in contract under art 97(1) CO.[471] However, X will have to prove that A and B or their auxiliaries made a mistake which constitutes a breach of contract, and that such breach caused her damage. C, D, and E all qualify as auxiliaries under art 101(1) CO.[472] **193**

As the transmission of E's staphylococcus infection caused X bodily harm, and as E is A and B's auxiliary, transmission as such could qualify as a breach of contract by A and B under art 101(1) CO. X would have no difficulty proving causation, as transmission was a *conditio sine qua non* of her damage. A and B could only avoid liability if they proved that E complied with the standard of care owed by A and B themselves, for which they bear the burden of proof.[473] However, they are unlikely to succeed due to the deficient hygiene standards in their practice. **194**

A and B's failure to maintain satisfactory hygiene standards also constitutes a breach of their contract with X. However, under this line of argument, X would have to prove that such failure more likely than not caused her damage.[474] Whether or not X will be successful in proving causation will depend on how large the risk of infection would have been had the usual hygiene standards been maintained. It is not recognised in Swiss law that hospitals and responsible doctors bear the burden of proof with regard to causation in the case of deficient hygiene standards, although such a shift in the burden of proof has been suggested in legal doctrine.[475] **195**

---

468 On joint and several liability, see supra, no 66.
469 On the latter, see supra, no 129.
470 Cf supra, nos 125 ff.
471 On the requirements under art 97(1) CO, see supra, no 82.
472 On art 101(1) CO, see supra, no 85.
473 Cf supra, no 85.
474 Cf supra, no 56.
475 See *Kuhn* (fn 154) 601, 650 ff with further references. The Federal Court has not yet been called on to decide this issue.

196 A further possibility would be to extend the notion of mistake in treatment by arguing that treatment administered under deficient hygiene standards is not *lege artis*. If this line of argument were accepted, the treatment administered by C and D (ie the injections) would already constitute a breach of A and B's contract with X under art 101(1) CO. X could prove causation as the breach was a *conditio sine qua non* of her damage. A and B would be unable to avoid liability as C and D did not comply with the standard of care owed by A and B themselves (hypothetical fault.)[476]

197 X could also base her claim against A and B in tort under art 55(1) CO.[477] As it is certain that E caused X's injury, and as E is subordinated to A and B,[478] A and B will only be able to avoid liability if they can show that they exercised all due diligence in selecting, instructing and overseeing E. As it is established that the medical assistants were not instructed properly nor supervised with respect to hygiene, A and B will not succeed. Although A and B could avoid liability under art 55(1) CO by proving that X's damage would also have occurred if they had exercised due diligence,[479] it will be practically impossible for them to provide such proof.

198 C and D could only be liable toward X in tort under art 41(1) CO.[480] However, under orthodox rules of causation, X would have to prove whether it was C or D who administered the harmful injection. If she cannot provide such proof, neither C nor D will be held liable.[481] X would also have to prove that the doctor who gave the injection was at fault.

199 Although E caused X's damage, she could only become liable toward X under art 41(1) CO if X could prove that E acted negligently.[482] Such proof will only succeed if X can show that E knew or ought to have known of her staphylococcus infection and the associated risks.

200 Accordingly, A and B are likely to be liable toward X in contract and in tort. If X is unable to perform all of her household tasks because of her injury, she will be entitled to compensation on the basis of the average cost

476 Cf supra, no 85.

477 On the requirements for liability under art 55(1) CO, see supra, nos 48 ff.

478 Depending on how long C and D were working as locums in A and B's practice, it is possible that E might be considered to be subordinated to C and D, rather than to A and B. In that case, A and B would not be liable toward X under art 55(1) CO. On the issue of *de facto* subordination, see supra, no 48.

479 Cf supra, no 50.

480 But cf fn 478. On the requirements under art 41(1) CO, cf supra, no 47.

481 On this issue of alternative causation, see supra, no 60.

482 Cf supra, no 54.

of home help, regardless of whether she actually employs such help or whether help is given free of charge.[483] A and B will also be liable for non-pecuniary loss under art 47 CO.[484]

Variation 1

Although the source of the infection cannot be identified, A and B will nonetheless be liable toward X in contract if X can prove that she probably would not have suffered damage if A and B had maintained satisfactory hygiene standards. This will again depend on how large the risk of infection would have been had the usual hygiene standards been maintained.[485] **201**

As before, another possibility would be to extend the notion of mistake in treatment by arguing that treatment administered under deficient hygiene standards is not *lege artis*. In this case, A and B would be unable to avoid liability as C and D did not comply with the standard of care owed by A and B themselves.[486] **202**

In contrast, as the source of the infection cannot be identified, X cannot hold A and B liable under art 55(1) CO as she will be unable to prove that damage was caused by a subordinate.[487] **203**

As in the first scenario, C and D could only be liable toward X under art 41(1) CO if X succeeded in proving which doctor administered the harmful injection, and also that such doctor was at fault.[488] E will not be liable under art 41(1) CO as X is unable to prove that E caused her damage. **204**

Variation 2

In this scenario, the only person who might be held liable toward X is E, on the basis of art 41(1) CO. However, such claim will only succeed if X can prove that E acted negligently.[489] **205**

483 See supra, no 117.
484 On liability for non-pecuniary loss, cf supra, nos 124 ff.
485 See already supra, no 195.
486 Cf supra, no 196.
487 See supra, no 61.
488 See supra, no 198.
489 See already supra, no 199.

Medical Liability in Europe: Comparative Analysis

Bernhard A Koch

Introduction[1]

1 In a recent interview with a German newspaper, the EU Commissioner for Health and Consumer Policy, John Dalli, claimed that every tenth treatment of a patient results in further injuries to the patient that could probably have been avoided.[2] Facts supporting these allegations were not cited, however,[3] which does not come as a major surprise since statistical data on medical liability in Europe 'is scarce and not easy to obtain'.[4] Still, a more realistic estimation of how frequently preventable adverse events may occur to hospital patients is closer to two per cent.[5]

1 The jurisdictions covered will be addressed by two-letter codes as used in the index. AT therefore stands for Austria, BE for Belgium, CH for Switzerland, CZ for the Czech Republic, DE for Germany, ES for Spain, FR for France, HU for Hungary, IT for Italy, NL for the Netherlands, PL for Poland, SE for Sweden, and UK for England (not the United Kingdom as a whole, see UK no 1). A country code used in combination with a number refers to a marginal number of the respective country report in this volume. Internet hyperlinks are current as of January 2011.

2 Interview with 'Die Welt', 10 January 2011, <http://www.welt.de/print/die_welt/wirtschaft/article12063790/EU-Schaden-bei-jedem-zehnten-Klinikaufenthalt.html>.

3 This is also true for a corresponding statement found on the Commission's website: 'An estimated 8–12 % of patients admitted to hospital in the EU suffer from adverse events whilst receiving health care.' <http://ec.europa.eu/health/patient_safety/policy/index_-en.htm>.

4 *H Nys*, The Factual Situation of Medical Liability in the Member States of the Council of Europe, Report to the 2008 Council of Europe Conference 'The Ever-Growing Challenge of Medical Liability: National and European Responses', CONF-ML (2008) 02 (available at <http://www.coe.int/t/e/legal_affairs/legal_co-operation/steering_committees/cdcj/cj_s_med/CONF-ML _2008_ 02 E – Report Prof. Herman NYS.pdf>) 3.

5 *Nys* (fn 4) 5.

2 Data generated by the OECD Health Care Quality Indicators Project show the following picture in selected jurisdictions covered in this volume:[6]

Percentage of reported incidents	Foreign body left in during procedure	Catheter- related bloodstream infection	Post operative pulmonary embolism or deep vein thrombosis	Post operative sepsis	Accidental Puncture or Laceration	Obstetric trauma – vaginal delivery with instrument	Obstetric trauma – vaginal delivery without instrument
Belgium	0.007	0.178	0.470	1.717	0.281	2.682	0.602
France						1.556	0.338
Germany	0.005	0.128	0.587	0.391	0.120	7.905	2.257
Italy	0.002	0.006	0.220	0.144	0.013	2.370	0.710
Spain	0.005	0.189	0.281	0.440	0.183	2.611	0.505
Sweden	0.002	0.013	0.170	0.474	0.085	11.950	3.342
Switzerland	0.011	0.056	0.399	0.226	0.285	6.564	1.997
United Kingdom	0.005	0.090	0.754	0.276	0.129	5.731	1.837

Obviously, the fact that percentages are higher in one jurisdiction than in another does not necessarily mean that there are quality deficiencies, but primarily show that more incidents are being reported.

6 Table 6 of *S Drösler/P Romano/L Wei*, Health Care Quality Indicators Project: Patient Safety Indicators Report 2009 (OECD Health Working Papers No. 47, available at <http://www.oecd.org/els/health/workingpapers>) 34. Austria, the Czech Republic, Hungary, the Netherlands and Poland did not participate in this study, which is why data on those jurisdictions is missing in the following table.

Almost 80 % of all EU citizens perceive medical errors to constitute a serious problem in their countries,[7] even though less than half believe that this will affect them personally.[8] More importantly (and in stark contrast to the finding of Commissioner Dalli cited at the beginning), the vast majority expressed full trust in the medical professions not to make mistakes while treating patients.[9] **3**

Nevertheless, the number of claims filed against health care providers alleging that something went wrong during treatment seems to be on the rise in Europe, at least when looking at the past decades as a whole,[10] while the increase seems to be slowing down in the most recent years. The introduction of new (and easier) ways to file claims in some jurisdictions though may have led to certain peaks in their statistics in light of a backlog of older cases which would not have been pursued under the previous regime. **4**

Irrespective of claims statistics, the general public has certainly become more aware of the fact that (1) adverse developments after medical treatment are not necessarily governed by fate and (2) there are ways to pursue claims for compensation against health care professionals and institutions which are not predetermined to fail.[11] The media have undoubtedly played a supporting role in this development, but so too have changes in the legal systems which were not necessarily, or at least not exclusively, aimed at reacting to adverse events in medicine. After all, tort law has undoubtedly become more victim-friendly over the past decades, including for victims of other causes. This is why statistics pointing at higher total amounts paid out in compensation for medical malpractice in comparison to previous years have to be read in light of the fact that damages for personal injuries have increased generally, with awards for non-pecuniary loss being just one (albeit important) set of various examples. **5**

As the German report rightly highlights, it is quite paradoxical that not only has the likelihood that patients will be cured risen with the undeni- **6**

---

7 Special Eurobarometer 241, Medical Errors (2006, <http://ec.europa.eu/health/ph_information/documents/eb_64_en.pdf>). Among the jurisdictions covered in this book, CZ (60 %), ES (61 %), AT (63 %), BE and DE (72 %) as well as FR and SE (75 %) were below that average percentage; the remaining countries equal or above, some even significantly: HU (78 %), the L (82 %), UK (85 %), PL (91 %) and IT (97 %).

8 On average, only 40 % contributing to the Eurobarometer survey cited in fn 7 were worried that they might suffer a serious medical error themselves.

9 74 % have such confidence in dentists, 69 % in doctors and 68 % in other medical staff.

10 But see HU no 5 ('relatively low' and stable number of lawsuits).

11 Cf *Stanisława Kalus*, Liability for Medical damages in Polish law, in: B Heiderhoff/G Żmij (eds), Tort law in Poland, Germany and Europe (2009) 47, 48.

able advance of medical science, but, at the same time, the likelihood of claims filed against doctors and hospitals for adverse events has also dramatically increased.[12]

7 Higher numbers of claims in the medical field do not necessarily indicate that the quality of services is on the decline, however – as statistics show in Austria, for example, the percentage of cases that are submitted to the patient advocacy,[13] which even they do not deem worthwhile pursuing, currently stands at almost 85 %, as compared to below 70 % a decade ago.[14]

8 Against this background, the following comparative report attempts to give an overview of the situation in thirteen selected European jurisdictions on the basis of the country reports prepared for each of them. The structure of the questionnaire to which they replied will be followed here as well in order to facilitate further references to each of these contributions. It will be impossible to depict each jurisdiction's specialties in this necessarily condensed analysis, but the aim is to at least sketch out the range of variations that one may encounter when looking at medical malpractice problems from a comparative perspective.

General Questions

A. The Health Care System Framework

I. General Introduction

1. The health care system in overview

9 Statistics paint a rather diverse picture of key health care data in the jurisdictions under survey.[15] The number of practising physicians per 1,000 population in 2008, for example, varies from 2.16 to 4.6.[16] In the

12 DE no 46.

13 See AT no 98 on the patient advocacies in Austria.

14 See the activity reports of the patient advocacy of Lower Austria at < http://www.patientenanwalt.com/publikationen/taetigkeitsberichte/taetigkeitsberichte-zum-thema-noe-ppa.html>.

15 All figures in the following are taken from the OECD database StatExtracts <http://stats.oecd.org/Index.aspx?DataSetCode=HEALTH>.

16 AT 4.6, BE 2.97, CZ 3.6, FR 3.34, DE 3.89, HU 3.09, IT 4.19, PL 2.19, ES 3.6, CH 3.88, UK 2.61. The data for FR, DE, IT, ES and CH include not only physicians who provide services directly to patients, but also those who work in the health care administration, for example.

same year, the density of hospital beds per 1,000 population ranged from 3.3 to 8.2.[17] On average, doctors were consulted between 5.9 and 11.4 times per capita.[18] There seems to be somewhat less diversity, though, when it comes to the duration of hospital stays.[19]

All jurisdictions under survey maintain both public and private health **10** care institutions,[20] but apart from those jurisdictions which assign claims arising in public health care institutions to a separate procedural path and/or distinct body of substantive law,[21] this difference apparently has no effect on the outcome of disputes about medical malpractice.[22] This seems somewhat odd at first sight in light of the fact that, with the growing influence of the state over the past century in the field of health care, liability still remains in essence private at its core in most jurisdictions.[23] On the other hand, at least providing health care services to individual citizens as such does not appear to be a task necessarily assigned exclusively to state authority, as contrasted to the establishment and (co-)financing of a functioning system as a whole. This is why only problems that are related to the latter seem to be obvious candidates for state liability, whereas medical errors are probably not.[24]

---

17 AT 7.7, BE 6.7, CZ 7.3, FR 6.9, DE 8.2, HU 7, IT 3.8, NL 43., PL 6.6, ES 3.3, CH 5.2, UK 3.4.

18 AT 6.9, CZ 11.4, FR 6.9, DE 7.8, HU 11.3, NL 5.9, PL 6.8, UK 5.9. Judging from data stemming from earlier years, only SE seems to fall outside that range (with on average 2.8 consultations per capita in 2006 and earlier).

19 The 2008 average length of stay for acute care ranged from 5.2 to 7.7 days, whereas the average length of stay for a normal delivery was only 1.8 days in the UK compared to 5.2 in Switzerland.

20 AT nos 3–4 (but difficult distinction, as marked by a combination of both ownership and status criteria); BE no 3 (about 70 % private); CH no 3; CZ no 7 (mostly private); DE no 20 (proportion of public hospitals 'continuously declining'); ES no 1; HU nos 1 ff; NL no 71; PL no 4; SE no 5; UK no 10.

21 France, Spain and Switzerland, see infra no 18.

22 AT nos 5, 79; BE no 45; CZ nos 29, 98; DE no 177; HU no 9; IT nos 7–9, 54; NL nos 9, 71; PL no 72–73 (though strict liability only exceptionally applies to public hospitals: PL no 56); SE no 42; UK no 44. But see also HU no 1 about possible complications arising out of the specific problems in this jurisdiction, where doctors provide services partly as private practitioners, partly as employees of a public hospital, which makes it difficult to identify the proper addressee of claims arising out of malpractice in such a setting.

23 See also *E Hondius*, General Introduction, in: E Hondius (ed), The Development of Medical Liability (2010) 1, 4.

24 Cf PL no 72. This is not suggesting necessarily that this is seen differently in Spain and Switzerland, even though they apply different substantive law to claims against public health care providers (infra no 102) – the status of these institutions also seems to play a significant role, not only with respect to budgetary reasons, but also in light of a differing regulatory environment.

11 Another significant feature distinguishing health care systems is the way in which primary health care is organized. Out-patient care seems to be mostly private, and if so, predominantly provided by individual general practitioners[25] with the exception of Poland, the Netherlands and the UK, where private clinics or group practices are at least as common.[26] Public health centres take the lead instead in offering primary health care in Italy, Spain and Sweden.[27]

12 The picture changes when it comes to specialists' services, which are offered predominantly by private doctors individually in only five countries, by private group practices in one, and by public centres or hospitals in the remaining jurisdictions.[28]

13 While group practices or doctors teaming up otherwise are presumed to be more favourable for patients, also with respect to maintaining quality standards and therefore potential liability issues,[29] there seems to be no empirical data available to support this, and it is hard to imagine how trustworthy information could be gathered at all as it seems difficult to link eg claims frequency in out-patient care exclusively to the structure of the health care providers.

14 The following table[30] gives an overview of how primary health care is actually delivered as compared to specialists' services, showing only the predominant (though not necessarily exclusive) modes.

---

25 Eg AT nos 6–7 (group practices only recently allowed); BE no 1 ('vast majority of physicians work as independent, self-employed health professionals'); DE no 18–19 ('out-patient field is dominated by the small-business structure of individual physicians' offices'). See also *Paris/Devaux/Wie* (fn 31) 29.

26 *Paris/Devaux/Wie* (fn 31) 29.

27 ES no 3; SE no 5. As to Italy, see *Paris/Devaux/Wie* (fn 31) 29 f.

28 *Paris/Devaux/Wie* (fn 31) 30.

29 Cf DE no 19. See also *Paris/Devaux/Wie* (fn 31) 29: 'Generally, group practice is deemed to increase patient accessibility and professional working conditions, as well as the effectiveness and efficiency of health care delivery as several health professionals work together in collaboration …'

30 Data is based upon the OECD survey on health system characteristics 2008–2009 as published in *Paris/Devaux/Wie* (fn 31) 30. '1' stands for solo practices, '2+' for group practices, clinics, centres or hospitals.

Country	Primary care services				Specialists' services			
	public	private	1	2+	public	private	1	2+
Austria		x	x			x	x	
Belgium		x	x			x	x	
Czech Republic		x	x		x			x
France		x	x			x	x	
Germany		x	x			x	x	
Hungary		x	x		x			x
Italy	x			x	x			x
Netherlands		x		x		x		x
Poland		x		x	x			x
Spain	x			x	x			x
Sweden	x			x	x			x
Switzerland		x	x			x	x	
United Kingdom		x		x	x			x

II. Social Welfare Provision

2. The role of public health care

When looking at the financing of primary health care in these countries, one can essentially differentiate between three different models:[31] 15

- In one group of countries (Italy, Spain, Sweden, and the United Kingdom),[32] health care is provided to all residents and primarily financed from taxes.
- Another group of countries (Austria, Belgium, the Czech Republic, France, Germany, Hungary, and Poland)[33] has implemented a compul-

31 See *V Paris/M Devaux/L Wei*, Health Systems Institutional Characteristics. A Survey of 29 OECD Countries (OECD Health Working Papers No 50, 2010, available at <http://www.oecd.org/els/health/workingpapers>) 8.

32 BE no. 7; ES no 7; IT no 4, SE nos 7, 10; UK nos 2, 5.

33 AT no 10; BE no 7; CZ nos 3 ff; DE nos 2, 4, 22; HU no 1; PL no 1. See also ADECRI (ed), The French Social Protection System (2005, available at <http://www.adecri.org/images/

sory social insurance scheme, financed at least in part through income-related contributions.[34] Almost (but not necessarily) the entire population is covered.[35]

- The Netherlands[36] and Switzerland[37] pursue a more (but not entirely) privatized model by requiring residents to buy health insurance from one of several private suppliers, though subject to state control and regulation, ruling out in particular the insurers' possibility to deny coverage. Premia are supplemented with contributions from state sources in order to finance the system.

16 A second way to look at the 13 national health care systems presented by this study is to focus on how centralized health care coverage is organised.[38] In this respect, the range goes from jurisdictions with one all-encompassing national health service (England, Hungary and Italy)[39] or at least several regional health services (Spain and Sweden)[40] to either one central health insurer (such as in Belgium or Poland)[41] or several insurers from amongst which people can either choose (Czech Republic, Germany, the Netherlands, Switzerland)[42] or not (Austria, France)[43].

17 Since primary health care is invariably covered irrespective of the cause of the patient's condition, those who finance it are typically also the first ones to absorb the immediate financial consequences of medical malpractice, which is particularly noteworthy as they will most likely already have paid for the treatment causing it in the first place.[44] Patients themselves (as victims of malpractice) will therefore only be able to sue for losses

stories/the_french_social_protection_system.pdf>) 13, 55 ff; and <http://www.cleiss.fr/docs/regimes/regime_france/an_0.html>.

34 The Czech system is different inasmuch as the premia for the non-employed are paid by the state. Insofar, the Czech system has elements of the first model mentioned.

35 In Austria, 98.7 % are covered, in Belgium 99 %, in France 97.5 %, in Germany 83.3 %, in Hungary 100 %, and in Poland 99 % (*Paris/Devaux/Wie*, fn 31, 10).

36 'A less fortunate side-effect is that the new system has left a number of people uninsured.' NL no 11.

37 CH nos 10 ff.

38 *Paris/Devaux/Wie* (fn 31) 9 f.

39 HU no 8; IT no 1; UK nos 2, 10. On Hungary, see also <http://www.eum.hu/english/main-policy-objectives/the-organisation-and>.

40 ES no 2; SE no 4; on Sweden see also *K Essinger*, The Swedish Medical Injury Insurance (2009, available at <http://www.patientforsakring.se/resurser/dokument/engelska_artiklar/Report_on_the_Swedsih_Medical_Injury_Insurance.pdf> – note the typo in 'Swedish' in the link) 1.

41 BE no. 10; PL no 1.

42 CZ nos 4, 85; NL no 11; CH no 11.

43 AT no 10; ADECRI (fn 33) 17.

44 Cf CZ no 100.

exceeding the cost of further treatment financed by their social (or private) health insurance provider,[45] which is important to keep in mind when comparing the amounts awarded for medical malpractice in the various jurisdictions.

3. Differences in treating patient's claims

When contrasting medical malpractice cases to other instances of personal **18** injuries, the basic principles of liability applied to both are invariably the same throughout the jurisdictions under survey.[46] However, this also means that those jurisdictions which generally differentiate between torts caused by public institutions on the one hand and harm caused by private institutions or individuals on the other hand tend to do the same in the field of medical liability, depending on where they draw the line.[47] This is the case in Spain and Switzerland, both with respect to the substantive law on which the patients' claims are based as well as procedural rules.[48] While the same was true in France until the 2002 *loi Kouchner*, this legislation harmonised the bases of liability claims, though it did not change the pre-existing split between general civil courts competent to hear cases brought by patients harmed in private health care institutions or by practitioners on the one hand and administrative courts for cases arising eg in public hospitals on the other hand.[49]

In those jurisdictions where there is no such public-private divide in **19** medical malpractice cases, and therefore in the majority of countries examined here,[50] there may still be more or less subtle differences to other personal injury cases in practice even though – as said – the same principles of liability apply.[51] Apart from the impact of various ways of alternative

45 See, eg, NL no 5. Potential recourse claims by the latter are addressed infra at no 21.

46 This is even true for Sweden, despite the fact that in practice almost all cases are handled within its no-fault patient insurance scheme: SE no 13.

47 See also PL no 83 on the question (ultimately answered in the negative) of whether medical services provided by public hospitals have to be classified as *acta iure imperii* (in which case – ordinary – state liability would apply).

48 CH nos 25, 45, 95 ff; ES nos 4–5, 66 ff. See also infra no 102.

49 FR no 26.

50 AT nos 13, 79; BE nos 9, 45; DE no 31; HU nos 9, 50; IT nos 7–9, 54; PL no 9 (but differences with respect to mandatory insurance cover); UK no 6 (though certain peculiarities for NHS treatment once the NHS Redress Act 2006 will be implemented).

51 Certain procedural specialities are indicated, for example, by the English report: UK no 7 (special pre-action protocol for clinical negligence claims, public funding still available for pursuing medical negligence cases). See also DE nos 33–34.

dispute resolution that may be available to patients only,[52] courts may, for example, be more inclined to apply (generally available) mechanisms to improve the claimants' position in cases where they are victims of medical malpractice, not (necessarily) out of sympathy for patients, but rather because of the peculiarities of the factual setting, such as the specific reasons for the difficulties in proving causation.[53]

20 In Sweden, medical malpractice cases fall under a no-fault compensation scheme and for that reason are handled quite differently in practice as compared to other tort matters not covered by a similar regime in Sweden.[54] However, even within this insurance scheme, certain principles of tort law (in particular the assessment of damages) apply as if the case had been brought before a court of law.[55]

4. Right of recourse

21 If a social or private insurer or a health fund provides monetary support or benefits in kind to a victim of medical malpractice, the payor invariably has a right of recourse against those liable to the victim for this adverse event.[56] However, the enforcement of such right does not seem to be a matter of course in most jurisdictions,[57] even though there may be a certain tendency in the more recent past, at least in some countries, to increase the percentage of cases where recourse claims are actually collected upon.[58] In England, on the other hand, National Health Service (NHS) bodies will 'not seek to recover their costs either in part or in full from the health care professional concerned' who negligently caused harm to a patient.[59]

---

52 See infra G (nos 132 ff) and, eg, AT no 13; BE no 9.

53 Cf AT no 13.

54 SE no 11. See also infra nos 104 ff.

55 SE no 12.

56 AT nos 11, 14, 17, 20; BE no. 11; CH no 27, 32; DE nos 37 ff; ES nos 9, 16; FR no 5; HU nos 11, 13; IT nos 10, 13; NL nos 10, 12; PL nos 10–11; SE no 14 (but only in cases of gross negligence or intent); UK nos 8–9.

57 Cf eg HU no 12; IT no 11 ('no cases … are known'). But see CH no 28.

58 AT no 14; DE no 40; FR no 5.

59 NHS Indemnity <http://www.nhsla.com/NR/rdonlyres/1CFE5864-05C3-4770-982C-7003294B8161/0/NHSIndemnity.rtf>, no 6. See also UK no 12.

III. Private Insurance

5. The role of private health insurance

'Health insurance is the second largest non-life-business line, accounting for 25 % of European non-life premiums.'[60] There are nevertheless regional differences, ranging from countries where private health insurance plays a 'marginal' role[61] or only concerns 'a very small share of the market',[62] to jurisdictions where considerable (or at least increasing) portions of the population take out at least some additional cover.[63] **22**

This is also where private health insurance has to be differentiated – some policies only address the latter (ie extra benefits and services not already absorbed by the state or social insurance), whereas others fill the gaps in the social insurance systems and offer basic health care coverage (though possibly already combined with the additional protection taken out separately by those otherwise covered by social insurance). **23**

In order to get a full picture of the financing of health care, it is important to note that apart from (direct or indirect) contributions to their base cover and possible extras paid via private health insurance (PHI), people in all jurisdictions may have to contribute directly via out-of-pocket payments (OOP) in order to receive certain health care benefits.[64] The following table puts this into perspective:[65] **24**

60 CEA Statistics No 42: European Insurance in Figures (November 2010, <http://www.cea.eu/uploads/DocumentsLibrary/documents/1290503264_european-insurance-in-figures.pdf>, 16 (also emphasizing that 'health continues to be one of the most dynamic non-life business lines, mainly because of rising demand due to ageing populations and increasing medical costs'). Two thirds of European health premiums are generated on the Dutch and German market (not surprising for the former in light of its privatisation of the health insurance regime, though).

61 IT no 12; PL no 14 (private health insurance 'of very little importance', with policies typically excluding liability of the insurer for medical malpractice).

62 ES no 10; probably also UK no 10.

63 AT no 16 (one third of the population); BE nos 12–13 ('recently grown steadily'); HU no 13 ('increasingly important role'). See also PL no 13, where indirect cover via employers offering health plans seems to play a significant role. Similarly in Sweden, where private health insurance 'used to be quite uncommon … but is now on the increase': SE no 16.

64 Eg DE no 23; PL no 2; SE no 9. A rather peculiar variety of it are the voluntary 'gratuities' paid by Hungarian patients to their doctors (no 3).

65 Source: Excerpts from Table 9 in *Paris/Devaux/Wie* (fn 31) 22; 'n/a' stands for 'data not available'.

Country	Share of OOP in inpatient curative care	Share of PHI in inpatient curative care	Share of OOP in basic medical and diagnostic services	Share of PHI in basic medical and diagnostic services
Austria	2.5 %	14.4 %	4.0 %	0.0 %
Belgium	17.9 %	5.9 %	39.1 %	2.6 %
Czech Republic	0.6 %	0.7 %	9.3 %	0.1 %
France	2.6 %	5.3 %	9.2 %	17.9 %
Germany	1.9 %	9.8 %	10.1 %	9.5 %
Hungary	7.3 %	0.1 %	14.1 %	0.4 %
Italy	n/a	n/a	n/a	n/a
Netherlands	0.3 %	0.0 %	2.5 %	1.6 %
Poland	0.6 %	2.8 %	n/a	n/a
Spain	3.8 %	5.2 %	3.0 %	6.5 %
Sweden	2.7 %	0.0 %	15.9 %	0.0 %
Switzerland	6.1 %	14.5 %	28.7 %	10.9 %
United Kingdom	1.9 %	n/a	2.0 %	0.0 %

25 Summing up, the interplay of public and private resources in the financing of health care is quite diverse, as shown by the next table:[66]

Country	Public expenditure			Private expenditure		
	Total	General gov't	Social security	Total	OOP	PHI
Austria	76,4 %	31,6 %	44,8 %	23,6 %	15,4 %	4,6 %
Belgium	75,1 %	12,4 %	62,7 %	24,9 %	19,0 %	5,6 %
Czech Republic	85,2 %	8,3 %	76,9 %	14,8 %	13,2 %	0,2 %
France	79,0 %	5,2 %	73,8 %	21,0 %	6,8 %	13,4 %

66 Source: Excerpts from Table 12 in *Paris/Devaux/Wie* (fn 31) 28 (data referring to 2007 or last available year). 'General gov't' refers to state payments taken from tax monies, 'OOP' are out-of-pocket payments, and 'PHI' stands for private health insurance.

Country	Public expenditure			Private expenditure		
	Total	General gov't	Social security	Total	OOP	PHI
Germany	76,9 %	9,0 %	67,8 %	23,1 %	13,1 %	9,3 %
Hungary	70,6 %	12,4 %	58,2 %	29,4 %	24,9 %	1,1 %
Italy	76,5 %	76,4 %	0,1 %	23,5 %	20,2 %	0,9 %
Netherlands*	81,4 %	5,8 %	75,6 %	18,6 %	6,0 %	6,2 %
Poland	70,8 %	12,3 %	58,6 %	29,1 %	24,3 %	0,5 %
Spain	71,8 %	66,7 %	5,1 %	28,2 %	21,1 %	5,9 %
Sweden	81,7 %	81,7 %	0,0 %	18,3 %	15,9 %	0,2 %
Switzerland	59,3 %	16,5 %	42,8 %	40,7 %	30,6 %	9,2 %
United Kingdom	81,7 %	81,7 %	0,0 %	18,3 %	11,4 %	1,1 %

6. Liability insurance

Jurisdictions are split when it comes to mandatory liability insurance for health care professionals: some require it[67] while others do not[68] or rather, not yet, since even in the former countries, a statutory requirement to insure against liability risks is a rather recent development.[69] **26**

Generally, markets are often claimed to have narrowed in many jurisdictions with typically fewer insurers offering to underwrite medical liability risks at increasing premia.[70] **27**

> 'The increase in the amount of damages for medical malpractice is one of the main reasons why insurance companies' business in this branch has been less profitable or unprofitable since 2000 in most countries. Many markets have reported escalating losses. … Moreover, re-pricing

67 AT no 18 (since 2010, minimum cover: € 2 million); CH no 33 (all-encompassing since 2007); ES no. 17 (since 2003, no minimum cover); FR no 7 (since 2002); HU no 14; PL no 15 (since 2004, 2007 and 2009 respectively, minimum cover for individual practices € 140,000, for health care establishment € 275,000, for doctors with certain specialisations € 100,000, for doctors not falling in the former group € 25,000, and € 50,000 for dentists); SE no 18.

68 BE no 14 (legislation not yet in force); DE nos 44–45 (but duty foreseen by professional codes of conduct; statutory requirement only in a few states regarding medical boards of registration); IT no 14; NL no 13; UK no 12.

69 See fn 67.

70 Cf, eg, DE no 50; FR no 9; NL no 13. But see, eg, AT no 18 (indicating sufficient supply in Austria).

the risk often leads to increases in premiums that are hardly affordable for physicians and other medical professionals. In fact, since 2002 insurers and reinsurers in some jurisdictions have decided to reduce their exposure to, or withdraw completely from, the medical malpractice market. These withdrawals have adversely affected the market by causing a massive contraction in capacity in some countries and driving up premiums to even higher levels. … In most countries, the growth in premiums for medical malpractice combined with reduced scope of coverage is particularly problematic for certain types of riskier specialties. These include notably general surgeons, obstetricians/gynaecologists, neurosurgeons, plastic surgeons, anaesthesiologists, orthopaedists and public and private establishments.'[71]

28 Lack of or at least problems with supply in the insurance market, however, is not a good starting point for introducing mandatory insurance.[72]

29 A particular problem linked to the way liability insurance is being offered in any given jurisdiction relates to the impact of the conduct of those covered in the aftermath of the harmful event. To what extent are eg doctors allowed to speak to their patients and talk about the incident? At what point – if any – are they admitting fault, and are they thereby violating duties arising out of the insurance policy? Some jurisdictions, by specific statutory exclusion, rule out such a consequence at least for true statements of fact[73] and thereby effectively foster the relationship between doctors and their patients.

IV. Professional Standards

7. Applicable professional standards

30 Professional standards for health care personnel are most commonly defined in rather general and broad terms in the legislation governing

---

71 *J Simon/B Jansen*, Economic Implications of Medical Liability Claims: Insurance and Compensation Schemes, Report to the 2008 Council of Europe Conference 'The Ever-Growing Challenge of Medical Liability: National and European Responses', CONF-ML (2008) 04 E (available at <http://www.coe.int/t/e/legal_affairs/legal_co-operation/steering_committees/cdcj/cj_s_med/CONF-ML _2008_ 04 E – Report J. SIMON.pdf>) 8, identical wording in OECD (ed), Medical Malpractice. Prevention, Insurance and Coverage Options (Policy Issues in Insurance No 11, 2006, available at <http://www.oecd-ilibrary.org/finance-and-investment/medical-malpractice_9789264029057-en>) 16 f.

72 See also OECD (fn 71) 44.

73 Eg AT no 18; NL no 15.

requirements and further conditions for these professions, or in codifications of patients' rights.[74] In some countries, the lawmakers have introduced at least some further specifications for certain aspects of health care.[75]

Nevertheless, details of what care is really owed during a specific procedure or treatment from a medico-scientific perspective are typically – if at all – specified in guidelines or rules developed within the medical profession,[76] even though they may subsequently be raised to a normative status or at least inspire regulations by the competent authorities.[77] Courts may, however, consider these as more or less persuasive evidence for interpreting the legal standard of due care.[78] This neither means, however, that an expert opinion submitted in a pending case and deviating from written standards will be irrelevant, nor that the former will always override the latter.[79] **31**

8. Quality and/or risk management systems

All jurisdictions under survey obviously require certain standards for health care professionals and institutions before entering the market[80] and foresee disciplinary sanctions for established breaches of proper professional standards.[81] Apart from that, some legal systems have intro- **32**

---

74 See, eg, AT no 21 (plans to develop national quality standards not yet implemented: no 22); BE no 16; CH no 37; DE no 59; SE no 20.

75 CH no 37; HU no 17 (66 detailed professional standards and protocols issued by the Ministry of Health for various treatments); NL no 16–17 (though 'one of the drawbacks of enactments by the legislator is its lack of expertise in the medico-professional area'). See also AT no 22 (plans to develop national quality standards, but not yet implemented).

76 BE no 16; CH nos 38–39; DE nos 10 ff; ES no 22, 24; FR no 11; PL no 22. Cf *Hondius* (fn 23) 7, 12 (quoting Lord Scarman who observed: 'the law imposes the duty of care; but the standard of care is a matter of medical judgment'). A different set of guidelines are those defining ethical rather than 'hands-on' standards, cf UK no 14 ('Good Medical Practice' guidelines of the General Medical Council) or the guidelines of the Swiss Academy of Medical Sciences at <http://www.samw.ch/en/Ethics/Guidelines/Currently-valid-guidelines.html>. Cf also the recent plan by the European Committee for Standardization to elaborate European standards for aesthetic surgery services (<http://www.cen.eu/cen/News/PressReleases/Pages/Aestheticsurgery.aspx>).

77 See fn 75.

78 BE no 16 (cf in particular the case at fn 7: anaesthetist disregarding safety standards approved by his peers); DE no 60; ES no 22; FR no 11; HU no 18; NL no 17 ('important guidelines'); PL no 24.

79 Cf, eg, BE no 16; HU no 18.

80 See, eg, BE no 17; DE no 55; NL no 1; PL nos 21, 25.

81 See, eg, CH no 37; DE nos 6, 58; PL nos 22, 24, 32; UK no 14.

duced continuing systematic quality control systems for hospitals and doctors, either by way of a mandatory procedure,[82] by way of incentives,[83] or a combination of both[84]. Others are at least considering such a regime (even though it has not yet been adopted).[85] Still others do not foresee mandatory formalized quality checks proactively for the time being and instead seem to rely on compliance with legislative quality standards once accreditation hurdles are cleared, coupled with sanctions ex post if deviations are established.[86]

33 Irrespective of (or in addition to) a statutory requirement, some health care providers voluntarily install some sort of quality control mechanism or sign- up for auditing or professional certification,[87] if only for reasons of competition.

B. Tort Liability

9. Fundamentals of tort liability

34 In those jurisdictions which strictly differentiate between tort and contractual liability, the former is relevant only when a patient was treated without her consent, if an employee of the contractual partner such as a hospital is sued individually, or if a third party outside the contractual relationship was harmed.[88] In light of France's specific legislative solution, the general 'non-cumul' rule does not play such a significant role in the medical malpractice arena any more.[89] In countries where liability arising from tort or contract share common grounds or are otherwise not mutually exclusive, on the other hand,[90] tort law principles are more

---

82 AT no 24; CH no 43 (but not implemented yet); DE no 63; NL no 18; PL no 27 (regular inspections by Health Fund); SE no 21 (details however only suggested in handbooks).

83 Eg. in France and the UK, see *Paris/Devaux/Wie* (fn 31) 63 f. See also UK no 15.

84 BE no. 10, 18; HU no 19; UK nos 14–15 (mandatory revalidation of license, regular 'risk management assessment' by the NHS Litigation Authority with an impact on the contributions payable by the institution scrutinized). For France, see FR no 13 and <http://www.has-sante.fr/portail/jcms/c_418544/to-improve-quality-of-care-in-health-care-organisations-hcos-and-in-general-medical-practice>.

85 BE no. 21; IT no 19 (but no legislative initiative yet).

86 BE no 17; ES nos 24–25 (though subject to regional deviations); NL 19.

87 AT no 25; CH no 43; DE no 66; HU no 19; IT no 19.

88 Cf BE no 22 (see also no 35 'The patient has no option as to whether he should proceed in contract and/or in tort.').

89 FR no 14.

90 Eg AT no 68; CH no 83; DE nos 160–161; ES nos 57–58; HU nos 42–43; IT no 47; PL no 31; SE no 24; UK no 40.

generally applicable, even though in jurisdictions with at least strategic advantages for claims based on violations of contractual duties,[91] delicts are still the less common starting point for claimants.[92] The reverse is true in Hungary, however, where patients can choose between the contractual and delictual liability regime, although they tend to select the latter due to its standard presumption of fault.[93]

While all jurisdictions share the same core elements of a tort claim, there are nevertheless some deviations, both when it comes to the interplay of these elements in general and in medical cases in particular. **35**

(a) **Damage.** When it comes to the basic trigger of a tort law examination, the damage claimed, divergences between the systems under survey in filtering out those losses that are compensable in tort are not peculiar to medical malpractice cases: While personal injury as a concept is the same throughout all jurisdictions, the most evident differences come from those jurisdictions that distinguish a biological (*danno biologico*) or existential loss (*danno esistenziale*) as an extra-pecuniary loss (*danno extra-patrimoniale*) from the classic pecuniary and non-pecuniary losses.[94] Even though Italy is the first to come to mind in this context, of course, the concept has clearly spread beyond the Appenin peninsula.[95] **36**

One specific question which may be of particular relevance also in the medical malpractice scenario is whether patients can claim compensation for the mere fear of a future deterioration of their condition, eg if the wrongdoing by the doctor is clear but has not yet had any measurable **37**

91 Eg AT no 69; CH nos 83 ff; IT nos 46–47.

92 But see UK no 40 ('in theory' both claim in contract and in tort, but 'will in practice amount to the same thing').

93 HU no 44; see also infra no 58 at fn 140.

94 IT nos 68 ff; infra no 125. On these concepts, see, eg, *G Christandl*, Eine kurze Darstellung der neuesten Entwicklungen im italienischen Nichtvermögensschadensrecht unter besonderer Berücksichtigung des danno esistenziale, <http://www.personaedanno.it/cms/data/articoli/files/000180_resource1_orig.doc>.

95 Cf ES no 97 (*daño corporal*). Even though the Germanic legal family would fiercely deny any traces of *danno biologico* in their damage nomenclature, the recognition of the loss of earning capacity (as opposed to actual loss of income; infra nos 116 f) is at least one step in that direction. The separate (and cumulative) indemnification of violations of personality rights as in the Czech Republic, for example (CZ nos 122, 127), also complements the picture.

adverse effect on the patient's physical or mental health. This seems to be possible in at least some jurisdictions, if only under certain conditions.[96]

38 **(b) Bases of liability.** While problems of causation will be addressed specifically further below,[97] linking the loss to the defendant does not per se establish the latter's liability. The traditional normative approach to reaching that decision is the examination of the objective and/or subjective[98] blameworthiness of her conduct,[99] even though this dogmatic foundation of fault liability has somehow become lost over time.[100]

39 It comes as no surprise that all jurisdictions require doctors to meet the objective standard of care owed by experts in their corresponding field, so a specialist, for example, needs to know more about her own field of specialisation than a general practitioner,[101] though it is typically (but not necessarily) the average specialist of her kind rather than the most outstanding physician of all times who sets the threshold.[102] While this is

96 AT no 94; but see UK no 23 (unless fear amounts to an immediate recognized psychiatric condition). See also the following contributions to WVH Rogers (ed), Damages for Non-Pecuniary Loss in a Comparative Perspective (2001): *H Koziol*, Austria, nos 45 f; *H Cousy/D Droshout*, Belgium, no 29; *S Galand-Carval*, France, no 41; *U Magnus/J Fedtke*, Germany, no 14; *MH Wissink/WH van Boom*, The Netherlands, no 30; *M Martin-Casals/J Ribot/J Solé*, Spain, nos 34 ff. Cf *BA Koch*, Comparative Report, in: B Winiger/H Koziol/BA Koch/R Zimmermann (eds), Digest of European Tort Law 2: Essential Cases on Damage (2011) 25/30; *C von Bar*, The Common European Law of Torts II (2000) 73 ff.

97 See infra 11 and 12.

98 Cf AT no 28; NL no 24.

99 As summarized by *P Widmer* in European Group on Tort Law, Principles of European Tort Law (2005) Introduction to Ch 4 no 1 (p 64), fault is 'the most traditional, most widespread and – apparently – most important criterion of imputation or foundation of responsibility: the blame addressed to the of a damaging event for not having observed due care in order to avoid damage'.

100 Cf *P Widmer*, Comparative Report on Fault as a Basis of Liability and Criterion of Imputation, in: P Widmer (ed), Unification of Tort Law: Fault (2005) 331, 357: 'If there is one conclusion that may be drawn as a kind of synthesis and common finding from the comparison of the different legal systems, it is that fault – which "officially" is still deemed to be the essential und most convincing criterion of liability – has become a mere phantom, an empty shell which serves as camouflage for a criterion of imputation which has almost nothing to do anymore with an individual blame towards the tortfeasor'. See also NL no 24.

101 Cf, eg, PL no 24, pointing at 'high expectations upon physicians on account of their long period of professional education and because of the particularly significant character of the patients' legal interests.'

102 AT no 29 ('prudence of a conscientious average doctor in the actual situation'). But see HU no 45 ('utmost care') and PL no 24: 'The model of due care must not be limited to care expected of an "average physician".'

universally true in all countries covered,[103] there are nevertheless at least slight differences when it comes to identifying the exact level of expertise.

An important aspect of fault concerns the up-to-dateness of the doctor's knowledge, which overlaps with the problem of competing schools of medicine, suggesting differing procedures or treatment for the same diagnosis made for the patient at hand.[104] **40**

Generally, the focus is on the state of medical science at the time of the doctor's conduct in question.[105] In Spain, the doctor must 'use all remedies and techniques known to medical science and required by the *lex artis* in order to heal the patient'.[106] English law seems to be slightly more generous in this respect: any competing school of thought is correct as long as it is still 'adopted by a respectable body of opinion in the profession',[107] unless 'no longer supportable by logical analysis'.[108] **41**

A variant of fault for which a doctor may be held liable arises if she knowingly undertakes to perform an operation or other treatment for which she is not sufficiently qualified (what is referred to as *Einlassungsfahrlässigkeit* in German legalese).[109] **42**

A special problem that at first sight seems to concern the common law world only stems from the fact that medical treatment without consent **43**

---

103 Eg AT no 28; BE no 23; CH no 37; DE no 82; ES no 29; UK no 18. As to Sweden, see *U Hellbacher/C Espersson/H Johansson*, Patient Injury Compensation for Healthcare-Related Injuries (2007, available at <http://www.patientforsakring.se/resurser/dokument/engelska_artiklar/Patient_Injury_Compensation_for_Helthcare-Related_Injuries.pdf >) 12 ff ('experienced specialist or other experienced practitioner in the field'). See also IT no 39: if treatment requires skills beyond ordinary qualifications, liability only for gross negligence unless the doctor's specialisation corresponds to such extraordinary level of expertise.

104 A typical formula is eg AT no 29: the doctor has to choose a method of treatment that is 'in accordance with the practice of well-respected doctors who are familiar with this method, even if other experts may have chosen a different technique. In such case, the doctor has to take the safest measures according to the state of medical science in order to prevent known risks of such treatment'. Cf the citation in ES no 29: 'skilled professional in medicine who acts in accordance with state-of-the-art knowledge of medical science'.

105 Eg AT no 60; BE no 35.

106 ES no 29.

107 UK no 19 (so-called *Bolam* test).

108 UK no 19 (*Bolitho*). Cf *Hondius* (fn 23) 12, comparing the *Bolam* test with the Dutch statutory standard (see NL nos 66 f): 'At first sight, the two tests are virtually identical. In fact, there is a gulf between them. The "standards of reasonably competent medical men at the time" are radically different from "conscientious health care providers", because in the latter case it is the court which decides, not the medical community as in the first case.'

109 Cf AT no 124; UK no 18.

meets the definition of battery (trespass to the person), depending upon the outcome,[110] which as a consequence of the doctor's conduct is hard to explain to the latter. But even 'fault' as a technical term in other jurisdictions is hard to spell out in discussions with medical professionals, as they tend to perceive this term in the blame-laden meaning of (or at least similar to) criminal law.

44 Apart from the actual treatment as such, liability may also arise, for example, due to deficiencies in the organisation of a hospital or private practice, such as a shortage of adequately qualified personnel on duty due to a flawed work plan, or a lack of equipment or other necessary resources required to run a hospital of the type it advertises to be.[111] If so, a hospital may be held liable for conduct attributed to it directly via its organs rather than vicariously for the conduct of its employees.[112]

10. Burden of proof

45 **(a) In general.** As a general rule throughout all jurisdictions, it is up to the claimant to prove the facts supporting her case. In turn, the defendant has to prove those facts which support her defence arguments.[113] However, in medical malpractice cases, it can be particularly troublesome for patients to collect evidence supporting their claims, which is probably one of the reasons why the informed consent doctrine[114] has gained such a disproportionate importance in practice[115] – after all, it shifts the focus of the evidence to a matter that is more easily proven. Here, the interplay of the patient's precondition and other aspects of her physical condition with the impact of specific medical procedures combined with the effects of pharmaceuticals hardly plays any role at all.

46 Problems of proof in a medical malpractice lawsuit have prompted most courts to be at least slightly more generous to patients as compared to other personal injury claimants, which is why the toolbox of alleviating or

---

110 UK no 21.

111 Cf, eg, AT no 66; PL no 66.

112 Cf infra Cases 3 (no 180), 5 (no 194) and 6 (no 204).

113 AT nos 31, 32, 35; BE no 24; CH no 54; CZ no 59; DE no 86; ES no 34; FR no 17; HU no 22; IT no 24; NL no 27; PL no 37; SE no 26.

114 See infra nos 85 ff.

115 Cf, eg, CH no 57.

even shifting the burden of proof[116] comes into play seemingly more often in such cases.[117]

Without shifting the burden of proof onto the defendant yet, claimants are still better off if it suffices for them to produce prima facie evidence supporting eg causation. This means that they need not establish every single link in a chain of alleged events, but if some of them are typically connected according to the experience of life, the claimants' evidence needs only to lead to the start of that typical course of events, which in itself need not be specifically proven. **47**

Similarly, if there is a possible explanation for a certain result at first sight, claimants need not submit evidence to support this, rather it is up to the defendants to prove that there may have been at least one other equally likely reason. In the iconic malpractice scenario of a needle or swab remaining in the patient's body after an operation, this *res* is indeed *ipsa loquitur*, ie it speaks for itself that the surgical team obviously neglected to remove it before closing the wound.[118] However, if the surgeon or hospital can prove that it had already been forgotten during an earlier operation not within their own responsibility (eg because the object was not produced by the hospital's supplier), at least the presumption that it was them who left it in the patient's body is thereby rebutted.[119] **48**

A presumption of a certain consequence in the claimant's favour subsequently needs to be rebutted by the defendant, sometimes having the same consequence as a complete reversal of the burden of proof.[120] However, unlike in the latter case, claimants still need to produce something to trigger this consequence, although they do not need to amass sufficient evidence to surpass the standard of proof hurdle set by the main theme. **49**

Under certain conditions, the burden of proof can be reversed entirely, however, which means that the claimant can lean back once she has raised an allegation eg of the defendant's fault, waiting for the latter not only to argue, but also to come up with counter-evidence to prove that she was not **50**

---

116 On the following examples of that toolbox, see *I Giesen*, The Burden of Proof and other Procedural Devices in Tort Law, in: H Koziol/B Steininger (eds), European Tort Law 2008 (2009) 49.

117 An exception thereto is Spain, where the reverse seems to be true: ES no 34 (but see nos 36–37).

118 Cf BE no 26; NL no 28.

119 They may, however, typically still be liable, though due to their apparent failure to detect and remove the needle or swab during their own operation where they could have detected it, which will shift the focus of the story to be proven by the claimant.

120 Cf, eg, CH no 55 (malpractice inferred from adverse outcome of the treatment per se).

at fault. The topic with respect to which the burden of proof was reversed is then entirely within the defendant's sphere, and only if she can convince the court of the contrary will the claimant have to come forward with further evidence rebutting that produced by the defendant.

51 **(b) Loss.** Patients in all jurisdictions need to convince the court that they have indeed suffered compensable damage.[121] 'Indeed, it is difficult to conceive how the law could be otherwise.'[122] The only slight deviation therefrom is the exact calculation of the loss – some procedural laws tend to be somewhat more generous than others by allowing for approximate guesses.[123]

52 **(c) Causation.** The first (and most important) question before addressing the burden of proving causation is the standard of proof required (which is of course also relevant in other areas). The range goes from a mere preponderance of the evidence ('more likely than not')[124] via 'high probability'[125] to 'almost certainty'.[126] While no judge will pin this down to a specific percentage of likelihood,[127] it nevertheless makes a tremendous difference to the outcome of a case whether patients need to remove all possible doubts or can succeed despite significant (but ultimately not entirely convincing) uncertainties. After all, this outcome in most jurisdictions means either all or nothing, ie full liability of the defendant or none at all.[128]

53 Whether a jurisdiction is either at the end or rather at the beginning of the scale just mentioned makes the burden of a patient to prove causation more or less burdensome, and it is her burden after all in general.[129]

---

121 AT no 31; BE no 24; CH no 54; CZ no 59; DE no 86; ES nos 34–35; FR no 17; HU no 22; IT no 24; NL no 27; PL no 37; SE no 26; UK no 23.

122 UK no 23.

123 Eg AT no 31; DE nos 98, 193; HU no 22; NL nos 59, 77, 78; PL no 37.

124 CH no 59 (but specifically in medical malpractice cases); IT no 30; SE no 32; UK no 22 ('balance of probabilities').

125 AT no 32; PL no 40.

126 BE no 25; FR nos 18, 50; CZ no 66; ES nos 35, 39 ('subjective certainty').

127 Cf R *Wright*, Proving Facts: Belief versus Probability, in: H Koziol/B Steininger (eds), European Tort Law 2008 (2009) 79 (nos 31–32).

128 Cf, eg, DE no 90. Only few jurisdictions resort to proportional liability at least under certain circumstances: AT no 39; NL no 47; UK nos 28 f. See the forthcoming publication by the European Group on Tort Law on this topic: I *Gilead et al* (eds), Proportional Liability (2011).

129 AT nos 32 ff; BE no 24; CH no 54; CZ nos 59, 66; DE no 89; ES no 35; FR no 17; HU nos 22, 24 (but see no 25); IT no 24; NL no 27; PL no 37; SE no 26; UK no 24.

However, some jurisdictions lower the standard of proof (and therefore move to the beginning of the range) particularly in cases of medical malpractice in order to make it easier for patients to proceed.[130]

Jurisdictions also apply other tools to improve the position of patients as claimants. Their burden of proving causation is reversed, for example, in Austria and the Netherlands, if the treatment created a specific risk and the worsening of the patient's condition can only be explained by the assumption that this must have materialised.[131] **54**

Spain, which seems to go the other way altogether at first sight,[132] still offers at least one line of reasoning which is in the patient's advantage: where the consequences of a treatment are disproportionately negative and beyond a typical risk thereof, causation and fault are inferred, thereby also effectively shifting the burden of exoneration to the defendant.[133] Recent developments indicate, however, that the rigor of the Spanish courts as regards the causal link may gradually be loosened with the increasing recognition of judical presumptions and other adjustments. **55**

A rather unique approach is followed by German courts, which even reverse the burden of proving causation once they are convinced of a particularly blameworthy conduct of the doctor.[134] Also, if a physician is neither herself fully qualified for the treatment that she performs nor supervised by an expert as required under the circumstances, it is rebuttably presumed that she failed to meet the standard of such a specialist.[135] **56**

A different approach is looking at the proximity of the evidence to either party's sphere: whoever is in a better position to prove a certain fact or its absence is bound to do so, even if this is to the benefit of the opposing party.[136] This is obviously of particular relevance in the medical field, where the exact steps taken by the health care personnel during a specific treatment can typically be substantiated more easily by themselves rather **57**

130 AT nos 32–33; CH no 56 (preponderance of the evidence).

131 NL no 41. Cf also AT no 33.

132 ES no 35: 'courts are *stricter* when evaluating the proof causation than in other tort law areas' (emphasis added). Cf also CZ no 178, reporting that medical experts in the Czech Republic 'are usually very reluctant to authoritatively and conclusively confirm' the patient's allegations concerning causation, which effectively means that the patient will lose her case as long as there is no other evidence available.

133 ES nos 35–42. See ES nos 43 ff on the loss of a chance.

134 DE nos 91 ff; cf AT no 34.

135 DE no 99.

136 ES no 38; IT no 25; see also NL no 31–35 (burden of proof effectively lowered in certain cases by requiring the opposing party to substantiate her defense by supplying information on all factual aspects of the claim).

than by the patient concerned. A related, though not entirely identical, argument concerns the absence of a piece of evidence that should have been submitted to the court. If the doctor or hospital cannot furnish the court with the documentation that should be part of the patient's file, whether it was never produced, is (allegedly) not to be found or is destroyed, the courts in several jurisdictions will reverse the burden of proof on what this evidence should have revealed to the disadvantage of these defendants.[137]

58 **(d) Fault.** Fault (or at least the facts allowing the court to make the proper legal evaluation of the conduct for which the defendants are charged) also has to be proven by the claimants in most jurisdictions, if only as a general rule.[138] In some countries, this burden is shifted onto the defendants either in all tort cases generally[139] or under certain specific conditions in medical malpractice scenarios only.[140] Again other jurisdictions at least lower the burden of proving fault.[141]

11. Uncertain causation[142]

59 If those on whom the burden of proof rests have submitted all the evidence they have, but uncertainties remain with respect to causation, the law has to draw the consequences and either deny the claim altogether or offer at least partial indemnification. Apart from the case where only one possible cause is at stake, whose likelihood does not exceed the required standard of proof, which will invariably be dismissed, there are (at least) two different more interesting scenarios to distinguish:

(1) Two or more health care professionals are proven not to have met the required standard of care, however, it remains unclear which one of them actually caused the harm.

---

137 AT no 34; CH no 58 (at least lower standard of proof); DE no 86; ES no 38; IT no 25; PL no 41; but not in CZ (no 136). See also Case 5 below (no 199).

138 AT no 35; BE no 24 (criminal law's presumption of innocence applied in tort cases based on offences); CH no 54; DE no 87; ES no 36; FR no 17; IT no 24; NL no 27; PL no 41 (general rule); SE no 26; UK no 25.

139 CZ nos 52, 60 (but breach of duty must be proven by the claimant); HU nos 20, 22 f.

140 AT no 37 (if protective law infringed); DE no 88 (risks within the control of the hospital or its staff).

141 NL no 32; ES no 36 (theory of 'disproportionate damage' – extraordinarily harmful consequences of a treatment outside a typical risk indicate negligence).

142 See also infra Cases 1 (nos 161 ff) and 3 (nos 182 f) as well as the country reports thereto.

(2) At least one health care professional is proven to have done something wrong, but there may be other reasons why the patient's condition deteriorated, including – unlike (1) – causes within the latter's own sphere, in particular the precondition which brought her into treatment in the first place.

In the first group of cases, at least if the possible causes are alternative, most jurisdictions tend to resolve the problem by attributing joint and several liability to all potential tortfeasors.[143] This is not necessarily so – some jurisdictions like Switzerland would dismiss the case entirely because neither conduct will meet the required standard of proof if considered individually.[144] A more novel approach would be to split the loss between the defendants, thereby shifting the insolvency risk to the claimant. While such proportional liability is being recommended,[145] it is clearly not yet the majority approach.[146] **60**

In the second variation, the picture is slightly more colourful in the jurisdictions under survey. Austrian courts would opt for proportional liability,[147] for example, as would English judges if proof of causation is deemed impossible.[148] Other countries would rather follow the classic all-or-nothing route.[149] In Spain, there is a tendency to dismiss the case (unlike in other cases of tort law), 'especially if there is no hospital or public administrative institution among the defendants', arguing that complications of a medical treatment are always possible despite proper conduct.[150] In those jurisdictions that have adopted the loss of a chance doctrine, this peculiar problem of causation may be circumvented altogether.[151] **61**

143 Eg DE no 100; FR no 20; HU nos 34–35; IT no 23.

144 CH no 60 (unless concerted action). See also ES no 41: possibility that nurses other than the defendant may have caused the harm against the claimant.

145 Cf Art 3:103 Principles of European Tort Law. See also § 1294 para 2 of one of the two proposals for a tort recodification in Austria, English translation at B *Steininger*, Austria, in: H Koziol/B Steininger (eds), European Tort Law 2007 (2008) 134, 158 ff.

146 Cf NL nos 47–48; UK no 26.

147 AT no 39.

148 UK no 28 (in *Fairchild* scenarios), otherwise *Wilsher* outcome (UK no 26).

149 Eg CH no 59 (if likelihood of other causes at least equal); DE no 90. As it is felt to be unjust, Hungary reports a 'clear tendency ... for shifting the risk of uncertainty in causation to medical health care providers': HU no 25.

150 ES no 40.

151 Eg BE no 27; see the next section.

12. Loss of a chance

62 The *perte d'une chance* doctrine effectively promotes proportional liability by shifting the focus when determining either the loss or its causation. In the former (and in comparison, probably prevailing) perspective, the victim does not claim the whole damage sustained, eg the personal injuries actually suffered, but rather the loss of the chance to have avoided such harm, which in the medical malpractice scenario is the chance to be cured by proper treatment or not to suffer any further harm by a complication arising out of it.[152] This is a distinct damage in itself which is quantified by a percentage of the actual loss corresponding to the likelihood of the chance. From this point of view, there is no problem of causality as the defendant is claimed to have set the *conditio sine qua non* for this peculiar loss.[153] The latter perspective starts from the actual loss suffered and argues that the defendant could have avoided causing such harm with a certain probability,[154] which then serves as the multiplier for calculating the ultimate amount of compensation due.

63 One argument at least against the first perspective re-interpreting damage is that the chance lost is not really a legally protected interest, at least not in the scenarios of interest here:[155] the patient after all argues that she lost the opportunity not to see her condition deteriorate, which clearly has no economic value in itself. Furthermore, as long as it remains uncertain whether the doctor really caused the deterioration of her condition, the theory of a loss of a chance cannot be of any help since it is exactly this chance which must necessarily remain doubtful as well.[156]

---

152 Cf FR no 50 (ad Case 1): 'lost opportunity not to have suffered such severe handicaps'.

153 *H Koziol* in: B Winiger/H Koziol/BA Koch/R Zimmermann (eds), Digest of European Tort Law I: Essential Cases on Natural Causation (2007) 10/29 no 3.

154 Cf *J Spier/O Haazen*, Comparative Conclusions on Causation, in: J Spier (ed), Unification of Tort Law: Causation (2000) 127, 151, who argue that 'the distinction between loss of a chance and alternative causation is somewhat arbitrary'.

155 Originally, the theory developed on the basis of cases concerning the lost chance of gaining something, such as winning a trial or during gambling, or making a profit out of an expected contract, all calculable losses made impossible by the misconduct of the defendant: *J-S Borghetti*, La réparation de la perte d'une chance en droit suisse et en droit français, (2008) 16 European Review of Private Law (ERPL) 1084, 1086.

156 *H Koziol* (fn 153) nos 5–7.

Despite such concerns, the theory is recognized and applied in practice in Belgium,[157] France,[158] Italy[159] and Spain[160] and is gaining influence in other countries as well.[161] Further jurisdictions remain reluctant[162] or refuse to adopt it.[163] 64

13. Multiple persons involved

(a) Vicarious liability for employees and other auxiliaries. It comes as no surprise that hospitals or doctors are liable for their staff in all jurisdictions under survey.[164] It is not equally universally true, however, that these auxiliaries can be held liable themselves (even if under separate 65

157 BE no 28, but see no 29: 'highly controversial' in cases of uncertain causation, 'theory ... clearly under pressure', but no change of jurisprudence yet.

158 FR no 19. See also *J-S Borghetti* (fn 155) *passim,* in particular 1089 ff, pointing at the fact that French law has never developed such a distinct notion of damage which would raise the concerns mentioned in no 63.

159 IT nos 32 ff ('possibility to achieve a different therapeutic result' missed, interpreted as an autonomous right).

160 Loss of a chance is typically seen as a matter of damage in Spain, not as a causal issue, and interpreted as a separate compensable head of non-pecuniary loss *sui generis*: ES nos 43–44, 110. However, since the percentage of the chance seems to have no impact upon the calculation of damages, at least in medical malpractice cases (ES nos 45–47), it remains doubtful whether it is really applied as conceived rather than a standard item of non-pecuniary loss. See also *J Solé Feliu*, The Reception of the Loss of a Chance Doctrine in Spanish Case-Law, (2008) 16 ERPL 1117, in particular at 1125 f: 'By qualifying the loss of a chance as a specific non-pecuniary loss head of damages, what Spanish courts really do is ... try to mask the true problem of causation under the cloak of damages.'

161 'Gradual acceptance' in the Netherlands (NL no 50); no clear position in England, though probably 'more No than Yes' (UK nos 31 ff). But see also *K Oliphant*, Loss of Chance in English Law, (2008) 16 ERPL 1073, 1074: 'Damages for loss of chance are, however, well established in English law in the context of lost economic gains.' *Idem* at 1080: 'English law has not so far embraced liability for loss of chance in relation to physical injuries, even if the door leading to them has yet to be firmly closed.'

162 CZ nos 70, 72 (not yet approved, but possible in personality rights cases); HU no 27 (but increasing the risk of loss may trigger liability, therefore moving towards loss of a chance seen as damage; 'tendency towards accepting it'). See also *A Menyhárd*, Natural Causation as Prerequisite for Liability in Hungarian Tort Law, (2008) 16 ERPL 1110.

163 AT nos 39, 42 (not necessary due to the possibility of proportional liability in cases of uncertain causation; see supra no 60); CH no 63; DE no 102; PL no 47; SE no 28. On the Austrian perspective, see also *BA Koch*, Der Verlust einer Heilungschance in Österreich, (2008) 16 ERPL 1051. On Germany, see *F Bien*, Schadensrechtliches Alles-oder-nichts-Prinzip und Beweislastumkehr beim groben Behandlungsfehler – Zum Umgang der deutschen Rechtsprechung mit Kausalitätszweifeln im Arzthaftungsprozess, (2008) 16 ERPL 1095.

164 AT no 44 (but limited in tort 'to rather rare cases' of dangerous or unfit helpers); BE no 30; CH nos 48–50, 65 (exculpation by proving proper organisation and lack of *culpa in eligendo, instruendo et custodiendo*); CZ nos 51, 73; DE nos 76–77; ES no 49; FR no 20; HU no 30; IT nos 23, 37; NL no 61; PL no 50; SE no 29; UK no 35.

conditions): while some jurisdictions confirm this (although it may be an unattractive route for claimants with an eye particularly to the deep pocket argument),[165] others have introduced limitations[166] or exclude such direct claims altogether in order to protect the employees.[167] A further argument for the latter is that the employers are in a better position to insure risks related to tasks they have undertaken. Similarly, employers who have indemnified the patients cannot seek unlimited recourse internally from their auxiliaries in all jurisdictions.[168]

66 **(b) Liability of an employed senior (supervising) doctor personally.** A related problem is addressed by the question of whether patients can directly seek indemnification from an intermediary employee of a hospital or other health care institution who acted as a supervisor during their treatment without personally participating in the tasks ultimately assigned to (and ill-performed by) subordinate doctors. This question is answered in the affirmative in several jurisdictions,[169] while some deny such a possibility.[170]

67 **(c) Operation performed in a hospital by a non-employee.** A different scenario is given if an external doctor not employed by the hospital uses the latter's resources, including parts of its staff, to perform an operation or other treatment on her patient.[171] In light of the foregoing, patients have to identify a suitable defendant. There are (at least) four different sub-scenarios:

- The external doctor herself made an error during the treatment.

68 Obviously, that doctor can be held liable individually. But jurisdictions are split when it comes to deciding whether she is the only possible

165 CH nos 66, 78 (but 'less attractive route'); DE no 150; ES no 49; IT no 36; NL no 61; UK no 35 (but 'theoretical').

166 AT nos 49–50; SE no 29 (only exceptionally, otherwise barred because employer expected to take out insurance cover).

167 CZ no 68; FR no 73; HU no 30 (immunity of the employee from claims falling within the scope of her employment); PL no 51.

168 Limitations apply eg in AT nos 51 ff, CZ no 73 (capped at 4.5 times average monthly salary of employee); HU no 30; PL no 53.

169 DE nos 104 ff; ES no 49; IT no 36 (unless instructions disregarded); PL no 50; SE no 30. Cf BE no 72 (quoting the 'captain of the ship' theory).

170 CH no 65; CZ nos 68–69.

171 Cf infra Case 1. This is uncommon in the Czech Republic, though: CZ no 75.

defendant,[172] or whether the hospital may be sued alternatively, even if it is not the doctor's employer. The latter solution, which is surprising at first sight, was introduced in order to facilitate the identification of the proper defendant for a patient who may not be in a position to immediately spot the proper addressee of her claim.[173]

- Hospital staff assisting the external doctor did something wrong while acting under the latter's instructions.

Disregarding the possibility to sue the staff members directly, which follows the general rules outlined above,[174] the question is whether patients have to focus on the external doctor alone,[175] whether they can only sue the hospital as the employer of the staff member at fault,[176] or whether they can choose between the two alternatively.[177] Again, the solutions offered by the jurisdictions under survey are diverse. **69**

- Nursing staff of the hospital did not handle the patient properly while the latter was recovering in the ward or in her room.

Apart from possible direct liability of the nursing staff, which again follows the general rules addressed earlier,[178] jurisdictions are in accord in this scenario that it is only the hospital as the employer that can be sued by the patient as long as they did not act upon the specific instructions of the external surgeon.[179] **70**

- Another external doctor (eg an anaesthetist) brought in by the external surgeon violated a duty of care.

While there can be no doubt that this second external doctor may face personal liability, the two more interesting options for patients include the surgeon and the hospital. While some jurisdictions will not allow either of the two alternatives to the first option, some will allow claims against the external surgeon despite the fact that it was neither her personal conduct that triggered the patient's harm nor her instructions to or supervision of **71**

172 AT nos 46–47, 63; CH no 68; DE no 130; PL no 55; UK no 35.

173 BE no 32 (statutory rule, unless express exclusion of liability by hospital beforehand); IT no 45; NL no 61, 63.

174 See no B13(a) no 65.

175 CH no 68; DE nos 130, 132; PL no 55; SE no 30.

176 CZ no 69; HU no 33; UK no 35.

177 AT no 47, BE nos 30, 32; DE no 152; NL no 61.

178 See no B13(a) no 65.

179 AT no 46; BE nos 30, 32; CH no 68; CZ no 69; DE nos 105, 153; ES no 49; HU no 33; PL no 55; SE no 30; UK no 35.

the other specialist.[180] In those jurisdictions which introduced a statutory basis to sue the hospital despite wrongdoing by the external surgeon,[181] patients will have that option also in this scenario.[182]

14. Strict liability

72 All jurisdictions have introduced product liability regimes based on the EC Directive's model.[183] There will consequently be strict liability for defective medical products or equipment,[184] and – unless covered by a separate statutory regime[185] – also for pharmaceuticals.[186] Nuclear medicine may be governed by the respective jurisdiction's nuclear liability regime.[187] More general clauses of strict liability may also play a certain role in medical scenarios in some countries.[188]

73 A special range of problems addressed by a specific regime in some countries are infections incurred during a hospital stay. Apart from the Swedish no-fault regime, France and Spain have also introduced provisions to that effect.[189]

C. Contractual Liability

15. Basics of contracts in the health care sector

74 Patients can by and large choose a hospital or private practitioner (though possibly limited to those who are accredited by or otherwise linked to a social insurance provider, typically via a contract),[190] and their mutual

180 AT no 47; DE no 132; NL no 64 (disputed).
181 Supra at fn 173.
182 BE no 32 (unless express ex ante exclusion); NL 61.
183 Even Switzerland has followed it: CH no 72.
184 A separate basis for liability may apply: see CZ no 77; ES no 52.
185 CZ no 80; DE no 157.
186 AT no 55; BE no 33; CH no 72; CZ no 80; DE no 157; FR no 15; HU no 38; NL no 94; PL no 57; SE nos 31 (medical product or apparatus), 34 (pharmaceuticals, but separate compensation scheme); UK no 37.
187 Eg AT no 56; DE no 157.
188 Cf HU no 36 (general clause applied in at least one case); NL no 63 (keeper of movable defective objects; in the medical context these might be needles or catheters, for example).
189 FR nos 15–16; ES no 52; SE no 31.
190 BE no 1–2, 10 (free choice of doctor, but channelled by incentives such as lower out-of-pocket payments if accredited physician is selected); DE no 143; ES no 7; HU no 6; PL no 8; SE no 5.

relationship is in most jurisdictions contractual[191] or at least treated as if it were,[192] even if these contracts may be subject to more or less far reaching statutory restrictions[193].

Apart from contracts for private treatment, this is neither true in England, however, where patients are directly eligible to receive benefits from the NHS due to its special nature,[194] nor in Spain or Switzerland for services rendered via the public health care system.[195] Equally in the Czech Republic, contract law seems to play no significant role in medical liability practice.[196] In France, the 2002 *loi Kouchner* has rendered the characterisation of the patient's relationship with the hospital or practitioner moot for purposes of liability.[197] **75**

If the patient's claim for compensation is indeed based upon a breach of contract, however, the starting point for the assessment of its validity is the scope of this contract. **76**

The personal scope of a contract (in particular the inclusion of third parties within the protective scope of the doctor-patient relationship)[198] varies according to each jurisdiction's way of addressing third parties in contract law in general, which is especially relevant for England.[199] **77**

The scope of contractual duties varies with the type of contractual arrangement: options include a pure doctor-patient contract to a variety of arrangements including or exclusively with a hospital, which may serve as anything ranging from hardly more than a hotel (though perhaps with special room service) to a fully-fledged health care service centre.[200] Further individuals or entities may come into play, such as additional individual doctors, therapists, midwives, nurses, but also insurers and other funds. This makes it sometimes difficult to discern who owed what to the patient, which in **78**

---

191 BE no 34; CH no 77; DE no 28.

192 Cf AT no 58; HU no 7; IT nos 8, 44. But see CZ no 82 (reluctance to interpret the tripartite relationship between the patient, the health care professional or institution and the public health insurance fund as contractual, rather a matter of social welfare).

193 BE no 37–38; HU no 41; NL no 65–67 (special contract type in the Civil Code); PL no 60.

194 UK nos 5, 39.

195 ES nos 7, 56; CH no 80. In private health care, however, medical services are provided on a contractual basis: ES no 54; CH no 77.

196 CZ nos 81 ff (see also no 84: 'almost all medical malpractice litigation stems from general tort law').

197 FR no 25.

198 Cf eg AT nos 61, 67. See infra no 83.

199 UK no 41. But see also CH nos 88, 152: 'The concept of contracts with protective effect for third parties has not hitherto been recognised in Swiss law.'

200 Cf the examples given by AT no 63; BE no 36; CH nos 78–79; ES no 55; IT no 43.

turn may complicate the latter's efforts to pursue a claim against a wrongdoer who is yet to be identified among the many parties involved.[201]

79 When focussing on the duties defining the medical treatment promised, all jurisdictions are in accord that the 'success' owed is of course not the healing of the patient,[202] but rather the provision of medical services according to the applicable professional standards of care.[203] Further duties include the obligation to properly inform the patient inter alia of possible risks of the treatment in advance.[204]

16. Differences to tort law

80 In countries where patients can pursue their claims either in tort law or on the basis of their contractual relationships alternatively,[205] the choice between the two depends upon the differences between them. Unless one of them is more favourable to the claimant, at least strategically, the selection will be irrelevant for the outcome of the case.

81 Apart from France, where delictual and contractual liability have been merged,[206] the latter is true in Belgium, England, Germany, Hungary, the Netherlands and Spain, where there are little if any practical differences between the two routes to compensation.[207]

82 Predominantly in the remaining countries, at least some significant differences can still be found which ultimately may tip the scales in favour of either path:

- In several countries, the burden of proving fault is reversed in favour of the claimant if she rests her case on the violation of a contractual duty instead of a delict.[208]

---

201 Cf supra nos 67 ff.

202 A foregone success owed may, however, be at stake, for example, in cases where the wrong limb was amputated.

203 Eg AT no 59; BE no 35; DE nos 80, 87; ES nos 28, 55; HU no 42.

204 See infra nos 85 ff.

205 Supra no 34 at fn 90.

206 FR no 22.

207 BE no 39 ('little practical difference'); DE no 160 ('in principal identical'); ES no 57 ('differences … not substantial'); HU no 43 ('differences … irrelevant'); NL no 68 ('hardly of any consequence'); UK no 40 ('no practical difference').

208 AT no 63; CH no 84 (but little practical impact); IT no 46; PL no 62; but see DE nos 87 f: corresponding rule does not apply in cases of medical malpractice unless risks within the control of the hospital or staff.

- Some jurisdictions are more generous when it comes to attributing the conduct of helpers and auxiliaries to their principal if the latter is sued under a contract theory.[209]
- The claimant's choice may make a further difference with respect to what will be indemnified, even though the variations in this regard are not all in her favour: in some countries, only foreseeable losses are deemed compensable under contractual liability.[210] A contract claimant may recover for pure economic loss,[211] whereas certain or even all non-pecuniary losses may only be indemnified in tort law.[212] Only the latter may allow the ad hoc mitigation of damages unlike contract law.[213]
- An important strategic difference concerns the timing of the claim: some reporters point at different prescription periods in contract law as compared to torts.[214]

17. Contractual claims in the absence of direct contracts?

The question of whether victims who are not themselves parties to a treatment contract can use the latter as a basis for potential claims against the health care professionals or the hospital who provided the treatment depends upon the jurisdiction's general approach towards third parties in contract law. Some countries see no problem at all in extending the protective scope of a contract to non-parties,[215] others find a workaround in construing a quasi-contractual relationship with the doctor or health **83**

209 AT no 69; CH no 85; HU no 42; but see DE no 160 (difference between full-fledged vicarious liability under § 278 BGB for contract claims and mere *culpa in eligendo vel custodiendo* according to § 831 BGB for tort claims 'is of no practical effect').

210 BE no 40 (unless intentional breach of contract); IT no 46 (but foreseeability requirement not relevant in personal injury cases such as medical malpractice: no 47).

211 DE no 160.

212 PL no 64 (non-pecuniary loss not compensated under contractual liability); CH no 86 (relatives can only claim their own non-pecuniary loss in tort).

213 HU no 42.

214 CH no 83 (one year for torts, ten years for contracts); ES no 57 (one year for torts, fifteen years for contracts); IT no 46 (five years for torts, ten for contracts); PL no 64.

215 AT no 71; DE no 163; NL no 69 (jurisprudence apparently more reluctant than academia). Cf supra no 77.

care institution even in the absence of a formal contractual agreement.[216] Still others are more restrictive.[217]

84 The case of an unconscious patient who requires emergency treatment to which she obviously cannot consent is often considered as negotiorum gestio (or benevolent intervention into another's affairs)[218] but still treated according to the principles that would govern a regular treatment contract.

18. Informed consent[219]

85 (a) **The informed consent doctrine.** In many jurisdictions under survey, the doctrine of informed consent has a growing or already well-settled impact upon medical malpractice claims.[220] After all, pointing the finger at the alleged omission of a doctor to properly instruct the patient about the upcoming treatment is significantly easier for the latter than claiming that the doctor did something wrong during the actual treatment. In fact, a deviation from medical standards during the performance of the treatment is irrelevant altogether – the patient may be indemnified irrespective of whether or not the doctor had been at fault or done everything right.

86 Among the thirteen countries under survey, only four[221] so far have ratified the 1997 European Convention on Human Rights and Biomedicine,[222] which in its Arts 5–9 lays down basic principles of the patients' right to information.[223] These and other jurisdictions have defined the scope of

---

216 IT nos 48–49. Cf ES no 55, where the Supreme Court holds that health insurers may be held liable for the '"contractual appearance" to ensure that the health care services will be provided under safe conditions'.

217 BE no 41; CH nos 88 (with the exception of patients lacking capacity to act who are within the protective scope of a treatment contract even if not a party thereto); ES no 59; UK no 41.

218 Eg AT no 58 (in fn 99); DE no 162; HU no 39. Cf BE no 42.

219 See also infra Case 4.

220 Cf AT no 72 ('of utmost importance for medical malpractice claims').

221 Czech Republic, Hungary, Spain, Switzerland.

222 CoE Convention for the Protection of Human Rights and Dignity of the Human Being with regard to the Application of Biology and Medicine, <http://conventions.coe.int/Treaty/en/Treaties/Html/164.htm>.

223 Art 5 provides:
'An intervention in the health field may only be carried out after the person concerned has given free and informed consent to it.
This person shall beforehand be given appropriate information as to the purpose and nature of the intervention as well as on its consequences and risks.
The person concerned may freely withdraw consent at any time.'

necessary information either in rather broad statutory language[224] or in a slightly more specific way.[225]

The doctrine of informed consent is of no apparent practical importance in Sweden, even though it is theoretically possible to bring it up in a tort case.[226] This rarely ever happens, however, due to the patient insurance scheme. The latter therefore also prevented the meteoric rise of this side-track of medical malpractice law as seen in other countries since Swedish patients have comparatively easier access to compensation anyhow. **87**

In the Czech Republic, lack of adequate information does not seem to play a major role in medical malpractice litigation either. After all, the burden of proof is not shifted onto the defendant,[227] but remains with the patient who has to prove that she did not validly consent.[228] **88**

(b) Burden of proof. If the patient rests her case on an alleged violation of duties of information preventing her to validly consent, the burden of proof typically rests upon her.[229] If instead she focuses on the tortious violation of her bodily integrity as a consequence of the treatment, arguing that it was wrongful in the absence of her valid ex ante approval, some jurisdictions see this differently: her consent then serves as a justification for the impact of the treatment on her body and thus as a defence for the doctor or hospital.[230] The burden of proof consequently shifts to the latter,[231] which gives the informed consent doctrine a significantly different strategic advantage. This is of course even more so true in those jurisdictions which shift the **89**

Art 6 aims at the protection of persons unable to consent, Art 7 addresses mentally disabled persons, Art 8 governs emergency situations, and Art 9 deals with previously expressed wishes of patients who at the time of the treatment could not be heard.

224 AT no 74 (even criminal law provision, whose violation also has implications on the tort law claim); HU no 47. See also the country-by-country overview in European Patients' Forum (ed), Patients' Rights in the European Union (<http://www.eu-patient.eu/Documents/Projects/Valueplus/Patients_Rights.pdf>).

225 BE no 42 (but no sanction attached to statutory rule in itself: no 43); CH no 91 ('statutory rules in particularly sensitive areas', in addition some cantonal provisions); ES no 62; FR nos 25, 76; NL no 66; PL no 67; SE no 38. On Sweden, see also *Hellbacher/Espersson/Johansson* (fn 103) 41 ff.

226 *Hellbacher/Espersson/Johansson* (fn 103) 42 ff.

227 See the next paragraph.

228 CZ no 97. Such proof seems to be difficult in court practice which apparently takes any slight evidence of risk disclosure for granted.

229 Eg AT no 73; BE nos 42–43; UK no 73. But see infra at fn 232.

230 Eg AT no 73; CZ no 88; DE nos 164–165; HU nos 48–49; IT no 51; PL nos 61, 68; SE no 38.

231 AT nos 73, 76; DE no 174. But see BE no 43 (patient has to prove absence of valid consent).

burden of proving that the patient was adequately informed to the health care institution or professional either way.[232]

90 The prime counter-argument refuting proof that adequate information was indeed missing is the fact that the patient would have gone ahead with the treatment even if all risks had been duly disclosed to her. As this argument obviously favours defendants, it typically falls on them to prove this, even if it had been their duty as well to establish proper information (which they failed to achieve).[233]

91 (c) **What needs to be disclosed?** All jurisdictions are in accord that the patient's needs to be informed about her diagnosis, the therapy recommended for her as well as the risks attached to it.[234] It is equally common to explain alternatives to the suggested treatment to the patient.[235] Further details expressly listed by some of the country reporters include the degree of urgency of her treatment,[236] its duration,[237] patient- and treatment-specific contraindications[238] as well as the impact of the treatment upon the patient's future lifestyle.[239] Perhaps not all jurisdictions would, however, consider details about the identity and qualifications of the staff assigned to the patient as necessary information for the patient,[240] at least if the latter has no choice in selecting these individuals. It is also interesting to note that French law requires doctors and hospitals to inform their patients about risks of the treatment discovered *after* it was performed upon them.[241]

92 While this is not expressly confirmed by all reporters,[242] one is left with the impression that courts tend to weigh up several factors when deciding

---

232 CH no 89; FR no 25 (statutory rule).

233 Eg AT no 78; CH no 90; but see DE no 172 (patient must show 'genuine decisional conflict'). In Belgium, where the burden of proof is already upon the patient (see fn 231), it is upon her to prove that she would have refused further treatment after full and adequate disclosure of all risks; BE no 43; similarly CZ no 172; UK no 73.

234 AT no 73; BE no 42; CH no 93; CZ no 91; ES no 62; FR no 25; HU no 47; IT nos 51–52; NL no 70; PL no 70.

235 AT nos 144–145 (risk decisive); BE no 42; CZ no 91; HU no 47; NL no 70. Cf DE no 272: no duty to disclose alternatives as long as chosen method 'at least equivalent to the alternative treatments in terms of prospects of success and risk'.

236 BE no 42; FR no 25.

237 BE no 42; HU no 47.

238 BE no 42; ES no 62; HU no 49 (in fn 38); IT no 52.

239 HU no 47.

240 But see AT no 65; CZ no 91 (but in practice typically not given); HU no 47.

241 FR nos 25, 76.

242 Cf AT no 77.

about the range of details in general and risks in particular that need to be disclosed to the patients upfront.

Certainly the urgency of the treatment is among those factors – the less vital the intended treatment is for the patient, the more risks she needs to know beforehand in order to have a sufficient basis for deciding whether or not to proceed.[243] On the other hand, in an emergency situation the first responders obviously need not delay their life-saving measures by trying to inform the patients about the potential risks thereof (if they are capable of grasping that information under the circumstances at all).[244] **93**

One side-aspect thereof is whether there is a probability threshold determined by statistical data below which risks no longer need to be disclosed. This is universally denied, even though the exact percentage of likelihood as typically determined by a medical expert may play at least a minor role in the overall assessment.[245] **94**

This leads to the question of whether patients need to learn about remote risks at all. While some jurisdictions answer this in the affirmative,[246] others seem to be more generous[247] or limit this to 'extremely serious' risks,[248] at least in cases of voluntary treatment like plastic surgery.[249] Belgium seems to have undergone quite a significant change in this respect in recent years: while Belgian courts originally required doctors to inform their patients only about 'normal and foreseeable' risks, this has now been extended to all risks 'relevant' for the patient's decision, which may also include exceptional risks.[250] **95**

Information may be withheld altogether if it might seriously harm the patient or it would otherwise be in the patient's best interests.[251] Ultimately, the individual needs of the actual patient and not of some imaginary average reasonable and knowledgeable individual are decisive **96**

243 See also infra at fn 249.
244 BE no 42; CZ no 89; ES no 65; FR no 25; IT no 51.
245 AT 79 (plays a role, but not decisive in itself); CH no 93 (generally not used); UK no 42 ('impossible to state any statistical formula for what must be disclosed'). Cf also BE no 70: 1 % likelihood as rule of thumb, even less frequent risks only if very serious consequences.
246 AT no 77; FR no 25; UK no 42 (see in particular fn 61).
247 Eg PL no 70 (very rare complications need not be disclosed).
248 Eg HU no 49.
249 ES no 62 (in case of medically-indicated treatment infrequent or atypical risks need not be disclosed if exceptional; more far-reaching duties for voluntary treatment); NL no 70 (only 'common, foreseeable risks', but more if treatment not urgent).
250 BE no 44.
251 AT no 77; CH no 94; NL no 70.

when it comes to determining what she needs to know and with what risks she can be burdened in order to make an adequately informed decision.[252]

97 **(d) Formalities.** Adequate information needs to be given to the patient well ahead of the commencement of the treatment so that she still has sufficient time to weigh the pros and cons thereof and to come to a reasoned decision as to whether or not to go ahead with it.[253]

98 It seems self-evident that the patient needs to be informed in a way that is intelligible to her which, for those who do not speak the same language as the doctor, means that she needs the assistance of an interpreter to the extent possible.[254]

99 Jurisdictions are split when it comes to the form of the information. Some require that the patient expressly agrees to the treatment and do not accept a merely implied consent as others do.[255] Among the former, some even insist on a written declaration, though only if the planned treatment is invasive, while they do not impose a form requirement for non-invasive measures.[256] Yet others do not insist on any form at all.[257]

D. Public Liability

19. Key differences from cases involving private hospitals or doctors

100 In most jurisdictions under survey, neither substantive nor procedural laws provide for different rules that would apply to public healthcare

---

252 CH no 92; DE no 172; ES no 64; HU nos 47, 49; UK no 42 (in fn 60).

253 AT no 75; equally CH no 92.

254 See also Case 4 below. As to Hungary, cf *S Defloor et al*, Patient Rights in the EU – Hungary (European Ethical-Legal Papers N°11, 2007, available at <https://www.kuleuven.be/cbmer/viewpic.php?TABLE=DOCS&ID=550>) 13.

255 Eg BE nos 42, 69. See also HU no 47: 'accessible manner that accords with his age, knowledge, experience and physical and emotional status'.

256 ES no 64; PL no 68 (but lack of writing has only evidential consequences); as to Hungary, see *S Defloor et al* (fn 254) 14 (writing or oral statement in the presence of two witnesses in case of invasive procedures).

257 AT no 75 (even the opposite – writing insufficient, oral explanation or at least some possibility to ask questions is required, though writing still remains useful as evidence); BE no 69 (writing only if requested; 'clear indication that the legislator … wanted to discourage the use of written consent forms in daily medical practice'); CZ no 93 (but writing required for refusal of treatment); NL no 70 (written only if requested).

institutions only and deviate from those applicable to private entities and practitioners.[258]

In France, with the adoption of the *loi Kouchner* in 2002, substantive law dissimilarities were abolished. However, claims against public entities still have to be filed with the administrative court system, so procedural differences remain.[259] **101**

Both procedural and substantive differences are still reported from Spain[260] and Switzerland,[261] however, with respect to treatment provided by public health care institutions as compared to their private counterparts: **102**

- In Spain, public entities are strictly liable for damage that 'results from the normal or abnormal operation of public services.'[262] However, this applies only in cases of a breach of a statutory rule or some organisational defect. Claims can only be brought against the public entity and not against the health care professional who actually caused the harm. Cases are heard before the competent administrative courts.
- In Switzerland, not only do the applicable rules depend upon whether institutions were established under either public or private law, but on top of that regional diversity comes into play: apart from federal, also cantonal public law may apply, depending upon which territorial authority is in charge of the public health care institution. For medical malpractice claims, cantons may provide that their own liability regime pre-empts corresponding federal private law which would govern instead. 'To date, all Cantons have made use of their power to legislate in this area'.[263] Differences concern inter alia the fact that, like in Spain, liability is channelled towards the state (excluding the possibility of direct claims against the staff members) and does not depend upon fault. Also, the respective cantonal statute of limitations applies. As to procedure, courts with general jurisdiction over private law matters may (but need not necessarily) be competent to hear cases on cantonal public law liability.[264]

---

258 AT no 79; BE no 45; CZ no 98; DE no 177; HU no 50; IT no 54; NL no 71; PL nos 56, 72–73 (but no-fault liability only applicable to public hospitals under exceptional circumstances); SE no 42.

259 FR no 26.

260 ES nos 56, 66 ff.

261 CH nos 95 ff.

262 ES no 66.

263 CH no 98.

264 CH no 103.

E. Alternative compensation regimes

20. Funds and/or other alternative compensation regimes

103 In the majority of countries covered, no fund or other alternative compensation regime exists that would absorb at least parts of the losses patients sustain due to medical malpractice or other adverse events related to the provision of health care.[265] However, some countries have installed specialized funds dealing with specific health care problems. These include funds for victims of a vaccination campaign[266] or for HIV or hepatitis C infections during blood transfusions.[267]

104 In five of the countries presented in this volume, fund solutions covering medical malpractice losses have been introduced instead which range from rather limited concepts, as in Austria,[268] to a more far-reaching regime, as in France, which served as a model for Belgium and Poland[269] and finally, to a fully-fledged no-blame[270] compensation scheme as exists in Sweden.[271]

105 The first two varieties are only designed as backup systems in case classic tort law does not offer a successful path towards compensation, whereas the Swedish model systematically encompasses all claims including those where patients would also be compensated under tort law.[272] Neither of the three prevents patients from opting for the classic court route instead, however, even though the fact that this may be a dead end serves at least as a theoretical prerequisite for payments out of the Austrian and French funds. While the Austrian provincial funds are only accessible for hospital

---

265 BE no 46 (but plans for Scandinavian-type no-fault insurance scheme, not put into force, may be replaced by a French-style regime); CH no 104 (2002 proposal not yet implemented); CZ nos 99 ff (ad hoc financial aid foreseen by statute never applied); DE no 178; HU no 51; PL no 74; UK no 44.

266 UK no 45; IT no 56; cf AT no 57 (state liability regime).

267 AT no 84; ES nos 74 ff; FR nos 27 ff; IT no 56.

268 AT nos 80–82.

269 FR nos 27 ff. The French system is critically reviewed by *S Taylor*, Providing Redress for Medical Accidents in France: Conflicting Aims, Effective Solutions? (2011) 1 JETL 57. As to Belgium and Poland see infra nos 145–146.

270 *Essinger* (fn 40) 2.

271 SE no 43. See also *Hellbacher/Espersson/Johansson* (fn 103) *passim*.

272 The French model at least has the potential of serving as a more far-reaching solution inasmuch as it offers compensation to those suffering more serious harm irrespective of fault, which may attract also those patients who would have a valid claim in tort but instead of litigating it prefer to be indemnified via the fast-track route offered by the ONIAM.

patients,[273] their French and Swedish counterparts are open to all patients, including those harmed by private practitioners.[274] Unlike the Austrian,[275] both the French and the Swedish scheme also include other adverse events in the health care area which may or may not be covered by separate regimes elsewhere,[276] such as nosocomial infections,[277] the afore-mentioned HIV or hepatitis C infections in the course of blood transfusions or complications during vaccination campaigns.[278]

All three models are financed in a distinct way: the Austrian funds are filled **106** by contributions from all inpatients, ie by the potential claimants themselves,[279] which moves this model towards something like a mandatory state-run first-party insurance, though not based upon actuarial principles and without granting the 'insured' a claim for payments, not even under certain conditions, as payments out of this fund are entirely discretionary. In France, the financing of the ONIAM regime is controlled the by the state directly, budgeted in the law that also assigns state funds to the social security system.[280] In Sweden, on the other hand, the traditional core of the patient insurance scheme is just that – it started off as a voluntary joint effort of the regions and four major insurers, and even though it was redesigned inter alia due to competition law issues, it is still effectively building upon the fact that the health care providers have to take out medical malpractice insurance, and the combined premia constitute the funds out of which payments are made. However, the state via its regions covers around 90 % of the Swedish health care, and the premia these pay into their own insurance company are therefore ultimately (though indirectly) financed from tax monies.[281]

273 AT no 80 (in fn 155).

274 While in Sweden claims arising out of a treatment by a private dentist or one of the few private practitioners unaffiliated to one of the regions (the latter being in charge of most medical services) still fall under the same Patient Injury Act, they have to be addressed to a different claims handler institution; see *Hellbacher/Espersson/Johansson* (fn 103) 14.

275 In Austria, special funds have been created to cover HIV or hepatitis C infections; AT no 84.

276 As just mentioned supra no 103.

277 FR no 30. For details on the Swedish system in this respect, see *Hellbacher/Espersson/Johansson* (fn 103) 33 ff.

278 FR no 32; on the ex gratia payments to Hepatitis C victims in Sweden, see <http://www.patientforsakringen.se/Hepatit-C.html>.

279 AT no 80.

280 FR no 27.

281 See *Essinger* (fn 40) 2: 'The premiums to the insurance company are paid directly from the regions according to the number of inhabitants in the region. The premium is not risk based per region or hospital. There are no government subsidies to the insurance. The premium is paid from the regional income tax. The cost for the insurance is 10 dollars per inhabitant and year.'

107 Claimants in all three systems must prove that the worsening of their condition was caused by the treatment,[282] so none of the regimes offer a workaround for problems in this particular respect that may prevent patients also from pursuing a tort action. However, once their injuries are linked to the treatment as such, the conduct of the health care personnel involved need not be assessed any further. In particular, it is not necessary to link the patient's condition to the conduct of any specific professional, let alone the latter's fault. The Swedish model requires that the patient's 'injury could have been avoided', which is purposefully stated in a way that avoids blame terminology. It nevertheless effectively aims at misconduct, though not necessarily of a blameworthy kind.[283]

108 Furthermore, again all three regimes require that the patient suffers from an abnormal consequence of the treatment, which excludes payments out of the fund in cases where the patient's present condition is a mere natural consequence of her pre-condition or an unavoidable outcome of the treatment.[284] 'Catastrophic' losses, ie rare and particularly severe consequences of a treatment, even if foreseeable, are still covered in Austria[285] and France,[286] however, but not in Sweden.[287]

109 A further prerequisite for compensation in Austria and France not mirrored in Sweden, as already mentioned, is that tort liability cannot or at least may not be established without requiring that the patient gave it a try, though.[288] If in the course of handling the patient's application it turns out that a doctor or hospital can be held liable, the French claims handling procedure foresees

---

282 AT no 81; FR no 29 ('directly attributable to acts of prevention, diagnosis or care'). For Sweden, see *Hellbacher/Espersson/Johansson* (fn 103) 17: 'In order for an injury to be considered compensable there must first be a causal relationship between the injury and the medical service. The patient is charged with the burden of proof of showing that such a causal relationship exists.'

283 The 'two most common reasons for rejecting patient compensation claims since the onset of the patient insurance system' are either lack of a causal link between the treatment and the adverse condition complained of or the fact that the latter is an unavoidable consequence of the former. *Hellbacher/Espersson/Johansson* (fn 103) 16.

284 AT no 81; FR no 29. On Sweden, see *Hellbacher/Espersson/Johansson* (fn 103) 19 ff (including the examples on p 21).

285 AT no 81.

286 Cf *Taylor* (fn 269) 60.

287 *Hellbacher/Espersson/Johansson* (fn 103) 47 f: a provision allowing compensation for extraordinary consequences of a treatment despite other requirements missing was dropped. A reform commission in the meantime proposed to re-introduce it into the statute, however, apparently to no avail so far.

288 AT no 81; FR no 29.

that the file is passed on to the competent liability insurer, who in turn has to make a reasonable offer of indemnification to the patient.[289]

Unlike Austria and Sweden[290], the French compensation scheme requires **110**
that the treatment caused harm with a certain minimum degree of gravity.[291]

Compensation is calculated on an ad hoc basis in Austria, though typically **111**
following regional guidelines which in turn were at least inspired by the tort system. The French regime comes with its own 'référentiel indicatif d'indemnisation'.[292] The Swedish system incorporates the standard rules of tort law,[293] though subject to limitations: not only are there lower limits (in the form of deductibles).[294] but also caps on the overall amounts that can be paid out under this scheme.[295] Maximum limits of compensation were also introduced for the Austrian funds.[296] In all three systems, not only pecuniary, but also non-pecuniary loss will be indemnified, though subject to the limitations of the fund regime itself and/or due to restrictions resulting from the respective jurisdiction's general rules on the compensability of losses or on tort remedies.

The success rate of these models with respect to its effect on medical **112**
malpractice litigation is quite diverse: 99.9 % of all claims in Sweden are resolved within the patient insurance scheme, with only a handful of cases brought before the ordinary court system each year.[297] In France, on the other hand,[298] 'ONIAM is called on to defend an increasing number of actions contesting its decisions',[299] and the percentage of claims litigated in court is clearly far beyond the Swedish figure.[300]

---

289 FR no 47.

290 See *Hellbacher/Espersson/Johansson* (fn 103) 20: 'Neither the severity nor the rarity of the injury has any bearing on the patient's right to compensation.'

291 FR no 29.

292 Text available at <http://www.oniam.fr/textes/referentiel_oniam_20090701.pdf>.

293 SE nos 44, 49.

294 In 2011, patients have to bear the first SEK 2,140 (approx € 240) themselves: <http://www.patientforsakringen.se/Vilken-ersattning-kan-du-fa.html>.

295 The maximum in 2011 stands at SEK 42.8 million (approx € 4.8 million) per event and SEK 8.6 million (approx € 960,000) per patient; see § 10 of the Patient Injury Act.

296 AT no 82 (in fn 163).

297 *Essinger* (fn 40) 5.

298 Data on Austria is missing inasmuch as the activity reports of the hospital funds only list those cases which have already been previously filtered by the patient advocacies; furthermore, they do not keep track of the fate of the claims left unsettled.

299 *Taylor* (fn 269) 72.

300 See the data provided by ONIAM itself in its most recent report of activities (<http://www.oniam.fr/rapport/RapportOniam2009sem2.pdf>) at pp 13 ff: ONIAM was involved in 1,203 court cases at the end of 2009. Considering that the number of claims received during that calendar year was hardly more than double (3,615), this is quite

F. Extent of Liability/Remedies

I. Pecuniary loss

21. Introduction to indemnifying pecuniary loss

113 All jurisdictions under survey pursue the principle of full compensation.[301] It is therefore hard to imagine that a panoramic view will detect any fundamental differences concerning the various heads of compensable loss and the way that they are being indemnified, even though there may of course be differences in detail, particularly when it comes to calculating the exact amount of damages.[302] This is not the place, however, to offer a comprehensive analysis of all possible deviations beyond the few aspects addressed immediately in the following.[303] Some detailed glimpses at the practice in all countries will be given in the course of the case analyses below.[304]

114 What is more important in this context is the fact that victims of medical malpractice are subject to the same rules and practices of the law of remedies as any other tort (or contract[305]) claimant.[306]

115 One should therefore also keep in mind that some jurisdictions allow judges (only) in tort law to reduce the ultimate award ad hoc for equitable reasons, which is equally extended to medical liability, of course.[307]

---

remarkable, even if one has to discount in a direct comparison cases that were filed in previous years but are still pending. In the second half of 2009, for example, 270 new cases were filed in the court system, as compared to 1,752 filings in that same period.

301 Eg ES no 82; FR no 36; HU no 53; NL no 75; PL no 76.

302 Cf *BA Koch/H Koziol*, Comparative Analysis, in: BA Koch/H Koziol (eds), Compensation for Personal Injury in a Comparative Perspective (2003) 407, 419 ff, pointing inter alia at differences regarding fictitious treatment costs not actually spent and other facets. Differences with respect to damages for wrongful death, where further complications arise due to the fact that it is not the immediate victim who claims compensation, are further elaborated by *C Wendehorst*, Wrongful Death and Compensation for Pecuniary Loss, in: H Koziol/B Steininger (eds), European Tort Law 2006 (2008) 35.

303 A comprehensive analysis of almost thirty European jurisdictions is given by B Winiger/H Koziol/BA Koch/R Zimmermann (eds), Digest of European Tort Law 2: Essential Cases on Damage (2011). See further *U Magnus*, Comparative Report on the Law of Damages, in: U Magnus (ed), Unification of Tort Law: Damages (2001) 185.

304 Infra nos 153 ff.

305 Cf nos 74 ff, in particular no 82.

306 AT no 90; CH no 113; CZ no 112; DE no 180; FR no 33; HU no 54; NL no 73; PL no 75; SE no 44 (but see the limitations applying to the patient insurance scheme, supra no 111).

307 CZ no 111; ES no 57; NL nos 76, 81; for Sweden see ch 6 § 2 *skadeståndslag*, English translation in: K Oliphant/B Steininger (eds), European Tort Law: Basic Texts (2011) 261.

22. Loss of earnings vs loss of earning capacity

One area where at least dogmatic differences remain between the legal systems analysed concerns a specific variety of future losses. While all jurisdictions invariably offer compensation for both past earnings (eg during treatment and rehabilitation) and future income calculated on the basis of what the claimant was paid during his previous employment, the picture is more diverse when the patient was in fact not salaried at all before the damaging event. Some jurisdictions stick to offering compensation for loss of (hypothetical) earnings,[308] while others shift the focus and are more or less willing to indemnify the claimant's reduced or lost earning capacity as such.[309] **116**

One specific aspect thereof concerns patients who had worked in the family household before and are now no longer able to do so (or not to the same degree as before). Some jurisdictions will indemnify this loss itself by awarding the equivalent of the labour market value of such household work,[310] others award only the cost of obtaining a substitute (and therefore not the loss of housekeeping capacity itself)[311] or nothing at all.[312] **117**

23. Periodic payments or lump sum?

The second aspect chosen as an illustration for deviations in detail concerns practicalities of how compensation is actually paid out. If a patient has lost her source of income, for example, she may be compensated either by way of a lump sum payment, with all future income capitalised, or by way of an annuity, for example corresponding to the frequency of the foregone payments she would have received from her employer. The former has the advantage of a once-and-for-all settlement, reducing the risk of future **118**

---

308 DE nos 192 ff (earning capacity not compensable, but potential workaround via possibility for court to determine future loss of earnings on a broader factual basis); HU nos 55–56 ('presumed loss of earnings', if necessary based on average earnings); SE no 46.

309 AT no 91 (due to objective approach to calculating the loss); BE no 49 (as damages *ex aequo et bono*); CH nos 114 ff (but 'merely abstract loss of earning power is not indemnified'); CZ no 114 (but only via alternative route – non-pecuniary loss of social dignity or other personality right); ES nos 84 ff ('most common practice'); FR no 34; IT no 62; NL no 78; PL no 85 (but '[s]ome pecuniary consequences of the loss must be proven'); but see UK no 47 (doubtful). Cf infra Case 3 (no 184).

310 Eg AT no 91 (labour market value); CH no 117; CZ no 114 (but only via alternative route – non-pecuniary loss of social dignity or other personality right); IT no 62.

311 UK no 47.

312 SE no 46. An extensive comparative survey of these specific problems is given by E Karner/K Oliphant (eds), Loss of Housekeeping Capacity (2011). Cf infra Case 6 (no 212).

insolvency of the defendant and – often overlooked – allowing the claimant to get on with her life without being reminded of the damaging event periodically. An annuity, on the other hand, may come closer to compensation of what the claimant actually lost, as eventualities such as life expectancy will have an immediate impact on the overall payments.[313]

119 Some jurisdictions therefore favour periodic payments,[314] though with an exceptional possibility to opt for a lump sum award instead,[315] others instead prefer the latter option as a rule.[316] Still others stay neutral in this regard and allow both options alternatively.[317]

24. Caps and thresholds

120 No tort law under survey provides for caps or thresholds restricting the extent of compensation that may be awarded to the patient.[318] The only slight exceptions to both concern product liability, where Spain has introduced upper limits,[319] and where all Member States had to implement the EC Directive's lower threshold for property losses.[320]

121 However, for those jurisdictions that have installed a more or less general compensation fund regime, limitations apply as already mentioned.[321] This is particularly noteworthy for Sweden, where the patient insurance scheme in practice (though not in theory) effectively replaced tort liability.

---

313 Cf *Koch/Koziol* (fn 302) 430 f.

314 AT no 92; CZ no 117; DE no 198; PL no 88.

315 AT no 92; CZ no 118 (requires written agreement between parties); DE no 199 (if 'compelling reasons'); PL no 88 ('for important reasons and upon the victim's request').

316 ES no 87 (but increasingly also periodic payments); IT no 65 (despite statutory rule to the contrary); UK no 49 (now general discretion of courts to award periodical payments, though lump sums still common and many awards would be a mixture of both).

317 BE no 50 (at request of claimant); CH no 118; FR no 35; HU no 57 (courts 'resistant to awarding lump sum compensation'); NL no 80 (choice of claimant, in practice mostly lump sum); SE no 47 (but annuity if 'of essential importance for the support of the victim': ch 5 § 4 *skadeståndslag*).

318 AT no 93; BE no 51; CH no 121; DE no 200; FR no 36; HU no 61; IT no 66; PL no 89; UK no 51. A statutory limit for compensating non-pecuniary loss of personality rights in the Czech Republic is 'not … conclusive anymore': CZ no 119 (free discretion).

319 ES no 93.

320 This will, however, play a role if, for example, the patient's clothing was ruined in the course of a treatment with a defective apparatus.

321 Supra no 110 f.

II. Non-pecuniary loss

25. Introduction to indemnifying non-pecuniary loss

(a) **Classifications.** Apart from Poland,[322] victims can be indemnified for non-pecuniary loss[323] under either tort or contract law. Some specialties are worth mentioning, however: **122**

In the Czech Republic and in Poland, an interference with a patient's bodily integrity can at the same time constitute a classic tort and a violation of a personality right,[324] which gives access to a separate line of remedies. Court practice in the Czech Republic thereby effectively allows a double indemnification of non-pecuniary loss under both headings cumulatively,[325] whereas the Polish practice strictly distinguishes between the two.[326] **123**

Similarly in Sweden, an alternative basis for awarding non-pecuniary loss is given if the medical professional had acted criminally, in which case the so-called *kränkning* may be indemnified, which is independent from the immaterial consequence of the bodily injury.[327] This may also become an option for patients whose consent to the treatment was based on insufficient information.[328] **124**

---

322 PL nos 64, 91 (in contract cases only available if breach of contractual duty also constitutes a tort).

323 Within the meaning of the definition by *WVH Rogers*, Comparative Report of a Project Carried Out by the European Centre of Tort and Insurance Law, in: WVH Rogers (ed), Damages for Non-Pecuniary Loss in a Comparative Perspective (2001) 245, 246: 'By this expression we understand what is also referred to as non-patrimonial loss, that is to say, loss which is not damage to a person's assets or wealth or income and which is therefore incapable of being quantified in any objective financial manner by reference to a market. What remains, however, is a very broad field. It covers, for example, not only physical bodily injury and injury to physical and mental health, except in so far as these matters produce loss of income or generate expenses (which are pecuniary or patrimonial losses) but also anxiety and mental distress and "symbolic" losses which the law may regard as flowing from matters like interference with personal liberty or reputation.'

324 In the case of Poland, the separate claim in medical malpractice cases can be based upon the violation of a right as embodied in the Patients' Rights Act; PL no 93. See also UK no 21.

325 The forthcoming new Civil Code shall overcome this duality; CZ no 127.

326 See the case cited in PL no 93 fn 45, which is also reported by *E Bagińska*, Poland, in: H Koziol/B Steininger (eds), European Tort Law 2008 (2009) 499, 511 ff: damages based on the violation of the patient's rights cannot be awarded if not claimed specifically.

327 SE no 52.

328 SE no 53.

125 Since the Italian *Codice civile* originally foresaw damages for pain and suffering (*danno morale*) only under very narrow conditions,[329] a work-around developed in doctrine and subsequently also endorsed by court practice offers compensation under a different theory – instead of suffering ensuing from bodily harm, the focus of the alternative route is on a violation of the victim's personal integrity in addition to (and separate from) the attack on her physical integrity (*danno biologico*).[330] While the latter is referred to as *danno extra-patrimoniale* (valued objectively, as compared to the traditional *danno morale*, which is *danno non-patrimoniale* assessed subjectively), neither is aiming at the compensation of material harm, so both would have to be counted as damages for immaterial harm under the traditional dichotomy.[331]

126 'Psycho-physical or biological damage' is also recognised as a separate non-pecuniary head of damage in Spain.[332] Further 'specific personal detriments' are indemnified as separate categories such as aesthetic damage.[333] The latter is also true in Austria, but categorised as pecuniary damage there.[334]

127 **(b) Assessment of the loss.** Damages for non-pecuniary loss are typically compensated by a lump-sum payment[335] calculated by way of an equitable assessment of the circumstances of the case.[336] Tables typically drawn up by practitioners and/or academics serve as unofficial and non-binding, but still

329 Art 2059 Codice civile allows damages for non-pecuniary loss only if expressly allowed by statutory law, which essentially was only true for torts that also constituted a criminal offence. This narrow interpretation was given up by the Italian Supreme Court in the case cited IT no 67 fn 106. On this decision, see also *E Bargelli*, Italy, in: H Koziol/B Steininger (eds), European Tort Law 2003 (2004) 267, 267 ff. Nevertheless, the meanwhile long-established *danno biologico* continues to be available to tort victims.

330 IT nos 67 ff; on the development see also *FD Busnelli/G Comandé*, Italy, in: WVH Rogers (ed), Damages for Non-Pecuniary Loss in a Comparative Perspective (2001) 135. This development bears some resemblance to the Czech alternative route via an infringement of personality rights; supra no 123.

331 *Busnelli/Comandé* (fn 330) 138. Cf the definition supra fn 323.

332 ES no 97. But see *M Martín Casals/J Ribot/J Solé*, Spain, in: WVH Rogers (ed), Damages for Non-Pecuniary Loss in a Comparative Perspective (2001) 192, 193 ff, distinguishing the Italian *danno biologico* from the Spanish *daño corporal*.

333 ES no 98.

334 AT no 88.

335 Eg AT no 95; CZ no 117; ES no 100; but see DE no 210.

336 Eg AT no 94 (but no subjective criteria like specific sensitivity used, only objective ones like type of injury); CH nos 125, 130; DE nos 205–206; NL no 82; PL no 92.

persuasive guidelines.[337] In the Czech Republic, an official point system was decreed, although it led to unsatisfactorily low awards.[338]

The amounts awarded differ dramatically throughout the jurisdictions surveyed. The maximum amounts reported vary from € 50,000 to € 680,000.[339] **128**

26. Who can claim compensation for non-pecuniary loss?

Apart from claims passed on by way of inheritance,[340] the death of a direct victim may also generate a claim for bereavement damages by her relatives or other persons close to her.[341] While this is true in most jurisdictions covered here,[342] Germany, the Netherlands and Sweden deny this and only consider to indemnifying relatives if they have suffered a nervous shock and therefore have incurred a medical condition of their own.[343] In non-fatal cases, however, only few jurisdictions allow claims for the non-pecuniary loss of relatives who experience the consequences of a serious bodily injury of the (surviving) direct victim.[344] **129**

---

337 AT no 95 (base amounts per degree of non-pecuniary loss plus commercial publication); CH no 130 fn 340; DE no 209 (survey by commercial publishers); ES no 101; IT nos 70–72 (but statutory point system for *danno biologico* caused by traffic accidents; more flexibility for *danno morale*, even though previously perceived as fraction of *danno biologico*); NL no 83; SE no 50 (charts developed for traffic insurance, but also used in other areas); UK no 52 ('flexible judicial tariff system'). Belgian practice tends to use a so-called 'tableau indicatif' compiled by practitioners for guidance (current version available at <http://www.fcga-gmwf.be/documents/AN_INDEMNISATION.pdf>). Even if in the absence of such tables, courts still aim at harmonious ranges of awards by looking at previous awards: HU no 63.

338 CZ no 124.

339 AT no 95 (€ 250,000); CH no 132 (€ 150,000); CZ no 129 (€ 680,000); DE no 210 (€ 500,000 plus monthly pension of € 500); ES no 101 (€ 300,000); HU no 63 fn 59 (€ 50,000); NL no 83 (€ 150,000); PL no 94 (€ 125,000); UK no 52 (€ 310,000).

340 Eg BE no 54; IT no 75. Jurisdictions are split as to whether or not to allow claims for non-pecuniary loss acquired by way of inheritance even if not raised by the deceased herself; see *Rogers* (fn 323) 259 f.

341 See generally *WVH Rogers*, Death and Non-Pecuniary Loss, in: H Koziol/B Steininger (eds), European Tort Law 2006 (2008) 52, 56 ff.

342 AT no 96 (but qualified fault required); BE no 54; CH nos 126, 135; CZ nos 125 (statutory lump sum), 131 f (additional award via infriction of personality right possible); ES no 102; FR no 38; HU no 65; IT no 73 (own danno biologico); PL no 95 (introduced by statutory amendment); UK no 53 (flat rate statutory claim for selected relatives).

343 DE nos 211 ff (only close relatives); NL nos 85 f (statutory proposal to introduce lump-sum damages for bereavement failed); SE nos 54 f (but psychological injuries presumed under objective criteria, court practice therefore *de facto* close to awarding damages for mere bereavement).

344 CH nos 127, 136; CZ no 131 (claim based upon violation of own personality right, eg right to family life); ES no 102.

130 The range of eligible people is defined by family ties, the closeness of the relationship and whether or not the claimant had shared a common household with the direct victim; the ways these factors are used (either selectively or combined) differ from country to country.[345]

131 With the exception of the Czech Republic and England, where statutory lump sums apply,[346] compensation for bereavement is assessed on a case-by-case basis similar to other non-pecuniary losses. Again, the amounts awarded differ significantly.[347]

G. Procedural Matters

27. Specific rules of jurisdiction or procedure

132 Most jurisdictions do not provide for special rules that apply solely to medical malpractice claims.[348]

133 An exception thereto can be found in England, where a special pre-action protocol[349] was drawn up by the Clinical Disputes Forum, which in turn was installed in the course of the Woolf reforms.[350]

---

345 While spouses, parents and minor children are invariably deemed eligible, if anyone at all, it is not equally universally true that, for example, grand-parents or others may successfully claim damages for bereavement. Cf the reports cited in fn 342.

346 CZ no 125 (€ 9,600 for all eligible claimants but siblings, who receive € 7,000); UK no 53 (€ 14,000 for all eligible claimants alike).

347 Taking the example of parents, awards range from € 3,750 (non-cohabitant parents in Belgium, double for cohabitants, see the *tableau indicatif* cited in fn 337) to € 20,000 (AT no 96 fn 196).

348 AT no 97; BE no 55; CH nos 138 ff (apart from division between ordinary or administrative courts, see no 102); DE no 214 (but heavier duty on lower courts to establish the facts, triggering more extensive judicial investigations); FR no 39; HU no 66 (statutory rules on mediation in the health care sector, but no experiences with it yet); IT no 76; PL no 97; SE no 57.

349 The protocol defines best practice for pre-action conduct. As Lord Woolf argued in ch 10 of his final report on 'Access to Justice' (<http://www.dca.gov.uk/civil/final/contents.htm >), pre-action protocols 'are intended to build on and increase the benefits of early but well-informed settlements which genuinely satisfy both parties to a dispute. The purposes of such protocols are:
(a) to focus the attention of litigants on the desirability of resolving disputes without litigation;
(b) to enable them to obtain the information they reasonably need in order to enter into an appropriate settlement; or
(c) to make an appropriate offer (of a kind which can have costs consequences if litigation ensues); and
(d) if a pre-action settlement is not achievable, to lay the ground for expeditious conduct of proceedings.'

350 See their website at <http://www.justice.gov.uk/civil/procrules_fin/contents/protocols/prot_rcd.htm>.

One might also consider the fact that claims against public health care providers may have to be filed in a separate (administrative) court system.[351] However, this is not a peculiarity of medical litigation, but rather true for all actions against public entities in jurisdictions where this applies. **134**

Three reports point at special rules already introduced or at least forthcoming that apply to a broader category of tort cases than just medical malpractice cases exclusively, but still differing from general procedural law. In the Czech Republic, separate rules (such as different courts of first instance) apply to personal injury claims either aiming at damages in tort or based upon a violation of personality rights. Both may be triggered cumulatively by medical malpractice as well, but this is not a requirement for these special rules to apply.[352] The Polish report presents the new class action regime, with the first case filed interestingly originating in the health care system, but not a malpractice case.[353] In the Netherlands, a new rule will permit litigation of only one specific aspect of a personal injury case before a judge, thereby facilitating settlements where just one key aspect is in dispute.[354] **135**

28. Special institutions handling malpractice claims

Some jurisdictions have so far abstained from setting up special institutions to which patients can turn if they believe that they have been wronged.[355] **136**

In other countries, classic ADR options are available, such as mediation in Hungary[356] or arbitration in Spain.[357] **137**

Again others have introduced some ombudsman-like institution which effectively serves as mediator between claimants, medical professionals and institutions as well as insurers.[358] A special role is taken by the NHS **138**

---

351 Supra nos 101–102.

352 CZ nos 133 ff.

353 PL nos 98–99 (a hepatits C infections case).

354 NL no 87.

355 BE no 56; IT no 77; PL no 98; UK no 55 (until NHS Redress system in force, see infra no 148).

356 HU no 67 (costs borne by either side).

357 ES no 105: Courts of arbitration installed by local bar associations may even have special sections specifically for medical malpractice disputes, as is the case in Madrid, for example.

358 Cf AT no 98 (patient advocacies); NL no 3 (independent confidential advisor for patients of certain health care providers).

Litigation Authority in the UK, which handles all negligence claims raised against NHS bodies and thereby effectively filters out all but 2% of all cases that would otherwise have gone to court.[359]

139 More or less independent claims handlers can be called upon in yet other jurisdictions, most of them without decision-making power, however:

140 The French *Commissions Régionales de Conciliation et d'Indemnisation* (CRCI), introduced in the course of the 2002 reforms, offer two different tracks, depending upon the seriousness of the patient's adverse condition.[360] If it exceeds the minimum gravity as defined under the statute,[361] patients can initiate a five-stage procedure of amicable dispute resolution, ultimately resulting in an offer of compensation issued either by ONIAM itself or by an insurer, the latter if the commission concludes that the health care professional or institution can be held liable. If the harm complained of falls short of the minimum threshold, conciliation is the only option with the CRCI, though it is rarely ever used.[362]

141 In Sweden, most patients typically submit their cases to *Patientförsäkringen LÖF*,[363] which handles claims for the insurer of all Swedish regions and therefore the vast majority of health care services.[364] Furthermore, a Patient Claims Panel (*Patientskadenämnden*) upon request by a patient offers advisory opinions in cases falling under the Patient Injury Act. Despite the fact that these are mere recommendations, they are in practice commonly followed.[365]

142 The Austrian hospital compensation funds typically have set up a commission which decides upon applications filed. The Lower Austrian fund, for example, requires that claims first have to be assessed by the patient advocacy[366] before they can be forwarded by the advocacy upon the patient's request to the commission.[367]

---

359 See the NHSLA's website for further details: <http://www.nhsla.com>.

360 FR nos 40 ff.

361 Supra fn 110.

362 *Taylor* (fn 269): 'The conciliation services have been used very little by patients. … The low take-up may be because the conciliation role of the Regional Commissions is not well known by the public and, to the extent that it is known, it is often perceived as a wasteful detour.'

363 See their website <http://www.patientforsakring.se/index.html> for further information.

364 See also supra no 106.

365 SE no 58.

366 Supra at no 138 and AT no 82.

367 See the rules of the commission at <http://www.patientenanwalt.com/fileadmin/dokumente/04_publikationen/taetigkeitsberichte/noe_patienten_entschaedigungsfonds/Gesch%C3 %A4ftsordnung_09__Dez_2010_.pdf>.

In Austria, the Czech Republic, Germany and Switzerland, the respective professional representation bodies of physicians have installed conciliation panels which can issue non-binding (but still highly persuasive) recommendations in complaints lodged against their members.[368] The Dutch Hospital Dispute Settlement Commission does the same for harm suffered in an affiliated health care institution, though limited to small claims up to €5,000.[369] 143

H. Outlook

29. Reform plans

Despite the fact that discussions about a possible reform of the laws governing medical malpractice have been going on in all countries,[370] most of them do not show any reform activity at present.[371] 144

In Belgium, after the failure of a Scandinavian-style compensation scheme, new legislation in 2010 aims at introducing a system modelled on the French solution.[372] 145

The latter is apparently also true in Poland, where a new law proposes the introduction of a compensation scheme, though limited to certain medical errors in hospitals only.[373] 146

The new Czech draft Civil Code will probably include provisions on the treatment contract as well as on medical liability.[374] 147

The English NHS Redress Act 2006 foresees an 'optional mechanism for the extra-judicial settlement of claims',[375] which will apply to lower value claims (probably up to the equivalent of approx € 24,000). However, details are not yet clear due to the delays in implementing this legislation. 148

---

368 AT no 99, CH nos 141 ff; CZ no 137 (see also <http://www.clkcr.cz/dokumenty.php?item.id=72179>); DE no 216.

369 NL no 88.

370 Eg AT no 103; DE no 221; NL no 89; PL no 99.

371 AT no 103; CH nos 148 ff (but specific aspects such as liability for medical trials in discussion); DE no 221; ES no 107; FR no 48; HU no 68; IT no 78; NL no 89; SE no 59.

372 BE no 57. Cf supra nos 104 ff.

373 PL nos 101–109. The draft presented there has just been adopted on 28 April 2011; see <http://orka.sejm.gov.pl/proc6.nsf/ustawy/3488_u.htm>.

374 CZ no 141.

375 UK no 6.

Cases

Preliminary remarks

149 The following case hypotheticals have been selected among actual German court decisions. Their facts have been slightly adjusted to the format and needs of a questionnaire, and occasionally supplemented with one or another detail in order to address additional aspects, particularly with an eye to compensable losses.

150 The facts of all cases are necessarily filtered in two ways. First of all, they build upon court decisions which necessarily do not reveal the full story, and the statements of fact have subsequently been reinterpreted for purposes of the questionnaire, so evaluating the conduct of those involved is only possible to a very limited degree. Readers should therefore not expect final outcomes of the hypotheticals, neither in the country reports nor in the following, but instead rather pointers to which directions and turns the jurisdictions might take on the way to the solution.

151 Dates and years of the actual cases were left unchanged. Nevertheless, both the responses by the country reporters as well as the comparative remarks below will disregard the aspect of prescription that may time-bar at least some of the claims if filed now, even if otherwise given. Therefore, the responses to the six hypotheticals as well as their comparative analyses below build upon the current legal situation and not necessarily on the historic laws in force at the time of the real cases.

152 Some tort laws of the jurisdictions covered experienced significant changes over the past decade since the publication of the first medical malpractice study in 2001.[376] This includes legislation altering tort law in general in particular in Germany, where the *Zweite Schadensrechtsänderungsgesetz* of 2002 significantly expanded the recoverability of non-pecuniary loss in particular.[377] Also important amendments to the Swedish *Skadeståndslagen*, entering into force on 1 January 2002, deserve to be mentioned, which inter alia regulate the compensability of claims for non-pecuniary losses incurred by relatives of the direct victim.[378] Furthermore, some countries have passed legislation dealing specifically with medical

---

376 See, eg, the overview by *BA Koch*, Personenschäden in Europa – Aktuelle Trends, in: HAVE (ed), Personen-Schaden-Forum 2007 (2007) 305.

377 On this legislation, see *J Fedtke*, Germany, in: H Koziol/B Steininger (eds), European Tort law 2002 (2003) 206 ff.

378 *H Sandell*, Sweden, in: H Koziol/B Steininger (eds), European Tort law 2002 (2003) 393 ff. Cf supra no 129.

malpractice. The French *loi Kouchner* of 2002[379] is the most significant example in this respect. Other projects were at least introduced and are awaiting implementation.[380]

Case 1[381]

A and B had a joint gynaecological practice and both were also affiliated doctors in a hospital run by C. A and B always stood in for each other whenever one of them was away, in particular on holidays.

X was attended by B in the joint practice during her pregnancy with twins. On 24 February 1989, X was admitted to C's hospital because of preterm contractions and treated by B and other doctors with intravenous tocolysis. On 15 March 1989, A took over X's treatment acting as a locum for B during his holiday.

On 17 March 1989, the midwife D, who was employed by C, took a CTG starting at 6:35am, the results of which were so abnormal that she ought to have sent for a doctor immediately. However, she only informed A by telephone at 7:20am. A did then come around briefly but did not take the medical action required at this point in time. Instead he immediately thereafter treated another patient although there was no necessity for him to do so. During his subsequent round of the patients at 8:30am, he should have carried out further investigations on the basis of said CTG and ordered a caesarean section; he omitted however to do so. At 9:40am X was transferred to the delivery room, where A also appeared at 10:00am. At 10:06am, Y was born with Apgar scores of 1, 2 and 5. Y's twin brother was subsequently delivered stillborn.

Y suffers from serious, permanent impairments, in particular spastic tetraplegy (paralysis of all four limbs), central hypotension (muscular atony) as well as optic atrophy with extensive visual impairment (blindness). Y cannot sit on her own or stand or walk. She must be fed. She suffers from secondary damage like deformation of the spine. She also has a cognitive disability, in particular she is unable to speak. Y lives in her parents' household and is looked after there by day by professional nursing staff. The associated costs are nonetheless greater than if Y lived in a care home. X looks after her in particular during the night and at weekends.

It cannot be ascertained whether, prior to the events which happened around the time of her birth, Y already had a pre-existing problem which could at least partially have contributed to her present condition. While it is probable that a considerable part of her impairments happened before the delivery, it is also possible that A and D's conduct were the sole cause of Y's impairments.

Y seeks an order for A, B and C to pay for the pecuniary damage sustained up until now and which will be sustained in the future as a result of the alleged mistakes in treatment during

379 FR nos 14 ff.

380 Supra nos 145 ff.

381 Based on OLG München 20. 6. 2002, 1 U 3930/96, OLGR München 2003, 269–270.

the pregnancy and the birth, insofar as such has not been passed on to the social insurance agencies or other third parties. Furthermore, she seeks damages for non-pecuniary loss from the defendants.

X seeks an award of compensation for the care that she herself provides to Y, assessed according to the standard wage of a qualified nurse, as well as damages for her own non-pecuniary loss from the distress arising from the stillbirth of her son and the serious damage sustained by her daughter Y.

1. Who may be liable?[382]

(a) A

153 A may be held liable for his faulty conduct in tort[383] subject to further conditions – apart from the crucial aspect of causation, which will be addressed separately below, the relevant standard of care according to which his conduct has to be assessed will be decisive.

154 The theories upon which the claims can build may vary, though: all tort laws will offer an adequate basis for wrongdoers to be held liable for their own faulty conduct.[384] If A is deemed an employee of the joint practice (supposing it were a separate legal entity)[385] or of the hospital,[386] however, he may not be accountable himself in those jurisdictions where employees are immune from liability if it is channelled to their employer instead.[387]

155 Furthermore, it is not equally self-evident that A personally may also be held vicariously liable for D. If the claim is based upon a tort theory, the narrow interpretation of vicarious liability in some jurisdictions alone may prevent him from having to account for the conduct of others,[388] while actions based upon a violation of A's contractual duties may be more successful in this respect if he used the help of D to fulfil these

382 Y may recover under the Swedish patient insurance scheme without identifying an individual defendant as in the following: SE no 62.

383 Eg CH nos 151, 153; DE no 233; ES no 108; HU no 70; PL no 111; UK no 59 (though private maternity services unlikely in England).

384 Eg FR no 51 ('obviously liable').

385 See infra no 157.

386 CZ no 146; FR no 52.

387 FR no 52. Cf supra no 65.

388 AT no 44; DE no 227.

obligations. Therefore, if checking the CTG by D was part of the contractual duties of A, he will typically be vicariously liable for D's conduct.[389] This in turn depends upon the question of whether A himself was in a contractual or at least a quasi-contractual relationship with X and/or Y despite the fact that the contract was concluded by B.[390]

(b) B

Since B apparently did not do anything wrong himself according to the facts, he may not be held liable for personal misconduct.[391] However, the crucial question – again – is whether the wrongdoing of others might be imputed to him. Also in his case this depends upon whether the claimants pursue a contract theory or sue B in tort, with more far-reaching vicarious liability in the former than the latter case in some jurisdictions. These would therefore deny B's liability for A in tort and only allow a contractual claim.[392] The latter may also be extended to D's conduct if she was performing a contractual duty of B.[393] **156**

(c) A & B

If the joint practice of A and B is a separate legal entity, it may be the contractual partner of X instead of A and/or B individually.[394] In this case, the practice itself will be vicariously liable for all misconduct by its affiliates and employees who helped to perform its contractual duties.[395] **157**

---

389 AT no 45; DE nos 224, 229.

390 Confirmed by BE no 59; DE no 224 (appearance of joint practice leads to joint and several liability of A and B); IT no 79.

391 Eg CH no 154; CZ no 154; ES no 108; NL no 90; PL no 111; but see BE no 59.

392 AT nos 48, 105; CH nos 151 (no duty of supervision or other authority over B or D), 158–159. B's liability for A also confirmed by IT no 79 (*obbligo di protezione* vis-à-vis the claimants). See also BE no 59: B only liable for A if *culpa in eligendo*. Similarly FR no 53; ES no 108.

393 AT no 104; CH no 159; DE nos 224, 229.

394 AT no 104; CZ no 146.

395 Eg NL no 90. But see CZ no 147: No error during ambulatory part of care, and services of A and B individually at the hospital would in Czechia be attributed to the latter, therefore only C is a potential defendant.

(d) C

158 Apart from a potential claim based upon flaws in its organisation and therefore direct liability,[396] hospital C will be vicariously liable[397] for D's deviations from the standard of care expected from midwives under the circumstances.[398] This may not be the case in those jurisdictions which put more emphasis on the actual control and supervision of D's activities and which therefore would shift vicarious liability to A instead if it was him who was in charge.[399]

159 C will not be liable for the conduct of external physicians such as A acting temporarily on its premises under a special arrangement,[400] unless A is deemed an employee of C[401] or a special provision holds the hospital liable for all services provided there.[402]

(e) D

160 D may be held liable for her own fault in all jurisdictions[403] but for those which keep her immune from personal liability in an employment relationship.[404]

2. Causation

161 The crucial question for both X and Y in their quest for compensation is whether those sued caused their losses. The particular complication in the instant case is that Y's condition may have been triggered by a precondition, but it is also possible that the conduct of the health care professionals involved was the sole cause.

---

396 BE no 58; ES no 108.

397 AT no 106; CH no 155; DE nos 225, 228 (even in tort); ES no 108; FR no 55; HU no 70; IT no 79; NL no 90; PL nos 110 f. See also CZ no 146 (vicarious liability for A).

398 On this standard, see BE no 58 in particular.

399 CH no 155.

400 Eg CH no 155; DE no 225.

401 CZ no 146.

402 IT no 79; NL no 90.

403 Eg DE no 229; ES no 108.

404 FR no 54 (unless 'fault of exceptional gravity'). See also no 65.

While it is universally agreed that the tortfeasor must take the victim as she finds her,[405] including a special precondition of hers which might turn the impact of the tortfeasor's conduct from a harmless to a harmful event or at least worsen its detrimental effect, all jurisdictions start from the basic rule that the tortfeasor must have set a *conditio sine qua non* for at least part of the victim's loss, unless an exception to this but-for-test applies.[406] **162**

In the majority of countries where the all-or-nothing rule governs, liability will be denied altogether if causation, ie such a *conditio sine qua non*, cannot be proven with a probability exceeding the threshold of the required standard of proof. If this is the case here, as it seems likely, neither X nor Y can recover the losses sustained.[407] **163**

Some jurisdictions avoid this outcome by shifting the burden of proof under specific conditions, which effectively means that (full) liability of the defendant(s) can be established despite the same uncertainties prevailing.[408] **164**

Other legal systems would allow at least partial recovery on the basis of the loss of a chance-theory.[409] The claimant's loss is then reinterpreted from her overall physical condition to the 'lost opportunity not to have suffered such severe handicaps'.[410] **165**

Proportional liability is also endorsed by yet other jurisdictions, splitting the loss between claimants and defendants according to the likelihood of either side's contribution to causing the loss. This solution avoids the harsh consequences of the all-or-nothing rule in cases of causal uncertainty.[411] **166**

---

405 Eg BE no 60; NL no 91. Cf also Art 4:101 par 2 PEL Liab Dam: 'In cases of personal injury or death the injured person's predisposition with respect to the type or extent of the injury sustained is to be disregarded.'

406 Eg CH no 153; NL no 91.

407 CH no 153; CZ no 151; IT no 81; PL no 112 ('unambiguous causation'); SE no 61 (also for claim under patient insurance scheme); UK nos 59–60 ('material contribution' by defendant required). But see IT no 83: 'Regardless of the applicable criteria of causation, there is a "policy" trend in Italian jurisprudence towards the affirmation of the medical staff's liability, in such cases in order to grant to the family of the newborn (who has suffered severe damage) a *de facto* "indemnity".'

408 DE nos 231–232 (grossly negligent behaviour by defendants shifts burden of proving causation upon them); HU no 70 ('shifting the risk of uncertain causation to the medical service provider is a clear tendency in Hungarian court practice', exoneration if proof that conduct with utmost care and no contribution to loss); NL no 91 (*omkeringsregel*).

409 ES no 110; FR no 50; IT no 82; NL no 91.

410 FR no 50.

411 AT no 112; NL no 91. This would also be the solution endorsed by the Principles of European Tort Law, cf Art 3:103 and 3:106 PETL.

3. Compensable losses

167 Should the causation problem be resolved in favour of the claimants, the question remains which losses will have to be compensated either in full or in part, depending upon the solution found.

168 There is unanimity that all medical costs (to the extent not yet covered by the health care and/or social insurance provider) and increased expenses have to be indemnified.[412] The same is true for the nursing costs, even if the total exceeds the amount that would be incurred at a care home: as long as the difference is not excessive and unreasonable, these expenses can be recovered.[413] As to Y's probable inability to earn a living on her own later on, her lost earning capacity will be covered in at least most jurisdictions.[414]

169 Reporters further agree that Y is eligible for payments indemnifying her non-pecuniary loss, which – depending on the jurisdiction – is either limited to damages for pain and suffering and loss of amenities[415] or extended to the 'extra-patrimonial' infringement of her personality rights[416] or the harm to her health (*danno biologico*).[417] The amounts that she can expect differ significantly in comparison.[418]

170 Turning to X, it is not universally true that she could claim compensation for her own pecuniary loss such as lost income or her investment into taking care of her daughter, as is possible in some countries.[419] Some jurisdictions instead insist that these items are claimed by Y rather than X herself.[420]

---

412 Eg AT no 108; CH no 156; DE no 234; ES no 110 (unless compensation for loss of chance, in which case the lump-sum award will be considered damages for non-pecuniary loss); FR no 57; HU no 69; IT no 84; PL no 113; SE no 61.

413 AT no 108; CH no 156; CZ no 149; DE no 234; HU no 69; PL no 113; SE no 61; UK no 61. But see NL no 92: duty to mitigate loss may reduce claim in some circumstances; alternatively, the judge may reduce the claim but 'not below the sum covered by liability insurance'.

414 AT no 108; DE no 234; PL no 113; UK no 61 ('educated guess'). But see also infra no 184.

415 CH no 156; ES no 110; HU no 69; NL no 92.

416 CZ no 153.

417 IT nos 68, 84.

418 AT no 109 (€ 200,000 plus € 30,000 for disfigurement); CZ nos 149, 153 (up to € 600,000, plus up to € 40,000 for violation of her personality rights); DE no 235 (€ 350,000–500,000); PL no 115 (up to € 125,000); UK no 61 (in excess of € 235,000); see also supra no 128.

419 AT no 110; CH nos 158, 160 (but only if contract claim); CZ nos 149–150; ES no 110; FR no 58; HU no 69; NL no 93.

420 CH no 162 (if tort claim); PL no 114; SE no 63 (would be pure economic loss, not recoverable in tort); UK no 61.

Furthermore, irrespective of who may claim it, the question remains how the services of X in looking after her daughter are valued. Some legal systems would calculate the value on the basis of the wages that a professional nurse could earn, arguing that it should not be to the tortfeasor's advantage that X chose to render such services herself instead of buying them on the market.[421] Others are more restrictive and would only allow compensation based upon the salaries of an unqualified carer.[422]

Finally, while X will be able to claim damages for her own pain and suffering in presumably all jurisdictions if she has sustained a medical condition of her own (such as a nervous shock when she learned about her daughter's condition or because of the stress related to taking care of her handicapped daughter),[423] it is not universally agreed that she may claim damages for witnessing her daughter's condition per se,[424] not even in those countries where she could be compensated for the bereavement due to the death of her other twin child at birth.[425] 171

Case 2[426]

The gynaecologist A gave his patient X at her own wish and at her own expense the long-acting contraceptive implant 'Implanon' in January 2002. This is a plastic tube about 3mm wide and a few centimetres long, which is inserted under the skin above the inside of the elbow. In July 2002, A diagnosed that X was in the 16th week of pregnancy. It was no longer possible to locate the 'Implanon' implant and its active agent could no longer be detected in X's blood.

X was unable to take on a position she had been offered because of the pregnancy and having to care for the child. Y, the father of the child, who the plaintiff had known for about half a year at the time of the conception, acknowledged paternity. However, he does not live with the plaintiff. He fulfils his maintenance payment obligations towards their son Z.

---

421 AT no 110; CH no 160 ('average cost of home care'); DE no 234 (but depends upon further facts); HU no 69; NL no 93 (but maximum as long as 'normal and common' to get professional help instead); UK no 61 (periodical payment).

422 CZ no 150.

423 Eg CZ no 150; DE no 236; SE nos 63–64; UK no 63 (but uncertain, typically only granted for sudden events).

424 Granted in CH no 161; CZ no 153 (based on violation of personality rights, however, up to € 40,000); HU no 69; IT no 84; but denied in AT no 111 (not yet recognized); DE no 236; PL no 115; UK no 61.

425 AT no 111 (up to € 20,000); HU no 69; IT no 84; PL no 115 (between € 7,500 and € 17,500); UK no 61 (statutory amount of approx € 14,000, cf UK no 53).

426 Based on BGH 14. 11. 2006, VI ZR 48/06, VersR 2007, 109.

X now seeks compensation from A for the damage sustained up until now and which will be sustained in the future as a result of the parental obligation to support the child both in her own right and on the basis of the assigned right of the father Y.

172 This is a case of wrongful conception, as it is commonly referred to. Parents sue a medical professional for the loss sustained because of the unwanted conception and subsequent birth of a healthy child, arguing that the defendant's negligence, eg in the course of a sterilisation, or her failure to warn them of the risks of a birth-control method[427] ruined their efforts to prevent this. It is equally imaginable that the producer of a contraceptive is sued for the consequences of its failure.[428] 'In such cases, the parents typically attempt to claim for the pecuniary losses constituted by the whole costs of bringing up the child until it reaches adulthood, and/or loss of income sustained during pregnancy and childrearing. The parents' argument is that, as no child was wanted, therefore all costs associated with its birth and childrearing should be recoverable.'[429] Wrongful conception cases are different from wrongful birth cases inasmuch as in the latter cases the child is born handicapped and the parents would have legitimately terminated the pregnancy had they known of the disability, even though they wanted to have a child originally. The second type therefore typically deals with incorrect prenatal diagnosis.[430] A third variety is known as wrongful life cases, which are based on the same factual situation as in the second type, but instead of the parents, the handicapped child itself claims compensation for its own existence.[431]

173 Jurisdictions are split when it comes to wrongful conception cases like the one here. In the majority of countries including Belgium, the Czech Republic, Germany, Italy, the Netherlands, Poland, Spain, and Switzerland,[432] such claims are successful, even though not necessarily under all

427 Cf CZ no 157; NL no 94.

428 Cf NL no 94.

429 *M Hogg*, Damages for Pecuniary Loss in Cases of Wrongful Birth, (2010) 2 JETL 156.

430 See also *E Bagińska*, Wrongful Birth and Non-Pecuniary Loss: Theories of Compensation, (2010) 2 JETL 171.

431 On this third type, see *A Ruda*, 'I Didn't Ask to be Born': Wrongful Life from a Comparative Perspective, (2010) 2 JETL 204. See also *B Steininger*, Wrongful Birth and Wrongful Life: Basic Questions, (2010) 2 JETL 125.

432 BE nos 61–62 (with jurisprudence being 'rather reluctant', however); CH nos 163 ff; CZ nos 155 ff; DE nos 238 ff; ES nos 112 ff; IT nos 86 ff; NL nos 94 ff. On Poland, see the case reported by *E Bagińska*, Poland, in: H Koziol/B Steininger (eds), European Tort Law 2006 (2008) 373, 386 ff (Sąd Najwyższy 22.2.2006, III CZP 8/06).

circumstances, and for all heads of damages;[433] whereas they are being denied in the remaining jurisdictions such as Austria, England, France, Hungary and Sweden.[434] In England, however, loss relating to the pregnancy and giving birth as such may be recoverable, ie the harmful impact of the doctor's negligence on his patient's (the mother's) bodily integrity.[435]

The prime problem with such cases is the fact that they are overloaded with ethical concerns unrelated to the fundamentals of tort law, and the struggle to reconcile these conflicting policy arguments has no obvious solution. Arguments in favour of granting the claim primarily come from the tort law side of the ring, where it is a desirable goal to hold someone liable for her fault. On the other side, family values and the wish of society to promote procreation[436] play a decisive role. **174**

The tort law perspective is in a dilemma, though: since the birth of a child itself cannot and shall not be called a 'damage', it has to be redefined as the economic consequences of this event. Apart from the difficulty that such pure economic loss is not universally compensable, a causation problem arises: 'The medical negligence may be a sine qua non of such costs, but its causal significance can arguably be said to have been eclipsed by the subsequently arising parental duty of support.'[437] The reasons for that maintenance duty do not support shifting it to a third-party tortfeasor. This dilemma becomes even more obvious in those jurisdictions like Austria which do allow compensation for wrongful birth, but deny it in wrongful conception cases.[438] **175**

In legal systems which allow a claim for wrongful conception, parents[439] are indemnified not only for their pecuniary, but also for their non- **176**

433 Cf, eg, BE no 62: Granting the claim is easier in cases where the reason for the parents against a (further) pregnancy is the possibility that the child might suffer from a genetic disorder. See the overview by *BA Koch* (fn 96) 20/30.

434 AT no 114; FR nos 61 ff; HU no 72; SE no 65 ('unlikely'); UK no 65.

435 UK no 65.

436 This is even true in jurisdictions allowing abortion, which apparently 'is not ... a decisive factor in the decision to disallow such claims': *Hogg* (fn 428) 160. Furthermore, abortion is just a right and not a duty, so defendants fail with their argument that the unwanted pregnancy could have been terminated: DE no 242; NL no 95.

437 *Hogg* (fn 428) 161.

438 Cf AT no 119.

439 While the mother undoubtedly has a claim (if granted at all), it is not universally agreed that also the father can be compensated for his own losses: confirmed in DE nos 244 ff (father within protective scope of treatment contract) and CH no 166 (but only on tort theory/violation of personality rights, or if father was part of the contract, not as third party thereto); but denied in NL nos 94 ('doubtful'), 99.

pecuniary loss, the former typically including in particular all the costs of raising the child as well as a potential loss of at least one parent's income,[440] the latter pain and suffering of the mother during pregnancy and while giving birth.[441] This is not the case in the Czech Republic, though, where parents are only awarded compensation for the infringement of their personality rights rather than for the economic consequences of having a child.[442]

Case 3[443]

X was born on 26 August 1997 in the hospital run by A. About two to three hours after his birth, a blood sugar test was carried out and the results were under the norm threshold. After sugar had been administered orally and two control tests were carried out, X was discharged after about 8 hours.

X ought definitely to have been classified as a high-risk newborn at his birth. He should, therefore, not have been discharged at a few hours old, even subsequent to the short-term pickup in his blood sugar level due to the oral glucose. In the year 1997 it had long been established paediatric knowledge that overweight children with hypoglycaemia need to have their sugar levels monitored for a minimum of 24 hours. Because of the serious long-term effects which failure to treat such hypoglycaemia has for the child, the obstetrician who attends babies directly after the birth must also be familiar with the condition. It is not necessary for him to know in detail how to treat it but he is under a duty to seek the advice of a paediatrician.

In this case, however, no paediatrician examined the child and neither X's mother nor her midwife B were informed of the necessity to monitor his blood sugar level.

---

440 BE no 62; CH no 164; DE no 243; ES nos 112, 114 f (but maintenance costs not universally compensable); IT nos 86–87 (if based on infringement of right to procreation, 'solely to the extent to which it implies a "loss of income and personal consumptions due to the newborn"'); NL nos 96 f. See also *Hogg* (fn 428) 163.

441 BE no 62 (*dommage moral* for parents of girl who may be a carrier of a gene for a genetic disorder – 'atypical for Belgian jurisprudence'); ES no 113; IT no 88 (either for violating the psychological integrity of the mother or for infringing the right to procreation); NL no 98 (but denied by some courts). German courts allow damages for pain and suffering by confirming that causing an unwanted pregnancy and delivery constitutes bodily injury: BGH 18.3.1980, VI ZR 247/78, NJW 1980, 1452. See also *Bagińska* (fn 429) 182 ff.

442 CZ nos 155–156. This means that the award is much lower than the maintenance costs etc. Insofar, the Czech and the English jurisprudence seem to be in accord, as also in the latter the House of Lords in *Rees* had awarded a lump sum of around €18,000 in specific recognition of the interference with the mother's freedom to limit her family (cf UK no 65).
See in particular the argument brought forward by one court cited in no 155: granting the full claim 'would ridicule the situation of parents who lose a beloved child in an accident and receive only the 240,000 CZK statutory compensation for death'.

443 Based on HansOLG Bremen 13. 1. 2006, 4 U 23/05, OLGR Bremen 2006, 745–748 = MedR 2007, 660–663.

B took over the care of X in his mother's home. She visited him still on the 26 August 1997 and after his mother told her of the hypoglycaemia after the delivery, she recommended that he be given tea with grape sugar and she also gave him a homeopathic sedative the next day. On the basis of her education and experience as a midwife and independently of any references from the birth clinic, B ought to have recognised the risk posed to X and have acted accordingly without delay. She should have sought the advice of a paediatrician by the afternoon of 27 August at the latest.

On the morning of the 28 August the parents went to the paediatric clinic run by C because X looked as if he was dead; they arrived at 8:30am.

In C's clinic there was neither a consultant in attendance nor were there any directions as to when either the nurse handling admissions or a doctor who was still inexperienced had to call in an experienced doctor. There were not even any directions that or whether the nurse handling admissions had to call on a doctor at all. Neither were there any binding regulations to the effect that a detailed case history (questioning of the mother) had to be carried out and recorded, that the child be thoroughly examined or that a consultant then be brought in within a reasonable length of time. Moreover, in the case of alarming findings, valuable time should not be wasted, as in this case, with having to phone around to see which ward could admit the child before treatment could be started.

In the absence of such organisational structure, it happened that more than one and a half hours passed from when the child and his parents reached the hospital to when X had his first blood sugar level check and blood gas analysis. In these first one and a half hours, the nurse handling admissions, D, only initiated a breast-feeding attempt. An exact case history was not taken by the inexperienced doctor E, who arrived at about 9:00am in admissions. Questioning the mother could have led quickly to a complete diagnosis. Without having documented such a detailed case history, E proceeded to only organise the first examination at about 10:00am; however, she clearly did not believe the alarming result. The very first recording of a blood sugar test in the documentation of the case was at 10:25am. At this point in time, the child had a serious hypoglycaemia of 17 mg/dl, on re-check 20 mg/dl (a usual result would be 40–45 ml/dg). Yet despite this, still no immediate action was taken. X was only admitted to a ward after 11:00am, where he was finally examined by a consultant physician. According to the patient's file, the next acid-base status was not evaluated until 11:15am. Shortly thereafter, X suffered cardiac arrest during the consultant's attempt to place an IV line and had to be resuscitated. Ever since then X has been severely disabled. He cannot perform any targeted movements and can only communicate at the basic level. In addition, he is practically sightless.

Even in the year 1997 such an organisational structure fell below the medical standard for a full-service hospital such as the C clinic. Evaluation of the condition of a newborn baby who has been brought in by his parents without a doctor's referral cannot be left solely in the hands of a nurse handling admissions, even if said nurse is experienced. Equally, the fact that the child was not immediately examined by a doctor and no precise medical history was taken and documented failed to meet the required standard. Moreover, it ought to have been ensured that a doctor on duty, who was inexperienced, be required to secure a specialist's standard of care for the final assessment of the patient's condition. Those responsible for the organisational structure of the medical service may not rely on an admissions nurse, even when experienced, to reliably recognise the health problems of a newborn brought in without a doctor's referral. If the clinic cannot be attended at all times by an experienced doctor who can attain the required standard of care, there must be directions requiring that a child at least be examined thoroughly and a detailed medical history taken. Then, the advice of an experienced doctor must still be sought.

Even in the event that there was pre-existing damage to X's brain by the time he had arrived in the paediatric clinic, it is no longer possible to establish the extent of such damage. The longer hypoglycaemia is allowed to continue, the higher the risk of such damage. In retrospect it is no longer possible to establish what degree of damage had already been sustained and to what extent more damage was sustained during X's treatment in the C clinic. On the basis of how things continued it can be assumed with a very high degree of probability that the organic damage was sustained in the C clinic.

X seeks compensation from the defendants A, B, C and E on the basis of joint and several liability for all damage sustained up until now and which will be sustained in the future and which is a result of the care provided in the aftermath of his birth from 26 August until 28 August 1997. Besides the costs of nursing care and the expenses caused by his increased needs, he seeks compensation for his prospective loss of capacity to earn in the amount of € 2,000 per month (as of his 21st year of life capitalised until his 65th year of life). Additionally, he seeks compensation from the defendants for non-pecuniary loss.

1. Who may be liable?[444]

177 There is universal agreement among all reporters that all of the defendants could be held liable if problems of causation are resolved in the claimant's favour. The only exception concerns E, who cannot be held personally accountable in those jurisdictions where employees are immune from lawsuits if their employer is vicariously liable for them, or whose liability as an employee may be limited.[445] Otherwise she will be liable in tort (as she is not in a contract or quasi-contractual relationship with X).[446] The fact that she was inexperienced at the time does not lower the standard of care which she has to account for.[447]

178 As far as A is concerned, contractual liability is confirmed for most countries.[448] This is neither true in England nor in Sweden, however, where patients typically do not contract with their health care provider,[449]

444 X may recover under the Swedish patient insurance scheme without identifying an individual defendant as in the following: SE no 70.

445 Supra no 65 (limited in AT, SE; immune in CZ, FR, HU, PL).

446 AT nos 124, 132; CH no 172; IT no 89; UK no 67 (but liability 'academic' as NHS indemnity scheme would pay).

447 Eg CH no 172; FR no 67.

448 AT nos 122 ff; BE no 64; DE nos 254–257; ES no 116 (if private health care; cf ES no 54); IT no 89; NL no 100; PL no 118 (if private health care; cf PL no 59).

449 SE no 35; UK no 39.

nor in Switzerland, where X cannot be brought into the protective scope of his mother's contract with A.[450] Tort liability is an option in all jurisdictions[451] but Italy, where medical malpractice claims are always deemed contractual.[452] The French liability regime is detached from both alternatives, but also allows a claim against A.[453]

The same is correspondingly true for midwife B, with the difference that she has to account for her own conduct if she is not employed by another as indicated by the facts.[454] **179**

As far as C is concerned, all reporters agree that while this hospital may have to account for its employees, including D and E, it will also be directly liable for its own lack of proper organisation.[455] **180**

To the extent more than one of the defendants can be held liable, ie if causation is established for the conduct of two or more of them, they will all be jointly and severally liable, with a possibility to seek recourse among themselves.[456] **181**

2. Causation

As in Case 1, it is not self-evident that all four defendants have at least contributed to causing X's condition, which is why the Spanish reporters **182**

---

450 CH no 168.

451 AT nos 125 ff (but vicarious liability for staff probably not given due to restrictions of § 1315 ABGB, see AT no 44); DE no 255 (presumption of § 831 BGB probably not rebuttable for A); SE no 67; UK no 66.

452 IT no 22.

453 FR no 65 (negligence 'self-evident'; cf FR no 22).

454 AT no 123; BE no 65 (wrongful prescription of homeopathic sedative); CH no 169 (though different to the case against A inasmuch as the mother of X may have entered into a contract with B for the benefit of X, which would allow him to sue on a contract theory); CZ no 160; DE nos 254–256, 258; ES no 117; FR no 65 (negligence 'self-evident'); IT no 89; NL no 100; PL no 120 (if employed as presumed by the reporter, B will be liable in recourse towards their employer); SE no 67.

455 AT no 128; BE no 66; CH no 170 (liable both under tort and contract law, as parents may have concluded contract with C in X's favour); CZ no 159; DE nos 254–256, 259; ES no 118; FR nos 65–66; IT no 89; NL no 100; PL no 119; SE nos 67, 68; UK nos 66–67.

456 AT no 132 ff, in particular 137 ('in light of the dangerousness of each contribution … very likely that all four defendants … liable jointly and severally for the entire damage due to the impossibility of resolving individual quotas'); CH no 173; CZ no 165; DE no 265; ES no 120; FR nos 70, 73 (but B and E immune if employees of A and C respectively, see also supra no 65); HU no 73; IT nos 89–90; NL nos 100–101; PL no 118 (only A and C because employees immune); SE nos 67–68; but see UK no 69 (C most likely defendant, handled by NHSLA). On the way various legal systems deal with multiple tortfeasors, see *WVH Rogers*, Comparative Report on Multiple Tortfeasors, in: WVH Rogers (ed), Unification of Tort Law: Multiple Tortfeasors (2004) 271.

in light of their jurisdiction's rather rigid approach to causal uncertainties doubt that X will be successful.[457] The opposite seems to be true in the Netherlands, where the legal system offers ample ways to resolve problems of causation, in particular, by dividing the consequences of such uncertainties between both sides of the dispute.[458]

183 The fact that all four have to account for conduct which was evidently faulty and prone to cause harm will help the claimant in at least some jurisdictions, however, to overcome causal uncertainties.[459]

3. Compensable losses

184 While the pecuniary losses claimed seem to raise no problems of compensability in general,[460] one specific item thereof does, and this is X's loss of earning capacity. Since X is still a young child who had no income so far, some jurisdictions deny that he could claim compensation for some fictitious future earnings[461] and instead compensate the costs of covering his actual needs[462] or otherwise shift the focus of this particular loss by reinterpreting it.[463] Some country reports specifically point at the possibility of obtaining declaratory relief now and raising monetary claims later once X's risk of not being able to generate income himself materialises.[464] Still others would already indemnify X's loss of earning capacity now.[465]

---

457 ES nos 116 ff, in particular no 119: high standard of proof required, referring to the Spanish Supreme Court's ruling that 'there is no place, in the area of causal relationship, for mere deductions, guesswork or probabilities, but evidential certainty is required'.

458 NL nos 100 ff (in particular by acknowledging proportional liability or loss of a chance).

459 AT no 135 ('dangerousness of each contribution' makes it 'very likely that all four defendants' can be held liable); DE no 261 ('gross negligence, therefore reversal of the burden of proving causation'). Cf also HU no 73: 'According to court practice which clearly tends towards shifting the risk to the hospital (doctor) in cases of uncertain causation and increased risk of worsening the patient's condition, the court would require each of the defendants to prove that they complied with the required standard of conduct (ie they acted according to the utmost professional care) concerning all the possible causes. They would also be required to prove that their omissions could not have increased the risk of deficiency or the worsening of the condition of X.'

460 Cf eg CZ no 162; DE no 266; ES no 120; IT no 91; SE no 69; UK no 70.

461 ES no 120 (too 'distant and merely possible'); FR no 74.

462 HU no74; PL no 121.

463 Eg CZ no 162 (loss of social dignity or violation of personality rights, otherwise not compensable).

464 AT no 136; DE no 267.

465 BE no 67 (but courts split); CH no 173 (projection as to how X's career path and income would have developed in comparison with family members, but rather 'conservative' with very young victims, lump sum or periodic payments, also retirement damage); IT no 91; SE no 69 (capitalised periodical payments for lost future income 'within the

X's non-pecuniary loss seems to be unproblematic;[466] however, the amounts suggested vary considerably, if only in those jurisdictions tending to award damages in the upper range in this respect.[467] **185**

Case 4[468]

The Iranian citizen X came to live in the Federal Republic of Germany in April 1987, at which time he did not speak German; his mother tongue is Persian. Four months later it was also not possible to communicate with him through English.

X was referred on 9 June 1987 to the neurosurgical department of A clinic, subsequent to treatment as an in-patient in another hospital because of problems over a long period of time including severe pains in his legs and an occasional weakness of the right leg. In the clinic, a disease of the spinal cord (myelopathy) with transverse spinal cord symptoms was diagnosed and an operation recommended.

In the course of his examination upon admission to the A clinic on 9 June, a weakness of the right leg when going up stairs was noted. After he had been examined comprehensively, surgery to treat a process which was causing the compression of the bone marrow was proposed.

On 24 June 1987, X and B, a doctor who worked at the A clinic, signed a form for 'consent to a medical procedure'. This included inter alia the declaration 'I have been informed that it is intended that the above-mentioned procedure be performed on me, about the type, purpose and manner of proceeding as well as about its main advantages and disadvantages and the risks also in comparison to other methods of examination/treatment/operation and I was informed orally/by the leaflet ... with respect to the option of not carrying out the procedure ... Particular problems of mine were discussed in detail, especially infection, deterioration, paralysis, secondary bleeding.' The words in italics were added in handwriting by B. This doctor had already noted in his admissions report: 'The case history was taken through the patient's interpreter. The patient himself can hardly speak German'. It could not, however, be established whether and how B had used a Persian dictionary during his talk with X. In any case, no interpreter was present during this consultation with the patient.

If X had been informed in a manner understandable to him about the risk of paralysis associated with the operation, he would have found himself in a state of conflict as to the decision and would probably not have had surgery at all. His symptoms were not so serious as to make an operation absolutely necessary.

---

scope of Swedish tort law'); UK no 70 (but largely speculative, average net wage 'if all else fails', family circumstances may lead to increase).

466 Eg CH no 173; ES no 120; FR no 74; HU no 75; SE no 69. In Italy, not only *danno morale*, but also *danno biologico* can be claimed: IT no 91 (cf supra no 125).

467 Cf AT no 137 (€ 200,000–250,000); CZ no 162 (€ 400,000–480,000 plus 40,000 for violation of personality rights); DE no 266: € 500,000; UK no 70 (close to € 240,000).

468 Based on OLG Oldenburg 25. 6. 1996, 5 U 170/95, VersR 1997, 978 = ArztR 1997, 205. The hypothetical was already used as case 2 in *M Faure/H Koziol* (eds), Cases on Medical Malpractice in a Comparative Perspective (2001).

On 25 June 1987, the operation was carried out by the surgeon C as a laminectomy of the 9th and 10th thoracic vertebrae. Alternative to the dorsal approach which was selected for the operation, it would also have been possible to make a transthoracic opening (through the breastplate). Both paths of access are possible from a medical point of view. Both involved a risk of death as well as of paralysis. The risk of death is higher in the case of the transthoracic opening. However, in the case of the dorsal approach the risk of paralysis is higher. The fact that there was a choice of these two approaches was, however, not discussed in the preoperative consultation.

After the operation, X suffered complete paralysis of the lower extremities accompanied also by almost complete loss of sensitivity and a bladder/rectum malfunction. The operation led to complete motor and vegetative paralysis with partially retained sensitivity. X can no longer control his anal sphincter muscle. He can no longer perform intentional movements with either of his legs. There is a definite loss of sensitivity below the level of the navel; the right side is worse affected. X will need a wheelchair for the rest of his life. He is henceforth dependent on care and assistance in many areas of life.

Nonetheless X, who was 47 when he underwent the surgery, already suffered from myelopathy with paralysis symptoms. As of the 9th thoracic vertebra, the pyramidal pathways and the posterior bundle were most affected. While this myelopathy did not continually restrict his movement, his well-being had been seriously impacted during the five years prior to the operation. He had also had to use crutches sometimes. Without an operation this state would at the least have remained unchanged.

X seeks inter alia compensation from A and C for the conversion of his house to provide wheelchair access, for the purchase of a new car with wheelchair access and for additional increased needs arising from his paralysis. Moreover, he also seeks appropriate damages for non-pecuniary loss.

186 All country reporters agree that X was not properly informed because of language problems.[469] Even if the law does not provide for a duty to call in interpreters in order to assist in the information process,[470] it is the outcome (or rather the foregone result) that seems to count, ie the fact that X was *de facto* unable to weigh the pros and cons of the suggested treatment when at least formally expressing his consent thereto.[471]

187 It is not equally clear that the omission to inform X about the alternative treatment method would also have affected the validity of his declaration of consent. While some confirm this or point to general statutory language requiring disclosure of alternatives,[472] others are less convinced[473] or even

---

469 AT nos 138–140; BE no 69; CH no 175; CZ no 175; DE no 270; ES nos 121 f; FR no 77; HU no 77; IT no 93; NL no 105; PL no 125; SE no 72; UK no 72.

470 Eg BE no 68 (statutory provision purposefully stripped of references to language skills 'in order to prevent patients expecting to be informed always in their mother tongue').

471 Eg AT no 140; BE no 69 ('If the patient did not understand the information given by the physician, there is no valid informed consent.').

472 BE no 70; CH no 175; CZ no 175; FR no 76. See, eg, Art 7:448 para 2 lit c of the Dutch Civil Code.

473 DE no 272.

deny that X should have known in advance about the second possible approach, pointing in particular to the fact that this would have entailed at least equal – if not higher – risk.[474]

When it comes to the burden of proving lack of adequate information, jurisdictions are split and impose this either upon the claimant herself[475] or upon the doctor or hospital.[476] **188**

The use of the consent form neither harms nor helps the defendants – even if a written declaration had been required, the signature by X on a document that he could not understand does not turn it into a convincing piece of evidence.[477] **189**

X's pre-existing condition described by the facts does not seem to have an impact on the outcome;[478] at best it is relevant only for defining the deterioration of his state of health before and after the procedure.[479] **190**

Apart from those legal systems where liability is channelled to the hospitals, leaving employees therefore immune from personal liability,[480] surgeon C himself may also have to account for his failure to inform X.[481] **191**

As to the possible consequences of the failure to properly disclose all risks etc of the planned treatment, they range from damages for being deprived of information as such (which is a non-pecuniary loss in itself),[482] to compensation for the loss of a chance,[483] to the recovery of all harmful consequences of the (wrongful) treatment.[484] In the second and third variety, the basis of calculating the pecuniary loss includes all heads of **192**

474 AT nos 144–145; HU no 78.

475 BE no 69; CZ no 97; NL no 106; UK no 73.

476 AT nos 76, 143; CH no 175; FR no 76.

477 AT nos 142–143; BE no 69 ('no superior legal value', use of written consent forms even discouraged by legislator); DE no 271; UK no 72; but see CZ nos 171, 173.

478 DE no 273; UK nos 74 f.

479 AT no 148 (but liability only for the earlier beginning of the paralysis if it had happened anyhow); FR nos 81 f; SE no 74.

480 Supra no 65. Cf CZ no 168; HU no 78 (only personally liable if not employed, but independent doctor).

481 DE nos 271, 274; CH no 179; ES no 122. But see AT nos 149 f: C not necessarily required to inform X again after taking note of the consent form produced by B.

482 CZ no 174 (if causal link between lack of information and adverse effects not proven); IT no 53 (dispute in jurisprudence whether mere lack of adequate information suffices to trigger); PL no 126; excluded eg in FR no 79.

483 Ie the lost opportunity to refuse the treatment and thus avoid the risk; BE no 71; FR nos 78 ff. But see FR no 86: ONIAM may step in if no or only limited liability if minimum incapacity of X, but further required that no link to the victim's former condition or that the evolution of the harm was unforeseeable; cf supra nos 107 ff.

484 AT no 151; CZ no 175 (if claimant successfully proves lack of adequate information and causation); DE nos 275–276; ES no 123; HU nos 76–77; IT no 94; SE no 74; UK no 74.

damage claimed in the hypothetical case.[485] X's consequential non-pecuniary losses are also compensable in those jurisdictions which at least partially indemnify his pecuniary losses.[486]

Case 5[487]

X underwent surgery in a hospital operated by A because of fractures. Directly after the operation, X had pain and numbness in the left side of the hand and in the area of the fourth and fifth finger. He suffered damage to the nervus ulnaris and consequently had restricted movement in the left hand. He was no longer able to pursue his occupation as a bricklayer.

During the three-hour operation, X was placed in a supine position, his arms were cushioned and secured so that they did not stick out. The damaged arm was turned to his back, laid on a splint with a standard rubber cushioning, which was splayed out at an angle of 90 degrees to the patient's body.

According to an agreement between the national professional association of anaesthetists and the professional association of surgeons, the positioning of the patient on the OP-table during and after the operation as well as the monitoring of the positioning is the responsibility of the surgeon and the anaesthetist. The actual positioning is, in principle, the surgeon's responsibility. He must instruct the nursing staff on how to position the patient and equally, he must check such positioning before beginning the operation. The anaesthetist must point out any errors to the operating surgeon. The anaesthetist, on the other hand, is responsible for the positioning of those extremities which he requires for the monitoring and administration of the anaesthetic, infusions and medication, ie also for X's arm in this case. Equally, the anaesthetist must monitor the positioning of the extremities during the operation. While the patient is under the anaesthetic, the anaesthetist must observe the positioning and communicate any eventual change in position to the operating surgeon.

The surgeon B states that he was only able to make observations directly before the operation. Thereafter, his view of the patient's arm was blocked by the surgical drape, which is why B was unable to see any eventual changes in position.

It has been established that the damage to the nervus ulnaris could not have occurred as a direct result of the positioning at the beginning of the operation but can only have been sustained due to compression during the operation, which moreover must have lasted for some time. It is not possible to establish whether the arm was so unpropitiously positioned, partly because there is no corresponding reference in the documentation of the operation. Furthermore, it cannot be established whether the anaesthetist C monitored the proper positioning of the arm on a

---

485 Eg AT no 151; CH no 177 (but costs of new car only if required for work); CZ no 175 (only if reasonably incurred); DE no 275 (but not new car, only adaptation of existing vehicle); ES no 123; FR no 83, HU no 77; IT no 94; NL no 106; SE no 74; UK no 74.

486 AT no 153 (up to € 80,000); CZ no 175 (up to € 60,000); DE no 276 (€ 10,000–150,00); HU no 77; IT no 94 (plus *danno biologico*); UK no 75 (previous condition may lead to reduction of the award); see also PL no 116 (non-pecuniary loss for being improperly informed, citing inter alia an award of € 25,000 for a permanently disabled patient suffering a stroke, which risk had not been properly communicated to him).

487 Based on OLG Köln 2. 4. 1990, 27 U 140/88, VersR 1991, 696.

sufficiently cushioned abduction splint during the long operation, taking into consideration the shaking of the body caused by the surgical procedure, in order to make sure it was positioned so as not to suffer any damage. C was an intern at the point in time of the operation and was only three months into her residency. The responsible chief resident D had to supervise procedures in six operating theatres at the same time as X's operation and thus only appeared once an hour to check on anaesthetist C.

Besides damages for non-pecuniary loss, X seeks compensation from A and its employees B, C and D for his loss of income, including the loss of income from moonlighting at the weekend. He refuses to consider retraining as a sales person in a building supplies store.

Apart from that, X wants to be awarded the costs for a private medical injuries assessment which he commissioned from an 'institute for the assessment of medical injuries' to clarify the facts. He could have had the facts evaluated free of charge by an assessment commission at the medical council.

1. Who may be liable?[488]

As the responses to the country reports show, medical standards in these jurisdictions are not necessarily identical. In comparison to the German agreement between the anaesthetists' and the surgeons' professional organisations mentioned in the facts of this hypothetical case, the distribution of responsibilities seems to range in at least some countries from the 'captain of the ship' theory with the surgeon as the top person in charge,[489] to the joint sharing of tasks and duties,[490] to separate responsibilities according to the areas of expertise.[491] **193**

All agree, however, that hospital A can be held liable, in particular as the employer of all the doctors involved, as long as the further requirements of its vicarious liability such as the wrongdoing of at least one member of its staff and its causation can be established.[492] Some reporters also specifically point to the possibility of holding the carrier of hospital A accountable for its lack of proper organisation,[493] since particularly the way that anaesthetics were organised, with doctor D supervising several simultaneous operations, seems to be flawed.[494] **194**

488 X may recover under the Swedish patient insurance scheme without identifying an individual defendant as in the following: SE no 78.

489 BE no 72; see also FR no 89 (in the past).

490 ES nos 124 f.

491 FR no 90.

492 AT nos 152–153; BE no 74; CH nos 182, 187; CZ no 176; DE no 283; ES no 127; FR no 87; HU no 79; IT no 95; NL no 108; PL no 128; SE no 75.

493 AT no 154; DE no 283; ES no 127; FR no 93; PL no 128.

494 Cf BE no 73, referring to the Belgian 'Safety-First' norms on this point.

195 As far as the personal liability of the three doctors involved is concerned, this is ruled out by those legal systems which hold employees immune from personal liability if their employer is vicariously liable for their conduct.[495] In the remaining jurisdictions, they may be held liable in tort individually and in contract only if they were in a direct contractual relationship with the patient, eg as an external doctor merely using the facilities of hospital A.[496] Either way, courts need to be convinced, however, not only of the fact that their conduct deviated from professional standards, but also that this caused a deterioration of the patient's condition which would not have happened in the normal course of events.[497]

196 The former aspect is doubted by some reporters with respect to surgeon B, who does not seem to have neglected professional duties of care at least in those countries where the positioning of the arm was not his own shared responsibility.[498] Some jurisdictions, however, at least in the past would have held B as surgeon in charge of the operation vicariously liable for the conduct of all members of his team.[499]

197 As far as intern C is concerned, her personal liability is confirmed for all jurisdictions which do not prevent direct actions against employees.[500] However, while most legal systems would apply the standard of care expected from a fully-trained expert,[501] at least one would compare her conduct with the standard to be expected only from an intern of her degree of training.[502] In the latter jurisdiction, she will still effectively be held liable, however, for a deviation from the former (higher) standard, but for the reason that she assumed the tasks of a more experienced specialist without meeting the latter's qualifications.[503]

198 Chief resident D may also be personally liable, but the facts of the hypothetical case do not seem to give sufficient support for a definitive answer from most reporters.[504]

---

495 CZ no 176; FR nos 73, 87; HU no 30; PL no 51; SE no 75.

496 See also IT nos 44, 95: also employed doctors considered to be in a 'social contact' with the patient and therefore contractually liable.

497 Cf CH no 188.

498 AT no 157; FR no 88; DE no 281; ES no 126.

499 BE no 72 ('captain of the ship' theory); FR no 88.

500 Cf fn 494.

501 Eg DE nos 280, 282; ES no 126; NL no 108.

502 AT no 155.

503 AT no 155.

504 Cf AT no 156; CH no 188; ES no 126; FR no 92; IT no 95; NL no 108.

2. Lack of documentation

The fact that the positioning of the arm was not recorded in the documentation of the operation comes to the claimant's advantage in some,[505] but not all, jurisdictions.[506] 199

3. Compensable losses

Apart from his claim for damages for his non-pecuniary losses, which are of course compensable once liability is established,[507] certain aspects of his pecuniary loss deserve specific attention. 200

Not all jurisdictions would, for example, be willing to compensate X's proceeds of his moonlighting activities on the weekends. While some legal systems have no problem indemnifying X for this loss of 'tax-free' earnings,[508] others deem it illicit and therefore would deny damages for this part of his previous income.[509] 201

His refusal to retrain as a sales person in a building supplies store has no effect on his claim for lost income in some countries,[510] whereas others at least reduce it as long as such retraining is deemed objectively reasonable, pointing in particular at X's duty to mitigate his loss.[511] 202

The costs for the assessment of his injuries by a private institution, which he could have obtained free of charge from the medical council, may 203

505 AT no 158; see also NL no 107: substantive claim based on art 7:454 CC and the loss of a chance theory. Cf supra at fn 137.

506 CH nos 182, 185; CZ no 178 (and patient unlikely to prove causation otherwise).

507 Eg AT no 161 (up to € 50,000); CH no 191; CZ no 180 (up to € 10,000); DE no 285 (approx € 15,000); ES no 128; HU no 80; NL no 109.

508 AT no 159; CH no 189; CZ no 180 (but difficult to prove); ES no 128; IT no 95 ('at least in the abstract'); NL no 109 (reduced by applicable tax and social insurance premiums); PL no 134 (but courts split); UK no 78; cf also *WVH Rogers*, England, in: U Magnus (ed), Unification of Tort Law: Damages (2001) 53, 73 f.

509 BE no 75; DE no 288; FR no 94; cf also Art 2:103 PETL.

510 ES no 128; FR no 95; HU no 80; NL no 109 (but 'problems under social security law').

511 AT no 160 (but burden of proof upon tortfeasor that claimant refused reasonable alternative); BE no 76; CH no 189; CZ no 180; DE no 286; IT no 95 (earning capacity reduces X's claim for lost income); SE no 76; UK no 78 (failure to seek alternative employment 'unreasonable').

nonetheless be recoverable in some jurisdictions,[512] while others deem this at least doubtful,[513] or exclude it altogether.[514]

Case 6[515]

In June 1999, X went to A and B's joint orthopaedic practice, in which C and D worked as locums at the time. C gave X an injection in the neck area on 9 and 11 June 1999, D did the same on 15 June 1999.

In the aftermath, a syringe abscess developed, making it necessary for X to be treated as an in-patient for two weeks. The syringe abscess derived from a staphylococcus infection. The infection originated from the medical assistant E employed by A and B, who was suffering from hay fever at the time and assisted with the administration of the injections. Other patients at the practice acquired similar infections during the same time period, the first cases were on 2, 8 and 10 June 1999. It is not possible to establish whether it would have been possible for the doctors to recognise the staphylococcus infection of the medical assistant E.

An investigation by the Health Authority in mid-June 1999 revealed that the hygiene standards in the doctors' practice for the medical assistants were not communicated and supervised by the doctors to the extent necessary. Disinfectants were not kept in their original containers but moved to others. Vials with substances for injection were used over several days. Furthermore, disinfectants for working surfaces, which had a long exposure time, were wrongly used as disinfectant for skin. Additionally, it was not usual for the medical assistants to disinfect their hands before drawing up a syringe and working surfaces were not disinfected every day as required but only once a week.

X was the manager of a catering business and initially resumed this work. However, as she suffers on-going pain, insomnia and depressive moods as a result of the syringe abscess, she is unable to work. Besides appropriate damages for non-pecuniary loss, she seeks compensation from A, B, C, D and E for her pecuniary damage, in particular also costs for cleaning assistance. However, since the infection her daughter has been helping her with household tasks, which she performs for her mother in addition to her own.

Variation 1: The carrier of the bacteria cannot be identified. It could have been the medical assistant E, another patient in the waiting room or someone who accompanied patient X.

Variation 2: No hygiene shortfalls in the doctors' practice can be proved, the usual standards were observed.

---

512 AT no 162 ff (as long as reasonable and within market price limits); ES no 129 (as costs subject to limitations of procedural law); IT no 97; NL no 109 (but 'double test for reasonableness'); SE no 77 (as trial expenses); UK no 78 (if reasonably incurred) PL no 131 (no duty to use medical council instead).

513 BE no 77.

514 CH no 190; CZ no 181; HU no 80.

515 Based on BGH 20. 3. 2007, VI ZR 158/06, NJW 2007, 1682 = VersR 2007, 847 (cmt *Jungbecker*) = BGHZ 171, 358 = MDR 2007, 951 = ArztR 2008, 153.

1. Who may be liable?[516]

(a) A & B

Assuming that A and B are the joint employers of C, D and E, they may be vicariously liable for the latters' conduct.[517] The facts of this case may also speak for another basis of a claim against A and B, now in their function as owners of the joint practice: they may have to account for flaws in implementing proper hygiene standards at their practice, which looks more at the result than at some specific conduct of any individual employee that may have led to it.[518] **204**

In Germany, at least under facts as in the instant case, a reversal of the burden of proof may apply if a risk has materialised that originated in the doctors' practice 'and could have been fully controlled if it had been organised appropriately'.[519] **205**

Also other jurisdictions offer alleviations for the claimant, such as a presumption of fault in Belgium and France, triggered by the apparent violation of a safety obligation (if – as here – an infected medical device was used). Again, the focus is on the result rather than on the conduct producing it.[520] In the Czech Republic as in Spain, A and B may be subject to strict liability.[521] **206**

(b) C & D

Individual liability of C and D is excluded if they are employees of A and B's joint practice and the legal system channels liability vis-à-vis third parties to the latter.[522] **207**

516 X may recover under the Swedish patient insurance scheme without identifying an individual defendant as in the following: SE no 81. If her invalidity exceeds 25 %, she will be entitled to benefits from ONIAM (which in turn can seek recourse from the practice): FR nos 110 ff.

517 AT no 169; CH nos 193 ff; CZ no 188 (if no proof that syringe was infected, but caused by contact with E); DE no 289 f (but only in contract, not in tort; reversal of burden of proof applies); ES no 130; HU no 81; IT no 98; PL no 135; SE no 79.

518 CH no 195 (but tricky proof of causation); ES no 130; FR no 107; PL no 138.

519 DE nos 293 ff.

520 BE no 78; FR nos 99 f.

521 CZ no 183 ff (if infection caused by object, ie contaminated syringe); ES no 132.

522 CZ nos 68, 182; FR no 73; HU nos 30, 81; PL no 51. See also no 65.

208 In other countries, the requirements for holding C and D liable are hard to fulfil; both causation and blameworthiness of their conduct are at least doubtful.[523] However, due to shifts in the burden of proof, claimants may be more easily successful in some jurisdictions.[524]

(c) E

209 The medical assistant who carried the infection when in contact with claimant X may be a slightly more promising target of a tort claim than C and D, though obviously not from a deep-pocket perspective. While E – like her co-employees – is immune from personal liability in some countries,[525] X may possibly succeed in proving causation and fault, particularly if she can convince the court that E knew about the risk and still failed to take precautionary measures.[526]

2. Variation 1 – alternative causes

210 If the origin of the infection cannot be identified with the required standard of proof, but there are alternative potential carriers, jurisdictions are split when it comes to attributing the risk of pinpointing the true cause. Some leave it with claimant X, which means that she would lose her case in the absence of sufficient proof of who caused her loss.[527] The majority of legal systems would rather place the risk with the defendants, however, at least under certain (further) conditions,[528] and perhaps not exclusively, ie share the risk by imposing proportional liability.[529]

---

523 AT no 169; CH no 198; ES no 130.

524 DE no 298; FR nos 99 f.

525 Cf fn 521.

526 CH no 199; ES no 130. But see AT no 169.

527 CZ no 189 (X would have to prove that particular contact with E caused infection); DE nos 301 f; NL no 111.

528 AT no 171 (if high probability that only causes within their sphere relevant); BE no 79 (no need to identify carrier of bacteria as long as proof that a safety obligation has been violated in the practice; external cause to be proven by defendants); CH nos 201 ff; ES no 132; FR no 101 (infection during medical act, source of microbe irrelevant); HU no 82 (risk shifted to medical service provider in Hungarian court practice); IT no 100; PL no 138 (reversal of burden of proof); UK no 81 (if proper hygiene procedures would probably have prevented the infection).

529 AT no 171 (if qualified fault and significant risk attributable to A & B); UK no 81 (*Fairchild* scenario, but doubtful).

3. Variation 2 – no hygiene shortcomings

If one left out one part of the main facts of this hypothetical case, ie the investigation showing flaws in implementing adequate hygiene standards at the practice, this would not necessarily change the outcome of the case against A and B in some countries. They would still be held liable in several jurisdictions,[530] whereas others would no longer deem them accountable for X's loss.[531] **211**

4. Compensable losses

Apart from her loss of income,[532] X may recover the costs for cleaning assistance, even if actually performed by her daughter, in most jurisdictions,[533] though opinions are divided as to whether she could claim the equivalent salaries of a professional cleaner[534] or less, down to the costs of an unqualified worker.[535] **212**

Her non-pecuniary losses are compensable as well, of course.[536] **213**

Conclusions

'Although the development of medical liability looks spectacular, it should not be exaggerated.'[537]

When looking at developments throughout Europe in the field of medical liability, there have seemingly been more changes in the last two or three decades of the 20th century than in the first decade of the 21st. This may at least in part be explained by the fact that once the patients' rights movement came on track,[538] legal systems have sometimes gone out of their way **214**

530 Eg HU no 83; IT no 101; presumed fault: BE no 80 (safety obligation violated); PL no 139; strict liability: CZ no 188 (as long as it is still proven that the actual syringe was infected); FR nos 102 f (but not in public hospitals: fault-based).

531 AT no 172; CH no 205; DE nos 303 f; ES no 133; NL no 112; UK no 82.

532 Eg AT no 170; CZ no 190; DE no 299; ES no 131; HU no 81; IT no 99; PL no 137; UK no 80.

533 But see IT no 99 (X would have to prove actual loss).

534 AT no 170; CH no 200; DE nos 299 f; ES no 131; FR no 108; HU no 81; PL no 137.

535 CZ no 190; UK no 80 ('less than commercial rate').

536 Eg CH no 200; CZ no 190; DE no 299 (around € 25,000); ES no 131; HU no 81; IT no 99; PL no 137; UK no 80.

537 *Hondius* (fn 23) 9.

538 *Hondius* (fn 23) 10 f.

to improve the situation of patients who might have been harmed during treatment but who could not successfully be remedied with tools from the traditional toolbox of classic tort or contract law. Reversals of the burden of proof and alleviations of the standard of proof are just indications thereof which can be witnessed in almost all countries, though not necessarily everywhere to the same degree.[539] The boom of the informed consent doctrine, which quite often appears to be just a fast-track detour to liability if medical errors are suspected, but cannot be proven, is another example of this trend.

215 However, now that these points have been clarified, novelties in the outcome of medical malpractice cases seem rather to come from adjustments of tort law as a whole.[540] This is best witnessed when looking at the changes concerning non-pecuniary loss over the past decade alone. Some jurisdictions have significantly increased the overall level of damages awarded for such losses and/or have expanded the range of potential claimants – third-party losses such as damages for bereavement are nowadays recognized in legal systems where this was not heard of before the millennium.

216 Exceptions are of course possible as always – the most prominent example being the 2002 *loi Kouchner* in France,[541] which may at least in part inspire changes in the laws of at least some jurisdictions in the next decade to come, such as already in Belgium or Poland[542].

217 A harmonisation of medical liability – without even touching upon the question whether this is desirable at all[543] – is far from sight, but not surprisingly so: the social, economic and other factors characterising health care in the various countries are in themselves ample reason to proceed at least cautiously when considering the approximation of the laws governing medical malpractice, let alone their legal peculiarities.[544] Models useful in one society may not be ideal for others.

---

539 Cf supra nos 45 ff.

540 One noteworthy development within medical liability law proper is the jurisprudence on wrongful conception, wrongful birth or wrongful life, of course. Cf supra Case 2 and the contributions to (2010) 2 JETL cited in fn 428 ff.

541 FR nos 14 ff.

542 BE no 57; PL nos 101 ff. But see supra no 144.

543 *Hondius* (fn 23) 21 ff, 25 f.

544 See also *H Koziol*, Deficiency of Regulation and Approach to Solutions: Conclusions from the Comparative Research, in: M Faure/H Koziol (eds), Cases on Medical Malpractice in a Comparative Perspective (2001) 311.

This study intended to give a snapshot of where 13 European jurisdictions stand today with respect to medical liability, as compared to a decade ago. As could be seen, differences still persist and are unlikely to be overcome in the nearer future. It would come as a great surprise if the next study ten years from now would paint a radically different picture. **218**

Index

The numbers refer to the marginal notes and the letters refer to the reports: AT stands for Austria, BE for Belgium, CA for the Comparative Analysis, CH for Switzerland, CZ for the Czech Republic, DE for Germany, ES for Spain, FR for France, HU for Hungary, IT for Italy, NL for the Netherlands, PL for Poland, SE for Sweden and UK for England.

Kolibri 360 GmbH
Ferdinand-Jühlke-Straße 7
99095 Erfurt, Deutschland
produktsicherheit@kolibri360.de